About the Author

Dr. Lisa J. Cohen is a licensed clinical psychologist who works as a teacher, scientist, and clinician. She is Associate Professor of Clinical Psychiatry at Beth Israel Medical Center/Albert Einstein College of Medicine in New York City, where she also serves as Director of Research for Psychology and Psychiatry. Dr. Cohen teaches topics in clinical psychology to graduate and undergraduate students in psychology and to psychiatric residents. Her scientific research has covered a number of domains, including obsessive compulsive disorder, child trauma, personality pathology, psychological testing, opiate addiction, bipolar disorder, and schizophrenia. She has authored or co-authored over 70 articles in professional journal and 14 book chapters. In her private practice, she provides psychotherapy to individuals and couples, combining psychodynamic and cognitive-behavioral techniques. She also works as a supervising psychologist on an inpatient psychiatric unit, where she oversees the provision of group therapy and psychological testing to psychiatric patients with serious mental illness, such as schizophrenia and bipolar disorder.

Also from Visible Ink Press

The Handy Anatomy Answer Book
by James Bobick and Naomi Balaban
ISBN: 978-1-57859-190-9

The Handy Answer Book for Kids (and Parents)
by Judy Galens and Nancy Pear
ISBN: 978-1-57859-110-7

The Handy Astronomy Answer Book
by Charles Liu
ISBN: 978-1-57859-193-0

The Handy Biology Answer Book
by James Bobick, Naomi Balaban, Sandra
  Bobick and Laurel Roberts
ISBN: 978-1-57859-150-3

The Handy Dinosaur Answer Book, 2nd Edition
by Patricia Barnes-Svarney and Thomas E
  Svarney
ISBN: 978-1-57859-218-0

The Handy Geography Answer Book,
  2nd Edition
by Paul A. Tucci and Matthew T. Rosenberg
ISBN: 978-1-57859-215-9

The Handy Geology Answer Book
by Patricia Barnes-Svarney and Thomas E
  Svarney
ISBN: 978-1-57859-156-5

The Handy History Answer Book, 2nd Edition
by Rebecca Nelson Ferguson
ISBN: 978-1-57859-170-1

The Handy Law Answer Book
by David L. Hudson Jr.
ISBN: 978-1-57859-217-3

The Handy Math Answer Book
by Patricia Barnes-Svarney and Thomas E
  Svarney
ISBN: 978-1-57859-171-8

The Handy Ocean Answer Book
by Patricia Barnes-Svarney and Thomas E
  Svarney
ISBN: 978-1-57859-063-6

The Handy Philosophy Answer Book
by Naomi Zack
ISBN: 978-1-57859-226-5

The Handy Physics Answer Book, 2nd Edition
by Paul W. Zitzewitz, Ph.D.
ISBN: 978-1-57859-305-7

The Handy Politics Answer Book
by Gina Misiroglu
ISBN: 978-1-57859-139-8

The Handy Religion Answer Book
by John Renard
ISBN: 978-1-57859-125-1

The Handy Science Answer Book®,
  Centennial Edition
by The Science and Technology
  Department Carnegie Library of
  Pittsburgh
ISBN: 978-1-57859-140-4

The Handy Sports Answer Book
by Kevin Hillstrom, Laurie Hillstrom and
  Roger Matuz
ISBN: 978-1-57859-075-9

The Handy Supreme Court Answer Book
by David L Hudson, Jr.
ISBN: 978-1-57859-196-1

The Handy Weather Answer Book, 2nd Edition
by Kevin S. Hile
ISBN: 978-1-57859-215-9

Please visit the Handy series website at handyanswers.com

THE
HANDY
PSYCHOLOGY
ANSWER
BOOK

Lisa J. Cohen, PhD

VISIBLE
INK
PRESS

Detroit

THE HANDY PSYCHOLOGY ANSWER BOOK

Visible Ink Press®
43311 Joy Rd., #414
Canton, MI 48187-2075

Visible Ink Press is a registered trademark of Visible Ink Press LLC.

Most Visible Ink Press books are available at special quantity discounts when purchased in bulk by corporations, organizations, or groups. Customized printings, special imprints, messages, and excerpts can be produced to meet your needs. For more information, contact Special Markets Director, Visible Ink Press, www.visibleink.com, or 734-667-3211.

Managing Editor: Kevin S. Hile
Art Director: Mary Claire Krzewinski
Typesetting: Marco Di Vita
Proofreader: Sharon R. Gunton and Sharon R. Malinowski
ISBN 978-1-57859-223-4

Cover images: iStock.com.

Library of Congress Cataloguing-in-Publication Data

Cohen, Lisa J.
    The handy psychology answer book / Lisa J. Cohen.
        p. cm. — (Handy answer book series)
    Includes bibliographical references and index.
    ISBN 978-1-57859-223-4
    1. Psychology—Popular works. I. Title.
    BF145.C59 2011
    150—dc22   2010042165

Printed in the United States of America

10 9 8 7 6 5 4 3 2

Contents

INTRODUCING THE BASICS ... 1

The Basics ... Psychology before Psychology ... Psychology in Other Cultures ... History and Pioneers ... Sigmund Freud ... John B. Watson and B.F. Skinner ... Jean Piaget

MAJOR MOVEMENTS IN PSYCHOLOGY ... 31

Behaviorism ... Gestalt Psychology ... Psychoanalytic Theory ... Jungian Analytical Psychology ... Humanistic Theories ... Attachment Theory ... Sociobiology and Evolutionary Psychology ... Neurobiological Theories ... Cognitive Science ... Psychology as a Science ... Psychological Tests ... Intelligence Testing

BRAIN AND BEHAVIOR ... 95

Basic Concepts in Neuroscience ... The Major Structures of the Brain ... Brain Development ... From Brain to Mind ... The Brain as Mapmaker ... Sensation and Perception ... Motor Behavior and Intentional Action ... Cognition and Behavioral Control ... Emotions ... Emotion and the Limbic System ... Emotions in Mammals ... Frontal Control of the Limbic System ... Neurotransmitters and Other Brain Chemicals ... Impact of the Environment on the Brain

PSYCHOLOGICAL DEVELOPMENT ACROSS THE LIFESPAN ... 147

Freud's Psychosexual Stages ... Erik Erikson's Psychosocial Stages ...

v

Introduction

I have been fascinated with psychology ever since I was a child. I wanted to understand what made people do what they do, what the story was behind their behavior. I wanted to strip back the outer cover and see the machinery within. Many years later, I am still fascinated with psychology. Psychology is ultimately the foundation of all human endeavor. Why do we think, feel, and act the way we do? Why do we love, hate, eat, work, or dance the way we do? How does our three-pound brain produce the incredible intricacies of human behavior? How much of our psychology is due to genes and how much to our environment? These questions are addressed every day in thousands of laboratories and consulting rooms across the country and across the world. And the answers to such age-old questions are closer at hand than at any point in history. While I do not believe we will ever fully understand the extraordinary mystery of the human mind, we certainly can learn—and *have learned*—a tremendous amount about our mental processes. Moreover, such discoveries can help reduce the suffering and improve the lives of millions of people.

Interestingly, the major players in the field of psychology used to be far better known to the general public. Fifty years ago, the average person on the street was more likely to be familiar with the likes of Sigmund Freud, B.F. Skinner, or Jean Piaget. There was a widespread appreciation of the importance of the field of psychology and its relevance to everyday life. In contemporary times, there is far less general awareness of the contributions of the field of psychology. Perhaps psychology—that is, the *scientific discipline* of psychology—has been a victim of its own success. Certainly talk shows and magazines are filled with psychological topics. Dr. Phil, Dr. Laura, and Dr. Joyce Brothers remain household names. But I would suggest that the entertainment value of popular psychology has overtaken the appreciation of serious science.

Meanwhile, psychology is flourishing within the walls of academia. Psychology remains an incredibly popular major in college and graduate school. But within the university, the seriousness of the field has overtaken its inherent entertainment value. Thus psychology has split into two vectors: popular psychology, which is entertaining but not rigorous, and academic psychology, which is serious but not easily accessible to the non-specialist.

This book is intended to find a middle ground, to provide a rigorous and scientifically grounded book that is nonetheless accessible and engaging to the general public.

The first section of this book gives an overview of the fundamentals of psychology. We cover the history and pioneers of psychology, the major theoretical movements, the science of psychology, the brain and its relationship to behavior, and psychological development across the lifespan. These are the areas traditionally covered in textbooks.

In the second half of the book we address how the scientific methods of psychology have been applied to questions of everyday life. Here we see how the science of psychology has immediate relevance to a broad spectrum of human activities. What can psychology tell us about love, marriage, family, and sexuality? What can psychology tell us about happiness or our relationship with money? Chapter 7 explores the psychology of the group and how group dynamics play out in the work place, the public sphere, and in the problems of prejudice and racism. Chapters 8 through 10 look at abnormal psychology. Chapter 8 addresses clinical psychology, covering such topics as psychopathology, psychiatric diagnosis, psychotherapy, and psychiatric medication. Chapter 9 looks at the psychology of trauma, and chapter 10 at forensic psychology, where psychology intersects the law.

As part of the "Handy Answer Book" series, this book is structured in a question-and-answer format. Approximately 1,000 questions are answered with one- or two-paragraph answers. The goal is to break down complex topics into bite-size ideas. While the questions were carefully selected to create a narrative flow, this is also the kind of book that you can open at any point and browse. If you want, you can read the book from cover to cover, but you can also flip through to find questions that particularly jump out at you.

Although I want the reader to feel free to jump around, the nature of science is that it is cumulative. In other words, the most recent developments rest upon the shoulders of earlier work. Because of this, the sections in the second half of the book will sometimes refer to topics and people introduced in the first half. If readers run across an unfamiliar idea, person, or issue, they can look the topic up in the index, which will then point them to other areas in the book where the issue is discussed.

I have applied the same scientific standards when writing this book that I use when writing scientific articles for professional journals and have worked hard to only include conclusions that are supported by solid if not multiple references. In professional papers, you cite your sources in the middle of the text, right where you are referencing them. While this practice is necessary for scientific accuracy, it does not make for easy reading. Therefore we put the reference list at the back of the book. Readers who are interested in learning more about any particular area can look up the relevant references for more information.

This book is intended for the general public. Anyone who has a passing interest in psychology could pick up this book to learn more about the field. Did you study psychology in college and always maintained an interest in it? Have you had personal experience with psychological problems, either in yourself or in your family? Are you thinking you might like to pursue a career in the mental health field? Or do you just wonder about why people behave the way they do? Then *The Handy Psychology Answer Book* is for you.

Although this book is intended for the general public, it can also be used to supplement traditional textbooks. If you want a quick review on Attachment Theory or on Behaviorism, if you want to remind yourself of the basics of brain-behavior relationships, or if you want a quick introduction to key psychological theories, this book can be helpful for you.

Whatever your reasons for picking up this book, I hope that you can put it down with a better appreciation of just how fascinating psychology can be and how important it is to everyday life.

Lisa J. Cohen, Ph.D.

ACKNOWLEDGMENTS

Many people contributed to the writing of this book. I'd like to acknowledge Drs. Igor Galynker, Nancy Maruyama, and the Division of Biological Psychiatry for their continual and extremely helpful feedback on various chapters. Thanks to Drs. Ramin Mojtabai, Alessandra Strada, and Ed D'Angelo for their comments on the accuracy or lack thereof of sections on neurobiology, humanistic psychology, and classical thought. I would also like to acknowledge Vanessa and David Evans, Alex and Josh Cohen, David and Marina Vergara, Julie Cohen Evans, Katia Segre Cohen, and Sylvia Cohen for their insights into adolescent slang past and present and into the mysterious world of children's thought. Thanks as well to Dennis Mack for creative ideas as well as legal advice. To Roger Janecke and Kevin Hile, there would be no book if it weren't for you. Finally, to Ed, for tolerating with such good grace my many, many hours absorbed at the computer.

INTRODUCING THE BASICS

THE BASICS

What is **psychology**?

Psychology involves the systematic study of mind and behavior. This extremely broad domain includes questions of motivation and information processing, normal and abnormal behavior, mental health and mental illness, the individual and the group, and people functioning in the context of their lives.

How does **psychology relate** to **everyday life**?

Psychology relates to every part of everyday life. The questions of psychology relate to how and why we love and suffer and desire, how we raise our children, how and why we succeed or fail at work. Psychology also relates to why we are so fascinated with celebrities and why their marriages so often fail. While the science of psychology may seem abstract at times, the implications touch every arena in which people think, feel or act.

How does **psychology interact** with **biology** and **sociology**?

The human mind does not function in isolation. It exists within both a biological and a social context. Therefore psychology serves as an interface between biology, specifically the biology of the brain, and sociology, the study of the behavior of groups.

What do **psychologists do**?

Psychology is a remarkably varied field, involving both the performance of scientific research and the application of its findings. Psychologists work as scientists, clini-

1

cians, teachers, authors, consultants, and evaluators. They perform empirical research, provide therapy and assessment, and evaluate mental status or disability in numerous settings, such as the government, schools and the judicial system. Psychologists also consult on wide-ranging problems for businesses, schools, the military, the police force, sports teams and even rock bands. As the study of human behavior, psychology can potentially apply to any field of human endeavor.

What is the **difference** between **psychologists** and **psychiatrists**?

The responsibilities of psychologists and psychiatrists often overlap; both psychologists and psychiatrists can diagnose and evaluate mental illness, provide psychotherapy, and conduct research. Nonetheless, their background and training differ considerably. In general, psychologists are students of the mind and behavior while psychiatrists are experts in mental illness. Psychologists are trained in academia and their highest degree is the doctorate (Ph.D. or Psy.D.) in psychology. They do not prescribe medicine, unless they are certified by the few states that have prescription privileges for psychologists. Moreover, not all psychologists are involved with clinical work. In contrast, psychiatrists are trained in the medical field. They are all physicians, having completed medical school and having obtained an M.D. (or D.O.). Their training is almost entirely clinical and focuses on the evaluation and pharmacological treatment (i.e., medication) of severe mental illness.

What are the **divisions** of the **American Psychological Association**?

The APA is divided into the following interest groups, known as divisions.

1. General Psychology
2. Teaching of Psychology
3. Experimental Psychology
5. Evaluation, Measurement, and Statistics
6. Behavioral Neuroscience and Comparative Psychology

7. Developmental Psychology

8. Personality and Social Psychology

9. Social Issues

10. Aesthetics, Creativity and the Arts

12. Clinical Psychology

13. Consulting Psychology

14. Industrial and Organizational Psychology

15. Educational Psychology

16. School Psychology

17. Counseling Psychology

18. Psychologists in Public Service

19. Military Psychology

20. Adult Development and Aging

21. Applied Experimental and Engineering Psychology

22. Rehabilitation Psychology

23. Consumer Psychology

24. Theoretical and Philosophical Psychology

25. Behavior Analysis

26. History of Psychology

27. Community Psychology

28. Psychopharmacology and Substance Abuse

29. Psychotherapy

30. Psychological Hypnosis

31. State, Provincial, and Territorial Psychological Association Affairs

32. Humanistic Psychology

33. Intellectual and Developmental Disabilities

34. Population and Environmental Psychology

35. Psychology of Women

36. Psychology of Religion

37. Child and Family Policy and Practice

38. Health Psychology

39. Psychoanalysis

40. Clinical Neuropsychology

41. Psychology-Law

42. Psychologists in Independent Practice

43. Family Psychology

44. Lesbian, Gay, and Bisexual Issues

45. Ethnic Minority Issues

46. Media Psychology

47. Exercise and Sport Psychology

48. Peace, Conflict, and Violence

49. Group Psychology and Group Psychotherapy

PSYCHOLOGY BEFORE PSYCHOLOGY

When was the field of **psychology established**?

The study of mental processes as a science is relatively new as it is dependent on the scientific revolution. Wilhelm Wundt (1832–1920) is credited with first establishing psychology as an independent science. He opened the first scientific laboratory to study psychology in 1879 at the University of Leipzig. Wundt was interested in investigating human consciousness through systematic introspection; collaborators would be trained to report their own sensory experience in response to physical stimulation.

What came **before psychology**?

Modern psychology is a child of the scientific revolution. Without the systematic application of reason and observation that forms the foundation of the scientific method, there would be no modern psychology. Nonetheless, contemporary psychology is not without precedents, and within Western history there are many precursors, ancestors so to speak, of psychology as we know it today. Ancient Greek philosophy, medieval Christianity, and post-Renaissance philosophers of the past several centuries all addressed the core questions of psychology in ways that both differed from and anticipated much of what we know today.

What did the **ancient Greeks** have to say about **psychology**?

Twenty-five hundred years ago, ancient Greek philosophers turned their remarkably sophisticated inquiries away from the whims of the gods and toward questions of the natural world. Questions about humanity's place in the world naturally followed. What is knowledge and how do we gain it? What is our relationship with emotions? While some of their answers to these questions appear bizarre by modern standards, much of it remains strikingly current.

What is the **Greek root** of the **word "psychology"**?

The word *psychology* derives from the Greek words *psyche*, meaning soul, and *logos*, meaning a reasoned account in words. It is important to note, though, that the Greeks' conception of the mind was quite different from ours. In general, the Greeks understood the mind in more concrete ways with less emphasis on the complexity of subjective experience.

Did **Homer** have a **Concept of the Mind**?

Homer's legendary epics, the *Iliad* and the *Odyssey*, date back to the eighth century B.C.E. Although Homer's epics are timeless stories of passion and drama, his understanding of human psychology is radically different from our view today. There is no real concept of consciousness in Homer, no sense of the characters' behaviors being motivated by their own internal feelings or thoughts. Instead characters' motivations are *imposed* on them through the whims of the gods. Athena *makes* Odysseus do whatever he does. Abstract ideas of mental life, of consciousness, do not exist and awareness is understood in concrete, bodily terms. For example, the Greek word *noos* (later spelled *nous*), which later came to mean consciousness, was more concretely understood as vision or sight. The word *psyche*, which in later years referred to the soul or the mind, in Homer's day meant only blood or breath, the physical markers of life.

When did the **Greeks** turn to **questions of psychology**?

The pre-Socratic philosophers—i.e., those who predated Socrates—lived in the early fifth century and sixth centuries B.C.E. Philosophers such as Alcmaeon, Protagoras, Democritus, and Hippocrates introduced concepts remarkably pertinent to modern ideas. Shifting focus from the gods to the natural world, they attributed mental activity to nous (the later spelling of noos), which some even located in the brain. Several of these philosophers believed that our knowledge of the world is only learned through the sense organs. As we can only know what we see, hear, smell or touch, all human knowledge is necessarily subjective and will differ from individual to individual. This belief in the relativism of human knowledge is a radical idea that remains pertinent to modern psychology.

Do all the ancient **Greeks' ideas hold up** in the light of modern science?

Not all of the ancient Greeks' ideas make sense from a contemporary point of view. Hippocrates, for example, believed that mental illness is caused by imbalances between bile, phlegm, and blood and Alcmaeon believed that perceptions reached the brain through channels of air. Nonetheless, the attempt to find biological explanations of psychological processes is extraordinarily similar to modern views.

What are the four bodily humors?

Hippocrates (460–377 B.C.E.) was a brilliant physician who introduced the notion of the four bodily humors, a concept that would influence medical theories for almost 2,000 years. Hippocrates based his physiological theory on the ideas of another pre-Socratic philosopher, Empedocles (c. 492–c. 432 B.C.E.), who believed the entire world to be composed of earth, air, fire, and water. The bodily elements of black bile, yellow bile, blood, and phlegm corresponded with each of Empedocles's four elements. Although Hippocrates attributed all mental processes (such as joy, grief, etc.) to the brain, he believed that both mental and physical health rested on a harmonious balance of the four bodily humors. Over five centuries later, the Roman physician Galen (130–201 C.E.) expanded Hippocrates's ideas to create a typology of personality. The melancholic personality (from black bile) tended toward the depressed; the choleric (from yellow bile) tended toward anger, the sanguine (from blood) tended toward the vigorous, courageous, and amorous, and the phlegmatic (from phlegm) tended to be calm and not easily perturbed. Each personality type resulted from an excess of its respective bodily humor. Although modern science has disproved this theory, Galen's terms are still used to describe personality traits.

What did **Plato** and **Aristotle** have to say about psychology?

Plato (428–347 B.C.E.) and Aristotle (384–322 B.C.E.), the two most famous Greek philosophers, have had far-reaching influence on Western thought. While neither is best known for his psychological ideas, both have had impact on Western conceptions of the mind. Plato believed that the truth lay in abstract concepts, or forms, that could be grasped through reason alone. The data we get from our senses is impermanent and therefore illusory. The notion of an inborn mental ability to grasp concepts and categories is consistent with modern cognitive psychology and neuroscience, although the dismissal of "sense data" is not. Aristotle was much more enamored of the natural world and believed knowledge to come from systematic logical reasoning about our observations of nature. He maintained that the capacity for logical reasoning is innate but the content of our knowledge can only be grasped through our senses. In this way, Aristotle anticipated the foundations of modern science.

Did **Plato's ideas anticipate Freud** in any way?

Plato also had ideas about emotions and emotional control that anticipated Freud's theories of the ego and the id. Plato's three-part division of the soul into appetite, reason, and temper (also known as the spirited part of the soul) has been linked to Freud's division of the mind into the id, ego, and superego. Plato also believed in controlling

Does life have a purpose?

Aristotle believed that everything on Earth has a purpose, a *telos*. The acorn is intended to grow into an oak, a knife is intended to cut, a baker is intended to bake. As human beings are the only animals that reason, it is our telos to reason; it is our purpose. If we live according to our purpose, we will be living virtuously and will consequently be happy.

There are two types of telos: *intrinsic* telos and *extrinsic* telos. Intrinsic telos suggests that the aim of the organism is inherent in its nature, an acorn is innately programmed to grown into a tree. Extrinsic telos refers to a purpose imposed by an external force, such as a deity.

For Aristotle, everything has a purpose. The acorn is intended to grow into an oak tree, for example, and people are meant to think and reason (photo: *iStock*).

Not all modern views hold that life has a purpose, however. In the Darwinian view of natural selection, genetic variations happen by *chance* and persist only if they turn out to be adaptive, if they promote the survival of the species. We reason not because it is our *telos* but because we happen to have evolved that way. Our capacity to reason helped our species to survive.

The teleological view is more consistent with other modern views, though. Abraham Maslow (1908–1970), the humanistic psychologist, believed that we are predisposed to strive for a state of *self-actualization*, in which our personality is fully flowered and we reach our full emotional potential. It is, in effect, our *telos*.

Sigmund Freud, as well, may have been influenced by teleology. He studied with Franz Brentano, who was a scholar of Aristotle.

the bodily passions in order to turn one's desire toward loftier goals, as described in his metaphor of the soul as a charioteer with a pair of winged steeds. One steed is immortal like the steeds of the gods and aspires toward contemplation of spiritual beauty. The other steed is mortal and plunges toward earth and toward animalistic passions and desire. The chariot must rein in the steed of animal appetites in order for the soul to gain true happiness. We can link the earthly steed to the id and the charioteer to the ego. More loosely, we could tie the immortal steed to the superego.

It was once common in Europe for people to believe that mental illnesses were the result of possession by devils and demons. In the Middle Ages, Satan was often blamed for most of the suffering in the world.

Did the Roman statesman **Cicero** have anything to add about the **mind**?

The Romans were better known for their practical accomplishments in the fields of law, engineering, and warfare than for their philosophical works but some contributions are worth noting. Cicero (106–42 B.C.E.), the famous Roman orator, gave a detailed description of the passions. He grouped the passions into four categories: discomfort, fear, pleasure or joy, and desire (*libido* in Latin). We can wonder whether Freud's use of the term libido was influenced by Cicero.

What happened to the **Greeks' ideas** after the **fall** of the **Roman Empire**?

The ideas of the Greek philosophers were disseminated throughout the Roman Empire and remained influential until its fall in the fourth century C.E. By then Christianity was the official religion of the Roman Empire, and following the fall of Rome, the Christian church was essentially the sole surviving institution. Although many aspects of pagan philosophical thought were integrated into church teaching (e.g., Plato's idea of the immortal soul), anything that did not fit with Christian theology was considered heretical. In Christendom, meaning most of Europe, this state of affairs remained largely unchanged until the dawn of the modern era. Thus questions of psychology were addressed through medievalChristianity.

How were questions of **psychology** seen in **medieval Christianity**?

In general, medieval Christianity focused more on the next world than on our happiness within this one. True happiness would only be found in Heaven, not on earth, and

> ## How does the belief in demonic possession relate to psychology?
>
> The idea of the devil was pervasive throughout the Middle Ages and pre-scientific Europe, and all manner of illness and misfortune was attributed to Satan or lesser devils and demons. Mental illness, in particular, was seen to be caused by demonic possession. It was believed that Jesus exorcised demons, a task that was performed by priests by the time of the Middle Ages. Even today some people believe in demonic possession.

entrance to Heaven could only be found through religious piety. Free will was emphasized by St. Augustine (354–430 C.E.), the most influential Christian theologian in the first millennium C.E. Every individual has the free will to choose whether or not to follow God. Sex and the passions of the body were considered sinful, unless performed within a marriage for the purpose of childbearing. Belief in the devil was also widespread and mental illness was often seen as a result of possession by the devil.

What was happening in the **Muslim world** during the **Middle Ages**?

Within one century after the death of the Islamic prophet Mohammed (570–632), Muslim armies had conquered almost all of the southern and eastern Mediterranean, encompassing essentially the southern half of the former Roman Empire. In contrast to northern Europe where the advanced culture of the Greco-Roman world was largely lost for a millennium, the literature of the ancient scholars was preserved in medieval Islam and several centers of learning were established across the Arab world. Avicenna (980–1031), who was known in Arabic as ibn Sina, was committed to the synthesis of classical literature with Islamic doctrine.

Despite a traumatically peripatetic life, Avicenna succeeded in writing one of the most influential texts in the history of medicine, known as the *Canon of Medicine*. As a physician, he was very familiar with psychological illness. He endorsed the doctrine of the four humors in the tradition of Hippocrates and Galen as well as the brain's role in psychological disturbances. His theory about inner senses addressed the relationships between perception, memory, and imagination. He even speculated about what parts of the brain control different psychological functions.

When did more **modern approaches** to **psychology begin**?

After the European Renaissance (fifteenth to sixteenth centuries) brought a sea change of cultural and intellectual values, attention was drawn away from the world beyond and back to this world. Philosophers started to revisit the questions asked by the ancient Greeks and then built upon those ideas to create a new way of seeing the mind. While psychology per se did not exist yet, philosophy was beginning to lay the groundwork for what would later become psychology. Philosophers of note included René Descartes (1596–1650), Benedict de Spinoza (1632–1677), Thomas Hobbes (1588–1679), and John Locke (1632–1704).

What was **Descartes's contribution to the history of psychology?**

Fundamentally, Descartes's contribution to psychology was to make the concept of mind front and center of his philosophy. His famous phrase *Cogito ergo sum* (*I think therefore I am*) links the mental function of thinking to the proof of his very existence. A naturalist who carefully observed the natural world and even dissected animals, he was extremely interested in the relationships between mental and bodily processes. In fact, Cartesian dualism, the notion that the mind and the body are separate entities, continues to inspire debate to this day.

How did **Descartes understand** the workings of the **brain** and the **nervous system**?

Influenced both by his knowledge of physiology and the hydraulic (i.e., water-based) mechanics of the day, Descartes had a complex mechanical understanding of mental and physical processes that anticipated Freud's own hydraulic model. Descartes wrote that impressions of the outside world are made on our sensory organs (i.e., eyes, ears, nose) causing animal spirits (a life giving fluid filled with purified blood) to press on our brain. The brain then sends the fluid down to our body through our nerves, causing muscles to expand and move. In this way critical functions like digestion, respiration, and even psychological processes such as sensation, the appetites and passions, take place. He also identified the pineal gland, which lies at the base of the brain, as the site where the non-physical mind and the physical body interact.

How did **Spinoza contribute** to the history of psychology?

Benedict de Spinoza (1632–1677) was a sephardic Jew living in the Netherlands in the seventeenth century. Now seen as one of the first modern philosophers, he was excommunicated in 1656 from the Jewish community for what was then considered heretical writings. Spinoza believed our primary psychological drive to be the promotion and protection of our own well-being and survival, an idea that anticipated evolutionary psychology. He also believed our three primary emotions to be pleasure, pain, and desire, all of which signal the state of our well-being. This anticipated Freud's pleasure principle. Finally, Spinoza taught that our cognitive appraisal of any situation will determine our emotional response. In other words how we think about an event will shape how we feel about it. Therefore we can change our emotions by changing our thoughts. This is the basic principle behind cognitive therapy, pioneered in the mid- twentieth century by Aaron Beck and Albert Ellis.

What is folk psychology and how does it deal with the issues of everyday life?

It was not only the philosophers who grappled with the questions of psychology. As the issues of psychology are so relevant to everyday life, we would expect many people to come up with ideas about psychological principles. Folk psychology, often expressed in aphorisms or proverbs, captures some of these ideas as they were passed down through the generations. Below are just some of the common sense sayings that people have used over the years to communicate the wisdom of folk psychology.

- Let sleeping dogs lie
- Old dogs can't learn new tricks
- Look before you leap
- A stitch in time saves nine
- A penny saved is a penny earned
- Penny wise, pound foolish
- A fool and his money are soon parted
- Spare the rod, spoil the child
- When the cat's away, the mice will play
- The apple doesn't fall far from the tree
- If wishes were horses, beggars would ride
- Pride goeth before a fall
- Nothing ventured, nothing gained
- Shallow brooks are noisy
- Loose lips sink ships
- If you love someone, set them free
- Absence makes the heart grow fonder
- Hunger is the best sauce
- Out of sight, out of mind
- Every cloud has a silver lining
- Three's a crowd
- Never go to bed mad
- He who laughs last, laughs best
- One man's meat is another man's poison
- God helps those who help themselves

What were **Thomas Hobbes's** views about the **relationships** between **ideas**?

Thomas Hobbes (1588–1679) was most famous for his political philosophy and for his view of life in "the state of nature" as "solitary, poor, nasty, brutish, and short." But he also had ideas about cognition and memory. Hobbes believed that all our knowledge comes from our sense impressions. Memories are the residues of the initial sense impressions, somewhat like waves that continue even after the wind ceases. He noted that ideas get linked together in memory when the sense impressions first occur close in time. This concept of *associative* memory became the basis of behaviorism, a psychological movement that arose in the twentieth century.

How did **John Locke build** on earlier **ideas**?

John Locke (1632–1704), who was also mostly known as a political philosopher, divided ideas into two classes: sensation, our initial sense impressions; and reflection, the mind's actions on the initial sense impressions. Thus he distinguished between *perception* and *cognition*. Further, he considered our complex ideas (abstract concepts such as justice, love, whiteness) to derive from combinations of simple ideas. The notion that cognition develops from the simple to the complex anticipates Piaget and other twentieth- century cognitive psychologists.

PSYCHOLOGY IN OTHER CULTURES

How have **other cultures** addressed **psychological issues**?

Psychology addresses the basic human questions about life. Why do we act the way we do? Why do we feel what we do? Why do we suffer? Why do we love? Why do we desire what we desire? Modern psychology is unique in that it investigates these primordial questions through the lens of the scientific method. Nonetheless, throughout history and across cultures, people have grappled with these questions and come up with their own answers.

How is **shamanism relevant** to psychology?

Shamans are individuals from traditional, pre-modern societies who mediate between their community and the world of the spirits. In order to travel to the domain of the spirits they enter a trance-like state, often by dancing, music, or a psycho-active plant. Shamanism is a widely spread practice, ranging from the Mongolian steppes to indigenous people of the Americas. While shamanistic practices will vary across cultures, in all shamanistic societies, it is presumed that the world is peopled by spirits and that proper ceremonial communion with these spirits will heal mental and physical illness, bring favorable weather conditions, regulate social harmony, etc. There is an emphasis on the ecstatic trance state as a condition of personal transformation. Moreover, an individual's internal mental states are seen to be caused by—or at least subject to— outside forces, such as the spirits of ancestors, animals, or aspects of nature.

What **psychological concepts** do **Eastern religions** have?

By Eastern religions, we generally are referring to the cultures of Asia. There are a number of religious traditions in Asia, many going back thousands of years. Buddhism and Hinduism are the largest and best known of the Eastern religions.

What tenets of **Buddhism** are **relevant** to **psychology**?

One of the primary tenets in Buddhism is that suffering comes from the illusion that our selves are separate, individual, and complete. People who are emotionally attached to what Westerners might call the ego, or to the idea of the self as a self-contained, isolated entity, are bound to suffer. Happiness or bliss can only be found by relinquishing attachment to the limited and mortal self in favor of the infinite reality of which we are all a part. Meditation and other contemplative practices are the best ways to access the spiritual knowledge that lies within all of us.

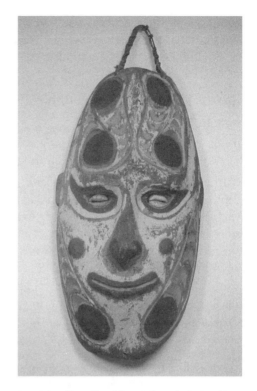

A mask from Papua New Guinea similar to the kind used by shamans. Shamanism is common in many cultures where people believe that the world is filled with spirits.

What aspects of **Hinduism** are **relevant** to **psychology**?

Hinduism is an ancient religion whose beginnings date back 6,000 years. Although there is tremendous variation in Hinduism, there are some consistent strains. As with Buddhism, which originally derived from Hinduism, there is an emphasis on an all-encompassing, multi-dimensional spiritual unity to which we all belong. The many deities in Hinduism are simply manifestations of this cosmic divinity. Suffering comes from ignorance and enlightenment comes from knowledge of the oneness of all reality and of the illusory nature of separateness and individuality. Contemplative practices are also important in the Hindu religion.

How do the **tenets** of **Eastern religions** relate to modern **Western psychology**?

Eastern ideas about the self and self-transcendence have been embraced by many Western psychologists. These ideas are consistent with Western psychological theories

13

about narcissism, which involves an excessive attachment to the ego. Contemplative practices have also been explicitly integrated into contemporary psychotherapies, such as Mindfulness Training and Dialectical Behavioral Therapy.

How do the three major **monotheistic religions** address **psychological questions**?

While there are major differences between the three monotheistic religions—Christianity, Judaism, and Islam—they all believe in a single God who is the source of all truth, morality, and happiness. Thus in all three religions, human psychology is defined and shaped by the relationship to God. Happiness is found by getting close to God, by submitting to or obeying Him and living according to His dictates. Likewise, suffering comes from distance from God. Christianity has a well-developed concept of sin, which reflects a rejection of God's path. Christianity also speaks of the devil, to whom much destructive and socially unacceptable behavior is attributed. Finally, truth is revealed by God, either through the central religious texts or through prayer. There may be variation in the interpretation of God's truth, but His truth is absolute; there is no truth outside of it.

HISTORY AND PIONEERS

What was the **scientific climate** at the **birth of psychology**?

By the time psychology came into its own as an independent discipline, the scientific revolution was two centuries old. Much more was known about the nervous system, the brain and the chemical and electrical processes in the body than could have been dreamed of by the earlier philosophers. The scientific method had continued to evolve and technology allowed for sophisticated instruments of measurement. Thus when psychology burst on the scene in the late 1800s, its proponents were eager to prove this new field as worthy a science as any other discipline.

Why is **Wilhelm Wundt** considered the **father of psychology**?

Although Wilhelm Wundt (1832–1920) was not the first to address psychological questions with scientific means, he was the first to establish a scientific laboratory devoted specifically to psychology. This was done in 1879 at the University of Leipzig. Ernst Weber (1795–1878), Hermann Helmholtz (1821–1894), and Gustav Fechner (1801–1887) had all made important contributions to our understanding of sensation and perception prior to this, but none of them considered himself a psychologist per se. Wundt, in contrast, was specifically focused upon establishing psychology as a science.

What is phrenology?

Not all of the early forays into psychology were based on solid science. *Phrenology* was started by Franz Joseph Gall (1758–1828) in the beginning of the nineteenth century. Gall believed that specific psychological traits could be localized to specific parts of the brain. When any of these individual traits were prominent, that part of the brain would grow larger relative to the rest of the brain and would push outward against the skull. These enlarged brain areas would then cause bumps in the skull. Consequently, careful examination of the shape of the skull could reveal the person's psychological profile.

Gall based his conclusions on empirical techniques (i.e., he measured the skulls of hundreds of people), but his biased methods allowed him to pick and choose his

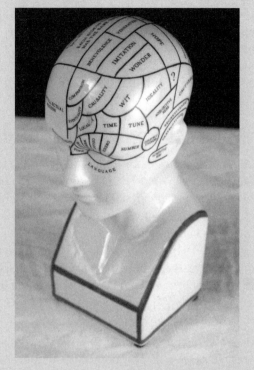

Phrenologists busts became very popular in the nineteenth century. (istock)

findings to fit his theories. Phrenology became very popular over the next century, and phrenology busts were quite common. Phrenology only fell out of favor in the twentieth century after modern science advanced enough to prove it wrong. As with *eugenics*, it was sometimes used to justify racist and socially prejudiced theories. Similarly, it was adopted by the Nazis to prove Aryan supremacy. On a more positive note, it challenged neuroscientists to study the important question of *localization of function* to ask which parts of the brain support different psychological functions.

Interested in the nature of sensation, he combined objective measures with rigorously trained introspection. Researchers were taught to carefully monitor their own perceptual and sensory experience. Wundt's focus was on mapping the mechanics of sensation with mathematical precision. He also taught hundreds of students and was responsible for training many of the major figures in the first few decades of the field. His focus on identifying the components of the mind was termed *structuralism*.

Why is **William James** considered the **father of American psychology**?

James (1842–1910) was among the first professors of psychology in the United States. Hired by Harvard in 1872 as a professor of physiology, he took on the new title of professor of psychology in 1889. Like Wundt, he was an avid promoter of the new field of psychology. Just as Wundt did, James taught many students who would disseminate his ideas into the wider world. Although his interests eventually took him far beyond psychology, his publication *Principles of Psychology* had a long and powerful influence on the development of the field.

How did **James differ from Wundt** in his approach to psychology?

In general, James had a hard time with the atomistic approach to studying psychology exemplified by Wundt's lab. Although he ran his own lab using similar methodology, he felt that the psychophysiology practiced by Wundt and others focused only on the smallest and ultimately least interesting of mental phenomena. He believed that treating moments of consciousness as discrete isolated units was at odds with the real nature of experience, which is continuous. He believed in the flow of consciousness. He was also more interested in holistic concerns, such as the meaning and continuity of the self. How do I know that I am me? What gives me the continuous sense of self across time?

This conflict between a holistic vs. atomistic approach marks a theme that persists throughout the history of psychology as well as the natural sciences in general. Do we study something by breaking it down into its smallest parts or do we try to grasp it as an organic whole? Like Wundt, however, James was an advocate of introspection as a method of studying consciousness, something the behaviorists would later reject vigorously.

How did **James's functionalism differ** from **Wundt's structuralism?**

James was particularly interested in how the mind affects behavior, how it helps us *function* in the world. He was less interested in simply identifying the components of the mind, which was more in keeping with Wundt's structuralism. In fact, later in his career, James abandoned psychology for a school of philosophy called pragmatism. Pragmatists maintained that the value of a belief was less in its accuracy than in its effectiveness, the degree to which it helped people function in their environment.

Who was **Francis Galton?**

Francis Galton (1822–1911) was never formally trained as a psychologist but, an extremely innovative and creative man, he made enormous and long-lasting contributions to the methods of psychological research. In mid-life, after a wide range of endeavors, which included explorations in Africa and new discoveries in meteorology, he became preoccupied with the question of the heritability of intelligence. Is intelligence passed on in families, much like height or hair color? That his own family tree was filled with gifted intellectuals is probably relevant to his choice of study. He was a child prodigy and was the grandson of Erasmus Darwin (a noted physician and botanist) and a first cousin of Charles Darwin.

What were the **contributions** of **Francis Galton**?

In his search to prove the heritability of intelligence, he made several astounding methodological innovations that are still in wide use today. These included the statistical technique of correlation (a mathematical test to see how much two traits increase or decrease together), the comparison of identical and fraternal twins, the use of self-report questionnaires and word association tests, the phrase "nature

Francis Galton (1822–1911), a former child prodigy and cousin of Charles Darwin, made long-lasting contributions to the methods of psychological research. Less commendable were his contributions to the theory of eugenics. (*Mary Evans Picture Library*)

and nurture" and the concept of "regression towards the mean." This last idea derives from Galton's observation that when measurements are repeated over time, the extreme values tend to move toward the middle. For example, very tall parents will often have less tall children. His less illustrious contribution was the field of eugenics.

What is **eugenics**?

Galton's interest in the heritability of intelligence was not only academic. He wanted to apply it to social policy so that only families with high intelligence would breed and the less fortunate would be discouraged from reproducing. These ideas were expressed in several books and later spread to numerous academic departments and international societies. The fact that he greatly discounted the impact of environment on intellectual development, specifically the effect of social class, racial discrimination and access to education, inevitably set the stage for prejudicial and racist applications of this theory. Moral questions regarding the civil rights of the genetically "less fit" were also neglected. Eugenics had significant impact on American immigration policies in the 1920s, justifying the restriction of Eastern and Southern European immigrants. Eugenics fell out of favor after the Nazis championed it in support of their genocidal policies.

What influence did **Emil Kraepelin** and **Eugen Bleuler** have on views of **mental illness**?

Even though both Kraepelin and Bleuler were psychiatrists rather than psychologists, their contributions to psychiatric diagnosis have profoundly impacted the entire men-

How can social prejudice impact psychological measurements?

The early history of psychology and the social sciences in general is littered with examples of gross social prejudice. In the early nineteenth century, Franz Joseph Gall (1758–1828) introduced the study of phrenology, which mapped various personality traits onto different parts of the brain. Although Gall tried to ground his theories in the scientific measurement of skulls, he let his preconceptions shape his collection and analysis of the data.

Later proponents of phrenology tried to use it to justify ethnic and class discrimination. Likewise, Herbert Spencer (1820–1903), a proponent of Social Darwinism, interpreted Darwin's theory of natural selection as a justification for social inequality. The studies of Francis Galton (1822–1911) on the heritability of intellectual giftedness led to the theory of eugenics, which promoted selective breeding of the social elite and discouraged childbearing within socially disadvantaged groups.

Not surprisingly, when psychological tests were first developed, they also fell prey to the confusion between scientific objectivity and social prejudice. The first intelligence tests were full of socially biased items that unfairly favored affluent, American-born English speakers over poor, uneducated immigrants and non-white minorities. While psychological science has developed more sophisticated methodology to minimize the effect of experimenter bias of any kind, it is important to realize that as long as science is conducted by human beings, it is subject to human error. The beauty of science, however, lies in its ability to correct its own mistakes through further research.

tal health field. Psychiatry came into its own as a distinct medical field in the early nineteenth century. Concerned with severe mental illness, early psychiatry had little overlap with early psychology, which focused more on normal mental processes. With the later development of clinical psychology, however, psychiatry and psychology became more intertwined.

The German psychiatrist Emil Kraepelin (1856–1926) first distinguished between manic depressive illness and dementia praecox, or what was later called schizophrenia. He saw manic depression as a milder form of illness with a more optimistic prognosis. In contrast, dementia praecox was seen as a progressively deteriorating illness with little hope of cure. Of course, there were no medicines available in the nineteenth century to effectively treat these conditions.

The Swiss psychiatrist Eugen Bleuler (1857–1939) was the director of the renowned Burghölzli psychiatric hospital. Bleuler coined the term *schizophrenia* from the Greek words for "split mind." He believed schizophrenia encompassed a group of diseases, which he subdivided into hebephrenic, catatonic, and paranoid subtypes. He also introduced the term *autism* to describe the schizophrenic's withdrawal from the outer world.

SIGMUND FREUD

Who was **Sigmund Freud**?

Sigmund Freud (1856–1939) was a Viennese neurologist who became one of the most influential figures of the twentieth century. As the inventor of psychoanalysis, he introduced concepts of the unconscious, the impact of childhood, repressed emotions, and even the entire field of psychotherapy to the wider world. While aspects of his theories remain controversial, much of his work has become such an integral part of our culture that it is taken for granted.

What are the **major tenets** of his **theory** of **psychoanalysis**?

Unlike the other pioneers of psychology, Freud was more interested in the abnormal than the normal. As a physician, he tended to the sick; thus, he developed his theories of the mind through investigations of psychopathology. Although it is difficult to neatly summarize his ideas because they changed and evolved over more than four decades of work, there are several key concepts. These include the dynamic unconscious, the instincts of libido and aggression (or Thanatos), and the importance of childhood conflicts on adult psychopathology and even personality.

What was **Freud's view** of the **unconscious**?

Unlike the early psychologists, who were almost entirely concerned with conscious thought, Freud was fascinated by the idea that our emotions, wishes, and thoughts could operate wholly outside of consciousness. Moreover, unacceptable wishes and impulses would be pushed back into the unconscious to protect the person from anxiety. However, these repressed desires would rarely sit calmly

Sigmund Freud, the father of psychoanalysis, was one of the most influential figures of the twentieth century (*Library of Congress*).

out of awareness, but rather come back to do mischief, generally in disguised form. These partially expressed impulses formed the symptoms that psychoanalysis was designed to cure.

What was **Freud's theory** of the **instincts**?

Freud believed in two primary drives or motivations in life: libido and aggression. Libido, defined as sexuality although more accurately thought of as broad sensual pleasure, was his primary focus. He added the death instinct, Thanatos, after living through the carnage of World War I. In later years, Thanatos was frequently interpreted as the aggressive drive. Freud asserted that an instinct functions like an electrical charge that needs to be expressed through behavior.

However, he felt society forbids the free expression of sexuality and aggression. Psychopathology, or what he termed *neurosis*, involves the conflict between our instinctual drives and our need to inhibit them. Because the instinct still presses for expression, much like water rushing downhill, it will be displaced into another channel of expression, resulting in a symptom, such as an obsession, compulsion, or a hysterical complaint (a physical symptom without any true physical cause). His fluid-like conception of the instincts was later referred to as the *hydraulic model*.

While this theory may appear odd from today's point of view, it is easy to see that he was attempting to fit his observations of his patients' behavior into the scientific models of his day.

Where does **childhood** come in with **Freud**?

Freud believed that the primary areas of instinctual gratification, the erogenous zones, moved across childhood in predictable stages. His theory of the psychosexual stages included the oral, anal, phallic, and genital stages. Each psychosexual stage had specific psychological characteristics to it. For example, the anal stage was characterized by stinginess, concern with money, and/or wish for control. If the child was either undergratified or overgratified in any stage, the child could fixate at that stage, becoming, in effect, psychologically stuck.

Neurotic symptoms would reflect the person's characteristic psychosexual stage. For example, obsessions and compulsions reflected regression to the anal stage. While Freud's instinctual theory has been much criticized, the notion that developmental problems at any point in childhood can hinder later development and result in adult psychopathology must be seen as one of Freud's greatest contributions.

What was **revolutionary** about **Freud**?

Freud was revolutionary for several reasons. For one, he brought to light the way unconscious passions can rule our lives–the battle between animalistic passions and

How did Sigmund Freud's theories make their way into a classic Alfred Hitchcock film?

Alfred Hitchcock's classic suspense film *Psycho*, which came out in 1960, provides an excellent example of how Sigmund Freud's theories have permeated popular culture. In the famous shower scene, Marion Crane (played by Janet Leigh) is stabbed to death by a knife wielding Norman Bates (played by Tony Perkins). At the end of the movie we learn that Bates's excessive attachment to his mother has lead him to murder her in a fit of jealous rage, following his discovery of her romantic involvement with another man. Attempting to keep his mother alive, however, he preserves her body in the basement. At the same time, he takes on her identity as his own alter ego. Finally, while dressed up as his dead mother, he murders Marion Crane to eliminate any possible rival for his attentions. Such unmistakably Oedipal themes are clearly indebted to Sigmund Freud and psychoanalytic theory.

the constraints of civilization. His particular emphasis on sexuality opened discussion on a formerly taboo subject. Secondly, he drew attention to the effect of childhood experiences and trauma on adult emotional adjustment. Thirdly, his invention of the method of psychoanalysis spearheaded the entire discipline of psychotherapy.

While psychoanalysis per se is no longer the preferred method of psychotherapy, many forms of psychotherapy can be seen as the direct descendants of Freud's couch. Finally, he brought the emotional and the irrational into the realm of science. While poets, artists and philosophers had addressed the concerns of psychoanalysis before, few people had considered these questions in scientific terms.

How **original** were **Freud's ideas**?

Freud did not operate in a vacuum. Many of his ideas came out of earlier philosophical works. For example, the German philosopher Arthur Schopenhauer (1788–1860) wrote about the primacy of unconscious sexual instincts as early as 1819. Moreover, Freud was not the first clinician to practice psychotherapy. By 1909, Freud's approach to psychotherapy was just one among many competing forms of psychotherapy. Contemporary psychotherapy in the early twentieth century was very crude, however, and still focused largely on hypnotism and suggestion. Ultimately it was psychoanalysis that had the widest impact on the later development of psychotherapy.

What was **controversial** about **Freud**?

Freud was famous (or infamous) for his fights with detractors and is still a somewhat controversial figure. From the beginning Freudian theory tended toward the dogmatic.

21

Although Freud was flexible in his own thinking, and he reworked his own theories multiple times, he was less tolerant of the divergent views of his followers. He rejected both Carl Jung and Alfred Adler, who questioned the primacy of libido as the motivating force.

In Freud's time, his theories were particularly controversial for their emphasis on sexuality, which was rarely discussed openly in Victorian times. His emphasis on child sexuality was thought frankly perverted. By the mid-twentieth century, however, Freudian theory was criticized mainly for its lack of scientific data. Although he aspired to make psychoanalysis a science, he never tested his theories with the methods of empirical research, preferring instead to rely on his clinical observations.

How has **Freudian theory influenced** contemporary **culture?**

Freud has had enormous influence on contemporary culture, so much so that we often barely notice. Any attention to the unconscious meaning of slips of the tongue, jokes, or dreams can be traced directly to Freud. Awareness of the impact of childhood experiences on adult emotional adjustment, the importance of sexuality, and the value of talking out our feelings, let alone the now international industry of psychotherapy, all owe their debt to Freud. Freudian ideas also captured the imagination of a wide range of famous artists and writers throughout the twentieth century, such as the surrealists, Virginia Woolf, and Alfred Hitchcock.

JOHN B. WATSON AND B. F. SKINNER

Who was **John B. Watson?**

John Watson (1878–1958) spearheaded the triumph of *behaviorism* in American psychology. Reacting against the emphasis on introspection promoted by both Wundt and James, he believed that the only object of psychological study should be *observable behavior*. He criticized the introspective approach as imprecise and dependent on unverifiable, and therefore unreliable, subjective judgments. Influenced by the Russian psychologist Ivan Pavlov's work on associative conditioning, he reduced all of psychology to stimulus-response chains.

Having also spent the beginning of his career studying rats in mazes, Watson further broke down the division between animal and human research, stating that stimulus-response behavioral chains in animals did not meaningfully differ from those in humans. In other words, the only worthwhile subject of study in psychology was how animals or people behaved in response to carefully observed stimuli. Moreover, he felt, the purpose of such study was the prediction and control of behavior.

This viewpoint was articulated in a 1913 publication entitled "Psychology as the Behaviorist Sees It." While behaviorism became less restrictive in later years, this celebration of observable behavior and disdain for subjective experience dominated American academic psychology until the middle of the twentieth century.

What was **unusual** about **Watson's personal life**?

Watson had an unusually dramatic and difficult life. Born into poverty with an alcoholic, womanizing, and violent father who abandoned the family when Watson was only twelve, Watson seemed more likely to enter a life of crime than to become a pioneer in the field of psychology. He was, in fact, arrested twice before he managed to convince the president of a South Carolina college to admit him as a freshman at the age of sixteen.

The brash confidence displayed by his appeal to the college president was characteristic of the ambition and audacity that would later propel his career. He excelled academically and quickly progressed from student to graduate student to assistantship to professor at the University of Chicago and then, by age thirty, to chairman of the psychology department at Johns Hopkins University. At age thirty-seven he was made president of the American Psychological Association.

Unfortunately, he remained a compulsive womanizer and during a particularly indiscreet extramarital affair, his wife found evidence of his dalliance and showed it to the president of the university, who promptly demanded his resignation. In 1920 such scandal could ruin one's reputation and it ended Watson's career as an academic psychologist. Ever resilient, however, he eventually obtained a position at the J. Walter Thompson advertising agency, applying his psychological expertise to advertising campaigns on a wealth of household products. He married the woman with whom he had been having an affair and had two children with her. Unfortunately, she died quite young, which was, by many accounts, a devastating loss for him.

We can speculate about the relationship between Watson's painful childhood and his choice of psychological theories. Is it entirely a coincidence that an emotionally troubled child would grow up to shun exploration of the mind? Nonetheless, whatever personal appeal behaviorism might have had for Watson, its dominance in American academic psychology cannot be attributed to the psychological conflicts of a single individual.

Who was **B.F. Skinner**?

Burrhus Frederick (B.F.) Skinner (1904–1990) was a famous champion of behaviorism. He wrote several books, including *Walden Two* and *About Behaviorism*, in which he spelled out his views on psychology, in particular the view that observable behavior was the only valid object of scientific study. Like John Watson before him, he had a flair for public relations and knew how to get his ideas into the public eye.

Skinner made numerous long-lasting contributions to behaviorism. He was interested both in the theory of behaviorism and its application to everyday problems. His

B.F. Skinner (1904–1990) was famous for his work in behaviorism.

two most important contributions include the principles of operant conditioning and the techniques of behavioral modification. He was also interested in educational methods and in techniques of animal training. Although Skinner's radical behaviorism has been out of fashion for several decades, many of his core ideas survive. While they cannot explain all of human psychology, they do offer important insights into a broad range of behavior. Moreover, the techniques he proposed are still fundamental tools in a dramatically broad range of disciplines.

What is Skinner's concept of **operant conditioning**?

Building on Edward Thorndike's earlier Law of Effect, Skinner elaborated the way animals and humans learn from rewards and punishments. If a behavior is followed by a reward, it is likely to be repeated. If it is followed by a punishment, it is less likely to be repeated. Through research on rats and other animals, Skinner explored in great detail how the timing, frequency, and predictability of rewards and punishments affect behavioral change. These basic concepts of operant conditioning were viewed as the foundation of all learned behavior in both humans and animals. While we now know that there are many complex forms of thought that operant conditioning cannot explain, these principles do tell us a tremendous amount about basic forms of learning and memory.

What was **Skinner's contribution** to **behavioral modification**?

Another critical contribution that Skinner made was to translate his laboratory research on rats and other animals into a new form of psychotherapy termed *behavioral modification*. Although John Watson had declared the purpose of behaviorism to be the prediction and control of behavior, he did not have much success in formulating specific techniques to be applied to everyday life.

In contrast to Watson, Skinner worked out rules about how to change human behavior through the manipulation of *reinforcement contingencies*, in other words, the manipulation of rewards and punishments. Skinner favored the use of rewards

Did Skinner raise his daughter in a Skinner box?

Skinner also developed a form of crib/playpen that he termed an "air crib" (also called a "baby-tender" or an "heir conditioner"). This was a large, well-lit and temperature-controlled chamber for a small child. He raised his second daughter Deborah in this chamber for the first few years of her life. Contrary to popular thought, this was not a classic Skinner box, where rats have to press levers to obtain food; it was more like a roomy bassinet. Although critics assumed his daughter had been damaged by a bizarrely technical approach to child rearing, Skinner always maintained that his daughter had not suffered and had, in fact, grown up to be a well-adjusted, college-educated artist.

over punishment to modify behavior, as he felt a reliance on punishment created more problems than it solved. He initially developed his behavior modification techniques for use with psychotic psychiatric patients, but variations of his techniques have been applied to work with juvenile delinquents and emotionally disturbed children. Similar techniques have been adapted for use with animal training, child rearing, and many other disciplines.

What is the **Skinner box**?

Another innovation created by B.F. Skinner is called the *Skinner box*. This was an adaptation of Thorndike's puzzle box, used by scientists to observe how an animal learns to escape the box. Skinner's innovation was to connect the animal's behavior (e.g., a rat pressing a bar) to a counting mechanism so that the number of times the behavior was performed would be automatically recorded. This way the frequency of the behavior could be compared across different reinforcement conditions. For example the number of times a rat presses a bar when each bar press is rewarded with a food pellet can be compared with the frequency of bar pressing when the rat is not rewarded with food pellets.

What were **Skinner's contributions** to **educational practices**?

Skinner was also interested in applying operant conditioning principles to education. He introduced the concept of *programmed learning*, in which the material to be taught is presented in a sequence of small steps. Thus learning progresses step by step, with positive reinforcement given after each step is mastered. Although this approach has been criticized for its restricted focus on parts rather than the whole and for failing to foster creative thinking, it still serves as the basis for most forms of computerized training.

JEAN PIAGET

Who was **Jean Piaget**?

Jean Piaget (1896–1980) was a Swiss psychologist who pioneered the study of cognitive development. Ironically, Piaget never received formal training in psychology. In fact, he received his doctorate in the natural sciences. Along with Freud and B.F. Skinner, however, Piaget is one of the most influential figures in all of psychology. Piaget showed a talent for scientific research from a very early age. He published his first scientific paper on the albino sparrow at age ten, although the publisher had no idea of his extraordinary youth. For four years in his early teens, he classified mollusks in the Neuchâtel Natural History Museum in Switzerland. He published several more scholarly papers from ages fifteen to eighteen. Around the same time, Piaget visited his godfather, Samuel Cornut, who felt that Piaget's education was weighted toward the natural sciences. Cornut introduced him to philosophy, sparking Piaget's interest in epistemology, the philosophical study of knowledge. Questions such as "What is knowledge?" and "Where does knowledge come from?" would form the foundation of his later work.

Jean Piaget (1896–1980) made fundamental contributions to our understanding of children's intellectual development (*AP/WideWorld*).

How was **Piaget influenced** by working with **intelligence tests**?

Early in his career, Piaget went to work for Theodore Simon in Paris. Simon, along with Alfred Binet, was the author of the Binet-Simon intelligence test, the first successful test of its kind. Piaget's job was to record the answers of five- to eight-year-old children in order to determine expected scores for each age group. Although he was hired to record the correct answers, he became far more interested in the children's mistakes, in the typical patterns of error at each age. This sparked his interest in the development of children's intellectual understanding of the world around them. He had found his life's work. For the next sixty years, Piaget studied children's behavior in great detail. From this data, he generated a voluminous body of writings on the subject and changed the way we look at intellectual development.

What did **Piaget discover**?

Piaget's greatest contribution was to change psychologists' focus from what we know to how we know. He studied how the mind organizes and transforms information—how it shapes information. The mind is not a blank screen; it is not a camera or a mirror that simply reflects what it sees. It is an active participant in knowledge. The mind takes in information and actively organizes it. As such, it *constructs* a view of reality through this shaping and transforming of information. This concept is referred to as Piaget's *constructivist* view of knowledge. Moreover, the way that the mind organizes information changes across child development. So younger children do not simply know less than older children or adults; they know *differently*.

Why is **Piaget's** work **important**?

Freud told us about desire, the behaviorists told us about behavior, and Piaget told us about the way we think and how that develops across childhood. Perhaps more than anyone else, he has told us about how we make sense of our environment, the processes by which we interpret it. His work has been profoundly influential to many branches of psychology: developmental, cognitive, educational, and even clinical.

What did **Piaget** think about the **nature/nurture** debate?

There is an age-old debate, dating back to the earliest Greek philosophers, of whether knowledge is innate—that is we are born with it—or whether it is learned through experience. Piaget's solution to this ancient dilemma was to propose that knowledge is *both* innate *and* learned. *What* we know is learned and *how* we know is based on innate capacities.

How do **children learn** by **action**?

Although other forms of information may be important, Piaget believed the initial and fundamental way that children learn about the world is through action. Through action, children explore and encounter their environment. The memories of these encounters are encoded in their minds as knowledge. These memories then shape their interpretation of later experiences, which in turn modifies their knowledge about the world. For example a child is given a rattle. By chance the child shakes it and it makes noise. Interested, the child shakes it again. Later, another rattle is produced, which the child immediately shakes, now having a rudimentary concept of rattles as something to shake.

What is a **schema**?

A *schema* is a representation or a map of a pattern of events. It is essentially the building block of knowledge. Infants' initial knowledge of the world is through action

27

What is object permanence?

Jean Piaget's notion of object permanence refers to the ability to hold an image of an object in the mind even when it is not concretely present. Piaget developed this concept while studying the behavior of his own children. He noticed that before the age of eight or nine months, if he removed an object of interest from his child (e.g., a rattle), the child would not search for it. Once it was out of sight, it was out of mind. After the development of object permanence, however, the child displayed searching behavior. For example, if Piaget removed the toy from the child and hid it behind a pillow, the child would move the pillow to find the object. This searching behavior shows that the child can think about the object even when it is not present.

schemas or *sensory-motor schemas*. This means the child can only know the world through immediate sensation or direct action, such as bringing the thumb into the mouth or seeing bicycle wheels go round and round. Around nine months of age, these action schemas begin to exist in the mind alone. In other words, the child can think about the event when it is not actually occurring. The *mental* life of the child has begun. A mental representation of an event is called a *conceptual schema*. One sign of this is called *object permanence*, which occurs around nine months of age when an infant will look for an object after it is hidden from view, such as searching for a rattle after it is hidden behind a pillow.

What are **assimilation** and **accommodation**?

Assimilation and accommodation are the two ways that children gain new knowledge. In assimilation, the new is fitted into the old; in accommodation, the old is adapted to the new. This is the way that schemas develop. Accomodation means that a schema will become modified by new information. For example, an infant is handed a rattle that is shaped differently than any previously encountered rattles. Because of the different shape, the infant has to grasp it in a different way. Thus the schema of grasping the rattle has just *accommodated* to the new action.

Assimilation is the complement of accommodation and refers to the way new information is adapted to previously existing schemas. For example, when presented with the new rattle, the infant tries to grasp it and shake it. This reflects an attempt to *assimilate* the new action with the pre-existing rattle schema. Throughout development, both processes occur simultaneously.

How have **Piaget**'s theories been **criticized**?

Piaget has been criticized for relying almost exclusively on the intellectual content of knowledge. Piaget paid little attention to the impact of culture, emotion, observational learning, and verbal instruction on cognitive development. Indeed, later research has shown that children's (and adults') knowledge of the world is greatly impacted by all of the above factors. Nonetheless, this does not invalidate Piaget's contributions; it simply shows that his work is limited in scope. He cannot explain all of children's mental life, but he did tell us a tremendous amount about early cognitive development.

What **role** did **Piaget's children** have in the development of his theories?

Much of the fundamental ideas of Piaget's work were based on his intense, methodical observations of his own three children, Jacqueline, Laurent, and Lucienne. Their mother was a trained psychologist herself and helped in these studies. In fact, she had been one of Piaget's students. Although we can question what emotional impact this intense attention may have had on these children, Piaget's investigations were never invasive or even particularly experimental. Relying on a naturalistic approach, for the most part he observed their natural behavior, questioned them about their understanding of natural events, or minimally modified their environment, for example by manipulating toys.

MAJOR MOVEMENTS IN PSYCHOLOGY

What are the **major theories** in psychology?

Across its fairly short history, psychology has had several major theoretical movements. Perhaps the most important are Behaviorism, Gestalt Theory, Psychoanalytic and Psychodynamic Theory, Humanistic Theories, Attachment Theory, Sociobiology, Neurobiological Theories, and Cognitive Science. Some of these movements were natural outgrowths of earlier ones. Others were reactions against earlier approaches. Most contemporary psychologists do not limit themselves to any one theoretical view. Nonetheless, these movements have shaped psychology's history and continue to influence contemporary psychologists' orientation to research and practice. Thus, it is important to understand the major movements in the history of psychology to truly appreciate modern findings.

BEHAVIORISM

What is **behaviorism**?

Behaviorism is the school of psychology that considers observable behavior to be the only worthwhile object of study. Behaviorists believe mental phenomena are impossible to measure objectively and thus impossible to prove. They therefore focus on the processes underlying behavioral change, specifically classical (or *associative* or *Pavlovian*) conditioning and operant conditioning. These basic learning principles operate in humans and animals alike, or at least in mammals and birds.

Major figures of behaviorism included John B. Watson (1878–1958), Edward Thorndike (1874–1947), and B.F. Skinner (1904–1990). Although Freudian psychoanalysis, educational psychology, and other mental schools of psychology continued in tandem, behaviorism was the dominant force in American psychology until well into the middle of the twentieth century.

What was Thorndike's **Law of Effect**?

Edward Thorndike (1874–1947) was originally a student of Henry James, although his research veered far from James's fascination with consciousness. As a side note, he was also the author of the Thorndike dictionary. Thorndike turned to the study of chickens while still a graduate student and then expanded his research to observations of cats and dogs. By placing an animal in a puzzle box, or an enclosure with only one means of escape, he could study how the animal learned to escape the box. He observed that animals initially stumble on the escape route (e.g., stepping on a peddle or biting a string) through trial and error. With repeated trials, however, animals take less time to find their way out.

Based on this research, Thorndike formulated two laws of learning. *The Law of Effect* states that the *effect* of an action will determine the likelihood that it will be repeated. In other words, if the response generates a satisfying effect (the cat pulls the string and the door opens), the cat is more likely to pull the string again. If the action generates a negative impact, the animal is less likely to repeat the action.

This concept forms the bedrock of B.F. Skinner's later theory of operant conditioning. Thorndike's *Law of Exercise* likewise contributed to theories of associative conditioning. Here he stated that the strength of an association between a response and a stimulus will depend on the number of times they have been paired and the strength of their pairing. Thorndike thus took the *associationism* of philosophers such as Thomas Hobbes and placed it into a scientific paradigm.

What is the **black box theory** of the mind?

In this view, the mind is no more than an opaque black box inserted between stimulus and response. As no one can see inside of it, it is not worthy of study. This extreme *antimentalism* of the behaviorists has been frequently criticized and was finally put to rest by the cognitive revolution in the 1960s. While the behaviorists made invaluable contributions to psychology regarding the fundamental principles of behavioral change, their devaluing and dismissal of subjective experience was extremely limiting.

How do **behaviorists understand learning**?

Behaviorism is best described as a theory of learning and, in fact, is often referred to as *learning theory*. However, the mental process of learning had to be translated into behavioral terms. Thus learning occurs when a new behavior is repeatedly and consistently performed in response to a given stimulus.

What famous experiment did Ivan Pavlov perform using dogs?

Ivan Pavlov (1849–1936) was a Russian scientist who was originally interested in the digestive processes of animals. When trying to study how dogs digest food, he noticed the animals' tendency to salivate at the sound or sight of their keeper shortly before feeding time. In other words, they salivated in the absence of actual food. Initially, this phenomenon was a nuisance, interfering with his study of digestion, but later it became the focus of his research. Pavlov's studies provided the basis of the theory of classical conditioning, also known as associative or "Pavlovian" conditioning.

Pavlov developed his famous theory of classical conditioning after watching dogs salivate right before mealtime at the mere sight or sound of their keeper (*iStock*).

Where does **emotion** fit in?

Although strict behaviorists avoided all emotional terms, learning theory fully depends on emotion. In Thorndike's Law of Effect and the theory of operant conditioning that followed, the likelihood that a behavior will be increased or decreased depends on its emotional impact. Behavior is increased when it elicits positive emotion (reward) and reduced when it elicits negative emotion (punishment). While it is more difficult to speak of emotions in animals, modern scientists assume that the simple emotional processes involved in learning theory—that is, forms of pleasure and pain—apply to both animals and humans.

What is **associative** or **classical conditioning**?

Associative conditioning, also called classical or Pavlovian conditioning, refers to a form of learning in which a person or animal is *conditioned* to respond in a particular way to a specific stimulus. If a neutral stimulus is paired with an emotionally meaningful one, than the neutral stimulus will become *associated* with the second stimulus and elicit the same response. For example, if a child learns to associate a particular perfume with a beloved grandmother, the child will develop a positive response to the perfume. In contrast, if the child learns to associate going to the doctor with getting a painful shot, then the child will learn to fear the doctor. This basic concept is used in child rearing, advertising, political campaigns, the treatment of addictions, and much of animal training.

What is the **difference** between the **conditioned** and the **unconditioned stimulus**?

The unconditioned stimulus is the stimulus that elicits a natural and unlearned response. For example, the child does not have to learn to feel pain from the shot. A dog does not have to learn to feel pleasure when fed. The conditioned stimulus is a formerly neutral stimulus that now elicits a response through its pairing with the conditioned stimulus. The perfume that the child associates with his grandmother is a conditioned stimulus. The doctor that the child associates with the shot is also a conditioned stimulus.

What is the **difference** between the **conditioned** and the **unconditioned response**?

The *unconditioned* response is the innate, unlearned response, for example loving the grandmother or feeling pain at the shot. The *conditioned* response is the learned response, for example loving the grandmother's perfume or fearing the doctor.

How is **classical conditioning relevant** to **everyday life**?

Classical conditioning pervades everyday life. When we develop food aversions (e.g., a hatred of fish), phobias (a fear of dogs), positive associations (an association of Paris with a romantic vacation) our behavior reflects classical conditioning. It is therefore no accident that so many advertising campaigns hire young, beautiful, and skimpily clad models. The advertisers want consumers to associate their product—be it a washing machine, paper clip, or automobile—with youth, beauty, and sex.

How is **classical conditioning relevant** to **animal behavior**?

As (non-human) animals lack higher cognitive abilities, such as complex reasoning, symbolic thought, or language, associative conditioning is a primary way that animals learn. Does your cat love to sit on the couch and purr? Does she associate the couch with affection and attention? Does your dog start to bark and wag his tail when you put on your shoes? Does he associate your shoes with his walk?

What is **operant conditioning**?

In operant conditioning, pioneered by B.F. Skinner (1904–1990), behavior is influenced less by the stimulus with which it is associated than by the effect of that behavior. Operant conditioning builds on Thorndike's Law of Effect. If the effect of the behavior is

> ## Who is Little Albert?
>
> **S**tarting in 1920, John Watson conducted a series of experiments on a baby named Albert B. to investigate classical conditioning in human beings. While these experiments successfully support the principles of conditioned learning, Watson was chillingly insensitive to the emotional impact of his research methods on the baby.
>
> When Albert was about nine months old he was exposed to a series of white fuzzy items, including a white rat, rabbit, dog, monkey, and masks with and without white cotton hair. The presence of the rat was then paired with a loud noise created by banging a hammer against a steel pipe. This was repeated several times until little Albert grew terrified at the mere sight of the rat. Later experiments showed that Albert's fearful reactions had generalized to other fuzzy white items, including a rabbit, dog, and Santa Claus mask. This generalized fear was still present several months after the original experiment.
>
> Today human subjects review committees are required in all research institutions in order to protect the rights of research subjects.

positive, then it is reinforced, and the behavior is more likely to recur. If the effect of the behavior is negative, then it is punished and therefore less likely to be repeated.

What are **reinforcers**?

Reinforcers are *consequences* of a behavior that increase the likelihood that the behavior will be repeated. For example, if a child is given an ice cream cone as consolation after throwing a temper tantrum, the temper tantrum has been *reinforced*. Reinforcers can be either positive or negative.

What is the **difference** between **positive** and **negative reinforcement**

Positive reinforcement is also called *reward*, and refers to the positive consequence of a behavior, which increases its likelihood of recurring. For example, employees are paid to do their job and performers who perform well are applauded. Negative reinforcement, to be distinguished from punishment, involves the *removal* of a negative condition as a consequence of the targeted behavior. If you lose weight by dieting, that is negative reinforcement.

In the 1980s, a man with a saxophone and a small kitten on his shoulder frequented the New York City subways. He would play a harsh note on the saxophone as loudly as possible and offer to stop only if the passengers gave him money. This man was utilizing

One example of positive reinforcement is a mouse receiving cheese for successfully navigating a maze (iStock).

the principles of negative reinforcement (though it might also be called blackmail).

How **effective** is **punishment**?

Punishment involves the introduction of a *negative consequence* to a behavior with the intent of diminishing the frequency of the behavior. When a child is grounded for getting into a fight, this is punishment. The parents are trying to diminish the targeted behavior. Likewise, the criminal justice system relies on punishment to maintain an orderly and lawful society. Punishment can be extremely effective but it also has drawbacks. Although the early behaviorists avoided mental considerations, it is now clear that punishment, if done too frequently, creates anger, fear, and resentment and can breed an oppositional mindset, in which people try to cheat the system instead of willingly following the rules. B.F. Skinner distrusted punishment as well, stating that it had only short term effects and it did not teach alternative behavior.

How is **operant conditioning relevant** to **everyday life**?

Operant conditioning is in evidence in almost every aspect of daily life. When we are paid for our work, evaluated for a merit raise by our managers, thanked by a friend for being considerate, penalized for paying taxes late, or even given a parking ticket, operant conditioning is in play.

How is **operant conditioning** relevant to **animal life**?

Most of animal training involves operant conditioning. When we spray our cat with a squirt gun after he jumps on the kitchen counter or give our dog a treat after he rolls over, we are using operant conditioning. Even pigeons can be shaped to do a particular behavior, such as peck at a lever, by successively rewarding behavior that more closely approximates the desired behavior.

What is **extinction**?

When the association starts to erode between the stimulus and the response (in classical conditioning) or between the behavior and the reinforcement (in operant conditioning), a behavior becomes *extinguished*. A behavior is extinguished when it is no

> ## How is classical conditioning related to drug addiction?
>
> Classical conditioning is central to the process of drug addiction. Addiction treatment often focuses on the management of craving. Craving, or the urge to use the problem drug, can be very strong and frequently leads to relapses in people striving for sobriety. Craving is triggered by cues, both external and internal, via the process of classical conditioning. In other words, the person encounters a *reminder* of drug use (such as drug paraphernalia or the bar where the person used to drink) and the association stimulates craving. This is basically the same conditioning process Pavlov noticed with his dogs. External cues include environmental factors (people, places, and things). Internal cues include emotions, thought, or physical sensations that previously led to drug use.

longer performed. This can be a positive thing if the behavior was undesirable to begin with. It can also be negative if the behavior was valued. In general, the behavior should eventually extinguish if it is no longer accompanied by either the prior reinforcement or the unconditioned stimulus. If you stop paying people to go to work, they will probably stop going. If you stopped taking your dog for a walk after you put on your shoes, the dog will eventually stop barking and wagging his tail each time you put them on. The association between sneakers and walk will be extinguished.

How do **reinforcement conditions** affect **learning**?

Although the principles of conditioning are very simple, they are less simple in practice. A number of factors affect the effectiveness of conditioning. *Timing* is important, specifically the time separating the unconditioned and conditioned stimulus. If the sneakers go on too soon before the dog is walked, it will be hard to associate the shoes with the walk.

Relatedly, the reinforcement should closely follow the behavior for the act to be connected with the consequence. This is why news of global warming has had so little effect until recently, although we've known about it for decades. The consequences were not immediate. This is also why it is so difficult to instill healthy habits in the young, when the consequences of their self care will not be evident for decades. The *schedule* of reinforcement also affects learning. Should the behavior be reinforced every time it occurs? What kind of reinforcement makes a behavior most resistant to extinction?

Why is **intermittent reinforcement** more **resistant** to **extinction**?

Intermittent reinforcement, in which the behavior is only reinforced intermittently, best protects a behavior from extinction. If people do not expect the behavior to be

How is intermittent reinforcement used in gambling?

In gambling, the behavior of betting is rewarded *intermittently* and *unpredictably*. When the gambler's bet is not rewarded, the gambler continues to bet, expecting that another win will follow sooner or later. If the gambler had been rewarded for every bet, it would take fewer losses for the gambler to disassociate betting with winning and for the act of gambling to be extinguished. Thus casinos take advantage of an intermittent and unpredictable reinforcement schedule in order to keep gamblers gambling as long as possible.

reinforced every time it occurs, they will be less likely to stop the behavior when it is not reinforced. It will take longer for them to give up on the behavior. Further, when intermittent reinforcement is *unpredictable*, it is even more resistant to extinction.

What **problems** with **behaviorism** started to show up even among the faithful?

As the reign of behaviorism continued, the limits of the paradigm became more evident. Animals kept behaving in ways that could not be explained by behaviorist theory alone. For example, Skinner had thought that any animal could be taught any behavior with the appropriate reinforcement schedule. But this did not turn out to be the case. The same behavior was learned easily by some animals, with difficulty by others, and not at all by still others. Rats could easily learn to press a bar for food, while cats would do so only with difficulty. These findings suggest that the genetics of each animal species set the parameters of what could and could not be learned. There were limits to what could be taught.

How did **Tolman's contributions** mark the beginning of the **end** of the **behaviorist era**?

Edward Chase Tolman (1886–1959) was a devoted behaviorist who studied maze-running behavior in rats (a favorite topic of behaviorist researchers). Despite his expectations, he repeatedly observed behavior in rats that he could not explain solely by stimulus-response connections. He noticed that rats in a maze would often stop, look around, and check out one path, then another before choosing a particular route. He could only explain this behavior (and many other similar behaviors he observed) by inferring some kind of mental process. The rat seemed to have a mental picture of the layout of the maze and that directed its behavior. In this way, Tolman introduced the mind into the behaviorist stronghold. Even rats running mazes evidenced mental processes, some form of thinking about the problem.

How were **mental processes** evident even in **rats** running **mazes**?

Tolman introduced the notions of expectancy, of mental maps, into behaviorism. Rats and other animals did not simply respond to the number of rewards for each behavior, automatically repeating the most frequently rewarded behavior. Some kind of thought process mediated between stimulus and response. More specifically, the rats appeared to develop a set of expectations about how events would play out based on their prior experiences. They then made decisions by matching their expectations against information from the new situation. This kind of mental map is essentially identical to Piaget's concept of mental schemas and has become a critical concept in many areas of psychology, including cognitive, developmental, and clinical psychology.

What was the **Cognitive Revolution**?

In the 1950s and 1960s several lines of development converged to create the explosive shift in academic psychology known as the *cognitive revolution*. Research in various other fields of study, such as anthropology, linguistics, and computer science, had been moving toward the scientific study of mental processes. Within psychology, studies of memory, perception, personality traits, and other mental phenomena continued to gain ground.

Even orthodox behaviorists were stumbling onto mental processes. As these lines of development came together, the mind once again became a worthy object of study. The black box model of psychology was rejected and cognition, or thought processes per se, became the object of intense interest. Major contributors included Ulric Neisser, Howard Kendler, and George and Jean Mandler. With the renewed interested in cognitive processes, there was also a resurgence of an earlier movement that had started in Europe but migrated to the United States after World War II, namely Gestalt psychology.

GESTALT PSYCHOLOGY

What is the **basic concept** of **Gestalt psychology**?

Gestalt psychology, which started in the early twentieth century, provided an important counterpoint to the academic psychology of its time, specifically Watson's behaviorism and Wundt's structuralism. Its full impact, however, would not be felt until many decades after its birth. Gestalt psychology originated in 1910 with Max Wertheimer's study of the perception of motion.

The core idea behind Gestalt psychology is that the mind actively organizes information into a coherent whole or a gestalt. In other words, the mind is not a passive recipient of sensory stimuli but an active organizer of information. Furthermore, knowledge does not come from a collection of isolated bits of information. Rather the

39

mind creates a *whole* out of the *relationships* between separate parts. Gestalt psychology is a *holistic* theory.

What is a **gestalt**?

A gestalt refers to a perceptual whole. The gestalt is created out of the *relationships* between the parts. Our perceptual knowledge of the world is based on our recognition of these relationships. For example, let us consider what we recognize as a table. Although a table can be large or small, metal or wood, dark or light, we recognize an object as a table if it has a flat, horizontal plane with one or more supports underneath it. Its gestalt is determined by the relationship among its parts.

How do **Gestalt** ideas **pertain** to **perception**?

Gestalt psychology countered the assumption that perception is based solely on the stimulation hitting our sensory organs. As the sensory stimulation coming in differs depending upon the circumstance, we would not be able to recognize an object or person as the same across different situations if our mind did not actively organize our perceptions to recognize the *gestalt*. For example, we recognize our neighbor as the same person even if he loses weight, changes his clothes, or cuts his hair. Clearly the sensory information differs in each circumstance yet somehow we still recognize our neighbor as one person.

Who were the **pioneers** of **Gestalt theory**?

Max Wertheimer (1880–1943) is recognized as the father of Gestalt theory. His interest was first piqued when he noticed the illusion of motion while sitting on a train. Although the landscape outside the train was stationary, it seemed to be moving backwards as the train sped by. Most of us have had the same experience. To Wertheimer, however, this phenomenon offered a unique window into the workings of the mind. When he began his investigations at the University of Frankfurt in 1910, two slightly younger psychologists, Wolfgang Köhler (1887–1967), and Kurt Koffka (1886–1941) came to work with him. Together they studied the illusion of movement through various experiments. Their research into the *phi effect*, as Wertheimer named it, was the beginning of a life-long, shared commitment to Gestalt research and theory. By the mid-1930s, all three men had relocated to the United States, Koffka before Hitler's rise to power, and Wertheimer and Köhler in direct response to it.

Why is **Gestalt theory important**?

Arguably, Gestalt theory is important more for its profound philosophical implications than for the specifics of its research findings. For one thing, by demonstrating its principles with solid empirical research, Gestalt theory put the *mind* back into academic psychology. Secondly, gestalt theory introduced a *holistic* paradigm, which was in

What does Gestalt theory tell us about optical illusions?

The Gestalt theorists were fond of optical illusions as they illustrated how the mind actively organizes perceptual information. The fact that we can see something that is not really there shows that our perceptions are more than an exact copy of reality. In the photo to the right, a field of rounded dots can seen as either convex (rows of buttons) or as concave (rows of holes). Notice that you can perceive either buttons or holes but you cannot perceive both at the same time. In order for your perception to switch, you have to look at something other than the dots, such as the flat area between the dots.

A field of dots can appear to be either convex or concave, depending on one's perception of them (*iStock*).

sharp contrast to the associationist approach found in both behaviorism and Wilhelm Wundt's structuralism. In associationism, complex knowledge is seen to derive entirely from *associations* between simple memories. Gestalt theorists rejected this view as overly simplistic as they believed that complex knowledge also develops holistically, through recognition of patterns and identification of the whole.

How did the **holistic view** of Gestalt theory go **against** the **scientific worldview** of the time?

In the late nineteenth century and early twentieth century, when psychology was coming into its own as a science, there was tremendous admiration for the accomplishments of physical science. This was a time of extraordinary technological changes. The telephone, the motor car, the moving picture—all of these were relatively recent inventions and all of them radically changed society. Science was exploding across the industrialized world and there was a widely shared assumption that the only worthwhile way to understand reality was through the methods used in the physical sciences. And these methods largely reflected an analytic approach to reason.

In other words, the way to understand complex phenomena (such as human psychology) was to break it down into its smallest parts (such as stimulus-response associations). Complexity in and of itself had no interest; it simply reflected a grouping of smaller parts. The whole could be *reduced* to the sum of its parts. Gestalt theorists challenged this reductionist assumption. They were interested in *synthetic* reasoning. How do you put the parts back together again? How do you make a whole out of the relationships between parts? Their core position was that "the whole is greater than the sum of its parts."

How did **William James's functionionalism** anticipate Gestalt theory?

Gestalt theory had much in common with James's interest in the holistic flow of consciousness. Like Wertheimer and his colleagues, James did not believe we can understand reality simply by breaking it down into its elemental parts. In order to understand the whole of reality, we must look at it as a whole. Gestalt theorists felt that James did not go far enough, however, in his rejection of reductionistic assumptions. But this may not be fair to James, who after all died in 1910, the same year that Wertheimer first became fascinated with the perception of movement.

What **other principles** of **perception** come from **Gestalt theory**?

Gestalt psychology proposes a series of rules by which the mind organizes perceptual information. These include the rules of proximity, similarity, simplicity, and closure. The first two rules suggest that objects that are placed closely together (proximity) or are similar to each other (similarity) will be grouped together into a gestalt. The mind will combine them into a whole. Closure reflects the tendency to fill in the gaps of a gestalt. If we see a circle with sections missing, we will still see it as a circle. Further, the mind will group parts into a whole according to the simplest solution.

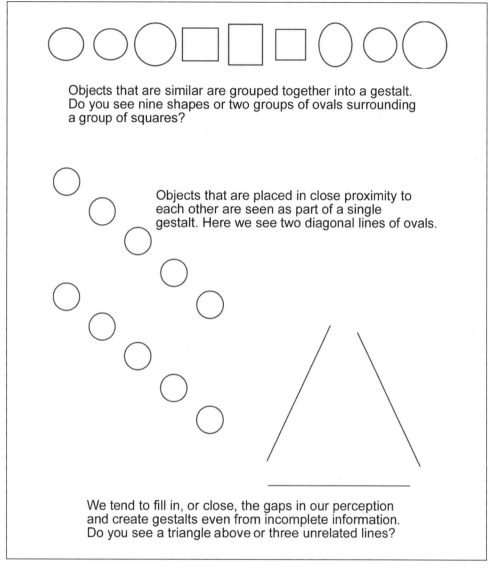

Objects that are similar are grouped together into a gestalt. Do you see nine shapes or two groups of ovals surrounding a group of squares?

Objects that are placed in close proximity to each other are seen as part of a single gestalt. Here we see two diagonal lines of ovals.

We tend to fill in, or close, the gaps in our perception and create gestalts even from incomplete information. Do you see a triangle above or three unrelated lines?

This graphic explaining Gestalt principles also uses Gestalt principles. Notice how you associate each picture with the text near it. This is an example of proximity.

What were **Wolfgang Köhler's** studies on **insight learning**?

Wolfgang Köhler (1887–1967) was one of Wertheimer's closest associates. From 1913 to 1920, Köhler was director of the Anthropoid Research Station on the island of Tenerife, which is in the Canary Islands off the coast of Northwest Africa. He had intended to stay in Tenerife for only a short while. With the outbreak of World War I, however, he was unable to leave for several years. While in Tenerife, Köhler conducted

43

an important series of studies on chimpanzees' problem-solving behavior. He set up rooms where bunches of bananas were placed just out of the chimpanzees' reach and then watched how they solved the problem of reaching the bananas.

Although not all chimpanzees were able to successfully solve the problem—evidently chimpanzees, like human beings, vary in their intelligence—those that did so exhibited similar behavior. For one, they would often try to reach the bananas simply by jumping or reaching for them. Upon failing to grasp the bananas, they would often show frustration, screaming, or kicking the walls of the room. Eventually, after surveying the entire room, they would suddenly derive a solution involving the use of nearby objects as tools. One chimp might drag a box under the bananas and then climb on top of it to reach them. Some chimps stacked multiple boxes to attain their goal. Another might put two sticks together to create a stick long enough to reach the food.

What did these **studies show**?

These studies showed two things. For one, the animals arrived at their solutions only after surveying the entire environment. They did not just focus on a single object but took the entire *field* into account. Secondly, the problem was not solved through trial and error via rewards and punishments as the behaviorists would have predicted. Instead the animal arrived at a complete solution all at once. In other words, the chimps did not solve problems in a piecemeal fashion, but rather in a holistic way. Köhler referred to this holistic form of problem solving as *insight learning*.

How did **Wolfgang Köhler** study **insight** learning using **apes**?

Wolfgang Köhler (1887–1967) conducted a famous series of studies on chimpanzees' methods of problem solving. He placed a bunch of bananas just out of the animals' reach and then watched how they figured out how to get to the bananas. At first frustrated, the chimps eventually reached an insight about how to use available objects as tools. This insight often came suddenly in a sort of A-Ha! moment. In one case, a chimpanzee put two sticks together to create a tool long enough to reach the bananas. Another chimp stacked three boxes on top of each other to reach the fruit hanging from the ceiling. Besides showing us the remarkable ingenuity of these animals, this work supported the Gestalt notion that the mind actively creates complete solutions to problems. This is in contrast to the behaviorist assumption that problem solving can only proceed piecemeal by trial and error.

What is the **difference** between **Gestalt psychology** and **Gestalt psychotherapy**?

Gestalt therapy, a school of psychotherapy founded by Fritz Perls in the 1940s, is completely distinct from *Gestalt psychology*, the body of research and theory derived from Max Wertheimer's experiments with perception. Gestalt therapy is commonly considered part of humanistic psychology and incorporates principles from the philosophical schools of phenomenology and existentialism as well as psychoanalysis and Gestalt psychology.

PSYCHOANALYTIC THEORY

What is **psychoanalytic theory**?

While behaviorism dominated American academic psychology throughout the first half of the twentieth century, psychoanalysis dominated clinical psychology—the study of *abnormal* psychology—during the same period both in Europe and the United States. Psychoanalysis was so prominent because it provided a comprehensive theory of psychopathology and a psychological method of treating mental distress. It is fair to say that most, if not all, subsequent theories of psychopathology and psychotherapy owe an enormous debt to psychoanalysis.

Although many schools of psychotherapy were formed in *reaction against* psychoanalysis, they were still defined in *response to* it and therefore must be seen as its descendants. Psychoanalytic theory actually includes a broad range of theoretical writing, starting with Sigmund Freud's original contributions in the late nineteenth century. Since Freud, psychoanalysis has broken into numerous schools including ego psychology, interpersonal psychoanalysis and the object relations school, all of which developed in the mid-twentieth century. More recent schools include self psychology and relational theory.

Did **Freud change his theory** over time?

Freud changed his theories several times over the course of his long career. He initially proposed the seduction theory to explain hysteria, a common disorder of the late nineteenth century involving physical complaints without an actual physical basis.

45

The seduction theory posited that hysteria resulted from early sexual experience, what we would now call childhood sexual abuse. This explanation was abandoned in the late 1890s, however, and Freud focused instead on unconscious sexual fantasy. In other words, the symptoms were caused by the patient's disguised wishes rather than memories of real events. Freud also moved from a *topological* theory, focusing on the relationship between conscious and unconscious processes to a *structural* model, focused on the id, ego, and superego. Finally, in the 1920s Freud added the instinctual force of Thanatos, the death instinct, to his theory of instincts.

What is Freud's **topological model**?

In Freud's topological model, the mind is divided into three sections, the *unconscious*, the *pre-conscious* and the *conscious*. In the unconscious, the individual is not aware of the contents of the mind. Here forbidden and dangerous wishes reside, safely out of awareness. In the pre-conscious, mental content is capable of entering into consciousness but is not currently there. There is no block between conscious and pre-conscious as there is between the conscious and the unconscious. The conscious part of the mind contains all the mental content that is in our awareness. It is very small compared to the unconscious.

What is the **structural model**?

The structural model overshadowed the topological model's focus on the conscious/unconscious division of the mind. While Freud still believed in unconscious processes, he became more and more interested in the compartmentalization of the mind into the *id, ego,* and *superego*. The id, translated literally as "the it", contains the animalistic passions that must be subdued in order for civilization to function. The id works on the pleasure principle, where wish equals reality and desire is not subject to restraint. The ego, Latin for "the I," mediates between the id and reality. The ego operates on the reality principle and recognizes that the world does not always obey our desires. The superego is the source of our morality. It is formed through our internalization of our parents' rules and discipline. A strict superego results in inhibited, moralistic behavior. A weak superego results in self-indulgent, poorly disciplined, or immoral behavior.

What is **Freud's theory of libido**?

Throughout his career Freud maintained a theory of libido as the primary motivating force behind all human behavior. In fact, he parted ways with some of his favorite protégées after they proposed competing theories about human motivation. Libido can be loosely translated as the sexual instinct, but really refers to all aspects of sensual pleasure. In Freud's view, instincts press for release as part of the pleasure principle. Pleasure is only attained when tension is reduced through release of instinctual energy. If the instinct is blocked from release, it will seek another outlet, much like a river run-

Sigmund Freud's office in London, where he immigrated in 1939. Patients lay down on his famous couch while Freud sat behind them in his chair. *(photo by Lisa J. Cohen)*.

ning downstream. This mechanistic view of human motivation was called the hydraulic model and reflects the scientific models of the day.

What did **Freud** say about Thanatos, the **death instinct**?

Following the carnage of World War I, Freud added Thanatos to his theory of instincts. Thanatos, the death instinct, explains human destructiveness. Because pleasure can only be found through the reduction of tension, there must be a drive to reach a state of total quiescence, a state of no tension at all. This is the equivalent of death, hence the death instinct. We now realize that pleasure comes from the build-up of tension as well the release of tension.

Why was **Freud** so **focused** on **sex**?

While the focus on sex may seem odd to modern eyes, it is important to consider Freud in the context of his own time. He was an extremely ambitious man who aimed to build an all-encompassing scientific theory to explain human behavior. In keeping with nineteenth-century mechanics, he looked for one single force that could explain all of human behavior. He was also a product of the Victorian period—a prudish, sexually inhibited time when sexual repression in the European upper middle-class was probably rampant. It is possible that many of the psychological symptoms his female clients exhibited truly were related to repressed sexuality. Over time, however, much of Freud's theories, including the theory of libido and of psychosexual stages, were translated into emotional and interpersonal terms.

What is the **Oedipal period**?

Freud believed that the libidinal instincts moved through a series of developmental stages, corresponding with different erogenous zones at different ages. In the phallic stage (approximately ages four to seven), the little boy goes through the Oedipal crisis, which results in the formation of his super-ego. Around this age, the little boy falls in love with his mother. Recognizing his father as his rival, he feels murderous rage toward his father, controlled only by his fear of his father's greater strength. His fear that his father will cut off his penis in retaliation is termed *castration anxiety*.

As a solution to this dilemma, the little boy identifies with his father, realizing that he will grow up to be a man just like him and then have a wife all his own. This internalization of the father and the father's authority is seen to be the foundation of the super-ego and of a boy's moral development. Freud was not as sure how to account for female moral development and assumed women to have weaker super-egos due to their obvious immunity to castration anxiety. While the specifics of this theory have been roundly criticized by feminists and developmental psychologists alike, Oedipal behavior is often observed in children this age, who can show strikingly romantic behavior to older relatives of the opposite sex.

How is **Freudian theory** seen **today**?

Since the inception of psychoanalysis, Freud has always had passionate loyalists and detractors. Psychoanalysis has been trashed as all hocus-pocus; Freud's writings have also been treasured as the bible and seen as infallible. To some extent this is still the case today. However, many advances in our understanding of behavior and of the brain have shown that Freud was often onto something, although he was wrong in many of the specifics. Modern neuroscience, for example, has revealed the frontal lobe and the limbic system to function dramatically similarly to the ego and the id.

How has **psychoanalytic theory changed** over the years?

There have been many developments in psychoanalysis. In contemporary psychoanalysis, the schools of object relations, self psychology, and relational theory have translated Freud's original ideas into interpersonal terms. The emphasis has shifted from sexual instincts to consideration of how early childhood relationships affect adults' capacity to relate to others and manage emotions. Principles from attachment theory and ideas about self-reflective functioning (as found in the work of Peter Fonagy and Mary Target) have also informed contemporary psychoanalysis. Arguably, the integration of psychoanalytic concepts with advances in neuroscience currently forms the cutting edge of psychoanalytic theory.

JUNGIAN ANALYTICAL PSYCHOLOGY

Who was **Carl Jung**?

The Swiss psychiatrist Carl Gustave Jung (1875–1961) was one of Freud's closest collaborators until he broke off to form his own school of analytical psychology. While clearly grounded in Freudian psychoanalysis, Jungian analytical psychology moves away from the dominance of libido and toward a mystical understanding of the human unconscious. Interestingly, Jung came from a long line of clergymen. His father was a minister in the Swiss Reformed Church.

Fairly early in his career, Jung worked in Zurich at the renowned Burghölzli clinic under Eugen Bleuler, a prominent psychiatrist and the originator of the term "schizophrenia." Here Jung became involved in research with word association, detecting unconscious meaning through the way people grouped words together. This work led him to Freud's psychoanalytic research and the two men met in 1907. An intense and dynamic collaboration followed but ended acrimoniously in 1913 following a 1912 publication in which Jung was critical of Freud's work. From

Carl Gustave Jung (1875–1961) was a protégé of Freud who broke away in 1913 to found his own school of Analytical Psychology (*Library of Congress*).

1913 on, Jung referred to his own work as *analytical psychology* to differentiate it from Freudian psychoanalysis.

What was **Jung's relationship** with **Freud**?

Jung was a favorite protégé of Freud until they broke off their relationship over doctrine. Jung rose quickly within the psychoanalytic world, becoming editor of a psychoanalytic journal and president of the International Psychoanalytic Association. Freud favored him in part because as a non-Jew, he offered a bridge to the wider non-Jewish scientific community in Europe. Jung's relationship with Eugen Bleuler also offered the promise of greater scientific respect for psychoanalysis, which was something Freud craved. Jung grew increasingly uncomfortable, however, with Freud's insistence on sexuality as the sole motivating force. He agreed with Freud's energy-based conception of psychological motivation—that normal and abnormal psychological processes were a product of energy flow—but he believed sexuality to form only a small part of human motivation.

Temperamentally, the two men differed as well. Jung had a mystical bent, nurtured perhaps through his family's religious heritage, and a life-long interest in the occult. Freud was a fervent rationalist, believing religion to be little more than an infantile form of neurosis. It is unlikely Freud would have had much respect for the occult either, except perhaps as clinical material.

How did **Jung's view** of the **unconscious** differ from Freud's?

Like Freud, Jung believed the mind was divided into the conscious and unconscious parts and that the conscious part comprised a small fraction of the total psyche. Jung also believed, like Freud, that repressed and forbidden ideas were banished to the unconscious, intentionally kept out of consciousness. Unlike Freud, however, Jung

Mandalas are religious designs used in the Hindu and Buddhist traditions (*Fortean Picture Library*).

divided the unconscious into the *personal unconscious* and the *collective unconscious*. The personal unconscious contained personal experiences that had slipped out of consciousness, due either to simple forgetting or repression. The contents of the personal unconscious came from the individual's life experience. The collective unconscious, however, held the entire, evolutionary heritage of humanity. It contained the entire library of our typical reactions to universal human situations. It was not limited to the individual's life but encompassed the great, impersonal truths of existence.

What are the **personality traits** that **guide** our conscious **awareness**?

Jung developed a typology of personality traits that has had wide influence on personality psychology. He divided the conscious mind into both functional modes and attitudes toward the world. The functional types refer to ways that people process information. Believing the mind to be composed of opposites in continual tension with each other, he proposed two polarities, *thinking* vs. *feeling* and *intuition* vs. *sensation*. Each polarity was mutually exclusive from the other one. You could not process the world through feeling and through thinking at the same time. One side of the polarity was always dominant, the other relegated back to the unconscious. *Extroversion* vs. *introversion* described the attitude toward the outside world. The extrovert attends primarily to external reality, to other people and objects. The introvert is turned inward, preoccupied with internal, subjective experience.

What **personality tests** are derived from **Jung's theory** of personality?

The Meyers-Briggs test is a well known personality test that is often used in the workplace to identify employees' different personality styles. This test uses all three polarities mentioned above, extroversion vs. introversion, thinking vs. feeling, intuition vs. sensation, and adds one more, judgment vs. perception. Extroversion is also measured on scales associated with the Five Factor Model of personality, such as the NEO personality inventory. This test, formulated to identify dimensions of personality in non-pathological adults, uses 240 items to quantify five areas: neuroticism, extroversion, openness to experience, agreeableness, and conscientiousness.

What are **archetypes**?

Archetypes are patterns of experience and behavior that reflect ancient and fundamental ways of dealing with universal life situations. Archetypes reside in the collective unconscious. There is a mother archetype, a child archetype, an archetype of the feminine, of the masculine, and many more. Archetypes can never be directly known in consciousness but can only be glimpsed through the images that float up from our unconscious in dreams, creative works of art, mythology, and even religious symbolism. Through interpretation of this visual symbolism, we gain greater knowledge of our deepest selves.

What was Jung's relationship with mysticism?

Jung was always drawn to mysticism and late in life he traveled extensively to learn about the spiritual practices of other cultures. He visited the Pueblo Indians in New Mexico, he traveled to Kenya and India and he collaborated on studies of various Eastern religions. He viewed the symbolism in all the religious traditions as expressions of universal archetypes. Jung's view of mental health was also religiously tinged. Our happiness is dependent upon our communion with a universal reality that is part of us but yet larger than us. In his concept of the collective unconscious, he combined psychology, evolutionary biology, and the spiritual traditions of many diverse cultures.

HUMANISTIC THEORIES

What is **humanistic psychology**?

Humanistic psychology refers to a group of psychological theories and practices that originated in the 1950s and became very popular in subsequent decades. Similar to the Gestalt psychologists, the humanistic psychologists reacted against the constraints of the dominant psychological schools of their time but the humanistic psychologists had better timing. They arrived on the scene just as the dominance of behaviorism and psychoanalysis was beginning to fade. In fairly short order, they became powerful counterpoints to the orthodoxies of both schools.

In general, humanistic psychologists wanted to inject *humanity* back into the study of human beings. More specifically, they objected to a mechanical view of psychology, to the portrayal of human beings as passive objects at the mercy of either stimulus-response chains or unconscious drives. They insisted that people are active participants in their own lives. Humanists emphasized free will and the importance of choice. They also valued the richness of subjective experience and concerned themselves with the qualities of lived experience, of human consciousness.

Finally, they challenged the emphasis on pathology in psychoanalysis. In contrast to Freud, they believed that people are inherently motivated toward psychological growth and will naturally move toward health with proper encouragement and support.

What philosophical and psychological **schools influenced humanistic psychology**?

In Europe, the ravages of World War II and the Holocaust brought the question of *meaning* to the fore. How can life have meaning and purpose in the face of such senseless slaughter? The philosophical movement of Existentialism came out of these circumstances and provided a backdrop for the humanistic psychologists. Phenomenology, an earlier branch of European philosophy, also influenced the humanistic psychologists with its focus on the rich complexity of subjective experience. With regard to psychological schools, the functionalism of William James also played a role, as did the holistic theories of the Gestalt psychologists.

What is meant by **third force psychology**?

In 1950s America, where humanistic psychology originated, the field of psychology was dominated by the twin giants of behaviorism and psychoanalysis. Behaviorism dominated academic psychology and psychoanalysis dominated clinical psychology. Humanistic psychologists wanted to create an alternative to these two great forces: *a third force* in psychology.

Who was **Abraham Maslow**?

The American psychologist Abraham Maslow (1908–1970) was one of the founding fathers of humanistic psychology. Maslow wrote a number of books and also made several important theoretical contributions. He is perhaps best known for his concept of the hierarchy of needs. Maslow believed that human psychological needs are multidimensional and that there is no single motivating force to explain all of human behavior. He believed these needs could be organized hierarchically with the most fundamental needs related to biological survival. Once our fundamental biological needs—such as thirst, hunger, and warmth—are met, our needs for safety come into play. Following satisfaction of safety needs, psychological needs for emotional bonds with other people become important. Once those are met, we become concerned with self-esteem and the need to feel recognized and valued in a community. Finally, after all these more basic needs are met, we encounter the need for self actualization, a kind of creative fulfillment of our human potential.

This triangle illustrates Maslow's hierarchy of needs.

What did **Maslow** mean by **self-actualization**?

Although Maslow was not the first to use the term self-actualization, his name is most frequently associated with it. *Self-actualization* refers to a state of full self-expression, where one's creative, emotional, and intellectual potential is fully realized. We recognize what we need to feel fully alive and we commit ourselves to its pursuit. Although Maslow was criticized for promoting what was seen as a selfish pursuit of pleasure, he stressed that it is only through development of our truest selves that we attain full compassion for others. In his view, self actualized people make the strongest leaders and the greatest contributions to society. This concept illustrates humanistic psychology's concern with personal growth and psychological health in contrast to psychoanalysis' emphasis on psychopathology and mental illness.

What did Maslow mean by **peak experiences**?

A *peak experience* occurs in a state of total awareness and concentration, in which the world is understood as a unified, integrated whole where all is connected and no one part is more important than another. This is an awe-filled and ecstatic experience, which is frequently described in religious or mystical terms. It is not simply a rose-colored distortion of life, however, where all evil and tragedy is denied. Rather it is a moment of full comprehension, where good and evil are fully accepted as a part of a complete whole. Like William James and Carl Jung before him, Maslow believed the mystical and ecstatic aspects of religion were proper subjects of psychological study.

What is the difference between **D-love** and **B-love**?

Maslow also distinguished between two different kinds of love. *D-love* or deficiency-love refers to a kind of grasping, possessive love. In this state, we cling to the loved one out of desperate dependency and see the loved one as a means to fill come kind of deficiency in ourselves. *B-love*, or being-love, reflects a love based on full acceptance of the other person. In B-love, we love other people simply for who they are and not for what they can do for us. Naturally, B-love is seen as the healthier and more sustainable kind of love. Maslow was very focused on the importance of rising above selfish desires in order to embrace other people for their own sake rather than as means to a goal. Interestingly, Maslow described his own mother as an extremely disturbed woman who was incapable of valuing anyone for any reason outside her own personal agenda.

What **impact** did **humanistic psychology** have on the practice of **psychotherapy**?

A number of schools of psychotherapy came out of the humanistic movement and many more were influenced by it. Carl Rogers's person-centered psychotherapy, Fritz Perls's Gestalt therapy (named after Gestalt psychology but more closely tied to humanistic psychology), Victor Frankl's logotherapy, and Rollo May's existential psychoanalysis are all children of humanistic psychology.

Who was **Carl Rogers**?

Carl Rogers (1902–1987), another key figure in humanistic psychology, has had enormous influence on the practice of psychotherapy. His school of person-centered psychotherapy, originally known as client-centered psychotherapy (and often simply referred to as Rogerian therapy), placed the client's subjective experience at the forefront of the therapy. He believed the therapist's role was less to untangle psychopathology than to promote the client's personal growth through empathic listening and *unconditional positive regard*. While Rogers has been criticized for a relative disregard of negative emotions and interpersonal conflict, *therapeutic empathy* is now universally recognized as an essential ingredient of psychotherapy.

What did Rogers mean by **unconditional positive regard**?

Rogers made a distinction between loving a child for his or her intrinsic worth and loving the child dependent upon some condition: "I will love you if you are a good student, beautiful, obedient," etc. Children who feel loved unconditionally grow up to have faith in their own intrinsic worth. In contrast, children who experienced their parents' love as conditional, as contingent on some kind of performance, will often suffer long-lasting damage to their sense of self. These notions are similar to Maslow's concepts of B-love and D-love.

What **contributions** to psychotherapy research did Carl **Rogers make**?

Rogers was a pioneer in the scientific investigation of psychotherapy. He believed the methods of empirical research could and should be applied to the practice of psychotherapy. He was the first to record psychotherapy sessions despite vehement opposition from the psychoanalysts who believed the privacy of the therapy hour should never be violated. Rogers also systematically measured improvement by administering psychological tests pre-and post-treatment and then compared the results of subjects in therapy with those in a control group. These methods became fundamental tools in psychotherapy research, which has since blossomed into a discipline all its own.

ATTACHMENT THEORY

What is **attachment theory**?

Attachment theory was one of the first movements to provide empirical support for the key concepts of psychoanalytic theory, specifically that early childhood relationships with caregivers have profound impact on later personality development. Similar to Carl Rogers, attachment theorists believed that scientific methods could be usefully applied to the study of emotional and interpersonal phenomena. Thus attachment theory was the first movement to bring scientific methods to bear on psychoanalytic ideas. Not surprisingly, this occasioned resistance at first but over time attachment theory has been accepted by most psychoanalytic schools.

Attachment refers to a biologically based drive in the child to form an enduring emotional bond with the caregiver, generally the mother. Attachment theory originated with John Bowlby who wrote a trilogy of books entitled *Attachment and Loss* (1969, 1973, 1980). Bowlby's theory was greatly expanded by Mary Ainsworth (1913–1999), who developed an experimental procedure to study attachment. It was Mary Ainsworth who put attachment theory into the lab.

Who was **John Bowlby**?

John Bowlby (1907–1990) was a British psychoanalyst who became concerned with the devastating impact of early mother-child separations, which he frequently witnessed when working in post-World War II England. Disturbed by the dismissal of real-life events in the psychoanalytic world view, Bowlby's insistence on the real-time influence of the mother's presence often put him at odds with his colleagues. Bowlby was also interested in ethology, the study of animal behavior, and eventually synthesized both psychoanalytic theory and ethology into his theory of infant-mother attachment.

What was John **Bowlby's concept of attachment**?

Generally, attachment is seen as a biologically-based, evolutionarily adaptive drive for the infant to seek protection from the mother. When the child is frightened or is separated from the mother, the *attachment system* is activated and the child will seek proximity or physical closeness to the mother. The child will reach toward the mother, cry to be picked up, or crawl close to the mother. In Bowlby's view, the child is motivated to attain a sense of felt security, a subjective experience of safety and well-being–perhaps a kind of cozy contentment. When the child feels secure, the attachment system is deactivated and the *exploratory system* is turned on. At these points, the child will venture away from the mother to explore the world, to play. If the relationship with the mother is disrupted through separation or loss, the child will experience

This little boy's crying and reaching for his mother are what Bowlby referred to as attachment seeking behaviors.When a child is separated from his or her mother, the attachment system is activated and the child displays attachment seeking behavior to re-establish contact (*iStock*).

great sadness and distress, which can have long-lasting and even lifelong impact, depending on the severity of the loss.

What was **Bowlby's** concept of the **internal working model**?

Although his description of the infant attachment system was largely behavioral, Bowlby addressed the psychological aspects of attachment through the notion of the child's *internal working model* of attachment. This is a kind of mental map or script of the caregiver and the self. Through repeated attachment experiences, the child develops expectations about the availability and responsiveness of the mother (or caregiver). The child develops a working model of how the mother-child interactions will play out and then modifies attachment behavior according to these expectations.

How did **Mary Ainsworth** create a scientific means to **measure attachment**?

Although John Bowlby was always interested in translating his concepts into empirical research, his colleague Mary Ainsworth (1913–1999) is credited with taking attachment theory into the lab. While Bowlby had initially been interested in the universal effect of mother-child separation, Ainsworth was interested in individual differences in the quality of attachment based on the nature of the mother-child relationship. Her initial research was in Uganda, where she had traveled with her husband in 1954. By observing twenty-eight Ugandan babies, she noted individual differences in the quality of mother-infant attachment.

This research would be further developed in Baltimore at Johns Hopkins University, where she and her husband moved after leaving Uganda. Here she studied mother-child interactions both in their homes and in the laboratory during an experimental procedure she termed *the strange situation*. Based on the child's responses to separations and reunions with the mother, the child could be classified into secure and insecure attachment categories. Ainsworth also found that attachment status in the lab correlated with the mother's behavior toward the child in the home. Ainsworth's publication of this data in her 1978 book *Patterns of Attachment* was a milestone in attachment research. This fairly simple experimental paradigm would dramatically change psychological research into child development.

What is the **strange situation** and what does it show?

The strange situation is a twenty-minute procedure in which infants of twelve to eighteen months and their mothers are introduced to a room full of toys attached to an observation room by a one-way mirror. A sequence of separations and reunions follow. There are eight episodes to the strange situation, the first lasting only thirty seconds and the rest up to three minutes. The baby's reactions during the two separation and reunion episodes are carefully observed through the one-way mirror. Based mainly on these behaviors, the baby is classified as either securely attached or into one of three insecurely attached categories.

What does it mean to be **securely attached**?

A securely attached child (B baby in Ainsworth's system) showed interest in the toys when the mother was in the room. Some but not all babies showed mild to moderate distress in the separation episodes. Most importantly, in the reunion episodes, the child directly sought out contact with the mother. If the child was distressed after the separation, contact with the mother was effective in soothing the child. This pattern of behavior is seen to reflect the child's felt *security* in the mother's availability and responsivity to the child's attachment needs.

What does it mean to be **insecurely attached**?

A child who is insecurely attached is viewed as feeling *insecure* about the mother's emotional availability or responsivity to the child's attachment cues. The child then modifies his or her attachment behavior to adapt to the mother's behavior. There are several categories of insecure attachment. Ainsworth originally proposed two categories, avoidant and resistant attachment, but another category, disorganized attachment, was added later.

What are the ways that **insecure attachment manifests**?

Avoidant children, whom Ainsworth originally classified as A babies, show overly independent behavior. They tend to show more interest in the toys than their mother and little distress during the separation. Most importantly, they turn away from their mother upon reunion; hence they are *avoidant*. Resistant babies (or C babies) may be seen as overly dependent. They are less likely to engage with the toys when with their mother is present and may show great distress upon separation. Upon reunion, they show proximity-seeking behavior with the mother (crying, reaching, etc.) but also *resist* the mothers' attempts to soothe them. They may push their mothers away, arch their backs when picked up, or angrily kick their mothers. While avoidant and resistant classifications are considered a variant of normal attachment, disorganized attachment is more likely to be found in children who are victims of abusive or otherwise pathological parenting. These children do not show a consistent strategy of dealing with attachment and may even show fear toward their parent.

Are **insecurely attached children less attached** to their parents than are securely attached children?

No. Biology ensures that all children are powerfully attached to their caregivers. There is no choice in this matter. Children vary in the *security* of their attachment, which basically means how safe they feel in their relationship with their attachment figure, how secure they are that their caregiver will respond to their needs. But this does not mean they vary with regard to the power of their attachment to their caregivers.

The way mothers respond to their babies' emotional cues affects the quality of the infants' attachment. Parents of securely attached infants are reliably and sensitively responsive to the child's emotional communications. Parents of insecurely attached children fail to respond sensitively to their children's emotional cues or at least do so inconsistently (*iStock*).

What kind of **parenting** results in **securely attached** babies?

In Ainsworth's sample, securely attached children were more likely to have mothers who were reliably sensitive and *responsive* to the child's cues as measured in the home environment. Mothers who were more sensitive to their infants during feeding, play, physical contact, and episodes of emotional distress in the first three months of life were more likely to have securely attached infants at twelve months.

What kind of **parenting** results in **insecurely attached** babies?

Mothers of avoidant babies were shown to be *reliably unresponsive* to the babies' cues in Ainsworth's home studies. Avoidant attachment behavior is considered to reflect a down regulation of attachment in response to a reliably unresponsive mother. Mothers of resistant babies were found to be *unreliably responsive* to the child's attachment cues in the home setting. Thus resistant attachment may be seen as a strategy to maximize their mother's attention by ratcheting up their attachment system. Disorganized attachment is more often found in children who have been abused or whose mothers have significant emotional pathology. These babies cannot find a consistent strategy to deal with their parents' erratic or even frightening behavior. Thus their attachment behavior is disorganized.

How might the **principles** of **behaviorism** apply to **attachment theory**?

The three major attachment classifications, secure, insecure-avoidant, and insecure-resistant, can be seen to reflect predictable responses to different reinforcement schedules. They can be explained by the laws of operant conditioning. Avoidant attachment reflects the *extinction* of attachment-seeking behavior after these behaviors have consistently failed to elicit a response from the mother. The children in effect give up on the mother's response. Resistant attachment reflects the opposite pattern, in which there is an increase of behavior in response to an *intermittent reinforcement schedule*. The child learns to crank up the attachment behaviors in order to maximize the likelihood of the desired response from the mother. Secure attachment reflects a consistent reinforcement schedule. The child has learned that attachment-seeking behaviors will be consistently and predictably rewarded, so the child simply performs them when needed and stops when they are no longer needed.

What implications does **attachment style** have for **later child development**?

Alan Sroufe and his colleagues conducted several studies looking at the impact of attachment status on later childhood development. Children who were classified as securely attached were more likely to have better relationships with peers and teachers in later childhood than those classified as insecure. Insecure-resistant children showed overly dependent behavior with teachers while insecure-avoidant behavior showed overly independent behavior. These children were less likely to seek help from teachers when problem solving even if they could not solve the problems by themselves.

Is your **attachment status fixed** by the time you're **one year** old?

Attachment research is sometimes interpreted as implying that personality is entirely formed by the time that a child is one year old. Attachment strategies are conservative, that is they are resistant to change, but they are *not* fixed. If the family environment remains stable and the parent-child interaction patterns do not change dramatically, it is likely that the child's general approach to attachment will remain stable. On the other hand, if the family environment changes dramatically or if the parent chooses to change his or her way of relating to the child, the child's attachment status can change.

When is **attachment status** more likely to **change**?

Changes in parental circumstances can impact attachment status, either positively or negatively. A single mother getting married or a father losing his job can make the parents more or less available to the child and thus impact the child's attachment status. Studies of low income families show greater changes in children's attachment classification over time than is found in middle-class families. This may be because lower income families have less buffer against changes in the environment than do families with greater financial means.

What is the **adult attachment interview**?

In order to study attachment in adults, Mary Main and colleagues developed a semi-structured interview called the Adult Attachment Interview (AAI). A semi-structured interview provides specific questions as well as open-ended, follow-up questions. There is a script to follow but the interviewer can deviate from it to clarify information. The interview takes about an hour and a half and asks questions about the subject's childhood relationship with his or her parents. The way the subject talks about childhood attachment is more important than what they say about their parents. Of most importance is the coherence of their narrative, specifically between their abstract generalizations about their childhood attachment relationships (e.g., "My mother was loving, involved.") and the specific memories generated to illustrate these generalizations (e.g., "I remember making chocolate chip cookies with her in our kitchen."). The narrative is coherent if the story makes sense; if it is riddled with contradictions, it is not coherent.

How can the **three child attachment styles** be **mapped** onto Mary Main's three adult attachment styles?

Main developed three attachment classifications to correspond with the three infant classifications. She labeled them D,E, and F to match Ainsworth's A, B, and C. Dismissing adults (D) were hypothesized to correspond to avoidant babies (A); Enmeshed adults (E) to correspond to resistant babies (C); and Secure adults (F for Free) to correspond with secure babies (B). The enmeshed classification was later changed to preoccupied.

What are some examples of **adult attachment interviews**?

These (simulated) excerpts below illustrate typical responses for each of the adult attachment classifications on Mary Main's Adult Attachment Interview. Note how the dismissing adult presents an idealized view of her relationship without any specific memories to back it up. The securely attached adult is much more coherent. She acknowledges contradictions and mixed emotions but can reflect objectively on the relationship. The preoccupied adult, in contrast, is flooded by her attachment-related memories and is unable to integrate emotion and thought into a coherent narrative.

Dismissing

Interviewer: Could you tell me five adjectives that describe your childhood relationship with your mother?

Mother: Oh, I don't know. I guess she was normal, she was fine. I guess she was loving. She was practical and a good teacher.

Interviewer: Could you give me an example for each of those words?

Mother: Well, you know, she was always there. I don't remember any problems or like anything that was really wrong. She was a good teacher—she always wanted to make sure we got good grades.

Secure

Interviewer: Could you tell me five adjectives that describe your childhood relationship with your mother?

Mother: Hmm, that's a little complicated. My mother was very warm and very loving but she could also be controlling. So we had a very close relationship but it was also conflictual at times, especially when I was a teenager.

Interviewer: Could you give me an example for each of those words?

Mother: I remember a lot of affection. I remember curling up with her on the couch in the evenings, watching TV. But I also remember getting in fights with her, more when I was older, when I wanted to go out with my friends. She would insist that I be home earlier than any of my friends had to. Hmm, maybe she was just being responsible, but at the time I thought she was unreasonable.

Preoccupied

Interviewer: Could you tell me five adjectives that describe your childhood relationship with your mother?

Mother: It was loving, absolutely, so loving. She was wonderful, fabulous. But you know, sometimes she was really selfish, totally insensitive, like only out for herself.

Interviewer: Could you give me an example for each of those words?

Mother: It was unbelievable, you know. Whenever she got insecure, her dander got up and she would just never listen to my side of things. I think she had real problems with self-esteem. And all I wanted, all

63

Securely attached adults tend to be more sensitive to their infants' emotional cues (*iStock*).

I wanted, was like, "Listen to me, Mom!" But not that I didn't love her. Of course I did and still do and I know she loves me more than anything in the world. So that's what makes it fabulous, just fabulous. It would destroy me if anything happened to her.

How do **securely attached adults** act?

Adults who are securely attached value attachment and can speak about attachment relationships with feeling but will also be thoughtful and reflective. They can take some distance from their feelings and be reasonably objective about their experiences. On the AAI, secure adults give a coherent account of their childhood relationships with their parents and their generalized descriptions of the relationship are supported by specific memories. In the same way that a securely attached child balances dependency and exploration, a securely attached adult balances emotion and thought.

What characterizes **dismissing adults** ?

A dismissing adult corresponds to an avoidant infant. Attachment is devalued and dismissed by these adults with a concomitant emphasis on thought separated from emotion. An idealized picture of childhood attachment relationships is presented though it is not backed up by supporting memories. The adult may describe his or her mother as "fine, normal, and a good mother" but only provide memories such as "Well, you know, she was always there. She was just a normal mother." The impression is of a cool, distant relationship with minimal recognition of the child's emotional need for the parent.

How do **preoccupied adults** behave?

Preoccupied adults correspond to resistant infants. In contrast to dismissing adults who attempt to minimize the effect of attachment, preoccupied adults cannot turn their attention away from attachment; they are *preoccupied* with it. These adults are flooded with memories of attachment relations but cannot take the distance necessary to create a coherent, objective narrative. They provide contradictory, rapidly alternating views of their attachment relationships ("She was loving, no she was really selfish.") accompanied by a gush of vivid memories ("I remember on my senior prom. It's always about her. It was my night but she kept inserting herself. I wanted to wear my blue heels but she said they made my legs look fat.") In this case emotion predominates over rational thought.

Does a **parent's attachment style** necessarily **translate** into a **child's** attachment style?

There is a strong relationship between security of attachment in parents and security of attachment in their children. Secure adults are more likely to raise secure children and insecure adults are more likely to raise insecure children. However, the type of insecure attachment in adults is less strongly correlated with the type of insecure attachment in their children. Some dismissing mothers may have resistant children and some preoccupied mothers may have dismissing children.

What is **self-reflective functioning** and how does it relate to attachment?

Peter Fonagy and Mary Target have added to the attachment literature with their dual concepts of *self-reflective functioning* and *mentalization*. They propose that security of attachment in adulthood involves the capacity for self-reflective functioning, which means the ability to reflect upon one's emotional experiences in a thoughtful and coherent way. The ability to *mentalize* emotional experiences involves the capacity to represent one's own and others' mental experiences; that is, to understand and grasp the nature of emotional experience. In their view, the child's security of attachment is not only dependent on the mother's sensitive *behavior* but also on her psychological sensitivity. When the mother can keep her child's subjective experience in mind, she teaches the child that emotions both can be understood and communicated. The child's development of self-reflective functioning is therefore dependent upon the mother's mentalization of the child's experiences. Fonagy and Target have applied these concepts to their work with adults with severe personality disorders, many of whom sorely lack both self-reflective and mentalization abilities.

SOCIOBIOLOGY AND EVOLUTIONARY PSYCHOLOGY

What is **sociobiology**?

By the final third of the twentieth century, evolutionary concepts were increasingly penetrating psychological theories. For example, both attachment theory and Jungian psychology borrow from evolutionary biology. The field of sociobiology explicitly applies the principles of evolutionary theory to the understanding of social behavior. This approach assumes that at least some part of social behavior is genetically based and therefore has been acted upon by evolution. In other words, when a behavior has survived across thousands of generations, it most likely serves an evolutionary purpose. This approach was first applied to the study of non-human animals; it wasn't until the 1970s that evolutionary theory was rigorously applied to the study of human social behavior.

What is **evolutionary psychology**?

Evolutionary psychology is an outgrowth of sociobiology that focuses specifically on the evolutionary roots of human behavior.

Who is **Edward O. Wilson**?

Edward O. Wilson (1929–) is considered the father of sociobiology. A professor of entomology (the study of insects) in the Harvard biology department since 1956, he has maintained a lifelong interest in the social behavior of animals. His original specialty was the social life of ants. Wilson's great contribution was to state that the evolutionary explanation of animal behavior could be applied to the study of human behavior. He did not mean that culture and environment had no influence, only that our behavioral repertoire has its origins in our genetics and has been shaped by the processes of natural selection.

When he first published his classic text *Sociobiology: The New Synthesis* in 1975, it was met with much resistance. To many people it was politically offensive because it seemed to dismiss the importance of environment. As with Eugenics and other earlier movements that proclaimed the heritability of human behavior, it seemed to endorse social inequality as the natural order of things. Over the last few decades, however, sociobiology and evolutionary psychology have become more widely accepted. With advances in brain imaging technology and other methods of studying biology, our understanding of the biological underpinnings of human behavior has grown dramatically. Likewise, our appreciation of the complex interplay between genes and environment has also advanced, so that it is now accepted that a focus on the genetic basis of behavior does not have to mean that environment is irrelevant.

How is **Darwinian evolution relevant** to psychology?

Darwinian evolution is the central explanatory framework for all of biology. All of biological science is understood within the context of evolution. Likewise, human beings are biological animals and our behavior is inextricably tied to our biology. Thus a clear understanding of evolutionary principles is critical to the understanding of human psychology.

Charles Darwin's theory of evolution has proved key to an understanding of biology, and this has translated, as well, to how scientists understand human psychology (*iStock*).

If our **behavior** is **genetically determined**, where does **learning** come in?

Both sociobiology and evolutionary psychology assume our behavior is grounded in our genetics. Genetics determine the range of possible behaviors, the parameters of our behavior. Much of our behavior, however, simply cannot develop without extensive training. For example, we cannot learn to read unless we are taught the necessary skills and unless we are exposed to reading materials. With the proper circumstances, our genetic make-up allows us to *learn* to read. In contrast, no amount of training will ever lead a cat, a dog, or a pigeon to read. Likewise, no amount of training will ever allow a human being to fly (without artificial support). Thus genetics determine the *potentiality* of our behavior but genetics alone cannot determine the specific outcomes for any given individual.

What is **natural selection**?

Natural selection refers to the effect of the natural environment on the likelihood that genetically based traits will be passed on from one generation to the next. The process goes like this: First there must be variation in a particular trait within a population. Secondly, the trait must have some genetic basis. Thirdly, one version of the trait is better *adapted* to the environment than another version. Consequently, the animals with the more adaptive trait will bear more young, thus passing more of their genes onto the next generation.

Let's consider the example of light and dark moths first recorded by Charles Darwin. There were two varieties of moths in England, light-colored moths and dark-colored moths. Originally, there were more light-colored moths than dark ones, as the dark ones stood out against the light-colored tree bark and were easy prey for the local birds. At this point, light color was more adaptive than dark color.

During the Industrial Revolution in England, however, the trees became covered with soot. This meant the dark-colored moths were better adapted to their environ-

Why was Charles Darwin such an influential figure in science?

Charles Darwin (1809–1882) is easily one of the most influential figures in modern science. His theory of evolution has influenced every scientific discipline involved with living organisms. Prior to the theory of evolution, the variety of life on earth was seen as a product of God's creation. All creation occurred according to the book of Genesis with no changes since. To suggest that animals had changed over time implied that God's creation was less than perfect. Thus the theory of evolution challenged Christian theology about the very origins of life.

Because of this, Darwin's theory was highly controversial in its day. In some circles it remains so today. Scientifically, however, Darwin's basic premises have never been seriously challenged. Darwin was not the first proponent of a theory of evolution. In fact, his grandfather Erasmus Darwin (1731–1802) contributed to early work on the subject. What was missing in Darwin's day was an exact explanation of the mechanism of evolution and appropriate supporting evidence. Darwin gathered evidence for his theory on his famous sea voyage on the H.M.S. *Beagle* in 1831, in which he traveled from England to the coast of Africa to the southern tip of South America and back. It took him more than twenty years, though, to synthesize his observations into a coherent theory.

By the time Darwin published his famous essay "On the Origins of Species by Means of Natural Selection" in 1859, the scientific community was ready to receive it. It was an immediate sensation. Darwin's theory of genetics, however, was not well developed. The monk Gregor Mendel did not publish his study of pea plants until 1866 and his work was not appreciated until the beginning of the twentieth century. The current view of evolution reflects a synthesis of Darwin's theory of natural selection and Mendelian genetics.

ment than the light-colored moths, as they no longer stood out against the soot-covered tree bark. Now it was the light-colored moths that were easy prey for the birds. Hence, the population of dark-colored moths grew relative to the population of light-colored moths as more of the former survived to reproduce and pass their genes on to the next generation. Thus *natural selection* acted on the moth population as a result of their coloring. Of note, Darwin's concept of natural selection does not explain how variation in the population comes to be, only how one trait comes to be more frequent in the population than another trait.

How is **reproductive success** relevant to **evolution**?

Evolution occurs through the process of *reproductive success*. Those organisms that pass their genes onto the next generation have *succeeded*; their genes and the traits associated with them have survived into the next generation. In evolution, success really means survival. If a trait is common in a population, this means that the genes of previous generations with that trait have survived to the present.

What does **evolutionary fitness** mean?

Evolutionary fitness is the ability to pass on one's genes to the next generation. If there is a larger proportion of gene A in the present generation than in the previous one, then the organism with gene A has demonstrated evolutionary fitness. Conversely, if the proportion of gene B has decreased across generations, then the organism with gene B has poor fitness.

How does **evolution affect behavior**?

We generally assume that animal behavior is *adaptive*, that it has evolved because it confers fitness on the organism whose genetic make-up produces the behavior. For example, we assume that the mating dance of pigeons—in which they strut back and forth, jut their necks in and out and emit loud cooing noises—is adaptive. It increases male pigeons' access to females and thus to reproductive success. This display behavior may make the male look bigger and stronger than he actually is. Females are more likely to select such males as mates because selection of large and strong males may confer an evolutionary advantage for the females' offspring. Male displays of strength and size are very frequent strategies for access to females, evident in an extremely wide array of species, including our own. If we consider human males' predilection for muscle cars and bodybuilding, we can see how the principles of sociobiology might indeed be relevant to the behavior of humans.

What does **survival of** the **fittest** mean?

Survival of the fittest means that those individuals of a species with genetic traits that are best adapted to the particular environment are most likely to mate and pass those traits on to the next generation. Importantly, survival of the fittest does not mean that the most aggressive and dominant will pass their genes on to the next generation. Dominance is one evolutionary strategy, but it is not the only one. For example, in some fish species, male fish can disguise themselves as females and then sneak into the dominant male's territory to mate with his females. In this case, fish that are not the most dominant nevertheless reproduce successfully. Moreover, in many circumstances, cooperation and altruism can be useful evolutionary strategies—as effective, if not *more* effective, than competition and aggression.

What is **LaMarckian evolution**?

Jean-Baptiste LaMarck (1744–1829) was a French biologist who contributed to pre-Darwinian theories of evolution. In keeping with the ideas of Charles Darwin's grand-

What is Social Darwinism?

Social Darwinism refers to a loose group of theories that arose in the late nineteenth and early twentieth centuries, following publication of Charles Darwin's theory of evolution. This was a time of European imperialism, intense immigration into the United States, and growing masses of urbanized poor due to the industrial revolution. Thus, social prejudices spread among the European and American elite who convinced themselves that the conquered and the impoverished were somehow deserving of their status. Likewise, the idea of survival of the fittest was used to justify this viewpoint. Darwin did not intend evolution to be racist or a justification of social inequity. His theory was an explanation of how animals adapted to their environments. It was not a moral prescription for society. But his work was misinterpreted to mean that only the strongest and most worthy will survive and that social disadvantage was a reflection of genetic inferiority. Galton's theory of eugenics is a good example of Social Darwinism.

father, Erasmus Darwin, LaMarck believed in the *inheritance of acquired characteristics*. In other words, an animal adapts to the environment and these changes are then passed onto the animal's offspring via some form of heritability. Genetic change takes place because of the animal's behavior. The classic example involves the long neck of the giraffe. It was thought that giraffes stretched their own necks by reaching up to eat the leaves off the top of tall trees. This trait was then passed on to later generations. Similarly, mountain goats grew a thicker coat in a cold climate and then passed this trait onto their offspring.

Although LaMarckian evolution has a kind of intuitive appeal, there has never been any evidence to support its central premise, that acquired behavior is directly coded into the genes. In Darwinian evolution, genetic changes occur through random mutation. Some of these genetic mutations will improve the animal's adaptation to the environment, though most will not. Those genes that do improve adaptation are more likely to be passed on to the next generation. Hence the environment influences reproductive success but does not act upon the genes directly.

How do **evolutionary theorists** understand **altruism**?

Altruism, which involves helping others at some cost to the self, has long been a puzzle to evolutionary theorists. How is altruistic behavior evolutionarily adaptive? It is certainly common enough in the animal world. Worker bees and drones live their entire lives in service to the queen bee. They do not even reproduce. Alarm calls are also altruistic. When an animal sounds the alarm, warning others of the presence of a predator, the animal increases its visibility to the very predator it is warning against.

Likewise, altruistic behavior is widespread in human beings. We give money to charity, take care of other people's children, and may even donate a kidney to a relative in need.

Although altruistic behavior may cost the individual animal, it may still confer reproductive success if it helps other animals that share the same genes. Thus, we would expect altruistic behavior to be most common among close relatives, which is universally the case. What is also found is that the cost and risk of altruistic behavior decreases as the biological relationship grows more distant. Think about it. Most of us are willing to donate used clothes to children in another country. This is a low cost and low risk

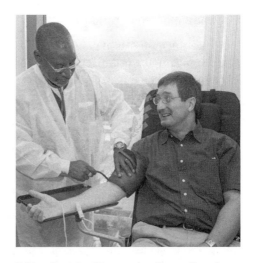

Helping others when it in no way benefits oneself—such as donating blood—is called altruism. Scientists, believing that evolution has been based on self-preservation, have long wondered what the advantages could be of altruism (*iStock*).

investment. But would you be willing to sell your house and donate the proceeds to a complete stranger? Would you be willing to donate a kidney to a stranger? Or would you be more likely to donate your kidney to your sister, especially if she was likely to die without it?

How do **evolutionary theorists** understand **sexual behavior** of males and females?

Because sexual behavior has such direct impact on reproductive success, sociobiologists have given a good deal of thought to the evolutionary significance of various forms of sexual behavior. In many species, males and females may have different strategies for reproductive success. Females devote an enormous amount of time and energy to bearing and raising their young. The more complex the species, the more this is the case.

For example, humans, chimpanzees, and dogs provide much more maternal care than turtles do. Therefore it is in the evolutionary interest of many females to be highly selective in their choice of mates and to seek males that can contribute to care of the young. Males, on the other hand, do not bear young and are not physically bound to the care of the young. They can develop a wide array of successful reproductive strategies. They can inseminate a large number of females but give little resources to the care of their offspring (e.g., buffalo, wildebeests), or they can inseminate fewer females, have more offspring with them and give much more time and energy to the care of their young (e.g., trumpeter swans, gibbons). Some males (e.g., gorillas, fur seals) compete for exclusive access to a group of females, devoting considerable energy to protecting their harems from encroachment from rival males.

Are **men** inherently **polygamous**?

Across history, human males have exhibited all of the above reproductive strategies. They are monogamous, promiscuous, or polygynous. Some even have harems. Whichever strategy is selected is dependent on numerous environmental contingencies, such as population density, scarcity of resources, culture, religion, social status, etc. While human females are not immune to the temptations of multiple partners, polygamous societies with *polygynous* marital patterns (men with multiple wives) are far more common than those with *polyandrous* marital patterns (women with multiple husbands).

What is **sexual selection**?

Because females invest so much more energy into reproduction than males do, females are high-energy resources and hence very valuable to males. Consequently males are likely to evolve strategies to compete for them. *Sexual selection* means that any physical trait or behavioral pattern that increases access to mates will be evolutionarily advantageous. Sexual selection is most pronounced in polygamous species, where a sort of winner-take-all system results in clear winners and losers.

One of the most common competitive strategies for males involves physical size and strength. Across many, many species larger males have more offspring. Likewise dominant males can jealously guard access to multiple females, creating harems that they defend aggressively. However, in these circumstances non-dominant males will be excluded from access to females. Therefore, the non-dominant males have developed alternative strategies.

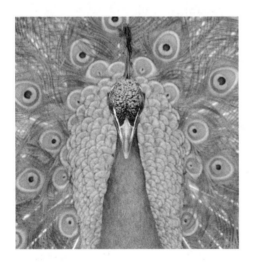

In the competition for sexual partners, many species have adapted in amazing biological and behavioral ways. Peacocks, for instance, have evolved so that they have stunning feathers to attract peahens. Humans, too, have developed their own competitive strategies (*iStock*).

In several species, including stickleback fish, prairie chickens, and elephant seals, smaller and non-dominant males disguise themselves as females to gain access to the dominant males' territory and the females within. These strategies work in direct male-to-male competition. But females are also often highly selective. Males have to compete for female favor as well. It is likely elaborate display rituals that are evident in many birds reflect behaviors evolved to enhance female preference. Such rituals often do two things. They can advertise the males' size and strength, often in exaggerated form. They can also attempt to persuade the female of the resources the male can make available for child rearing. For example, male scorpion flies give a high

---

So, is evolution only about competition?

Natural selection works on the *comparative* advantage of genetic traits. Perhaps because of this, evolutionary theorists have tended to emphasize the competitive nature of social relations. But this paints a very incomplete picture. Social behavior in all highly social animals involves much more cooperation than competition or antagonism. If social life was entirely a Hobbesian free-for-all, there would be little reason for humans and other animals to seek each other out. Just as evolution results in competitive and aggressive behavior, it also results in the capacity for strong social bonds, parental devotion to children, affection, cooperation, empathy (in humans at least), and many other traits that support cohesive social groups.

---

calorie gift to their prospective mates. Female scorpion flies, in turn, prefer males who make larger gifts. Perhaps the tendency for human males to buy women expensive jewelry and take them out to high-priced restaurants is a related phenomenon.

Do **females compete** for males?

Although male-to-male competition can be very dramatic in the animal world and consequently has received more attention from sociobiologists, female-to-female competition certainly exists. Some female birds roll other females' eggs out of the nest or otherwise interfere with their reproduction. In complex social groups, females can compete for status. In large monkey troupes, for example, high-status females and their offspring have many advantages over lower status females. The presence of monogamy can also affect female-to-female competition.

Monogamy is more common when a prolonged or intensified period of dependence in the young favors paternal investment in child rearing. When males are monogamous, they are likely to be more selective in their choice of a mate as they invest more in each partner. Hence females may need to compete for males. In these cases, females who show signs of greater reproductive fitness are often more successful in attracting males. We can certainly consider how this might apply to human females, who characteristically spend considerable energy and time maintaining and enhancing their physical attractiveness to males. Across human cultures, the standards for female beauty almost universally relate to youth and physical health, which corresponds to a long period of fertility.

If we consider the size of the beauty industry, which produces women's makeup, jewelry, clothing, skin creams, hair products, and many other forms of female adornment, we can see how evolutionary pressures may be in play within our own culture.

What are the **controversies** of **sociobiology**?

Sociobiology was extremely controversial in its early days in the 1970s and 1980s. To say that a behavior had a genetic basis seemed to imply that it was morally desirable or inevitable. Further, the emphasis on genetics was seen to invalidate the importance of environment. We now know that environment and genetics interact in almost all of human behavior. While genetics may set the outer limits of behavior, environment has huge influence on the expression of behavior and even on the expression of genes themselves. Genes can be turned on and off according to environmental influences. The biggest problem with evolutionary explanations of human behavior, however, involves the profound difficulty distinguishing between *proximate* and *ultimate* levels of causation.

What is the difference between **proximate** and **ultimate causation**?

The *ultimate* level of causation refers to the behavior's evolutionary significance; how the behavior enhances reproductive fitness. The *proximate* cause refers to the immediate cause of a behavior, whether that be hormonal, neurological, cognitive, interpersonal, or cultural. For example, the proximate cause of humans eating more cookies, cake, and ice cream involves the psychological tendency to desire and enjoy foods with high sugar and fat content. The ultimate cause involves the high caloric content of both sweet and high fat foods, which promotes physical survival in resource-scarce environments.

Such environments were typical until only just recently. However, distinguishing between proximate and ultimate causes in human beings is extremely difficult, far more difficult than it is in simple animals, like insects, whose behavior is much more closely tied to their genetics. This is because one of the most important evolutionary strategies of human beings involves our remarkably developed intelligence. No other animal on earth can learn information of such complexity and modify its behavior in such diverse ways. Therefore, due to our remarkable behavioral flexibility, it is very difficult to distinguish what behavior is learned and what is genetically based.

How do scientists **test** the **evolutionary significance** of **behavior**?

In the absence of rigorous scientific research, sociobiologists can potentially fall back upon speculation, which can easily be biased by prevailing prejudices. Women are *supposed* to be subordinate to males; males are *supposed* to be aggressive. Therefore it is critical that rigorous scientific research support any claims as to the evolutionary significance of human behavior.

Sociobiology relies on careful animal studies in which the frequency of any given social behavior can be correlated with some marker of evolutionary significance. For example, the frequency of altruistic behavior in baboons can be correlated with the degree of biological relatedness between animals, which will then translate into the

Studies comparing identical twins, fraternal twins, and non-twin siblings have been used in an attempt to tease apart the role of genes and environment in various psychological traits (*iStock*).

proportion of shared genes (50 percent for parents and children, 50 percent for full siblings, 25 percent for half siblings, 12.5 percent for cousins).

In humans, twin studies have been used to differentiate the effects of genetics from the effects of environment. Additionally, anthropological studies that compare social behavior across different cultures are also used in an attempt to separate the effects of genetics and environment. These studies become harder to do with time, however, as globalization leaves fewer cultures truly independent of each other.

How do **twin studies** help illuminate the **role of genetics**?

Twin studies have largely focused on IQ tests, comparing monozygotic (identical) and dizygotic (fraternal) twins. Monozygotic twins grew from the same fertilized egg and share 100 percent of their genes. Dizygotic twins grew from two separate eggs and therefore share only 50 percent of their genes. Twins reared together and twins reared apart have also been compared. These studies show that intelligence does have a significant genetic component, as monozygotic twins score much more similarly on IQ tests than do other types of siblings. However, these studies have been criticized because while the percentage of genes that differ from one subject to another has been carefully measured, the degree that environments differ between subjects is not clear at all. Moreover, there is considerable evidence showing that many environmental factors, such as socio-economic status, years of education, and mother's level of education also have very strong influences on IQ.

75

NEUROBIOLOGICAL THEORIES

What are **neurobiological theories** of psychology?

Neurobiological theories of psychology investigate the links between the brain and the mind. The assumption is that all psychological processes can be linked to specific patterns of brain activity and that understanding the *neurobiological substrates* of behavior can only enhance our understanding of human psychology. With the remarkable technological advances of recent years, our ability to study the workings of the brain and its relationship to psychological processes has grown at an extremely rapid pace.

What is **neuropsychology**?

Neuropsychology involves the study of specific psychological functions that can be directly linked to brain processes. Alexander Luria (1902–1977), one of the fathers of neuropsychology, studied brain-injured soldiers in World War II to determine how different kinds of brain damage impacted intellectual functioning. Modern neuropsychological research helps identify the specific psychological functions that are associated with specific patterns of brain activity. For example the encoding of information into long term memory is mediated by a brain area called the hippocampus.

How do **neurobiological theories** of psychology dovetail with **evolutionary psychology**?

Animal models are a critical aspect of neurobiological research because, for obvious ethical reasons, scientists can perform much more invasive procedures on animal brains than on human brains. In fact the ethics of animal research is a controversial and difficult area. Studies of animal brains shed important light on the workings of the human brain but they also highlight the ways that brains differ across species. When the brains of various animal species are compared, we can generate hypotheses about how our own brains developed across evolution. For example, the frontal lobe, which is associated with planning and other complex cognitive functions, is proportionately larger and more convoluted (providing more surface area) in animals with higher intelligence. This suggests that the frontal lobe grew in size across human evolution as intelligence became an increasingly important evolutionary strategy.

How do advances in **brain imaging technology** affect **neurobiological theories** of psychology?

Only a few decades ago, it was not possible to observe the human brain in action. Autopsies after death and neuropsychological studies of brain-injured patients were the main methods of neurobiological research. With the advent of brain imaging tech-

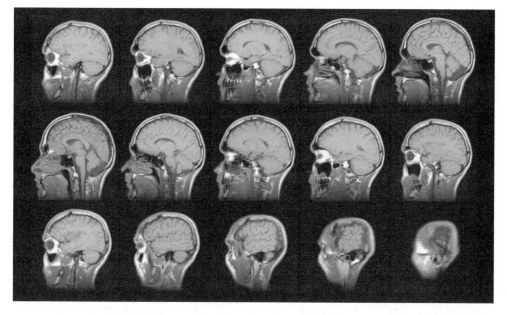

This photograph shows a Magnetic Resonance Imaging (MRI) brain scan for a 22-year-old man. The scan includes twenty vertical slices starting from the man's right ear and running through to his left ear. Brain imaging technology allows us to view the workings of a living brain, an extraordinary accomplishment possible only in the last few decades (*iStock*).

nology, however, it became possible to obtain snapshots of the living human brain. Computerized tomography (CT scans) and magnetic resonance imagery (MRI) allowed pictures of brain anatomy. Positron emission tomography (PET) and single photon emission computed tomography (SPECT) scans allowed investigation of the actual workings of the brain via recorded patterns of glucose uptake or blood flow.

More recently, functional MRI (fMRI) allows rapidly repeated images of brain activity, permitting study of brain activity over time. In effect, brain imaging technology has moved from still photos to moving pictures. Moreover, subjects can be scanned while performing various actions, opening up an enormous array of research possibilities that will take many years to fully exploit.

COGNITIVE SCIENCE

What is **cognitive science**?

Cognitive science can be seen as an outgrowth of the cognitive revolution. Cognitive scientists use tools of evolutionary psychology, linguistics, computer science, philosophy, and neurobiology to investigate mental phenomena from a scientific vantage point. One of the aims of cognitive science is to create complex computer programs to model psychological and brain processes. Cognitive scientists address a broad range of psychological problems including memory, language, learning, and decision making. Theories of *neural networks* address how the vast network of brain cells, or neurons, work together to create complex behaviors. Out of these investigations, many remarkable technological innovations have developed, including voice recognition software and advances in robotics.

What is **artificial intelligence**?

Artificial intelligence (AI) is a computer-based model of intellectual processes. AI scientists build computer programs to simulate human intelligence. Their implicit assumption is that psychology can be reduced to mathematical algorithms, the set of mathematical rules from which computer programs are built. As of yet, AI has been restricted to relatively simple aspects of human psychology, such as visual perception and object recognition. Nonetheless, AI models have become increasingly sophisticated and have taken on the complex problem of learning. How can a computer program modify itself in the face of new information? Pattern recognition software depends on a kind of teaching. The programs are designed to respond to incoming feedback from the outside world. Responses that are reinforced are strengthened and those that are not reinforced are weakened. In this way, AI is similar to the both behaviorist and evolutionary models of psychology.

Can the **mind** be reduced to **mathematical equations**?

Computer models of human psychology are based on mathematical rules. It is a philosophical question whether the mind can ever be wholly explained by a finite set of mathematical equations. A new branch of philosophy called neurophilosophy endorses this view while the holistic tradition of William James, the Gestalt theorists, and the humanistic psychologists would argue that the whole is more than the sum of its parts. As of now, there is no definitive answer to this question. Another controversy regarding cognitive science and artificial intelligence involves the concept of *qualia*. This refers to the subjective quality of a mental process, the yellow of yellow, the sadness of sad. AI may well be able to model the neurological processes underlying the perception of the color yellow, but can it explain how these neuronal firing patterns produce the experience of yellow? At present, we simply do not know the answer to these fundamental philosophical questions.

PSYCHOLOGY AS A SCIENCE

What is the **purpose** of **psychological research**?

Psychological research provides the absolute foundation of modern psychology. It is the bread and butter, the bricks and mortar, of the science of psychology. Research allows us to study the questions of psychology in a rigorous and systematic way so psychology can be more than a collection of subjective opinions and anecdotal observations.

Is psychological research ever **completely objective**?

Arguably, no. Human behavior is too complex, and influenced by too many factors to ever presume 100 percent certainty in our conclusions. Even the best studies depend to some extent on subjective judgments. Therefore we aim for the most rigorous methods possible, accounting for possible confounds, biases, and limitations in our research. That is also why we employ the peer review method for quality control before publishing our studies in journals, so that other experts in the field can independently and anonymously review each paper. Empirical research is the most rigorous method we have but it is not a crystal ball. Luckily, the best way to refute erroneous research is more research. Research can be used to correct its own mistakes.

What is a **variable**?

A variable is the building block of psychological research. It is the fundamental unit of a study. Any trait or behavior that we wish to study is translated into a variable so that we can measure it with numbers. We use the term *variable* because we are studying traits that *vary* across individuals or across time. If we want to study the relationship between red hair and school achievement, we must first *operationalize* our traits of interest, that is turn them into variables. We will code hair color as 1 = red hair, 0 = not red hair. We will operationalize school achievement by using grades, translating A through F into a 13-point scale, (A+ = 13, A = 12, A- = 11, B+ = 10, etc.). Having translated our traits of interest into numerical variables, we can now use mathematics to calculate the relationships between the variables. This, in effect, is the nuts and bolts of psychological science.

What are the **major methods** used in psychological **research**?

A number of different methods allow flexibility in the way we conduct psychological research. In *experimental* studies the variables are controlled and manipulated to give the maximum precision to our observations. The drawback of such control is that we cannot know how well the behavior observed in the artificially controlled environment will generalize to everyday life. In an *observational* study, we systematically observe behavior in its natural environment. We sacrifice a degree of control and precision for naturalism. *Cross-sectional studies* assess behavior at one point in time. *Longitudinal studies* observe behavior over a period of time, sometimes over decades. In *quantitative studies*, behavior is quantified into numbers. Even though quantitative research is the most common form of psychological research, *qualitative research* has gained more attention recently. This involves careful observation without the use of numbers.

79

How have laws changed to protect people from abusive scientific experiments?

The history of scientific research with human subjects has been fraught with abuses. Examples abound, including the Nazis' murderous experiments on concentration camp victims and the infamous Tuskegee experiments of the 1930s in which poor and uneducated African American men with syphilis were deliberately deprived of available treatments.

Psychological research is not excluded from this disturbing history. Examples include Stanley Milgram's work in the 1960s, in which subjects were falsely led to believe that they were causing pain, injury, and even death by administering electric shocks to another person. John Watson's treatment of Little Albert provides another example.

Starting in the 1940s, a series of national and international laws were instituted to protect the rights of human subjects in research studies. In 1947 the Nuremburg code laid down an international code of ethics regarding human experiments. In the 1960s, a series of laws was passed in the United States further developing these protections. The establishment of independent review boards to oversee the safety and ethics of human research in all American research institutions dates from this period.

Currently, Institutional Review Boards (IRBs) or Human Subjects Review Committees must approve all studies conducted with human subjects. Most academic journals require IRB approval of any study submitted for publication.

Do all psychological **studies** use **numbers**?

Most psychological studies are quantitative and rely on the translation of psychological traits and behaviors into variables that can be analyzed statistically. Qualitative research, however, also has a place in psychological research. In qualitative research a smaller number of subjects are observed or interviewed intensively. The observations are recorded not in numbers but in a long, detailed narrative. From these narratives, the researcher identifies themes that can be explored with greater precision in later quantitative research. Thus, qualitative research is *hypothesis generating* vs. *hypothesis testing*. It is more broad-based and open-ended than quantitative research but less precise and reproducible. It is best understood as a *preliminary* type of research.

How do the **methods** of the **social sciences differ** from those of the **hard sciences**?

In general, the role of math is different in the social sciences than in the hard sciences. In the hard sciences, especially physics, mathematics is used to identify fixed laws of nature. Once a mathematical equation is identified to explain the behavior of an object, the equation can be used to predict the behavior of the object with extraordinary precision. Consider the equations that send rockets into space. Thus, mathematics in the hard sciences is *predictive* and *deterministic*.

All of the object's behavior can be predicted by the equation. Aspects of modern physics, such as quantum mechanics and Heisenberg's Uncertainty Principle, do contradict this certainty, however, although only in the realm of the extremely small (e.g. the sub-atomic particles) or the extremely large. In psychology, the topics of study are so complex that it is not possible to predict all human behavior with mathematical equations. Whether that will ever be possible is debatable, but it certainly has not been done yet. What does that mean for the role of mathematics in psychological science? In psychology, mathematics is *probabilistic*. We estimate the likelihood that certain statements are true or not. Further, these estimates are based on the aggregate, on the behavior of groups. Therefore, while we may be able to say a lot about the likely behavior of groups, we are unable to predict the behavior of any given individual with certainty. For example, based on samples showing increased beer drinking among male college students compared to females, we can predict that, in general, male college students will drink more beer than females but we cannot predict the behavior of any given college student.

Why is **sample selection** important?

In psychological research, we try to draw conclusions about a larger population from observations of a small sample. We cannot study all male college students or all people with schizophrenia so we study a sample of the population of interest and then try to apply our findings to the larger population. For this reason it is critical to make sure the sample is similar to the larger population. There are many ways the sample can vary from the larger population. The way we recruit our study subjects may bias the sample right from the start. For example, if you want to study illegal behavior, you are likely to find your sample in the judicial system. Right off the bat your sample is biased toward people who have been arrested, leaving out the people who never got caught. If you want to study people with depression, you are likely to study people in the mental health system and your sample will be biased toward people who seek treatment. Because it is virtually impossible to remove all problems from sample selection, researchers must carefully describe their samples so that the applicability to a larger population, or the study's *generalizeability*, can be assessed.

What are **statistics** and how do they work?

Millions of psychology majors grit their teeth and roll their eyes at the very thought of statistics. Nonetheless, statistics are a fundamental part of psychological research. Statistics provide a mathematical technique to measure the relationships between two

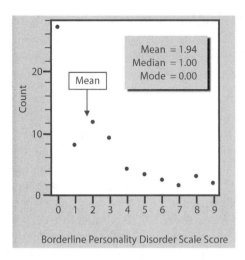

Mean = 1.94
Median = 1.00
Mode = 0.00

Mean

Borderline Personality Disorder Scale Score

This is a graph showing how 69 people scored on a test measuring traits of a personality disorder. The vertical axis represents the count, or the number of people who attained each score. The horizontal axis represents the scale score. In this graph, the vast majority of the subjects scored on the low end of the scale while a few people had much higher scores. When the distribution of scores is concentrated toward one end of the scale, we say there is a *skewed* distribution. In a *normal* distribution the majority of scores are in the middle with a few scores moving out toward the far ends of either side. When the distribution is skewed like this, the mean, median, and mode separate from each other.

or more variables (traits of interest such as intelligence, aggression, or severity of depression). Statistics can show how these variables relate. It can show the strength of their relationship and the probability that the relationships found in a given study are likely to be true findings, rather than a statistical fluke, i.e., due to chance. The most common statistics are measures of central tendencies, specifically: the mean, median, and the mode; measures of group differences such as the t-test, ANOVA, and MANOVA; and measures of covariation, such as correlation, factor analyses, and regression analyses. Measures of covariation assess the degree to which two or more variables change in relation to each other. For example, height and weight covary (or are *correlated*) while age and ethnicity do not. In general tall people weigh more than shorter people while ethnicity does not change with age.

What are measures of **central tendency**?

These are ways to characterize a population or a sample. The *mean* is the average score. It is calculated by dividing the sum of scores by the number of scores. For example, the average of the series {4, 7, 8, 9, 9} equals 7.4, (4 + 7 + 8 + 9 + 9 divided by 5). The *median* refers to the number that falls in the middle of the sample; half of the scores lie above it and half lie below. In this case the median is 8. The *mode* refers to the most common score. In this case the mode is 9. Each measure of central tendency has different advantages and disadvantages.

What is the difference between the **median** and the **mean** and why does it matter?

The mean is very sensitive to extreme values, also known as outliers, and so can give a distorted view of a population when some values are much higher than the rest. The median is not affected by outliers and thus can be a more stable measure of central tendencies. For example, the mean of 8, 8, 9, 12, 13, and 102 is equal to 26.4 but the median is equal to 10.5. This distinction is very important when describing characteristics such as national income. Due to a small percentage of people with very large incomes, the average or mean income in the United States is higher than the median income. Because of this the U.S. Census only reports median income. The mean, on the other hand, is more useful in statistical analyses.

What does **correlation** mean?

Correlation is one of the most common ways of evaluating the relationship between two variables. If one variable increases at the same time another one increases, the two variables are *positively correlated*. For example, gregariousness and number of friends are well correlated. The more gregarious a person is the more friends they are likely to have. Less gregarious people are likely to have fewer friends. If one variable increases while another decreases, the two variables are *negatively correlated*. Age and impulsivity are negatively correlated. The older someone gets, the less likely they are to engage in impulsive behavior. Likewise younger people are more likely to engage in impulsive behavior. If there is no relationship between variables, they have no correlation. Month of birth and mathematical skills have no relationship. We do not anticipate that the month of birth would have any impact on a person's mathematical ability.

What are the **critical concepts** one needs to know when **interpreting** the results of **a study**?

We trust the scientific method to give us reliable knowledge. Nevertheless, research should never be taken at face value. There are many ways a study can be biased and it is extremely important to be able to interpret the results of a study critically. The issue of *validity* is of particular importance. Are the results valid or is the study flawed to the extent that the conclusions are not supported by the data? *Internal validity* refers to the integrity of the study methods. Is there a fatal flaw that is intrinsic to the design of the design? For example, a study comparing the effectiveness of two drugs used one drug that had passed its expiration date. In this case, drug B may be less effective than drug A simply because it passed its expiration date. *External validity* refers to the extent to which the results can be applied to a larger population. A study of attitudes toward religion that only includes atheists will have limited external validity. It may be an accurate measure of the subjects' religious beliefs but the study would not tell us much about non-atheists. In general, internal validity is more important than external validity.

What does a **study confound** mean?

A confound is something that biases the results of a study. It is a third, extraneous variable that accounts for the relationship between the two variables of interest. For example, much of the early literature on intelligence tests found that Americans of northern European descent had greater intelligence than immigrants from southern or eastern Europe. These results were *confounded* by language fluency as the immigrants were not fluent in English. We cannot conclude that the difference in test scores across ethnic groups is due to intelligence if it is confounded by language ability. There are statistical techniques to control for confounds, but they are not appropriate in all cases and it is always better, if possible, to avoid confounds in the first place.

What does it mean when a study is **generalizeable**?

If the results of a study can be applied to a larger population, we say the study is *generalizeable*. Another term for generalizeability is *external validity*.

PSYCHOLOGICAL TESTS

What **role** do **psychological tests** play in the science of psychology?

Psychological tests are the bread and butter—the currency—of psychological science. Research in psychology depends upon the measurement of psychological traits, which can only be accomplished with psychological tests. Nonetheless, psychological traits are inherently difficult to assess. They are not concrete objects that are obviously measured, like the number of green peas or the height of a giraffe. They are abstract and intangible traits like love or happiness or self-esteem that can neither be seen, touched, nor counted and may be interpreted differently by different people. Therefore a critical part of psychological research involves the construction of tests that can measure psychological traits in a systematic and reliable way.

What are the different **kinds of tests**?

There are many forms of psychological tests, all of which offer both advantages and disadvantages. Perhaps the most common form of test is a *self-report questionnaire*, in which a subject answers a series of questions that gives information about one or more psychological traits. These tests are quick and easy to develop, to administer, and to score, but they are limited by the likelihood of inaccuracies in the subject's self report.

Clinician-administered questionnaires allow the clinician to make the final scoring decision based on the subject's responses to each question.

Interviews, like questionnaires, involve a series of questions administered to the subject, but the interviewer has room to follow up each question with probes to obtain more information or clarify responses.

Projective tests, like the TAT or the Rorschach, ask the subject to complete a task (e.g., to tell a story based on a picture), which is intended to reveal characteristic ways of thinking, feeling, and behaving. The subject, however, is unaware of the information being revealed.

In *cognitive tests*, the subject completes various tasks that involve intellectual skills, like memorizing a list of words or arranging blocks to match a pattern.

Sensory or motor tasks likewise measure sensory skills, such as sensitivity to touch, or motor skills such as visual-motor coordination.

Tests in these last three categories are often called *objective tests* because they involve the assessment of objective behavior.

What are some **examples** of **test questions** that measure **emotional** or **behavioral traits**?

The two excerpts listed below give sample items from a psychological test measuring various emotional and behavioral traits. The first group of questions measures anger regulation and the second group of questions measures sustained initiative. The questions can either be read aloud by the examiner in an interview format or given to the subject to fill out as a self-report questionnaire. Note how the answers are translated into numbers, which can then be added together to form a total score.

How frequently have any of the statements listed below been true for you in the past five years?

(5) Daily	(4) Weekly	(3) Monthly per year	(2) Several times once a year	(1) Less than	(0) Never

— Sometimes I can be really irritable and other times nothing rattles me.
— There are times when the least little thing makes me furious.
— I can be really furious about something and then suddenly feel calm and back to normal.
— I hold onto a grudge for a long time.
— When I'm angry I cannot easily control my temper.

Some people have a difficult time getting themselves to do things they either should do or would like to do. Over the past five years, how frequently have any of the following statements applied to you?

(5) Daily	(4) Weekly	(3) Monthly per year	(2) Several times once a year	(1) Less than	(0) Never

— I've had a hard time getting around to things I have to do.
— I've had a hard time finishing things I've started to do.
— Although I'm motivated and excited when I start a project (job, hobby, school), I get distracted and bored easily.
— I give up on things when I get frustrated or bored.

— I arrive at work more than half an hour late.

— I arrive at work more than an hour late.

How are **tests** and **measurements developed**?

A good deal of work goes into test construction. First, the construct must be defined. What exactly are you trying to measure? Then, taking the most typical case of a self-report questionnaire, the items must be selected. Next, the test must be administered to several samples of people to prove that it is a consistent and reliable measure of the construct it is intended to measure. Two critical concepts in test construction are *reliability* and *validity*.

What does it mean to say a **test** is **reliable**?

The reliability of a test refers to its ability to measure a given trait consistently. If the outcome of a measure varies each time it is applied, the measure is not *reliable*. There are several forms of reliability, depending on the format and purpose of the test. *Inter-item consistency* means that the individual items of a test are inter-correlated, or they are well related to each other. This form of reliability is used with questionnaires in which multiple items are used to rate one trait. *Test-retest reliability* measures how well an initial administration of a test correlates with a repeated administration. This is only useful if the trait measured is unlikely to change much over time. *Inter-rater reliability* is used with semi-structured questionnaires and other instruments in which the rater must use complex subjective judgments in the scoring. An instrument has inter-rater reliability when two or more raters rate the same material the same way.

What does it mean to say a **test** is **valid**?

The *validity* of a test reflects the degree to which it is measuring what it says it is measuring. Validity is often measured by correlation with a similar measure of the same construct. For example, a depression rating scale could be correlated with another questionnaire that measures depression. Differences across groups can also be used to establish validity. Does a group of depressed psychiatric inpatients score higher on the depression scale than a group of healthy subjects? For that matter, do the depressed patients score higher on the depression scale than a group of inpatients with schizophrenia? With *convergent validity*, measures of similar constructs will rate the same material similarly. Two measures of depression should be positively correlated. With *divergent validity*, measures of different constructs will rate the same material differently. A measure of depression should not be well correlated with a measure of happiness.

Can you have **reliability without validity**?

A test can be reliable without being valid. For example a ruler is a reliable measure. It will always measure a given distance the same way. However, it is not a valid measure of depression, as the outcome of its measurements, no matter how consistent, have no relationship to depression. Although a test can be reliable without being valid, it cannot be valid without being reliable. If a test is inconsistent in its measurements, we cannot say it is measuring what it is intended to measure and, therefore, it is considered invalid.

What is the **Rorschach inkblot test**?

The Rorschach inkblot test is a well-known projective test. In fact, it was once so widely used that it was frequently portrayed in the popular media, often as a mysterious and somewhat menacing test that could magically see into people's souls. The Rorschach consists of ten cards with images of inkblots, some in black-and-white and some with color. These blots were created by Herman Rorschach (1884–1922), who first published the test in 1922. Just as people see images in clouds, subjects see images in the inkblots and they are asked to identify and describe these images. The responses are then coded for their content and form, which are seen as reflective of the subject's own mental processes. There are no set answers to this test; the subject must project his or her own thought processes onto the blot in order to make sense of it. The Rorschach is therefore called a projective test. Perhaps because Herman Rorschach originally developed his test with inpatient schizophrenics, this test is particularly sensitive to psychotic thought process.

What **criticisms** have been leveled at the **Rorschach**?

Although numerous scoring systems for the Rorschach have been developed since its original publication in 1922, in its heyday in the mid-twentieth century, the Rorschach was interpreted essentially arbitrarily, according to the whim of the clinician who was administering the test. Claims for the power of the Rorschach were also overblown and poorly supported by empirical research. Because of that, the Rorschach has been harshly criticized as unscientific. It was further disparaged because of its strong ties to psychoanalysis, a discipline also criticized as unscientific. Like the Rorschach, psychoanalysis involves the identification of emotional meaning in ostensibly neutral material.

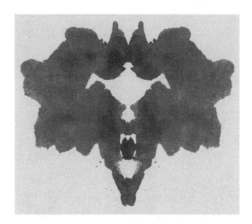

This ink blot design is very similar to those used in Rorschach tests. As an experiment, try to see what images you can find in the ink blot. What part of the blot do you use? Are your images based on the form of the blot, or the white space? (*iStock*)

How did **Exner's system** give the **Rorschach** scientific **legitimacy**?

In 1974, John Exner published the Comprehensive Scoring System for the Rorschach, in which he reworked earlier scoring systems into a comprehensive and systematic approach. He also provided considerable empirical research for his results, showing perfectly respectable reliability and validity. His system has been revised and updated multiple times. While there are still criticisms leveled at Exner's approach, many of them legitimate, he has undeniably provided a scientifically supported system with which to score the Rorschach.

What is the **Thematic Apperception Test** (TAT)?

The TAT is another projective test, almost as well known as the Rorschach. The TAT was developed by Henry Murray in 1938. It consists of 20 cards with evocative and ambiguous drawings involving one or more people. Usually, only ten cards are administered at a time. Subjects are asked to tell a story about what is happening in the picture, what led up to it, and what will happen afterward. Subjects are also asked to say what the characters are thinking and feeling. Because the images are ambiguous, the subjects' stories will reveal their personal ways of processing interpersonal relationships. Unfortunately, the TAT has not had the benefit of a John Exner to develop a modern scoring system. Therefore, without a reliable and valid scoring system, the TAT can only be used qualitatively and only in conjunction with other scientifically supported tests.

What is the **Minnesota Multiphasic Inventory** (MMPI)?

The MMPI is one of the oldest and best known self-report questionnaires. It measures various aspects of personality and psychopathology. The original version of the MMPI was developed in the 1940s. The second edition of the MMPI, known as the MMPI-2, is currently in use and was last revised in 1989. Eight basic syndrome scales are derived from 567 self-report items in a true/false format. These are Hypochondriasis, Hysteria, Psychopathic Deviancy, Paranoia, Psychasthenia, Schizophrenia, and Mania. Additional scales include Masculinity-Femininity, Social Introversion and three validity scales to assess response biases, such as under-reporting or over-reporting. There is also a shorter MMPI-A for adolescents.

INTELLIGENCE TESTING

What is an **IQ test**?

An IQ test is a test of cognitive skills that produces an IQ score. This refers to an *intelligence quotient*, which is an estimate of general intelligence. IQ tests have multiple subtests to tap different kinds of intellectual skills, such as memory, vocabulary, reasoning, attention, and copying skills. Tests therefore can include lists of vocabulary words to define, arithmetic problems, or drawings to be copied. All subtests have both easy and hard items, and the items become more difficult as the test goes on. The score is based on the number of items answered correctly.

What does it mean to say that an **IQ test** is **normed**?

Test *norms* allow comparison of any individual's score with those of the general population. In other words, when a test is normed, it is possible to know the *percentile rank* of any given score, which means the percentage of people who scored below it. In order to establish test norms, the test is administered to a large sample of people. The average (or *mean*) score and the standard deviation are then calculated. The standard deviation measures how much the individual scores vary from the average score. Are all the scores clustered tightly around the mean or are they all spread out? If you know both the mean and the standard deviation of a test, you can determine the percentile rank of any score. Thus IQ scores reflect a person's percentile rank according to the tests' norms.

What is the **Wechsler Adult Intelligence (WAIS)** IQ test?

The Wechsler Adult Intelligence Test is the most widely-used intelligence test. The first WAIS was published in 1958. The WAIS-IV, published in 2008, produces a Full Scale IQ based on scores from ten core subtests. These core subtests include Vocabulary, Similarities, Information, Arithmetic, Digit Span, Block Design, Matrix Reasoning, Visual Puzzles, Digit Symbol, and Symbol Search. Five supplemental tests include Comprehension, Letter-Number Sequencing, Picture Completion, Figure Weights, and Cancellation.

What are the **four index scores** of the **WAIS-IV**?

The WAIS subtests are grouped into four index scores, each measuring a specific cognitive skill. The Verbal Comprehension Index reflects the ability to express abstract ideas in words. The Perceptual Reasoning Index reflects the ability to process visual and spatial information; the Working Memory Index suggests the ability to hold and manipulate information in memory; and the Processing Speed Index indicates the ability to process information rapidly. These indices show that intelligence, as measured by the WAIS, has several very different components.

Does the **WAIS measure intelligence**?

Whether any one test can measure a concept as complex as intelligence has been a topic of considerable controversy. What we do know is that the WAIS does a good job of measuring a range of cognitive skills that are indicators of other measures of intelligence, such as academic and occupational success. WAIS subtests are also well correlated with many other cognitive tests and with studies on brain activity. In other words, compared with those who have lower scores, people with high scores on the WAIS are more likely to perform well in school and in their work life and to score well on other tests of thinking ability. They are also more likely to show greater activity in the areas of the brain associated with complex thought.

Is there **agreement** on what **intelligence means**?

There is some agreement that general intelligence does exist and that people vary in how much of it they have. Nonetheless, there is considerable disagreement as to the exact way to define intelligence. Loosely, we can define intelligence to refer to the ability to process information in a way that allows individuals to adapt to their environment. This definition suggests, however, that intelligence may vary according to the environment. If you live in a hunting and gathering society, your intelligence will have nothing to do with your ability to read abstract philosophy texts and much more to do with your ability to interpret your natural surroundings. In fact, someone who scores very highly on the WAIS would probably perform very poorly if he or she had been dropped into the Australian bush in the middle of the nineteenth century. Likewise, an aboriginal Australian from the nineteenth century with no formal education would perform extremely poorly on the WAIS, but would have an enormous store of knowledge and skills about surviving in the bush. Because the nature of intelligence is inherently dependent on an individual's environment, there are chronic problems with cultural bias in intelligence tests. It is arguably impossible to design an intelligence test completely free from cultural bias.

What are the best ways to **reduce cultural bias** in **IQ tests**?

While it is probably impossible to remove all cultural bias from IQ tests, there are ways to ensure that the test is relevant to as broad a sample of people as possible. This is especially important in highly diverse societies such as the United States. The WAIS-IV includes non-verbal tests such as Block Design and Matrix Reasoning that are not dependent on language and not too dependent on education. Further, the use of abstract, geometric shapes avoids culturally meaningful images. It is also important to exclude items that depend on knowledge that is relevant to only a small percentage of the population. For example, early intelligence tests included items on the make and model of specific cars, which would only be relevant to people who drive and who care about cars. Another important way to reduce cultural bias is to provide norms for different segments of the population. The WAIS-IV includes norms for different age groups and many other

Some people question the usefulness of IQ tests because it is difficult to create a test that is not skewed somewhat by cultural biases (*iStock*).

cognitive tests provide separate norms for people with different levels of education. Finally, translation of tests into several languages is also very important.

Are there **other kinds of intelligence** that the WAIS doesn't measure?

If we define intelligence as information processing that allows us to adapt to our environment, then the WAIS only taps a narrow range of such skills. Howard Gardiner has argued against the idea of a single, unitary intelligence, proposing instead the existence of multiple intelligences, including forms based in the body, and social and emotional forms of intelligence. Similarly, Daniel Goleman has written extensively about *emotional intelligence*, the ability to process emotional and interpersonal information effectively. Folk psychology speaks about street smarts, political acumen, business smarts, mechanical aptitude, and even common sense. None of these are directly measured on the WAIS, although we would assume the visual-spatial tests to have some relationship to mechanical aptitude. We do know, however, that people with very low intellectual skills—as measured by tests such as the WAIS—have significantly reduced interpersonal and self-care skills. On the other hand, we probably all know people with very high IQs who are sorely lacking in emotional and interpersonal skills and even common sense. Therefore we can conclude that the WAIS measures some aspects of intelligence that are related, but not identical, to other aspects of intelligence.

What were the **Alpha and Beta Tests** developed by the U.S. Army?

In 1917, immediately after the United States entered World War I, the American Psychological Association (APA) convened a committee to consider how best to contribute to the war effort. The committee concluded that the development of an intelligence test that could be administered to large groups would be most useful. Potential soldiers falling below a cut-off point would be excluded from the military, while high scorers could be selected for elite positions.

Under the guidance of Robert Yerkes, a Harvard psychologist and army major, the *Army Alpha*, a written test, and the *Army Beta*, a pictorial version for the 40 percent of soldiers unable to read the written test, were developed. These tests had broad impact on the discharge and promotion of soldiers. The use of such tests in WWI spawned an explosion of intelligence and aptitude tests after the war to be used in schools, the military, and other institutions.

Criticism of cultural bias soon followed, with complaints that the content of the Army tests favored affluent native-born Americans over less privileged immigrants, who could not be expected to know, for example, the engines of different luxury cars or the layout of a tennis court. Further, many questions were moralistic, as if disagreement with Anglo-American values reflected lower intelligence. Despite these very legitimate complaints, it must be kept in mind that intelligence tests aimed for a merit-based approach to job placement. In this way, the army at least tried to be more democratic than the explicitly prejudiced, family- and class-based approaches to employment that were typically used before. Today's intelligence and aptitude tests aim for much greater cultural sensitivity. Nonetheless, it is arguably impossible to develop a test that is completely culture-neutral.

Who devised the **first intelligence test**?

Frances Galton (1822–1911), the father of Eugenics, was one of the first scientists to study individual differences in intelligence. He presumed such differences were inherited, what we would now call genetic, and he aimed to separate the most intelligent individuals from the least in the interest of selective breeding. In keeping with Wilhelm Wundt's studies of sensation and perception, his initial intelligence tests comprised various measures of hand grip, reaction time to sensory stimuli, and other sensory-motor skills. James Cattell (1860–1944) carried this work forward and developed an intelligence test based on Galton's work. In his position as professor of psychology at Columbia University, he administered his test to hundreds of college freshmen. (Perhaps this was the beginning of a long tradition of using college freshmen in psychological research.)

By 1901, he had sufficient data to correlate students' grades with their intelligence test results. To his great disappointment, there was no relationship at all between the two variables. We might attribute these negative findings to two factors: a lack of construct validity, such that psychophysical measures have no relationship at all to academic performance, and restriction of range. College freshmen at an elite university will not vary that much in intelligence, so some correlations with intelligence may be masked by this fact.

What does **mental age** mean?

Alfred Binet (1857–1911), a French psychologist, furthered the work of Galton and Cattell with his concept of *mental age*. While observing his own children develop new cognitive skills as they grew, Binet recognized that intelligence could be measured *developmentally*. By comparing the test performance of a child with the age at which such performance was expected, he could calculate a mental age for each child.

What was the **Binet-Simon test**?

Influenced by a mandate from the French government addressing the needs of mentally retarded children, Binet and his colleague Théodore Simon decided to develop a test capable of distinguishing mentally retarded children from those of normal intelligence. They did this through multiple administrations and refinements of their measure, giving the test both to children of normal intelligence and those identified as mentally retarded. The first version of their test was published in 1905, with several revisions following in quick succession. By providing the expected scores for each age in the 1908 edition, Binet and Simon created the first empirically validated, standardized test. Within a few years, the Binet-Simon test had spread to countries on five continents.

What is the **Stanford-Binet intelligence test**?

Lewis M. Terman (1877–1956) at Stanford University revised and refined the Binet-Simon test to increase its sensitivity at the higher end of the scale. The Stanford-Binet test, published in 1916, was the first test to use IQ scores. An IQ score (or intelligence quotient) is derived from a large sample of test results. Terman set the mean IQ score at 100 and the standard deviation at 10. By translating raw scores into IQ scores, the percentile rank of each score could be calculated. For example, an IQ score of 100 falls in the 50th percentile, of 80 in the 2.5th percentile, and one of 130 in the 99th percentile. The Stanford-Binet was the primary IQ test used for many decades and is currently in its fifth edition. In 1958, two years after Terman died, David Wechsler published the Wechsler Adult Intelligence Test (WAIS), which is now the more widely used IQ test.

What were the **problems** with the **early IQ tests**?

The problem with Galton's approach was an utter lack of relationship between outside indications of intelligence, such as school performance, and the measures used. His tests had more to do with physical coordination and strength than intelligence and as such had no construct validity. Later tests also had problems with validity but these were more subtle. For the most part, they were extremely culturally biased, serving the anti-immigrant bias of the first several decades of the twentieth century. Here the biggest problem was generalizeability, meaning the applicability of the test to a larger population. There was no consideration of English-speaking ability or of culturally relevant knowledge. Some items only measured knowledge available to wealthy, English-speaking, and native-born Americans. Other items measured moral values more than strict intellectual skills. Later IQ tests addressed these problems by including non-verbal tests, considering cultural relevance when including items, and basing test norms on samples carefully constructed to match the demographics of the United States.

BRAIN AND BEHAVIOR

BASIC CONCEPTS IN NEUROSCIENCE

Why do we study the brain?

As early as 500 B.C.E., Alcmaeon of Croton identified the brain as the physical seat of the mind. Twenty-five hundred years later, modern science has proven this ancient Greek to be absolutely correct. There is no aspect of psychology that is independent of the brain. The very essence of our humanity—our thoughts, our feelings, our beliefs, and our values—all emerge from this three-pound lump of gray tissue. Psychology has no choice but to take the brain into consideration. Moreover, with the remarkable advances of neuroscience in the last few decades, we now know more about the brain and its relationship to the mind than at any other time in human history.

What do neuroscientists assume about brain evolution and how does that influence our understanding of the brain?

In order to understand brain research, it is important to consider three basic assumptions that neuroscientists make about brain evolution. For one, the brain is believed to carry traces of its evolutionary origins deep within its tissues. Just as we carry traces of our earliest childhood within our adult personalities, the brain carries the history of our whole species within its very anatomy. Secondly, the brain has evolved up and out, so that the lowest and deepest parts of the brain are the oldest. The outermost, uppermost, and the furthest forward brain regions are the youngest on the evolutionary scale. Thirdly, our brains have increased in complexity across evolution. The older structures tend to be simpler and more primitive, both in their anatomy and in the behavioral functions they control. Likewise, the evolutionarily newer structures tend to be more complex.

What are the **costs** and **benefits** of **complexity**?

As brain structures have evolved toward greater complexity, we can ask what benefits complexity may offer. Are there any costs? In general, complexity allows for more flexibility. Complex systems have a broader repertoire of responses with which to adapt to complicated or changing circumstances. However, complexity is expensive. Complex systems take more energy and are more fragile than simpler systems. With more parts involved, it is easier for something to go wrong.

How **costly** is our **brain**?

Although our brain only weighs about three pounds (two to three percent of the average person's body weight), it uses up about 15 percent of the blood that our heart pumps out and about 20 percent of our body's oxygen and glucose. In other words it uses up to ten times as much of the body's resources as would be expected for its weight.

What **terminology** is important in **brain anatomy**?

Although we will try to stick to plain English in this book, it is useful to know the basic terminology used in the discussion of brain anatomy. As the brain is a three-dimensional structure, specific terms are used to distinguish up from down, back from front, and inside from outside. The terms *anterior* and *posterior* are used to refer to front and back, respectively, as are the Latin words *rostral* and *caudal*. *Superior* and *inferior* refer to top and bottom, respectively, as do the Latin words *dorsal* and *ventral*. *Lateral* refers to outside, while *medial* refers to the inside.

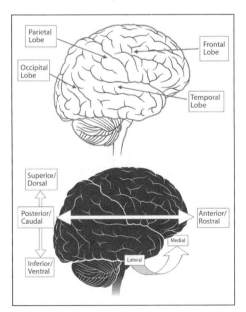

How do the **Latin terms** differ from the **English ones**?

The English terms are purely directional while the Latin ones are defined in reference to the body. *Rostral* and *caudal* are the Latin words for head and tail. Likewise, *dorsal* and *ventral* refer to the back and belly of a body (as in the dorsal fin of a shark). *Medial* means close to the body's midline while *lateral* means away from it. Nonetheless, when we speak about the brain, rostral and caudal are generally understood to mean front and back, dorsal and ventral to mean top and bottom, and medial and lateral to mean inside and outside.

Lateral view of the brain (*iStock*).

What does the word **phylogeny** mean?

The word *phylogeny* means evolution. To say something is phylogenetically old means that is old in evolutionary terms.

What have we **learned** from **animals**?

Our understanding of the human brain is heavily indebted to the study of animal brains. Although the use of animals in biological research raises moral questions about animal rights, there is no question that much of our knowledge about the human brain derives from research on animal brains. Legally and ethically, we can perform much more invasive procedures on animal brains than we can on living human brains. Additionally, comparison of the brains of many different kinds of animals gives us critical insight into brain evolution.

THE MAJOR STRUCTURES OF THE BRAIN

What are the **major structures** of the brain?

The brain is an intricate structure that looks like a boxing glove placed over a spiral of sea creatures. The outer layer of the brain is called the *cortex*, or the *neocortex*. It is a wrinkled surface that covers the top and sides of the brain. This is the part that looks like a boxing glove, albeit a wrinkled one. Underneath the cortex are the *subcortical* regions: the cerebellum and brain stem at the very base of the brain, the thalamus and related regions toward the middle of the brain, and the limbic system, which wraps around the thalamus. The basal ganglia are also in the middle of the brain, close to the thalamus.

What is the difference between the **cortex** and the **subcortical regions**?

The distinction between the cortical and subcortical regions of the brain is an important one. The cortex is a relatively recent evolutionary achievement and the cortical structures are much more developed in humans than they are in more primitive animals. Most of the more complex psychological processes, the ones we think of as uniquely human, such as language, abstract thought, and reading, are controlled by the cortex. The subcortical regions process more fundamental psychological and even physiological functions. The lowest parts of the brain, closest to the spinal cord, are the oldest parts and regulate physiological processes we share with more primitive animals, such as breathing, heartbeat, and digestion.

THE CORTEX

Why is the **cortex** so **wrinkled**?

The surface of the cortex is covered with folds and looks somewhat like a walnut. These folds are referred to as *convolutions*. The rounded parts of the convolutions are called *gyri*, gyrus in the singular. The grooves between the gyri are called *sulci* (sulcus in the singular). These extra folds allow for much greater surface area, which in turn greatly increases the number of neurons that can fit into the relatively small space of the human skull. The more neurons we have, the more powerfully we can process information. To illustrate this efficient use of space, imagine an accordion or pleated paper fan, first folded up and then stretched out from end to end.

What are the **four lobes** of the **cortex**?

The cortex is divided into four lobes, the *frontal, temporal, parietal,* and *occipital lobes*. The frontal lobe comprises the front half of the cortex. It extends from the central sulcus forward. The thumb-like segments of the cortex are the temporal lobes. The parietal lobes cover much of the back surface of the cortex, extending from the central sulcus back to the border with the occipital lobe (the parietooccipital sulcus). Finally the occipital lobes are at the lower back end of the cortex.

What is the **frontal lobe**?

The frontal lobe is considered the seat of our intellect. It covers about half the human cortex and is the most recently evolved part of the brain. More specifically it mediates our *executive functions*, a group of psychological functions that serve to control our behavior. These include planning, abstract thought, impulse control, and the control of behavioral sequences. As might be imagined, impairment in these areas can lead to significant problems functioning in the world. The frontal lobe has other functions besides executive functions, though. The most posterior region of the frontal lobe is called the motor strip and is involved with intentional movements. Additionally, Broca's area, on the left posterior side of the frontal lobe, mediates speech production, or the translation of thought into spoken words.

What do the **other cortical lobes** do?

The three remaining cortical lobes are all involved with some aspect of sensation and perception. The occipital lobe is involved with vision. The parietal lobe processes both touch and taste (in the somatosensory strip) and the temporal lobes are involved with hearing. Additionally, the parietal lobes are involved with attention and visual-spatial information, while the temporal lobes mediate language, memory, and the recognition of familiar objects.

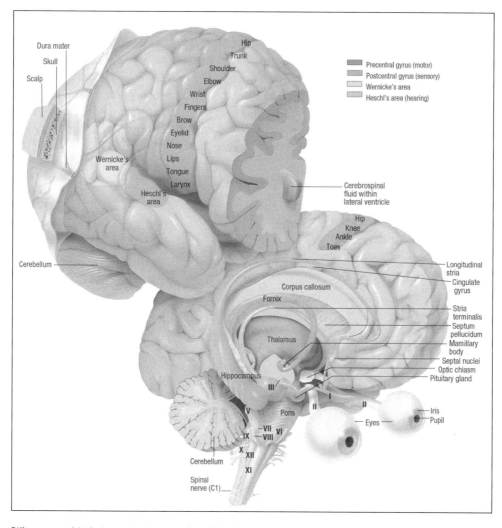

Different areas of the brain control different functions (*LifeArt*).

How do **Brodman areas** map the cortex?

In 1909, Korbinian Brodman (1868–1918) tried to standardize the discussion of brain anatomy by creating a map of the cortex. He first divided the cortex into distinct regions based on the way neurons were organized (cytoarchitecture). He then numbered these regions from one to 52. Only 45 Brodmann areas are found in the human brain, however; the other seven are found in the monkey brain. Although brain structure may vary somewhat across individuals, this system has been extremely helpful for neuroscientists, giving them a common language with which to talk about brain anatomy. Nonetheless, there is still variation in the terms used, as many brain structures have several different names.

99

Do **both sides** of the brain do the **same thing**?

The two halves of the brain are almost, but not quite, identical. With regard to the cortex, there is considerable difference in the functions they perform. This difference between right and left sides of the brain is called *lateralization*. The left side of the cortex is involved with language comprehension and speech production. The right side of the brain is involved with spatial and emotional processing and facial recognition. Because of lateralization, the impact of brain damage (for example due to stroke) will differ depending on the side of the brain affected.

BENEATH THE CORTEX

What is the **limbic system**?

The limbic system is the seat of our emotions. The term was first introduced by James Papez in 1937 and refers to a group of brain structures in the middle of the brain. The original Papez circuit included the hippocampus, the fornix, the mammilary bodies, the anterior nucleus of the thalamus, and the cingulate gyrus. Over time the boundaries of the limbic system were expanded, although the exact definition of the limbic system is still not universal. For our purposes, however, we can include the *amygdala, hippocampus, hypothalamus, septum,* and *cingulate gyrus*. These regions are all involved with emotional and motivational processing.

Where does the word **amygdala** come from?

The *amygdala* is a small, almond-shaped structure buried deep in the middle of the brain. Because of its oval shape, the amygdala was named after the Greek word for almond.

What do the **amygdala** and the **hypothalamus** do?

The amygdala seems to be an early responder to emotionally significant signals from the environment. It is particularly reactive to fearful stimuli. The amygdala activates the *hypothalamus*, which in turn activates the autonomic nervous system, in part through control of important hormones. The autonomic nervous system regulates the physiological components of emotion. For example, imagine that a vicious dog has broken free of its leash and is now lunging toward you. Immediately, your amygdala responds to the perception of danger. It sends signals to the hypothalamus, which then activates the autonomic nervous system, resulting in the rapid heartbeat, sweaty palms, and heavy breathing associated with fear.

What does the **hippocampus** do?

The *hippocampus* is a caterpillar-like structure on the medial (inner) side of the temporal lobe and is heavily involved with memory. Early brain anatomists believed it looked more like a seahorse and named it after the Greek word for seahorse (hippo = horse). While the hippocampus does not process emotion, per se, it is located near the other limbic structures and carries memories of emotionally meaningful events. What we interpret as emotionally arousing, therefore, is heavily dependent on our memories of similar experiences.

What do the **other limbic structures** do?

The *septum* is a small area that is involved with the experience of pleasure among other functions. The *cingulate gyrus* is a long structure that wraps around numerous other subcortical regions and has attentional, emotional, and cognitive functions. More specifically, it is involved with decision making.

What are the **regions** of the **brain** and their **functions**?

Brain Area	Major Function
Cortex or Neocortex	*Perception, Action, and Cognition*
Frontal Lobe	Intentional Action and Executive Functions
Parietal Lobe	Touch, Taste, Spatial Processing, Attention
Temporal Lobe	Hearing, Language, Memory, Object Recognition
Occipital Lobe	Visual Processing
Limbic System	*Emotion and Motivation*
Amygdala	Emotional Reactions
Cingulate Gyrus	Emotion, Attention and Cognitive Functions
Hypothalamus	Coordination Mental & Physiological Processes
Hippocampus	Memory
Basal Ganglia (Globus Pallidus, Putamen, Caudate Nucleus)	*Automatic Behavioral Sequences*
Brain Stem (Pons, Medulla Oblongata)	*Basic Physiological Processes: Digestion, Respiration, Cardiac Function*
Cerebellum	*Motor Coordination and Balance*

What are the **basal ganglia**?

The basal ganglia are centrally involved with action and motor behavior. The basal ganglia are actually a group of brain regions, including the putamen, globus pallidus, and caudate nucleus. This part of the brain is relatively old, phylogenetically, and handles the more automatic aspects of behavior. When we learn a new behavioral sequence, like riding a bicycle, we initially depend on the frontal lobes while we are concentrating on what we are doing. After the behavior is learned and becomes more

101

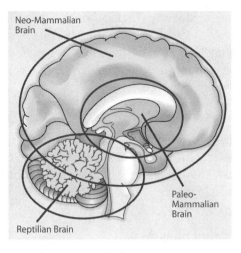

MacLean's triune system (*iStock*).

automatic, however, it is handled by the basal ganglia. Damage to the basal ganglia can severely disrupt motor behavior, as is found in neurological diseases like Parkinson's or Huntington's disease.

What is the **brain stem**?

The *brain stem* is the oldest and most primitive part of the brain. It regulates basic physiological processes necessary for life, such as breathing, temperature regulation, sleep-wake cycle, and cardiac function. The brain stem has been relatively conserved across evolution and therefore does not dramatically differ across animal species.

What is the **triune model**?

In 1964, Paul D. MacLean (1913–2007) divided the brain into three general regions, the *reptilian, palio-mammalian,* and *neo-mammalian*, which he believed to correspond with different periods of evolution. The neo-mammalian region of the brain refers to the neocortex, which includes the frontal lobe and most cortical regions. These parts of the brain are most developed in more complex and evolutionarily younger mammals, such as primates. The paleo-mammalian region incorporates the limbic system, which is found in all mammals. The reptilian area of the brain refers to the brain stem and the cerebellum, phylogenetically ancient regions that are found in some of the most ancient and primitive species (e.g., reptiles). Although MacLean's triune model has been criticized as overly simplistic, it does provide a useful way for non-specialists to picture the brain.

THE NEURON

What is a **neuron**?

A neuron is a brain cell, the basic building block of the brain. The entire brain is actually a huge network of interlocking, interacting neurons. There are about one hundred billion neurons in the human brain and several times that amount of glial and other smaller cells that support neuronal function. A neuron is composed of a *cell body*, an *axon,* and a profusion of branching *dendrites*.

What are the **input** and **output** **sections** of the cell?

Brain cells have both input and output sections. *Dendrites* are the tree-like extensions that reach out from the cell body. They are the input section of the cell and carry electrical information into the cell body from the axons of other neurons. *Axons* are the output section of the cell and carry electrical information from the cell out to other neurons. Axons can be extremely long, reaching from the brain all the way down to the base of the spine. While some axons branch into two sections, by and large there is only one axon per neuron. At the end of the axon, the cell branches into numerous axon terminals. One axon can have thousands of axon terminals. The majority of axon terminals connect with the dendrites of other cells, resulting in trillions of neuronal connections in the typical brain.

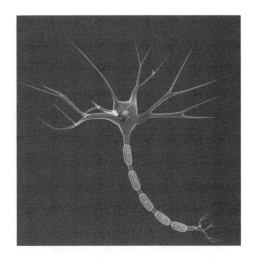

This computer graphic illustrates the basic structure of a neuron. The dendrites branch up away from the cell body. The axon reaches down from the cell body. Note the segmented sheath covering the axon. This is the myelin sheath, a fatty covering that increases the speed that an action potential travels down the axon. Note also the branching at the end of the axon. This is the axon terminal. (*iStock*)

What is a **synapse**?

The contact point between the dendrite of one cell and the axon terminal of another is called the *synapse*. Neurons communicate across synapses with chemical messengers known as *neurotransmitters*. The neuron sending the message is called the *pre-synaptic* neuron while the neuron receiving the message is the *post-synaptic* neuron. The gap between the neurons is called the *synaptic cleft*.

What are **neurotransmitters** and what do they do?

Neurotransmitters are the chemical messengers that neurons use to communicate with each other. When an axon meets up with the dendrite of another cell at the synapse, neurotransmitters are released into the synaptic cleft. Some of these neurotransmitters are *excitatory* and others are *inhibitory*. Both types of neurotransmitters change the electrical charge of the postsynaptic neuron.

How do **neurons fire**?

When a neuron fires, it sends an electrical impulse down the length of the axon to the axon terminals. Excitatory neurotransmitters make it easier for the post-synaptic

103

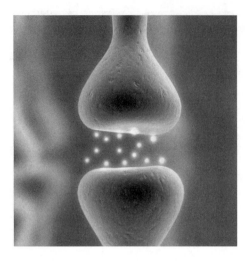

This graphic illustrates both the pre- and post-synaptic neurons and the synaptic cleft between them. The bright dots are neurotransmitters that have been released into the synaptic cleft (*iStock*).

neurons to fire; inhibitory neurotransmitters make it more difficult. Each cell receives excitatory and inhibitory inputs from many synapses. When the sum total of these inputs reaches a certain threshold, the neuron fires, sending an electrical impulse down the axon. This firing is known as an *action potential*. When the action potential reaches the bottom of the axon, the axon terminals release their own neurotransmitters, stimulating (or inhibiting) action potentials in the next group of neurons. In this way, wide networks of neurons communicate with each other in very little time. Action potentials commonly travel at speeds of 50 meters per second and can occur every five-hundredth of a millisecond.

What is the difference between **white matter** and **gray matter**?

Axons are coated by a fatty sheath known as *myelin* that speeds up the rate that the action potential travels down the axon. Because myelinated axons are white in appearance, brain tissue made up of these fibers is called *white matter*. In contrast, *grey matter* refers to brain tissue made up of dendrites and cell bodies (as well as glial cells and capillaries). The surface of the cortex is composed of grey matter.

BRAIN DEVELOPMENT

THE HUMAN BRAIN ACROSS EVOLUTION

How has the **human brain changed** across evolution?

Because we see the brain through the lens of evolutionary theory, it is important to consider how the human brain has changed across evolution. We make inferences about how our brain has evolved based on comparisons between human and animal brains. For one, our brain has become much larger relative to our body size. Evolutionarily older and more primitive animals have much smaller brains relative to their body size. Think of the dinosaurs with their tiny brains and huge bodies. In fact, our brains are about three times the size of the brains of our closest relative, the chimpanzee, although our bodies are not much bigger than theirs. Secondly, the brain has become much more complex. It is less the size of an animal's brain that determines its intelligence than the complexity of its neuronal networks. Billions of neurons create trillions of connections. Brain size and brain complexity, however, do tend to go together.

How has the **cortex grown compared** to other **animals**?

Another way that the human brain has changed across evolution is the growth of the cortex. The neocortex, the six-layer tissue that forms the outer layer of the human brain, is found only in mammals. Primitive cortices are evident in smaller mammals, such as hares, opossums, and armadillos, and more developed cortices are evident in higher-order mammals, such as elephants, dogs, and dolphins. In humans, the cortex wraps around the entire brain. The cortex allows for much more sophisticated processing of sensory information (e.g. sight, sound, touch). It also allows for more varied and flexible behavioral responses to internal and external stimulation.

Do the different **brain regions** ever perform **redundant functions**?

In some cases, the cortex and subcortical areas provide redundant or overlapping functions. For example, both the frontal lobe and the basal ganglia regulate motor behavior. But the behavior regulated by the basal ganglia is relatively crude and inflexible. Although fast and efficient, it is not easily adapted to changing conditions. Behavior regulated by the frontal lobe, on the other hand, is much more nuanced, flexible, and responsive to changing conditions. The frontal lobe is often slower, however, and consumes more energy than the basal ganglia. Thus we are happy to rely on our basal ganglia when walking down the sidewalk, but would prefer to employ our frontal lobe when performing surgery or defusing a bomb.

Has the **frontal lobe grown** across human evolution?

The greatest change in brain structure across human evolution relates to the frontal lobe. Frontal lobes are tiny in many smaller mammals, such as tree shrews and hedgehogs. In higher-order mammals, like cats and dogs, they are still smaller than in humans and also considerably less convoluted. As mentioned above, the convolutions on the cortex provide more surface area for dendrites to expand. Relatedly, our species has the most complex and sophisticated cognitive capacities on earth. That is not to say that other animals do not use some form of thought—chimpanzees use tools to solve problems and gorillas can be taught the rudiments of language. Nonetheless, as far as we know, no other species really comes close to us with regard to intelligence.

How has the **olfactory bulb changed** across human evolution?

One of the most striking differences between the brains of humans and other mammals involves the size of the *olfactory bulb*, which is the part of the brain involved with smell. In many mammals, the olfactory bulb is a major portion of the entire brain. In fact it is present in even the most primitive vertebrates, such as fish. In humans it is a tiny little orb sandwiched between our limbic system and the bottom of our frontal lobe. This contrast illustrates our reduced reliance on the sense of smell in favor of vision, hearing, and analytic thinking, all functions supported by the cortex.

THE BRAIN SINCE EARLY HOMINIDS

When did **human beings evolve** from early hominids?

About four to five million years ago, our ancestors and chimpanzees diverged from a common ancestor. The Australopithecus genus was one of the earliest forms of hominids. The homo genus followed, with several species, such as *Homo habilis*, *Homo erectus*, and *Homo sapien neanderthalensis* (neanderthals) preceding or even overlapping with modern humans. Modern humans (*Homo sapien sapiens*) evolved between 100,000 to 300,000 years ago.

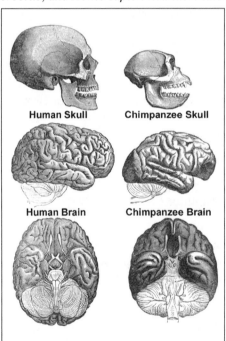

Human Skull   Chimpanzee Skull

Human Brain   Chimpanzee Brain

A comparison of chimpanzee and human brains and skulls. Chimpanzees are the closest genetic relative to humans (*iStock*).

How do we **compare** our **brains** with those of **extinct species**?

Because soft tissue decomposes quickly we cannot expect hominid brains to survive over the hundreds of thousands and even millions of years of evolution. Therefore, paleontologists must work with skeletal remains, using skulls and other bone fragments to draw inferences about the biology and behavior of early hominids. However, tools, animal bones, fossilized seeds, and even cave paintings (in the case of early modern humans) have been found alongside hominid skeletal remains, providing intriguing clues about the mental capacity of our predecessors.

How has **brain size changed** from early hominids?

Hominid skulls show a steady increase in cubic centimeters across evolution. Estimating from skull size and shape, *Homo habilis* had a brain size of 600 to 700 cubic centimeters (cc) and *Homo erectus* about 900 to 1,000 cubic centimeters. *Homo sapien sapiens* (modern humans) have a brain size of about 1,400 cubic centimeters. Concurrent with the increase in brain size, paleontologists find an increase in the complexity of tools found with hominid remains. Larger brains apparently translated into more sophisticated tool use. Additionally, larger brained hominids were adapted to more varied and/or harsher climates.

Has the **frontal lobe increased**?

Along with the increase in skull size, the shape of the skull also suggests enlargement of the brain and of the frontal lobe in particular. Australopithecine skulls do not look much different from ape skulls. There is a prominent jaw, a small sloping forehead and a relatively small brain casing. Modern humans, in contrast, have flatter faces, very steep foreheads, and small jaws. Our foreheads, which lie just in front of the frontal lobe, cover about 50 percent of our faces. Likewise our brain casing is greatly enlarged relative to the rest of our skull.

Is there **evidence** of **language** in **hominid skulls**?

Indentations on the inside of *Homo habilis* skulls (*Homo habilis* lived about two million years ago) suggest an enlarged area around the location of Broca's area, a central region for speech production in modern humans. While we cannot know if this area was connected to speech in *Homo habilis* brains, we can suggest that at least a precursor to modern language regions of the brain was present at a very early point in hominid evolution.

What does **pedopmorphy** mean?

Pedopmorphy refers to an evolutionary process in which adult animals maintain the traits of juveniles. One fairly easy way for genetic mutations to produce physical changes in the animal is to adjust the timing of maturation. No new physical structures or behaviors need to be introduced; the animal simply maintains its youthful traits instead of shedding them when it reaches maturity. There is evidence that many advances in human evolution involve pedomorphy. For example, we are one of the few mammals that retain a high level of playfulness throughout adulthood. Secondly, the shape of our skull mirrors that of juvenile apes. The skulls of juvenile chimpanzees look more like the skulls of adult humans than the skulls of adult chimpanzees. Adult chimpanzees have small sloping foreheads, prominent jaws, and more horizontally-aligned faces. Adult humans, on the other hand, have high foreheads, small jaws, and flat, vertically-aligned faces, similar to juveniles of both species. Of note, juvenile chimpanzees have a larger brain to skull ratio than do adult chimpanzees. In humans, this favorable ratio is retained into adulthood.

What does "phylogeny recapitulates ontogeny" mean?

This is a nineteenth century idea put forward by a German zoologist named Ernst Haeckel (1834–1919) that development in childhood exactly parallels evolution. *Phylogeny* refers to evolution and *ontogeny* to development across the lifespan. Haeckel believed that every stage in the development of a human embryo exactly parallels the stages of human evolution. Besides having a faulty view of human evolution (e.g., there was no cow stage in human evolution), this theory oversimplified the processes of embryonic development. While Haeckel's specific theory has been discredited, he was correct in pointing out important parallels between evolution and maturation. Careful understanding of our development across the lifespan does offer some clues as to our evolutionary history.

THE BRAIN IN UTERO

How does the **brain** develop **in utero**?

All vertebrates start life the same way. In their earliest stages of embryonic development, a flat plate is formed composed of three layers, the *ectoderm, mesoderm,* and *endoderm.* Cells in certain sections divide more quickly than cells in adjacent areas, causing the layers of cells to buckle and fold. In this way, curves and bends are formed and the different parts of the body begin to take shape. The outer layer of the flat plate is called the ectoderm and it is this layer of cells that will curl into the *neural tube,* out of which the brain and spinal cord will develop.

After an initial period of furious cell division, some cells are created that are postmitotic, that is, they stop dividing. These cells begin the fascinating process of migrating to their final destination. They do so by means of molecular and cellular signposts that guide their progress. After the cells arrive at their proper place, neuronal connections must be established. Axons are then sent out to travel across broad swaths of territory to create synaptic connections with other cells. Their journey throughout the brain is also directed by chemical signals that point them toward their destination. The establishment of specific synaptic connections between neurons is partially controlled by genetic factors during pregnancy. The refinement of these synaptic connections, however, takes place largely after birth and is highly dependent on experience.

What is the **neural tube**?

The neural tube is a long tubular structure that develops from the outer layer of the initial plate of embryonic cells. At the head of the neural plate, three bulges form distinct sections. These are called the *forebrain*, the *midbrain* and the *hindbrain*, also known as the prosencephalon, the mesencephalon, and the rhombencephalon. The table below lists the parts of the neural tube.

The Neural Tube and Its Corresponding Brain Regions

Neural Tube Regions		Final Brain Regions
Hindbrain	Metencephalon	Pons
		Cerebellum
	Myencephalon	Medulla Oblongata
Midbrain	Tectum	Inferior Colliculus
		Superior Colliculus
	Cerebral Peduncle	Various Neurotransmitter
		Cell Bodies
Forebrain	Diencephalon	Hypothalamus
		Thalamus
		Other Thalamic Regions
	Telencephalon	Neocortex
		Limbic System
		Basal Ganglia
		Cerebral White Matter

What does the **hindbrain** become?

The hindbrain divides into the metencephalon and the myelencephalon. These two sections subsequently develop into the *cerebellum* and *pons* on one hand and the *medulla* oblongata on the other. The pons and medulla oblongata are both part of the brain stem. Together with the cerebellum, they form the reptilian brain of Paul MacLean's triune model.

What does the **midbrain** become?

The midbrain divides into the *tectum* and the *cerebral peduncle*. These deep brain structures lie just above the brain stem. In primitive vertebrates such as amphibians, fish, and reptiles, the tectum serves as the main visual processing center in the brain. In primates, its function is more restricted as the majority of visual processing is done in the neocortex. The primate tectum helps to control eye movement. The cerebral peduncle includes several brain areas that contain the neurons that produce important neurotransmitters. For example, the substantia nigra is the origin of a major tract of dopamine neurons.

What does the **forebrain** become?

The forebrain develops into the evolutionarily newest parts of the brain and those most closely involved with mental life per se. The forebrain divides into the *diencephalon* and the *telencephalon*. In MacLean's model, the forebrain includes both the paleo-mammalian and the neo-mammalian brains.

What does the **diencephalon** turn into?

The diencephalon divides into the *thalamus*, the *hypothalamus,* and several related regions. The thalamus is involved with sensation. It is the relay station between the sense organs and their corresponding cortical regions. Olfaction (smell) is the only sense modality that does not run through the thalamus as it is processed directly by the olfactory bulb. The hypothalamus links the brain to the autonomic nervous system and serves a critical role in emotion, connecting the mental aspects of emotion with the body's physical response.

What develops from the **telencephalon**?

The telencephalon contains the most advanced parts of the brain. Although present in all vertebrates, it is most developed in birds and mammals. In humans the telencephalon develops into the *cerebral cortex, the limbic system, the basal ganglia,* and important *white matter regions*. The cerebral cortex includes the four lobes of the neocortex as well as those areas on the inside surface of the cortex that directly contact the subcortical regions. These include the cingulate gyrus, hippocampal and parahippocampal regions, as well as the insula, which is sandwiched between the temporal, frontal, and parietal cortices. The basal ganglia, amygdala, and septum also develop out of the telencephalon. Finally, cerebral white matter is made up of bundles of axons that travel across large sections of the brain. Important cerebral white matter structures that develop out of the telencephalon include the anterior commissure, the internal capsule, and the corpus callosum.

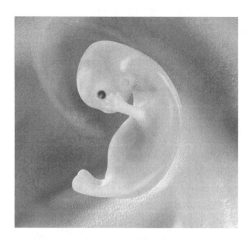

Given the extraordinary journey that brain cells must travel during fetal development it is amazing that so many babies are born without brain damage (*iStock*).

What impact does **brain injury** have during **fetal development**?

Because such extraordinarily complex structures develop out of very simple cell groupings, early problems in neuro-development can lead to severe birth defects. For

> ## What does it mean to say that the brain is plastic?
>
> **P**lasticity of the brain refers to the brain's ability to change with experience. As the very development of our brain is dependent upon our experience, we can say that the human brain is very plastic. In fact, brain development in humans is more experience-dependent than in any other species, reflecting the central role our capacity to learn has played in human evolution.

example, spina bifida is linked to defects in the neural tube. In fact, serious problems in the first trimester of pregnancy often lead to miscarriage, such that 80 percent of miscarriages occur in the first trimester. When we consider the enormous lengths the brain must travel in its journey to maturity, it is indeed remarkable that so many human beings are born without brain damage.

THE BRAIN ACROSS CHILDHOOD

How does the **brain change** across **childhood**?

The brain weighs about 350 grams at birth and about 1,450 grams by adulthood. The increase in weight is mainly due to growth in dendritic branches. This is because the basic structures of the brain are in place at birth, but the connections between neurons are still under developed.

How is our **brain development** dependent on our **experience**?

The synaptic connections between neurons are highly dependent on experience. In other words, the firing of neurons greatly influences the creation and strengthening of synaptic connections. When our brain responds to its environment—be it a sensory, perceptual, emotional, or motor response—we are activating all the neurons in the relevant brain circuitry and causing them to fire. This activation then strengthens the synaptic connections between them. As the saying goes, "Neurons that fire together, wire together."

How are **synapses formed** or **strengthened**?

Synaptogenesis (the creation of synapses) involves multiple steps. New dendrites are formed, thickening the dendritic branches of the neuron. New synapses are made when these dendritic branches make contact with other neurons' axon terminals. Additionally, an existing synapse can be strengthened by the creation of new receptor

111

How can I maintain a healthy brain?

A growing body of research has yielded clues as to the best way to maintain a healthy brain. This becomes especially important as the U.S. population is living longer. In fact, the average lifespan in the United States has increased 32 years over the course of the twentieth century. In the coming decades, therefore, we can expect far more people to live into their seventies, eighties, and nineties than ever before. There are many ways to promote the brain's health. General approaches to healthy living reduce cardiovascular disease, which is one of the main culprits in dementia. Nutritious meals, regular exercise, and avoidance of excessive alcohol, weight gain, and smoking are all important. Exercise, in particular, has been shown to protect cognition in older people, probably by promoting blood flow into the brain.

Good mental health is also important, as depression and excessive stress put strain on the brain. Mental stimulation is helpful, as well. Keep in mind that these factors all work together. Mentally active people with good social support are more likely to be happy and physically more active. Furthermore, you should not wait until you retire to start healthy behavior. It is important to instill good habits while still young. At any given time, our brain reflects our entire lifetime of experience.

sites on the post synaptic neuron (the dendrite). These new receptor sites increase sensitivity to the neurotransmitters released into the synaptic cleft.

What is **pruning**?

Experience affects brain development in two major ways. Activation of synaptic connections strengthens the connections but lack of activation causes these connections to die off. The atrophy (or dying off) of unused connections is known as *pruning*. In short, the brain has a "use it or lose it" policy. For example, a baby is born with the capacity to recognize all sounds of all languages on earth. With exposure to the child's native language, however, the synapses activated by those sounds are strengthened, but the neural networks related to other sounds weaken. Eventually the child's brain has been wired to respond only to its own native language. Although a strong capacity to learn new languages is retained throughout childhood, receptivity to new languages decreases with age.

What are **critical periods**?

The brain does not remain equally plastic throughout the lifespan. There are critical periods where the most growth takes place. The peak of synaptic growth occurs within the first two years of life but synaptogenesis continues at a rapid pace for the first ten years of life. If we think of how much learning takes place within the first two years of life—a child learns to walk, talk, manipulate objects, and begins to understand the social world—it is not surprising that this is a peak period of brain growth. Children also remain extremely open to learning throughout the first decade; they learn to ride bicycles, follow societal rules, and read and write. If these tasks are not learned in childhood, it becomes much more difficult to learn them later on.

What happens if **learning** does not take place during the **critical periods**?

Learning does not stop after the age of ten and the ability to form new memories continues throughout the lifespan. However, the brain networks laid down during critical periods are quite conservative and difficult to change. Consider how easy it is for children under ten to learn a new language and how comparatively difficult it is for their parents to do the same

As the rest of the body ages, so does the brain. The good news is that there are things everyone can do to keep both your mind and body healthier for longer periods of time (*iStock*).

thing. This is often the case in immigrant families, where the children's ability to learn the new language far outstrips that of their parents.

What role does **myelination** play?

Myelin is a fatty sheath that covers the surface of axon fibers and acts as a kind of insulation. *Myelination* increases the speed at which the action potential travels down the axon. The myelination of axon fibers is not well developed at birth. Myelination continues throughout childhood and myelination of the frontal lobe is not complete until the third decade of life.

How does the **frontal lobe change** across development?

The frontal lobe is one of the last areas of the brain to reach full maturity. In fact the frontal lobe does not complete synaptic formation and myelination until the mid-twenties. In this regard, ontogeny does recapitulate phylogeny; in both development and evolution the frontal lobe is a late comer. This is entirely consistent with our

113

observations about the intellectual abilities and social judgment of children and adolescents. While many brain functions, such as physical coordination and language abilities, are fully mature by adolescence, social judgment and abstract thought take considerably longer to mature.

How does the **brain** become **more complex** with development?

As new synapses are formed, the brain becomes more tightly networked. The mature brain has trillions of synapses forming neural networks of extraordinary complexity. This complexity allows for much greater intellectual power and sophistication. Although children have an advantage over adults in their ability to take in and retain new information, adults maintain a profound advantage over children in their ability to process complex information. Thus, while children's brains may be "little sponges", adult brains permit much greater understanding of the world around them.

How does the **brain change** across the **life span** of an individual?

Experience continues to shape the brain throughout the life span, though the changes tend to be more finely tuned later in life than in childhood and infancy. Nonetheless, the more you perform an action, think a thought, or feel a feeling, the more those circuits are reinforced. Circuits that are not reinforced fall off. As such, the "use it or lose it" adage holds across the lifespan. Of course, core circuitry that is laid down in childhood is conservative and difficult to change. That is why early learning and early emotional experience have such a profound effect on adult functioning.

THE AGING BRAIN

How does the **brain age**?

An unfortunate aspect of aging involves the gradual degeneration of most organs. The brain is no exception. There is an overall decrease in the speed, flexibility and efficiency of neuronal networks. There is atrophy and shrinking of many parts of the brain. However, the news is not all grim. Much can be done to preserve brain health in aging.

What is **cortical atrophy**?

Cortical atrophy refers to the shrinking of the neocortex that occurs with age. The gyri (convolutions) shrink, the sulci (grooves between gyri) and the ventricles (vessels filled with cerebral spinal fluid) expand, and there is about a 17 percent decrease in brain weight in both sexes by age eighty.

Do **cells die**?

Brain cells seem to have a preprogrammed life span and cell death occurs throughout the life span. However neuronal death is intensified in aging and neurogenesis, the production of new neurons, is slowed down.

What happens to the **dendrites**?

Another finding of aging involves the thinning of dendritic branching. This may account for some of the atrophy of cerebral gray matter. Fewer dendrites mean fewer synapses for neurons to communicate with each other, which in turn reduces the speed and efficiency of brain functions.

What impact does **brain aging** have on **mental functioning**?

The reduction in brain volume and density definitely has an impact on the aging adult's cognitive functions. These changes correspond with decreased processing speed, working memory, and psychomotor speed, and a reduced ability to commit new information to memory. However, many critical cognitive functions remain intact well into late life. Recognition memory, verbal skills, conceptual abilities, and general IQ stay stable for a long time despite decreases in speed and raw processing power.

What is the difference between **crystallized** and **fluid intelligence**?

Psychologists make a distinction between crystallized intelligence, which remains stable into old age, and fluid intelligence, which reduces with age. Crystallized intelligence involves verbal skills, conceptual skills, and fund of knowledge. Fluid intelligence involves immediate information processing skills, such as the speed at which information is processed, the amount of information that can be processed at a time, and the ability to commit new information to memory.

Are there any **benefits** of an **aging brain**?

Although reductions in processing speed and memory efficiency are evident by middle age, there are some ways the brain improves with age. By the seventh or eighth decade of life, a lifetime of experience is encoded in the brain's neural networks. A lifetime of synaptic strengthening suggests better connectivity across the brain, better integration of different brain areas. This translates into a more comprehensive understanding of the world in which we live. Moreover, enhanced cortical control of limbic responses supports a more thoughtful response to emotion. We know that impulsivity, violence, and recklessness decrease with age. We also value age and life experience when appointing people into positions of leadership. In late old age, however, such as the ninth or tenth decade of life, these strengths can be eclipsed by the degeneration of

Alzheimer' disease is in many ways more frightening than other diseases as it robs one of his or her memories and ability to do daily, simple tasks (*iStock*).

brain tissue and the elderly may become considerably constricted in their independent functioning. Nonetheless, there are more than a few people who remain healthy and vigorous even into their nineties.

Can the **brain regenerate**?

For a long time it was simply assumed that there was no production of new neurons after birth. More and more evidence shows that this is not the case. Certain areas of the brain, such as the hippocampus (an area critical for memory formation), produce new neurons throughout adulthood. We also know that dendritic branching and synaptic development can occur throughout the lifespan. *Neurogenesis* (the creation of new neurons) can be bolstered by physical exercise, diet, appropriate levels of rest and relaxation, mental stimulation, and by certain medications, such as antidepressants, that act on the neurotransmitter known as serotonin.

What is **Alzheimer's** disease?

Alzheimer's disease is an age-related brain disease, in which abnormal growths called *neurofibrillary tangles* and *amaloid plaques* destroy the brain's ability to function properly. These growths start in the hippocampus, where short-term memory is translated into long-term memory. Thus the cardinal feature of Alzheimer's is loss of memory. As the disease progresses, other areas of the brain are affected and other psychological abilities deteriorate, including spatial orientation, executive functions, and eventually speech. Alzheimer's disease is a form of *dementia*, which refers to any condition that involves a permanent loss of cognitive abilities. While it is one of the most common forms of dementia, it is not the only one, and other dementias, such as vascular dementia, can also cause cognitive decline in old age.

FROM BRAIN TO MIND

What can we know of how the **brain creates** the **mind**?

The brain is an extraordinarily intricate web of one hundred billion neurons. Somehow through the trillions of connections among these neurons, the phenomenon of the human mind emerges. Do we know how the mind comes out of the brain? Yes and no. We are learning more and more about what we call the neurobiological *substrates* or *correlates* of mental life. We are learning which parts of the brain are active when we do various mental functions. But correlation is not equal to causation. Just because two things happen together does not mean that we understand how one thing causes the other. The fundamental mystery of how billions of mindless brain cells, or neurons, somehow come together to create consciousness continues to elude us.

What is **qualia**?

The concept of *qualia* relates to the question of subjectivity—what is the yellow of yellow, the green of green? Although we know a tremendous amount about how the brain processes light waves, we still have no idea how our own *experience* of yellow comes to be. At present, many neuroscientists have agreed to put the question of qualia aside. By studying how different brain processes *correlate* with various mental processes, we can still learn an inordinate amount about the relationship of brain and mind. This next section addresses what we do know about the links between the mind and the brain.

THE BRAIN AS MAPMAKER

How does the **brain act** as a **mapmaker**?

One critical way that the brain processes information is to create *maps* of the world around it. From the brain stem up to the cortex, the brain processes information like a very detailed mapmaker. The brain passes information upstream in steps, moving from the lower-level, more simply organized regions to the higher-level, more complex regions. At each step, the new region maps the neural firing patterns of the region below. It does this by recreating the spatial lay-out of the neurons of the other region. In this way, the brain builds a series of representations of both internal and external reality. These maps then serve as guides for action. They help the brain to regulate the internal states of the body, respond to objects in the environment, and respond to the neural patterns underlying our own thoughts and emotions. Another term for map is *representation*. This term is used frequently in discussing the brain.

What does it **mean** to **map something**?

When an arrangement in space in one system mimics that of another system, the first system is *mapping* the second. For example, when you draw two intersecting lines to show a visitor how to get to your house, you are mapping the streets where you live. The brain uses time in its maps as well as space, however. The *sequence* of firing patterns over time is also captured in the maps of the brain, similar to the way in which a musical theme repeats throughout a symphony.

How does the **brain stem** act as a **mapmaker**?

The brain stem maps information both from the outside world and from inside the body. Nerves originating in the skin, muscles, skeletal system, blood vessels, and viscera (internal organs) all connect to neurons in the brain stem. The firing patterns of these nerves are then mirrored in the firing patterns of the brain stem neurons. In this way, the brain forms a representation of the internal state of the body, and this representation is updated on a moment-by-moment basis. Likewise, some types of sensory information, such as sound and touch, are sent to the brain stem in the initial stages of perception.

What does the **frontal cortex map**?

The frontal cortex maps the activity of lower areas of the brain as the frontal lobe is richly connected to other brain regions. By coordinating information from so many diverse areas of the brain, the frontal lobe can map both internal and external reality in great detail.

SENSATION AND PERCEPTION

What is the difference between **sensation** and **perception**?

Sensation is the immediate mapping of raw sensory data, such as light patterns, sound waves, or tactile stimulation. Perception is the next step in the process where all that raw data is synthesized into more complex maps. These maps are then linked via memory to similar maps drawn from past experience. This allows us to classify the images into known categories, for example furniture, food, or animal. Perception

> ## What is blindsight?
>
> **A** number of neurological disorders gives us clues as to the workings of the brain. *Visual agnosia,* also known as blindsight, is a neurological disorder that sheds light on how the brain makes sense of visual information. People with injuries to the visual association cortex will be blind in the conventional sense of the word. They will not be able to recognize any objects visually. Likewise, they will tell you that they cannot see anything. However, if you put a large object in front of their path, they will walk around it, all the while insisting that they do not see a thing. This suggests that fundamental information about the presence and location of visual stimuli does get through. This preliminary information is processed in the primary visual cortex. However, the coordination of visual information into coherent, recognizable shapes takes place in the association cortices. Therefore, injury in those regions results in visual agnosia. In effect, a visual agnosia is sensation without perception.

occurs when the initial sensory information is organized into a sufficiently complete whole (or gestalt) that it can be recognized as an object. At this point, we recognize that the pattern of light waves hitting our retina is actually a chair. Thus sensation works by analysis—by breaking down information into its smallest parts. Perception works by synthesis, by coordinating the parts back into a whole.

How does the brain **process sensory information**?

Our initial sensory information comes from physical stimulation from the outside world. This might come in the form of light waves or sound waves or physical pressure against our skin. This information is picked up by our sense organs, for example our eyes, ears, nose, skin, or tongue. Our sense organs then relay this information to the *primary sensory cortices* via the thalamus. The thalamus acts as a gating station, blocking information it identifies as unimportant and passing on information it deems important. This is true for all our senses except the sense of smell (olfaction) which goes directly to the olfactory bulb, bypassing the thalamus and the cortex. The primary visual cortex is in the occipital lobe, the primary auditory (hearing) cortex is in the temporal lobe, and the primary sensory cortex (for touch and taste) is in the parietal lobe. The primary sensory cortex is known as the *somatosensory strip*.

What do the **primary sensory cortices** do?

The primary sensory cortical areas register the most fundamental aspects of sensation, such as the orientation of a line, the location of a touch, the frequency of a sound wave. Information about these fundamental sensory properties is then passed onto the association cortices, where it is synthesized into a larger whole. In this way sensation moves toward perception.

Does the brain also **process** sensory information from **inside our bodies**?

Sensory information does not only come from outside the body. We also need sensory information about the state of our body. We need to know if we are feeling dizzy or sick to our stomachs, or if our heart is beating fast. This tells us important information about our health but also tells us about our emotions. Part of the way that we know what we are feeling is through sensory information about our internal bodily states. In fact, there are neurons throughout the gastro-intestinal system—so many that it is sometimes called our second brain. The brain stem, somatosensory strip and insula (a cortical area on the inside of the cortex) are involved with processing sensory information from inside our body.

How does the **brain process** perception?

It is important to understand that the brain does not work like a camera, simply photographing outside reality. As mentioned above, the brain *constructs* its own version of reality by constructing a map of the world around it. In the primary sensory cortices, neurons respond to patterns of stimulation, for example, with cells that fire in response to horizontal, vertical, or diagonal lines. This information is then sent to the *association cortices*, where the firing patterns of the different cells are coordinated with each other to establish a broader pattern. When this information is sent to the parts of the brain associated with memory, language, and emotion, we are both able to recognize and label an object as well as appreciate what meaning it might have for us. In this way, the brain constructs an interpretation or map of reality that is deeply connected to our personal experience and history.

What are **association cortices** and what role do they play in perception?

The association cortices are the cortical areas that synthesize the fundamental units of sensation into larger patterns and towards a recognizable whole. The visual association cortex is in the occipital lobe, just anterior to the primary visual cortex. The auditory association cortex is in the temporal lobe, close to the primary auditory cortex. The association cortex for touch is next to the somatosensory strip in the parietal cortex, in the brain regions known as S2 and S3.

After sensory information is processed in the *unimodal* (single sense) *association areas*, it is sent to the *multimodal association areas*, where information from different sensory modalities can be coordinated. For example, information about the sight of a chair as well as the sound and the feel of your body as you sit down in it is coordinated into the unified perception of a single object. Simultaneously, activation of the hippocampus and parts of the temporal cortex jog our memory, allowing us to place our perception in the context of our memories. Thus, this particular object is recognized as a chair.

Do different **people perceive** the same event **differently**?

As mentioned above, the brain does not record reality like a camera; it constructs a representation of reality through analysis and synthesis of sensory information. Therefore, each person's perception of any given event will be unique, which explains why people can have such differing memories of the same event. Even if the same sensory information is available to two different people, the unique history of each person's brain will ensure that the final perception of each individual will differ, colored by variations in the individuals' attention, memories, emotional states, etc. Moreover, the exact sensory information in any given event will never be identical for any two people because

What meets the eye is not always perceived the same from person to person. The external world that people see and hear and touch and smell is interpreted differently as it is filtered through each individual's emotions, memories, and cognitive processes (*iStock*).

the position in space of each person's body will necessarily differ. All these factors will continue to color the memory of the event at later times. This is well understood in legal contexts and is the reason that eye witness testimony can be highly problematic.

How does the **brain process vision**?

One-third of the brain is used to process visual information, which tells us just how important vision is to human beings. The processing of visual information starts in the eyes, the visual sense organs. On the retina, the inner back surface of the eye, there are a number of neurons that are specialized to fire in response to light. These specific cells are called *rods* and *cones*. Rods respond to night vision and process information in shades of black, white and gray. Cones fire in bright light and respond to color. The axons of rods and cones connect to other cells in the retina, where some preliminary visual processing is done. These neurons then connect to ganglion cells, whose axons bundle together, like wires in a cable, to form the *optic nerve*.

The optic nerve exits through the back of the retina and travels to the brain. All the ganglion cells that respond to the right side of the visual field will go to the left side of the brain. Likewise the ganglion cells that respond to the left side of the visual field will go to the right side of the brain. Any ganglion axon that needs to cross over

What is prosopagnosia?

An elderly man was admitted to a hospital. The staff soon noticed that he became agitated when walking by pictures hanging on the walls. These were framed prints encased in glass. When passing by the picture, he would catch a reflection of himself and then turn and start yelling, "Get away from me! Leave me alone!" He would ask the nurses plaintively, "Why does that man keep following me?"

This man suffered from a disorder known as *prosopagnosia,* which refers to the inability to recognize faces. This bizarrely specific disorder is due to lesions in the *fusiform gyrus*, a multimodal association region that is located at the bottom of the temporal lobe. The fusiform gyrus integrates perceptual information about faces into recognizable wholes. When this region is damaged, the person cannot perceive faces as a recognizable whole but only as a collection of visual parts. Some readers may be familiar with this disorder from Oliver Sacks's book *The Man Who Mistook His Wife for a Hat.*

to the opposite side of the brain is able to do so at the optic chiasm, in the middle of the brain. The two branches of the optic nerve next connect to the corresponding lobes of the thalamus. The thalamus is the gate keeper for sensory information. Based on feedback from the cortex, the thalamus lets some information through to activate neurons connected to the cortex but stops other messages in their tracks. Neurons in the thalamus send visual information up to the primary visual cortex in the occipital lobe, known as VI or Brodman area 17. From there, the fundamental features of the visual stimulus are processed. As discussed above, these neurons connect to association cortices where the basic visual features are then synthesized into larger patterns.

How does the **brain process sound**?

The ear is composed of three sections, the *outer ear*, the *middle ear*, and the *inner ear*. The outer flap that we normally think of as the ear is called the pinna. That and the ear canal, the long inner tunnel where our wax collects, comprise the outer ear. The ear canal ends in the ear drum, a thin membrane that stretches across the back end of the ear canal. The middle ear consists of three tiny, delicate bones that transfer sound vibrations from the ear drum to the cochlea, a fluid-filled spiral that translates sound vibrations into neural activity. The cochlea and the vestibular apparatus, which senses balance and motion, comprise the inner ear. Sound vibrations are captured by the pinna, channeled back to the middle ear by the ear canal, and communicated to the cochlea via the bones of the middle ear.

The fluid-filled cochlea is lined with hair cells, a type of sensory neuron that responds to sounds of specific frequencies. High frequencies (which translate into high pitched sounds) are recorded by hair cells at the opening of the spiral cochlea, middle frequencies in the middle of the cochlea, and low frequencies by hair cells at the end of the spiral. The hair cells send information to the spinal cord, which then connects to several regions in the brain stem. Here the auditory information is processed for the timing and intensity. These neurons connect to the inferior colliculus in the mid-brain, where some further analysis takes place. The inferior colliculus connects to the gate-keeping thalamus. Finally, the auditory information enters the cortex at the primary auditory cortex (A1), located in the superior and posterior (upper rear) temporal lobe. Association areas are nearby, including the regions that deal with language.

Why do some people hear **voices** that **aren't really there**?

One of the most common symptoms of schizophrenia and other psychotic disorders involves auditory hallucinations. This occurs when someone hears sounds that have no basis in external reality. People can hear voices talking to them—sometimes a single voice, sometimes an entire chorus of voices. The voices can maintain an ongoing commentary on the person's behavior, can make derogatory statements, call the person names, or even instruct the person on what to do.

The most elaborate auditory hallucinations are associated with schizophrenia. Researchers have found that the auditory cortex is active when a person is hearing voices. In this way the brain actually *is* hearing voices although the sensory information does not come from the ear but from inside the person's brain. It is believed that hallucinatory voices actually derive from the person's thoughts. The thoughts get translated into a kind of inner speech, which the brain hears as if it were hearing actual speech.

While inner speech is a common phenomenon, healthy brains can distinguish between inner speech and spoken words. In psychosis, however, the distinction between inner and outer reality is lost. For reasons we do not fully understand, antipsychotic medication restores the ability to make the critical distinction between imagined and external reality.

How does the **brain process touch**?

The sensory organs for all of our other senses are relatively small. Consider the size of the ears, nose, or eyes. The sensory organ that processes touch, however, covers our whole body. Our entire skin functions as the sensory organ for touch. Our skin is covered with many different sensory receptor cells. Some are specialized to

Animals such as dogs have a much more heightened sense of smell than humans, whose olfactory bulbs are correspondingly smaller and process less information (*iStock*).

sense changes in physical pressure, some to vibrations, some to pain, and others to temperature. These neurons send information to the cortex via a fairly long pathway, running through the spinal cord, areas in the mid brain, and the thalamus. The primary sensory area for touch is called the somatosensory strip (S1) in the anterior (front) area of the parietal lobe. Neurons responding to touch on different areas of the body are mapped along the somatosensory strip. This map is known as the *homunculus* ("little man" in Latin). Association cortices for touch (e.g., S2 and S3) are adjacent to S1.

How does the **brain process smell**?

The sense of smell is processed in the *olfactory system*, which is an evolutionarily ancient system, dating back hundreds of millions of years. The olfactory system responds to airborne chemicals, which waft into the nose. The olfactory nerve connects the olfactory receptor cells in the nose to the olfactory bulbs, two small structures on either side of the brain just below the frontal lobe. From the olfactory bulbs, axons bundled together into the olfactory nerves project to various parts of the limbic system. From there, neurons connect to other subcortical areas such as the thalamus, hypothalamus, and insula. Thus, the olfactory nerve sends information directly to the emotional centers of the brain, without the filtering role of the thalamus or the cortex. The olfactory bulb plays a much larger role in simpler and phylogenetically older animals than it does in phylogenetically younger and more complex animals like primates.

What about **taste**?

Our subjective experience of taste is actually a combination of taste and smell. If you sever the olfactory nerve, removing the sense of smell, your ability to taste your food will be much reduced. You will only be able to taste sweet, bitter, salt, and sour flavors. There is now evidence for a fifth type of taste category, however, which has been named *umami*. This is a Japanese word meaning delicious, savory, or meaty. Umami seems related to monosodium glutamate (MSG), a food additive used extensively in East Asian cuisine.

All of these taste categories have survival value. Sweet, umami, and salty tastes enhance our intake of carbohydrate, protein, and salt, respectively. Excessive amounts of bitter or sour taste alert us to decaying or toxic food. The relative amounts of the taste qualities of any food put in the mouth are sensed by the *taste buds* (gustatory papillae), tiny protrusions that cover the surface of the tongue. The taste buds are somewhat specialized to specific taste qualities, but generally respond to more than one aspect of taste (e.g., both salty and sweet). The taste buds carry information to the cranial nerves, which connect to neurons in the brain stem, which then connect to neurons in the thalamus. These project (or connect) to a particular area in the somatosensory strip specialized for the tongue.

MOTOR BEHAVIOR
AND INTENTIONAL ACTION

How does our **brain** generate **motor behavior**?

Physical action, also called motor behavior, is the output side of the input/output system of the brain. Sensation/perception is our input and action is our output. Our physical behavior ranges from simple reflexive movements up to intentional, planned, and complex movements.

What is the difference between **voluntary** and **involuntary movements**?

Voluntary movements are those movements that are potentially under conscious control. Examples include walking, standing up, raising our arm, getting dressed, shaking our head, etc. *Involuntary movements* are those movements that are not under conscious control or that generally happen automatically without conscious thought. Examples include breathing, heartbeat, posture, and motor coordination.

How does the brain **process involuntary movements**?

Different tracts of neurons are involved with voluntary and involuntary movements. Involuntary movements are processed largely through a group of brain cells known as *extra-pyramidal* neurons. They connect input from the cerebellum and the inner ear to the brain stem. The first two areas process information about coordination and balance. The brain stem sends this information to motor neurons in the spinal cord, which connect directly to the muscles involved. Thus, information related to involuntary movement does not go through the cortex and generally travels in a relatively simple, closed circuit.

How does psychiatric **medication** affect **extra-pyramidal neurons**?

Antipsychotic medication can disrupt the function of extra-pyramidal neurons. This can result in disfiguring side effects, such as tardive dyskinesia, a syndrome characterized by tremors in the extremities and facial muscles. The atypical antipsychotics, a new class of medication, have now become popular because they produce fewer extra-pyramidal side effects (e.g., restlessness, tremor, and muscular stiffness).

How does the brain **mediate voluntary movements**?

While sensory information moves more or less from the back to the front of the brain, motor information moves in the opposite direction. Goals for physical action are processed in the pre-frontal cortex, the seat of planning and goal setting. This information is sent back to the pre-motor cortex and the supplemental motor area, which

125

lie just in front of the primary motor cortex. *Coordination* of the specific movements appears to take place in these areas.

This information is then transmitted to the *primary motor cortex* (or M1), which lies just in front of the central sulcus, next to the somatosensory strip of the parietal lobe. The surface of the body is mapped along M1, creating a similar homunculus to the one found next door in the somatosensory strip. This region is linked to the actual *execution* of the movement. M1 sends information to the brain stem, which then activates motor neurons in the spinal cord. These in turn connect directly to the muscles.

Does **information** only **move** in **one direction**?

It is important to understand that the brain is continuously giving and receiving feedback. Information is always moving up and down the system and modifying both input and output. For example, the motor system sends out a signal to move and the left hand reaches out to grasp a glass. Simultaneously, the brain processes important sensory feedback. The hand is too far to the left of the glass, the pinky finger brushes against the back of a chair. This feedback is automatically incorporated into the ongoing movement, and the hand is moved half an inch to the right. The impact of this new movement is then encoded into new sensory information. For the sake of simplicity, our sensory and motor systems are presented here as if they act in isolation. In reality, though, the brain is a giant web of interacting systems giving itself constant feedback.

What **role** does the **cerebellum** play?

The *cerebellum*, which is Latin for "little brain," is the large, bulbous structure located below the back of the cortex. With rich connections to both the frontal lobe and the brain stem, it is integrally involved in motor control. The cerebellum mediates motor coordination, posture, and the smooth flow of movement. Damage to the cerebellum results in jerky, uncoordinated movements and problems with balance. More recent research has revealed that the cerebellum is involved with a range of cognitive functions as well.

Is **imagined movement** different than **actual movement**?

Surprisingly, the brain processes observed movement and imagined movement in much the same way it processes actual movement. Brain imaging studies have shown that the same areas of the motor cortex are activated when people witness an action in another person, imagine performing the same action themselves, or actually perform the action themselves.

What are **mirror neurons**?

Mirror neurons are a group of neurons found in the premotor cortex that respond both to witnessed movements in other animals and to the analogous movement in the

What is a phantom pain?

People who have lost their limbs to amputation often complain of feeling pain where the limb used to be. This phenomenon is known as *phantom limb pain*. Such an experience can be very distressing as it compounds an already devastating loss. Brain imaging studies have shown that phantom limb sensation is related to activity in the somatosensory strip and the sensory association cortices nearby. Neurons in the spinal cord still send pain signals to the parts of the brain that process sensory information from the amputated limb. This does not apply to just pain. For example, people who have lost their hands can imagine moving their fingers. When they do so, the corresponding area of the motor strip in the brain is activated as if the hand is still there.

People who have had a limb or other body part amputated can still experience sensations like pain because the nerves in the spinal cord corresponding to that area of the body can still send signals to the brain (*iStock*).

self. Similar neurons have also been found in the sensory association cortex in the parietal lobe. Some scientists have suggested that mirror neurons might be the basis of empathy. Mirror neurons were discovered when scientists implanted electrodes in monkeys' brains to measure the electrical activity of single neurons. The cells fired both when the monkey made a particular hand movement and when the experimenter made the same hand movement. The cells did not fire when the experimenter made a different hand movement.

Does the brain process **complex behavior** differently than **simple behavior**?

The frontal lobe is not the only source of complex goal-oriented movement. As discussed above, the frontal lobe is a recent evolutionary achievement and is most fully developed in humans. Prior to the evolution of the frontal lobe, however, animals needed some way to perform goal-oriented behaviors. Prey had to be hunted, hygiene maintained, food eaten, and social behaviors performed. In most animals, these behaviors were patterned into fairly fixed packets of behaviors that would be released rather automatically in the face of the appropriate stimulus. The mouse runs across the floor and the cat pounces. The part of the brain associated with these pre-set behavioral packets is known as the basal ganglia.

What role does the **basal ganglia** play?

The *basal ganglia* refers to a group of brain structures which include the *caudate nucleus*, the *putamen* and the *globus pallidus*. This is an evolutionarily ancient brain region that precedes the evolution of the cortex and is found in mammals, birds, and even reptiles. The basal ganglia mediates simple motor programs. These are packets of movements that serve a purpose—riding a bike, throwing a ball, etc. Some of these automatic behaviors are learned (e.g., riding a bike) and some are unlearned, based on genetics. The unlearned motor programs are also known as fixed action patterns. In humans, the basal ganglia is heavily involved with learned motor programs. Although complex behaviors are learned via the frontal lobe, with practice the behavior becomes more automatic and the basal ganglia comes into play.

What are **fixed action patterns** and what do they tell us about our "**animal instincts**"?

A *fixed action pattern* is a genetically-coded behavioral sequence that is triggered by specific stimuli. Fixed action patterns are analogous to animal "instincts" and are mediated by the basal ganglia. The behavior is fixed and relatively unmodifiable. There is very little goal correction; the behavior is a set response to a set stimulus.

What examples of **fixed action patterns** do we see in **animals**?

For example, cats smell their urine and start digging in cat litter to bury their waste. They rarely check the results of their efforts to see if they have met their goal; they simply respond in a preprogrammed way to a set stimulus, in this case the smell of their urine or feces. Grooming behavior in multiple animals provides additional examples of fixed action patterns. Birds preen themselves, cats lick themselves, and dogs shake themselves when wet. Additional examples include gnawing behavior in pigs and horses whinnying and shaking their heads.

What **fixed action patterns** do we see in **humans**?

In humans, we see reflexes at birth (rooting, swimming, grasping, and sucking). With development, however, these basal ganglia-mediated reflexes get suppressed by the frontal lobe. For the most part, thoughtful, intentional behavior replaces automatic stimulus-response chains. In adulthood, fixed action patterns can re-emerge if there is damage to the frontal lobe. *Frontal release signs*, which are associated with frontal lobe damage, include several reflexes that we normally see only in early infancy. Certain psychiatric conditions may also reflect pathological activation of fixed action patterns. For example, obsessive compulsive disorder (OCD) has been linked to basal ganglia-frontal lobe circuits. It is characterized by repetitive, stereotyped, and senseless behaviors, such as compulsive hand-washing, tapping, straightening, or organizing behavior.

COGNITION AND BEHAVIORAL CONTROL

How does **cognition** serve to **regulate behavior**?

What is cognition? How do we define thought? At base, *cognition* involves the representation of events and the mental manipulation of events outside of immediate reality. In other words, the use of imagination. If you can imagine the outcome of an action, you can evaluate whether or not it is worthwhile to take such an action. Or you can imagine alternative actions that can be taken. These abilities dramatically change the animal's relationship with action. With cognition, human beings are able to think before they act and to correct their mistakes. They are also able to plan future actions and to anticipate possible outcomes.

What does **goal-correction** mean?

Cognition also allows us to compare the actual outcome of an action with the desired outcome and then modify the action accordingly. This process is called *goal-correction*.

What are **executive functions**?

Executive functions are a set of mental abilities that are mediated by the frontal lobes. These include planning, analyzing, considering alternative actions, abstraction, changing sets, etc. These critical mental functions help people adapt to a complex and ever-changing environment. When the frontal lobe is damaged, people lose executive functions. They become more impulsive, disorganized, unable to plan, and unable to monitor and regulate their own behavior. In effect they become more childlike, regressing to a time when the frontal lobe was less developed.

How does **impulse control** relate to executive functions?

Impulse control is also critical. Specifically, this involves the linking of representations of events with memories or expectations of punishment. The person can consider the negative consequences of an intended action and inhibit or alter the action accordingly. People with poor impulse control often do poorly on neuropsychological tests that measure executive functions like abstraction, set switching, and planning. Impulse control is mediated by the *orbital frontal cortex*, which lies on the underside of the frontal lobe.

Who was **Phineas Gage**?

Phineas Gage (1823–1860) was a railroad worker living in the mid-nineteenth century who suffered a terrible accident while at work. An iron rod crashed through his head, tearing a large hole through his brain. Surprisingly, he survived this incident and in fact was relatively unharmed physically. His cognition and motor control were reasonably intact. However, there were marked personality changes that were very disturbing to those who had known him prior to the accident. While he had once been a sober and well-behaved citizen, after the accident he became rude, impulsive, and socially inappropriate. We now understand that he suffered from orbital frontal damage, with severe damage to the areas of the brain centrally involved with impulse control and social judgment.

EMOTIONS

What are **emotions**?

We can think of emotions as behavioral packets for social animals. They are a very quick and efficient way to respond to different circumstances in the environment. Such circumstances might include aversive conditions, such as danger or aggression, or rewarding conditions such as food, sex, safety, or social bonds. All emotional reactions involve coordination of several features. These include autonomic nervous system arousal, facial expression, muscular tension, and subjective experience. This packet of responses is almost like a computer macro that serves as preparation for a specific situation. For example, when people are angry their blood pumps faster, their face becomes flush, their brow furrows, their mouth purses, the large muscles in their arms and legs tense, and they have the distinct subjective experience of anger. In this way, their body is prepared not only for action, but for aggressive action in particular.

What **purposes** do **emotions** serve?

All emotions serve at least three purposes: they prepare the individual for appropriate action; they alert the individual of the salience (or significance) of the situation; they communicate to others how the individual is reacting. For example, in a situation of danger, the emotional response of fear alerts the individual to the danger of the situation, prepares the individual for physical flight, and communicates to other people via facial expression, vocalization, and physical posture that the individual senses danger.

What are the different **classes** of **emotions**?

The core emotions are generally recognized to be anger, fear, disgust, surprise, joy, and sadness. These are biologically encoded, unlearned human responses that are immediately recognizable regardless of linguistic or cultural differences. Many of these emotions, such as fear and anger, are also found in other mammals. However, the palette of human emotions is broader than these six core emotions. Self-conscious emotions—such as shame, embarrassment, pride, or guilt—are also part of the human emotional repertoire. These more complex emotions depend upon a certain degree of cognitive development and relate to one's place in the social group.

Do we always **know** what we are **feeling**?

Feeling something and knowing what we are feeling are two different things. In fact, the neuroscientist Antonio Damasio makes a distinction between *emotion,* which is the body's physiological response, and *feeling,* which is the conscious experience of emotion. Infants are born with emotional responses—they are literally born crying. In contrast, the ability to recognize and verbally label emotion ("Oh, I'm feeling sad.") is something that develops with age and is to some extent dependent on appropriate social feedback. Relatedly, the basis of psychodynamic psychotherapy is the idea that emotional maladjustment comes from lack of knowledge of one's own emotions. The inability to recognize one's own emotions is called *alexythymia.*

EMOTION AND THE LIMBIC SYSTEM

How is the **limbic system** involved in **emotion**?

Our knowledge of the neurobiology of emotion is far less developed than our knowledge of the role of the brain in cognition. But we do know that the group of brain structures called the *limbic system* is centrally involved with emotion. The limbic system refers to a group of subcortical brain structures that wrap around the thalamus. Although there is disagreement about the exact boundaries of the limbic system, the term is usually understood to include core brain structures involved in the processing of emotion.

What role does the **amygdala** play in **emotion**?

The amygdala is a small, almond shaped structure that lies just below the basal ganglia ("amygdala" is Greek for "almond"). The amygdala is a critical player in emotional reactions. It is an early responder to emotionally salient stimuli, particularly fearful stimuli. The amygdala has rich connections with other limbic areas as well as lower brain regions, such as the midbrain and the brain stem. In particular, it has many connections to neurons in the midbrain which manufacture neurotransmitters highly relevant to emotional life.

For example, the raphe nucleus generates serotonin, the ventral tegmental area dopamine, and the locus ceruleus norepinephrine. Most psychiatric drugs target one or more of these neurotransmitter systems. The amygdala also connects to the frontal and temporal lobes. In this way, the amygdala acts as a way station between the thinking and perceiving areas of the brain and the physiological control centers.

What is the **HPA axis**?

The HPA axis is one major route by which the hypothalamus can step on the gas pedal and rev the body up. The HPA axis includes the *hypothalamus, pituitary gland, and adrenal glands*. This triad is centrally involved in the stress response of the body. The pituitary gland is a small structure below the hypothalamus and the adrenal glands lie just above the kidneys. The hypothalamus secretes a hormone known as cortisol releasing hormone (CRH), which travels down to the pituitary gland, where it stimulates the release of adrenocorticotropic hormone (ACTH). This is turn travels down to the adrenal glands, where it stimulates the release of cortisol and other corticosteroids. These hormones activate the sympathetic nervous system. Cortisol influences many psychological responses, including stress, mood, and some forms of mental illness.

How does the **hypothalamus** act as the **gateway** to the **autonomic nervous system**?

One of the brain regions that the amygdala connects to is the *hypothalamus*. This important structure is involved with motivational drives such as hunger, sex, and thirst and also serves as a coordinator for the physiological centers of the brain. The hypothalamus is the master control center for the *autonomic nervous system*. This whole body system gears the body up for action by mobilizing the cardiovascular, respiratory, muscular, and gastro-intestinal systems.

The work of the autonomic nervous system is evident when we feel emotionally aroused. Our heart beats faster, we start to sweat, our stomach churns, and our breath grows rapid and shallow. (More specifically, this is the work of the sympathetic nervous system, which speeds us up. The parasympathetic nervous system slows us down.) The hypothalamus activates the autonomic nervous system in two major ways. The first is the more traditional route of synaptic connections between neurons. The second is through the release of hormones, free-floating chemical messengers that largely travel through the blood stream.

How does the **hippocampus** affect **emotional processing**?

The hippocampus is involved with memory, which is critical to our evaluation of any new stimulus. Have I encountered this person/situation/object before? Is this friend or foe? Although the hippocampus is not directly involved in emotion, it is located near the other limbic structures and has neuronal connections with several of them, including the amygdala, the hypothalamus, and the cingulate gyrus.

How does the **insula** provide information about **internal bodily states**?

The insula is involved with the representation of internal bodily states. It helps process sensory information from inside our bodies, for example butterflies in our stomach or cramps in our intestines. More specifically it has been associated with the processing of aversive food tastes and the related experience of disgust. The insula is located on the inside of the cortex, surrounded by the temporal, frontal, and parietal lobes. Brain imaging studies have shown that this region is activated in many different emotional states. This is because sensory information about the physical state of the body plays a critical part in the subjective awareness of emotion. Try to remember the times when you have felt intensely happy, angry, or frightened. Do you recall the sensation of changes in muscle tension, energy level, heartbeat, etc? Can you imagine experiencing intense emotions without feeling these bodily changes? In sum, the amygdala and hypothalamus primarily provide emotional *output*—they activate the emotional responses. In contrast, the insula gives emotional *input*. It helps translate biological emotion into conscious feeling by giving us information about what our body is doing.

EMOTIONS IN MAMMALS

How are our **emotions rooted** in our **mammalian history**?

Emotions are part of the evolutionary tool kit of mammals. Mammals are, for the most part, very social animals and emotions help in the core aspects of social functioning.

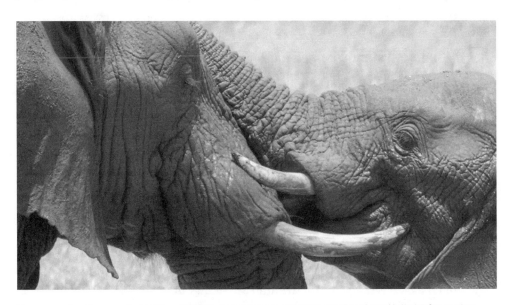

Many mammal species are very social. These elephants, for instance, are engaging in affectionate social behavior. Our emotions evolved in large part to help us negotiate the social world (*iStock.com*).

For example, emotions cement social bonds, in the interest of both mating and parenting. They support intra-species competition, as when animals compete for status, resources and mates. They also offer invaluable help in responding to and communicating danger and, finally, they give us information as to how other group members are responding to ourselves and to the environment.

What **emotions** are evident in **higher mammals**?

Core emotions are clearly evident in our household pets, our cats and dogs, which is why we grow so attached to them. Affection, aggression, fear, contentment, and excitement are all impossible to miss. When a dog wags its tail and assumes a play position, it is hard not to respond with positive emotion. Likewise, when our pet cat rubs against us and purrs, this typically elicits a similarly content and affectionate response.

How do **human emotions differ** from **animal** emotions?

Because of our greater brain complexity, our emotions tend to be more nuanced and complex, more influenced by cognition and by our considerations of the past and the future. Animal emotions are simpler, more directly tied to actions and to the here and now. Dogs may growl at a stranger, rub against a beloved and trusted owner, or wag their tails at a sign that they are about to be taken for a walk. In contrast, human emotion is much less tied to the present. We regret the past and worry about the future. And our emotional responses are not restricted to our immediate environment. Human beings might become depressed after reading a newspaper article on global warming, worry about what their friends think of their lovers, or feel jealous of a high school friend's success at work.

Has the **limbic system changed** much across evolution?

The limbic system, the seat of emotions, has not changed as much as the frontal lobe across evolution. Our cortex is quite different from that of our mammalian cousins; our limbic system is not. This is why we can make emotional attachments to animals of different species. Even though our intellectual brains are vastly different, our emotional brains are relatively similar.

FRONTAL CONTROL OF THE LIMBIC SYSTEM

How does the **frontal lobe control** the **limbic system**?

The frontal lobe serves to control the limbic system. Correspondingly, thought serves to control emotion. The frontal lobe is richly connected to brain regions throughout the limbic system and many frontal lobe neurons that connect to limbic regions have

> ## Are Freud's ego and id concepts rooted in biological fact?
>
> **M**uch of psychoanalytic theory has required modification since Sigmund Freud's original work. Nonetheless, Freud's concepts of the ego and the id have held up remarkably well over these past 100 years. The ego is the seat of the reality principle. It helps us adapt our wishes and urges to cold reality. The id, on the other hand, is the seat of our most primitive and animalistic desires. It is the source of our passions. As is suggested by Freud's famous phrase "Where id was, there shall ego be," the ego serves to control the id.
>
> Surprisingly, modern neuroscience has completely supported this notion. The id can be equated with the limbic system, the seat of our emotions. The ego can be equated with the frontal lobe, or, more specifically, the pre-frontal cortex, which mediates cognition and behavioral control. Just as the ego serves to control the id, the frontal lobe serves to control the limbic system.

inhibitory effects. Emotions are blunt instruments—they are very fast, but not very precise. The frontal lobe helps us refine our emotional responses; to ensure that our responses are proportional to the situation. This is done with the use of thought, by interjecting thought between emotion and response.

Sometimes cognitive analysis of the situation may increase the emotional response. Think of the times when your initial response to a situation was muted but then escalated the more you thought about what happened. On the other hand, cognitive analysis frequently serves to dampen the emotional response by helping the individual consider the consequences of acting on emotions. (*If I punch him, he might punch back. If I quit my job, I won't be able to pay my rent.*) Cognition also helps people consider alternative explanations for a situation. (*Hmmm, maybe this wasn't an insult. Maybe he just didn't see me.*)

What role does the **orbital frontal region** play?

The *orbital frontal* region lies on the underside of the frontal lobe, just above the eyes. This brain region is particularly important for impulse control, for the inhibition of dangerous or reckless actions. People with damage to their orbital frontal cortex show disinhibited, impulsive, and socially unacceptable behavior. The case of Phineas Gage is a famous example of orbital frontal damage. Orbital frontal inhibition probably works through linking representations of future events with representations of past or future punishment.

What is the role of the **superior medial frontal cortex**?

New research suggests that a part of the frontal lobe, the *superior medial frontal cortex*, is involved with social cognition via connecting emotional memories with cogni-   135 tion. This part of the brain, which lies in the middle of the frontal lobe, has been linked to the perception of self, of others, and of mental states. Although this research is still fairly new, it may be quite radical, in that it provides the first evidence of the neurobiological substrates of certain aspects of personality.

Does an **immature frontal lobe** mean **poor emotional regulation**?

As the frontal lobe is the last to develop across childhood, and in fact is not fully developed until adulthood, emotional control also does not fully mature until adulthood. This is intuitively obvious if we think of the relative emotional immaturity of children and even adolescents.

What happens when the **frontal lobe deteriorates**?

When the frontal lobe deteriorates, we can see re-emergence of more primitive behaviors that had previously been inhibited by the frontal lobe. The *Babinski reflex* and frontal release signs are examples of this. Likewise, there is less control over primitive limbic responses. Consequently, the person loses social judgment, impulse control, and the ability to plan and to analyze situations effectively. This is why people with Alzheimer's disease or other dementias need continuous supervision. When the frontal lobe goes, the person in effect regresses to childhood.

What are **frontal release signs**?

The *frontal release signs* refer to a group of reflexive behaviors, controlled by the basal ganglia, which are normally evident only in earliest infancy. Examples of these behaviors include rooting (turning the face toward an object if it touches the cheek near the mouth) and puckering of the lips in response to touch of the skin above the upper lip. These instinctual behaviors promote nursing behavior in an infant.

The palmar grasp reflex helps an infant hold onto its mother. In this reaction, the infant grasps at anything that strokes its palm. The Babinski reflex, in which the foot arches away from tactile stimulation on the sole of the foot, is another of these early reflexes. With development of the frontal lobe, these crude automatic behaviors are suppressed. When there is damage to the frontal lobe in adulthood, however, these early reflexes may re-emerge. The presence of frontal release signs in adulthood, therefore, is a sign of significant brain damage.

NEUROTRANSMITTERS AND OTHER BRAIN CHEMICALS

What are **neurotransmitters** and why are they important?

Neurotransmitters are perhaps the main chemical messengers in the brain. They are the means by which neurons communicate with each other. It is through neurotransmitters that one neuron tells another neuron to fire. If we think of the neuronal networks of the brain as a vast economy, neurotransmitters can be seen as the currency of that economy. The exchange of neurotransmitters stimulates neurons to act.

How do **neurotransmitters** act at **synapses**?

Neurotransmitters are stored in sac-like vesicles in the axon terminals of the neuron. When the neuron fires, its axon terminals release neurotransmitters into the synaptic cleft, the space between the pre-synaptic and post-synaptic neuron. When the neurotransmitters bind to the receptor sites on the post-synaptic neuron, they impact the likelihood that the neuron will fire. Excitatory neurotransmitters increase the likelihood of firing while inhibitory neurotransmitters decrease it.

What are the **main neurotransmitters**?

Dopamine, norepinephrine, and *serotonin* are probably the best known of the neurotransmitters and the ones most frequently targeted by psychiatric medication. All three are classified as monoamines based on their chemical structure. *Glutamate* is a general excitatory neurotransmitter—it increases the likelihood that neurons will fire. *GABA* is a general inhibitory neurotransmitter—it decreases the likelihood of neurons firing. *Histamine* is known for its involvement in the allergic response. *Acetylcholine* is involved with memory and is targeted by anti-Alzheimer's drugs.

What are the major **classes** of **psychiatric medications**?

The table below lists the major classes of psychiatric medications, sample drugs in each class, and the primary neurotransmitter systems targeted by each medication class. Cognitive enhancers are a fairly new class of drugs, developed to treat Alzheimer's dementia.

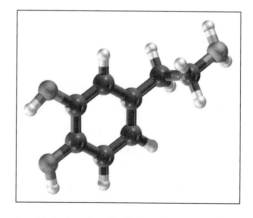

A model of a dopamine molecule. Dopamine is a neurotransmitter frequently targeted by psychiatric medications (*iStock*).

137

Class of Medication	Specific Drugs	Neurotransmitter
Typical antipsychotics	Haloperidol (Haldol) Chlorpromazine (Thorazine)	Dopamine
Atypical antipsychotics	Risperidone (Risperdal) Olanzapine (Zyprexa)	Dopamine, Serotonin, Histamine, Norepinephrine
SSRI Antidepressants	Fluoxetine (Prozac) Sertraline (Zoloft)	Serotonin
Tricyclic Antidepressants	Amitriptylene (Elavil) Clomipramine (Anafranil)	Serotonin, Norepinephrine
Benzodiazepine antianxiety medications	Diazepam (Valium) Clonazepam (Klonopin)	GABA
Stimulants	Methylphenidate (Ritalin) Dextroamphetamine (Dexedrine)	Dopamine, Norepinephrine
Cognitive Enhancers: Cholinesterase Inhibitors	Donepezil (Aricept) Tacrine (Cognex)	Acetylcholine
Cognitive Enhancers: NMDA Receptor Antagonists	Memantine (Namenda)	Glutamate

NMDA Receptor Antagonists

What functions does **dopamine** serve?

The *dopamine* pathways serve many functions. There are, in fact, several dopaminergic tracts. The *nigro-striatal* tracts originate in the substantia nigra in the midbrain and project to the basal ganglia. These tracts are involved with motor control (control of physical movements) and are the neurons damaged in Parkinson's disease. Antipsychotic drugs can also cause problems with this system, resulting in abnormal movements. The second major dopaminergic tract is known as the *mesolimbic* pathway. It originates in the ventral tegmental area (also in the midbrain) and projects to the nucleus accumbens and some areas of the limbic system. This tract is associated with the reward system. The third major dopaminergic tract is the *mesocortical* tract. Like the mesolimbic tract, this originates in the ventral tegmental area. It projects to the cortex, with particularly rich connections in the frontal lobe. This pathway is associated with psychotic symptoms and is targeted by many antipsychotic medications.

What is the **reward system**?

The *reward system* refers to a tract of dopamine-containing neurons that are centrally involved in the experience of desire. The object of desire is not important. This is an all-purpose motivation machine that is active in drug craving (cocaine, methamphetamine, alcohol, and cigarettes) and in gambling, eating, and sex. It may be active as well in many other activities that elicit strong motivation and desire. The reward system is composed of the *mesolimbic dopaminergic* tracts, which reach from the *ventral tegmental area* in the midbrain to the *nucleus accumbens* in the forebrain.

How is **serotonin** involved in **mood** and **behavior**?

Serotonin is an evolutionarily ancient neurotransmitter system and is found in animals as primitive as sea slugs. In humans, not surprisingly, it is involved with a very wide array of functions, ranging from the simplest to the most advanced. For example, serotonin is involved with hunger, sleep, migraine headaches, and sexual function. It is also involved with mood, anxiety, and anticipation of harm. People with low levels of serotonin demonstrate impulse control problems, while people with high levels of serotonin manifest excessive levels of caution and inhibition. The serotonin tracts originate in the raphe nuclei in the brainstem and project widely throughout the cerebral cortex. Certain serotonergic tracts also project downwards to the spinal cord.

Serotonin is targeted by the selective serotonin reuptake inhibitors (SSRIs), the widely used class of antidepressants. Examples of SSRIs include fluoxetine (Prozac), sertraline (Zoloft), and paroxetine (Paxil). SSRIs are also effective in the treatment of anxiety disorders and obsessive compulsive disorder.

What ways does **norepinephrine** impact **mental life**?

Norepinephrine appears to be related to arousal and attention. When norepinephrine, also known as *noradrenaline,* is released into the brain of an animal, the animal becomes more alert and vigilant to its environment. Likewise, norepinephrine may be involved in attention deficit disorder (ADD). Norepinephrine also activates the autonomic nervous system during the fight/flight response, affecting activity in the cardiovascular, muscular, and digestive systems. In fact, beta blockers, a class of medication used to treat high blood pressure, act on the noradrenergic system, the tract of neurons that release norepinephrine. In addition, the noradrenergic system is targeted by a class of antidepressant medication known as tricyclics. This suggests that norepinephrine may also be involved in mood.

How are **glutamate** and **GABA** important?

These two neurotransmitters have broadly distributed effects; they are found throughout the brain. Glutamate is the main excitatory neurotransmitter in the brain; it activates the nervous system and appears to be involved in learning and memory. New research suggests it is also involved with schizophrenia. In contrast, GABA is an inhibitory neurotransmitter; it calms the nervous system. GABA neurotransmitters are targeted by the benzodiazepines, antianxiety medications that also act as tranquilizers. Examples of benzodiazepines include clonazepam (Klonopin), lorazepam (Ativan), diazepam (Valium), and alprazolam (Xanax). Because of their enjoyably relaxing effect (as well as their addictive potential), these GABA-ergic medications are sometimes used as drugs of abuse.

What are **neuromodulators**?

Many of the brain chemicals known to influence psychological processes are not actually neurotransmitters. These alternative forms of brain chemicals are also known as *neuromodulators* because they modulate the action of neurotransmitters. Such chemicals may include *neuropeptides* or *neurohormones.* Examples include opioids, oxytocin, and vasopressin, which are involved in pain processing and social behaviors, respectively.

What are **opioids**, the natural pain killers?

Opioids are a form of neuromodulator that serves to dampen our pain response. They are our homemade analgesics, our natural painkillers. One way that opioids work is to

How did scientific studies of voles show the effects of oxytocin and vasopressin on behavior?

A series of studies comparing the montane vole and the prairie vole has given us important insights into the workings of oxytocin and vasopressin. Voles are small rodents found in several different habitats. The montane voles live in fairly isolated mountain burrows, while the prairie voles live in densely populated colonies.

Studies of the humble vole have demonstrated how oxytocin and vasopressin affect behavior.

Consequently, the two types of voles demonstrate very different social behaviors. The prairie vole, but not the montane vole, displays monogamous mating patterns and a generally high level of social behavior. Prairie voles also have higher levels of oxytocin and vasopressin. Vasopressin has been directly linked to social behaviors displayed by the male prairie vole but not his montane cousin. Specifically, male prairie voles display both partner preference and mate guarding. This means that they prefer to sit by their mates over other animals and they show aggressive behavior towards any male who comes near their mate.

When vasopressin is blocked in the male prairie vole's brain, the animal no longer demonstrates partner preference or mate guarding, although sexual and aggressive behavior are otherwise intact. Likewise, when oxytocin is blocked in the female prairie vole's brain, both partner preference and maternal behavior decline.

inhibit the effect of the neurotransmitter glutamate. As glutamate is an excitatory neurotransmitter, inhibiting glutamate serves to reduce brain activity, in effect to calm down the brain.

How are **opiates different** from **opioids**?

Opiates are essentially the plant form of opioids. Opiates are extracted from the sap of the opium poppy. Synthetic versions of this chemical are also called opiates. When ingested, opiates bind to the opioid receptors in the human brain. Thus the brain responds to opiates the same way that it responds to our own endogenous (internally created) *opioids*. Several very potent painkillers, such as morphine, heroin, and opium, are made from opiates. Because of the relaxing and euphoric effects of opiates, opiate-based medications are popular drugs of abuse.

What are the "love chemicals"?

Oxytocin and *vasopressin* are two neuropeptides that perform a wide range of important functions. For example, vasopressin is involved with kidney function. However, they are best known within the field of psychology for their involvement in social behavior. Oxytocin has been linked to childbearing and lactation and both oxytocin and vasopressin have been linked to parenting behavior as well as to sexual orgasm and the emotional connection formed during sexual activity. A famous series of studies on the social behavior of the vole (see Sidebar) suggests that these chemicals are less related to sexual behavior per se than to the formation of emotional bonds.

How do **psychiatric drugs** act on our **brain chemicals**?

The majority of psychiatric drugs act by altering one or more neurotransmitter systems. Typically the medications do not contain the actual neurotransmitters but instead contain various chemicals that regulate the action of neurotransmitters. For example, the SSRI antidepressants block the re-absorption of serotonin. This keeps the serotonin molecules in the synapse longer, giving them more time to bind to receptor sites and, therefore, stimulate the firing of the post-synaptic neuron. To visualize this process, imagine someone standing at your door, continuously pressing his or her finger on your doorbell.

How do **drugs of abuse** act on the brain?

Drugs of abuse and legitimate medications act similarly on our brain. In fact, a number of psychiatric medications are sometimes misused as drugs of abuse. Drugs of abuse tend to cause quicker and more intense pleasurable effects than other drugs. It is this "high" that makes these drugs attractive as recreational drugs.

How can **drugs of abuse change** the **brain**?

Because of the direct effect of illicit substances on neurotransmitter action, there is often a dramatic alteration of neurotransmitter receptor activity. For example, in response to foreign chemicals that mimic the activity of neurotransmitters, the neurons may decrease their own neurotransmitter production or activity. Receptor sites may die off. This change of the actual structure of the neurons contributes to the addictive process. When the brain makes less neurotransmitter or is less able to process it, craving sets in. Drug tolerance, the need for more and more of the same drug to achieve the same psychological effect, is likewise related to the changes in the structure of the neuron.

The list below shows which drugs affect which brain chemical systems:

- Marijuana: Cannabinoid receptors
- Cocaine: Dopamine
- Heroin: Opioid receptors
- Ecstasy: NMDA Glutamate receptors
- Alcohol: GABA

IMPACT OF ENVIRONMENT ON THE BRAIN

How does **learning change** the **brain**?

More and more research is revealing the powerful ways that learning and experience shape the brain. While this is most true in childhood, the brain continues to be modified by experience throughout adulthood. Although genetics are crucially important in prenatal brain development, much of postnatal brain development is dependent on learning. In fact, every time the brain fires, it is slightly altered. One way that memory takes place is through a process known as *long-term potentiation*. The neurons fire in a particular pattern and the connections between the neurons involved are strengthened. Experience can change the brain in other ways as well. The receptor sites at a synapse can increase or decrease. New dendrites can branch out as can new axon terminals to form new synapses with nearby neurons. In these varied ways, the brain is very *plastic*.

What does the **plasticity** of the brain say about the **nature/nurture** debate?

One of the oldest debates within psychology (dating back to Plato and Aristotle, at least) involves the importance of nature vs. nurture with regard to human psychology. How much of who we are is innate and how much is learned, a product of our environment? In modern terms, this is a debate between genetics and learning. How much is genetic and how much is learned? The growing body of evidence showing the plasticity of the brain, however, throws a wrench into this debate. If the brain is a function of genetics—and few people would contest the importance of genetics in the development of the brain—then how do we understand the plasticity of the brain?

The brain is both genetically determined and shaped by lived experience. One way to resolve this nature/nurture dilemma is to assume that genetics sets the outer boundaries of brain development. The basic structure of the brain is genetically determined. Even if you bring a child up among horses, the child will not develop the brain

143

Eric Kandel experimented with sea slugs to show how conditioning behaviors actually changes neuron synapses (*iStock*).

of a horse. However, the specific connections among neurons, the density of these connections, and the neuronal connections that die off are in large part determined by learning and environment.

How does the **environment affect** the **brain** in **childhood**?

An enormous amount of brain development takes place during childhood, particularly early childhood. Because of the central role of experience on brain development, the nature of environmental input in childhood is critical. Nutrition, education, verbal exposure, language, emotional, and interpersonal experience—all critically impact the formation of connections between neurons, the building of neural networks. This kind of environmental input affects which synaptic connections survive and which die off. In this way, early environment becomes hardwired into the child's brain. With time, these early environmental influences become increasingly difficult and sometimes even impossible to change.

How does **nutrition affect** the **brain**?

The brain essentially quadruples in weight from birth to adulthood. Although there is a peak period of synaptogenesis (creation of new synapses) in the first two years of life, synaptogenesis continues rapidly throughout a child's first decade. All this growth takes fuel. Just as the spurt in the body's growth during adolescence takes fuel (and most parents can attest to the enormous amount of food their adolescent sons take

> ## How did Eric Kandel demonstrate that learning physically changes the nervous system?
>
> The photograph (on the opposite page) is of a species of sea slug similar to the one that won Eric Kandel the Nobel Prize in 2000. Kandel's great contribution was to demonstrate in an animal with a very simple nervous system how learning changes the brain. By altering the way he touched the tail of the sea slug, Kandel trained the animal to either amplify or minimize a protective reflex. When he examined the sea slug's nervous system, he found that the neurons' synapses had been changed as a result of the conditioning.

in), brain growth also takes fuel. Therefore, if there is inadequate nutrition, brain growth in childhood will be hampered. Moreover, when children are hungry, their concentration is impacted and their ability to learn in school or in any other environment will suffer accordingly. Although it seems to make intuitive sense that the quality of food will also affect brain development during childhood, the research is less robust on the effect of specific diets on learning.

How does **language exposure affect brain** development?

The human brain is uniquely designed to learn and process language. This differentiates us from every other animal on earth. Children are born with the capacity to recognize sounds made in any language. With exposure to their native language, however, the neural circuits associated with sounds from their own language will be strengthened and those associated with the sounds of other languages will atrophy. In this way, children become hardwired to speak and understand their native language. Children can learn other languages, of course, but second languages are processed somewhat differently than are native languages. Moreover, as children grow older, it becomes more difficult to learn new languages.

How does **psychological trauma affect** the **brain**?

There is now considerable evidence that severe psychological trauma, and particularly childhood trauma, has long-lasting impact on the brain. Since the time of Freud, psychotherapists have been aware of the severe and persistent psychological damage caused by traumatic experiences, but neuroscience is now catching up with the clinicians. Trauma triggers the body's stress response, mediated through the HPA axis. Over-activation of the HPA axis, as can occur with chronic trauma such as child abuse, dulls its flexibility, sort of like a rubber band that has been stretched out of shape.

145

This results in people with either overactive or underactive stress responses. Frequently, they have both. When the stress response is underactive, people can be somewhat dissociated, as if they are not processing what is going on around them. When the stress response is overactive, people will be hyper-reactive to any possible threat. Another set of studies has suggested that there is a reduced volume in the hippocampus in people with trauma histories. This may relate to the distortions of memory that often accompanies trauma.

How does **interpersonal experience affect brain** development in **childhood**?

Psychologists have long understood the importance of early interpersonal relationships in child development. Several different branches of psychology—including psychoanalysis, attachment theory, and even cognitive therapy—explain personality development in terms of the profound impact of early interpersonal experience. While our understanding of the neurobiology behind these observations is relatively young, we are slowly gaining a richer understanding of how these potent early experiences shape the brain. For one, there is suggestion that representations of early childhood relationships are processed in the superior medial pre-frontal cortex.

Once these representations have been encoded, it is hard to change them. In this way, our view of relationships become somewhat hardwired. It has also been suggested that the emotional tone of early childhood experiences is preserved in the underlying neural circuitry. More specifically, neural circuits underlying positive emotions are strengthened or weakened depending on the degree of positive emotion experienced in childhood. Further, the circuits related to the stress response, particularly the HPA axis, are strongly influenced by the degree of stress experienced during childhood. Over time, this affects the flexibility and resilience of the body's stress response. We all know people who are entirely overwhelmed by stress. Their stress reactions are easily triggered and they can only calm down with difficulty. In some cases, this might be the result of abnormal levels of stress during childhood.

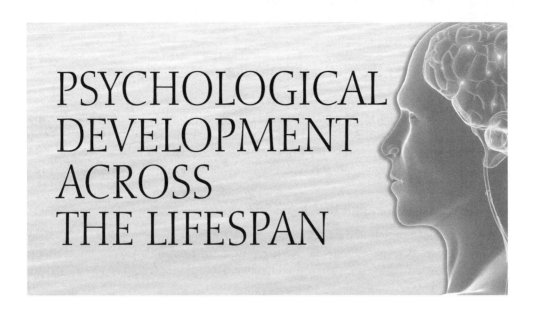

PSYCHOLOGICAL DEVELOPMENT ACROSS THE LIFESPAN

What are the major **developmental stage theories** according to Sigmund Freud, Eric Erickson, Jean Piaget, and Margaret Mahler?

The table below summarizes the various theories of how humans develop from infancy to late adulthood:

Major Developmental Stage Theories

Years	Freud	Erickson	Piaget	Mahler
1st Yr.	Oral	Trust vs. Mistrust	Sensory-Motor	Differentiation
2nd Yr.				Practicing Rapprochement
3rd Yr.	Anal	Autonomy vs. Shame & Doubt		The beginnings of emotional object constancy
Age 3–5	Oedipal	Initiative vs. Guilt	Preoperational	
Age 6–12	Latency	Industry vs. Inferiority	Concrete Operational	
Adolescence	Genital	Identity vs. Role Diffusion	Formal Operational	
Early Adulthood		Intimacy vs. Isolation		
Middle Adulthood		Generativity vs. Stagnation		
Late Adulthood		Integrity vs. Despair		

147

What are the **major theories** of **child development** and why are they important?

There are several theories in psychology that cover different aspects of child development. For example, Sigmund Freud developed a theory of the psychosexual stages of childhood, Erik Erikson translated Freud's psychosexual stages into a theory of emotional and social development, and Jean Piaget wrote about intellectual development.

Are there **theories** of **adult development**?

While the theories of child development are better known, there are also several theories of how adults change across the lifespan. Erik Erikson's psychosocial stages extend across the entire lifespan. Daniel Levinson and Roger Gould have also written about adult development.

FREUD'S PSYCHOSEXUAL STAGES

What are Freud's **psychosexual stages**?

We will start with Sigmund's Freud's theory of psychosexual stages as it is the oldest and best known developmental stage theory. Moreover, it influenced later theories, particularly Erikson's. Freud proposed five psychosexual stages: oral, anal, phallic, latency, and genital. Freud's general theory of psychology (often referred to as his *metapsychology*) is difficult to understand in modern terms. He wrote in the late nineteenth and early twentieth century and framed his concepts in the physical science of the day. It was very important to him that his work was seen as having scientific merit.

From a modern vantage point, however, some of his theories seem like he was trying to fit a square peg into a round hole. Each stage of Freud's theory refers to a part of the body known as an *erogenous zone*. This refers to the area of the body where libido (loosely translated as sensual pleasure) is most powerfully concentrated. Personality traits accompany each erogenous zone. For example, the anal stage is associated with either a rigid need for order or a messy lack of self-discipline. Later theorists interpreted his psychosexual stages less literally, seeing his ideas in more metaphorical terms. Erikson translated these ideas into social constructs.

What did Freud mean by the **oral stage**?

The oral stage occurs during the first eighteen months of life. During this time the child's primary erogenous zone is in the mouth. The personality traits associated with this stage include dependency and a kind of oceanic and all-encompassing emotional experience. When emotions are felt, they seem to take over the whole world. If we look at babies of this age, we can see why Freud called it the oral stage. For one thing,

In this picture the infant is mouthing a toy. Infants' tendency to put any object they can find into their mouths is highlighted in Freud's notion of the oral stage (*iStock*).

nursing is a central part of their life. Moreover, as any parent can tell you, babies love to put things in their mouth. Additionally, we expect dependency from children at this age. As they are incapable of surviving on their own, they have intense and continuous need of parental attention.

What did Freud mean by the **anal stage**?

The anal stage takes place from age eighteen months to approximately three years. At this point the child's erogenous zone transfers from the mouth to the anus. This is a time of toilet training, when the child is expected to exercise control over his or her feces. The quality of parental discipline during this process can influence the child's development through this stage. If the parent is too strict, the child might become anal retentive, focused too much on controlling and holding in feces. In personality terms, this translates to an overemphasis on control, self-discipline, neatness, and stinginess with regard to money. If the parents are insufficiently strict around toilet training, the child can become anal-explosive, inadequately focused on controlling feces. The associated personality traits include messiness and a lack of self-discipline.

What did Freud mean by the **phallic stage**?

The phallic stage takes place from around three to around six years of age. Freud believed this to be a critical phase in the development of *neurosis*, which he understood to reflect

149

a conflict between instinctual urges and societal restraints. In this phase, the erogenous stage moves from the anus to the phallus (or the penis). This is the first psychosexual stage in which gender becomes an important factor. The fact that half the population does not have a phallus evidently did not deter Freud from naming this phase after an exclusively male body part. The personality traits associated with this phase include initiative and aggressiveness, which is associated with the intrusive action of the penis during intercourse. If parents react to this stage with excessive punitiveness, the child will be overcome with guilt and suppress his or her own initiative and ambition.

How does the **Oedipal complex influence** the development of the **phallic stage**?

Freud put a lot of emphasis on the *Oedipal complex*, which he believed to be a universal drama that children undergo during the phallic stage. The Oedipal complex is best understood in boys, though Freud also proposed an *Electra complex* for girls. Both complexes are named after characters in classical Greek plays. Oedipus was the Greek prince who unwittingly killed his father and married his mother. When he realized

Freud based many of his ideas on themes from ancient Greek literature. This picture shows a bust of Sophocles, the famous Greek dramatist who wrote plays about Oedipus and Electra. Sophocles lived in the fifth century B.C.E. (*iStock*).

what he had done, he gouged out his own eyes in remorse. In little boys, the phallic stage brings an increased interest in their own genitals. Along with this, they start to become interested in their mothers as romantic partners. Recognizing their fathers as rivals for their mother's exclusive attention, they fantasize about getting rid of their fathers, even of killing them. However, they also love their fathers, so the tension between feelings of love and hate cause them much conflict and guilt. They project their guilt feelings onto their fathers and fear that their much larger and more powerful fathers will retaliate against them by cutting off their now highly valued penis. This fear is known as *castration anxiety*.

As a means of resolving their conflict, they identify with their fathers, aiming to become just like their big and strong fathers when they grow up. They also internalize the moral code of their father. This newfound respect for authority reflects the development of the *superego*, the part of the mind that adopts parental rules as the basis of a moral code. Freud attributed many aspects of adult personality to the successful resolution of the Oedipal complex. These include capacity for ambition, aspiration, guilt, and morality.

How did Freud account for **girls' Oedipal complexes**?

Freud had a hard time accounting for girls' Oedipal complexes. Because he tied psychological processes so tightly to specific body parts, he ran into trouble when he focused too narrowly on the penis. How can a girl have an Oedipal complex if she has no penis to be castrated? His solution was the Electra complex, named for a character in a Greek tragedy who conspired with her brother to kill their mother in order to avenge the murder of their father. In Freud's view, the little girl realizes that her mother does not have a penis. She loses respect for her mother and turns to her father, whom she now values more than her mother. She is tormented with *penis envy* herself and blames her mother for her own lack of a penis. She resolves this dilemma by identifying with her mother's childbearing abilities. She realizes that she will grow up to have a baby just like her mother and accepts that as consolation for her lack of a penis. Freud infamously concluded that because girls cannot be influenced by castration anxiety, they were likely to have weaker superegos than boys.

What does the **latency stage** refer to?

After the drama of the phallic stage, the child goes into a period of relative calm. This covers the period from about age six to puberty. The sexual or libidinal impulses go underground at this stage; they lie *latent*. Instead, libidinal energy is translated into nonsexual pursuits, such as school, peer relationships, games, etc. Libido does not rise up again until puberty.

What did Freud mean by the **genital stage**?

The genital stage begins at puberty, in the early teens. At this stage the genitals become the primary erogenous zone. Of note in this stage, Freud does not restrict his focus to male genitals only. The earlier erogenous zones do not disappear, however; instead they are integrated into fully mature genital sexuality. Oral and anal pleasure remain but they are subordinate to genital pleasure. Successful entrance into this stage allows the person to attain pleasure through sexual intercourse. The personality traits that have been associated with genital sexuality include the capacity for mature, reciprocal, and intimate relationships—the capacity for give and take.

How are **Freud's** psychosexual **stages** understood **today**?

Much has changed in psychoanalytic circles since Freud's day. In general, Freud essentially *equated* particular personality traits with specific body parts. Even though Freud's erogenous zones do play important roles in childhood (the mouth in infancy, toilet training during the toddler years, and genitals in adolescence), the psychological tasks of child development cannot be reduced to parts of the body. Moreover, although sensual and sexual pleasure does play some role in childhood, there are few psychologists today who would put sexual pleasure at the heart of childhood development as Freud did.

ERIK ERIKSON'S PSYCHOSOCIAL STAGES

What were Erik **Erikson's psychosocial stages**?

Erik Erikson (1902–1994) was a psychoanalyst who translated Freud's psychosexual stages into his own set of *psychosocial stages*. He also extended his stages into adulthood. In effect, he interpreted Freud's emphasis on sexual body parts as a metaphor for emotional and interpersonal processes. His eight psychosocial stages include: Trust vs. Mistrust, Autonomy vs. Shame and Doubt, Initiative vs. Guilt, Industry vs. Inferiority, Identity Development vs. Role Confusion, Intimacy vs. Isolation, Generativity vs. Stagnation, and Integrity vs. Despair. The first four stages take place in childhood while the last three stages cover adulthood.

What is the **Trust vs. Mistrust** stage?

The first four stages cover childhood and parallel Freud's psychosexual stages. *Trust vs. Mistrust* parallels Freud's oral stage and takes place during the first year and a half of life. This is when the child's fundamental sense of the safety and benevolence of the world is formed. If the child is well cared for and his or her needs are met, the child will experience the world as a generally safe and positive place. If the child does not receive this basic level of care, it sets the stage for a general experience of mistrust; the world will be seen as cold and dangerous. This fundamental world view forms the foundation of all later psychological development.

What is involved with the stage of **Autonomy vs. Shame and Doubt**?

The stage of Autonomy vs. Shame and Doubt parallels Freud's anal stage and takes place from about age 18 months to about age three. During this period there is new demand for self-control and for control of bodily functions. The process of toilet training is an important example of this. With these new demands, for the first time the child is exposed to the possibility of shame. Additionally, it is a time of greater independence, when the child demands greater autonomy. Depending on the parents' responses to the child's behavior, the child either develops a rudimentary sense of autonomy or becomes excessively constrained by shame and doubt.

What happens during the **Initiative vs. Guilt** stage?

The next stage, Initiative vs. Guilt, parallels Freud's phallic stage and takes the Oedipal complex into account. This stage takes place during the pre-school years, from about age three to age six. At this stage, the child has developed the capacity for initiative, to set goals and intentionally pursue them. However, the child also becomes aware that not all goals are socially acceptable, marking the beginning of moral development. The child's sense of right and wrong depends on a simplistic and black-and-white understanding of parental rules and prohibitions. Depending on parental reactions to this stage, the child will develop confidence in his or her own initiative, or become overwhelmed and stifled by guilt.

What did Erikson mean by **Industry vs. Inferiority**?

This stage parallels Freud's latency stage and takes place during middle childhood, from about age six to about age twelve. As Freud noted, children of this age are less emotionally tumultuous. This is a relatively calm time in a child's development, where the basic skills of self-regulation and interpersonal behavior have been mastered. This is a time for the child to learn how to participate in the wider world. In industrialized countries this mainly involves school-based education. When children feel successful in these endeavors, they develop confidence in their own industry, in their capacity to work. If they cannot master the tasks expected of them at this stage, they feel inferior and incapable.

What is involved with **Identity vs. Role Confusion**?

This stage takes place in adolescence. It is the first psychosocial stage to extend beyond childhood. One of Erikson's particular interests was the concept of ego identity. He was interested in the manner in which people develop a concept of themselves within their social world. In late adolescence, people are expected to leave the shelter of their family and start to take their place within the larger society, to take on an adult role in society. Part of this process involves the development of an identity. What kind of adult will I be? What kind of career will I have? What are my values? My beliefs? While it is important that adolescents not shut down this search too soon, thus imprisoning themselves into an overly rigid identity, they also need to narrow their options enough to choose an adult path. People who have trouble with this process struggle with a diffuse and confused sense of their role in society.

What does Erikson mean by **Intimacy vs. Isolation**?

Another of the challenges of early adulthood involves the capacity for romantic intimacy. Erikson believed that it was necessary to consolidate a personal identity before committing to a life partnership. We need to have a sufficiently solid sense of self before we can endanger it by merging our lives with another person. If the young adult cannot manage the task of intimacy, the cost is isolation. While Erikson mainly focused on heterosexual love and marriage, he also included the capacity to commit to a social group in his notion of intimacy. It is important to consider, however, that Erikson published his theory of psychosocial stages in 1950, when most people married and had families in their early twenties. The average age of marriage in the United States has increased significantly since then, as has the percentage of people who remain single or choose not to have children. Thus while Erikson's theories are still well regarded, they must be considered within the context of the culture.

What does **Generativity vs. Stagnation** refer to?

This stage takes place in mid-life. By this point, people have generally established a solid sense of self, a clear role in society, and a stable romantic partnership. Up until this point, people focus on themselves and on establishing their own adult lives. However, in this new stage, the adult turns his or her attention to the next generation, to helping other people establish their lives. This new need for *generativity* can be met through parenting, through mentorship of younger people in the workplace, or through other forms of contributing to one's community. The opposite of generativity is *stagnation*, a feeling of being stuck in a rut.

What does Erikson mean by **Integrity vs. Despair**?

This stage occurs in late life. At this point the adult is facing the end of life. In other words, the adult is facing the reality of his or her own death. Life is not infinite, it has an end and the end is getting closer. This is a time of reflection, a time to review one's whole life. Has it been what you expected? Were there things you were disappointed about? What was meaningful? If people can come to terms with their own life as lived, they can begin to accept the reality of death. They can reach a sense of integrity, of wholeness. If they cannot accept the reality of their life, if they are plagued by a sense of unfinished business or of disappointment, they can only face death with despair.

MARGARET MAHLER

Who was **Margaret Mahler**?

Margaret Mahler (1897–1985) was a Hungarian-born psychoanalyst who immigrated to the United States in 1938. In 1975, she published a book with Anni Bergman and Fred Pine called the *Psychological Birth of the Human Infant*. This book was very influential in psychoanalytic circles because of its use of the direct observation of children. In other words, Mahler applied the scientific method to clinical theory, something few psychoanalytic theorists had bothered to do previously. Mahler was roughly

Placing babies in a room with toys and their mothers, Margaret Mahler studied how young children go through the separation-individuation process (*iStock*).

contemporary with John Bowlby and Mary Ainsworth, the founders of attachment theory, who were also pioneers in this domain.

What is Margaret Mahler's theory of **separation-individuation**?

Like many psychoanalysts of her time, Mahler believed that the foundation of adult personality was created in the childhood relationship with the mother. Mahler was focused on independence, how the child grows from an entirely dependent being to one who is relatively independent, both physically and psychologically. She called this developmental process *separation-individuation*. Mahler was most interested in the child's growing ability to recognize both the self and the mother as independent and separate beings. It is the child's developing capacity to *represent* (or conceptualize) the mother that allows independence from the mother. When children can think about their mother when she is not there, they can comfort themselves with the memory of her presence. In Mahler's terms, the child has *internalized* the mother.

How did **Mahler differ** from previous psychoanalytic stage theorists?

Prior to people like Margaret Mahler and John Bowlby, psychoanalysis had largely relied on the process of reconstruction to understand child development. In other words, ideas of child development were based on observations of adult patients. In order to understand the problems of their adult patients, Freud and his followers *reconstructed* the childhoods of their patients. The most severe psychopathology was assumed to reflect regression to the earliest stage of childhood. Less severe psychopathology was assumed to reflect regression to later stages in childhood (like the Oedipal complex). There was very little direct observation of actual children. Although Mahler grounded her ideas in accepted psychoanalytic theory, she added the actual observation of real children. It is perhaps no surprise, then, that the parts of her theory that are based on real observation have had the most staying power, while the parts derived from purely theoretical assumptions have been much less influential.

How did **Mahler** study **infant behavior**?

Mahler wanted to observe the real-time interaction of mothers and babies during the first three years of life. She set up a laboratory, which eventually expanded to several adjacent rooms. There were areas with chairs for the mothers to sit comfortably. There were also rooms full of toys. This gave the babies the choice either to be close to their mothers or to separate from them in order to explore the rooms full of toys. The systematic observation of mothers and babies began when the babies were about four or five months old. Mahler assumed that the separation-individuation process did not start until this age.

What are the stages, or **sub-phases**, of **separation-individuation**?

Mahler proposed five overall phases of separation-individuation. The first two stages, which extend from birth to four to five months, are considered forerunners of the actual process of separation-individuation. The next three stages are termed sub-phases of the separation-individuation phase proper. *Differentiation* starts at four to five months and continues until about ten months. *Practicing* ranges from about ten months until sixteen to eighteen months. *Rapprochement* ranges from about eighteen months to about two years. After the child comes out of rapprochement, the child is in *the beginnings of emotional object constancy*, the final subphase of the separation-individuation phase, which extends from two years to about three years.

What are the **forerunners** of the **separation-individuation phase**?

As Mahler observed relatively few babies before the age of four to five months, her theory of the first two stages was based less on actual observation than on prior psychoanalytic theory. Her ideas about these two stages are heavily indebted to *assumptions* about infancy drawn from work with emotionally disturbed children and adults. The first phase is called the *normal autistic phase* and takes place from birth to two months. At this period the child is thought to be uninterested in the outer world; the child is withdrawn, only attending to inner bodily experiences. In the *symbiotic phase*, the baby's attention has moved out beyond the sensations of his or her own body to include a newfound interest in the mother. This is a time of tactile exploration of the mother, of molding to her body when held, and of direct eye contact. However, Mahler believed that symbiotic children do not recognize the distinction between their mother and themselves. They do not *differentiate* their mother from themselves and so live with an illusion of blissful fusion.

What is the **egg metaphor**?

Mahler liked to use the image of the egg to describe the child's development during these first two stages. In the normal autistic phase, children live as if inside their own egg. The eggshell is a barrier between the baby and the outside world. In the symbiotic phase, the egg extends to include the mother as well as the baby. The child's entire world includes only the mother and the self.

What did Mahler mean by **hatching**?

Drawing from the egg metaphor, Mahler used the term "hatching", to describe the baby's emergence out of what Mahler believed to be the self-absorption of earliest infancy. Around five months, the child starts to show increased awareness and interest in the surrounding world. It is as if the child is hatching out of the shell, finally entering the world psychologically as well as physically.

What is the **differentiation sub-phase**?

This is the first sub-phase of the separation-individuation process proper. It starts around four to five months and extends to about ten months. This is also the first of Mahler's stages that was fully based on direct observation of infants. The term *hatching* was applied to this stage. The child is showing increased interest in the outer world and is beginning the critical process of recognizing the separateness of the mother. This is also the beginning of physically moving away from the mother; the baby slides out of the mother's lap or crawls away from her. The psychological separation parallels the physical one. A number of behaviors demonstrate the child's growing awareness of the mother's identity as a separate person. One particularly charming behavior, which Mahler termed "custom's inspection", involves the child's purposeful investigation of the mother's face or even that of a stranger. The baby grabs at various parts of the adult's face, figuring out what does and does not belong to that person's body. The glasses, for example, come off while the lips do not. The child can also compare the features of the mother's face to that of the stranger. Stranger anxiety and separation anxiety also occur during this phase, both of which signal a new awareness of the separateness of the mother.

What is the **practicing sub-phase**?

This is the second observed phase and extends from about age ten months until sixteen to eighteen months. This is the period where children's *locomotor* abilities, or their

A toddler often experiences sheer joy over mastering the ability to walk (*iStock*).

capacity to move about on their own, take a giant developmental leap. Around eight months, a baby begins to crawl. By about ten months, children are frequently pulling themselves up by grabbing onto furniture and, at least temporarily, they are able to stand on their own. By about twelve months, the child is starting to walk. This dramatic motor development hastens the physical aspect of the *separation-individuation* phase. More and more, babies can now get about on their own.

What is the **child's love affair** with the **world**?

In the early practicing sub-phase, Mahler describes the child's "love affair with the world." The child appears to be simply delighted with the newfound power and freedom. Separation anxiety decreases as does sensitivity to minor knocks and falls. Frequently, we can see children of this age running gleefully away from their parents, as if on top of the world. Often they are running toward the street, with a horrified parent close behind. To children of this age, the world is their oyster. Danger does not exist. In fact, the greatest frustration comes from confinement. We have all witnessed this with joyful toddlers running around the supermarket, only to explode in screams when forced into their stroller.

What is the **rapprochement subphase**?

This period ranges from about eighteen months until about two years. Although Mahler locates this period prior to age two, parents might recognize this period as the Terrible Twos. In Mahler's view, the child has recovered from the elation of the practicing period to recognize the terrible dilemma of independence. Just as they can separate from their mothers, their mothers can separate from them. Mother is not an extension of the child's will, but a separate person who is not under the omnipotent control of the child. It is as if children realize that they are only three feet high—very small people in a very large world.

The child is caught in a conflict between the fierce desire for greater independence and the inevitable distress of recognizing the limits of one's control over the world. This same conflict is encountered again in adolescence and the resulting behaviors are fairly similar. Mahler describes great ambivalence in children in the rapprochement stage. A child will be very clingy toward the mother and then suddenly push her away. This is also the time of temper tantrums and of insistent self-assertion. The child discovers the word "No!" Certainly we have all heard toddlers of this age, shouting "No! No! No!" to any request or demand.

Temper tantrums are a hallmark of the toddler years. Although infants can certainly get very upset, they do not throw temper tantrums per se. While frustrating for the parent, the onset of temper tantrums is actually a sign of cognitive development. The child has become aware that he or she has a will and that this will is being thwarted (*iStock*).

What are **the beginnings of emotional object constancy**?

After the child resolves the conflicts of the rapprochement stage, the child enters the sub-phase of *the beginnings of emotional object constancy*. In this sub-phase, the child consolidates a representation of the mother, in which the mother can have both good and bad features at the same time. Children can feel both anger and love toward their mother without fearing the loss of their relationship. Even when they are angry at their mother, children can remember that they still love and need her. This integration of positive and negative features supports the child's *internalization* of the mother, an achievement that gives children much greater control over their emotions and their behavior. As the positive memory of the mother can now withstand the storm of the child's negative feelings, the child is less afraid of the loss of the relationship. The child is at *the beginnings of* emotional object constancy as the capacity to keep both positive and negative feelings toward someone in mind is a skill that is far from mature at two years of age. In fact, this hallmark of psychological maturity remains a challenge throughout the lifespan.

JEAN PIAGET'S THEORY OF COGNITIVE DEVELOPMENT

What is Jean **Piaget's theory of cognitive development**?

Jean Piaget (1896–1980) was a Swiss psychologist who produced an extremely influential body of work on the intellectual development of children. Unlike Freud   159 and Erikson, who developed comprehensive theories about personality development in children, Piaget had a more narrow focus. He was exclusively interested in the child's *intellectual* development. He wanted to understand the ways that children learn to understand their environment. It was Piaget's brilliant insight to recognize that children do not only differ from adults in the *content* of their knowledge; they also differ in the *structure* of their knowledge. They not only know less, they know *differently*.

Piaget proposed four stages of intellectual (or cognitive) development: sensory-motor, pre-operational, concrete operational, and formal operational. Although Piaget failed to consider the important roles of culture, language, or environment on cognitive development, his basic ideas maintain their tremendous importance and influence, particularly in the field of educational psychology.

What did Piaget mean by the **sensory-motor stage**?

The sensory-motor stage covers the first two years of life. It is roughly parallel with Freud's oral stage and Erikson's trust vs. mistrust stage. In this stage, the child only knows the world through direct physical contact. In other words, the child only knows the world through *sensory* experience (e.g., touch or sight) or *motor* action (e.g., kicking or grasping).

What does **object permanence** mean?

An important feature of the sensory-motor stage is the baby's inability to symbolize. In other words, the child cannot hold an image of an object in his or her mind when it is no longer physically present. When the object is "out of sight," it is "out of mind." Piaget's concept of *object permanence* illustrates this phenomenon. If you dangle an object in front of a young baby and then remove the object, the child will not search for the object when it is hidden from view. The child's attention will simply drift to the next interesting event. However, after the age of eight months (give or take), the baby will search for an interesting object hidden from view. If you hide the rattle behind a pillow, the child will move the pillow to look for the rattle.

What role does **language** play in the **pre-operational stage**?

Piaget thought that the development of language was a milestone in cognitive development. Language, or what he called the *semiotic function*, frees the child from the prison of the here and now. Not only can children think about things that are not immediately present, but they can also communicate about them to other people. The semiotic function shepherds the child out of the sensory-motor stage and into the pre-operational stage.

What did Piaget mean by the **pre-operational stage**?

The *pre-operational* stage takes place between the ages of two and seven. In this phase, the child has learned to symbolize. That is, the child can think about an event when it is not immediately happening. The child can represent the event mentally and is no longer dependent on immediate physical contact for knowledge of the world. This is an enormous step forward and frees the child's intelligence from the constraints of time and space. Nonetheless, the child's comprehension of space and time is still very immature. As we can imagine, the way a three-year-old understands the rules of nature is very different from that of an adult.

What does Piaget mean by an **operation**?

Piaget uses the term *operation* to refer to the ability to act upon an object in one's mind. Piaget believed that knowledge came from action. The child acts upon the world and therefore learns via direct experience how the world functions. When Piaget spoke about operations, he meant that the child was able to perform *mental actions* on the world, or on objects within the world.

Why are children between **two** and **seven years** in the **pre-operational stage**?

In the pre-operational stage, children can manipulate objects in their mind, but they cannot yet perform a complete operation. There are several aspects to this. For one, children cannot perform *reversible* operations. They cannot understand that an object can change shape and then change back again. Examples of this ability include the conservation of volume and conservation of substance. Secondly, children of this age cannot *decenter*. This means they cannot pay attention to more than one feature of the object at a time. They can pay attention to height or to width but not to height and width at the same time. Because of this, they cannot understand how a tall and thin object can have the same volume as a short and fat object. The taller object must be bigger. We see this when small children insist that a taller person must be older than a shorter one.

What did Piaget mean by **conservation of volume** and **conservation of substance**?

Piaget performed several experiments to study how children develop the concepts of *conservation of volume and substance*. In one experiment, he poured a specific amount of liquid into a tall beaker. Then he poured the same amount of liquid into a short and fat beaker. He asked the child which beaker had more liquid. Children in the pre-operational stage would insist that the tall and thin beaker had more liquid, although an older child could understand that both beakers have the same amount of liquid. In another experiment, the child is presented with two round balls of clay of the same size. In front of the child's eyes, one ball of clay is rolled into a long, thin

shape. When asked which is bigger, pre-operational children pointed to the long, thin one, even after witnessing it being formed out of the original round ball. These children could not conserve the volume or mass of the object as it was transformed. Piaget performed similar experiments to study conservation of number, quantity, and weight.

What about the **concrete operational stage**?

The concrete operational stage takes place from about age seven to about age eleven. It is concurrent with Freud's latency age and Erikson's industry vs. inferiority stage. By this stage, children have mastered the basic rules of the physical world. They understand the laws of space and time. This stage is marked by the *conservation* of volume, substance, number, and other physical features. Likewise, this stage is marked by the capacity for *decentration*. In other words, the child no longer gets hooked on only one feature of a situation. The child can

At age seven, Max is old enough to recognize that the tall, thin glass holds the same amount of milk as the short, wide bowl—in this case, one liquid cup. This understanding of *conservation of volume* is a hallmark of Piaget's concrete operational stage (photo courtesy Roger Jänecke).

coordinate several features of an object, such as height and width, into a more comprehensive understanding of how objects change and how they stay the same.

What are the **societal implications** for a **child** in the **concrete operational stage**?

As Piaget pointed out, by the time a child has reached the age of seven, he or she has mastered the fundamental rules of the physical world. This does not mean that children are now ready to leave their parents and live independently, but that they are ready to learn the basic skills necessary to function in their society. In the contemporary Western world, this means learning academic skills in school. In some tribal societies, boys of this age move out of their mother's huts into the long house where the men and older boys stay. In medieval Europe, boys began their apprenticeships at age seven. Thus, it is no coincidence that Erikson referred to this period as the stage of Industry vs. Inferiority. Now that the child has grasped the basic rules of physical reality, he or she must learn the rudimentary rules of work.

What about the **formal operational stage**?

The formal operational stage begins around the age of 12. This is the beginning of adolescence, a time of tremendous change in all areas of development. As Piaget points out, among the many changes associated with adolescence, there are significant cognitive changes as well. Primarily, the adolescent can effectively reason about the *possible*. While children in the concrete operational stage can reason about *actual* physical events, they are less effective when reasoning about potential or hypothetical events. In this way, concrete operational children are more restricted to the present or to the concrete.

What is **hypothetico-deductive reasoning**?

When asked to solve a problem, the adolescent can imagine many possible solutions to the problem. These imagined solutions are called hypotheses. Adolescents can then plan ways to test each of those hypotheses. This kind of reasoning from the hypothetical is known as *hypothetico-deductive reasoning* and is the same kind of reasoning used in scientific experiments. This newfound ability allows adolescents to use systematic planning when solving problems. In contrast, children in the concrete operational stage are more likely to problem solve through trial and error. They reason from the *actual*, not the *hypothetical*.

How do **Piaget's theories accord** with what we know about **brain development**?

Although Piaget's writings preceded our current discoveries about the brain, his observations about cognitive development are strongly supported by contemporary neuroscience. The intellectual skills that Piaget studied are mediated by the prefrontal cortex, the area of the brain involved with complex cognitive processes. The frontal lobe is the last area of the brain to develop in childhood and much of its development takes place within the first decade of life. In fact, there is a peak period of synaptogenesis (creation of synapses, the connections between brain cells) in the first two years of life—during Piaget's sensory-motor stage. Synaptogenesis continues at a rapid pace throughout the first decade of life, bringing us up to the doorstep of the formal operational stage. Myellination of the frontal lobe, or the insulation of brain cells by a fatty sheath that speeds up nerve impulses, is not completed until the mid-twenties, however, suggesting that cognitive development is far from complete in the teenage years.

What are the **social implications** of reaching the **stage** of **formal operations**?

Because of the adolescents' increased ability for abstract thought—that is, their ability to reason about the possible and the hypothetical instead of just the actual—they become capable of much greater independence than they were at younger ages. Adolescents can plan, consider possible outcomes of their actions, consider alternative solutions to problems, and otherwise negotiate their way in the world far more effectively than younger children can. They can also understand abstract concepts like religious or political belief systems in ways that younger children simply cannot appreciate. It is no coincidence that people first become aware of and interested in political movements in adolescence. While children may parrot their parents' political beliefs, they cannot truly reason out their own beliefs until they attain some degree of formal operational thought.

What roles do **environment** and **education** play in the attainment of **formal operations**?

Although Piaget downplayed the role of environment in cognitive development, much research has shown that adults vary considerably in their demonstration of the cognitive skills associated with formal operational thought. Piaget based his studies on adolescents in prestigious schools that specifically taught the skills of the scientific method. Thus, it is not surprising that adolescents and adults without the same educational advantages would not perform as well in the tests of basic physics that Piaget used to measure formal operational thought. However, there is evidence that adolescents and adults can show hypothetico-deductive reasoning in areas that are relevant to their day-to-day lives. For example, Kalahari bushmen show hypothetico-deductive reasoning when analyzing animal tracks. Thus the *concept* of formal operations appears to be valid, but the tests that measure it need to have *ecological validity*, that is they need to be appropriate to the situation at hand.

KOHLBERG'S STAGES OF MORAL DEVELOPMENT

Who was **Lawrence Kohlberg**?

Kohlberg (1927–1987) was a pioneer in the field of moral development. Influenced by Piaget, he developed a large body of research investigating moral reasoning. Like Piaget, he was interested in the way that children reason, and how this changes across development. In fact, Piaget himself had studied the moral development of children, but in a fairly limited way. It was left to Kohlberg to create the more elaborate theory for which he is now known.

What methods did **Kohlberg** use to **study moral development**?

Kohlberg relied on a method of vignettes. He wrote up scenarios that involved a moral dilemma and presented them to his research subjects. He asked people what they would do in each situation and then asked them to explain the reasoning behind their

How would you handle this moral dilemma?

Lawrence Kohlberg used this vignette in his research on moral development. He was less interested in the content of the answers—whether Heinz should or should not have stolen the drug—than in the nature of the reasoning people used to come to a moral decision.

In Europe, a woman was near death from a special kind of cancer. There was one drug that the doctors thought might save her. It was a form of radium that a druggist in the same town had recently discovered. The drug was expensive to make, but the druggist was charging ten times what the drug cost him to make. He paid $200 for the radium and charged $2,000 for a small dose of the drug. The sick woman's husband, Heinz, went to everyone he knew to borrow the money, but he could only get together about $1,000 which is half of what it cost. He told the druggist that his wife was dying and asked him to sell it cheaper or let him pay later. But the druggist said: "No, I discovered the drug and I'm going to make money from it." So Heinz got desperate and broke in to the man's store to steal the drug for his wife. Should the husband have done that?

(Kohlberg, 1963, p. 19 quoted in Crain, 1985, p. 119)

decision. He was much more interested in the way that people reasoned about their moral choices than in their actual conclusions. Like Piaget, he was more interested in the thought process than the content. Kohlberg's best known vignette involves a man named Heinz who broke into a pharmacy to steal a drug in order to save his wife's life. (See Sidebar).

What are **Kohlberg's stages** of **moral development**?

Kohlberg divided moral development into three levels: *preconventional, conventional*, and *postconventional*. Each level contains two stages for a total of six stages altogether. Kohlberg believed that all children go through the same sequence of stages in the same order. A fair amount of research supports this view for the first two levels of moral development. The scientific evidence for the third level, however, is less robust. Kohlberg was also interested in moral reasoning in adults. Indeed, research has shown that different adults are characterized by different stages of moral development.

What did Kohlberg mean by **preconventional morality**?

The first level, *preconventional morality*, is most commonly found in children under ten. There are two stages to level 1, *obedience and punishment orientation* and *indi-*

vidualism and exchange. In both cases, morality is determined by the consequences of the action to the person performing the behavior—whether the individual is punished or rewarded. In stage 1, the child equates what is right with what authority says is right. Often that is discernible by the punishment that follows. If you get punished, the behavior must be wrong. In stage 2, the child has learned that different people can have different perspectives—that is, there can be more than one view of right and wrong. However, morality is still determined by the consequences of the event, whether the actor benefits or not. Additionally, there is a sense of exchange between people. Behavior may be wrong because the other person may retaliate or may fail to cooperate in the future.

What did Kohlberg mean by **conventional morality**?

The second level is called *conventional morality*. This level covers stages 3 and 4, *Good Interpersonal Relationships* and *Maintaining the Social Order*. In both stages, morality of a behavior is determined by its effect on social relationships. At this point the person reasons in terms of how a behavior will affect relationships between people, not just the person performing the behavior. In stage 3, the person is concerned with the emotional impact on an interpersonal relationship. The focus is on issues of empathy, care, and relief of suffering. In stage 4, the person recognizes the need for rules that all members of society must follow. For example, people should not steal because society would become unmanageable if everybody stole.

What is meant by **postconventional morality**?

The third and final level is called postconventional morality. This level contains stages 5 and 6, which are termed *social contract* and *individual rights and universal principles*, respectively. In these stages, the person is interested in abstract concepts of justice and a just society. At stage 5, the person recognizes the necessity for social rules and laws, but also recognizes that laws themselves can be unjust. Therefore, there are times that a moral act may not be a legal act. At stage 6, the person considers the importance of abstract, universal principles of justice and believes that laws should be subordinate to general moral principles. For example the value of a human life should outweigh the law protecting private property. In his later research, Kohlberg abandoned stage 6, saying that too few people actually reached this stage.

What **criticisms** have been leveled at **Kohlberg's theory**?

Kohlberg's great contribution was to say that moral development is dependent on cognitive development. A certain level of abstract thinking is necessary for mature moral reasoning. However, Kohlberg has been criticized for his overemphasis on intellectual development, as if intellect alone could account for moral maturity. Specifically, he failed to recognize the importance of context. Moral reasoning reflects what is relevant to people in their own circumstances. For example, people in urban environments tend to score at stage 4, with an appreciation of the importance of impersonal rules that all people need to follow. In contrast, people from rural areas tend to score at stage 3, where moral judgments are based on consideration of interpersonal relationships. In urban areas, where personal ties are eroded, behavior is regulated by impersonal and formal laws. In small villages where everyone knows one another, behavior is regulated by the web of personal relationships.

What did **Carol Gilligan say** about Kohlberg's theory?

In 1982, Carol Gilligan published "In a Different Voice," which became a famous critique of Kohlberg's theory. Gilligan believed that Kohlberg's theory was biased by an exclusively masculine viewpoint. She noted that the bulk of his subjects were male and that his emphasis on abstract thought and impersonal laws reflected his masculine bias. Gilligan claimed that women are more likely to emphasize empathy, interpersonal relationships, and concern for the feelings of others and are, therefore, more likely to score at level 3. This does not mean that women are less moral than men, only that they reasoned from a different set of values. While Gilligan's critique raises important points about Kohlberg's prioritizing intellect over emotion, she also has been criticized for over-simplifying the process of moral reasoning in women. Subsequent research has shown that women are no more likely to score at level 3 than men. In general, both women and men take issues of justice and empathy into account when making moral decisions.

THE ROLE OF CULTURE

Is **childhood development** the same for **all cultures**?

Grounded in our fundamental biology, much of childhood is the same across cultures. All children grow from infants to toddlers to children to adolescents. All learn to walk and talk and play and eventually to take part in the work of their society. All children develop profound emotional attachments to their family and their primary caregivers. Moreover, all children have to develop an identity within their social group and to balance self-expression with self-inhibition. Within these broad outlines, however, there are many areas for cultural differences.

What are some of the **ways** that **cultures differ**?

While all children must learn to balance emotional expression with emotional inhibition, cultures vary widely with regard to the freedom of emotional expression. Some cultures value open expression of deeply felt emotion and others value emotional

A child's psychological development can be influenced considerably by the culture in which he or she is raised. Some cultures, for instance, frown on allowing too much free emotional expression, especially in public. Gender roles also vary widely from culture to culture (*iStock*).

restraint, believing public displays of emotion to be vulgar. Cultures also vary widely with regard to the emphasis on dependence vs. independence, individuality vs. group orientation, and respect for authority vs. individual freedoms. Additionally different cultures have disparate views on stability versus change and religious tradition versus scientific thought. Cultures also differ with regard to the perceived value of intellectual development, of physical prowess or athleticism, and of sexual modesty. Moreover, cultures vary tremendously with regard to gender roles. Not only do different cultures vary from each other, but there is considerable variation within cultures. People within the same culture can vary because of socioeconomic class, level of education, and where they grew up. All of these factors influence the environment in which a child develops.

When do **cultural differences** become **apparent**?

In earliest development, cultural influences take a backseat to the role of biology. With time, however, the impact of culture becomes more powerful. Cultural influences are subtle in the infancy, toddler, and preschool years. By middle childhood, cultural differences become more central as the child is educated in the specific ways of his or her culture. By adolescence, cultural differences are even more acute, as adolescents prepare to take on an adult role within their own culture.

How do **cultural differences complicate** our **theories** of psychology?

Psychology is the study of the human mind and aims to find universal rules of human behavior. As the science of psychology developed in Western Europe and America, many psychological theories have been limited by a kind of cultural myopia, a short sightedness. Aspects of psychological development that were assumed to be universal turn out to be culturally specific. This does not mean that all of our classic psychological theories are without merit, but we have to be cautious when assuming that what is true in one culture is necessarily true in another.

Are there **cultural differences** in **patterns of attachment**?

Attachment theory looks at the ways that children understand their emotional bonds with key caregivers. However, cultures vary as to the expression of emotion, the value of independence, and the emphasis on intimacy. Consequently, the patterns of attachment may vary across cultures. Security of infant-mother attachment has been assessed in several different cultures, including Japanese, German, and American populations.

Interestingly, the proportion of *securely* attached infants, that is, infants who appear to believe that their mother will be emotionally available, did not differ across cultures. Cultural differences were only found in the quality of *insecure* attachments. In other words, no one country was any more likely to have unhealthy mother-infant pairs, but the nature of insecurely attached mother-infant dyads differed across the three countries. For example, Japanese children were more likely to be classified anxious-resistant than were American children, showing much greater difficulty tolerating separations from their mother. In contrast, German children were more likely to be classified as anxious-avoidant than American children, reflecting their tendency to minimize their distress at separation from their mother. This brings to mind the Russian novelist Leo Tolstoy's famous saying that all happy families resemble one another, but each unhappy family is unhappy in its own way.

How have **cultural differences affected theories** of intellectual development?

Piaget found that high school students in elite schools in Geneva, Switzerland, were more likely to demonstrate formal operational thought (his highest level of intellectual development) than were adolescents and adults with less rigorous scientific training. This has been linked to the specific tests he used, which involved the solving of basic physics problems. As mentioned above, our intelligence develops through solving problems that are directly relevant to us. Tests that do not take *ecological validity* into account, therefore, are likely to be culturally biased. Ecological validity refers to the extent to which a given test is appropriate to the context in which it is being used.

INFANCY

How **important** is development in the **first year** of life?

More development happens in the first year of life than at any other time after birth. During the first year, the body almost triples in weight and becomes about one-third longer. Moreover, a newborn is unable to talk, crawl, move independently, or even hold his or her head up. By the end of the first year, the typical child can crawl, manipulate objects, and is beginning to walk and talk. In fact, much of human development in the first year of life happens before birth in other species. For example, horses and deer are ready to walk immediately after birth.

What are the major **developmental milestones** in the **first year**?

The major milestones in the first year of life include the social smile (two months), laughter (four months), the ability to sufficiently coordinate vision and grasp to play with an object (four months), the ability to sit up (six months), the ability to eat solid food (eight months), the ability to crawl (seven months), the ability to pull oneself up to a standing position (ten months), the ability to walk independently (twelve months), and the formation of words (twelve months).

What **physical** and **behavioral milestones** are typical during the **first year** of development in a child?

The table below reflects the approximate age when most children show certain developmental milestones. It is important to recognize, however, that children vary in terms of the timing of their development.

Milestones of the First Year of Life

Typical Age	Milestone
2 months	Hold head up
2 months	Social smile
4 months	Reach toward object
6 months	Sit up independently
7 months	Crawl
8 months	Separation anxiety
8 months	Stranger anxiety
10 months	Pull self up to standing position
12 months	Begin to walk
12 months	First words

What does a **neonate know**?

There is no question that neonates, or newborns, are born without much of the vast psychological tools that adults have at their disposal. In contrast to an older view of infants as helpless, passive blobs, however, a wealth of infancy research has highlighted the skills that newborn infants bring into the world. For the most part, these skills have to do with their sensory abilities. As this research shows, infants are born with a sensory toolkit that allows them to actively make sense of their world as soon as they are born—and to some extent even before birth.

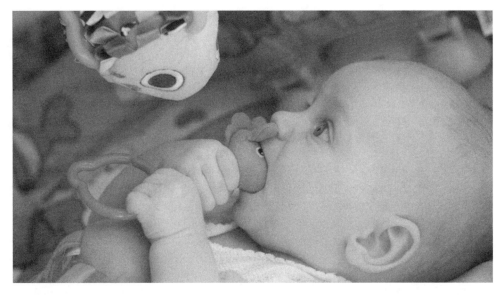

Infants have specific visual abilities that help them recognize and relate to their parents. They prefer curved lines and human faces over random features (*iStock*).

How do we study **infants' visual abilities**?

Infants are born with the capacity to perceive and even remember a good deal of visual information. But how do we know what infants are seeing? As they do not speak we cannot ask them. In the early 1960s a psychologist named Robert Franz started a revolution in infancy research by building a device that could monitor infants' viewing patterns by noting the reflections on their pupils. By determining which object was looked at the longest when two objects were presented simultaneously, Franz was able to infer which object the infant preferred.

What **visual skills** are infants **born with**?

Using Franz's method and modifications on it, infancy researchers have shown that infants prefer curving lines to straight lines, patterns to plain surfaces, contrast to sameness, the edges of a shape to the center of a shape, and relatively complex designs to relatively simple designs. Infants also prefer to look at images of faces rather than scrambled facial features. Finally, infants can only focus about eight to ten inches from their face. All these visual tendencies prepare infants to interact with their mother, specifically to recognize and make sense of her face.

What other **sensory skills** do **newborns** have?

Infants are born with the capacity to recognize their mothers' voice, which they have been able to hear throughout the last few months of pregnancy. Infants show prefer-   171 ence to female voices over male voices and high-pitched voices over lower-pitched ones. Baby talk—or the use of high-pitched, simplified, repetitive, and highly melodic speech patterns—is found across different cultures and different languages. By using baby talk, adults and older children reflexively adapt their speech patterns to infants' capabilities. Babies are also born with a developed sense of smell and the ability to discriminate sweet tastes from salty, bitter, or sour ones.

What evidence is there of **infants' capacity** to **remember**?

There is a good deal of evidence supporting newborns' ability to learn. Babies recognize their mother's voice immediately after birth and within several days can recognize the smell of their mother's breast milk. Within the first day of life infants can be trained to suck longer on a nipple to hear a woman's voice rather than a man's voice. Babies also look longer at novel images and turn away sooner from images that they have already seen multiple times. Eight-day-old babies also respond differently to their mother if she wears a mask, looking at her more frequently during feeding as if recognizing something is not right. Thus, infants are born with the capacity to store sensory information in memory and to make distinctions that are critical for their survival.

What **reflexes** are **infants born** with?

Below is a list of primitive reflexes that infants are born with. Most of these disappear within the first year of life. It is likely that these reflect vestiges from our evolutionary past.

Reflex	Description
Babkin	The mouth opens in response to pressure on the palms.
Rooting	The baby turns toward the stimulus if the cheek is stroked. This prepares the child for nursing.
Grasping	The fingers curl around and grasp onto any object that touches the palm.
Moro	When the infant is put down suddenly or startled, the arms and legs extend outward.
Stepping	The feet make stepping movements when the infant is held upright with the feet touching a flat surface below.
Swimming	Babies wave their arms and legs and hold their breath when underwater.
Babinski	When the bottom of the foot is stroked, the foot jerks upward and opens up.

What do we know about the **subjective experience** of the **infant**?

Daniel Stern is an infancy researcher who has written several influential books on infant psychology. In 1985 he published a book titled *The Interpersonal World of the*

Infant, in which he asked the fascinating question: What is it *like* to be a baby? He was not only interested in what an infant can and cannot do, but what it feels like to experience the world from the infant's perspective. Stern concluded that, to the infant, the world was less like a smooth movie than a series of largely unrelated snapshots. The infant is first aware of the patterning of stimulation, the musical arrangement of sight, sounds, smells, and touch. With time, these patterns of stimulation consolidate into objects, and the objects settle into predictable routines. From this process, children develop an understanding of themselves in the world and of their relationship with other people.

What other aspects of **social life** develop in the **first year** of life?

Babies are born with the propensity to seek out interpersonal contact and to slowly learn to make sense of the ebb and flow of social life. Babies learn to recognize faces and facial expressions, to take turns in a kind of proto-conversation, and to read intention and meaning in the behavior of others. By four to six months, babies recognize discrete facial expressions in their caregivers. By about one year, they engage in social *referencing*. In other words, before they explore a new toy or approach a stranger, they look back at their mother to check her read on the situation. If the mother shows anxiety or fear, the baby will back off. If the mother looks calm and confident, the baby will approach the new situation with interest.

What about emotions? How do **emotions develop** in the **first year** of life?

Emotions are a critical psychological tool for the infant's survival. By expressing emotion, infants communicate essential information about their comfort and well-being as well as their immediate needs. Although infants are born with an emotional system in place, it is fairly crude at birth. Newborns only demonstrate two kinds of emotion, distress and calm. These are global emotional states with none of the nuance of the emotional repertoire of an adult. Within the first six months, however, the infant begins to

This tiny baby is discovering a brand new world. Note her rapt attention and how well adapted she is for face to face interaction (*iStock*).

173

show signs of discrete emotions. Through their facial expression, vocalization, and body movements, infants express joy, sadness, anger, surprise, and fear.

What about **temperament**?

Throughout this chapter we have discussed the formative role of the environment in the development of an infant. However, there is also a body of research that looks at infant characteristics that may be inborn and not learned, a product of nature rather than nurture. Such characteristics are known as *temperament*. In 1956, Alexander Thomas and Stella Chess initiated a decades-long study of temperament. This study followed infants throughout childhood and adolescence into early adulthood. They identified nine dimensions of temperament related to activity level and response to stimulation and stress.

These nine traits include: activity level, rhythmicity, approach/withdrawal, adaptability, attention span and persistence, intensity of reaction, threshold of responsiveness, and quality of mood. More recently, Mary Rothbart simplified Thomas and Chess's definition of temperament into two general categories, reactivity and self-regulation. Her specific temperament dimensions included activity level, smiling and laughter, fear, distress to limitations, soothability, and duration of orienting.

How **stable** is **temperament** over time?

Several studies have shown only low to moderate stability of temperament over time. This means that children may change in terms of how they respond to stimulation and how well they can self-soothe or exhibit some form of self-control. Temperament is least stable in the first two years of life. After the age of two, however, temperament is more stable.

Is **temperament genetically** based?

The pioneering research on temperament was conducted decades before the current revolution in genetic research. At the time there was no real way to separate the effects of environment from the effects of genes. Now, however, there is more and more evidence of genetic contributions to various personality traits. Individual differences in sociability and shyness, impulsivity, anger control, and anxiety have all been shown to have a genetic basis. Therefore the concept of a genetically based temperament that is first evident in early childhood and persists into adulthood is supported by current research.

Does **environment** affect **temperament**?

Although temperament is presumed to be largely inborn, there is clear evidence that it is affected by the environment. Some of the temperament dimensions listed by both Thomas and Chess and Rothbart are highly influenced by parental behavior, particularly the dimensions related to positive and negative emotion. Moreover, even genetically based traits can be strongly influenced by the environment. Therefore, how parents, family, and the general community respond to a certain temperament in a child can modify the expression of that temperament.

For example, highly anxious and fussy children are more vulnerable to developing anxiety disorders and depression. If such children are gently encouraged to expand their tolerance for social stimulation, they can avoid disabling social anxiety. While they will probably never become gregarious extroverts, they can still develop social competence. Likewise, extroverted and sensation seeking children are vulnerable to disorders of impulsivity, such as substance abuse and aggressive and/or illegal behavior. With appropriate guidance and limit setting, however, such children can learn to effectively control their impulses.

TODDLER YEARS

What **role** does **language** play in the **toddler** years?

One of the cardinal features that distinguishes toddlers from infants is the use of language. Why is language so important? Language is a vehicle for symbolic thought. Unlike furniture or food, words are not useful objects in and of themselves. Words are useful only in their ability to *symbolize* something else. Why is that important? The capacity for symbolic thought removes the child from the prison of the here and now. Words take the child into the future and the past and to any place that can be imagined. Of course, words are also critical tools for communication. Prior to language the parent has to guess the child's wants and needs. After children can talk, they can tell their parents what they want.

Are there **precursors** to **language**?

The precursors to language start in the first few months of life. First the child must develop the capacity for complex vocal sounds. At two months, babies start cooing, or producing vowel sounds. At four months, they start babbling, which involves combinations of consonant and vowel sounds. Over the rest of the first year, the babbling becomes increasingly complex and tailored to the native language of the child. Around ten months, their babbling becomes strikingly melodic, mimicking the intonation and rhythm of their native language.

There is also unmistakable emotional content. In fact, it can be quite amusing to listen to a ten-month-old baby clearly communicate emotion and intent in the complete absence of intelligible words. For example, an 11-month-old baby crawled into his mother's chair, which she had recently vacated. He picked up her coffee cup, and looked at her adult friend who had just been conversing with his mother. Putting his elbow on the table, he immediately started babbling. "Ah bah *doo* be dah. Doo doo *bah* me *mah*!" he said with evident purpose. "He thinks he's talking," his mother explained. "He wants to join the conversation."

How does **language develop**?

By the end of the first year, the child has developed a vocabulary of single words. At this point, words may have *overgeneralized* meanings. "Kitty" may refer to any four-legged animal. "Bus" may include any vehicle of transportation that has wheels. By the end of the second year, word usage is more accurate and the child is combining words into two-word sequences. This is known as *telegraphic speech*, where only the most meaningful information is expressed, (e.g., "More juice," "Want candy"). At this point, the child has a vocabulary of about 200 words. Over the next year, the child combines more and more words together, eventually forming full sentences. Words are learned at a rate of about one to three words per week.

What are the typical **stages** of **language development**?

The table below outlines the typical times that language skills develop:

Age	Skill
2 months	Cooing—producing vowel sounds ("Oooh")
4 months	Babbling—consonant-vowel combinations ("Ba ma")
7 months	Babbling—with sounds of native language
10 months	Sound and intonation of native language ("Ba MA ba ba")
1 year	First words ("Mama," "Papa," "No," "Shoe")
2 years	Vocabulary of 200 words, two-word utterances, telegraphic speech ("Want juice," "Mommy up!")
3 years	Sentences
4 years	Grammatical sentences, often with mistakes ("I holded the bunny")
6 years	Vocabulary of 10,000 words

How does a child develop the **concept** of the **self**?

Another critical development during the toddler years is the development of a representation of the self. This is not to say that babies have no awareness of themselves prior to this period. From birth, infants have some sense of their physical selves based in part on the correspondence between their movements and physical sensations. When they kick the blanket, they feel the cloth on their feet. However, infants lack a *concept* of the self, a mental image of "Me."

In the toddler years, the child develops a mental concept of the self as a unique individual who has goals and desires, who acts upon the environment, who interacts with other people, and to whom other people have emotional responses. This gigantic psychological leap is evident in the first use of personal pronouns (I, me, mine), the emergence of self-conscious emotions (shame, embarrassment) and the recognition of the mirror image.

When do toddlers start **using personal pronouns**?

Around age two, the toddler starts to use personal pronouns. They refer to themselves as "I" or "me" and they refer to anything they possess (or wish to possess) as "mine." Prior to using personal pronouns, toddlers might refer to themselves as "baby" or by their own name. Alternatively, they would use only verbs and nouns to express their desires ("want juice"), rather than identifying themselves as the source of the desire, as the one who desires.

How does **possessive behavior** relate to a toddler's new **self-concept**?

The concepts of self and of personal property are young and fragile to a toddler and they often defend their newly recognized territory with great emotion. Consequently, they can become very possessive. At this point, caregivers must introduce the concept of sharing. Toddlers must begin to learn about self-control and social expectations. It is very difficult, however, for a toddler to accept the idea of deliberate self-sacrifice and parents must not have unrealistic expectations of generous behavior in their newly assertive toddler.

How do **self-conscious emotions** reflect the **emergence** of the **self**?

The emergence of self-conscious emotions is another consequence of the concept of the self. One cannot feel shame if there is no self to feel bad about. The emotions of shame, embarrassment, pride, and jealousy are recognizable from about eighteen months on. Shame or embarrassment is evident when children lower their eyes, hide their face, or hang their head. While such emotions may be painful for the child, they are critical tools for socializing behavior. Humans are profoundly social animals, and a child needs to learn to inhibit various impulses and emotions in order to successfully function in a social world. Self-conscious emotions create an inborn motivational system to avoid social disapproval and to seek out social approval.

What is the **mirror test**?

The mirror test is a famous test that is used to investigate the child's concept of self. A mark is put on a child's nose. When the child is put in front of a mirror, he or she will either touch the reflected marking in the mirror image, or will touch the actual marking on his or her own nose. Children who touch their own nose recognize the image in the

The mirror test tells us about the development of the child's concept of the self. In the first year, babies do not recognize themselves in the mirror image. A baby is interested in the mirror but does not relate the reflection to the self. In contrast an older child is well aware that the image in the mirror is her own reflection (*iStock*).

mirror as their own reflection. Most children can pass this test by eighteen months. Interestingly, the mirror test has also been conducted on several species of great apes. Only a fraction of chimpanzees, orangutans, or gorillas pass the mirror test, even as adults. In general, chimpanzees appear to do better than the other ape species on this test.

How do **toddlers discover** their **will**?

Along with a newly developed concept of the self comes a stronger sense of one's own *will*. The toddler has discovered that he or she is an individual person with individual goals. In contrast, infants respond to the world with generalized distress or contentment. If bad things happen, they are unhappy. They become content again after the circumstances change. In this regard, their emotional reactions are largely passive. With development, however, children become less passive and more proactive. They learn to pursue what will bring pleasure, and to avoid what will cause displeasure. This desire to impact the environment in line with the child's emotional responses is the basis of the *will*. The child learns *intentions*. Unfortunately, once children discover their own will, they encounter the limits of their control. Willing something to be true does not make it true. Moreover, one's will is not necessarily aligned with the will of others.

Why do toddlers have **temper tantrums**?

Once toddlers develop awareness of their own will, they inevitably encounter the frustration of their will. This is very upsetting to the child and frustration can escalate into a full-fledged temper tantrum. A temper tantrum should be distinguished from the distress expressed by a younger baby. A temper tantrum is more than a simple reaction to negative circumstances; it is an angry, defiant protest. The temper tantrum occurs not only because the child is frustrated over a particular event, but because the child is outraged at the very *existence* of frustration. In these moments, children are enraged that they should have to be frustrated at all, that their will can actually be thwarted.

It takes some time for toddlers to adapt to this cold, hard truth. During this time parents should be sensitive and patient with their child. While they should refrain from needless power battles, they should set appropriate limits, even if its causes the child to throw a temper tantrum. In this stage, the child is learning to adapt to the world as it is and not just how he or she might want it to be. Giving in to the temper tantrums of a child can undermine the child's development of frustration tolerance.

How is **toddler language** a window into children's **cognitive development**?

In the examples below, toddler language reveals key developmental processes. Vanessa speaks in full sentences at two and a half and has clearly discovered the first person possessive. Her emphasis on the word "my" reflects a critical step in the development of the sense of self. Her insistence on her privileged relationship with (if not ownership of) her mother also reflects the importance of mother-child attachment. Cognitively, she is in Piaget's pre-operational stage. She does not realize that she cannot be both granddaughter and grandfather to her own grandfather.

David's speech is still largely telegraphic. His emphasis on the sound that a bus makes ("Brrr") reflects the importance of sensory-motor experience in the development of language. His interest in the gender of the bus driver reflects his newfound fascination with grown men. At this age little boys first recognize their male gender. This is a fundamental step in their individuation from their mother; unlike their mother, they are boys not girls.

These interchanges took place when Vanessa and her mother, Julie, were visiting family after several months away.

Grandpa Baba: Vanessa, don't you look cute today!
Vanessa: (Pause.) Baba is MYYYY granddaughter and MYYYY grandfather!

Uncle Daniel: Do you want to talk on the phone to Susan?
Vanessa: Susan! Daniel is MYYYY uncle!

Uncle Daniel: Vanessa, *Julie* is my sister. I am Julie's *brother.*
Vanessa: (Pause. Clear consternation.)
JU-LEE … is … MYYYY mother!!!
JU-LEE … is … MYYYY mother!!!
(Repeat five times)

As is not uncommon with boys, when David was two years old, he was not as verbally advanced as his older sister Vanessa had been at the same age. This interchange took place as he watched his sister go off to kindergarten in a school bus.

David: Daya bye-bye brrrr *man*! Daya bye-bye brrrr *ma-an*!
Mom: (Translating) That means "Vanessa is going off to school in a school bus driven by a man."

What does the **toddler understand** about **gender**?

By the third year of life, the toddler can understand that they fit into various categories. In particular, they learn that they belong to a specific gender; they are either a boy or a girl. For little boys, this is a fairly momentous discovery as their newly discovered masculinity marks a dramatic break with their mother. While little girls are "girls" *like* Mommy; little boys are "boys" *unlike* Mommy. Many little boys of this age become fascinated with adult men, following them around like adoring puppies. This is not an early sign of sexual orientation, only the hero worship of a small boy toward a new role model.

PRESCHOOL YEARS (3–5)

What are the main **developments** of the **preschool years**?

Although the pace of development is not as dramatic in the preschool years as it is during infancy and the toddler period, development still proceeds at a rapid rate. There are notable changes in body structure. There is a loss of body fat, a lengthening of the legs and arms, and a flattening of the tummy. With a longer body, the child is no longer all head and belly. At this point the child looks like a "kid" and no longer like a baby. Additionally, there is continued rapid brain growth, particularly in the left hemisphere, the cerebellum, and the frontal lobe. This corresponds with rapid increases in language, motor coordination, and cognition and self-control, in that order.

What **cognitive developments** take place during the **preschool years**?

In general, cognitive development continues at a rapid pace during the preschool years. Improved language skills and the ability to count, play games, and even begin to read and write all reflect advances in the preschool child's cognition. The development of *symbolic thought* is of particular importance.

What **advances** in **symbolic thought** take place in the preschool years?

While the toddler learns to symbolize objects and events that are not present, the preschool child learns to *manipulate* objects and events in his or her own mind. In other words, the preschool child is capable of *imagination*. Not only can preschool children refer to something that is not present, they can change it in their mind. This significant shift opens the door to pretend play, to fantasy, and even to lying.

What is **magical thinking**?

The capacity for imagination develops ahead of logical abilities. Thus, preschool children are prone to a kind of reasoning known as *magical thinking*. This involves faulty reasoning about causation. The child develops hypotheses about causation that are unchecked by mature logic. For example, the superstitious saying "if you step on a crack, you'll break your mother's back" reflects magical thinking. Likewise, a child might attribute the rain to God's tears or thunder to giants moving furniture.

Another aspect of magical thinking involves *animistic thinking*, in which children attribute lifelike qualities, such as wishes, fears, thoughts, and intention, to inanimate objects. For example after the wind blows the door shut, a child might say, "Mr. Nobody shut the door." In keeping with their tendency toward magical thinking, children of this age are particularly drawn to fantasy stories. The clear enjoyment with which children this age engage in fantasy is particularly appealing to adults, thus encouraging the persistence of stories of Santa Claus and the Easter Bunny and other related fantasy figures.

Why do children see **monsters** in the **closet** at night?

The ability of preschool children to create fantasy precedes their ability to *distinguish* fantasy from external reality. The lack of clear distinction between fantasy and reality can be a drawback. A scary story can seem very real to a preschool child, even when reminded that it is only pretend. Many preschool children become afraid of monsters in their closet at night. Although they see that the closet contains only clothing when the lights are on, they fear that their shirts and pants can change into monsters as soon as the lights go out. This phenomenon relates to Piaget's concept of pre-operational thought. The child does not yet have a solid grasp on how objects change and how they stay the same. Such a changeable world can be very scary at times.

What kind of **pretend play** takes place in the preschool years?

In keeping with the new capacity for fantasy, children this age are very drawn to pretend play. They love to play dress-up, to pretend to be parents, to play house, or to imitate adult roles that they see in their life, such as a teacher, fireman, or doctor. While some pretend play is evident in the toddler years, it is much more elaborated in the preschool years. A toddler may pretend to talk on the phone or dress up in Mommy's shoes, but a preschool child enacts whole stories, with different children assigned different roles in the drama.

What does **"theory of mind"** mean?

Theory of mind refers to the ability to understand the nature of the mind, to recognize that people experience the world through their *beliefs*. The understanding that all people have unique mental perspectives develops gradually across childhood. In the preschool years, children master the concept of *false beliefs*. In other words, children grasp: that our beliefs are not equal to external reality; that one person's beliefs can be different from another person's beliefs and that our beliefs shape our actions. Development of this skill is a critical step in socialization, in the ability to manage interpersonal relationships. People with autism, a psychiatric disorder characterized by interpersonal skills deficits, are believed to lack adequate theory of mind.

These children are engaged in pretend play. The capacity for fantasy is one of the hallmarks of the preschool years (*iStock*).

What is the **false belief task**?

There are a number of false belief tasks that have been used to study the theory of mind as understood by a child of preschool age. In one such test, a child is shown two boxes. One is marked "band-aids" and the other is not. The child is asked which box contains band-aids. Most children point to the marked box. After this they are shown that the band-aids are actually kept in the unmarked box. When the question is repeated, they now point to the unmarked box. Next, the children are introduced to a puppet named Pam. They are then asked to point to the box where Pam believes the band-aids to be. While typical three-year-olds will point to the unmarked box, the typical four-year-old will point to the marked box, thus demonstrating an understanding of Pam's false belief.

In what ways does **self-control improve** in the preschool years?

One of the critical developmental challenges of the preschool years involves the mastery of emotions and impulses. Although seeds of this process are evident in the toddler years, we do not expect much in the way of self-control in a child under the age of three. In the preschool years, however, self-control dramatically improves. Children this age master various strategies for controlling their impulses and emotions. In the face of negative emotions, they learn to distract themselves or to change their goals (for example, abandoning a contested toy in favor of a new, available toy). They also use speech to regulate their actions, reminding themselves out loud how they are supposed to behave. Likewise, their understanding of their own emotions and the emotions of others increases. They use more feeling words and better understand how emotion motivates behavior. These developments have significant social implications.

What **role** do **friendships** play in the preschool years?

In keeping with the profound developments in self-control, social understanding, and emotional awareness, there is a new emphasis on peer relationships. Preschool children now have a basic capacity for peer-to-peer relationships. Although toddlers show interest in other children, they do not have the capacity to relate to other children without constant adult intervention. In contrast, preschool children are capable of enduring, emotionally important relationships with other children. Preschool children can make *friends*. This is not to say that preschool friendships are completely mature. Quite the opposite. At this age, friendships are highly unstable and prone to constant disruptions. Minor conflict often leads to a declaration of the end of the friendship: "Johnny isn't my friend anymore!" Luckily the bad times are generally short lived and once the storm passes, the friendship resumes: "OK, Johnny, you can be my friend again."

What are some examples of **preschool children's language**?

When the interchanges listed below took place, Josh was between four and five years old and his sister Alex was two years older. These quotes were recorded by their mother. Note how Josh, who is in the preschool stage, is drawn to fantasy and imaginative thinking. Despite his verbal skills, he does not yet fully understand the rules of logic or the difference between reality and fantasy. In contrast, his older sister, Alex, is in Piaget's stage of concrete operations. At this age, she understands the basic rules of transformation, how objects and people change, and how they stay the same.

Josh:	Dolphins can dance on their tails and flop onto their tummies.
Mom:	How do they dance on their tails?
Josh:	They have purple shoes on.
Josh:	When I grow up, I'm going to be a train.
Alex:	You can't be an animal or a machine. You have to be a man cause that's the way God made you. You can be whatever you want to be like a doctor or teacher, but you have to be a man cause that's the way it is.

(Josh and Alex are fighting over toys.)

Alex:	Josh, let's trade.
Josh:	OK, I want both.
Josh:	No, you can't eat that for breakfast. Breakfast comes from on top of the fridge.

By the age of six, both boys and girls tend to spend more time with same-sex playmates than with the opposite sex. (*iStock*).

How do preschool children **understand morality**?

With the gains in self-control and social competence, the preschool child also develops the beginnings of a moral sense. Concern with a dawning morality is frequently evident in pretend play, which is often populated with cops and robbers and bad people getting sent to jail. A child this age has a rudimentary concept of right and wrong and of good and bad. These concepts are largely based on adult behavior. If an adult tells them a behavior is wrong, particularly if they are punished for it, they learn that the behavior is considered "bad." A preschool child's concept of morality is very crude, however. It is simplistic, rigid, and sometimes self-serving. "OK, we can share, but I want both," a five-year-old boy told his sister when she suggested dividing a piece of cake in half.

With time the child begins to internalize parental standards, basing moral understanding not only on what parents say, but on the child's own personal standards of right and wrong. Moreover, as their cognitive development progresses, their moral understanding gains sophistication. How well the parents teach morality and instill discipline profoundly influences the child's ability to develop mature and effective moral standards. If parental discipline is overly rigid and harsh, overly permissive, or arbitrary and inconsistent, children will be hampered in their understanding of right and wrong. Children whose parents explain moral standards and point out the effect of aggressive actions on other people develop better social skills.

What **gender differences** are **evident** at this age?

By the age of four, boys and girls have developed notable differences in their play and in their choice of playmates. By the age of six, children spend eleven times as much time with same-sex as opposite-sex peers. Although there is always considerable individual variation, on average boys are more likely than girls to engage in rough-and-tumble play, verbal and physical aggression, and large group activities. Girls, on the other hand, prefer activities that involve verbal interaction and fine motor skills and are more sensitive to emotional reactions both in themselves and in other children.

Girls also express aggression differently. They are less likely to use physical violence, but more likely to attempt to undermine other's friendships, disrupting the network of personal relationships that are so important for girls. Gender-typed behavior is strongly influenced by environment and there is tremendous variation across cultures in the ways that the different genders are socialized. Nonetheless, there is also strong evidence of a biological basis to gender differences. Sex hormones, such as androgens and estrogen, seem to play an important role.

SCHOOL AGE CHILDREN (6–11)

What are the major **changes** in the **school-age** years?

The school-age years extend roughly from ages six through 11. Otherwise known as middle childhood, these are years of relative stability. The child has mastered the cognitive, linguistic, emotional, and social challenges of early childhood and is now capable of participating in the social world. School-age children are ready to join society, not as independent participants—children this age still need considerable adult supervision—but as junior members of the social world. They are capable of learning the fundamentals of adult work, of building and managing peer relations, and of understanding and respecting social rules. Many parents find these the easiest years of parenting, with the enormous demands of infancy and early childhood behind them and the upheaval of adolescence yet to come.

Why are the school-age years called the **latency years**?

Freud referred to this period as the latency period, in which the passions of the earlier psychosexual stages calm down, go underground so to speak, only to re-emerge in adolescence. Latency-aged children devote their energy to the mastery of skills, particularly those taught in school. Erikson's stage of Industry vs. Inferiority also speaks to this observation, suggesting that the latency years are focused on mastery, with powerful implications for a child's basic sense of competence.

What kinds of **motor development** take place at this age?

Children's physical growth during this period is regular and continuous. It is not a time of dramatic physical changes. Nonetheless, important changes do take place. The child continues to grow in height and weight, with most of their growth in the lower part of their body. Children become longer and leaner, continuing to stretch out from the rounded mass of head and belly characteristic of the infancy and toddler years. Motor coordination also develops. Children make considerable advances in both gross motor and fine motor skills. Improvements in coordination, balance, flexibility and power allow them to develop skills such as writing and drawing, as well as to engage in complex and physically demanding sports.

What kind of **cognitive changes** take place in this period?

School-age children are in Piaget's concrete operational stage. In other words, they can make sense of the physical world and understand how objects behave in space and time. While six-years-olds may still have some trouble with conservation tasks, by age seven most children have a basic understanding of these concepts.

Other cognitive skills are also important. School-age children have a more sophisticated sense of classification. They understand that objects can belong to different categories and that categories can be hierarchically arranged. For example, a child can collect baseball cards of left-handed pitchers or of third basemen in the American League. They can also rearrange these categories, to collect left-handed pitchers in the American League. Their understanding of number, of sequencing, and of spatial relationships also grows. Language also continues to develop and by the end of this stage children have an average vocabulary of 40,000 words.

Because of this ongoing cognitive development, children are ready to learn skills needed for adult life. In industrialized societies, this involves academic skills. Reading, writing, and arithmetic are three academic skills that school-age children have to master in industrialized and economically developed countries.

How do **children develop emotionally** during the school-age years?

Cognitive and emotional development move forward together. With their increased cognitive capacities, children have a growing understanding of emotions in both themselves and others. School-age children understand that people are motivated by their internal states rather than by situations alone. Children this age also master the concept of *mixed feelings*, that people can have more than one emotion at a time. Children advance in their ability to regulate their own emotions, to tolerate frustration, to delay gratification, and to distract themselves from distress. Their capacity for empathy is heightened. They understand that people suffer not only from momentary frustrations, but also from longstanding life circumstances. Thus, they can appreciate the concept of charity, which is beyond the grasp of a preschool child. Their self-conscious emotions also advance, heightening their social capacities, but also opening up new areas of psychological vulnerability.

What kinds of **social developments** occur in this period?

This is the age when children truly become social beings. Prior to the school-age years, children have primary formative relationships with their adult caregivers. In the preschool years, they develop friendships with other children, but are not unduly influenced by the inevitable crises of these relationships. In the school-age years, however, peer relationships become much more central. Entering this period, children have already mastered a rudimentary understanding of the minds of others, the difference between right and wrong, and some degree of frustration tolerance and impulse control. These critical skills continue to solidify in the school-age years, supporting the development of peer relationships. Children have internalized moral standards to some extent, and there is a basic concept of fairness and justice which persists even in the absence of an adult. Children have developed a repertoire of tools to manage conflict in peer relationships, such as sharing, compromising, helping, and seeing things from another's perspective.

How do **peer relations change** in the school-age years?

Peer relationships take on much greater importance in the school-age years than at any earlier point in childhood. Children develop enduring and close friendships that can last into adulthood. Children understand the concept of behavioral patterns and choose friends according to their personality traits, how they behave over time.

This is where children with poor social skills can run into trouble. While disruptive children may be off-putting in early childhood, the social impact is transient and can be easily rectified. Every day is a new day. In middle childhood, however, such behavior can have a detrimental impact on the child's ability to form and maintain friendships, which can have long lasting effects on the child's self-esteem.

Additionally, children are now relating to other children as part of a social group and not simply on a one-to-one basis. School-age children must therefore begin to negotiate the complexities of group dynamics. Such issues include in-groups and out-groups, group hierarchy and social status, leaders and followers, and conformity and resistance to group norms. Although such issues will be sharply accentuated in adolescence, they are first encountered during the school-age years.

Why are **rules** so **important** at this age?

Cognitively, academically, and socially, school-age children are trying to master the way that things are supposed to be. Children can now understand the concept of impersonal rules that all people have to follow regardless of their preferences. In effect, school-age children have an understanding of the social contract. They are also learning the rules of their new skills, how to read, write, and add and subtract numbers. Thus, the desire for stable and predictable rules is a central characteristic

While some rules might seem unreasonably strict, research shows that children need limits and rules as part of their normal, healthy development (*iStock*).

What do clapping games tell us about school age children?

The little girls' clapping game rhyme below dates back as far as the U.S. Civil War. More or less unchanged, this game is found in multiple countries and across the United States. The remarkable stability of these games reflects the importance of rules for school age children and contrasts dramatically with the ever-changing nature of adolescent slang.

Miss Mary Mack, Mack, Mack,
All dressed in black, black, black,
With silver buttons, buttons, buttons,
All down her back, back, back
She asked her mother, mother, mother,
For fifty cents, cents, cents,
To see the elephant, elephant, elephant.
Jump over the fence, fence, fence.
He jumped so high, high, high,
He reached the sky, sky, sky,
And he never came back, back, back,
Till the end of July, July, July.

of school-age children. This emphasis on rules shows up in their play, in their attraction to board games, video games, and clapping games. It shows up in their rule-based morality ("Ooh! You said 'stupid'! You're not supposed to say 'stupid'!") and their great sensitivity to perceived unfairness ("That's not fair! He went first last time!").

Why do kids bully?

Psychology has traditionally had a rather idealistic view of social life, assuming that aggression in children was a manifestation of some sort of psychopathology. Unfortunately, psychology has proven itself rather naïve in this regard. Current research has now caught up with Hollywood and television, showing that childhood aggression is often socially rewarded. While some aggressive children are maladjusted, emotionally troubled, and disliked by their peers, other children use aggression quite effectively to gain social status. Boys are more likely than girls to bully other children, using verbal and physical aggression. However, girls are still capable of using relational aggression, or social ostracism, to enhance their own status within a group.

With time, however, children who bully fall out of favor, alienating other children with their cruelty. As bullying is a common behavior among children—by some estimates 10 to 20 percent of children are bullies—the most effective means to reduce bullying is to promote a culture in which bullying is neither condoned nor tolerated.

Why are **some kids bullied** and not others?

Between 15 to 30 percent of children are repeatedly victimized by bullies, according to some estimates. Children who are shy, unassertive, and passive, with low self-esteem and an anxious temperament are particularly vulnerable to bullies. Overprotective parents actually increase their children's risk of being targeted by bullies by hampering their independence and self-confidence and enhancing their sense of passivity and dependency. While such children should never be blamed for the being victims, they can benefit from interventions that increase their social skills, assertiveness, and initiative.

How **important** is it for a child to **do well** in **school**?

A child's performance in school is critically important on a number of levels. For one, the academic skills learned in the school-age years form the foundation of all later learning. If a child never masters reading, he or she will be at a serious disadvantage. In our information-based society, a high level of literacy is vital for occupational or economic success. Perhaps even more importantly, though, a child's experience in school powerfully influences his or her self-concept. Children at this age are capable of comparing themselves to others in a meaningful way. They have some idea of social standing and of social categories.

Nonetheless, they still tend to think in global terms and have some difficulty distinguishing whether their behavior reflects particular circumstances or a general personality trait. In other words, did they fail the test because they need new glasses and couldn't read the blackboard or because they're bad at math? Thus, children's school experience leads to a global, generalized sense of their own competence. If they feel "bad at school," their lowered self-confidence will diminish their initiative and their persistence in the face of challenge. If they feel "good at school," their positive self-concept will enhance initiative, frustration tolerance, and self-discipline, and also encourage higher academic and occupational goals.

What are **learning disabilities** and why are they important?

Learning disabilities refer to a biologically based deficit in specific cognitive skills in the face of normal intelligence. For example, some children have particular difficulty in maintaining focused attention (e.g., ADHD), in reading letters in the correct sequence (e.g., dyslexia), or in organizing information in space (e.g., non-verbal learning disability). When these difficulties are undiagnosed, children can have repeated experiences of failure in the classroom. This can lead to low self-esteem and some associated negative behaviors, such as a defensive rejection of criticism.

Some children with undiagnosed learning disabilities feel so bombarded by criticism and feelings of failure that they simply shut out negative feedback, with predictable consequences. Children with learning disabilities may develop disruptive behaviors and have an increased risk of becoming involved in antisocial behaviors in adolescence. To some extent, this is related to biological deficits in impulse control, but it is also related to problematic reactions after repeated experiences of failure.

ADOLESCENCE (12–18)

What **physical changes** take place in **adolescence**?

Unlike middle childhood, which is a period of predictable and gradual change, adolescence is a time of abrupt and dramatic transformation. To start with, there are tremendous physical changes. The child becomes an adult and the body dramatically changes form, frequently leaving young adolescents surprised and disoriented by their new and alien body. "I didn't know where my feet were," one young man described his feelings, referring to the year he grew ten inches in about as many months. "And everyone wanted me to play basketball," he added.

What physical changes take place in adolescence? Both boys and girls undergo tremendous growth spurts. While the typical American ten-year-old is about 4'7", the median height for seventeen-year-olds is about 5'8" for boys and 5'4" for girls. The shape of the body changes as well, with lengthening of the trunk, arms and legs and enlargement of the hands and feet. The face also changes, with growth of the nose, jaw, and cheekbones. Often the ears and nose grow before the rest of the face. In North American girls, the growth spurt starts around ten and is completed by about age sixteen. In North American boys, the growth spurt begins around twelve or thirteen and is completed by about seventeen or eighteen. Most adolescents add about ten inches in height and gain about fifty to seventy-five pounds. Additionally, there are tremendous hormonal and physiological changes associated with puberty.

What **transpires** during **puberty**?

During puberty, the body transforms into a sexually mature state, with the adolescent now capable of sexual reproduction. This takes place about two years earlier in girls than in boys. Girls start puberty around age twelve and complete it in about four years. In both sexes, a flood of hormones is released by various glands in the body. Growth hormone and thyroxine stimulate the increase in body size.

For boys, most of the hormones are released by the testes. The androgen (or male hormone) testosterone leads to muscle growth, body and facial hair, and the development of male sexual characteristics. Boys also release a small amount of estrogen, which stimulates release of growth hormone. This in turn stimulates growth in body size and bone density. By the end of puberty, boys have developed greater muscle mass than girls and their shoulders have widened relative to their waist and hips.

In girls, hormones are released from the ovaries. Estrogen release results in maturation of the breasts, uterus, and vagina, an accumulation of body fat, and an increase in the hip to waist ratio. In girls but not boys, androgen release from the adrenal glands (right above the kidneys) results in increased height as well as the growth of pubic and underarm hair. Menarche, the beginning of menstruation, begins around age 12.5, although this can vary widely depending on many factors, including diet.

What kind of **changes** take place in the **brain** during **puberty**?

Adolescence is a time of dramatic changes in brain organization as well. Early in adolescence there is marked growth in brain gray matter, particularly in the frontal lobe. This is caused by a burst of *synaptogenesis*, the creation of synaptic connections between neurons. Following this growth spurt, however, there is increased pruning, which

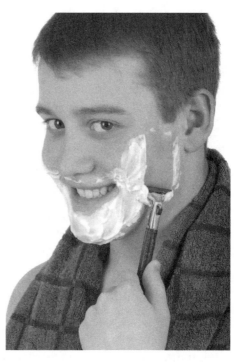

Everyone knows the body goes through tremendous physical changes during puberty, including hair growth and increased production of hormones that ready the body for sexual reproduction. Such drastic changes can be a lot to adjust to, making puberty a trying time in life (*iStock*).

refers to the dying off of unused synapses and dendrites. This enhances efficiency in the brain by ridding the brain of unused circuitry, like throwing out clothes that are never worn.

Myelination also continues, which enhances the speed and efficiency of electrical impulses traveling through the brain. This increase in brain connectivity and efficiency results in profound changes in cognitive abilities, bringing about a seismic shift in the adolescent's understanding of the world.

Additionally, there are changes in the density of neurotransmitters, the chemical messengers that help neurons communicate with each other. Changes in the level of excitatory neurotransmitters (such as glutamate and dopamine) relative to the level of inhibitory neurotransmitters (such as GABA) may make adolescents more reactive to emotional stimuli, possibly contributing both to the emotional turbulence and thrill-seeking tendencies commonly found in adolescents.

What **cognitive changes** take place in **adolescence**?

According to Piaget, adolescents are capable of formal operational thought. Primarily, this means that adolescents can reason from the possible instead of just the concrete and the tangible. School-age children can explain the behavior of objects that are directly in front of them. However, they are not yet skilled at *imagining* the different possible actions of objects and then reasoning from these imagined possibilities. In contrast, adolescents can reason from the possible, or hypothetical, instead of just from the concrete or tangible. Consequently, adolescents are capable of *abstract thought*. They can reason in terms of verbal concepts, such as social justice, political conservatism, or religious doctrine.

Additionally, adolescents are capable of *metacognition*, which refers to the ability to think about thought, their own thought as well as that of others. Likewise, adolescents are capable of grasping the rules of logic as concepts in and of themselves. They can critique the logic of another person's argument, a skill that was not available to them during the school-age period. This new logical ability is not always welcomed by parents faced with a child who is now capable of criticizing their reasoning. A two-year-old rebels by shouting, "No! No! No!" An eight-year-old pouts and cries, "That's not fair!" But a sixteen-year-old can point out contradictions in their parents' arguments.

How do the **cognitive changes** affect the **academic abilities** of adolescents?

The capacity for abstract thought, for logical analysis, and for metacognition prepares the way for an explosion of academic pursuits. Of course, these cognitive capacities are still in their earliest stages of development in early adolescence, and do not reach full flower until late adolescence. In fact, the capacity for abstract thought continues to grow well into adulthood. Likewise, full development of these cognitive abilities is heavily dependent on environment, on the adolescent's exposure to relevant education and experience. What differentiates adolescents from school-age children is the *capacity* for abstract thought, not always the performance of it.

Nonetheless, adolescents are capable of learning about *theory* in ways younger children simply cannot grasp. They can learn about religion, philosophy, mathematics, politics, and sociology. For the first time, adolescents can develop their own ideas about these topics, and not simply parrot the opinions of their parents. Although adolescents are capable of understanding these abstract concepts, their viewpoints still differ from those of adults. They tend toward grand generalizations, particularly in social and political ideas, with little appreciation for complexity and nuance. In fact, there is a saying about adolescents' understanding of politics that has been attributed to various people, including Winston Churchill and Victor Hugo. "Whoever is not a socialist in their youth has no heart. Whoever remains one in old age has no head." This is not to promote one political theory over another, but to illustrate how adolescents' understanding of abstract concepts is more simplistic than that of older adults.

Why are **adolescents** so **self-conscious**?

The shift in adolescents' cognitive abilities has far-reaching implications for their social lives as well as their view of themselves. Their ability to put themselves in others' shoes, to take another's perspective, continues to develop. Moreover, they recognize that there are *levels* of human behavior and motivation. What is shown to the public is not necessarily the whole picture. There can be feelings that are covered by a public mask. Hidden motivations can drive behavior. When they appreciate that they can see behind other peoples' surfaces, they realize their own interior lives might be equally visible. There is a tremendous feeling of exposure. It's almost as if everyone around them has developed X-ray vision and they are suddenly naked.

The intense self-consciousness of the typical adolescent is well known. Young adolescents, in particular, become extremely self-conscious about their appearance and are prone to mortifying feelings of embarrassment. The wrong shoelaces, pant length, hair style—all of these can trigger a crisis of self-consciousness as well as peer ridicule. These difficulties are at their height in early adolescence, in the first half of the teens. By the late teens, adolescents' self-consciousness diminishes. Older adolescents recognize that regardless of the visibility of their personal quirks and foibles, such matters are of little or no interest to the rest of the world. Most people are far too wrapped up in their own concerns to waste precious energy and attention on another person's minor imperfections. Older adolescents also realize that their inner struggles and failures are far from unique. Thus, there is little reason to feel shame, since these experiences are widely shared.

What role does **identity development** have during adolescence?

Erikson considered adolescence to be a critical time for identity development. For the first time in their lives, adolescents are challenged to develop a view of themselves that is separate from their relationship with their parents. They can no longer simply see themselves as somebody's child. They will have to find a role within adult society, which is no simple task in our complex, modern society. Moreover, adolescents' cognitive development allows them to understand abstract notions of values and of religious and political beliefs. The beliefs they endorse become an important part of their identity.

This process of identity formation also relates to an excessive concern with peer acceptance. When one's identity is in flux, the reactions of other people become that much more important. In other words, people who are unsure of their own identity tend to give their peers more power to define who they are, while those with a stable self-identity are less easily influenced by the opinions of others.

What happens when there are **social barriers** to **identity formation** in adolescence?

In all cultures, it is a developmental task of adolescence to move toward an adult role in society. What happens when such roles are not available? Perhaps the society is in disarray, due to war or political or economic chaos. Alternatively, certain subgroups of the population may be barred from productive participation in society, due to poverty, lack of education, and/or racial or ethnic prejudice. When constructive social roles are not readily available, destructive or antisocial group identities become viable alternatives. For example, disenfranchised youths (particularly young males) may be inducted into street gangs or criminal organizations. As such, psychological development in adolescence is heavily dependent on the surrounding culture, more so than at any earlier period.

What kinds of **emotional changes** do **adolescents** undergo?

For many reasons, adolescence is a time of intensified emotions. The upsurge in hormones, the changes in brain function, and the adolescent's own psychological reactions to massive physical, cognitive, and social changes all contribute to this emotional upheaval. In fact, brain imaging research has shown that the amygdala, an emotional center of the brain, is more responsive to emotional stimuli during adolescence than at any other time in life.

Adolescents are known to be moody, dramatic, and to react intensely to seemingly minor problems. Likewise, this is a time of increased vulnerability to mental illness. In fact, many psychological and psychiatric disorders have their start in adolescence, including depression, eating disorders, drug abuse, and even schizophrenia. This is not to suggest that all adolescents develop emotional problems; quite the opposite, in fact. Nonetheless, adolescence is typically a time of some emotional upheaval, which can set the stage for the development of psychopathology in vulnerable individuals.

How does a child's **relationship with parents** change during adolescence?

Adolescence is a time of radical transformation of the parent-child relationship. Both parent and child must find a way to renegotiate the relationship so that the child's growing independence is not stifled, but the child is not allowed too much freedom. Although the stereotype of battling parents and teens is exaggerated and most adolescents have reasonably harmonious relationships with their parents, there is clearly an increase in conflict between children and parents when children reach their teens. Parents and adolescents conflict over the teen's desire for greater privacy, for reduced discipline, for greater freedom to choose friends and to spend time with them away from home. Adolescents fare best when their parents can loosen the reins but not let go entirely. Moreover, the adolescent's increased logical abilities allow for reasoned discussions between parents and children about what should and should not be allowed.

Why does **adolescent slang change** over the years?

In contrast to school aged children's preference for the routine and predictable, adolescents prize the new and contemptuously dismiss the old and familiar. We can contrast the rapid changes in adolescent slang with the conservative nature of school aged children's games. Listed below are slang terms used by adolescents at four different periods during the last century:

Years	Slang	Definition
1940s		
	doll	attractive woman
	dollface	attractive woman
	jerk	idiot
	dope	idiot
	drip	idiot
	rugged	attractively masculine man
	hep cat	"cool" male
	swell	positive
	keen	positive
	golly	exclamation of surprise/admiration
	gee	expression of mild astonishment
1960s–70s		
	lady	girlfriend
	uptight	uncool/rigid
	far out	awesome/amazing
	bad	good
	hip	cool
	groovy	great/awesome
	foxy	attractive woman
	fine	attractive
	bogart the joint	hog the marijuana
	stoned	intoxicated
	take a hit	inhale from a joint
1980s		
	crib	house/home
	rents	parents
	bogue	from bogus
	bogus	negative
	excellent	pronounced like *egg* salad

Years	Slang	Definition
1980s		
	dope	a drug, usually marijuana
	radical	positive
	rad	short for radical
	fresh	positive
	dude	young male
2000s—often influenced by text messaging		
	lol	laugh out loud
	bff	best friends forever
	g2g	got to go
	brb	be right back
	idk	I don't know
	ttyl	talk to you later
	jk	just kidding
	omg	oh, my God
	sweet	great!
	wicked	positive
	call you out	disrespect someone
	def	positive
	dope	positive
	tramp stamp	wide tattoo on the small of a woman's back
	tool	idiot

How do **peer relationships** change during adolescence?

In modern Western society, peer relationships have enormous influence during adolescence. Relationships with peers, acceptance by peers, and the adolescent's role and status in peer groups become of utmost importance. Peer relationships can be a source of great fun and excitement, but can also bring pain and humiliation when they do not go well.

What lies behind this greatly enhanced emphasis on peers? For one, in the movement away from dependence on parents, the adolescent turns toward peers as replacements for the family. Secondly, the adolescent's increased perspective-taking capacities and greater understanding of emotional life allow for a level of intimacy with peers that was not possible earlier. As adolescents gain better understanding of their own motivations and emotional experience, they have greater capacity for empathy.

The ability and desire to share intimate experience creates intense bonds between friends. Initially, these intimate relationships are largely with friends of the same gen-

Why do adolescents dress so strangely?

Adolescents are in the process of establishing their own identity while also establishing independence from their parents. Adolescent fashion trends often reflect these dual goals. Many styles that become popular with adolescents reflect rejection of basic adult norms and assumptions about self-presentation. For example from earliest childhood, parents teach their children that clothes should be neat, clean, orderly, and attractive, and should promote a socially acceptable image. In contrast, consider the adolescent fashions of the 1960s in which clothes were ripped and tattered and hair was long and shaggy. In the hip-hop style, which has lasted with some changes since the 1980s, clothes are baggy and fit poorly, modeled after the beltless pants of incarcerated prisoners. The goth style promotes a morbid image of violence and religious transgression. These rebellious styles often exude a good deal of vitality, and frequently become absorbed (and diluted) into mainstream fashion.

Parents often are puzzled, and even worried, when their teenage children begin to dress unconventionally or change their appearance in other ways, but this is actually a very common expression of the search for self-identity (*iStock*).

der. The tendency toward *chumship*, or intense same-sex friendships, in early adolescence is slowly supplanted by romantic relationships in later adolescence, although same-sex friendships retain great importance throughout adolescence.

Why is it so **important** to be **popular**?

More than ever before, adolescents are highly attuned to the dynamics of the social group. We are all familiar with the phenomena of cliques, popularity, peer pressure, and terms such as "coolness" and "geekiness." These all represent aspects of adolescent social organization. Just as wolf packs organize into hierarchies of social status, so do human societies. In adolescence, when children move away from their parents toward membership in a new social group, these markers of social organization become acutely important. Boundaries between the in group and the out group and between the elite and low status individuals are communicated fluently through a system of ever-changing symbols. Group etiquette and rituals are reflected in language, clothing, cars, electronic gadgets, and taste in music.

Adults are constantly astonished at the importance placed on a seemingly trivial distinction in shoe style, haircut, or method of folding a baseball cap, but woe to the adolescent who misses out on such distinctions. Why are adolescents so painfully obsessed with these signs of group acceptance and social status? If these are universal aspects of human social organization, why don't adults place the same importance on popularity and peer acceptance? Adults are not immune to consideration of social status. Consider the market for luxury cars and designer clothes, as well as the importance of occupational and financial success to many adults' self-esteem. However, adults can put such issues in greater perspective.

Unlike adolescents whose acute self-consciousness makes them magnify any social gaffe into world-shattering proportions, adults are more forgiving of their own and others' social imperfections. They are also better able to distinguish between social relationships that truly matter to them and those that have less relevance to their daily lives.

What **role** does **sexuality play** in adolescence?

One of the greatest changes adolescents undergo involves sexuality. In puberty they transition from pre-sexual children into sexually mature individuals who are capable of conceiving and/or bearing children. In general, sexual maturity precedes emotional maturity, and young teens are often faced with feelings and social demands that they are not emotionally ready for. The age of puberty has come earlier and earlier over the past century. Initially, this development reflected improvements in nutrition and adolescent health. In more recent years, however, the earlier timing of puberty may have more to do with changes in the environment, specifically with hormones in the food. Moreover, in our highly complex, industrialized society, the full adult role is reached far later than in simpler societies. Thus, the period during which an adolescent is sexually mature but not yet inhabiting a fully adult role has greatly lengthened over time.

Adolescents receive many conflicting messages about sexuality. Boys may be under pressure to prove their manhood, and possibly to be sexually active before they feel ready for it. Likewise, the intense sex drive of the adolescent male along with their concern with promoting a masculine identity may lead to irresponsible and dangerous sexual behavior, or behavior that is inadequately sensitive to the needs of the partner. Girls, in particular, face conflicting sexual messages. There is pressure to engage in sexual activity in order to "be cool," to maintain male attention, or to prove that one is not a child. There is also pressure to avoid being labeled as promiscuous.

Despite many changes in sex roles over the past few decades, the sexually promiscuous female is often still stigmatized. Alternatively, adolescents may feel ready to engage in sexual behavior but face restrictions on their behavior from parents, peers, or culture. Sexual mores for adolescents have undergone many changes in recent decades. Because of this cultural flux, sexual development in adolescents can present many challenges. Adolescents benefit most from careful, thoughtful, and open discussion with adults about the risks and rewards of sexual activity.

Why are **adolescents** so **reckless**?

Adolescents are known for a level of recklessness and disregard of danger not found at any other age. They drive cars at fast speeds, drive while intoxicated, imbibe massive amounts of alcohol or illicit drugs, break laws, get into fights, have unsafe sex, and engage in many other high-risk behaviors. As the saying goes, adolescents seem to believe they are immortal. While this phenomenon is well recognized, it is not fully understood. Probably several factors contribute. For one, the myelination of the frontal lobe is not complete until the mid-twenties. Thus, the parts of the brain responsible for impulse control and the consideration of consequences are not fully developed. Further, the surge of testosterone, particularly in males, probably increases thrill-seeking behavior.

There is evidence that the emotional parts of the brain are more reactive as well. The combination of increased thrill seeking with inadequate impulse control can be a combustible mix. Social factors also come into play. The heightened emphasis on peer approval in adolescence, along with the desire to establish independence from parental authority, encourages adolescents to forcefully and publicly assert their independence. Caution and self-control can thus become a sign of childish dependency, a potential source of great embarrassment, and a target for peer ridicule. Common sense can become "uncool."

Does **culture influence** our **understanding** of **adolescence**?

Although there are many biological influences on adolescent psychology, adolescence does not take place in a cultural vacuum. The very concept of adolescence is a relatively recent one. Earlier in our history, there was less recognition of a transitional period between childhood and adulthood. Marriage, childbearing, and occupational maturity took place during the teen years. Although there was recognition of the special characteristics of "youth" (a period extending roughly from adolescence into early adulthood), most people took on an adult role within their society in their teens. As our society has become more complex, more and more time is needed to prepare for adult participation in society. Consequently, adolescence has come to be seen as unique period to be distinguished from both childhood and adulthood.

Whay are adolescents so drawn to social networking sites?

Adolescents are known for their emphasis on peer relationships and identity formation. With recent advances in telecommunications and Internet technology, adolescents can now remain in almost constant contact through text messaging or Internet social networking sites.

Two of the most popular websites, Facebook and MySpace, allow participants to craft and promote a social identity by posting pictures, videos, and text on their own Web pages. Additionally, they can add comments to their friends' Web pages.

The following quotes were culled from various high school students' pages on Facebook. (Any identifying information has been removed or changed to protect confidentiality.) Note the playful and dramatic tone as well as the abbreviations, careless spelling, and emphasis on music, clothing, and technical gadgets.

- IM NORMAL I SWARE!!!
- well arent u just a ray of sunshine!!
- "boys with accents = hottness"—BLN
- omg so whenever me and Alyssa get ready for any outing we listen to really loud fun music on Z100 and the same for sleepover parties and fun nights at eachothers houses
- we're like insane when it comes to music
- i like all music…. unless its the really boring kind with like no rythem at all lol
- anything thts fun to danse to but also the really cute slow songs that everyone loves
- "The creepy man asked if we needed a ride so we ran away and got lost"
- rich fat man: whats an ipod touch?
- Sarah: its like an iphone without the phone
- Megan: yeah u could talk to it but no one would talk back
- I don't have ANY dresses!! Like seriously … not like in the spoiled way like omg my dolce is out of style. I totally need a new dress
- AmeliAAAAAAAAAAAAAAAAAAAAAAAAAHHHHHH

Do **cultures vary** with regard to the **emphasis on peers**?

Cultures vary significantly with regard to the emphasis on peers. In cultures that place high value on interdependence and family ties and less value on self-sufficiency and independence, peer relationships are less central to adolescent development. Additionally, there is greater respect for authority and less tolerance for nonconformity. As a significant emphasis is placed on individuality and independence in the United States, peer relationships have assumed tremendous importance in the lives of many adolescents. Relatedly, there is more tolerance of challenges to authority, rebellion, and nonconformity in American culture than in more traditional cultures.

EARLY ADULTHOOD (19–40)

What are the **psychological challenges** of **early adulthood**?

Early adulthood is a less tumultuous period than adolescence. Nonetheless, it has its own share of challenges and gratifications. At this point, the individual is clearly an adult. He or she is biologically, cognitively, and socially prepared to take on an adult role within society. This movement toward greater independence and responsibility entails several steps. Young adults must achieve some degree of emotional and financial individuation from parents. This does not mean that they need to cut ties with their parents, only that the nature of their relationship should change from that of dependency to greater equality.

Young adults need to achieve some degree of financial independence. Many young adults are still in school, even in their mid to late twenties, and thus are hampered from earning a full living. Nonetheless, they are working toward financial independence and often have an independent source of income, even if they cannot work full time. Additionally, they should be learning to budget, pay bills, pay taxes, and otherwise handle their money independently.

This is also a time of embarking on new intimate attachments. Long-term romantic relationships are established, and most people get married during this period. Many people also become parents in early adulthood, and thus undertake enormous responsibility for the lives and development of their dependent children.

Finally, this is a time of establishing a career path. Although social roles in Western society have become much more flexible in recent decades and young adults typically make multiple changes in their work and romantic life, choices still need to be made that have far-reaching consequences. For example, the choice to marry and have children with a particular partner will have lifelong implications, even if the marriage ends in divorce. Likewise, the choice to pursue higher education or a particular career path has extensive influence on later life.

What does **separating from parents** entail?

The separation from parents is a focal aspect of early adulthood. This may take different forms in different cultures and subcultures. In cultures that emphasize independence and self sufficiency, there may be less contact with parents and less dependence on them for advice, guidance and determination of values and beliefs. In cultures that emphasize family ties and traditional relationships, there is less expectation of physical separation and greater respect for parental opinions.

However, in any culture, a young adult is expected to engage with parents on a more egalitarian basis. Young adults must take on more responsibility for the support of themselves and others, and they are more capable of independent decisions. In Western society, young adults are expected to differentiate their own desires, beliefs, values, and goals from those of their parents. Often this is a complicated process, as many parental attitudes are not explicit and have been unconsciously absorbed over time.

Young adults adjust best when they can maintain close relationships with parents but also retain the ability to evaluate parental opinions critically but fairly, accepting what is helpful and disregarding what is not. Ultimately, an important psychological task of this period is to achieve an understanding of parents as three-dimensional humans, limited and flawed but precious for their unconditional love.

What does it entail to **embark** on an **occupational role**?

One of the cardinal features of young adulthood is the assumption of adult responsibilities within society. In modern Western society, this generally involves taking on a role in the work force, deciding on and embarking upon an occupational path. At earlier points in history, there was little choice in one's occupation. Men often did what their fathers did and women got married and raised children.

In modern industrialized societies, however, this is no longer true. For most members of society, there is a smorgasbord of occupational choices, and young adults can often feel bewildered by the sheer number of options. One's choice of occupation has far-reaching implications for one's personal identity, social role, financial well-being, and general quality of life. Unfortunately, there is little definitive information upon which to make such important decisions. Consequently, young adults make choices based on stereotyped views of success and career gratification, with little life experience of their own to guide them. The perceived number of options is also a function of education and social class.

Not all adolescents will feel that high-status and high-income professions are available for them. Nonetheless, the choice to complete high school and even to enter some form of post-secondary education is possible for many members of Western society. Thus, across socioeconomic groups, young adults must grapple with the task of choosing an occupational path.

What specific **challenges** are involved with the **beginning** of **committed romantic partnerships**?

Although the average age of marriage has increased in the West over the last few
decades, this is still a time where the majority of people commit to romantic partner-

ships. Commitment to marriage or other forms of long-term romantic relationships brings a host of challenges. The very act of commitment is often an ambivalent one, especially for young adults who have grown used to freedom and independence. The same social changes that have demanded longer and longer periods of preparation for adulthood have stretched out the period when a young person has no one to account to besides himself or herself. Thus, the necessary compromises and sacrifices of commitment can present considerable problems. Moreover, even in those people eager to find a committed relationship, it often takes time and experience to identify those traits in a potential partner that are most important to sustain a long-term relationship.

Many young people complain of being single but continue to pursue lovers who offer little potential for a successful relationship. Once a committed relationship is attained, there are numerous relationship skills that need to be developed. Couples need to learn how to balance alone and together time, communicate needs effectively, and manage conflict constructively. In our constantly changing society, however, there are few fixed rules for relationships, making it more difficult for the young adult to master the skills necessary for a successful relationship. The difficulty of these tasks is reflected in the divorce rate. According to 2005 statistics from the U.S. Center for Disease Control, about 7.5 out of every 1000 people get married each year and about 3.6 out of every 1,000 people get divorced. While this is the lowest divorce rate since 1970, it is still remarkably high. Likewise, people who marry very young, specifically before the age of twenty-three, have the highest likelihood of divorce.

What are the challenges of **becoming a parent** in **early adulthood**?

The transition to parenthood demands one of the largest psychological transformations in adulthood. Although young adults may be living entirely independently, with an established career and a mature set of social relationships, they may still think of themselves as "a kid" and not "a real adult." When a person becomes a parent, this illusion is shattered. A small, helpless baby is utterly dependent on the new parent and there is no more hiding from the reality of adult responsibilities. Most people find that, for the first time in their lives, their responsibility to another person is as great, or greater, than their responsibility to themselves. While this level of self-sacrifice can be very stressful for new parents, especially very young ones, many experience it as an opportunity for tremendous growth and maturity. It can be life enhancing to be less self-centered. However, as with most aspects of early adult development, our changing culture has taken away clear guidelines.

Although many parents happily take advantage of the flood of available books and articles on parenting, new parents face inevitable uncertainty when making decisions about how to raise their children. At the same time, many new parents renegotiate their relationship with their own parents, gaining new appreciation for their knowledge and experience. Families tend to get closer when a new baby arrives as grandparents become involved with the new family, often helping out with childcare.

What happens if these **challenges** are **not met**?

The transition out of adolescence into young adulthood presents challenges on a number of levels. Young people must establish a multi-faceted adult identity, commit to deeper and more mature relationships, and take on financial, emotional, and social responsibilities. In so doing, the young adult opens up opportunities for great satisfaction and fulfillment, for greater control and empowerment, and for improved social status and respect. However, each of these developments entails sacrifices. In effect, growing up means giving up: the security of depending on parents, the freedom of a life without commitment and responsibility, and the illusion that it is possible to avoid failure. These present real psychological challenges and few young adults progress smoothly along each line of development.

It is normal to have some spottiness across different developmental lines. However, it is far more problematic if there is little movement across any area of development. In this case, young adults may become progressively more depressed as the distance between themselves and their peers becomes more and more apparent with time. In fact, popular culture has addressed this issue through movies such as *Reality Bites* and *Clerks*, both of which came out in 1994. In both these movies, young adults idle aimlessly, frustrated with their lack of forward momentum, but unable to accept the inevitable compromises necessitated by an adult role in society.

What is the **social clock**?

The social clock is a term introduced by a psychologist named Bernice Neugarten. This refers to age-based expectations about when certain life goals should be achieved. These might include the age of marriage, bearing children, attaining a first job, buying a house, and/or completing education. Although the settings for a social clock will vary across cultures, Neugarten suggests that all cultures have some form of age-based expectations of task performance. Adults who perceive themselves to be falling behind the social clock can suffer painful blows to their self-esteem. In our current culture, in which social mores are in a constant state of flux, the realities of daily life may not match the social clock. For example, many women expect to marry and have children on a timescale similar to that of their mothers. However, as the proportion of never-married adults aged thirty to thirty-four is six times greater than it was in 1970, it is likely these social clocks may need to be reset. In fact, according to the 2007 U.S. census report, the proportion of never-married people aged thirty to thirty-four was over 28 percent.

Who was **Daniel Levinson**?

Daniel Levinson (1920–1994) was one of the first psychologists after Erikson to develop a theory of adult development. In 1978, he published a book called *Seasons of a Man's Life*, which was based on extensive interviews with men in several different occupations. In 1987 he published a book entitled *Seasons in a Woman's Life*, using

> ## Why is college graduation so traumatic for some young adults?
>
> College graduation marks an abrupt transition between adolescence and young adulthood. Particularly for those students who attend residential, four-year colleges, the end of the relatively sheltered and structured college experience can be quite disorienting. In general, the transition between adolescence and adulthood can be anxiety-provoking. People at this stage of life often feel considerable anxiety about taking on the risks and responsibilities of creating an adult life structure. Fear of failure or of being trapped in a dead-end or soul-crushing career can feed a desire to prolong the carefree, aimless days of adolescence.
>
> Two popular American movies that came out in the 1990s address the emotional difficulties some young adults have in making the transition from adolescence to early adulthood. *Clerks,* starring Brian O'Halloran and Jeff Anderson, and *Reality Bites,* starring Winona Ryder, Ethan Hawke, Janeane Garofolo, and Ben Stiller, both play with the humor and pathos of this stage of life.

similar methodology with a sample of women. Even though his samples were small and largely limited to upper-income people, his thoughts about adult development are worth considering.

What is Daniel **Levinson's theory** of **adult development**?

Levinson proposed that adult development goes through a series of predictable stages, known as *seasons* or *eras*. These include: early adulthood (age twenty-two to forty), middle adulthood (age forty to sixty) and late adulthood (age sixty and up). He also proposed the notion of cross-era transitions, in which the adult negotiates the psychological challenges of transitioning from one stage to another. Cross-era transitions last about five to seven years. Levinson suggests that the first stage, early adulthood, is characterized by the creation of the initial *life structure*. This is a period of great excitement and satisfaction, but also of notable uncertainty and anxiety. To Levinson, adult development involves a series of fluctuations between the creation and rearrangement of life structures. A life structure refers to the entire design of a person's life, including psychological traits, social relationships, and work life. A life structure is most satisfying when personal needs can be harmonized with external societal demands.

What did **Levinson** say about **early adulthood**?

In the novice phase of early adulthood (roughly age seventeen to thirty-three), the young adult is creating the initial life structure. This is a very difficult task for people with so little life experience, and choices are based more on a dream of what life should be than on personal experience. At the age thirty transition, people have the opportunity to evaluate their life as lived so far. For the first time in their life, they have a past as an adult as well as a future. They can compare their actual experiences with their original life dream, and consider what part of their life structure needs to be revised. In the culminating phase (33 to 45), the initial life structure is brought to fruition. The adult experiences both the gratifications and the disappointments in life as it has turned out to be. This era ends when the adult transitions into the next major life era, middle adulthood.

Which of Eric **Erickson's psychosexual stages** pertain to **early adulthood**?

Erik Erikson suggested that young adulthood was a time when people struggled with intimacy vs. isolation. He believed that this stage depended upon a successful resolution of the previous stage, identity vs. isolation. Erikson believed that it is necessary to have a stable personal identity, a secure sense of self, in order to establish a committed, intimate relationship. In an intimate partnership, one has to open up one's identity to another person. To some extent, intimacy involves the merger of one's sense of self with that of the other person. If a secure sense of self has not been achieved, it remains too threatening to loosen the reins and let another person in. When people are afraid of losing themselves in a relationship, intimacy and commitment will be avoided. Such people may engage in many short-term relationships or avoid monogamous relationships. Interestingly, later research has supported Erikson's ideas. People who are more secure in their values and goals are more likely to remain faithful in intimate relationships and to be more ready for a serious commitment.

What are the **developmental tasks** of **early adulthood** according to **Roger Gould**?

Roger Gould (1935–) is a psychoanalytic writer who has written a good deal about adult development. In fact, the popular book *Passages* by Gail Sheehy was based heavily on his research. Like Levinson, Gould conceptualized adult development as unfolding in a series of predictable stages. Gould was particularly interested in the way adults understand their life choices and how that changes across the lifespan. Gould proposed that the early adult years (age eighteen to thirty-five) were characterized by several psychological illusions that are slowly relinquished over time. He was particularly interested in the *illusion of absolute safety*.

One of the cardinal experiences of all human beings involves the fear of death. Our drive is toward life and we are terrified at the prospect of the annihilation of life, of death. In childhood, the illusion of absolute safety is maintained through dependence on idealized parents who are seen as omnipotent protectors, all-powerful guardians against death. In early adulthood, the illusion of absolute safety is transferred to the fantasy of the one right path. This path will lead to "the prize," to absolute safety. Young adults anxiously and desperately seek this one true path, ever fearful of making a mistake, of going down the wrong path. It is only in midlife, when mortality becomes an emotional as well as an intellectual reality, that the illusion of the one right way can be abandoned.

MIDDLE ADULTHOOD (40–60)

What are the overall **themes** of **middle adulthood**?

In all of the previous life stages, the individual is moving toward maturity. In middle adulthood, the adult has reached maturity. The adult is fully a grown up. At this stage in life however, middle-aged adults must confront the beginnings of physical decline. There is still considerable vigor and vitality in middle adulthood as well as considerable potential for psychological growth. Nonetheless, the signs of a declining body are unavoidable. Middle-aged adults confront a loss of physical strength and energy, minor aches and pains that occur more easily and take longer to go away than ever before, and various losses in sensory and cognitive abilities. There are significant consolations to middle adulthood, however. Decades of life experience promote general wisdom, the capacity to understand the world as a whole, integrated system. There is greater emotional maturity as well, an understanding of one's self and others in more tempered and thoughtful ways. In middle adulthood, we are older but wiser.

What kind of **physical changes** occur in **middle adulthood**?

While middle-aged adults retain the physical abilities necessary to conduct their daily lives, there are unmistakable signs of aging. There is a loss of lean body mass, including both muscle and bone, and a concomitant gain in body fat. On average, women's abdomens increase by about thirty percent and men's by about ten percent from early to middle adulthood. There are also changes in the layers of the skin, such that elasticity is lost, the skin loosens and wrinkles form. Gray hair is caused by a reduction of melanin in the hair follicles.

There are also important changes in the reproductive system, especially for women. Menopause occurs on average at age fifty-one but most women experience considerable hormonal changes for several years before. These changes affect sleep, temperature regulation, bone density, and sexual function. It is important to note that physical health in middle adulthood is strongly influenced by health-related behaviors. A healthy diet (i.e., one rich in fruits, vegetables, whole grains, and lean proteins), regular exercise, and avoidance of smoking and excessive alcohol can greatly moderate the effects of aging.

What **sensory changes** occur in **middle adulthood**?

Presbyopia, which means "old eyes" in Greek, refers to a common condition encountered in middle adulthood. The lens of the eye becomes less flexible, reducing the ability of the eye to focus on close objects. People in their forties frequently have difficulty reading due to presbyopia. They must hold reading material at arm's length to focus on the letters. Consequently, many people this age buy reading glasses for the first time. There are also changes in hearing, although these are not as noticeable as the changes in vision. Loss of sensitivity to high-pitched sounds can begin in middle adulthood although hearing loss is generally more pronounced in later adulthood.

How does **cognition change** in **midlife**?

When discussing cognition in midlife, it is important to distinguish between fluid vs. crystallized intelligence. *Fluid intelligence* refers to raw processing power, specifically aspects of attention, memory, and processing speed. *Crystallized intelligence* refers to learned skills, including funds of information, verbal knowledge, and knowledge of social conventions. Fluid intelligence declines in midlife. The raw ability to process new information slows down. Consider the ease in which a teenager or young adult learns new technology compared to the difficulties middle-aged adults often face mastering the same task. On the other hand, crystallized intelligence increases steadily throughout middle adulthood. In fact, aspects of complex reasoning, verbal ability, and spatial processing peak in middle adulthood and only slowly decline thereafter.

In what ways does **cognition improve** in midlife?

While the speed of information processing slows down considerably, this loss is made up for by a much greater understanding of the world in general. Adolescents and younger adults can process isolated bits of information more efficiently than older adults, but they have little context with which to understand it. Older adults have a richer, broader, and more integrated understanding of the world at large. Moreover, the ability to recognize how events can fit into familiar patterns can help compensate for the loss of fluid processing skills. For example, if a chess master can recognize familiar configurations of chess pieces, there is less need to memorize the positions of each chess piece on the board.

What **emotional changes** transpire in **middle adulthood**?

There is a universally recognized trend in middle adulthood to be calmer, less impulsive, and less emotionally reactive than at younger ages. Middle-aged adults often feel stress, due to the numerous responsibilities they face, but they are relatively free of the existential angst that characterizes earlier periods. Their greater understanding of the world as a whole allows them to put events into perspective. When you can take the long view of a situation, it tends to take the sting out of any particular incident. This reduces emotional volatility. Moreover, middle-aged adults have a larger world view, which allows them to better understand the implications of any given event, to appreciate the possible consequences. This consideration of consequences tempers impulsivity.

Why does time seem to speed up as we age?

One of the dramatic experiences of middle adulthood involves the change in the subjective sense of time. To a small child, an hour seems like an eternity. The future does not exist. By early adulthood, time has sped up considerably from early childhood but the young adult still experiences time as relatively static. While the future exists in theory, only the present feels real.

In contrast, by mid-life every year is a much smaller fraction of the adult's entire life span. Time seems to flow faster and faster, almost as if the person is walking on a moving sidewalk and the surrounding landscape is speeding up with every step. Because of this, middle aged adults have a less static sense of time. They experience themselves and their world in a sense of flux. The present is a moving target and the future is just around the bend. Likewise, middle aged adults are often surprised by the speed that the present retreats into the past. "That was twenty years ago? Already?" "These clothes are out of style? But I just bought them!"

What **impact** does **mortality** play in **middle adulthood**?

A critical aspect of psychological development in midlife involves a change in the relationship with death. As several theorists have noted, in adolescence and early adulthood, mortality is often theoretical at best. Adolescents are known for their illusions of immortality, resulting at times in a reckless disregard for danger. In early adulthood, death is recognized in the abstract. While young adults do not believe they are immortal, neither does death feel entirely real.

In middle adulthood, death becomes much more real. Many people of the prior generation die: parents, aunts and uncles, older friends and colleagues, and the parents of friends. Some people of the adult's own generation die as well. In the context of these direct encounters with mortality, death can no longer remain an abstraction.

In some people, the confrontation with mortality in midlife can lead to panic and a frantic denial of aging and death. More optimally, it can lead to greater perspective of what really matters in life and a realignment of priorities. Of note, this discussion applies to people in modern Western societies, who remain largely shielded from death prior to midlife. In societies where early death is more prevalent, however, it is likely that mortality is experienced quite differently.

How does the view of **one's options in life** change during this period?

In early adulthood, we have a sense of open horizons. Regardless of what is happening in the present, goals and ideals can still be reached in the future. There will always be time to get married, have children, or start a career. In midlife, the adult confronts the narrowing of options. Time is limited. Life's possibilities are finite. Even though it may be possible to change tracks, it may not be worth the cost in time, money, or sheer energy. And some opportunities are simply closed. A woman cannot give birth after menopause. For some people, there might be feelings of being trapped. For others, there may be anger and disappointment at lost opportunities. Optimally, the confrontation with limitations in one's life promotes greater psychological maturity. Difficult decisions must be made, disappointments must be accepted, and priorities must be realigned to make the best of life as it is, not as we think it should be.

How does the **view** of the **self change** in middle adulthood?

In midlife, the sense of self is much more defined than it was in earlier periods. A good deal of life has already been lived, and the unfolding of that life has cemented the adult's sense of who they are, where they have been, and where they are likely to go. Because of this, middle-aged adults are likely to have a greater sense of self assurance than are adolescents and younger adults. To the extent the adult has had experiences of success, of mastering challenges, and accomplishing goals, there are gains in self-confidence.

In midlife, one also has to confront one's own limitations. The dreams of youth must be reconciled with the reality of life as lived. To the extent that the discrepancies between ideals and reality can be accepted, there is greater self-acceptance and more stable self-esteem. There can be a sense of liberty from the tyranny of youthful expectations. However, for those who cannot accept that life does not always turn out the way we want, there can be considerable depression along with a great sense of anger, frustration, and shame.

How is **middle adulthood** often a time of **peak responsibilities**?

Midlife is frequently a time of peak responsibilities, both at home and in the workplace. Adults at this stage of life often have ongoing parenting responsibilities with children still living at home. At the same time, their parents are aging and frequently need care. Due to their greater experience and psychological maturity, middle-aged adults are ideally positioned to assume greater responsibility in the workplace. Many move into positions of management at work. Assumption of such supervisory roles brings to mind Erikson's stage of Generativity vs. Stagnation, the psychosocial stage of middle adulthood. In Erikson's view, generativity involves providing care and guidance for the next generation and for society as a whole.

What are the typical **challenges** of **parenting** during middle adulthood?

In early adulthood the challenges of parenting typically involve taking on the enormous responsibility of day-to-day care of children. In middle adulthood, however,

One of the cardinal challenges of middle adulthood involves the confrontation with mortality and the loss of the youthful body. Changes in modern technology, such as plastic surgery, collagen injections, and Botox injections, can prolong physical beauty. Over-dependence on such techniques, however, can promote a denial of aging. This in turn undermines the psychological maturity derived from acknowledgment and acceptance of the inevitable limits in life (*iStock*).

the parent will need to learn how to let go. If the children are adolescents, the parent will need to offer some supervision to the child, but also allow them a good degree of freedom from parental control. Finding the right balance is a difficult challenge as many adolescents are prone to recklessness and their judgment is far from mature. Allowing their children greater independence can also be a loss for parents, who have devoted more than a decade to the task of child rearing. Parents in midlife need to find areas of fulfillment in their life that are independent of their parenting role. This is to ensure that the parent's dependence on the parental role does not interfere with the child's developmental need for greater independence.

What **changes** take place in the **relationships** between middle-aged adults and their **parents**?

The vast majority of adults in middle adulthood will experience the aging and even death of their parents. As their parents' physical and cognitive abilities deteriorate, adult children must take on a caretaking role. The extent to which the children take on such responsibilities will vary from family to family but some degree of role reversal between parent and adult child is largely unavoidable. The financial, medical, and supervisory aspects of elder care can be extremely complex, particularly in modern, industrialized societies in which both women and men work outside the home.

Psychologically, the role reversal between elderly parent and middle-aged child can be difficult. Besides the obvious stress of the new responsibilities, there is a sense of sadness at the loss of the parental figure. Even though the middle-aged adult is fully mature and handles significant responsibilities, it is still upsetting to realize there are no more "grown-ups" to fall back upon. It is the children who are the grown-ups now, not the parents.

What does **Roger Gould** say about middle adulthood?

In Gould's view, the confrontation with aging and mortality in midlife punctures the *Illusion of Absolute Safety*. This demands a renegotiation of the adult's relationship with work, marriage, family, and many other aspects of life. With regard to work, people who have dedicated their lives to the pursuit of success realize that even when such goals are accomplished, they fail to bring the "prize" dreamt of at an earlier period. Fame, power, and wealth cannot confer immortality. A restlessness and dissatisfaction can occur, to be resolved only when the motivation for work comes from pleasure in the task rather than the expectation of magical transformation and ultimate salvation.

When Gould was writing in the 1970s, this dynamic mainly applied to men (and affluent men at that). In women, the illusion of absolute safety was more likely to manifest in a sense of self as helplessly dependent on a man. Although many women felt trapped by their lack of autonomy, the acceptance of greater self-determination was anxiety-provoking. It stripped away the comforting illusion of the male as the omnipotent protector. No matter how people cling to the illusion of absolute safety, the desire to protect oneself from awareness of death inevitably brings great psychological costs. Remaining ignorant of a disturbing reality forces people to constrict their own self-experience, impoverishing their personality. Fortunately, midlife provides an opportunity for people to enhance their psychological potential by shedding their denial of mortality.

LATER ADULTHOOD (60 AND OLDER)

What **physiological changes** occur in **later adulthood**?

The physiological changes that began in middle adulthood intensify in late adulthood. Primarily a nuisance in middle adulthood, they begin to truly interfere with everyday functioning in late life. But it is important to distinguish between different stages of this last phase of life. Gerontologists, people who study aging, speak of the young-old and the old-old, meaning those in their sixties and early seventies and those over the age of seventy-five. Some also speak of the oldest old, those over eighty-five. The young-old, by and large, are still very vigorous. In the older age group, however, the decline in body functions can significantly constrict life activities.

What kind of bodily changes occur in late life? There is some belief that aging starts in the cells. There is decreased cell regeneration and deterioration in cell DNA and RNA. Brain cells also deteriorate, with decreased neurogenesis (new neuron growth) and general shrinkage of brain tissue. There is musculoskeletal deterioration, with continued loss of muscle mass and bone density. Thickening of the lens of the eye continues to reduce vision. Hearing, in particular, takes a hit, with 65 percent of people age eighty or above showing an inability to hear high-pitched sounds. Difficulties making sense of conversation can leave the elderly feeling socially isolated.

Additional changes take place in the gastrointestinal, cardiovascular, respiratory, and endocrine systems. Chronic diseases become much more common at this stage in life, particularly diabetes, hypertension, and arthritis. The news is not all bad, however. There are many lifestyle factors over which people have considerable control that can maximize health and well-being. Perhaps even to a greater extent than at younger ages, exercise, diet, positive mood, stimulating mental activities, and positive social relationships can promote optimal functioning.

What are the **psychological challenges** of **later adulthood**?

Late adulthood, which can last up to thirty years (and beyond in some cases), is the last stage of life. Although this stage can cover many years, it still marks the closing of the life story. Adults at this stage must review their life as lived and come to some sort of emotional closure about how their life has unfolded. Adults in late life must also confront the unavoidable reality of mortality and hopefully come to accept the inevitability of death. People in this stage cope with numerous losses: physical vigor and sometimes health, roles and responsibilities of an earlier age, and loved ones who have died.

Luckily, older adults are often well-equipped emotionally to handle these daunting psychological challenges. Many studies show that psychological maturity continues to grow across the lifespan. In general, adults in late life have a more positive outlook, are less prone to negative emotional reactions, and are less egocentric than younger people. The storied wisdom of the old is both a function of life experience and a buffer against life experience.

Is **depression** more **common** in **later life** than at younger ages?

Depression is actually less common in later life than at younger ages but is arguably more debilitating when it does occur. Adults in late life incur a significant amount of losses, including their job, health, and status and role in society. They also suffer the death of loved ones. Such losses can certainly precipitate depression. Additionally, medical conditions that are more frequent in late life, such as stroke and dementia, can cause depressive symptoms. The nature of geriatric depression is somewhat different from that found in younger people.

Elderly people often express their depression through somatic complaints (complaints about physical problems) and frequently have sleep problems and markedly reduced energy, initiative, and appetite. Sometimes there is considerable weight loss. The resulting self-neglect can put the elderly depressed person in real danger. Likewise, suicide is a serious problem. In fact, the risk of suicide is five times higher in white men over the age of sixty-five than in the general population. Nonetheless, despite their exposure to multiple losses, in general, the elderly have a lower rate of depression than do younger groups. This has been attributed to the greater emotion regulation and coping skills of older adults.

What are the **benefits** of **getting older**?

Provided there is adequate financial, medical, and social support, adults in late life can benefit from both a reduction in stressful responsibilities and ongoing gains in psychological maturity. Many researchers talk of wisdom, which is loosely defined as better emotional regulation, judgment, understanding of the ways of the world, and empathy for others. With increasing age, there is generally a reduction in impulsive, impetuous behavior and emotional volatility along with an improved ability to see things from others' perspectives. In many cultures, the elderly are valued for their wise advice. If the older adult is in relatively good health, particularly in the earlier stages of late adulthood, there is enhanced opportunity for enjoyable leisure activities.

What do the **theorists** of **adult development say** about this period?

Erikson described the psychological challenge of the last stage of life as Ego Integrity vs. Despair. By this he meant that adults at this stage are facing the end of their life. Many decisions have been made, life has been largely lived, and it has brought both disappointments and rewards. When people can see their life as a whole and accept both its disappointments and gratifications as part of a complete narrative, then they can achieve ego integrity. When older adults cannot accept their disappointments and thwarted dreams, they fall into despair. Life will soon be over and there are no more chances.

Erikson's wife, Joan, later wrote about an additional stage for the very old, which she termed *gerotranscendance*. In this stage, in the ninth or tenth decade of life, people begin to look beyond their own individual lifespan. Very close to their own death, they start to transcend their identity as a single, isolated person and begin to see themselves as part of a larger whole that will live on after their own death. Accordingly, research has shown that older adults are more involved in religious activities than are younger people. Several other theorists, such as Heinz Kohut, Daniel Levinson, and Bernice Neugarten, also write about the need in late life to come to terms with both the positive and negative aspects of one's life as lived as well as the losses of aging, the diminished role of the self, and the impending end of life.

What is the **psychological impact** of **retirement**?

Sixty-five is the traditional age of retirement. For those who have spent the majority of their waking hours at work over the previous four decades, this is an enormous transition. For some people—particularly those who have not cultivated interests or social relationships outside of work—retirement represents a significant loss, and there can be difficulties with emotional adjustment. For others, retirement offers the opportunity to explore new interests and old passions, spend more time with friends and family, and give back to the community through volunteer work or socially meaningful part-time work. The extent to which people plan out a new life structure in advance influences their adjustment to retirement. Of course, much also depends on the financial resources and physical health of the retired adult, which in turn depends on social policies regarding retirement financing and healthcare.

Across developed countries the average lifespan has lengthened considerably. Projections show that the proportion of the population that is above sixty-five and eighty-five will grow tremendously in the decades to come. For example, according to U.S. census data, in 1900 people aged sixty-five and older comprised four percent of the population while those aged eighty-five and over comprised only 0.1 percent of the population. By 2050, these rates are projected to be 20 percent and 4.8 percent, respectively. This raises concerns about the ability of governments or corporations to fund retirement pensions. Lessening that concern are the same factors that account for the increased lifespan in the first place.

The advances in medical technology, nutrition, and lifestyle that have increased longevity also increase the vigor and productivity of seniors, particularly the "young-old" in their sixties and early seventies. In fact, many people reenter the work force soon after retirement, in volunteer or part-time positions, if not full-time jobs.

How does the **relationship with mortality change** in this phase of life?

While mortality becomes real in middle adulthood, it becomes immediate in late adulthood. Middle-aged adults deal with the death of their parents and other people in their parents' generation. Elderly adults deal with the death of people in their own generation, their spouses, siblings, and longtime friends. While middle-aged adults confront the reality of future death, adults in late life recognize their own death may be coming soon. Of course, the period of late life plays into this. Healthy adults in their mid-sixties can expect to live into their eighties (eighty-one for males and eighty-six for females according to the U.S. Census Bureau), while people in their ninth and tenth decade of life are looking at a much shorter time horizon.

What **factors contribute** to a **positive adjustment** to later adulthood?

A number of factors contribute to a positive adjustment to late adulthood, many of which serve a similar function at earlier stages of adulthood. For one, social support retains its critical importance. Although the size of people's social circles tends to decrease with age, and many older adults spend less time with acquaintances in favor of family and close friends, the quality of social relationships has a powerful impact on the sense of well-being. Secondly, engagement in meaningful and satisfying activities, such as hobbies, creative work, volunteer work, or even part-time jobs, are crucial sources of satisfaction for adults in late life.

Involvement in productive work of some kind enhances self-esteem and a sense of belonging. Particularly after retirement, it is important to have some form of structured and meaningful activity with which to replace the purpose, structure, and identity formerly derived from the work role. Finally, physical exercise is tremendously beneficial. Even thirty minutes a day of walking can have clear, measurable benefits. Physical exercise promotes cardiovascular health, muscle strength, and bone density. This gives older adults mobility and functional independence, which has a strong impact on life satisfaction.

Further, improved cardio-vascular health protects brain function and cognition. There is considerable evidence that physical exercise is protective against dementia. In fact, exercise has been shown to increase the amount of a chemical called *brain-derived neurotropic factor* (BDNF), which in turn promotes the growth of new brain cells.

How does the **role** of **older adults vary** across **cultures** and historical **time periods**?

In many traditional cultures, the elderly are highly esteemed members of the community. Their advice is sought in many matters and valued for its wisdom. People live in large, extended families and grandparents often contribute to the care of grandchildren. When people grow too old to take care of themselves, younger family members (mostly women) provide care. In most modern, industrialized societies, however, there has been a dramatic change in the structure of the family. To a large extent, the nuclear family has replaced the extended family. People are more mobile, move residences more often, and adult children can live hundreds if not thousands of miles away from their parents. Further, working women do not have the time to provide full-time care for aging parents.

Thus, the place of the elderly in society has undergone great disruption. Two movements have emerged in response to these changes. For one, there has been growth of government-sponsored elder care services, including nursing homes, adult homes, home health aides, and adult day care centers. Secondly, there has been an extension of activities previously associated with earlier periods of life, such as travel, sports, continuing education, and paid or unpaid work, far into late life. Seniors today are likely to be more active—physically, economically, and socially—than their parents were.

How does **cognition change** in **late life**?

As with middle adulthood, fluid intelligence (processing speed, working memory, complex attention) continues to decline. Crystallized intelligence (fund of information, verbal skills, vocabulary) remains intact for much longer. This relates to the growth of wisdom discussed above. Eventually, perhaps in the ninth or tenth decade of life, crystallized intelligence also starts to decline. Although we do expect some intellectual decline with normal aging, severe intellectual decline is not a part of normal aging, but rather a symptom of dementia.

What is **dementia**?

Dementia involves the loss of intellectual abilities, generally including memory, spatial skills, and executive functions (planning, abstract thought, self-monitoring, etc.). The two most common forms of dementia are *Alzheimer's disease* and *vascular dementia*. The biology of Alzheimer's is characterized by the buildup of *amyloid plaques* and *neurofibrillary tangles* in and around the neuron (brain cell). Alzheimer's starts with memory impairment and then generalizes to a broad range of cognitive impairments, sufficiently severe to leave people unable to care for themselves. Vascular dementia is caused by *cerebrovascular* events, such as strokes, which involve major disruptions of the blood supply to the brain.

Dementia is fairly rare in the mid-sixties (about ten percent) but becomes quite common by the eighties and nineties. By some estimates, 50 percent of all people over 85 have Alzheimer's disease. Consequently, virtually all families will be touched by dementia at some point. The social implications of this are enormous. People with severe dementia demand round-the-clock care, which puts tremendous strain on families, both emotionally and financially. Given the growing population of elderly people across the industrialized world, significant resources will be needed for elder care in the coming years.

What is the nun study?

The nun study is a fascinating examination of aging and Alzheimer's disease conducted in a convent for retired nuns in Mankato, Minnesota. Religious orders make marvelous settings for epidemiological research studies (studies of health and disease patterns in whole populations) because of the relatively uniform lifestyle found in these environments. With many potentially complicating variables held constant, such as smoking, alcohol use, quality of health care, and income, it is much easier to have confidence in the research results.

David Snowdon, the study's lead researcher, began the study in 1991 with a population of 678 nuns. He administered tests of cognitive function and health status. Remarkably, the convent had preserved the essays the nuns wrote upon entering the convent in their teens or early twenties. Finally, the nuns gave their permission for their brains to be autopsied after death. This is critical, as the only way to definitively diagnose Alzheimer's disease is through brain autopsy.

Although the study is ongoing, several noteworthy findings have already been published. For one, essays written in the nuns' adolescence and early adulthood gave clues as to who was more likely to develop Alzheimer's disease later on. The nuns who used more complex grammar and ideas and more positive emotion words were less likely to develop Alzheimer's disease 60 years later. More educated nuns also had a lower chance of developing Alzheimer's. From this data alone, however, we cannot distinguish between cause and effect. Do the essays reflect the earliest manifestations of Alzheimer's or good habits that ultimately protect against the disease?

The autopsy data give clues to this $64,000 question. Although the degree of brain damage due to neurofibrillary tangles and amyloid plaques did correlate with the degree of cognitive decline, it was not a 100 percent correlation. In other words, there were nuns with considerable amounts of brain damage who showed little to no dementia. In fact, 58 percent of the nuns with mild and 32 percent of those with moderate brain pathology did not show memory impairment.

The researchers concluded that there was something known as *cognitive reserve* that protected against functional deterioration in the face of brain disease. They believed that various factors contributed to cognitive reserve by promoting richer neuronal networks (or enhanced communication between brain cells) and greater *cerebrovascular* health. Such factors seem to include education, positive mood, mental stimulation, and healthy diet (specifically the vitamin folate). Cerebrovascular health is very important because the presence of strokes dramatically reduced the cognitive performance of nuns with Alzheimer's disease.

THE END OF LIFE: DEATH AND DYING

What is **thanatology**?

Thanatology refers to the study of death. Because of a number of societal changes, there is now more interest in the nature and quality of death and dying, at least in the developed world. Such changes include the growth of the elderly population, cultural shifts toward greater openness about distressing topics, and longer intervals from the onset of terminal illnesses to death. Thanatologists work closely with the health care system to improve the process of dying both for the dying patient and the surviving family.

What contributes to a **"good death"**?

A number of studies have examined the factors that influence the quality of the dying process–the factors that contribute to a "good death." All studies suggest there are multiple components involved. Probably first and foremost is the issue of physical pain and discomfort. For both dying patients and their families, it is critically important that the last days are physically comfortable. In response, the medical discipline of palliative care has arisen to address the comfort of the terminally ill.

Other domains include the social, psychological, and spiritual realms of experience, as well as the degree of preparation for death. Social factors pertain to the involvement, support, and cohesion of (or, conversely, conflict between) family members. Psychological factors include a sense of closure regarding life as lived and the awareness and acceptance of death. Ideally, the person will feel relatively at peace at the time of death. Spiritual needs are particularly acute at this time and religious beliefs about life after death or the connection of the individual to the larger whole can be profoundly comforting. Preparation for death also includes planning in advance for the medical, legal, and financial issues that are likely to follow.

What role does **hope** have in the **dying process**?

Many thanatologists speak of the importance of hope in the dying process. In the beginning of a life threatening illness, people hope for recovery, to survive the illness, or at least to prolong life. As the reality of death grows closer, it is important to transform the nature of hope. The hope of avoiding death can be translated into the hope of finding and achieving a sense of meaning, of reaching the conviction that one's life has had value, and that death will be faced with dignity and integrity.

What are Elizabeth **Kübler-Ross' five stages** of **grief**?

Elizabeth Kübler-Ross (1926–2004) was one of the first thanatologists to publish a stage theory about the grieving process. Her work was based on studies of the terminally ill. While her model has been criticized, her descriptions of the five stages of grief are still highly influential and provide a good overview of the variety of emotional experiences people undergo while grieving. The five stages of grief are as follows: denial, anger, bargaining, depression, and acceptance.

The first stage is denial. When people first learn of their terminal illness, they go into shock and try to deny that it is real. The next stage involves anger. People learning of their own impending death are frequently angry. This anger may be expressed at doctors, at family, or even at themselves. It is as though they are looking for a place to put their anger at their illness. The next stage involves bargaining. They try to bargain with doctors, friends, family, and even God. By holding onto the belief that they can change the outcome of their illness through "good" behavior, they try to maintain a sense of control. When the reality of death finally sinks in, the result is depression. Ultimately, the person absorbs the intense and devastating shock of their terminal illness. At this point, they reach the stage of acceptance, in which they can face death with a degree of resolution and psychological peace. Later research has shown that not all dying patients go through each stage, nor do they go through them in the same sequence. Nonetheless, many people do experience the states of mind that Kübler-Ross describes.

What do **other theorists** have to say about **grief**?

Several theorists have followed Kübler-Ross's work with their own work on the process of grieving. In a series of publications from the 1960s to the 1980s, John Bowlby (the father of attachment theory) collaborated with Colin Murray Parkes to condense Kübler-Ross's five stages into four phases of grief. Their work differed from Kübler-Ross's original work, however, in that their focus was on the bereaved rather than the dying.

Their four phases are as follows: Shock and disbelief, searching and yearning, disorganization and despair, and rebuilding and healing. Thus, the bereaved must undergo a process of recognizing the loss, experiencing the acute pain of the loss, and then slowly rebuilding life and relationships so as to continue on without the loved one. J. William Worden developed a similar approach, speaking less of the phases than the tasks of grief. In his view, the bereaved must go through four stages: accept the reality of the loss, work through the pain of grief, adjust to an environment in which the deceased is missing, and emotionally relocate the deceased and move on with life. Other theorists, such as Robert Neimeyer and Alan Wolfelt, write of related issues, such as the need to rebuild an identity independent of the lost relationship and to transfer the relationship with the deceased out of daily life and into memory.

Is there **research** on the **grief process**?

Although there are a fair number of theories about the process of grief, there has been less in the way of actual scientific data about the normal course of grief. In 2007, Paul

Maciejewski and colleagues published a study of 233 bereaved adults conducted over a twenty-four-month period. They administered measures of yearning, disbelief, anger, depression, and acceptance at three time points in the first two years after the loss. Their results showed that disbelief peaked soon after the death and then consistently declined afterward. Yearning, which was the most pronounced and long lasting of the negative emotional responses to loss, peaked at about four months. Anger peaked at about five months, and depression at about six months. Acceptance continuously grew throughout the mourning period.

Surprisingly, even from the start, acceptance was rated higher than all other grief reactions. The high levels of acceptance may be explained by the large percentage of people who were over 65 at the time of the loss and whose loved ones died after a long illness. Furthermore, the study only included people whose losses were due to natural causes. Presumably, younger people and those whose loved ones died due to unnatural causes may have more difficulty with accepting the loss. Although this study may not pertain to all types of losses, it does give a good sense of the typical grief reaction to the most common kinds of losses.

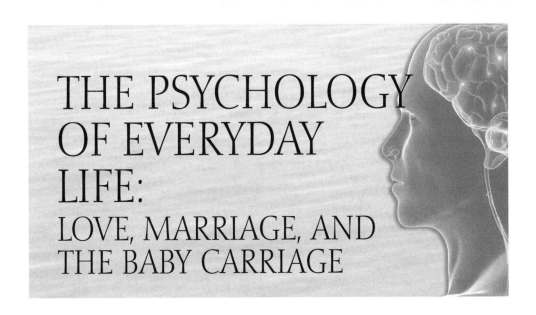

THE PSYCHOLOGY OF EVERYDAY LIFE:
LOVE, MARRIAGE, AND THE BABY CARRIAGE

LOVE

How do we **define love**?

What is love? How do we define it? Is love one thing or a set of many things? Are there different types of love? Is love the same for different types of relationships? Even as far back as the ancient Greeks, people have struggled with the nature of love. Poets have written about love perhaps as long as poets have been writing. Psychologists may lack the eloquence of poets, but through empirical research, we can study the nature of love systematically. We can observe people in different situations, interview them about their life experiences, and develop questionnaires to investigate people's attitudes and behaviors. This way, definitions of love are drawn not only from personal opinion, but from scientific investigations.

What do we **mean by love**?

There are many kinds of love: people can love their cats, their 1957 Chevy, or the smell of the air in early April. For our purposes, we are going to restrict the discussion of love to an emotional state that one person feels in relationship with another person.

How are **factor analyses** used in the **study** of **love**?

Is love one entity or is it made up of many different parts? One way to explore the structure of love is through *factor analysis*. This is an important statistical technique that shows how different items group together. It is used to investigate if a single idea is made up of separate sub-categories. Researchers create questionnaires based on a series of items, words, or scenarios related to love. They then ask research participants

What arguments were given about the nature of love at Plato's symposiums?

In ancient Greece, a symposium was something like an extended drinking party, which often involved speeches and philosophical discussions. Plato's symposium described such a dinner party in which the famed philosopher Socrates joined several of his friends to discuss the nature of love. Participants discussed love from various angles, including medical, humorous, erotic, and spiritual points of view. The comic poet Aristophanes declared that people were once twice as large as they are now but were cut in half by the Gods who saw such beings as a threat. Ever since this time, we have wandered the earth searching for our other half. Socrates stated that the love of wisdom and truth was the highest form of love, transcending erotic and romantic love.

Socrates felt that love of wisdom and truth was more important that romantic love (*iStock*).

to rate their love relationships using these questionnaires. Through factor analyses, researchers can then identify clusters of items that intercorrelate (or group together). Do people who score high on item 1 also score high on items 2, 3, and 4? These clusters, or *factors*, can then be labeled as components of love.

Are there **different types** of **love**?

Some researchers suggest that there are many types of love. Others suggest one core feature to love that cuts across different types of relationships. For example, in 1977 using factor analysis of 1,500 items related to love, John Lee categorized six major types of love: eros (erotic desire for an idealized other), ludus (playful or gamelike love), storge (slowly developing attachment), mania (obsessive and jealous love), agape (altruistic love), and pragma (practical love). In their own 1984 factor analytic study, Robert

Sternberg and Susan Gracek identified one overarching factor, which they termed interpersonal communication, sharing, and support (later called intimacy). In other words, many items on the scale grouped into this single component of love.

What is the **triangular theory** of **love**?

Drawing from previous research, Robert Sternberg proposed the *triangular theory of love* in a 1986 paper. In this model, all love is composed of three elements: *intimacy, passion,* and *commitment*. Intimacy involves closeness, caring, and emotional support. Passion refers to states of emotional and physiological arousal. This includes sexual arousal and physical attraction, as well as other kinds of intense emotional experiences. For example, parents can feel passionate love toward their children. Commitment involves a decision to commit to loving the other and trying to maintain that love over time. Using different combinations of these three elements, Sternberg described eight different kinds of love: nonlove (low on all three elements), liking (high on intimacy only), infatuated love (passion only), empty love (commitment only), romantic love (intimacy and passion), companionate love (intimacy and commitment), fatuous love (passion and commitment), and consummate love (all three together). While this approach may not capture the full complexities of love, it does seem to make intuitive sense.

How does **love differ** for **lovers**, **family**, and **friends**?

Is love the same for different kinds of relationships? Do we love different people differently? Research suggests that the feeling of intimacy, emotional connection, and closeness is central to all types of love. What may differ across relationships is the degree of passion, as well as the level of commitment. We can speculate that all love relationships would have high levels of intimacy; romantic love would have high levels of passion; and familial and long-term romantic relationships would have high levels of commitment. In fact, Sternberg and Gracek found that the intimacy component of love cut across all close relationships, with similar ratings for family, friendship, and romantic relationships. In a 1985 study by Keith Davis, spouses or lovers did not differ that much from close friends on liking (similar to Sternberg's concept of intimacy), but did differ on loving (which they conceptualized as liking plus passion and commitment).

What does **evolution** have to do with **love**?

In the past decade or two, evolutionary explanations of human psychology have become increasingly popular. Psychologists ask how various psychological phenomena evolved. What function have specific psychological patterns served in human evolution? More specifically, what function did love serve in human evolution? Evolutionary explanations for love can be divided into theories of *mating behavior, attachment,* and *infatuation.*

What makes a man attractive to the opposite sex?

Generally, young, physically fit, and muscular men with no signs of disease or malformation are considered attractive. Large pectoral muscle-mass and broad shoulders suggest upper body strength. Across evolution, these traits probably aided in *sexual selection*. In other words, traits that we associate with masculine beauty provide an evolutionary advantage. Masculine beauty advertises to women the man's ability to provide physical protection as well as to pursue or compete for food and other resources.

Masculine beauty also signals the man's ability to compete with other men for women. An appreciation of male beauty would help women choose mates that enhance their own reproductive success, both by ensuring better support in child care and by contributing genes that maximize their children's own reproductive fitness. While we know that culture strongly affects our notions of masculine beauty—for example with regard to hairstyle, fashion, and bodily adornment—we can still conclude that there is a biological basis to basic notions of male beauty and that such patterns have evolutionary significance.

Physical beauty sends signals to women that a man has an evolutionary and competitive advantage over less healthy and fit males (*iStock*).

What are the **evolutionary theories** of **mating behavior**?

A number of researchers have suggested that evolutionary pressures resulted in different reproductive strategies for men and women. In other words, the best way to pass genes onto the next generation may be different for men than for women. Men can reproduce quickly with little cost in time or energy. However, they have less control over the outcome of their mating, whether their offspring will grow to sexual maturity and be able to pass their genes onto the next generation. Thus, it is in their evolutionary interest to hedge their bets and spread their genes as widely as possible, particularly with females who show "fertility markers," such as youth and beauty. Women, on the other hand, put tremendous time and energy into reproduction, through pregnancy, lactation, and child rearing. It is in their interest to mate with fewer men and be more selective in their choice of a mate, focusing on the resources he can provide for child rearing.

This model, which is often referred to as the *theory of sexual selection*, has received considerable empirical support. For example, in a 1989 study by David Buss, 10,000 men and women across thirty-seven different cultures were interviewed about what they looked for in a mate. Men stressed physical attraction and women stressed high status, wealth, and ambition. Moreover, studies show that both homosexual and heterosexual men are more likely to engage in promiscuous and casual sex than either heterosexual or homosexual women. In fact, homosexual men are more likely to engage in promiscuous sex than heterosexual men, presumably because the sexual behavior of heterosexual men is limited by the preferences of their female partners.

Is **attachment** important in **evolution**?

The sexual selection theory has been criticized, however, for its neglect of emotional attachment. People seek out a romantic partner not only for sexual satisfaction, but also for emotional support and fulfillment. In both Buss's and Sternberg and Gracek's studies, attachment-related traits, such as kindness and understanding, were listed by both sexes as the most important considerations in romantic relationships. Moreover, these findings appear to be valid across cultures, as Buss collected his data from thirty-seven different cultures. According to Cindy Hazan and Lisa Diamond, attachment bonds between sexual partners, otherwise known as romantic love, may be just as important to evolution as sexual selection.

Is **romantic love** related to **parental love**?

The attachment bond between mothers and fathers may have developed out of the evolutionarily older bond between mother and infant. The fact that many more animal species show strong bonds between mothers and infants than show bonds between mothers and fathers suggests that the parent-child emotional bond is an earlier and more wide-spread evolutionary development than the romantic bond. In other words, romantic love probably evolved out of parental love.

What **evolutionary purpose** does **romantic love** serve?

Researchers propose that romantic love evolved to promote paternal investment in the raising of dependent children. Children who benefited from the care of both parents were more likely to survive to adulthood and pass their genes onto the next generation. Therefore, the capacity to seek out and maintain a strong bond with a mate (i.e., romantic love) provided an evolutionary advantage. Even in today's world, considerable research shows that paternal involvement brings powerful advantages for children, providing financial, cognitive, and emotional benefits. Moreover, studies show that children also benefit from a strong and harmonious relationship between their parents.

What is the **evolutionary function** of **falling in love**?

We can draw a distinction between the general feeling of love and the heady, intoxicating experience of being *in love*. The experience of falling in love is a widespread one, something that most people have experienced at some point in their life. Psychologists describe this emotional state as involving the idealization of the partner and a yearning to spend time with him or her. There is also great sexual desire for the partner and heightened emotional arousal. In their 2000 paper, Cindy Hazan and Lisa Diamond speculated that this mental state serves to keep the lovers focused and preoccupied with each other long enough for a more sustainable form of love to develop. These authors theorize that the attachment aspect of love, similar to what Sternberg considered the intimacy component of love, is what keeps long-term relationships alive. However, it takes time to develop. So infatuation, or the intoxicating state of being in love, serves as a sort of scaffold over which attachment and intimacy can develop. This suggests that infatuation is inherently short lived. Indeed research supports the short life of infatuation; several studies suggest the average length of romantic infatuation is about two years.

Physical beauty in a woman signals her youth, health, and fertility—in other words, her reproductive fitness (*iStock*).

What makes a **woman physically attractive** to men?

While fashions in female beauty can vary across culture and throughout history, there are certain constant features that are attractive to men. Signs of youth, health, and fertility always form the basis of notions of female beauty. For example, round breasts and a low waist-to hip ratio are universal signs of femininity and fertility. Smooth, unwrinkled skin and the lack of gray hair signify youth. The beauty industry makes an enormous amount of money enhancing women's signals of fitness and fertility. By enhancing the red color in her lips and cheeks, a woman can appear to have greater blood flow to her face, a sign of physical health and vigor. Likewise, millions of women dye their hair to maintain a youthful appearance.

What do we know about the **neurobiology of love**?

The anthropologist Helen Fisher has conducted a series of studies on the neurobiology of love. In a 1998 article, she proposed a three-part system. This system is composed of the *sex drive, attraction*, and *attachment*. The sex drive is associated with sex hormones, specifically *estrogens* and *androgens*. Attraction is similar to romantic infatuation. This euphoric preoccupation with the desired mate is mediated by two kinds of neurotransmitters, *dopamine* and *norepinephrine*. Dopamine is associated with the reward circuitry and is involved with many kinds of desire. Norepinephrine is involved with arousal, as well as attention and focus. Attachment is associated with the hormones *oxytocin* and *vasopressin*.

These hormones, known as neuropeptides, are evolutionarily ancient chemicals that are involved in a broad range of social behaviors. Oxytocin is released during nursing and childbirth and is also released in both males and females during sexual intercourse and after orgasm. Dr. Fisher speculates that these three systems are relatively independent of each other. Combining these systems in different ways allows human beings to engage in a broad repertoire of mating and reproductive strategies. In other words, people can highlight sex, attachment, or infatuation at different times or with different people.

Do **views** of **love vary** across **cultures**?

We can presume that the components of love proposed by Sternberg can be found in all cultures. Intimacy, passion, and commitment are most likely cultural universals. Evidence of this comes from many sources, including cultural anthropology, psychological research, and love poetry from across the world. What does appear to vary across cultures, however, is the emphasis placed on the different components of love and on different types of relationships. In *collectivist* cultures like those found in Asia and Africa, relationships with family may take priority over relationships with lovers and friends. In *individualistic* cultures, like those of Northern Europe and North America, friendships and romantic relationships compete with family for priority (and often win). Likewise, the concept of duty (similar to Sternberg's concept of commitment) is absolutely central to Chinese Confucianism. In contrast, judging by the mountains of romance novels, love songs, and beauty products found in North America, it is the passionate side of love that is prized in this culture.

MARRIAGE

FIRST COMES LOVE,
THEN COMES MARRIAGE,
THEN COMES [INSERT NAME]
IN THE BABY CARRIAGE.

Why talk about marriage?

This playground chant illustrates the long-standing cultural expectation that romantic love inevitably leads to marriage. While this progression may have been the norm for most of American history, current social trends have veered away from this single path. In 2007, according to the U.S. Census Bureau, fifty-six percent of the population over age fifteen was married. This means, however, that forty-four percent of the population was not. With the growth of single-parent households, single-person households, non-married cohabiting couples and same-sex couples, is it outdated to study the institution of marriage? Although the legal institution of marriage is no longer the sole option for adult relationships, it is still extremely widespread. The vast majority of people will be married at some point in their lifetimes, with estimates as high as ninety percent. Likewise, marriage as an institution is extremely widespread, essentially a cultural universal. For these reasons, marriage merits discussion in its own right. Furthermore, much of the material discussed below, such as what contributes to the success or failure of a marriage, is also relevant to non-marital relationships.

Are there health benefits to marriage?

In general, marriage confers benefits for both emotional and physical health. Married people tend to report higher life satisfaction and lower psychological distress than single people, meaning those who never married, or are widowed or divorced. This must be qualified, however, by the quality of the marriage. *Unhappily* married people report greater emotional distress than single people. Thus, it appears that being married has benefits over being single, unless one is unhappily married. It is also not clear whether the benefits are solely due to marriage per se or to the benefits of any long-term, committed relationship. Research is very clear that social support is a critical protective factor against emotional and physical stress. It is no surprise, therefore, that single people who establish solid social support networks often report high life satisfaction.

What makes a marriage last?

As marriages progress, the passion that may have characterized the early days tends to mellow into a deep bond of intimacy and commitment. Therefore, the relationship qualities that promote intimacy and commitment are most important to a long-lasting marriage. Strong communication, the ability to manage conflict constructively, shared experiences and values, and high levels of warmth and affection all contribute to successful marriages. In addition, financial stability, positive ties to the extended family, and positive role models in the families of both partners (rather than frequent divorces and marital acrimony) are associated with long-term marriages.

What makes a **marriage fail**?

Research suggests that marriages of people in their early twenties or younger are more likely to fail than marriages between older partners. Further, overly hasty marriages, such as those that take place within six months after meeting, are less likely to succeed. Additionally, insecure financial status, distant or acrimonious relationships with the extended family, and the absence of positive marital examples in the extended family are associated with poor marital outcome. As described in a 1993 paper by John Gottman, marital failure can also be predicted by the quality of the interactions between a couple. Couples who displayed high levels of defensiveness, contempt, stonewalling, and criticism, as well as facial expressions of disgust were more likely to end up separated or divorced several years later.

How important are **common interests**?

Contrary to popular belief, opposites do *not* attract, at least not that much. People are most likely to be attracted to partners who are similar to them. Research shows that spouses tend to share a great deal of similarities with regard to interests, personality, attitudes, ethnic background, educational goals or attainment, and even height. Relationships tend to work better and last longer between partners who are fairly similar to each other. Partners should not expect to share all interests, values or attitudes, but it is helpful to have considerable overlap.

How important is **communication** in marriage?

Effective communication is a critical ingredient to a successful marriage. In fact, most marital therapies focus on enhancing communication. While it is not necessary and can even be destructive to hash out every little bump in the marital path, it is critical that recurrent problems or personally meaningful issues be discussed directly. People cannot be expected to automatically know what their partner wants or needs or what is making the other person unhappy. When there is insufficient communication, misunderstandings can arise, resulting in unnecessary conflict. Additionally, inadequate communication can lead to emotional distance as partners can grow apart. If this continues unabated, one partner can end up seeking emotional and sexual intimacy outside the marriage.

Arguments between spouses can be disturbing, but they are perfectly normal when they occur on occasion. If arguments dominate a marriage, however, the results will be detrimental to a happy union (*iStock*).

Is it **normal** to **argue** during **marriage**?

It is certainly normal to argue during marriage. Marriage constitutes one of the most intimate and long-lasting relationships in one's entire life; spouses' lives are profoundly intertwined. Therefore, it is inescapable that there will be a degree of conflict. While some conflict is entirely expectable, if the marriage is dominated by conflict, marital satisfaction will suffer. The good days should definitely outnumber the bad days. Moreover, the method of handling conflict is very important. Healthy conflict management enhances the marital bond, but destructive modes of dealing with conflict can severely damage the marriage.

Are there **good** and **bad ways** to **fight** in a marriage?

There are definitely good and bad ways to fight (or argue) in a marriage. In general, people should address their concerns directly, keep their focus on the specific behaviors or circumstances that cause the problem, clearly state emotions, needs and thoughts, acknowledge responsibility for one's own contribution to the problem, and encourage the other person to express his or her viewpoint. Ineffective strategies include blaming, stonewalling, emotional explosiveness, name-calling, defensiveness, and resurrection of every complaint since the beginning of the relationship. Research shows that these behaviors serve to escalate the conflict rather than resolve it. It is also a problem when people become more invested in *winning* the argument than in *resolv-*

ing it. While no one can be perfectly mature at all times, and it is expectable that everyone will regress to immature behavior occasionally, it is vitally important to cultivate constructive conflict management skills. A robust literature shows that poor conflict negotiation is a key ingredient in marital unhappiness and, ultimately, divorce.

What is the **impact** of **avoiding conflict** in a marriage?

Although too much conflict is clearly damaging to a marriage and husbands and wives must learn the important art of letting little things go, it is also harmful to a marriage to completely avoid conflict. When people continually avoid difficult topics, misunderstandings can grow and couples can start to grow apart. By tiptoeing around the difficult issues, couples introduce distance into their relationship. In so doing, they deprive their relationship of the shared experience and mutual knowledge that provide the emotional foundation of marriage.

What are some **dos** and **don'ts** in **marital spats**?

Based on clinical and research literature, the table below is a helpful guide to some of the things one should or should not say when arguing with a spouse:

Do	Don't
Focus on resolving the problem	Focus on winning the argument
Discuss a specific problem	Attack the entire relationship
Stick to the present as much as possible	Bring up a list of past grievances
Focus on behavior not character	Make the problem about your partner's personality flaws
Clearly state your own feelings and thoughts	Expect your partner to read your mind. Stop talking out of pride. Refuse to admit that your partner "got to you"
Accept responsibility for your own contribution to the problem	Defensively refuse to acknowledge any contribution to the problem, invalidating your partner's every point
Acknowledge the other person's feelings	Invalidate your partner's emotional experience
Suggest solutions	Expect your partner to "fix it" or "change" without specific suggestions
Invite the other person's suggestions	Insist on dictating the solution
Keep the problem between you and your partner	Bring other people into the argument, declaring how many friends and family agree with you

How **important** is **sex** to a **marriage**?

For most marriages, sex is a very important ingredient. A healthy, mutually satisfying sex life can enhance intimacy and passion and provide an important buffer against the inevitable strains and stresses of marriage. An unsatisfying sex life can both cause difficulties in a marriage and be a symptom of relationship problems. It is important to note, however, that not all couples require the same degree of sexual activity. Moreover, sexual activity tends to decrease as couples age. What is important is that the sexual relationship works for both members of the couple.

How do **sex roles vary** across marriages?

A distinction is frequently made between *traditional* vs. *egalitarian* sex roles. In traditional sex roles, the man is the provider and the head of the household. It is his responsibility to financially support his family and to protect them from danger. He is the final authority in the family; his wife is ultimately subordinate to him. The woman's role is to take care of the family. She performs domestic services, including cooking, cleaning, shopping, and childcare. In more egalitarian marriages, neither paid work nor household responsibilities are exclusively the domain of one partner or the other. Partners have equal power and authority in the family and neither partner is subordinate to the other. With the dramatic social changes that have occurred since the 1960s, sex roles in Western society have become considerably more egalitarian. To some extent, these social changes have even impacted non-Western industrial societies, such as India and Japan. Nonetheless, many studies show that men still tend to make more money than their wives and wives do considerably more housework than their husbands.

What impact do **changing sex roles** have on marriages?

The impact of changing sex roles on marriage is complex. In the 1970s when the women's liberation movement reached full force, there was a strong increase in divorce rates. Divorced rates peaked in the 1980s and leveled off by the 2000s. It is likely this peak in marital turmoil had more to do with the disruptions in sex roles and to couples' difficulty adjusting to changing expectations than with the specific nature of the new sex roles. As both men and women become accustomed to women's greater participation in the workforce and their greater autonomy, it seems marriages have become more stable. Nonetheless, greater individualism in general tends to lead to higher divorce rates, as people prioritize their personal satisfaction ahead of family ties. On the other hand, several studies have found that greater equality in sex roles correlated with higher marital satisfaction even in fairly traditional cultures.

Egalitarian sex roles appeared to increase marital harmony, which correlated with higher marital satisfaction in both partners. Accordingly, a 2006 study by Mariet Hagedoorn and colleagues showed that marital partners who perceived their marriage to be equitable reported less psychological distress than those who perceived it to be inequitable. Interestingly, even the partners who believed they benefited more from the inequity than their spouse reported greater psychological distress.

How have the **rates** of **marriage changed** over time in the **United States**?

Despite the remarkable changes in sex roles over the last four decades, the overall marriage statistics have not changed as dramatically as one might predict. In 1950, according to the U.S. Census Bureau, an estimated 32 percent of the population over age fifteen had never married, 68 percent were currently married, 4 percent were widowed, and 2 percent divorced. In 2007, an estimated 33 percent of the population had never married, 56 percent were married, 2 percent widowed, and 8 percent divorced.

The institution of marriage has changed considerably in America over the last couple of generations. For one thing, people are getting married at an older age (*iStock*).

Has the **age** of **marrying changed** over time in the **United States**?

According to the U.S. Census Bureau, people are marrying approximately five years later now than they did in the mid-twentieth century. The median age of first marriage in 1950 was 22.8 years for men and 20.3 years for women. In 2007, it was 27.5 years for men and 25.6 years for women.

Do **approaches to marriage** vary across cultures?

The distinction between collectivist cultures and individualistic cultures is frequently made in cross-cultural studies. In collectivist cultures, found in many Asian countries such as Korea, India, and China, an individual's identity is tied to his or her social group. In individualistic countries, such as the United States, Canada, and Australia, the individual's independent identity is prioritized. People from collectivist cultures expect love to grow as the marriage unfolds over time. When choosing a spouse, there is less emphasis on romance and infatuation. Instead, people emphasize practical concerns, such as income potential, parenting ability, and compatibility with the extended family. In contrast, people from individualist countries emphasize the passionate side of love when looking for a spouse. They focus on feelings of excitement and physical attraction. Using Sternberg's triangular theory of love, Ge Gao measured the role of intimacy, passion, and commitment in ninety Chinese and seventy-seven American couples in a 2001 study. Ratings of passion were higher in American than Chinese couples, but ratings of intimacy and commitment did not differ. People from individualist countries also tend to have fewer children and a higher divorce rate.

PREGNANCY

What are the **psychological challenges** of **pregnancy**?

Becoming a parent entails one of the biggest psychological transformations of one's life. Luckily, nature gives women about forty weeks to prepare for this change. During this time both parents can make the necessary practical arrangements to prepare for the arrival of the baby. Simultaneously, they undergo a process of psychological transformation wherein they adjust to the enormous responsibility of parenting. Both mother- and father-to-be must reconfigure their identity from that of their *parents' child* into their *child's parent*. Furthermore, they must gird themselves for the loss of autonomy that inevitably comes with parenthood. After a child is born, a parent is no longer a single, unitary person, responsible only to himself or herself. From now on, every decision will be made from the vantage point of a responsible parent. As any parent can tell you, even when the children grow up and leave home, the sense of parental responsibility never completely goes away.

What are the **changes** in **identity** the **first-time parent** undergoes?

For the pregnant woman, especially, the sense of identity is drastically altered by the knowledge that another person is growing inside her. The woman's body no longer belongs to one person, it now contains two people. Likewise, the woman's identity expands from beyond a self-contained sense of self, to a broader, more encompassing identity that incorporates her new child. If we think of the enormous investment of time, energy, and resources that parents unthinkingly bestow on their children, we have to be impressed. Parents routinely spend inordinate sums of money, make extraordinary sacrifices and, at times, even give up their life—all for the sake of their children. In no other arena are humans so powerfully altruistic. Evolutionary biologists sum this up to the evolutionary imperative to pass on one's genes. On the psychological level, this drive manifests in a transformation of identity; what was one becomes two. The parent sees the child not as a wholly separate person but, to some degree, as an extension of themselves.

How does the **relationship** with the **parent's own parent impact** the psychological challenge of pregnancy?

In pregnancy, the parent comes face-to-face with the experience of nurturing a helpless, dependent infant. Consequently, old feelings and memories of *being* parented will inevitably be stimulated. This may happen on a conscious level, in which expectant parents actively reflect on their own childhood relationship with their parents. It may also happen on an unconscious level, with the impact of childhood experiences only visible through fantasies, attitudes, and expectations about the new baby. If the child-   237

Families tend to become closer when new babies arrive (*iStock*).

hood relationship was largely positive, expectant parents can gain a new appreciation for the level of work and devotion provided by their own parents. They become more understanding of what their parents went through.

If the relationship was problematic, these difficulties may interfere with the preparation for parenthood. The expectant parents may have heightened insecurities about their ability to function as a parent, exaggerated fears of the baby's demands, or of their ability to meet the emotional needs of their baby. Alternatively, there may be a constricted ability to imagine and anticipate the future relationship with the baby at all. Regardless of the quality of the original parent-child relationship, pregnancy is a time for expectant parents to reflect on their own experience of being parented, and consider what they would and would not like to repeat with their own children.

How do **parents' relationships** with their **own parents** tend to **change** with a pregnancy?

Overall, families tend to become closer when a new generation is born. Mothers and daughters, in particular, come together as new mothers need considerable support and information during this period. Early adulthood is often a time during which adult children and their parents lead fairly independent lives, as young adults aim to establish their separate life and identity. In pregnancy, however, that trajectory is reversed. Expectant parents need furniture, baby clothes, maternity clothing, advice, and even help with everyday tasks if the pregnancy becomes physically demanding. At this point, grandparents often step back into a caretaking, or at least supportive, role. In some cases, this can lead to control battles, but frequently the shared devotion to the new baby enhances the relationship between new parents and their own parents.

What **physiological challenges** does the **pregnant woman** undergo?

Pregnant women undergo massive physiological changes throughout their pregnancy. There is tremendous hormonal upheaval and an obviously dramatic shift in bodily size and shape. For some women, the bodily changes are sources of pride and excitement. For other women, however, there is fear of the weight gain and of a permanent loss of their figure. In the first trimester of pregnancy, most of the fundamental bodily and neurological structures are laid down. This entails tremendous hormonal surges, which often result in nausea and morning sickness for the mother. Although women have not gained much weight yet, there is often considerable discomfort. In the second trimester, the morning sickness generally resolves and the fetus grows to sufficient size that the mother starts to *look* pregnant. She starts to "show." This is also the time of *quickening,* when the baby starts to kick. In the third trimester, most of the fetal bodily structures are already developed. At this point, the fetus just needs to grow. During this period, women suffer the most discomfort from the changes to their bodily size and shape. They lose a good deal of mobility and often have difficulty sleeping.

What is the **impact of hormones** on the experience of pregnancy?

The hormonal surges have both physical and emotional effects on the pregnant woman. In the first trimester when the hormone surges are at their peak, women suffer from nausea and morning sickness. They also suffer from mood swings and emotional volatility. Such emotional upset can be disruptive to the marital relationship, as their partners are most likely to take the brunt of it. By the second trimester, this tends to cool down. In fact the second trimester is known as the most enjoyable part of pregnancy. The mother is past the physical discomfort and emotional upheaval of the first trimester, yet still relatively physically nimble.

What **role** does **oxytocin** play in the psychological make-up of the expectant mother?

The role of oxytocin and a related chemical called vasopressin have received increasing attention in scientific circles. Oxytocin is integrally connected with pregnancy, childbirth, lactation, and parenting. We can speculate that the surges of oxytocin that occur during pregnancy help condition the mother to nurture her baby. Research has linked oxytocin to attachment, so we can assume that increased oxytocin release during pregnancy will enhance the mother-infant bond. It may also contribute to the intense preoccupation with the new baby that mothers develop during pregnancy.

What are the **challenges** that **fathers undergo** during their partner's pregnancy?

During pregnancy, fathers must start to develop an attachment to the child they have not yet met and, at this point, can only know through their imagination. For many men this task can be quite challenging, as they do not go through the same massive bodily changes that women do. The baby may not seem quite real to them. This appears to be verified in a 2006 study by Lindsey Gerner, where the strongest predictor to paternal-fetal attachment was the number of ultrasound visits. Evidently, the sonograms helped the babies feel more real to the fathers. Additionally, new fathers often

What is "couvade"?

A fascinating cross-cultural phenomenon, termed couvade, speaks to how some men process the psychological challenges facing expectant fathers. Couvade has been witnessed in many different cultures, and may have even been recorded by Marco Polo during his world travels. In couvade, an expectant father takes on some of the physical symptoms associated with pregnancy. Such symptoms include gastro-intestinal problems, sleep disturbances, and even weight gain.

It has been shown that some men empathize so much with their pregnant wives that they may experience some of the physical symptoms of pregnancy (*iStock*).

This appears to serve several psychological purposes. By exhibiting some of the physical symptoms of pregnancy, the expectant father simultaneously draws closer to his wife, demands recognition of his role in the pregnancy process, and psychologically prepares himself for the new baby's arrival. Some authors suggest there are biological causes for this phenomenon as well as psychological ones. Indeed, there is evidence that during pregnancy, men undergo hormonal changes that are similar in quality if not quantity with their pregnant partners. Studies have shown increased prolactin and estradiol and decreased testosterone during and immediately after pregnancy in both males and females.

feel intimidated by the enormous responsibility of parenthood, anxiously doubting their capacity to handle it.

While women generally express such anxiety in terms of their ability to nurture, men often focus upon financial concerns. Many men are intensely concerned with their capacity to provide financial support for their growing family. Finally, an expectant father's experience of pregnancy may be highly dependent on the state of the relationship with the mother. Several studies note relationships between a father's marital satisfaction and his involvement and satisfaction with pregnancy and child rearing. This suggests that, although involvement with their children is a profoundly meaningful experience for most men, the father-child relationship is highly influenced by the marital relationship. The mother-child relationship is probably not influenced to such a great extent. This highlights a pattern that will hold throughout parenthood;

both for the marital relationship and the child, it is crucial that the focus on the new baby not overshadow the needs of the marriage.

PARENTING

How important is **parent-child attachment**?

For many parents, the love they feel for their children is the most intense love they have ever felt. Some parents talk about falling in love with their baby. It is not a rational feeling; it does not come from choice or deliberation. It is a profoundly powerful experience that changes the new parent's life. From the perspective of evolutionary theory, this blind parental love makes perfect sense. Children are wholly dependent on their parents; they require enormous investments of time, energy, and treasure over many years. If parents did not feel such intense love for their children, they would be hard pressed to make the sacrifices necessary for their children to survive, let alone thrive.

What are the **biggest stresses** in the **first year** of the **baby's life**?

Despite the profound rewards of welcoming a new baby into the home, the first year of the baby's life brings considerable stress. Probably most dramatic is the disruption in sleep. Additionally, there is a tremendous loss of personal time as an infant demands near-constant attention. Even finding the time to take a shower can pose a challenge at times. There are financial changes, as well, if a working woman stays home to look after her baby. If she goes back to work, child care arrangements must be made. Finally, parenting an infant involves marked changes in routine. Meals, social life, laundry, and many other aspects of daily life must now be arranged around child care. Eventually, parents establish new routines, but the transition period can be a time of notable stress.

How do **people vary** in their understanding of **gender roles** in **parenting**?

While nature has prepared women to be integrally involved in child care, there is much more variability with regard to the role of the father. Most fathers are involved in the support and protection of their family, but the degree to which they are involved in the day-to-day process of parenting can vary considerably across cultures and across historical periods. In modern Western society, changes in sex roles over the last several decades have radically changed cultural views about fathers' roles in child care. Although women still do the majority of child care, fathers are now expected to assume more child-care responsibilities than their own fathers may have done. This shift in roles can lead to some confusion as partners may have differing views and expectations about a father's role. A number of studies address that fact that new fathers seem to lack clarity about their role as a parent. These studies show that new fathers often feel uncertain about their relevance to the whole process, may have difficulty appreciating the degree of stress their partner is undergoing, and often have unrealistic attitudes about parenting techniques.

What **impact** does the **new baby** have on the **marriage**?

The birth of a baby has an enormous impact on a marriage. Just as the lives of the individual parents are permanently transformed by the birth of a child, the marriage is transformed as well. Parenthood undoubtedly brings the couple closer together; they now share the awesome and profound experience of bringing a new life into the world. Nonetheless, the arrival of the new baby brings considerable pressures to the marriage. For one, infants are extraordinarily time-consuming and the demands of a neonate can feel relentless. Secondly, it takes several months before infants develop regular sleep patterns. Sheer exhaustion can easily increase parents' irritability and emotional volatility. The disruption in routine is also difficult on a marriage.

What factors help a **marriage transition** into **parenting**?

Research has shown that couples that have the most realistic expectations of what life will be like once the baby is born have the easiest adjustment to parenthood. Additional protective factors include clarity and agreement about each parent's role, the establishment of routines, and protected time to devote to the marriage (e.g., weekly date night). Social support and financial stability also help the marital transition to parenthood.

What are the major **issues** relating to **discipline**?

Discipline is an essential aspect of parenting and inadequate discipline can be very detrimental to a child's development. Parents must aim to find the balance between appropriate limit setting and empathic acceptance of the child's developmental level. Finding the right balance is no easy task. Nonetheless, parents must search for the correct path between being too strict and controlling on one hand and being too permissive on the other hand.

Parents should discipline their children in order to set limits on behavior, but too much or too little can be detrimental (iStock).

Why is **limit setting** so important in parenting?

Limit setting is a critical aspect of parenting because children cannot be expected to regulate themselves. They need to be taught. Many parents feel it is easier to give in to the child's protests and avoid the fight than to tolerate the child's upset and anger. This is unfortunate as parents must tolerate some discomfort in the short run in order to raise well-regulated children. Children without limits feel they have too much power in the relationship with their parents and this makes them feel unsafe. Although they do not like feeling frustrated and they certainly like to get what they want, they also sense that they are ill-qualified to be in charge of their own lives, and depend upon an adult to step up and take control.

How does **limit setting** promote **frustration tolerance**?

Reasonable limit setting teaches children how to control their emotions and impulses. Without this necessary skill, a child will not be able to function effectively in a social setting. Therefore, when parents jump in to rescue their children each time they exhibit frustration or anxiety, they are depriving their children of the opportunity to learn to manage negative emotions. This undermines the development of crucial problem-solving and emotion-regulation skills. A child's family may be willing to be indulgent; the outside world is far less likely to be as tolerant of the child's whims. Thus, if children are not raised to adapt to the world outside their family, they are headed for a considerable amount of frustration, anxiety, and interpersonal problems. These problems can easily continue into adulthood as the previously indulged child is poorly equipped to negotiate the inevitable frustrations encountered in the realm of work and adult relationships.

What are the **dangers** of being **too strict**?

On the other hand, there is danger in being too strict and too controlling. When parental discipline feels excessively harsh, arbitrary or self-serving, parental authority loses legitimacy. The child may develop an antagonistic relationship with authority, responding to a wide range of authority figures with rebellious opposition or fearful resentment. Likewise, such children may have great difficulty translating parental discipline into self-discipline, which is the ultimate goal of all parental discipline. In adulthood, this might manifest in a refusal to exercise self-control or in problems with procrastination. Alternatively, overly controlled children can become excessively passive, their initiative and autonomy significantly constrained.

What is Diana **Baumrind's classification** of **parenting** styles?

A line of research initiated in the 1970s by Diana Baumrind delineates different styles of parenting. After observing parents interacting with their preschool children, Baumrind identified three types of interaction: acceptance and involvement, control (meaning the exercise of parental control), and autonomy granting (allowing children to make their own decisions). Four different styles of parenting were identified based on these behavioral patterns. *Authoritative* parents are high on all three types of behaviors, balancing parental control and recognition of the child's autonomy. *Authoritarian parents* are high on parental control but low on acceptance-involvement and autonomy granting. *Permissive parents* are low on parental control and high on autonomy granting. They are high on acceptance but not always high on involvement, as such parents can be inattentive as well as over-indulgent. *Uninvolved parents* are low on all three types of behavior. Of the four parenting styles, authoritative parents produce the best results, with the most upbeat, self-assured, and socially and emotionally competent children.

When does **corporal punishment** turn into **abuse**?

For centuries, corporal punishment was an acceptable and expected part of child rearing. In recent decades, however, corporal punishment has been branded outdated and needlessly violent. Nonphysical forms of discipline such as time-outs are recommended instead. A good deal of research supports the greater effectiveness of non-physical forms of discipline. However, the use of corporal discipline varies across cultural subgroups. Some research has shown that, within African-American communities, children raised with corporal discipline were less likely to display acting-out behavior, to get in trouble at school or with the police. It seems that corporal discipline can be effective when it is mild, predictable, performed for the purposes of discipline and not done out of anger. Corporal punishment becomes abusive when it is excessively harsh, causes ongoing pain or physical injury, is unpredictable or arbitrary, and is motivated by parental rage rather than the need to instill appropriate standards of behavior.

How important is **consistency** in **parenting**?

Maintaining a consistent stance toward children is a challenging task for many parents. It is often hard for parents to hold firm to a decision about what is and is not allowed rather than bend to the pressures of the moment. This can be highly problematic as children need very clear messages about what the rules are and where the boundaries lie. Moreover, inconsistent enforcement of rules creates its own complications. According to the theory of behaviorism, *intermittent reinforcement* makes behavior more resistant to extinction. To illustrate, let's imagine that a child is demanding a certain privilege to which the parent initially says "no." If the parent ultimately gives in to the child's demands, the child learns that "no" does not mean "no" and that parents can be manipulated. When the child next encounters the word "no," the automatic response will be to ramp up his or her demands in the expectation that the parent will eventually give in.

How **important** is **affection**?

Of course, parenting is not all about discipline. Fundamentally, it is about love. Physical affection plays a critical role in child development, shaping the growing child's ability to tolerate intimacy and physical touch. Moreover, a large body of research documents the importance of warmth and affection in neurobiological development, par-

What has research shown about the importance of tactile stimulation in early development?

A series of studies conducted by Michael Meaney and colleagues has shown how early childhood experiences actually affect the workings of our genes. Through ingenious studies with rats, he showed how maternal care had a potent effect on genes related to the stress response. This process works through chemicals known as *epigenetic markers*, which land on genes and alter gene expression. In other words they work to turn specific genes off and on. Importantly, they do not alter the DNA sequence but rather the expression of specific genes. The genetic blueprint is not changed, only what parts of the blue print get built.

Rats that are raised by mothers that lick them frequently displayed lower stress levels as adults than rats that were raised with less parental tactile stimulation (*iStock*).

Rats raised by high-lick mothers, who provide more tactile stimulation to their rat pups, were compared to those raised by low-lick mothers. High-lick rat pups had lower levels of the epigenetic markers known as methyl groups than pups raised by low-lick mothers. They also displayed much less stress and tension and were better able to calm themselves.

These same epigenetic markers came into play in human beings. The researchers autopsied the brains of people who had died either by suicide or car accident. They found that people with a history of childhood abuse had more epigenetic markers than those without. It appears that, in both rats and humans, parental care affects the production of epigenetic markers, which in turn modulates the reactivity to stress. Nurturing early environments reduce reactivity to stress while neglectful or abusive environments heighten the stress response.

ticularly affecting the flexibility of the stress response and capacity for positive emotions. The classic work of Rene Spitz illustrates the tragic effects of emotional deprivation. Dr. Spitz studied infants in an orphanage who were separated from their mothers during World War II. Although they were kept warm, clean, and well fed, these babies were left with essentially no affection, touch, or personal attention. This gross deprivation profoundly stunted and distorted the infants' cognitive, motoric, and physical development. They even had a very high death rate.

What **roles** do **parents** play in **teaching** their **children** to manage **emotion**?

Another area in which parents play a crucial role is the development of emotional competence. Children have to learn to recognize, label, and regulate their own emotions. Unlike the ability to walk or speak, this is not a skill that children will learn on their own with little effort on the parents' part. Thus the sensitivity of the parents to a child's experience and expression of emotion has a profound impact on the child's developing emotional competence. A 1996 study by John Gottman, Lynn Katz, and Carole Hooven found that the quality of parenting when a child was five predicted to a range of outcomes both at age five and at age eight.

The parenting styles measured included *emotional coaching*, in which parents teach children to label and then manage their emotions, *praising-scaffolding*, a kind of supportive teaching, and *derogatory parenting*, which involves intrusiveness, criticism, and mockery. The outcomes included the child's emotional regulation, peer relationships, school achievement, physical health, and vagal nerve tone—a physiological measure of stress reactivity. As might be expected, high levels of emotional coaching and scaffolding-praising and low levels of derogatory parenting were associated with positive outcomes. Emotional coaching, in particular, predicted to positive emotional functioning, at age five and at age eight.

What are the main ways that **parenting styles vary** across cultures?

While parenting in all cultures entails love, devotion, teaching, and discipline, there is considerable cultural variation in other aspects of parenting. In general, more traditional, collectivist cultures (e.g., found in Asia and Africa) employ parenting styles that promote interdependence, respect for authority, and behavioral control. Individualistic cultures (e.g., found in North America and North-Western Europe) promote independence, less hierarchical relationships, and greater freedom of self-expression. Cultures also vary with regards to physical affection. For example, Northern European cultures have traditionally been more reserved about emotional expression and physical affection than Southern European cultures.

FAMILIES

What is a **family**?

The U.S. Census defines families as groups of people related by birth, adoption, or marriage. More informal definitions include groups of people who live together in long-term committed relationships. For example, many homosexual couples live together for decades without the benefit of legal recognition. In general, however, the definition provided by the U.S. Census reflects the conventional understanding of the term "family."

How have **family structures changed** in the past few decades?

While the basic unit of the family has proved remarkably resilient, there have been considerable changes in typical family structure across the last few decades, at least in the developed Western world. For one thing the percentage of single households has increased dramatically. As people are marrying later and divorcing more frequently, people are living alone for longer periods of their life. Nonetheless, married couples with or without children still comprise the most common family structure. According to the 2000 census, married couples account for more than half of U.S. households, while single people accounted for more than one quarter. Unmarried partners of both the same and opposite sex, three generational families, and single parents with children also make up a large segment of American households. Furthermore, blended families—such as combinations of previously divorced families—are also very common.

What has recent U.S. Census **data** shown about **married life** in **America**?

The data in the table below describes the percentage of men and women in 2004 who have never married or who have been divorced. As the table shows, the traditional nuclear family is only one of many lifestyles favored within the United States.

Unmarried People in the United States in 2004

Gender/Age Group	% Never Married	% Divorced
Men 25–29	53.6	5.1
Men 30–34	30.3	13.1
Men 35–39	20.2	20.7
Women 25–29	41.3	7.0
Women 30–34	22.3	17.1
Women 35–39	16.2	25.6

How common are **single-parent families**?

While two-parent families are still the most common type of family structure for families with children, there has been a huge increase in children born to, or raised in, single-parent families over recent decades. According to statistics from the U.S. Census, the proportion of single-parent families tripled between 1970 and 1990. In 2008, 70 percent of children in the U.S. lived with two parents, 23 percent lived with their mother only, 3.5 percent with their father only, and 3.8 percent lived with neither parent. However, there are considerable ethnic differences in the frequency of single-parent households. For example in 2008, 17 percent of European-American children, 51 percent of African-American children, 10 percent of Asian children, and 24 percent of Hispanic children lived with their mother in a single-parent family.

What **impact** on **children** do the different **family structures** have?

There is a fair amount of evidence that children in single-parent families have more emotional, academic, and social problems than children in two-parent families. However, this data is confounded by the fact that many single-parent families have greater levels of poverty, less education, and are more likely to live in high-crime neighborhoods. What is clearly important is that parents need adequate social support, financial resources, and protection from inordinate stress in order to provide a stable and nurturing home for their children. The incidence of homosexual parents with children has also risen in recent decades. Research shows that such children do not differ from children of heterosexual parents in emotional and social adjustment. Nor do they seem to differ in sexual orientation, with the vast majority developing heterosexual orientations. However, the social environment in which children of homosexual parents are raised does make a difference; accepting environments promote positive adjustment while environments that do not accept gay families can take a huge psychological toll on children.

How do **family structures vary** across **cultures**?

The most common way that family structures vary across cultures involves the role of the extended family. Modern industrialized and Western cultures favor the nuclear family over the extended family. Young married couples move away from their parents to start their own new family in a separate home. In many traditional cultures, the boundaries between the extended family and the nuclear family are much more diffuse. Multiple generations often live together in a single household and grandparents, uncles, and aunts play influential roles in the couple's marriage and in the rearing of their children.

What is meant by the term **family systems**?

Great insight into the ways that families function has come to us from the family therapy literature. Coming of age in the 1960s and 1970s, family therapy broke away from the discipline of individual therapy to form its own theories and general philosophical outlook. The core idea, influenced by the seminal work of the biologist Ludwig von Bertolanffy, was that families should be looked at as systems and not as a static collection of isolated parts. In other words, families are best understood as a dynamic whole—almost as living organisms—rather than as an unrelated pile of objects.

What does the **2000 U.S. Census** tell us about **household arrangements** in America?

According to the 2000 U.S. Census, 273.6 million people lived in 105,480,101 households. An additional 7.8 million people lived in institutions such as group homes, prisons, or college dorms. As the table below shows, Americans are living in a wide array of residential arrangements, although married couples still predominate. The second most common household arrangement is a single person living alone.

American Households in the 2000 Census

Household Type	% of Households
Single	25.8
Three generations	3.7
Married	51.7
Married with children	23.5
Single with children	9.3
Single female with children	7.2
Single male with children	2.1
Unmarried partners	5.2
Of the opposite sex	4.6
Of the same sex	0.6

How is a **family** a **system**?

A system is a whole made up of interacting parts. While families are composed of individual family members (e.g., mother, father, children), the nature of the family is determined by the interactions between family members. The pattern of interactions among family members creates the *structure* of the family system. Families are also composed of subsystems, such as the siblings or the parents. Because the family is a system, the members cannot be seen in isolation. If you change one part, you change the other parts as well. Moreover, activity in one part of the system may reflect dynamics in the rest of the system. For example, children may act out at school to force their estranged parents to unite to discipline them.

What is meant by **boundaries** in a **family**?

Salvador Minuchin (1921–) is one of the pioneers of family therapy. He developed a school of family therapy called *structural family therapy*. In this approach, Minuchin emphasizes the importance of *boundaries*. Boundaries refer to the lines between different family members or subsystems that mark the limits of influence, information, and decision-making power. For example, there needs to be a clear boundary between parents and children. Children do not need to know about the sex lives of their parents or the details of their financial situation. Moreover, children should not have undue influence on their parents' marriage.

What is the difference between **rigid, firm,** and **permeable boundaries**?

In a family, boundaries should be firm, but permeable. If the boundaries are too rigid, there is no communication or mutual influence across generational or interpersonal boundaries. This leads to authoritarian or disengaged family systems. If the boundaries are too permeable, then there is insufficient respect for privacy and different family members inappropriately interfere with each other's decisions. This leads to an enmeshed family system. Ultimately, firm but permeable boundaries are optimal. For example, parents should listen to the opinions and the preferences of their children, but still make the final decisions.

What is the importance of **generational boundaries**?

One of the most important boundaries in families with children involves the boundaries between parents and children. When the boundary between generations is too permeable, children have too much information and too much power. The demands of immature minds excessively influence parental decisions, or even the parental marriage. This not only throws the family off kilter because the adults are not in control, but it also leaves the children feeling insecure and unprotected. When the boundaries are too rigid, the children may have no influence on parental decision making. Children may feel overly controlled or unimportant. Ideally, the generational boundary should be firm but permeable. However, this is the ideal and not always the reality. It is never easy to know exactly where the boundaries should be. While parents should not expect to always get it right, they should nonetheless strive to maintain appropriate generational boundaries.

What is meant by **triangulation**?

This concept is associated with another pioneer of family therapy, Murray Bowen (1913–1990). In *triangulation*, a third person is brought into a two-person relationship as a means of diffusing tension between the original dyad. For example, a parent may align with a child in an argument against the other parent. When parents triangulate a child into their marital relationship, the generational boundaries are violated and the child is unduly burdened.

How are the **boundaries** between the **family** and the **outside world** defined?

Families not only have boundaries between different family members or subsystems (internal boundaries), but also have boundaries with the outside world (external boundaries). Such boundaries refer to the degree of influence, time, and information given to

It can be a great help when extended family pitches in with raising the children, but such involvement also introduces the risk of some conflict (*iStock*).

people outside the family. For example, families with few relationships outside the immediate family have rigid external boundaries. Those who have too many people flowing in and out of their home, or who let non-family members unduly influence their family life have overly porous boundaries. Optimally, families should have firm but permeable boundaries so that there are strong and positive relationships with people outside the family, but clear distinctions between those who do and do not belong to the family system.

How do **marital problems** play out in the **family dynamics**?

Because families are seen as integrated systems, problems in any subsystem can influence the functioning of the family as a whole. In a typical nuclear family, the marital subsystem has more power than other subsystems. Minuchin is very attuned to power hierarchies within families. In families with children, parents are necessarily on top of the hierarchy, with the most power over the system as a whole. When there are problems between the parents, this affects the rest of the family. For example the children might develop behavioral problems in response to the marital difficulties of the parents. Certainly if the parents cannot act as a coordinated team, this disrupts the family as a whole.

What are the **benefits** and **drawbacks** of **extended family involvement**?

Most families with small children have extensive contact with grandparents, uncles, and/or aunts. Such involvement of the extended family offers considerable benefits, but

251

also potential drawbacks. One important benefit involves a sense of community, of belonging to a larger social group. Secondly, extended family members can provide very valuable assistance, offering practical, financial, and emotional support. For example, many grandmothers babysit while mothers are at work. Thirdly, no parent is free of personality flaws. Extended family members can provide alternative role models and relationships for children. For example, a mother may be loving but also very anxious. A more carefree uncle can provide a different example of how to manage stress. Potential drawbacks include conflicts between parents and extended family members. This is where appropriate boundaries come into play. For optimal adjustment, family members must work out ways to manage conflict and clarify the boundaries around issues such as decision making, privacy, and amount of time spent together.

How do **family dynamics change** across development?

Family dynamics change tremendously as children grow and develop. In the beginning when children are young, parents have much more control and authority. The family spends more time together as children are not capable of independent social lives. The extended family is often more involved at this time as well, as parents need considerable support with child care. As the children grow older and more independent, parents must loosen the reigns. Family members are less exclusively involved with each other and more involved with the outside world. Parents depend less on extended family for help in child care.

Eventually, parents and adult children establish more egalitarian relationships, a transformation that can be quite challenging at times. Parents must allow their grown children more independence and adult children must take on responsibility for their own lives. As the grown children start their own families, parents become grandparents and the family relationships are reconfigured again. The final reconfiguration comes toward the end of the parents' lives, when the grown children assume more of a caretaking role with their aging parents.

How are **generational boundaries negotiated** in **single-parent** families?

When the family therapy pioneers were writing in the 1960s and 1970s, single-parent families were not nearly as common as they are today. Hence their emphasis was on the more traditional nuclear families. However, as single-parent families make up a significant fraction of today's families, we need to consider how to adapt the family systems concepts to these families. In single-parent families, there is often a loosening of generational boundaries between the single parent and an older child, who may be recruited to serve as a parental helper. This is adaptive as long as the parent remains solidly in control and the older child remains in the role of the child and is not recast into a co-parent. Likewise, the child should not be cast in the role of substitute spouse, responsible to meet the emotional needs of the parent.

There is also likely to be more involvement of extended family members with single-parent families. This can be an extremely important source of support for the family, but also raises issues about the boundaries of control, involvement, and decision-making power between the parent and the grandparents, aunts, uncles, etc., who contribute to the upbringing of the children. For example, how much does a young single mother make her own decisions about her children and how much does she bow to the advice of her mother?

DIVORCE

How has the **frequency of divorce** changed over the last few decades?

Two generations ago, divorce was fairly rare and even considered a source of embarrassment and shame. With the massive social changes of the 1960s and 1970s, particularly the women's movement and the sexual revolution, the cultural attitude toward divorce shifted dramatically. The social stigma of divorce more or less disappeared and children of divorced parents were no longer marked by shame. In the 1970s the divorce rate shot up, peaking in the late 1970s and early 1980s. By 1990, it was predicted that 50 percent of all marriages would end in divorce. While the divorce rate has come down in the past twenty years, divorce is still extremely common. In 2004, 25.4 percent of forty-year-old men and 30 percent of forty-year-old women had been divorced.

How have the U.S. **divorce rates changed** over the last half century?

The table below lists the percentage of 30-year-old adults who have ever been divorced, based on U.S. Census data. Note how the divorce rate increases from the 1960s into the mid 1980s but steadily declines from then on. This effect appears to be separate from the declining marriage rate. In other words, we cannot say that there are fewer divorces simply because there are fewer marriages. While the marriage rate for 30 year olds steadily declined across the same period, the divorce rate clearly peaked before it declined.

Percent of Americans Divorced by Age 30

Years	Men	Women
1965–1969	7.3	11.5
1970–1974	11.6	14.0
1975–1979	16.2	20.8
1980–1984	16.0	21.6
1985–1989	15.0	20.4
1990–1994	13.3	19.9
1995–1999	12.9	17.4
2000–2004	10.7	14.1

What are the most frequent **contributors** to **divorce?**

One of the most potent predictors of divorce is the age of marriage. According to a 1990 U.S. Census report, couples married before the age of thirty were more likely to get divorced than those married at thirty or older. In fact, this worked in a step-wise fashion. Women married before age twenty had a higher rate of divorce than those married from age twenty to twenty-four, who in turn had a higher divorce rate than those married between ages twenty-five to twenty-nine. Whether a baby was conceived or born before the marriage also contributed to the divorce rate, such that couples who conceived or gave birth after marriage were less likely to get divorced. Other risk factors for divorce include financial instability, distant or acrimonious relationships with the extended family, and lack of positive marital role models.

What kind of **relationship problems contribute** to divorce?

Lack of warmth and affection and poor conflict management in a marriage increase the likelihood of divorce. It is not so much the amount of conflict that puts a marriage at risk. Rather it is the nature of conflict. As mentioned above in the section on marriage, a 1993 study of marital interaction by John Gottman found that couples who displayed high levels of defensiveness, contempt, stonewalling, and criticism, as well as facial expressions of disgust were more likely to end up separated or divorced several years later.

What is the **psychological impact** of divorce?

Divorce entails tremendous loss and, like any loss, stimulates a grieving process. When people get divorced, they not only lose the marriage—one of the most intense and intimate relationships of their lives—they also lose much of their married life. Most importantly, divorced parents can no longer live full time with their children, and co-parenting, custody, and visitation issues are perhaps the most stressful and conflictual issues in a divorce. There are also added financial pressures, because incomes that supported one household now must support two. When people get divorced, they lose the social life they shared as a couple, as well as their identity as part of a married couple or part of a family. Not surprisingly, research shows an elevated rate of depression, physical illness, and even suicide among divorced people, particularly divorced men.

How **long** does it take people to **recover** from a **divorce?**

For most people, life returns to some sort of normalcy within a few years. People get over the acute grieving process, and depression, hostility, and regret subside. People adapt to the new routines of child custody and build new relationships with new partners. However, lingering feelings of hostility and of difficulty accepting the end of the

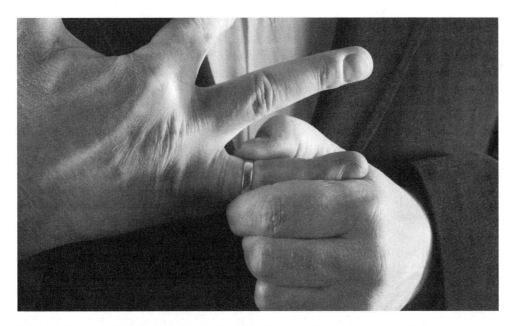

Next to a death in the family, divorce is one of the most traumatic of life events. Steps should be taken to minimize the stress and emotional pain that accompanies the end of a marriage (*iStock*).

relationship may persist even five to ten years after the end of the marriage. A small percentage of divorced people may harbor strong negative feelings, such as anger, depression, and regret even more than a decade later.

What **factors** contribute to a **hostile** and acrimonious **divorce**?

Given the inherently antagonistic nature of divorce, the chances of the process degenerating into a hostile battle are quite high. It takes considerable willpower to contain one's negative feelings and move through the divorce in a civil manner. One or both partners are leaving the marriage in the first place due to their dissatisfaction with it. If one partner initiated the divorce, the spouse who is left behind may have strong feelings of betrayal and abandonment. Secondly, there is the division of property and finances. This is an area rife for disagreement and conflict. Thirdly, if there are children, decisions around custody arrangements frequently elicit strong feelings. Parents may feel great loss at having to sacrifice time spent with their children. Unfortunately, parents often contaminate their co-parenting arrangements with their anger at each other.

What are the **processes** involved with **adjusting** to **divorce**?

The establishment of a clear divorce agreement and custody arrangement marks an important step in adjusting to divorce. Some psychologists suggest the antagonistic nature of the legal system increases conflict between divorcing couples. Nonetheless, it is critical to come up with a binding solution to financial and custody disputes. Once a legal solution is in place, the rancor generally settles down, although some people report ongoing hostility around co-parenting arrangements. Some divorced couples establish friendships after their divorce, but this seems to be relatively rare. The most common outcome is a relatively amicable but not overly involved relationship. Not surprisingly, couples without children generally have considerably less contact after divorce than those with children.

What happens when there is **ongoing conflict** and hostility?

A percentage of divorced couples maintain a high level of conflict and hostility after the divorce. Frequently, this involves disputes over co-parenting. Such ongoing hostility is very psychologically costly, especially for the children. Sometimes continued hostility leads to disengagement between the non-custodial parent (generally the father) and the children. Increased hostility can also keep the partners overly involved with each other. In fact, some researchers believe that ongoing conflict reflects the partners' inability to accept the end of the relationship, as if it is better to have negative contact than none at all. In both cases, ongoing hostility is harmful for all involved, and divorced couples benefit by finding ways to reduce hostility and to resolve conflict in healthier ways.

What **impact** does **divorce** have on **children**?

Clearly divorce has a large impact on the children. There is some disagreement in the research literature as to how much of an impact it makes. Is it a transient stressor that will lose its negative impact after the children and parents adjust to their new life? Or does divorce cause long term damage? There is a fair amount of data that shows that over time, children of divorce do not look much different from children of married couples on many psychological measures. However, there is also data that show children do exhibit an increase of emotional and behavioral difficulties when their parents get divorced. It is therefore useful to ask what factors are protective for children of divorce and what factors are most harmful.

How can parents best **protect** their **children's emotional health** during a divorce?

There is no way for a child to be entirely protected from the dislocations and losses inherent in divorce. When a family breaks up the child is pulled out of an intact family and will necessarily spend less time with one or both parents. Often there are major changes in the child's life; there may be a move to a new house or a new school. There may be new babysitting arrangements. The parents are going through a highly challenging time and it is very difficult to fully shield the children from the parents' ups and downs. However, most children will eventually adjust if they can maintain close relationships with both parents and if the parents can control their anger and hostility and learn to cooperate in the raising of their children. In order to thrive, children need love, predictability, and stability. Children are best protected against the negative impact of divorce when both parents remain committed to providing a safe and stable environment for their children, regardless of their feelings for each other.

What **behaviors** are most **damaging** to **children** during a divorce?

In a 2000 paper, Mary Whiteside and Betsy Jane Becker analyzed the research literature on children of divorce. They found that the child's adjustment was impacted both by the relationship with each parent and by the parents' relationship with one another. For example, both a positive father-child relationship and maternal warmth predicted to a child's well-being. However, the degree of cooperation and hostility between parents also influenced the child's emotional adaptation. Moreover, the relationship between the parents affected their behavior toward their children. In sum, a hostile, non-cooperative relationship between divorced parents has a long-term, destructive effect on children.

What are some common **mistakes** that **parents make** during a **divorce**?

Although most parents assume they will only act in the best interest of their children, in the heat of the divorce many parents act against their better judgment. Based on the clinical and research literature, here is a list of what not to do. In short, do not triangulate your child into your battle with your spouse.

Common Parenting Mistakes Made During a Divorce

What Not To Do	Example
Put down your former spouse in front of your child	"Your father is such a selfish jerk."
Bribe your child out of competition with the other parent	Spend large amounts of money in an attempt to woo children away from the other parent.
Pump your child for information about the other parent	"Is she still seeing that man?" "How often is he coming over?"
Use your child to punish your former spouse	Withhold custody payments out of anger at the custodial parent
Make your child choose between parents	"Wouldn't you rather spend Christmas with me?"
Confuse your feelings about your former spouse with your children's feelings about their parent	"Joey doesn't seem to want to see his father anymore, so I'm not making him."

How important is it to **stay together** for the **children's sake**?

Most research shows that children benefit from divorce when their parents' marriage was highly acrimonious or when there was domestic violence, severe alcoholism, or other highly problematic behavior. Not all marriages are worth saving. However, given that the divorce rate reached an estimated peak of 50 percent by 1990, it is reasonable to conclude that many of those marriages could have been saved if both partners had been more committed to working out problems and persevering through the hard times. As there are clear negative effects of divorce for both adults and children, we can conclude that divorce should not be taken lightly. Couples should try to save their marriages; they should work on improved conflict resolution and seek out couples' therapy if necessary. However, these efforts may not succeed and couples may choose to end their marriage anyway. If parents decide on divorce, it is incumbent on them to proceed through the divorce process in a thoughtful and emotionally controlled way. If they do not, they cause unnecessary emotional pain for their children.

SEXUALITY

What do we **mean** by **sexuality**?

Before exploring the research on sexuality, it is important to clarify what we mean by the term. Here we will define the word very broadly. Sexuality refers to all thoughts, feelings, and behaviors associated with sexual arousal. This includes sexual fantasies, sexual orientation, the physiology of sexual arousal, and actual sexual behavior.

What is **sexology**?

Sexology is the systematic study of sex and sexuality. Although there were many scholars of sexuality in the nineteenth century—some of the most famous are Richard von Krafft-Ebbing, Havelock Ellis, and Sigmund Freud—most of these investigators were physicians and were concerned with illness and pathology. There were many studies of perversions—what we now call *paraphilias*. It was not until the middle of the twentieth century that sexology included large-scale studies of normal sexuality. Most people credit Alfred Kinsey with pioneering the systematic and empirical study of normal sexuality in the twentieth century. William Masters and Virginia Johnson followed a few decades later with a revolutionary emphasis on sex therapy. Their innovation was to apply the principles of behavioral therapy to improve sexual functioning and enjoyment. Current sexologists study normal and atypical patterns of sexual behavior, desire, and attractions and address biological, psychological, relational, and societal influences on sexual health.

Why is it so difficult to talk about sex?

Sex is a universal part of life and is absolutely integral to our survival as a species. Nonetheless, sex is an extremely difficult and controversial topic to talk about. Many would argue that the scientific study of sexuality lags far behind scientific study of many other areas of human behavior. We do know that sexuality involves great passion and the relinquishment of everyday normal inhibitions. In the heat of sexual passion, people can violate critical social rules and betray important relationships. Probably because of this, all societies develop codes to regulate sexual behavior. Cultural, religious, and moral codes explicitly state when, where, and what kind of sexual behavior is socially acceptable. Breaking social rules about sexual behavior can bring severe consequences, even death in some cultures. It is possible that the evolutionary importance of sexuality may contribute to the intense emotional reaction most people have about the topic. In other words, people feel so strongly about sexuality because it is so central to our evolutionary survival.

Who was Alfred Kinsey?

Alfred Kinsey (1894–1956) was one of the pioneering sexologists of the twentieth century. Born into a devout Methodist family with a strict, repressive father, Kinsey's quest to bring human sexuality out of the closet and into the open, non-judgmental light of scientific inquiry was partly fueled by his own childhood experiences. He originally started his career as an entomologist, a student of insects. The obsessive attention to detail he put into the cataloging of millions of insect specimens carried over into his work in sexology. In 1947, he established the Kinsey Institute for Research in Sex, Gender and Reproduction, which is still in existence today. The 2004 movie *Kinsey*, written and directed by Bill Condon, portrayed the dramatic interplay between the personal and professional life of this influential figure.

How important is sex to a healthy relationship?

Most sexologists agree that a healthy and satisfying sexual life is very important to romantic relationships. Moreover, it pro-

Most people credit Alfred Kinsey with pioneering the systematic and empirical study of normal sexuality in the twentieth century (AP/WideWorld).

motes physical and mental health in both partners. However, couples can vary considerably with regard to the importance of sexuality in their lives. Some couples can maintain a close and satisfying relationship with little sexual activity. For many other couples, sexual intimacy is an important part of the relationship and disruptions to sexual life can either cause relationship problems or be a symptom of them. It is also important to note that sexual activity generally decreases with age, particularly in the last few decades of life. Because of this, older couples may place far less emphasis on sexual intimacy than do younger couples. Nonetheless, there are many older couples for whom sexual satisfaction is still important. As the elderly population increases and more people stay physically and mentally vigorous late into their life, it is likely that the topic of geriatric sexuality will gain more attention.

Do **men** and **women differ** with regard to **sexuality**?

In William Masters and Virginia Johnson's pioneering work on human sexuality in the 1960s and 1970s, it was assumed that the sexual response worked the same for both men and women. All people followed the four stages of sexual arousal: excitement, plateau, orgasm, and resolution. More recent work has shown that men and women differ dramatically in the nature of their sexuality. Compared to women, men masturbate more, use more pornography, are more reactive to visual cues, and experience sexual desire more spontaneously. Women, on the other hand, are less likely to become spontaneously sexually aroused and their sexual desire is much more reactive to their surrounding circumstances. For example, the quality of a woman's relationship with a potential sexual partner greatly affects her feelings of sexual attraction. In this way, science supports the cliché that women like to be wined and dined and men like sexy outfits.

What does **Roy Baumeister** propose with regard to **gender differences** in **sexuality**?

In a 2000 article, Roy Baumeister proposed that sexuality varies fundamentally between women and men. Men, he suggested, have a fixed, biologically determined sex drive that is relatively insensitive to context. Women, on the other hand, have a much more variable sex drive, far more responsive to the surrounding circumstances. He based these conclusions on a broad range of empirical findings. According to this research, women have greater variation both in the level of sexual activity and choice of gender over time. Moreover, in women sexuality is far more influenced by cultural factors, such as education, religion, and peer and parental attitudes.

What are the most common **sexual complaints** of **women**?

The sexual complaints most frequently encountered by sex therapists involve problems with sexual arousal, lack of sexual desire, pain during intercourse, and lack of orgasm. These complaints often co-occur; they are not necessarily separate from each other. Interestingly, a number of studies show that a woman's physiological response (e.g., blood flow to the genitals and vaginal lubrication) may not always correspond to her subjective sense of sexual arousal. While some physiological response may occur quite easily, the conscious sense of sexual excitement is much more tied to a woman's emotional state. Feelings of depression, anxiety, and emotional distance can dampen sexual desire while feelings of relaxation and intimacy heighten it. Negative emotions can be in response to current situations, but also a result of long-term emotional difficulties related to sex.

For many couples sexual intimacy is an important part of the relationship. Disruptions to sexual life can either cause relationship problems or be a symptom of them (*iStock*).

What are the most common **sexual complaints** of **men**?

The most frequent sexual complaints made by men include erectile dysfunction, rapid ejaculation, and delayed ejaculation. Men can also complain of lack of sexual desire. Erectile dysfunction and ejaculatory difficulty generally increase with age and may relate to the reduced testosterone levels associated with aging. Sexual desire decreases with age as well, although this does not have to be a problem if both partners are satisfied with their sexual life. Medical conditions, such as heart disease and diabetes, can also interfere with sexual function in men. These conditions become more frequent with age, but are also impacted by health behaviors, such as alcoholism, smoking, diet, and exercise. Emotional factors play a role as well, including depression, stress, and relationship problems. A range of deep-seated conflicts about sexuality, stemming from important childhood relationships, can further complicate sexual function.

How does **anxiety interfere** with sexual functioning?

There is clear indication that anxiety about sexual performance or experience can have an immediate and profound effect on sexual functioning. Many studies show that a woman's sexual excitement and pleasure is tied to feelings of relaxation. Fear of vaginal dryness, pain, or lack of response can immediately dampen a woman's sexual arousal. Likewise in men, fear of erectile dysfunction can create a vicious circle, in which anxiety about impotence can cause men to lose their erection, which in turn reinforces their anxiety.

What role does **conditioning play** in sexual response?

In associative or classical conditioning, people learn to respond to a situation in a particular way because they associate that situation with something that elicits the same response. For example, you might feel disgust at the thought of eating chicken if you got sick one time after eating rotten chicken. Conditioning plays a very important role in sexual response for both men and women. Expectations of failure, of discomfort, or of lack of response can dampen sexual arousal. Likewise positive expectations of pleasure and excitement can heighten sexual response. That is why classical conditioning techniques are incorporated into sex therapy. Sex therapists work to break the association between sexual activity and stress, performance anxiety or discomfort. They aim to replace such negative associations with positive associations of pleasure, comfort, and intimacy.

What roles do **hormones** play in **sexual response**?

There is considerable evidence that the male hormone, testosterone, plays an important role in sexual arousal. It seems to be more important in the sexual functioning of men than women, however. In women, the hormone estrogen affects sexual function, promoting vaginal lubrication and elasticity. After menopause, estrogen levels drop off dramatically in women, causing vaginal dryness and sometimes pain during intercourse. Hormone replacement therapy, which increases the level of estrogen, can moderate these negative effects although there are safety problems associated with long-term use.

How important is **sexual communication**?

Most sex therapists place considerable importance on sexual communication, which can be surprisingly poor in many couples. Many people assume that sexual needs and preferences should not have to be explicitly stated and thus shy away from direct communication. Some women are embarrassed to directly state their desires, fearing they would appear unseemly or critical of their partner. Likewise, many men feel pressure to know how to please a woman without necessarily being told. Enhancing sexual communication between partners can be a quick and easy way to improve the quality of a couple's sexual life.

What are the most **effective treatments** for sexual problems?

With the arrival of sildenafil citrate (Viagra) in 1998, medical treatments for sexual problems have become more prominent. Viagra improves erectile function by increasing genital blood flow. This is accomplished through a type of chemical called the PDE5 (phosphodiesterase type 5) inhibitors. Several other drugs of the same class have been developed that are also effective with erectile dysfunction. Unfortunately, no similar drugs have been found to help women. Premature ejaculation is treated with the SSRIs, a class of antidepressants that work on the serotonin system (e.g., fluoxetine [Prozac] or paroxetine

[Paxil]). Hormone treatments, which increase the levels of testosterone and/or estrogen, have also been tried but they have shown limited effectiveness and can have dangerous side effects. When treating sexual dysfunction, however, it is still critical to address psychological issues, which may include patients' attitudes toward sexuality as well as their body image, feelings of vulnerability, and/or performance anxiety. Couples' issues are also extremely important, and can involve emotional distance, poor communication, unresolved conflict, and mutual misunderstandings about each partner's sexual needs.

What is **sensate focus**?

Sensate focus is a specific behavioral technique that is used when there is considerable anxiety and stress associated with sex. In order to help people relax and learn to enjoy sexual intimacy, it is often useful to forbid them to actually engage in sexual activity. This takes the pressure off, removing the problem of performance anxiety or fear of discomfort. Instead, couples are instructed to express physical affection in nonsexual ways until they are completely relaxed. From there, they slowly increase sexual contact, moving in very small steps. In this way, negative associations are *extinguished*, to be replaced with positive associations. This technique has been highly successful with a wide range of sexual dysfunctions.

How do **values** about **sexuality** vary across **cultures**?

Cultures vary dramatically in their approaches toward sexuality. Some cultures are extremely sensual, but very restrictive about the conditions in which sexuality can be expressed. For example, many aspects of Muslim culture celebrate sensuality, but orthodox Islam is adamant about segregation of the sexes and the covering of women's bodies in public. Likewise, in orthodox Judaism, a husband is obligated to make love to his wife although women must cover their hair in public, and unrelated men and women cannot shake hands. Other cultures are restrictive about any aspect of sexuality, devaluing it as decadent and sinful. St. Augustine (354–430 C.E.), the early Christian theologian, wrote with great disgust about fleshly desire. Likewise, Alfred Kinsey (1894–1956) was partially motivated to study sexuality in response to the sexually repressive Christianity he experienced in his childhood. In contrast, other cultures are far more liberal about sexual expression. In many ancient cultures, sexual acts were incorporated into religious rituals. Phallic processions were often used in the worship of Dionysus, the Greek God of wine. These are parades in which a large phallic statue is carried by the participants of the parade. Similar processions have been found in Japan and other countries. These served as fertility celebrations, which were common in early agrarian societies.

How do **cultures vary** with regard to attitudes about **female sexuality**?

As with general attitudes toward sexuality, attitudes about female sexuality vary widely across cultures. Some attempt to control female sexuality is extremely widespread,

What are some ways in which cultures differ regarding sexual behavior and taboos?

While all cultures have some code by which they regulate sexual behavior, attitudes toward sexuality and sexual permissiveness vary tremendously across cultures. For one, the degree to which bodily exposure is socially acceptable differs widely. American law generally prevents public exposure of women's breasts or of either sex's genitals. In contrast, women sunbathe topless in many European countries. In orthodox Judaism, married women cover their hair when in public so as not to excite sexual desire in men who are not their husbands. Similar patterns are found in many Muslim countries in which women must cover their hair and most of their body when out in public.

There is also wide cultural variation in attitudes toward homosexuality. In many cultures, homosexuality is considered sinful and morally unacceptable. In other cultures, homosexuality is considered a normal rite of passage. Both in ancient Greece and in the Sambia tribe of Papua New Guinea, homosexual relations between young boys and older males were considered a normal part of development. In the United States today, the subject remains intensely controversial, with some people accepting homosexuality as a normal part of human sexuality and others still finding it religiously and morally objectionable.

however, ranging from social mores about "good girls" who "wait until marriage" (common in the United States throughout the 1960s), all the way to *clitorendectomies* and honor killings. Clitorendectomies, which are practiced in parts of Africa and the Middle East, involve the surgical removal of the clitoris, the part of a woman's genitals containing the bulk of sensory nerve endings. Removal of the clitoris greatly reduces a woman's capacity for sexual pleasure. Honor killings involve the murder of any female who brings shame onto her family through inappropriate sexual activity—whether or not she was a willing participant in such activity.

Is there an **evolutionary function** to **controlling women's sexuality**?

The remarkable pervasiveness of attempts to control female sexuality suggests it serves an evolutionary function, possibly the protection of paternity. While a mother can be very confident that her children are her own, men can never be 100 percent positive of their children's paternity. Controlling his partner's sexual freedom enhances a father's confidence (and that of his relatives) in the paternity of the children he is raising. Similar behavior is found in the *mate-guarding* of prairie voles and other animal species.

> ## What are some examples of sexual euphemisms that were used in Victorian England?
>
> In Victorian England, it was so taboo to speak openly about sex in "respectable company," that the language became rife with euphemisms. Two particularly striking turns of phrase involved the substitution of "white meat" for chicken breast and piano "limb" for piano leg.

How have **values** about **sexuality** in industrialized **Western societies changed** over the past several decades?

There have been many cultural changes in industrialized Western societies since the end of the 1960s, but the attitudes toward sexuality have undergone some of the most marked transformations. In general, attitudes toward sexuality have become dramatically more open, relaxed, and liberal. Premarital sex, masturbation, homosexuality, and the use of sexual aids are now commonly accepted practices when they used to be socially frowned upon if not actually illegal. Likewise, public discussion of sex is no longer considered taboo. Advertisements for the treatment of erectile dysfunction grace the pages of weekly magazines, and fairly graphic depictions of sexual encounters are easily found on cable television. For people born in the last few decades, it may be hard to appreciate the sea change in cultural mores that this represents. A look at television shows from the 1950s may help illustrate the magnitude of this shift. To the extent that the bedroom was shown at all in these programs, married couples slept in separate twin beds.

SEXUAL ORIENTATION

What is **sexual orientation**?

In recent years there has been a considerable increase in the research into sexual orientation. With this work has come much controversy as to the nature, stability, and even existence of sexual orientation. For our purposes, sexual orientation refers to the gender toward which a person's characteristic patterns of sexual attractions, fantasies, and behavior are oriented. It is important to consider someone's sexual attractions and fantasies in addition to their sexual behavior because external constraints have more direct influence on behavior than on internal psychological processes. For example, men in prison who have no access to women may engage in sex with other men even though their primary attraction is to women. Likewise, people may marry

265

Sexual orientation may be more clear cut in men than in women as men tend to be either straight or gay while women often fall somewhere in between (iStock).

because of social expectations although their primary sexual desires and fantasies involve members of the same sex.

Is **sexual orientation** a **category** or a **continuum**?

There is some controversy in the research literature as to whether sexual orientation exists as discrete categories or as a continuum. In other words, can we classify people into heterosexual, homosexual, or bisexual categories or do people vary along a continuum ranging from heterosexual to homosexual? Although there is a fair amount of evidence that people do not fall into absolute categories and some capacity for bisexual feelings, thoughts, or behavior exists in many people, there is other evidence that most people fall largely on one or the other side of the continuum. Recent studies suggest, however, that this distinction may be more clear-cut for men than for women.

What is the **Kinsey scale**?

Alfred Kinsey saw sexual orientation as falling on a continuum. He published a scale in 1948 which is still in use today. This seven-point scale ranges from 0 = exclusively heterosexual to 6 = exclusively homosexual. In a study of 4,506 subjects published in 2000 by Steven Gangestad, Michael Bailey, and Nicholas Martin, 5 percent of men and about 3 percent of women scored three or above on the Kinsey scale. About 9 percent of men and 19 percent of women scored a 1 or 2 on the scale. That left about 85 percent of the men and 78 percent of the women to score 0 = exclusively heterosexual.

What did a **2000 study** of men and women show about **sexual orientation**?

The data in the table below is drawn from a 2000 study by Steven Gangestad and colleagues, in which 1,759 men and 2,747 females were rated on the Kinsey Scale of sexual orientation. As you can see, the vast majority of subjects were rated as exclusively heterosexual, but 15% of men and 22% of women reported some degree of homosexual tendencies. In general, men are more likely to fall at the extreme ends of the scale, while women are more likely to fall in the middle.

Scores on the Kinsey Scale

Score*	No. of Men	Percentage	No. of Women	Percentage
0	1,502	85	2,142	78
1	136	7.7	451	16
2	31	1.8	75	2.7
3	12	0.7	33	1.2
4	12	0.7	16	0.6
5	20	1	15	0.5
6	46	2.6	15	0.5
Total	1,759		2,747	

*0 = exclusively heterosexual; 6 = exclusively homosexual.

How **prevalent** is **homosexuality**?

Estimates of the prevalence of homosexuality vary, but range somewhere between 3 percent and 13 percent, depending on the definition of homosexuality used. The number of people engaging in homosexual behavior is likely much smaller than the number of people experiencing homosexual attraction or fantasies. In a 1995 study by Randall Sell, James Wells, and David Wypij, about 3 percent of females and between 5 percent to 11 percent of men across the United States, the United Kingdom, and France reported homosexual behavior in the past five years. About 8 percent of males and 10 percent of females reported homosexual attraction but not behavior since age fifteen. Combining measures of attraction and behavior, about 18 percent of both men and women reported either homosexual attraction or behavior since the age of fifteen.

What are the **causes** of **homosexuality**?

Not surprisingly, there is considerable controversy over the causes of homosexuality. This is partly because the issue is very complex and partly because of the political implications of the question. There is a fair amount of evidence of a biological basis for homosexuality, at least for some people. Three biological models of homosexuality consider prenatal hormones, brain anatomy, and genetic influences. There is also support for social, psychological, and situational factors that contribute to homosexual feelings or behaviors.

What is the **neurohormonal theory** of homosexuality?

According to the neurohormonal theory, exposure to prenatal sex hormones influences sexual orientation in adulthood. Evidence for this comes from animal studies that show animals exposed to abnormal levels (either too high or too low) of androgens in utero can show behavior typical of the opposite sex. Additional evidence comes from studies of girls with a condition called congenital adrenal hyperplasia (CAH), which results in exposure to high levels of androgens both in the womb and immediately after birth. Women with CAH report elevated levels of typically masculine interests and activities, and increased frequency of homosexual or bisexual fantasies and behavior.

What are other **biological theories** of homosexuality?

There is also some evidence of subtle brain differences between homosexual and heterosexual men. In 1991, Simon LeVay published work suggesting that a certain part of the *hypothalamus*, the region of the brain that controls hormone function, may be smaller in homosexual men than in heterosexual men. His study has been criticized however, because many of his homosexual subjects were HIV positive. The genetic component of homosexuality has also been explored, largely through twin studies. The correspondence in sexual orientation between identical and fraternal twins gives information as to the genetic heritability of sexual orientation. If identical twins are more similar in their sexual orientation than fraternal twins, this suggests that genetics play an important role (because identical twins share 100 percent of their genes while fraternal twins share only 50 percent). The evidence for this has been mixed. Some studies show a strong genetic influence while others do not. It is possible that the genetic influence is most powerful in people who are strongly, if not exclusively, homosexual. Genetics may be less important in people with milder homosexual tendencies.

What are some of the **non-biological causes** of homosexuality?

As societies dramatically vary in their attitudes toward homosexuality, we have to assume that cultural attitudes toward homosexuality will affect the prevalence of homosexual behavior. While some people with strong homosexual desires will likely act on them regardless of cultural mores, it is likely that people with milder homosexual tendencies will be more influenced by their cultural context, inhibiting or exploring their desires according to notions of what is acceptable. The availability of heterosexual partners also affects the likelihood of homosexual behavior. In rigidly sex-segregated settings, such as prison, homosexual behavior is quite frequent.

So far, we have addressed the social influences on sexual *behavior*, not feelings, fantasies, or desire. Recent research suggests that for women more than for men, sexual attraction often follows feelings of intimacy. In this case, sexual desire is influenced by the quality of the relationship. Likewise, in some cases, painful, negative relationships with members of the opposite sex can turn people away from heterosexuality and toward the same sex.

How does **gender-typical behavior relate** to sexual orientation?

Michael Bailey and colleagues have conducted a series of studies looking at the relationship between *gender nonconforming behavior* and sexual orientation. By gender nonconforming behavior, Bailey means interests, activities, toys, and even body movements that are associated with the opposite sex (e.g., girls who play football, boys who play with dolls). A number of studies show that gay and bisexual men and women recall a higher degree of gender nonconforming behavior than do their heterosexual counterparts. However, these *retrospective* studies may be biased by selective recall. *Prospective* studies are really needed. In that vein, a study of childhood home videos supported a relationship between gender nonconforming behavior in childhood and homosexual tendencies in adulthood. It is important to note, however, that there was a lot of variation among these subjects and not all children with gender nonconforming behavior grew up to be homosexual and not all adults with homosexual tendencies showed gender nonconforming behavior in childhood.

Do **men** and **women differ** with regards to **sexual orientation**?

An explosion of research into female sexuality supports the notion that sexual orientation in women is different from that in men. Men seem to be more categorical in their sexual orientation; they are more likely to be either heterosexual or homosexual. Women, on the other hand, tend to be more flexible in their sexual orientation, less categorically heterosexual or homosexual. This is supported by studies using the Kinsey scale, in which women are more likely than men to fall in the middle of the scale, while men are more likely to fall on either end.

Fascinating new studies of the physiological response of men and women to various sexual images adds support to this theory. Meredith Chivers, Michael Seto, and Ray Blanchard measured genital response to different sexual images. While physiological response in men was, for the most part, oriented toward *either* adult women or men, women responded sexually to a much broader range of images. In fact, women had a (small) physiological response to images of bonobo chimps mating. Moreover, the physical response in women was often at odds with their verbal descriptions. In other words, what women said they responded to did not always correspond to their actual physiological arousal.

These findings are consistent with the distinction mentioned earlier between the physiological responses in women and their conscious emotional experience. These findings also align with Baumeister's theory that sexuality in men tends to be relatively fixed and unvarying while sexuality in women is more fluid and more responsive to situational factors.

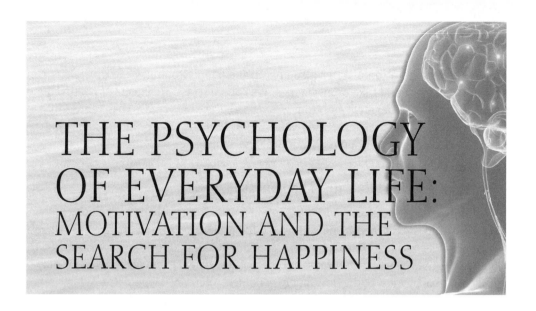

THE PSYCHOLOGY OF EVERYDAY LIFE: MOTIVATION AND THE SEARCH FOR HAPPINESS

THE PSYCHOLOGY OF HAPPINESS

Why **study happiness**?

Traditionally, psychology has devoted far more attention to negative emotions than to positive emotions. Perhaps because of the medical origins of clinical psychology, psychological research has concentrated on healing the sick and reducing suffering. While it is hard to argue with those aims, this focus has meant that the study of happiness and of positive emotion has been relatively neglected until recently. So why study happiness? Well, if all we do is reduce sadness and relieve depression, then the goals of life become no more than the absence of misery. Surely, we would all like more from our lives than that. By studying happiness and positive emotion, psychology can learn how people can best enhance their life and work towards fulfillment and self-development.

What is **happiness**?

How do we define happiness? Happiness can be defined as a mental state characterized by consistently positive emotions. Positive emotions can include curiosity, joy, contentment, excitement, interest, and/or pleasure. Life satisfaction is also considered in many happiness studies. Most researchers are more interested in the effects of *chronic* happiness, or the ongoing propensity to experience positive mood, than in the immediate effects of a momentary happy feeling.

What **function** does **happiness** serve?

Happiness researchers believe that positive emotions signal to us that we are in good shape. Our needs are being met, we have adequate resources, and we are reaching our goals. Positive emotional states also encourage people to engage with the environment, to seek out and take on new goals. We can contrast the effects of positive emotions with those of negative emotions, such as depression or fear. These emotions signal to the individual that something is not right, that the environment is not safe, and that the best course of action is withdrawal and avoidance.

How much does the **intensity** of **happiness** matter?

Apparently, the consistency of positive emotions matters more than the *intensity* of them. In a 1991 study by Ed Diener and colleagues, the proportion of time that people felt positive emotions was a better predictor of their evaluation of their overall happiness than the intensity of their positive emotions. In other words, happy people tend to feel mildly or moderately happy most of the time, but may not feel intensely happy all that often.

How do we **measure happiness**?

Because happiness is a subjective state, the only way to directly measure happiness is to ask people how they feel. There may be physiological indications of positive mood, such as low levels of stress hormones, but there are no objective measures of happiness per se. Self-report measures pose a number of problems, however. People may not always know exactly how they feel. Alternatively, they may bias their reports according to how they want to see themselves or what they feel is socially desirable. Nonetheless, self-reports of happiness have yielded meaningful data in a large body of research. Researchers also distinguish between rating overall happiness (How happy are you in general?) and tracking moment-by-moment emotional states. The second type of rating allows researchers to connect emotional reactions to the specific activities people are engaging in at the time.

What does **happiness do**?

Certainly many things can make us happy (or unhappy), but a consistently positive mood also brings significant benefits in and of itself. Let us consider what happiness does for us. In 2005, Sonja Lyubomirsky, Laura King, and Ed Diener published a meta-analysis on research looking at the relationship between positive mood and life functioning. They found that people who are generally happy also demonstrate adaptive psychological traits, such as optimism, resilience in the face of frustration, and enhanced goal seeking. In other words, happy people are upbeat, resilient go-getters. These traits in turn are related to a wealth of positive outcomes, including increased popularity, social engagement, pro-social (helpful) behavior, coping skills, and even physical health.

What **effect** does **happiness** have on our **health**?

How can we tell if happiness leads to better health? Any study of this question is plagued by the chicken and egg problem. Which came first, happiness or good health?

> ## What is a meta-analysis?
>
> **A** *meta-analysis* is a statistical analysis of a group of different studies. It is a way of examining the effect of one variable on another variable across a whole body of literature—and not just a single study. For example, if we want to look at the effect of happiness on coping skills, we can perform a meta-analysis on all the available studies on this topic in order to determine the overall *effect size* of this relationship. Meta-analyses give us much more robust and reliable information than data from individual studies.

There are many studies showing *cross-sectional correlations* between happiness and health. In other words, at any given point people who are happier are also healthier. While these studies show a clear relationship between positive mood and physical health, we cannot know which came first. Unlike cross-sectional studies, however, *longitudinal* studies can show whether high levels of positive mood actually *precede* healthy outcomes. For example, in a recent study of five thousand people, high levels of positive mood predicted to fewer hospitalizations five years later and a lower incidence of stroke six years later.

What **effect** does **happiness** have on our **social life**?

The chicken-egg problem also applies to studies on happiness and social relationships. Many cross-sectional studies show strong correlations between happiness and successful friendships, marriages, and family relationships. Longitudinal studies, however, demonstrate that the tendency toward happiness *precedes* strong relationships. In other words, happy people are more likely to get married, have successful marriages, and even have more friends. For example, in an Australian study carried out over fifteen years by Gary Marks and Nicole Fleming, people who scored high on happiness scales were more likely to be married in the following years than those who did not. Similar results have been found with German and American samples. Moreover, a 1989 study published by Bruce Headey and Ruut Veenhoven showed that happiness levels predicted quality of marriage. Over a six-year period, people with higher levels of happiness earlier in the study were more likely to have a happy marriage later in the study.

What **effect** does **happiness** have on our **work life**?

Does research show the same effect of happiness on our work life? Here too, most research is cross-sectional. Thus, at any given time people with high levels of positive mood tend to have better jobs, higher income, and more autonomous and meaningful work than less happy people. Obviously, the chicken-and-egg problem is relevant here as well. Certainly, many people (if not most) have experienced the negative emotional effects of working at an unpleasant job at some point in their lives. Longitudinal research, however, shows that high levels of positive emotion early in life predicts occupational and financial success many years later. For example, Ed Diener and colleagues found in a 2002 study that college students who displayed more cheerfulness in their first year of college made more money sixteen years later than did their less cheerful counterparts. This effect was found regardless of family income. In fact, the effect was particularly pronounced with students from higher-income families. Presumably, these students had fewer barriers to occupational success than students from lower-income families. Consequently, their emotional state had that much more influence.

What **does** and **does not lead** to **happiness**?

Clearly our mood is not simply a function of our own personalities. We are also subject to the circumstances in which we find ourselves and the effects of our own choices. What kinds of things truly contribute to sustained happiness and which do not?

The research on what *makes* us happy is far more complicated than the literature on the benefits of happiness–on what happiness does for us. The earlier happiness researchers were quite pessimistic about the degree of control we have over our own happiness, assuming that we can do little to affect our happiness in any sustainable way. Later researchers had a far more optimistic view, however, suggesting that our activities and circumstances can definitely impact our general level of happiness.

What is the **happiness set point**?

In the early 1970s Phillip Brickman and Donald Campbell introduced the notion of the *happiness set point*. In this view, our general level of happiness is genetically determined and largely untouched by life events. While significant life events may knock us above or below our set point, the effect is only temporary and we return to our baseline in relatively short order. Although most happiness researchers have since tempered this extreme stance, a fair amount of evidence suggests there is some merit to this idea.

According to the theory of the happiness set point, material wealth will only give us a temporary boost in happiness before we return to our normal mood (*iStock*).

What is the **evidence** supporting the **happiness set point**?

For one, twin studies suggest there is a large genetic component to happiness ratings, suggesting our level of happiness

How did a 1978 study help support the theory that we are born with a "happiness set point" that is largely unaffected by events in our lives?

A famous study conducted by Philip Brickman, Dan Coates, and Ronnie Janoff-Bulman in 1978 compared people who had come into enormous good fortune (lottery winners), people who had suffered tremendous misfortune (paraplegic and quadriplegic accident victims), and their neighbors. The findings from this study have been used to justify the idea of the *happiness set point*. The authors found that lottery winners were only slightly (and not statistically significantly) happier than their neighbors and that paralyzed accident victims were only modestly less happy than their neighbors. On a 0–5 scale of happiness, lottery winners scored an average of 4.00, accident victims 2.96, and neighbors 3.82. All three groups believed they would be equally happy in the future but, compared to the other two groups, accident victims believed they had been happier in the past.

Does sudden good fortune, like winning the lottery, make us happier? One important study concluded: not by much (*iStock*).

is at least partly pre-wired. In other words, the happiness ratings of identical twins, who share 100 percent of their genes, are more similar than those of fraternal twins, who share only 50 percent of their genes. Secondly, external conditions often have little to do with happiness levels. For example, demographic characteristics, such as age, gender, and income, have been shown to have weak correlations with life satisfaction. Even physical attractiveness has little to do with happiness. Moreover, research on people suffering negative life events, such as the loss of a spouse or a disabling accident, pointed to significant recovery in life satisfaction over time despite an initial drop in happiness ratings. Likewise, a famous 1978 study of lottery winners by Brickman and colleagues showed little difference in happiness ratings between lottery winners and a comparison group.

> ### How much does our neighbors' material success affect our satisfaction with our own possessions?
>
> **M**oney clearly matters to some extent and not having enough money definitely has a negative effect. But we can also ask how much money is enough? It is likely that social comparison plays some role here. We may be perfectly happy with our cute little cottage as long as our neighbors and friends live in similar houses. When our peers start moving into spacious mansions, however, we become dissatisfied with what we have. The term "social comparison" refers to the way we evaluate our own belongings through comparison with our neighbors' belongings.

What is the **hedonic treadmill**?

The concept of the *hedonic treadmill* is closely related to the concept of the happiness set point. If we are destined to return to our happiness set point over time, then positive life events can only give us a temporary lift. People who are constantly in search of a higher state of happiness may deny this to themselves, repeatedly pursuing temporary pleasures as if the effect will not, in fact, be temporary. It is as if they are continuously marching on a treadmill, thinking they are going forward when they are really staying in place.

What is the **current view** on the **happiness set point**?

In a 2005 paper, Ed Diener, Richard Lucas, and Christie Napa Scollon revisited the concept of the happiness set point. In their view, external events *do* affect our overall sense of wellbeing—we are *not* immune to our environment. Nevertheless, over time we do tend to adapt to our circumstances, both good and bad. Moreover, in a 2007 study by Richard Lucas, two fairly large groups of disabled people showed a distinct downturn in their life satisfaction following the onset of their disability, with little to no recovery over time.

What **factors** seem to **affect** our general **level** of **happiness**?

In recent years happiness researchers have looked at several factors that may influence our level of happiness. More specifically, researchers have studied the contributions of genetics, demographic characteristics, interpersonal relationships, money, attitude toward life, and sense of control.

How much do **genetics** contribute to our level of **happiness**?

Genetics probably contribute a fair amount to our general level of happiness, up to 50 percent according to a 2005 review by Sonja Lyubormirsky, Kennon Sheldon, and David

Schkade. However, this figure should be considered with some caution. Most genetic studies use samples that do not vary dramatically in their environment or life circumstances. When people's environments are fairly similar, the influence of genetics is heightened. When there is a broad range of environmental conditions, however, the role of genetics is less important. Therefore, because most genetic studies do not include samples from a wide range of environments, the importance of genetics may be exaggerated.

How much do **life circumstances** contribute to **happiness**?

According to this same review of the literature by Lyubormirsky and colleagues, life circumstances such as income, social status, and demographic characteristics (e.g., age, gender, ethnicity) matter, but not as much as we might expect, accounting for 10 to 20 percent of overall happiness scores. Estimates similar to this have been reported in other happiness studies.

How important are **interpersonal relationships** to **happiness**?

Supportive social relationships likely play a very important role in happiness, judging by many studies showing strong correlations between these two domains. There is also a large body of literature attesting to the powerful effect of social support on our resistance to stress and physical illness, as well as our general wellbeing.

Do our **attitudes affect** our level of **happiness**?

Several lines of research point to the importance of the way we *engage with life*, in effect, our attitude toward life. Lyubormirsky and colleagues suggest that 40 percent of our overall happiness depends on our active attempts to foster our own happiness through our thoughts, activities, and goals. This viewpoint is echoed by Martin Seligman in his work on *positive psychology*.

Does **money** make us **happy**?

Some research shows that people with higher incomes are happier than those with lower incomes, but other studies suggest that money has little effect on happiness. An ingenious 2006 study by Wendy Johnson and Robert Krueger sheds some light on these confusing findings. In their view, the *objective* amount of financial resources is less important than the *subjective perception* of financial status. In a study of 719 twin pairs, Johnson and Krueger found that people's perception of their financial circumstances—that is, whether they *believed* they had enough money—had only a modest relationship with their actual income and assets. Likewise, their satisfaction with their life was far less related to actual prosperity than to perception of prosperity. In other words, the degree to which people felt satisfied with their life had less to do with how much money they actually had and more to do with their *beliefs* about how much money they had—i.e., feeling that they had enough money.

Can meditation benefit your health and emotional well being?

A wealth of evidence suggests that happiness is mediated by an area of the brain known as the *left prefrontal cortex*. The frontal cortex takes up about half of the entire cortex, which is the outer covering of the brain. The prefrontal cortex is the most *anterior* (or forward) part of the frontal cortex (see Chapter 3 for more on brain anatomy). Brain imaging studies, electro-encephalogram (EEG) studies, and even research on the effect of strokes all support the role of the left prefrontal cortex in positive emotions.

Meditation has been shown to have a positive effect on mood (*iStock*).

Richard Davidson has conducted a number of investigations in this area. In one 2003 study conducted with John Cabott Zinn and a group of other colleagues, 25 subjects trained in meditation techniques were compared to a control group who had been put on a wait list. Meditation has been shown to have a strong impact on positive mood. Study subjects who completed the eight-week course in meditation showed a much greater increase in electrical activity in the left frontal regions than did wait-listed controls. Moreover, this group also showed a better immune response to a flu vaccine they received after their meditation course.

Is **sense of control** important?

In Johnson and Krueger's study, life satisfaction was also strongly related to beliefs about how much control people felt they had over their life. In fact, out of the twelve factors studied, perceived control over one's life was the single most important factor contributing to life satisfaction.

POSITIVE PSYCHOLOGY

What is **positive psychology**?

Positive psychology is a branch of happiness studies championed by Martin Seligman (1942–). Positive psychology came into its own in 2000, when Seligman was elected president of the American Psychological Association and was in a position to direct the field's attention. Unlike previous happiness researchers, Seligman is a staunch believer in the ability of each person to improve his or her general emotional well-being. His earlier seminal work on *learned helplessness* contributed to the development of cognitive behavioral therapies for depression. Consequently, Seligman brought a psychotherapist's point of view to the study of positive emotions, asking how psychologists can help people to feel better.

Why is **positive psychology** a **shift** from traditional **trends** in **psychology**?

Although Seligman has tested his techniques on depressed patients, positive psychology differs from traditional psychotherapy by its emphasis on happiness and wellbeing rather than on the relief of suffering and mental illness. Seligman is not the first to think about the human potential for happiness, however, and he acknowledges the influence of earlier writers such as Carl Rogers, Abraham Maslow, and Erik Erikson.

What are **Seligman's three aspects** of **happiness**?

Seligman actually rejects the use of the term "happiness," stating that it is too vague and unscientific. Instead, he breaks happiness or "the good life" into three components: positive emotion (the pleasant life), engagement (the engaged life), and meaning (the meaningful life).

What does **Seligman mean** by the **pleasant life**?

This refers to the experience of high levels of positive emotion regarding our present, past, and future. Positive emotions about our past include feelings of contentment, fulfillment, satisfaction, serenity, and pride. Positive emotions about our future include confidence, optimism, hope, faith, and trust. Positive emotions about our present include the ability to experience pleasure from immediate experience. This also involves the ability to *attend to* immediate experience and not be distracted by concerns about the future or past. Interestingly, this aspect of "the good life" appears to be the least important in that it has the lowest correlations with a person's ratings of life satisfaction.

What does **Seligman mean** by the **engaged life**?

The *engaged life* involves the ability to invest in and make connections with work, intimate relationships, and leisure activities. In the engaged life we are not isolated individuals, floating on a self-imposed island of alienation, but rather we are actively engaged with the world around us. Seligman believes that increasing life engagement involves identifying *signature strengths*—one's own particular strengths and interests—and then putting them to use. For example, people who are interested in art can take a painting class. Those who like animals can volunteer at an animal shelter.

Seligman believes that giving back to the larger community is an important part of happiness (*iStock*).

What is meant by the **meaningful life**?

In the *meaningful life*, people use their signature strengths to commit and contribute to causes larger themselves. The particular cause does not matter and might include politics, religion, community service, or family. In this way, people gain a sense of belonging to a larger group, cause, or institution and they enhance their sense of self-worth and life purpose. A series of studies shows the relationship between such commitments and life satisfaction. The importance of a meaningful life suggests that a life devoted to self-centered aims ultimately provides limited life satisfaction.

Which aspects of happiness are most important?

Multiple studies show that the engaged and meaningful life have stronger positive correlations with life satisfaction and stronger negative correlations with depression than does the pleasant life, although all three aspects of the good life relate to overall happiness.

How do **Seligman's findings accord** with **other** happiness **research**?

Seligman's findings that the pleasant life is least predictive of overall happiness compared to the engaged and meaningful life helps explain some of the contradictory findings in happiness research. It seems that *pleasure*, what we feel after we achieve a desired goal, is most likely to be short-lived. This is consistent with the notion of the hedonic treadmill, which presumes that any satisfaction derived from an achieved goal is bound to be temporary. Our way of *engaging with* our life, however—whether we are involved with other people in a meaningful way or meeting our own potential for growth—appears to have significant impact on our general happiness. Thus, if we want to increase our level of happiness, we are better off considering the way we live our life rather than solely focusing on the pursuit of pleasure.

What are the **virtues**?

Assuming that happiness has three components (listed above as the pleasant, engaged, and meaningful lives), Seligman and his colleagues believed it was important to identify personality traits that promote these positive modes of living. Consequently, they identified six overarching *virtues* which they claim to be culturally universal. These are: wisdom and knowledge, courage, humanity (which involves compassion and concern for others), justice, temperance (the capacity for self control), and transcendence (the ability to find connections with a larger universe).

What are the **character strengths**?

The six overarching virtues were broken down into twenty-four *character strengths*. These included: creativity, curiosity, open-mindedness, love of learning and perspective for wisdom and knowledge; authenticity, bravery, persistence, and zest for courage; kindness, love, and social intelligence for humanity; fairness, leadership, and teamwork for justice; forgiveness, modesty, prudence, and self-regulation for temperance; appreciation of beauty and excellence, gratitude, hope, humor, and religiousness for transcendence.

What does **Seligman's research** say about the **virtues** and **character strengths**?

Seligman and his colleagues have conducted research to see how universal these concepts are and how well they correlate with life satisfaction. A study conducted in forty different countries asked people to rate how much they could identify with each of the twenty-four character strengths. The rankings of the character strengths were notably similar from country to country, with kindness, fairness, authenticity, gratitude, and open-mindedness most commonly endorsed ("most like me"). Less frequently endorsed strengths included prudence, modesty, and self-regulation. The authors also noted that the strengths pertaining to emotional traits (zest, gratitude, hope, love) were more strongly associated with ratings of life satisfaction than the strengths relating to intellectual traits (curiosity, love of learning).

Are there **exercises** to **improve happiness**?

In a 2005 paper, Seligman, along with Tracy Steen, Nansook Park, and Christopher Peterson, reported results from an extremely simple and cost-effective intervention to increase happiness. They conducted their study through an Internet Website. Visitors to the Website were invited to participate in exercises designed to increase their happiness, with a warning that some visitors would be assigned to a *placebo condition*. Placebo conditions are routinely used as a comparison against the active treatment condition. Study participants were assigned to perform one of the following exercises for one week only. In the placebo condition, subjects had to write about early memories each night.

There were five treatment conditions: the gratitude visit (within one week participants had to write and deliver a letter of gratitude to someone who had never been properly thanked for their kindness); three good things in life (each day participants had to record three good things that happened and consider what caused them); you at your best (subjects were asked to write about a time when they were at their best, identify their signature strengths at that time, and then reflect upon what they wrote every day for a week); using signature strengths in a new way (participants were asked to identify their top five character strengths and to put them to use in a novel way each day for a week); and identifying signature strengths (participants had to identify their top five signature strengths and to use them more often in the following week).

All of the conditions, including the placebo condition, improved happiness scores and reduced depression scores immediately after the exercises were completed. One week after that, scores for the placebo condition returned to baseline and stayed there for the next six months. The effect of "you at your best" and "identifying signature strengths" also disappeared within one week after the exercises ended. The effect of "the gratitude visit" lasted somewhat longer, persisting for a month. Remarkably, the effects of "the three good things" and "using signature strengths" interventions lasted for the entire six months of the study period. It appears that people who maintained improvement had continued performing their exercises throughout the six-month study period.

What is **positive psychotherapy**?

In a 2006 publication, Seligman, Taayab Rashid, and Acacia Parks reported their results from their more formal study of positive psychotherapy (PPT). Here they adapted the exercises used in their Web-based study to more intensive forms of psychotherapy. The first study included forty mildly-to-moderately depressed undergraduate students. Nineteen students were assigned to two hours per week of group therapy for six weeks, while twenty-one were assigned to a no-treatment control group. Treatment involved a package of six exercises similar to the ones assigned in the earlier Web-based study. The last session focused on how to maintain therapeutic gains and continue the exercises after the study ended.

Statistical analysis showed that the students in the PPT group had lower depression scores and higher life satisfaction scores than the controls and that the improvement lasted for at least one year after the treatment ended. In a second study, more severely depressed patients were treated in individual therapy and compared to equally depressed patients in usual treatment (psychotherapy with or without medication). The individual therapy utilized many of the same techniques as the earlier two studies, but adapted the interventions to address the greater severity of depression. After a maximum of twelve weeks, patients in PPT showed more improvement than patients in treatment as usual, with greater reductions in depression and higher increases in positive emotion.

HAPPINESS ACROSS CULTURES

How do we **compare happiness** across **cultures**?

There is a growing body of literature that looks at happiness from an international point of view. Studying happiness across different countries can be very helpful for public policy planners, allowing them to identify the social and political factors that promote well-being. As with other happiness research, the best way to measure the subjective sense of happiness is to ask someone directly, "How happy are you?" Happiness researchers also ask people about their satisfaction with their life.

What **problems** are there with **international happiness studies**?

There are two main problems with this kind of research. The first involves potential cultural differences in the understanding of what happiness means. The second has to do with the selection of study subjects. The sample from each country should be representative of the entire population. For example, if the sample is too heavily weighted toward educated, urban dwellers—who are much more likely to take surveys than uneducated rural villagers—then the happiness ratings may not accurately depict that country's population. Cross-cultural happiness researchers are aware of these problems, however, and try to account for them in their study design.

What is the **World Database of Happiness**?

Ruut Veenhoven is a Dutch sociologist who has conducted cross-cultural research into happiness since the 1980s. In his World Database of Happiness, he has compiled data on happiness studies from countries all over the world into a publicly available Website (www.worlddatabaseofhappiness.eur.nl). There is also data on the correlates of happiness. For example, how much do political freedom and gender equality correlate with happiness? Veenhoven derives much of his findings from a ten-point scale ranging from 0 = most dissatisfied to ten = most satisfied.

What **factors** seem to **contribute** to **happiness** across nations?

On the whole, wealthier countries have happier citizens. Nonetheless, a country's wealth and its happiness ratings are not entirely aligned. Therefore money only accounts for part of the story. According to Veenhoven's studies, war, political instability, totalitarian governments, and economic chaos pull happiness ratings down. It also seems that democracy, security, gender equality, strong social programs, political stability, and greater political and economic freedom promote happiness in a country's citizens. Social cohesion, which Veenhoven refers to as "brotherhood," is also an important contributor to happiness.

How do the **wealthiest countries** do in terms of **happiness**?

Of the top ten wealthiest countries in terms of per capita income, only four (Iceland, Switzerland, Norway, and Luxembourg) ranked among the top ten happiest countries. The other six countries ranged from the fourteenth happiest country (Ireland) to the fifty-fifth (Hong Kong). Singapore ranked thirty-second in happiness ratings.

The United States is the fourth wealthiest country in terms of per capita income with an average income of $47,000 per year, yet we ranked twenty-seventh in happiness ratings, with an average happiness rating of 7.0.

How does **inequality** in **happiness** come into play?

Veenhoven is also interested in the inequality of happiness ratings within countries. In other words, how similar are the happiness ratings of various individuals within any given country? He constructed a measure called Inequality-Adjusted Happiness, which was based on the standard deviation of happiness ratings. The standard deviation is a statistical measure that reflects how much individual cases vary from the average. According to his calculations, the top five countries with both the highest and most equal happiness ratings were Malta, Denmark, Switzerland, Iceland, and the Netherlands. The middle five were the United States, the Philippines, Iran, South Korea, and India. The bottom five were Armenia, Ukraine, Moldova, Zimbabwe, and Tanzania.

Has **average happiness changed** over time?

According to Veenhoven's work, there have been increases in average levels of reported happiness over time. In wealthy countries, these changes have been slight, but in less developed countries, the changes have been pronounced. In the United States, however, there has been essentially no change in the reported levels of happiness over the past sixty years. These findings have been used by Richard Easterlin to support a theory that living conditions, which have risen steadily in the United States over the past sixty years, do not affect happiness. If we consider the findings on both developed and less-developed countries, we can see that happiness is most strongly related to living conditions when money is scarce and living conditions are less than optimal. After people reach a reasonable standard of living, however, affluence does not add much to happiness.

Are people in **wealthier countries happier** than those in poorer nations?

The list of happiness ratings below was collected from the World Database of Happiness, which compiles data on happiness studies from all over the world. These ratings apply to the years 2000 to 2008. The information on each country's income was gathered from the *CIA World Fact Book*. Per capita income refers to the average income of each country's citizens. As we can see from the table, the average happiness ratings, which range from 0 (least happy) to 10 (most happy), vary across the four income quartiles. On average, wealthy countries have higher happiness ratings.

Average Happiness Ratings on a 0 to 10 Scale			
7.27	6.31	5.90	5.39

Countries Listed in Descending Order of Per Capita Income			
1st Quartile	**2nd Quartile**	**3rd Quartile**	**4th Quartile**
Luxembourg	Cyprus	Turkey	Bolivia
Norway	Israel	Belarus	Honduras
Singapore	New Zealand	Panama	Paraguay
USA	Czech Republic	Costa Rica	Morocco
Ireland	South Korea	Brazil	Iraq
Hong Kong*	Portugal	South Africa	Indonesia
Switzerland	Slovakia	Montenegro	Philippines
Netherlands	Estonia	Macedonia	Nicaragua
Iceland	Saudi Arabia	Azerbaijan	Vietnam
Canada	Hungary	Columbia	Venezuela
Austria	Trinidad & Tobago	Thailand	India
Sweden	Puerto Rico*	Peru	Pakistan
Australia	Latvia	Dominican Republic	Moldova
Belgium	Lithuania	Ecuador	Nigeria
Denmark	Poland	Algeria	Kyrgyzstan
Finland	Croatia	Ukraine	Zambia
United Kingdom	Russia	Bosnia-Herzegovina	Ghana
Germany	Malaysia	Armenia	Bangladesh
Spain	Chile	El Salvador	Tanzania
Japan	Mexico	China	Mali
France	Argentina	Albania	Burkina Faso
Greece	Bulgaria	Egypt	Uganda
Taiwan	Iran	Guatemala	Rwanda
Italy	Uruguay	Jordan	Ethiopia
Slovenia	Romania	Georgia	Zimbabwe

*Hong Kong is actually part of China, and Puerto Rico is a territory of the United States, but they are listed separately as their local cultures are considered distinct.

According to the World Database of Happiness, Iceland ranks as the happiest country in the world (*iStock*).

What are the **10 happiest** and **10 least happy countries** and how does happiness relate to **per capita income**?

The table below lists the 10 countries with the highest happiness ratings and the 10 countries with the lowest ratings during the period from 2000 to 2008. On the whole, the happier countries are among the most wealthy, while the least happy countries have much less wealth. However, per capita income does not tell the whole story. Some countries that are listed as among the top 10 happiest have very similar, if not lower, per capita incomes than those of countries listed in the bottom 10. For example, Columbia has a per capita income of $8,900 while Bulgaria has a per capita income of $12,900. Likewise the per capita income of Mexico is not much higher than that of either Bulgaria or Macedonia.

Ten Happiest Countries and Per Capita Income

Country	Average Happiness Rating (0-10)	Per Capita Income	Rank in Per Capita Income
Iceland	8.5	$39,900	9
Denmark	8.4	$37,400	15
Puerto Rico*	8.3	$17,800	36
Switzerland	8.1	$40,900	7
Columbia	8.1	$8,900	58
Mexico	8.0	$14,200	44
Austria	7.9	$39,200	11
Finland	7.8	$37,200	16
Luxembourg	7.7	$81,100	1
Norway	7.7	$55,200	2

*Territory of the United States.

Ten Least Happy Countries and Per Capita Income

Country	Average Happiness Rating (0-10)	Per Capita Income	Rank in Per Capita Income
Macedonia	4.6	$9,000	57
Albania	4.6	$6,000	69
Bulgaria	4.4	$12,900	46

Country	Average Happiness Rating (0-10)	Per Capita Income	Rank in Per Capita Income
Georgia	4.4	$4,700	73
Rwanda	4.4	$900	96
Iraq	4.3	$4,000	78
Pakistan	4.3	$2,600	85
Ethiopia	4.3	$800	97
Zimbabwe	3.3	$200	98
Tanzania	3.2	$1,300	92

THE PSYCHOLOGY OF MONEY

What is the **theory of rational economic man**?

Ever since the 1700s when the seeds of modern economic theory first developed, economists have assumed that people have a very simple relationship with money. The *rational economic man* is seen to act more or less like a calculating machine. Financial decisions regarding how we spend, borrow, and save, are based on a rational assessment of our losses and gains. We compare the value of what we pay out to the value of what we take in and make decisions accordingly. If we make mistakes in these calculations, we eventually recognize them and correct our behavior.

What is **wrong with** the **theory** of rational economic man?

The problem with this theory is that it is often wrong. As the great financial crisis of 2008 has shown us, people's economic behavior is often anything but rational. Leading up to this crisis, the whole country gorged on unaffordable debt. In 2007, according to the U.S. Federal Reserve, the median savings rate for American households was just above zero and the median income for a large section of the population had remained flat for several years. Nonetheless, our household debt continued to grow, 11 percent between 2004 and 2007, and 34 percent in the three years preceding that. In fact, from 2004 to 2007, the median credit card balance rose 25 percent. In other words, we were spending more than we could afford. This was not due to the cost of living, as inflation had remained quite low. We were on a giant national binge. While psychology cannot account for the full complexity of economic events—larger political, legislative, environmental, and cultural factors play a central role—more and more economists are recognizing the critical importance of people's emotional responses to money.

What is **behavioral economics**?

Behavioral economics is a multi-disciplinary field, linking economics, psychology, and neuroscience. It developed as a reaction against the prevailing view of rational eco-

How much debt are Americans carrying?

The table below is based on data taken from the Federal Reserve and shows the nature and amount of Americans' debt in 2007. The third column shows the percentage of American families (perhaps more accurately referred to as households) that hold each kind of debt. The fourth column shows the median amount of debt of the households that hold debt. Remember the median refers to the amount that equally divides the top and bottom half of the population.

Irrational Economic Man: Americans and Debt (2007)

Type of Debt	Explanation	% of U.S. Households with Debt	Median Amount of Debt
Real Estate: Primary Residence	Home Mortgage or Home Equity	48.7%	$107,000
Other Real Estate		5.5%	$100,000
Installment Loans	Car, Education Loans	46.9%	$13,000
Credit Card Debt		46.1%	$3,000
Line of Credit	Not Home Equity	1.7%	$3,800
Other		6.8%	$5,000
TOTAL	All Kinds of Debt	77.0%	$67,300

nomic man. The focus of behavioral economics is the actual psychology of human financial decision making. How do people make decisions about money? What are their blind spots? Where does emotion come in? The first decade of the twenty-first century has brought an explosion of research in this area of study. Some of the scientists involved include Daniel Kahneman, Amos Tversky, Daniel Ariely, Read Montague, and Richard Thaler. There have also been a number of books written by science journalists, such as Jonah Lehrer and Jason Zweig.

What role does **evaluation of risk** and **reward** have in financial behavior?

Every financial decision involves risk and reward. The risk is the loss of money, for example, through a bad investment or through spending too much on something of little value. The reward is the possibility of making more money or the purchase of something we value.

How has **evolution** shaped our **evaluation** of **risk** and **reward**?

In order to survive, an animal needs to be highly attuned to both risk and reward. Examples of reward include food, sex, and social status; examples of risk include danger from predators, within-species aggression, and loss of resources. Our emotional life evolved as a means for us to quickly and efficiently recognize and respond to cues in the environment that are relevant to our survival. Our core emotions—such as desire, happiness, sadness, fear, and anger —help us process information about risk and reward. Because emotions and the parts of the brain that mediate them are relatively old on an evolutionary scale, we share many of our core emotions with other mammals, such as primates, cats, and dogs.

Anyone who has studied the stock market realizes that investors behave emotionally more than logically. Humans instinctively try to react quickly to potential risks, which tends to put logic second after gut reactions (*iStock*).

How important are our **emotions** in our **decisions** about **money**?

Although we may think we make financial decisions through thoughtful analysis, in truth it is our emotions that do the lion's share of the work. Brain imaging studies show that the emotional parts of our brain are extremely active when we make decisions about money. In fact, the emotional brain is frequently more active than the parts of our brain involved with thought. Therefore, in order to understand the psychology of money, we have to understand how emotion affects our decisions about money.

What role do **fear** and **desire** play in the psychology of **money**?

These are the primary emotions involved in financial decisions. Our fear motivates us to avoid loss, in this case the loss of money. Desire motivates us to pursue reward, such as money or the goods that money can buy. When desire for money becomes excessive and poorly controlled, we call it greed.

What **problems** do our **emotions** cause us when making **financial decisions**?

Even though our emotions have evolved over millions of years to help us adapt to our environment, they are not perfect tools and can often lead us astray. For one thing, our emotions are geared almost entirely toward the present. Our emotions can tell us a lot about our needs in the present, but they are not good at telling us what we will need in the future. For that, we need thought and careful analysis. Secondly, our emotions are stimulus bound, in other words they are highly and sometimes excessively responsive to cues in the environment.

How are we **biased** toward **immediate** consequences over **long-term consequences**?

There is clear evidence that the short term generally has far greater influence on our decision making than concerns about the long term. In fact, it takes considerable mental effort to put long-term consequences ahead of immediate gratification. Our use of credit cards provides a perfect example. A 2001 experiment by Drazen Prelec and Duncan Simester shows how the use of credit cards increases our spending, presumably because the money spent seems less immediate. The researchers set up an auction for basketball tickets, in which half the participants in the auction were instructed to pay with credit cards and the other half with cash. As expected, the bids made from credit cards were much higher, in fact twice as high, as those made with cash. In another study, Laurence Ausubel looked at consumer response to two commercial mortgages. The first mortgage offered a low teaser rate (4.9 percent for six months) that was followed by a lifetime rate of 16 percent. The second mortgage offered a higher teaser rate (6.9 percent) but a lower lifetime rate of 14 percent. Ausubel found that consumers chose the first mortgage almost three times more often than the second mortgage. Hence, they chose the mortgage that would save them money in the short run but cost far more money in the long run.

What does it mean to be **stimulus bound**?

Not only are we primed to put immediate considerations over long-term ones, we are primed to respond to *cues* in our environment that signal immediate risk or reward. These cues can then influence our appraisal of risk and reward–and sometimes throw us entirely off course. For example, when are people most motivated to stick to a diet: when they are in the store trying on bathing suits or when they are walking past an ice cream parlor?

What is the **anchoring effect**?

The anchoring effect refers to the way an irrelevant stimulus can have a strong effect on further decisions. For example, Dan Ariely and colleagues held an auction for a range of items. Before people were allowed to bid in the auction, they were asked to write down the last two digits of their social security number. Although the social security number had no logical relationship to the auction, people who wrote down higher numbers bid an average of three times more money for the same items than people who wrote down low numbers.

What is the **framing effect**?

In the *framing effect*, the way that information is presented influences our response to it. In other words, whether the risk or the reward is highlighted drastically affects our own appraisal of risk and reward. In a 2006 study, Benedetto de Martino and his colleagues ran an experiment in which people were handed fifty dollars and then given two choices. Their first option was to keep twenty dollars. They were then offered a gamble with a chance of keeping or losing the whole fifty dollars. In this scenario, only 42 percent chose the gamble. When the same choices were framed in terms of loss instead of gain (subjects would *lose* thirty dollars rather than *keep* twenty dollars), 62 percent of the subjects took the gamble. Decisions were strongly influenced by the way that risks and rewards were framed. As we can imagine, advertisers are well aware of this tendency and put it to good use.

How well do we evaluate the **probability** of **risk** and **reward**?

Our emotions are not very good at considering probability. We are highly attuned to the *intensity* of a risk or reward and get emotionally aroused by high value rewards or risks, but we do a poor job of balancing the intensity of a consequence with its probability. For example, many people are more afraid of a terrorist attack than of hypertension, although far more people in the developed Western world will die from heart disease than from a terrorist attack.

What is **loss aversion**?

This concept, introduced by Daniel Kahneman and Amos Twersky as far back as the 1970s, refers to our emotional reaction to cues of immediate loss. Emotionally, we are primed to hold onto what we have and to strenuously try to avoid loss. Consequently, we tend to avoid a choice that will lose us money in the short run, even if it will make us more money in the long run. It is important to remember that this tendency is stimulus bound. So we are not responding to the *actual possibility* of loss as much as the *cue* that signals the possibility of loss. In the absence of such loss cues, we can be sideswiped by reward cues, as happens when we overspend on our credit cards. Because of this, manipulation of cues will strongly influence our behavior.

The deMartino experiment on the framing effect described above supports our tendency toward loss aversion. Another experiment reported by Jonah Lehrer in his book on decision making shows the effect of loss aversion. A group of physicians was given a scenario involving an outbreak of a lethal disease. In the first condition, two options were described in terms of the number of people that would *live*. In option 1, 200 (of a group of 600) people would survive. In option 2, there was a one-third chance that 600 people would be saved and a two-thirds chance that no one would be saved. Only 28 percent of the physicians chose the second, riskier strategy. When the same options were described in terms of the number of people that would *die*, 78 percent of the physicians chose the risky strategy. Here we see how emotional biases affect the decisions even of highly trained people in responsible positions.

Why does "buy low, sell high" go against human nature?

This is the basic wisdom of the stock market: buy a stock when it is undervalued and sell it when it gains in value. This way you maximize your profit on the sale of the stock. Leaving aside the difficulty of predicting whether a stock is going to increase or decrease in value, this action goes against our basic emotional nature. As detailed in the section on behaviorism, we are primed to repeat behaviors that are rewarded and discontinue behaviors that are punished. When a stock is going up, our purchase is rewarded, so we are likely to want to buy. When a stock is going down, we are punished for our purchase, so we are less inclined to buy.

So does cognition play any role in financial decisions?

Of course we do use thought when making financial decisions. There is more to our psychology than just our emotions. We use cognition when we plan for the future, analyze complex situations, and calculate numerical amounts (after all, money is based on numbers). However, there are important limits to our analytic capacities and these limitations play out in our financial decisions.

What are the limits of our own analytic ability?

Despite the remarkable intellectual abilities humans do enjoy, there are clear limits to our ability to analyze economic information. For one, the frontal lobe, the area of the brain that mediates complex thought, has a limited amount of processing capability. The complex cognitive capacities that the frontal lobe provides take up a good deal of energy and calories, and incorporate a large amount of neurocircuitry. In other words, intellectual analysis of financial information is very "expensive." Consequently, our brain is highly dependent on energy-efficient shortcuts that allow us to process a lot of information very quickly. While these shortcuts allow us to function in the real world, they can also lead us astray. Three cognitive shortcuts that influence our thinking about money include: chunking, sensitivity to context, and the zero-sum game between our emotions and cognition.

How does chunking influence our decision making?

As was first pointed out by George Miller in 1956, we are capable of keeping only seven plus or minus two pieces of information in mind at a time. In order to expand the capacity of our memory, we group information into larger chunks. This is useful until we forget that the larger chunks were originally made up of smaller units. For example, as documented in a 2006 study by Andrew Geier, Paul Rozin, and Gheorghe Doros, people will eat more pieces of candy when using a large scoop than when using a smaller scoop. Further, as noted in Jonathon Lehrer's 2009 book on decision making, it is also well recognized that people will eat more food when their portion sizes or plates are larger. Instead of counting how many pieces of candy or ounces of food they are consuming, people count number of scoops or plates of food. When fast food restaurants offer jumbo-size servings they are taking advantage of this tendency.

How does our **sensitivity to context** affect our **decision making**?

People are not very good at evaluating the absolute value of an item. We tend to see value as relative. In other words, our estimation of the value of an object will vary tremendously depending on the situation. The economist Richard Thaler asked people if they would go twenty minutes out of their way to save five dollars on either a $15 calculator or a $125 leather jacket. Sixty-eight percent of people said yes for the calculator, but only 29 percent said yes for the leather jacket. Even though the amount of money was exactly the same, the five dollars *seemed* like it was worth more in the first condition, as it was a larger amount relative to the cost of the calculator. In the second condition, the five dollars seemed like it was worth less because it was smaller relative to the cost of the leather jacket.

How does **too much information** damage our **impulse control**?

There is somewhat of a zero-sum game between our intellect and our emotions. The brain depends on energy, just like a car depends on gas. If too much fuel is going to our pre-frontal cortex to support cognition, less fuel is available to the parts of the frontal lobe that inhibit our emotional impulses. This was shown in a 1999 experiment by Baba Shiv and Alexander Fedorikhin. Subjects were given two different memory tasks, an easy task (to remember two digits) and a difficult task (to remember seven digits). Remember we can only hold about seven digits in mind at a time. Subjects were then offered their choice of either chocolate cake or a healthy fruit salad. People with the easy task were more likely to take the healthy food while people with the difficult task were more likely to take the chocolate cake. The authors interpreted this to mean that energy expended to perform the harder memory task depleted the brain's ability to resist temptation.

What about the **social context**?

Our evaluation of worth and value is also powerfully influenced by social factors. Consider the amount of money people are willing to spend for high-status belongings. Is a purse really worth $1,000? Is a watch? How many people would pay $80,000 for a BMW if the logo was removed and nobody could tell it was a BMW? People pay outrageous prices for luxury brands not because they believe the products themselves are worth the money, but because the product takes on social meaning. In effect, people

Advertisers have long understood the importance of the emotional brain in making purchasing decisions, even before fMRI research. For example, a company selling lipstick associates the product with a life of beauty, youth, and glamour, even though it's unrealistic to believe lipstick will provide all these things (*iStock*).

are buying social status. This is why high-status people, such as movie stars or star athletes, are paid millions to endorse products such as athletic wear, cereal, or mattresses. Likewise, our sense of a fair salary, a reasonable price, and the worth of a purchase is often judged according to the social context. How much are our colleagues getting paid? How much did our neighbors pay for their car? Once again, advertisers are well aware of this tendency and have learned how to position their products to benefit from the social context.

THE BIOLOGY OF MONEY

What is **neuroeconomics**?

Neuroeconomics involves the study of the regions of the brain that are involved in our responses to money. As we learn more about the psychological processes underlying our financial decisions, we are better able to investigate which parts of the brain are active when we make financial decisions. We can now ask: What parts of the brain turn on when we see something we want to buy? How about when we see the price tag, or when we take a financial gamble? What about when we lose money?

How do **scientists study neuroeconomics**?

There are now many ways to look inside the brain. Older brain-imaging technologies like MRI, PET, and SPECT allowed us to take a snapshot of the brain. By recording blood flow or glucose uptake, we could map a pattern of brain activity at a given point in time. However, the development of fMRI brain-imaging technology has completely changed the game. Now, by recording the behavior of magnetized atoms, we can watch brain activity *over time*. We have moved from still shots to movies. This is critically important if we want to investigate brain activity during a *sequence* of mental processes. With fMRI technology, we can put people in scanners and watch how their brains respond while we run an experiment.

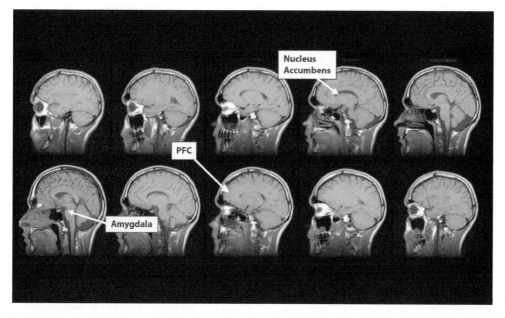

This is a photograph of an MRI brain scan. Arrows point to areas of the brain that are close to those regions involved with our response to money. The prefrontal cortex (PFC) is involved in our analysis of long-term consequences of financial decisions. The amygdala is particularly responsive to fearful cues, and the nucleus accumbens is a key player in the reward system, mobilizing us to pursue rewarding stimuli (*iStock*).

What **parts** of the **brain** are involved with **financial decisions**?

There are several areas of the brain that have been implicated in the mental processes involved with financial decisions. These divide fairly neatly into areas associated with cognitive or emotional processes. The *prefrontal cortex* is involved with careful analysis, quantitative reasoning, and consideration of future consequences; it is the seat of planning for the future. Several smaller areas deep within the middle of the brain mediate the emotional aspects of our financial life. The *nucleus accumbens*, a central point in the dopaminergic reward circuitry, is involved with desire and motivation to pursue reward. The *amygdala* is particularly sensitive to fearful stimuli. The *insula*, which is actually part of the cortex but is sandwiched inside the frontal, parietal and temporal lobes, is responsive to feelings of pain and disgust. The insula is activated when we lose money.

What **function** does the **prefrontal cortex** serve?

The prefrontal cortex is the most anterior (or frontal) part of the frontal lobe. The frontal lobe makes up the front half of the cerebral cortex, which is the wrinkled outer covering of the brain. The pre-frontal cortex integrates information from the rest of the brain, creating an overview of our current situation. Not only does the prefrontal cortex create a representation of our self in our environment, but it can create representations of future conditions. In this way, the prefrontal cortex supports our ability to plan, set future goals, and correct our behavior in pursuit of these goals. The prefrontal cortex is also involved with the precise, careful analysis of information, such as the calculation of cost over time.

Because the prefrontal cortex can create and hold representations of *possible* events and not just current events, our prefrontal cortex allows us to be more flexible in our thinking and even to come up with creative new solutions to problems. This is in contrast with the evolutionarily older parts of the brain involved with emotion. These areas are more *stimulus dependent*, more bound to cues in the present. The frontal lobe is also involved in inhibiting our emotional reactions; it inhibits the limbic system and other parts of the brain that mediate drive and motivation. In other words, the frontal cortex allows us to regulate emotion and impulse with thought.

What are the **drawbacks** with the **prefrontal cortex**?

As mentioned above, the frontal cortex takes up an enormous amount of energy, and mobilizes a large portion of the brain. Although the prefrontal cortex is powerful, it is slow and inefficient. Thus we would miss a good deal of information if we were solely dependent on our frontal lobe for reading our environment. Additionally, the prefrontal cortex does not address personal value.

It is our emotions that tell us the value of any given situation, whether and how something matters to us. In fact, without a sense of something's personal value, we are unable to make decisions. For example, people with lesions in their orbital frontal cortex cannot make decisions. This is a region that integrates information about our emotions into our reading of current and future events. Furthermore, if we think about a decision too much, it distorts our decisions.

In a 1993 study by Timothy Wilson and colleagues, undergraduate women were given the option to pick one of five posters. The subjects were divided into two groups. In one group, the subjects were instructed to rate from 1 to 9 how much they liked each poster prior to picking one. In the second group, subjects filled out a questionnaire about why they liked or disliked each poster before making their choice. Several weeks later, 75 percent of the second group regretted their decision, while none of the first group did. In this case, over-analysis interfered with effective decision making.

How much is the **prefrontal cortex** involved in **purchasing decisions**?

Because purchasing decisions are primarily about personal value, about how much we gain or lose, the prefrontal cortex does not seem to be the dominant player in our brain's response to purchasing decisions. According to a 2007 fMRI experiment by Brian Knutson, George Lowestein, and colleagues, the frontal cortex was less activated during purchasing decisions than either the nucleus accumbens (which processes

What did a 2007 experiment with wine show about the way people make decisions?

In a 2007 experiment by Hilke Plassman and colleagues, subjects were invited to participate in a wine tasting while sitting in an fMRI scanner. Three bottles of wine were poured into five different bottles, giving the impression that all five bottles contained different wines. The bottles' original labels were removed and replaced with new price tags. Even though some bottles with different prices actually contained the same wine, subjects clearly preferred the most expensive wine. Moreover, the prefrontal cortex was the area of the brain that most strongly responded to the price tag. This suggests that our prefrontal cortex is involved in evaluating our experiences according to what we think *should* be important, regardless of what we actually feel. In this way, if we rely too much on our intellect when making decisions, we might focus on the wrong features. A balance between thought and emotion is necessary for effective decisionmaking.

Do we judge wine based on the price tag? One study says we do, believing that a costlier wine must be better than a cheaper wine, even if the same wine is put in both bottles (*iStock*).

rewards), or the insula (which processes pain). This suggests that purchasing decisions are driven more by the balance of pain and desire than by a rational assessment of our options.

What function does the **dopaminergic reward system** serve?

The *dopaminergic reward system* is a circuit that runs through the middle of the brain. In the last decade or so it has received considerable attention because of its central role in a wide range of psychological phenomena. The dopaminergic reward circuitry starts in the ventral tegmentum, an area in the midbrain. This is where we find the cell bodies for the neurons that contain the neurotransmitter *dopamine*. This particular dopamine tract is called the mesolimbic dopaminergic tract, meaning it runs through the limbic system in the middle of the brain.

The dopaminergic neurons eventually connect to the nucleus accumbens, which is a critical node in the reward circuitry. The reward circuitry responds to reward cues and serves to mobilize the organism to pursue reward. Subjectively, we experience this kind of mobilization as desire, excitement, or craving. The reward system is centrally involved in our financial life. Whenever we experience desire for money or for the goods that money can buy, our reward system is activated.

How strongly does the **reward system** affect **motivation**?

It must be kept in mind that the reward system has a very powerful effect on motivation. When it is really firing, our desire can be overwhelming. In the most extreme state, we experience addictive craving, which can overpower any consideration of danger or future consequences. So, when we are caught up in the thrill of making money, our reward system can overpower the inhibiting (and cautionary) effect of the frontal lobe.

How does the **dopamine system** set **expectations**?

The dopaminergic reward system not only responds to the presence of rewards, it learns which cues signal reward and which do not. Therefore the reward circuitry is centrally involved with setting *expectations*. It is in the business of distinguishing which cues do and do not signal reward and in priming us to pursue a reward when it detects a relevant cue.

What are the **drawbacks** of the **dopamine system**?

The reward system has evolved over millions of years to help us recognize the presence of rewards and to motivate us to expend considerable energy to pursue and obtain them. However, it is not foolproof. For one, it responds to the intensity of a reward but not the probability. Secondly, it is over-responsive to novelty, or intermittent reinforcement. Thirdly, it does not do well with randomness.

What are the effects of the **lack of sensitivity** to **probability**?

The dopaminergic reward system is clearly reactive to the intensity of a reward. For example in an fMRI study by Brian Knutson, the nucleus accumbens was twice as activated in response to a promised reward of five dollars as to a reward of one dollar. However, this system does not process the probability of a reward, how likely it is for this reward to actually occur. This lack of discrimination between low-probability and high-probability rewards can explain our attraction to lottery tickets. Why does the purchase of lottery tickets skyrocket when the prize money hits the millions? Because, even though the intensity of the reward stimulates our dopaminergic reward system, the low probability of winning does not register. To the extent that our frontal lobe does process probability information, our reward system may overpower it.

How is the **reward system** reactive to **intermittent reinforcement**?

Our dopaminergic reward system is particularly sensitive to intermittent reinforcement. When a behavior is intermittently reinforced, the reward for a given behavior is irregular and unpredictable. Dopamine neurons are particularly sensitive to novelty and surprise, so when behavior is unpredictably reinforced, each experience of reward comes as a surprise. In fact an unpredicted reward is perhaps three to four times as activating as a predictable reward. This pattern contributes to our vulnerability to gambling, which is defined by intermittent reinforcement.

How does the **reward system** make us **susceptible** to **gambling**?

There is evidence that gambling activates the dopaminergic reward system and that people suffering from pathological gambling have abnormalities in this system. Jonah Lehrer relates one particularly telling example involving a woman who developed Parkinson's disease. Parkinson's disease is caused by cell death of the dopamine neurons in the basal ganglia. The treatment usually involves medication that increases the amount of dopamine in the brain. When this woman was treated with a dopamine agonist (a medication that increases dopamine activity), her Parkinson's drastically improved. Unfortunately, she also suddenly developed a serious gambling condition, which ultimately robbed her of her money, her house, and her marriage. When the medication was discontinued, her gambling problem disappeared.

How does the **dopaminergic reward system** respond to **randomness**?

Additionally, the dopaminergic reward system does not do well with randomness. This system has evolved to detect patterns and still tends to interpret patterns even when no pattern is really there. Consequently, we tend to overestimate our ability to predict future events from past events. We can see this when we consider how people demonstrate frequent overconfidence when picking stocks. If there is a good run in the stock market or in the real estate market, people tend to assume this run will continue forever. In truth, a streak of good luck can end at any time. When we assume that past fortune guarantees future fortune, we make foolish investments. Hence, we become overconfident at our ability to predict future events. This mechanism is a central contributor to financial bubbles.

What **role** does the **amygdala** play?

Amygdala is a critical part of the limbic system. The amygdala is particularly responsive to fearful cues, that is, cues of danger. When amygdala is activated, it stimulates activity in the hypothalamus, which in turn sends messages to the autonomic nervous system. This activates physiological stress responses, such as rapid heart beat, perspiration, shallow breath, etc. The amygdala is highly responsive to cues of financial loss.

Cues signaling immediate danger of loss activate the amygdala. This in turn stimulates an emotional reaction which may or may not reach consciousness, but will nonetheless affect our decision making. This reaction underlies our tendency to loss aversion. Like the nucleus accumbens and the dopaminergic reward system, the amygdala is highly attuned to immediate cues, but not very good at evaluating the meaning of the cues in the context of current and future circumstances. That role falls to the frontal lobe.

What is the role of the **insula**?

The insula is an area of the cortex that is sandwiched between the frontal, parietal, and temporal lobes. It communicates information about our internal bodily states to our cortex. In this way, it contributes to experiences of disgust and pain. The insula is activated when we experience the pain of losing money. For example, activity in the insula increases when we look at the price tags of our purchases and it decreases when we pay with credit cards as opposed to cash.

What **happens** in our **brains** when we make **socially conforming decisions**?

As social animals we feel an extraordinary pull to act within socially condoned ways and we resist behaving in ways that go against the group. In a study conducted by Gregory Burns and reported by the journalist Jason Zweig, people made correct choices in a cognitive test 84 percent of the time when they made the decisions by themselves, but only 59 percent of the time when they were exposed to incorrect decisions made by four peers. When the subjects conformed to the decisions of their peers, there was decreased activation in their prefrontal cortex, perhaps reflecting a reduction in independent thought. However, when they went against group norms, there was increased activation in the amygdala, suggesting a fear response.

GROUP DYNAMICS

Why are **group dynamics important**?

The study of group dynamics is important because *groups* are important. Our relationships with groups pervade almost every aspect of our lives. We are raised in families and educated in schools. Most of us work in a group setting and many of us live in families of our own. Moreover, we all live in a community, belong to one or more ethnic groups, and are categorized into a specific gender. Groups shape our daily life, powerfully influence our identity and self-esteem, and even shape our very perception of the world around us. Consequently, our psychology and the brain that creates it have evolved to promote our participation in groups.

Is a **group larger** than the **sum of its parts**?

The basic assumption of group dynamics is that there are characteristics of the group that cannot be reduced to the behavior of individual group members. In other words, the group has a personality of its own. We can see how this works when we consider that groups persist even after the individual members change. Individual group members may come and go, but the characteristics of the group continue. In effect, this is what is meant by culture; the norms and values and customs of the group—be it an institution, a society, an ethnic group, a religious group, or a corporation—exist apart from the individual members. This is not to say that groups do not change or that individual members do not matter, but that groups can develop an enduring identity and character that is independent of individual members.

How do we **define** a **group**?

There are various ways to define groups. Groups can be defined as a collection of people who share a common fate, who share a social structure, or who engage in face-to-face-interaction. In his 2000 book, Rupert Brown suggests the following definition: a group consists of two or more people who identify themselves as members of the group. Additionally, the group's existence must be recognized by at least one other person who is not a group member.

What role does **social psychology** play in the **study** of **group dynamics**?

Following the almost unimaginable slaughter of WWII, scholars in many fields became preoccupied by the notion of conformity. How could so many otherwise ordinary people participate in the atrocities of the Holocaust? Can the pressure to conform be so powerful that it can account for such extreme behavior? Questions such as these spurred investigation into the behavior of groups. A good deal of research on the structure and behavior of groups has been performed within a branch of psychology known as *social psychology*. Social psychologists conducted research on group norms, group identity, and on conformity. One of the pioneers of group dynamics was a social psychologist named Kurt Lewin (1890–1947).

Did **psychoanalysis** have any **influence** on the **study** of **group dynamics**?

While social psychologists were interested in the uniformity of groups—that is, the way that group members act in concert—some psychoanalysts became interested in the interactions *among* group members. From working in clinical settings, these clinicians recognized that group dynamics influenced the ways people relate to each other. Specifically, they noticed the ways that group members formed alliances with each other, split into different factions, and aligned with, and then rebelled against, group leaders. Wilfred Bion (1897–1979) was a pioneer in this movement. Another influential clinician in the group therapy movement is the psychiatrist Irvin Yalom (1931–).

What is **group identity**?

Group identity refers to the recognition of the group as a distinct unit by both members and nonmembers. Group identity is a critical part of a group's well-being and much of the behavior of a group will serve to promote and maintain group identity. For example, specific rituals, forms of dress, and speech patterns can help distinguish group members from nonmembers and thus promote group identity. We see this with teenage cliques, religious groups, and even military regiments.

This photograph shows Hasidic or ultra-orthodox Jews. Note the distinctive costume, including black felt or fur hats, long black coats, and long side curls, known as peyos. These outfits mark the boundaries between the in-group and the out-group and play a crucial role in maintaining group identity (*Shutterstock*).

How does **group identity** affect **personal identity**?

Individual group members reshape their own individual identity in keeping with their group membership. Our *social identity* is a function of our group memberships. By identifying with certain groups, we state that we share values, goals, and beliefs with that group. Moreover, our self-esteem is impacted by our status and value within the group as well as the group's status in relation to other groups. People who belong to low status or devalued groups suffer damage to their self-esteem. Likewise, people can gain self-esteem by joining a group that values them and/or is valued by others.

What are **group norms**?

Group norms refer to the rules and expectations governing the behavior of members of the group. For example, within a corporate setting, individual group members are expected to dress and act professionally. They should not wear overly casual clothes, engage in illegal behavior, drink alcohol, or behave in explicitly sexual or violent ways. They are expected to display a strong work ethic. In contrast, in adolescent street gangs, group members are expected to show unquestionable loyalty, present themselves as tough and ready for violence, and show little deference to conventional authority.

What happens when group **members violate** group **norms**?

When individual group members violate group norms, the group will act to bring their behavior back into compliance. Consider what would happen to a corporate   303 employee who shows up drunk for work, makes explicitly sexual overtures to his or her colleagues, and then destroys office furniture. The group (in this case the corporation) would act immediately to bring the employee back in line. Either that, or the employee would be expelled.

What is **group cohesion**?

Group cohesion refers to the degree that group members feel identified with and committed to the group. It is a reflection of the closeness and connection of the group as a whole. Cohesive groups have a strong group identity and tightly adhere to group norms. Early social psychologists believed that group cohesion reflected the degree to which individual members like each other. However, later researchers suggested that cohesion reflected the attachment of group members to the *idea* of the group rather than their attachment to specific group members. How much do group members agree with the goals and values of the group? How strongly do they feel about them?

What factors **enhance group cohesion**?

A variety of factors promote group cohesion. These include shared goals that have emotional significance to group members, as well as a history of success in reaching those goals. Leadership styles are also important. Effective leaders attend both to the goals of the group and to the social and emotional needs of the group. Finally, opposition to or contrast with an out-group can also promote group cohesion. In some cases, this can be harmless or even beneficial, as with rivalry between sports teams. However, this tendency can also have negative implications as groups can demonize out-groups or escalate inter-group tensions in an effort to promote group cohesion. This can take the form of racism, prejudice, or even wars.

What function do **initiation rituals** serve?

Initiation rites are found in diverse groups across many different cultures. Before being accepted to the group, an initiate must undergo various trials, most involving some degree of discomfort, pain, and humiliation. Such rites serve to increase initiates' loyalty and obedience to the group and to heighten the boundary between the in-group and the out-group. Social psychologists have theorized about the mechanism behind initiation rites. Some have suggested that *cognitive dissonance* plays a role. This theory, first presented by Leon Festinger in 1957, states that people tend to rationalize away contradictory thoughts. Therefore, an initiate might reason "if I went though all this trouble to join this group, I must really want to get in."

Are there **examples** of **modern initiation rites**?

Anthropologists have long spoken about initiation rites in pre-modern societies. For example, adolescent boys in the Fulani tribe in West Africa engage in whipping battles

Hazing rituals in fraternities can be seen as an example of a modern initiation rite. Pledges, or new initiates, are expected to undergo various trials which can include drinking massive amounts of water or alcohol. Although hazing practices have led to lawsuits and even deaths on occasion, the continuing popularity of this practice speaks to the psychological importance that initiation rites can have for group identity and cohesion (*iStock*).

with other adolescent boys as a rite of passage into adulthood. Related ordeals for adolescent males are found across different tribes in New Guinea. Many rites in modern Western culture may not be recognized as initiation rites per se although they may well serve that function. For example, boot camp in the marines, hazing in fraternities, and thirty-six-hour work shifts for medical residents may function as initiation rites. Initiates must go through painful and often humiliating trials before being accepted into an exclusive group.

How does **group conformity** shape **individual opinions**?

Although we may think we come to our opinions independently, research shows that people are profoundly influenced by group norms at all levels of thought and behavior. People feel tremendous pressure to conform to group norms and feel anxiety when they go against the group. An fMRI study by Gregory Burns showed increased activation in the amygdala when people made non-conforming decisions. The amygdala is a brain region associated with the fear response. Moreover, a large body of social psychology research illustrates how the pressure to conform can influence even our perceptions of physical reality. The presence of four peers stating a consistently wrong opinion can cause subjects to deny even obvious physical facts, for example, to call a color green when it is clearly blue.

305

What are some important experiments that have shown people's tendency to conform to group norms?

Two classic social psychology experiments illustrate the power of group norms. In a pioneering experiment by Muzafer Sherif in 1936, people were exposed to an optical illusion called the autokinetic effect. If you shine a pinprick of light in a completely dark room, the dot of light will appear to move. Sherif asked his subjects to estimate how much the light moved. He first tested people alone and then in groups of two or three. He found that when tested alone, individuals gave very different estimates of the light's movement. In groups, however, people's estimates tended to converge to the same answer. A group norm was formed that shaped people's perception.

In 1956, Solomon Asch published results of another classic experiment. Subjects were recruited to take part in an experiment of visual judgment. They were placed in small groups and shown pictures of several lines. The groups were asked to match a target line with one of three comparison lines. In fact, only one member of the group was an actual subject. The others were part of the experiment, with instructions to unanimously state the wrong answer two-thirds of the time. The real point of the study was to see whether the true study subjects, the "naïve" subjects, would answer correctly when their group members gave the wrong answer or whether they would conform to the group norm and agree to the wrong answer. In fact, the naïve participants did conform to the wrong answer (either fully or in part) 36 percent of the time. This study was important because it showed that people will alter their response according to group norms even when it is clear that the group is objectively wrong.

When is **conformity** most **pronounced**?

Conformity is most pronounced in new or ambiguous situations when people are least confident about their own opinions. When people are more knowledgeable or more secure about their opinions, they are less swayed by group-think. People are also more conformist when their group identity is new or tentative. This is particularly acute in adolescence, when the adolescent's entire social identity is new and insecure. Consider the intense pressure to conform that many adolescents feel regarding their choice of clothing, music, interests, and even friends. Most adults would consider these decisions to be either minor or personal, certainly not a target of intense social pressure.

How do **groups** react to **new ideas**?

In general, groups are conservative and slow to change. They are homeostatic. In other words, they work to regain their former state in the face of change. Consequently, group members tend to be far more responsive to majority opinions than to minority opinions. This has been shown many times in various adaptations of Solomon Asch's classic 1956 conformity experiment.

When does a **nonconformist** develop **influence**?

Groups are not entirely closed to new ideas and there are opportunities for minority influence. If the ideas of the majority are not strongly held and do not carry much personal or emotional weight, the group will be less closed to new ideas and minority opinions. Moreover, if the minority group is consistent in their positions, this has more impact than if they are not consistent. Further, majority influence seems to be most powerful in the immediate aftermath of the discussion and in public settings. As there is social cost to deviance, people tend to conform publicly. However, over time, perhaps when the source of the new ideas has slipped from memory, the new ideas are likely to show more influence. This may explain why totalitarian governments go to so much trouble to stifle dissent. They realize that even unpopular opinions can have considerable impact over time.

Are all **group roles** the **same**?

Although some uniformity of values, behaviors, and viewpoints is necessary within groups, group members are not all interchangeable. In many groups, there is role differentiation. For example, in a work setting, every employee has a specific set of tasks and responsibilities. Group roles are also differentiated according to status and in most groups there is some degree of a status hierarchy. In other words, some roles have more power and prestige than others.

Who was **Wilfred Bion**?

Wilfred Bion (1897–1979) was one of the pioneers of group psychotherapy. A psychoanalyst in the tradition of Melanie Klein (1882–1960), his main point was that the psychology of groups paralleled that of individuals. Like many before him, he was struck by the primitive quality of many group processes, the regressed and emotionally uncontrolled behavior that groups sometimes demonstrate. Using a very dense theory of emotional life, which may look bizarre to the modern reader, he nonetheless provided valuable insights about group dynamics.

Bion believed that the primitive quality of group psychology corresponded to the most primitive aspects of individual psychology. An immature or more primitive mind thinks only in extremes and in opposites (good/bad, love/hate). A mature mind can understand complexity, can see that people are a mix of good and bad. The world exists in shades of gray; it is not just black and white. In the same way that individuals can

307

regress to more immature modes of thinking, groups too can lose track of shades of gray and jump to extremes.

What is meant by **splitting**?

One of Bion's most valuable contributions was the concept of group *splitting*. This refers to the times when groups split into hostile factions that represent different parts of their shared experience. There are many examples of this. The part of the group that wants change can split against the part that wants to stay the same. The followers of one leader split against the followers of a rival. There may be a split between supporters and opponents of a controversial group member. These splits can become very antagonistic and a previously harmonious group can suddenly erupt into civil war. At some point just about everybody will encounter these kinds of splits in their everyday life, perhaps in a work situation, a family conflict, or even within a religious community.

It is important to recognize that these splits reflect a *group dynamic* and are not simply a product of individual behavior. When people can identify fractures like these as a group process instead of the fault of misbehaving individuals, they can reduce the inevitable blaming and finger pointing and work to restore the group's cohesion.

How is **splitting** related to **group polarization**?

Group polarization refers to the tendency of groups to take more extreme positions than individuals do when on their own. This has been attributed to various factors. The role of social pressure is clearly an important factor. Leon Festinger suggested that people compare their own positions with their peers, and then act to avoid deviating from the group norm. This pushes the group as a whole toward more extreme positions. Other researchers, such as Eugene Bernstein and Amiram Vinokur, have suggested that the greater amount of information gathered from group discussions leads groups to be more confident in their opinions than individuals who can only rely on their own knowledge. However, group polarization occurs even when group members do not share information. We can see how the process of group polarization can intensify splitting. Once a fracture has occurred within a group, the two new groups are liable to polarize into extreme positions. This, of course, only strengthens the split.

PREJUDICE AND RACISM

How do we define **prejudice** and **racism**?

Prejudice and racism reflect some of the negative aspects of group psychology. As they have caused enormous suffering across history, it is very important to understand how they work. Prejudice and racism both refer to a negative view of one group of people based solely on their membership in that group. Rupert Brown defines prejudice as a derogatory attitude, negative emotion, or discriminatory behavior toward members of an out-group *because of* membership in that out-group. Racism is a specific form of prejudice, involving prejudicial attitudes or behavior toward members of an ethnic group. The definition of race is somewhat variable, but commonly refers to an ethnic group originating on a specific continent, such as people of African, European, or Asian descent. Social psychologists have long been interested in the phenomenon of prejudice and have contributed much to our understanding of it.

What is **stereotyping** and how does it **relate** to **social prejudice**?

Stereotyping goes hand-in-hand with prejudice. The term *stereotype* as used in social science was first introduced by the journalist Walter Lippman in 1922. Previously, the term had been used in the printing business. When we stereotype people, we attribute a series of traits to them based on the one trait that signals their membership in a particular group. Common contemporary stereotypes are that Asians are hardworking and studious, Hispanics are macho, and that librarians are introverts. By definition, stereotypes are limiting and disregard each person's individuality. They also lend themselves to negative and derogatory assumptions. When that happens, the stereotype blends into prejudice. Certainly, prejudice is highly dependent on stereotypes. You are unlikely to say you hate Hmong Cambodians unless you have some set view of what you think they are like.

How does **our tendency** to **categorize** lend itself to **stereotyping**?

The tendency to classify our experience into categories is a fundamental and universal aspect of human cognition. We create concepts in order to make sense of the endless complexity we encounter in our environment. This is a necessary part of human thought, allowing us to process information efficiently and quickly. If we did not create categories, our entire life would be a buzzing mass of confusion. In social categorization, we place *people* into categories.

Social categorization is a critical part of our social life and is evident as early as infancy. Studies have shown that infants can distinguish people according to their gender, age, and degree of familiarity. People also reflexively distinguish members of in-groups (groups of which the subject is a member) from members of out-groups. Furthermore, people tend to minimize differences *within* groups and to maximize differences between them. Finally, people tend to evaluate out-groups more *negatively* than in-groups. In this way, social categories easily lend themselves to stereotypes in general, and to negative stereotypes in particular.

What impact does **stereotyping** have on people's **reasoning**?

Stereotyping creates automatic and unconscious biases that influence decision making. People frequently do not recognize that they are thinking in a stereotypical way, and assume that their views of various out-groups are based on solid information. Likewise, stereotypes are often quite persistent, even in the face of contradictory information. This occurs because people favor information confirming the stereotype and are more likely to ignore or disregard information contradicting the stereotype.

Furthermore, stereotypes are often self-serving and help people in powerful in-groups rationalize their privileged position relative to less privileged out-groups. For centuries women were depicted as emotional and childish and African Americans as lazy and unintelligent. More recently, homosexuals have been portrayed as sexually predatory (and thus a threat to our schools and our military).

Such views justify the exclusion of these out-groups from power and privilege. Stereotypes are not all powerful, however, and can be somewhat flexible. Our tendency to stereotype can also be shaped by cues in the environment. For example, when research subjects were cued to pay attention to gender, they thought in terms of gender stereotypes. This tendency was less evident when gender cues were removed.

What **impact** does stereotyping have **on the stereotyped**?

The impact of negative stereotyping on the stereotyped is quick, pervasive, and destructive. In laboratory experiments, people can begin to act in concert with their stereotype, even when the stereotype was arbitrarily assigned to them. In real life, when stereotypes are consistently encountered over a lifetime, people can easily internalize the negative messages. In fact, people have to struggle hard *not* to see themselves through the eyes of the stereotyper, and not to act in the way that they are perceived. A famous study by Kenneth and Mamie Clark in the 1940s showed the tragic impact of racial prejudice on the self-concept of African-American children.

How are **intergroup relations** relevant to an understanding of **social prejudice**?

Ultimately, social prejudice is about intergroup relations. People are prejudiced against other people because of their membership in a particular group. Understanding the dynamics of intergroup relations can help shed light on social prejudice.

What are the main **causes** of **intergroup strife**?

This is a difficult question and there have been many theories about the causes of intergroup strife. Unfortunately, there is no one theory that totally accounts for the relationships between different groups. One theory holds that social prejudice stems from frustration caused by deprivation of needed resources. Another view suggests that groups devalue each other when their goals are in conflict. Other research points to the nature of group identity in itself as a contributor to intergroup tension. As soon as people self-identify as part of one group, they tend to think more negatively about other groups.

How did Kenneth and Mamie Clark use dolls to demonstrate the effect of racism on African American children's self-concept?

During research conducted in the 1940s, Kenneth and Mamie Clark investigated the impact of racism on African American children's self-concept. Children were presented with two types of plastic baby dolls. The dolls were identical except for skin color; some were white and some were black. As expected, the children were all able to distinguish the race of the dolls. More importantly, the children tended to prefer the white doll over the black doll, attributing more positive characteristics to the white doll. Furthermore, when asked to draw a self-portrait, many of the children drew themselves with much lighter skin than they actually had. This research was used in the 1954 Supreme Court case *Brown vs. Board of Education*, Topeka, Kansas. In this landmark case, the U.S. Supreme Court declared racial segregation in public schools to be unconstitutional.

Research in the 1940s showed that black children seemed to prefer Caucasian over African American dolls, a finding that helped win a U.S. Supreme Court case that outlawed school segregation (*iStock*).

Is in-group **chauvinism natural**?

Some capacity for favoritism of one's own group over others appears to be a natural human tendency. In many studies, people attribute more positive traits to their own group than to other groups. This has been demonstrated cross-culturally. In 1976 Marilynn Brewer and Donald Campbell published a survey of thirty tribal groups in East Africa. Their subjects had been asked to rate their own tribe and other tribes on a series of traits. Twenty-seven of the thirty groups rated their own group more positively than any other group.

In-group favoritism or chauvinism can also be *created* in experimental research. In a series of classic studies published in the 1950s and 1960s, Muzafer and Carolyn Sherif and their colleagues recruited a group of twelve-year-old boys to attend a summer camp. The boys were divided into two teams which were then pitted against each other in competitive games. Following these games, the boys very clearly displayed in-group chauvinism. They consistently rated their team's performance as superior to that of the other team. Furthermore, 90 percent of the boys identified their best friends from within their own group even though, prior to group assignment, many had best friends in the other group. In some cases, the devaluing of the out-group started immediately after group assignment, even before the competitive games began.

How do **group goals affect** intergroup **relations**?

A major theory of intergroup conflict addresses the role of group goals. When the goals of two groups are in conflict with each other, there is likely to be an escalation of tension. Moreover, group chauvinism will kick in, and people will start to evaluate the other group in exaggeratedly negative terms while idealizing their own group. A number of studies show that perceived conflict of interest between groups heightens both a negative view of the out-group and in-group cohesion. As this tension escalates, the groups further polarize, taking more extreme positions against each other. The out-group becomes evil and badly intentioned, while the in-group remains morally decent and justified in their behavior. We can see this in many political situations, such as the current impasse between the Israelis and the Palestinians, who are fighting over the same land. On the other hand, when groups share goals, inter-group tension and group chauvinism decreases.

Do **shared goals improve** intergroup **relations**?

One important way to decrease intergroup prejudice is to introduce shared goals. In the summer camp experiments mentioned above, when the teams engaged in cooperative efforts toward shared goals, aggression towards the opposite team declined, as did in-group favoritism. Several other studies have shown a similar effect. However, success in meeting shared goals may play an important role. Failure can raise tensions again, especially if there is a prior history of conflict or competition between the groups. It is as if the groups want to blame each other for the failure.

Where does **deprivation** come in?

The earliest theory of intergroup aggression, as presented by John Dollard in 1939, focused on the role of deprivation. Groups grew angry because they felt deprived of their basic needs. This aggression was then expressed either toward the perceived source of their deprivation or toward a convenient target, in other words a scapegoat. Later authors, such as Leonard Berkowitz and Ted Robert Gurr, revised this theory. Intergroup aggression did not arise so much out of *actual* deprivation but more from *relative* deprivation. In other words, it was not how much people had that mattered, but how much they had *relative* to a norm or expectation of how much they *thought* they should have. This notion is consistent with research on the relationship between money and happiness. In either case, our emotional response is less about what we actually have than about what we believe we should have.

How are **norms** of **deprivation** developed?

So how do we develop norms of what we think we should have? To some degree, our norms are based on past experience. Groups whose conditions have deteriorated over time can become aggressive to other groups. A more powerful source of comparison, however, appears to be other groups. Groups who feel deprived relative to other groups around them are likely to become angry, which can lead to civil unrest. Further, in a 1972 paper by Reeve Vanneman and Thomas Pettigrew, a distinction was made between *collective deprivation* and *egoistic deprivation*.

In collective deprivation, people feel that their own group is deprived relative to another group. In egoistic deprivation, people feel deprived as an individual, but not in terms of group membership. Several studies have shown that feelings of collective deprivation are more strongly related to social prejudice. However, *double deprivation*, the feeling that one is deprived both as an individual and as a member of a group, leads to the highest level of social prejudice.

Where does **scapegoating** come in?

When *scapegoating* takes place, a stronger group takes out its aggression on a weaker group. In effect, the group displaces their anger at whatever difficulty they may be experiencing onto a convenient and defenseless target. This process refers to *between-group* scapegoating. Psychoanalytically oriented group theorists also talk about *within-group* scapegoating, which may be a somewhat different matter.

Although scapegoating cannot explain all of social prejudice, we can certainly think of examples when it played an important role. One example would be the rise of Hitler and Nazism in Germany that followed the devastation of World War I. Germany faced defeat, followed by extremely punitive conditions imposed by the Treaty of Versaille; this wrecked the German economy and unnecessarily humiliated a once-proud nation. In an attempt to rebuild German pride and group identity, Hitler used the Jews as a scapegoat, blaming them for all of Germany's troubles. The result was the Holocaust.

In another example of scapegoating, a 1940 study by Carl Hovland and Robert Sears looked at the relationship between the price of cotton and the number of lynchings of African Americans that took place in the American South between 1882 and 1930. A negative or inverse correlation was found: the number of lynchings increased as the economy declined.

How do we **reduce social prejudice**?

Given our diverse and multi-ethnic world, it is of great importance to understand ways to reduce social prejudice. In the 1950s, Gordon Allport introduced the intergroup-contact hypothesis. In this view, intergroup contact under positive conditions can reduce social prejudice. The necessary conditions include cooperation toward shared goals, equal status between groups, and the support of local authorities and cultural norms. Considerable research since then has supported these ideas. In a 2003 review, Stephen Wright and Donald Taylor also noted the effectiveness of identification with a *superordinate group*. In other words, different groups can come together as part of one overarching group, for example, as part of one community or of a common humanity.

A man marches to protest racism in schools. Research shows that inter-group tensions can be reduced by granting groups equal social status, sharing goals, and getting support from local authorities (*iStock*).

Do cross-group **friendships reduce** social **prejudice**?

Positive emotional experiences with members of different groups can also reduce negative stereotypes. Having close friends from different groups is especially effective in this regard. There may be several reasons for this. For one, it is near impossible to hold onto a simplistic, negative stereotype of someone you know well. Secondly, a close relationship promotes identification with the other person and of the groups they belong to. In other words, your relationships with other people become part of who you are. This is referred to as *including the other in the self*, a notion introduced by Stephen Wright, Arthur Aron, and colleagues.

MORALITY

How do **psychologists understand morality**?

Morality involves judgments between right and wrong. Morality is determined both by our reason, that is, by our cognitive analysis, and by our emotional response. Psychology tries to bring a scientific vantage point to the study of morality. Instead of determining what is and what is not moral—the *content* of moral decisions—psychological research studies the process of moral decisions and judgments. How do people determine what is and what is not morally acceptable?

Can **psychology determine** what **moral choices** should be?

In short—no. It is not the place of science to make moral decisions. Morality is ultimately about value, about what is right and what is wrong. Psychology is a science and therefore does not deal in the realm of value. That is the role of philosophy or of religion. However, psychology can provide information on how various behaviors affect other people, on the psychological impact of various choices. This information, in turn, can allow individuals and society to make *informed* moral decisions. Relatedly, we can study the process of moral choices and moral development; how people make moral decisions, what morality means to different people. Hopefully this can also help people enhance their moral decision-making abilities, so that they make more thoughtful, mature, and beneficial moral decisions.

How does **morality relate** to the **social group**?

Without morality, group life would not be possible. Morality is what holds groups together. It is the glue. If everybody simply acted out of self-interest with no concern either for other people or for the wellbeing of the group at large, the group would quickly dissolve into a free-for-all. Human beings have evolved with powerful self-protective and self-promoting motivations and drives. A good part of our motivations are entirely selfish; our desires, angers, and fears serve to promote our own individual interests, often at the expense of other people. Sometimes this erupts in horrific exploitation of, or even violence against, others. On the other hand, humans have also evolved as social animals. We are powerfully oriented toward social organization and most of our emotions serve social functions. Along with our self-serving motivations, we have also evolved moral capacities. Some sense that we must balance our own interest with the interests of others is deeply encoded in our genes.

In what ways does **morality** have an **evolutionary basis**?

Early students of morality, such as Jean Piaget (1896–1980) and Lawrence Kohlberg (1927–1987), focused on the intellectual aspect of moral development. They studied the role of reason in moral judgments. Carol Gilligan protested this narrow focus and emphasized the importance of compassion and caring. More recent psychologists, such as Steven Pinker, emphasize an evolutionary approach to human morality. In a 2008 article, Pinker noted that some of our most strongly held moral positions may not have any basis in reasoning or compassion. For example, many people react in horror when hearing scenarios in which an adult brother and sister engage in mutually consensual incest, a dog owner eats the family dog after it has died from natural causes, or a homeowner cuts up the American flag to use as a dust rag. (These scenarios were first described by the psychologist Jonathan Haidt.)

From research such as this, psychologists have concluded that evolution has inscribed in us the tendency to react with emotional disgust or horror at certain classes of situations. Such situations have evolutionary significance and involve behaviors that, over time, are destructive to our species. For example, the incest taboo is observed in many animal species and serves to protect variability in the gene pool. An aversion to eating members of our own family (and our pets become part of our family) has obvious benefits for kinship survival. In effect, we have evolved certain moral instincts.

What are the **five categories** of **moral instincts**?

Cross-cultural research has shown consistent themes to moral judgments, even across very different cultures. Jonathan Haidt suggested five general categories of moral concerns. These are *harm/care, ingroup/loyalty, authority/respect, purity/sanctity*, and *fairness/reciprocity*. Across cultures, people express disapproval and distress at the thought of harm coming to an innocent person. Betrayal of one's community is likewise judged negatively. A respect for authority and the value of fair treatment for members of the community also appear to be cultural universals. The purity/sanctity category relates to the emotion of disgust and involves moral judgments about dietary laws, sexual practices, urination, defecation, and other similar issues.

How do we account for the **extreme variation** in the **moral beliefs** of people?

It does not take much life experience to recognize that human beings can disagree passionately about moral choices. Contemporary debates about abortion and gay marriage show that people can hold completely opposite viewpoints with equal degrees of moral conviction. One way of understanding this is to assume that different people and different groups vary in the way they rank the five categories. For example, respect for authority is more highly valued in collectivist cultures than in individualist cultures, which might in turn prioritize fairness. This can explain the intense cultural divide between traditional Islamic cultures and Western European cultures over the 2005 controversy regarding a Danish cartoon about the prophet Mohammed. The Islamic side felt it was a moral transgression for the cartoonist to ridicule the Islamic prophet (authority/respect and ingroup/loyalty), while the Europeans felt the cartoonist had a moral right to free expression (fairness/reciprocity) without fear of violence (harm/care).

Do **political liberals** and **conservatives differ** in the way they understand **morality**?

Attitudes toward the five categories of moral concerns may also influence political beliefs. In a large Website-based study, Jonathan Haidt and colleagues found that, when

How has morality changed over the course of history?

Despite scientific evidence of a universal human tendency toward moral judgments, views on morality have changed dramatically across history. Things we now consider to be horribly immoral were not always seen that way. The ancient Greeks based their morality on the concept of honor, which was related to one's reputation for bravery and strength. In the quest for honor, it was perfectly acceptable to slaughter whole cities. More recently, in fact well into the nineteenth century, slavery was not considered immoral in the United States. Moreover, behavior once seen as highly immoral is no longer seen that way by many people. Pre-marital sex was seen as highly immoral only a few decades ago and now is widely considered acceptable. Likewise, there is far more tolerance of public disagreement with people in authority than there used to be. If we consider these changes in light of Jonathan Haidt's five moral categories, we can see that within Western society considerations of fairness/reciprocity have grown stronger while considerations of authority/respect and ingroup/loyalty have lessened.

The death of Hector.

An illustration of the Greek hero Achilles defeating Hector in battle. In ancient times, morality was based on concepts of honor, and killing other people was often seen as an honorable thing to do. That stands in stark contrast to today's sense of morality (*iStock*).

liberals and conservatives were compared with each other, liberals valued harm/care and fairness/reciprocity more than conservatives did, and conservatives valued authority/respect, ingroup/loyalty, and purity/sanctity more than liberals did. These differences held even after accounting for the effects of age, gender, education, and income.

How does **morality relate** to the **capacity** to **reason**?

The ability to analyze a situation with reason, or cognition, is a critical part of moral judgments. Earlier theorists of moral development, such as Piaget and Kohlberg, 317

If the only way to save five workmen on a trolley track is to divert the trolley onto another track, thus killing just one man on that track, would you divert the trolley? (*iStock*)

emphasized the importance of cognitive development in moral maturity. Two specific cognitive skills include: the ability to take another person's perspective (that is to put yourself in another's shoes), and the ability to recognize abstract rules that can be generalized across many situations. Similar ideas are reflected in many philosophers' ideas about morality. For example, Immanuel Kant (1724–1804), a famous German philosopher, introduced the concept of the *categorical imperative*, which refers to the importance of recognizing universally valid rules of behavior. Certainly the Golden Rule, to "do unto others as you would have them do unto you," assumes that we can take another person's perspective. As developmental psychologists have shown, these cognitive abilities develop slowly across childhood and continue to develop across adulthood. Because children have an immature capacity for either abstraction or perspective taking, they are not held to the same moral standards as adults.

How does **morality** relate to **empathy**?

Empathy is also a central part of our moral reactions. Our ability to feel another's pain, and to imagine our own pain if put in the same situation, underlies our concern for the well-being of others. People who are deficient in empathy, such as psychopaths or some people with autistic traits, can behave in immoral ways. The extent to which either empathy or rational analysis influences our moral decisions depends on the situation. If we have direct, personal contact with the people affected by our decisions, we are much more likely to be influenced by empathy and emotion than if we have

318

What is the "trolley problem"?

A series of studies have been done on the "trolley problem", which is a moral dilemma first thought up by the philosophers Philippa Foot and Judith Jarvis Thomson. The scenario involves a trolley that is hurtling down the track out of control after the trolley driver has become unconscious. If nothing is done, the trolley will hit five workmen on the tracks who don't see the oncoming trolley. You can save the workmen by throwing a switch that will divert the trolley onto another track. However, there is one workman on the other track. Will you throw the switch, sacrificing one man to save five others?

In these circumstances, most people say yes. From a purely rational standpoint, it makes sense. However, if the only way to save the five workmen is to throw a large man in front of the trolley, most people say they would not do it. When we have close contact with the person we are hurting, our moral decisions are likely to be based more on emotion than on reason alone. Likewise, when people considered these two scenarios during fMRI brain imaging, different parts of the brain lit up for each scenario.

less immediate contact with them, if the people involved feel more abstract. Research on the "Trolley Problem" has shown us how much circumstances influence whether empathy or reason will dominate our moral decisions.

What **parts** of the **brain** are involved in **moral responses**?

As discussed above, moral judgments involve both emotions and cognition, and the importance of either one will depend on the particular circumstances involved. Joshua Greene, Jonathan Cohen, and colleagues asked people to consider the trolley problem and similar scenarios while undergoing fMRI brain imaging. The authors divided their moral dilemmas into *moral-personal* and *moral-impersonal* scenarios.

The trolley scenario that required killing someone directly (i.e., pushing the large man in front of the trolley) is an example of a moral-personal scenario. The trolley problem that did not demand direct, physical contact with the man who would be killed (i.e., pulling the switch) is an example of a moral-impersonal scenario. When people thought about moral-personal scenarios, the medial frontal and anterior cingulate regions lit up. The medial frontal region is associated with the processing of interpersonal relations and, possibly, empathy. The anterior cingulate is associated with processing conflicting messages from different parts of the brain. When people considered the moral-impersonal scenarios, the dorsolateral frontal regions were most active. The dorsolateral frontal region is involved with rational thought and analysis.

319

This suggests that the farther away we are from the human cost of our actions, the more our moral decisions are based on cold rational analysis, rather than gut emotion. These kind of rational moral decisions are known as *utilitarian judgments*, and involve a kind of cost/benefit analysis.

At what **age** do children **start understanding moral issues**?

Children start showing a rudimentary sense of moral understanding around four years old, during the preschool years. Their initial sense of right and wrong is quite crude, and based mainly on what adults tell them or what behavior has brought punishment. A few years later, when children are about seven, they begin to grasp the importance of universal rules to govern behavior. Initially, they apply rules in simplistic and rigid ways ("Ooh, you said 'stupid'! You're not supposed to say 'stupid'!"). With time, they develop a better understanding of the purpose that rules serve. Nonetheless, some capacity to respond to the feelings of others is evident as early as infancy, and even four-year-olds can distinguish between prohibitions that serve a true moral purpose, such as protecting people from harm, and those that simply express a preference, such as not sitting on the couch.

What is **Lawrence Kohlberg's approach** to **moral development**?

Kohlberg (1927–1987) was a pioneer in the field of moral development. Influenced by Jean Piaget, he developed a large body of research investigating moral reasoning. Like Piaget, he was interested in intellectual development, in the way that the ability to reason changes across development. Kohlberg relied on a method of vignettes. He wrote up scenarios that involved a moral dilemma and presented them to his research subjects. His best known vignette involves a man named Heinz who broke into a pharmacy to steal a drug in order to save his wife's life. Based on his research, Kohlberg divided moral development into three levels, *pre-conventional, conventional,* and *post-conventional.* Each level contains two stages, for a total of six stages altogether.

The first level, *pre-conventional morality*, is most commonly found in children under ten. In this level, morality is determined by the consequences of the action to the person performing the behavior—whether the individual is punished or rewarded. In the second level, *conventional morality*, the morality of a behavior is determined by its effect on social relationships. The third and final level is called *post-conventional morality*. In this stage, the person is interested in abstract concepts of justice and a just society. Kohlberg believed that all children go through the same sequence of stages in the same order. A fair amount of research supports this view for the first two levels, but the scientific evidence for the third level is much weaker. Kohlberg was also interested in moral reasoning in adults. Indeed, research has shown that different adults are characterized by different stages of moral development.

Why is it so easy to rationalize immoral behavior?

Financier Bernie Madoff perpetrated the largest Ponzi scheme in history. Although Madoff was a widely respected member of his community and a devoted family man, he defrauded friends, family, colleagues, and many charities of approximately $50 billion. Did Madoff justify his behavior to himself as he did it? We do not know, but we can imagine he might well have. We do know, however, that people rationalize and justify their moral transgressions all the time. In fact, the very nature of cognition makes it inherently easy to justify behavior that is clearly against our moral code.

Cognition is never isolated from emotion. Emotion slants every thought we have and does so largely outside of consciousness. In other words, emotions bias our interpretation of events; we tend to interpret emotionally significant events in ways that are consistent with our emotions. Moreover, desire colors our thoughts as much as any other

A disgraced Bernard Madoff is led away by federal agents after being charged with creating a Ponzi scheme to rip off his customers of billions of dollars. How might an already successful, respected man like Madoff explain his behavior to himself? (*AP/WideWorld*)

emotion. If we want something to be true, we often convince ourselves it is true. That's why it is generally necessary to have some form of external check on our behavior; few people are up to the task of policing themselves.

How did **Carol Gilligan challenge Kohlberg**'s approach to moral development?

Carol Gilligan believed that Kohlberg's theory was biased by an exclusively masculine viewpoint. She suggested that his emphasis on abstract thought and impersonal laws reflected a typically masculine bias to favor thought over emotion. Gilligan claimed that women are more likely to emphasize emotions and interpersonal relationships than men and, therefore, more likely to score at stage 3 (the first stage in conventional morality). This did not mean that women were less moral than men, only that they made moral judgments in different ways. In effect, women made moral choices "in a different voice", which was the title of her 1982 book. While Gilligan's critique raises important points about Kohlberg's exclusive focus on intellect, she also has been criticized for oversimplifying the female style of moral reasoning. Other research has shown that women are no more likely to score at stage 3 than men. In general, both women and men take issues of justice and empathy into account when making moral decisions.

PSYCHOLOGY IN THE WORKPLACE

How do **group dynamics impact** the **workplace**?

It is in the workplace where we are perhaps most exposed to the ups-and-downs of group dynamics. Office politics, issues of leadership, productivity, and staff morale–all of these reflect group processes. The field of study that specializes in group dynamics in the workplace is known as organizational psychology.

What is an **organization**?

An organization is a group of people who join together in an organized manner for a common purpose. Although this can refer to any group united in a common purpose (for example, a religious, social, or community organization), in this context *organizations* refer to those groups that unite for the purpose of paid work.

How do **organizations differ**?

Organizations vary in two important ways: size and degree of hierarchy. Organizations can be very small (like a five-person start-up company), or enormous (like an international conglomerate with a workforce of thirty thousand people). Small organizations tend to be more informally organized, while larger organizations depend on greater standardization of policies and procedures. Organizations also vary in terms of the degree of hierarchy. In nonhierarchical organizations, there is no power differential between members. An example of this would be a cooperative or a Quaker religious community. In these entirely nonhierarchical organizations, decisions are made by consensus only. The decision is not made until the entire organization comes to agreement.

Hierarchical organizations organize decision making and power vertically. Subordinates report to superiors, who in turn report to their own superiors. This chain continues up the hierarchy until the very top. Strongly hierarchical organizations include the U.S. military and the Catholic church. Most work organizations fall somewhere between these two extremes. However, the majority of large commercial organizations have a fairly hierarchical structure.

What is **organizational psychology**?

Organizational psychology is the study of human behavior and relationships within work organizations. Organizational psychologists study how the structure of an organization influences company performance, productivity, and morale, as well as worker-worker relationships. While organizational psychologists are interested in individual traits and behaviors, they are also interested in the larger picture—how the group dynamics of organizations impact the organization's performance. Because large corporations have been the most frequent consumers of this kind of information, most organizational psychology research has been conducted in fairly traditional corporate environments. Nonetheless, the insights of organizational psychology can be fruitfully applied to a large array of work environments.

What are the **classic theories** of **organization**?

Classic theories of organizational psychology date back to the late nineteenth century. Writing in an age of massive industrialization, early theorists of organizational structure aimed to replicate the precision of a finely tuned machine. Frederick Winslow Taylor (1856–1915) introduced the notion of *scientific management*. He believed that the methods of empirical science should be adapted to engineer efficiency in the workplace. His work influenced the development of factory assembly lines. Another pioneer in this arena was Max Weber (1864–1920), a renowned German sociologist. While Taylor focused on the structure of tasks, Weber focused on the authority structure. Weber idealized the precision and control of a hierarchically organized bureaucracy. His aim was to standardize worker behavior and company policies into a completely impersonal, rule-bound system.

What about the **human element**?

Both Weber's and Taylor's organizational models treated the workplace as a machine. Workers were cogs in a wheel; their motivation and morale were of little importance to the functioning of the workplace. In fact, Taylor believed that workers had no intrinsic motivation to work. Rather, their performance could only be motivated by carrots (specifically, pay) and sticks (negative consequences for undesirable behavior). Likewise, Weber emphasized the rational and impersonal nature of bureaucratic rules as an antidote to irrational, emotional impulses.

A movement arose in reaction to this dramatically dehumanizing model. The *human relations approach* recognized that people are motivated by their emotional and social needs as well by monetary rewards. Organizations that neglect the human element miss out on a huge part of what makes people tick. The surprise results of a famous series of experiments known as the *Hawthorne studies* gave birth to this movement. Nonetheless, while a focus on emotional experiences of workers succeeded in raising worker morale, studies showed that it had little effect on productivity. A later version of this approach, the *neo-human relations school*, recognized that managers have to attend both to task performance and to the social-emotional aspects of work life.

What is the "Hawthorne Effect"?

In the 1920s and 1930s, a series of studies was carried out in the Hawthorne factory of the Western Electric Company in Chicago. The experiment was conducted from the vantage point of Frederick Winslow Taylor's theory of scientific management. The experimenters manipulated working conditions in a number of ways to determine what conditions would best enhance productivity. They attended to the temperature and level of humidity in the room, the hours worked, the amount of sleep the workers had, their meals, and various other variables.

After a year or two of this, performance greatly improved. This was at first attributed to the experimental manipulations (e.g., changing the level of light in the room). However, when working conditions were returned to their original state, the improvement continued. The experimenters finally realized that the improvement in worker performance was due less to changes in task conditions than to the human element inherent in the studies. While conducting these studies, the experimenters continually consulted the workers and paid careful attention to almost every detail of their work life. Because of this, workers felt valued and empowered, which greatly enhanced their work performance.

What does a **systems approach** involve?

The systems approach draws from Ludwig von Bertolanffy's 1967 work on general systems theory. In this view, organizations are seen more like living organisms than like machines. A system is a whole made up of interacting parts. Systems are composed of interacting subsystems (e.g., departments, divisions, work groups, teams). It is the relationships between the subsystems that make up the structure of the system. Therefore systems theory is particularly focused on *relationships* among individuals and groups within the work setting. While the classic organizational theories assumed that all members of the organization shared the same goals, systems approaches recognize that different subsystems can have very different interests and agendas.

What about **office politics**?

Although questions of productivity may be of most interest to upper management, most employees are interested in the daily life of the workplace. Office politics marks an inescapable and sometimes very difficult part of such day-to-day work life. In their 1998 review, Erik Andriessen and Pieter Drenth discuss the *multiple parties model*, which came of age in the 1970s and was influenced by a Marxist theory of management-worker relations. This approach emphasizes the competition for power that often goes on within an organization.

Where does **power** come in?

Power offers numerous privileges, in particular, greater control over one's life, which is highly correlated with life satisfaction. Power also offers social status, which for many people is an end in itself. There are several avenues to power in the workplace, including control over the distribution of rewards and punishments (authority), professional expertise, or the use of personal charm. Because the pursuit of power is such a potent and frequent motivator, there is often competition between different subsystems over access to power, or even access to the symbols of power.

Consider how different departments or divisions can fight over office space, control over budgets, hiring decisions, and even status symbols such as the corner office. Of course, such competition can occur among smaller units within these subsystems, such as individuals or coalitions of individuals. Likewise, in pursuit of power or in an attempt to maintain power, people frequently build alliances and coalitions. One's network of alliances is a powerful tool within office politics. However, it is important to recognize that much of this maneuvering is not conscious, and deliberate calculation may play a small part of this behavior.

Does the **degree of hierarchy affect** the motivation for **power**?

We can speculate that the quest for power is heightened in strongly hierarchical systems. When power differentials are more acute, people become more aware of having less power than other people and are more disturbed by their relative lack of power. As we know from a broad range of research, whether people are satisfied or dissatisfied with what they have is strongly impacted by social comparison, by the contrast between what they have and what others around them have.

How **important** is **leadership**?

Leaders are certainly important and a large body of literature shows how leaders can impact absenteeism, morale, turnover, group productivity, decision making, and even company profits. However when considering group performance, the qualities of the leader do not tell the whole story. Sometimes groups are largely autonomous, functioning with very little active leadership. Sometimes external factors, such as organizational structure and culture or larger economic conditions, can constrain a leader's impact.

Are there certain **personality traits** that make a **better leader**?

Earlier research studied the personality traits that contributed to effective leadership. Ultimately this research came up empty handed. The data was simply too contradictory to lead to any firm conclusions about what kinds of personality traits make for a better leader. What does seem important, however, is the fit between *leadership style* and the nature of the task. Different kinds of leadership are necessary in different situations.

Napoleon leads his troops in Egypt. Research is not clear about what qualities make a good leader, though charismatic leaders can be effective in times of turmoil (*iStock*).

What role does **charisma** play?

A repeated theme since the early days of Max Weber is the notion of the charismatic leader. A charismatic personality is not necessary in most managerial situations, but can come in handy in times of turmoil when workers need to be inspired and reassured about the need for significant changes in their values, goals, and group norms. This kind of leadership has been called *transformational* leadership.

What is the difference between **task-oriented** and **socio-emotional leadership** styles?

A task-oriented leader focuses on the most efficient ways to accomplish the goals of the group, whether that is to maximize sales, treat patients in a hospital, or produce the greatest number of widgets. The task-oriented leader does this by clarifying the group's goals, delineating each worker's responsibilities, and addressing any barriers to goal completion. A socioemotional leader addresses the overall morale of the group members. This includes consideration of group cohesion and morale, the emotions and needs of individual workers, and within-group relationships. Research shows that task orientation promotes efficiency, whereas a socio-emotional focus promotes worker satisfaction. However, worker satisfaction and worker performance are not always related. Therefore, most organizational psychologists conclude that leaders should attend to the demands of the task *and* to the socio-emotional needs of the work group.

How **important** is **structure** in the workplace?

One of the tasks of the leader is to create structure. Structure is a critical part of any organization, which needs rules, policies, and clear roles in order to function. However, it is quite difficult to achieve the right balance between structure and flexibility. Not enough structure prevents efficient, coordinated efforts toward the group's goals. It can also result in chaos, corruption, and abuse of power. Too much structure leaves the organization inflexible and poorly adapted to change or to variability in local conditions. Because of this, a parallel underground system can develop outside the rules of the formal structure. This is similar to the black markets that develop in countries whose economies are overly controlled.

How much should decision-making **power** be **shared**?

The extent to which decision making is shared with subordinates or concentrated at the top of the hierarchy differs across organizations. Thus, organizations can vary from strongly centralized decision-making practices to highly participatory decision-making practices. In participatory decision making, subordinates have much more input into how decisions are made. Research shows that greater participation in decision making improves employees' satisfaction with the decisions, but does not necessarily translate into better group performance. Therefore, research has investigated when participatory decision making is most useful, and when it is less important. When the workers are highly educated, intelligent, and have considerable expertise in their areas, participatory decision making is more effective. Additionally, when the task at hand is highly complex and knowledge about local conditions is important to the decision, participatory decision making is important. Finally, in times of crisis, when the decisions have very strong impact, participatory decision making is useful.

What did one study tell us about the fit between different **leadership styles** and different **decision-making conditions**?

In a 1973 publication, Victor Vroom and Philip Yetton considered the circumstances in which autocratic versus participatory decision making styles would be most effective. They believed that there is no one-size-fits-all leadership style, but that leaders have to adapt to different situations. They listed seven characteristics that might influence a decision, such as the amount of information needed to make the decision, the significance of the decision, employee support for the decision, and other related issues. They then made a decision tree based on the seven characteristics, resulting in 12 possible situations. For each situation, they listed which of five decision-making styles (AI, AII, CI, CII, or GI) would be appropriate. CII was listed for 9 of the 12 situations, while CI and GII were appropriate for 7 out of 12. Interestingly, the most autocratic styles, AI and AII, were only appropriate for three and five situations, respectively. In sum, this work suggests that consultative styles are appropriate for a broader array of circumstances than are autocratic styles.

Leadership Styles	
Autocratic I—AI	Leader makes decisions with out inquiries from subordinates
Autocratic II—AII	Leader makes decisions with inquiries of select subordinates
Consultative I—CI	Leader makes decisions after consulting all individual group members
Consultative II—CII	Leader makes decisions after consulting with the group as a whole
Group Method II—GII	Group makes the decision with leader as a participant

What **motivates** employees?

In his theory of scientific management, Frederick Winslow Taylor took an early behaviorist approach to motivation. He did not believe that employees had any intrinsic motivation to work, rather that people would only work for rewards (such as pay) or punishments (such as fear of being fired). The human relations approach considered the emotional and social needs of employees. Later organizational psychologists recognized that human motivation is complex. Influenced by Abraham Maslow's hierarchy of needs, various theorists came up with multifaceted theories of employees' motivational needs. In 1972, Clayton Alderfer proposed a three-part model of worker motivation: existence needs (basic physical needs), relatedness needs (for social connection and support), and growth needs (for realizing their own potential, similar to Maslow's self-actualization needs). In 1983, Wofford and Srinivasan suggested that worker performance reflected four factors: competence, motivation, role perception, and the limitations determined by the setting. A manager's job would be to address each issue as it became relevant.

What was **Frederick Hertzberg's approach** to motivation?

In 1959, Frederick Hertzberg (1923–2000) and colleagues published their survey of two hundred mid-level engineers and accountants in a Pennsylvania company. The subjects were asked about the high points and the low points of their work life. For high points, subjects frequently listed moments of accomplishment and recognition, increased challenge, promotion to a higher level of responsibility, and increased autonomy. For low points, subjects complained of problems with managerial and policy decisions of the company, recognition, salary, and relations with superiors.

Hertzberg interpreted these results to mean that causes of job satisfaction were *intrinsic* to the job (inherent within the work itself) while causes of job dissatisfaction were *extrinsic* (due to context). He integrated these insights into his *two-factor theory* of worker motivation, also known as the *motivation-hygiene theory*. Over the years, the study was repeated multiple times in different settings.

A consistent finding was that people attributed positive outcomes to intrinsic or internal causes (self-caused) and negative outcomes to extrinsic or external causes. In other words, we credit ourselves for our successes and blame others for our disappointments. Hertzberg's findings have been highly influential in organizational psychology.

What are some **dos and don'ts** that **managers** should adhere to?

Drawing from the literature on organizational psychology, group dynamics, and family systems, we can put together a list of pointers:

Manager Dos

Identify and support appropriate boundaries in your work group:

- Clarify sub-system boundaries. Identify each employee's responsibilities and clarify boundaries between different employees' roles, responsibilities, and decision making domains.
- Maintain in-group and out-group boundaries. Provide the buffer between your work group and outside systems.
- Clarify group hierarchy. Be clear about who makes what decision and who reports to whom.

Recognize positive behavior:

- Reward positive behavior. Verbal praise goes a long way. Over time, however, employees will need more than just verbal praise, such as increased pay and opportunities for growth and advancement.

Make sure employees' responsibility is proportionate to their control:

- Nothing causes burn-out quicker than responsibility without control.

Listen to your employees:

- Information needs to flow upstream as well as downstream. Solicit your employees' opinions and try to make them feel comfortable coming to you with problems.

Manager Don'ts

Pick favorites:

- Personal preferences are unavoidable but shouldn't affect your behavior toward subordinates. Rewards and punishments should be keyed to employees' behavior, not your likes and dislikes. The group needs the manager's behavior to feel predictable and fair.

Avoid setting limits when needed:

- If an employee is out of line, the manager has to respond and bring the employee's behavior back into line. Don't be afraid to be the bad guy or not to be liked.

If your behavior is fair and appropriate, in time it will be appreciated by all involved, even if the employee in question is unhappy in the moment. If you fail to set the necessary limits, the group as a whole will suffer and you will lose favor with your group.

Undermine group hierarchy:

- To the extent that a hierarchy is defined in your group, it should be followed. Do not undermine a supervisor by granting inappropriate power to his or her subordinates. If someone needs to be promoted, change the hierarchy formally.

Jump to conclusions when something goes wrong:

- Make sure you investigate the situation so you can diagnose the problem and assign responsibility fairly. Don't let your prejudices about different employees lead to unfair assumptions about what went wrong.

How are different **personality types suited** for different types of **jobs**?

There is a large body of research examining how different personality types fit different types of jobs. *The Strong-Campbell Interest Inventory* is a well known test that aims to match personal interests, personality types, and occupational choice. This and similar tests are used in vocational counseling to help people decide on a career direction. According to their interests, people are characterized according to six personality dimensions: realistic, investigative, artistic, social, enterprising, and conventional (RIASEC). The pattern of test scores is then matched to professions whose members have similar patterns of test scores. For example, mechanics and construction workers score high on realistic, biologists and social scientists score high on investigative, and clinical psychologists and high school teachers score high on social. Newer adaptations of this test, such as the Campbell Interest and Skill Survey and the Strong Interest Inventory, have also been developed.

What is the **Myers-Briggs Personality Test**?

Developed by Isabel Briggs Myers and her mother Katharine Briggs and first published in 1962, the Myers-Briggs Type Indicator has become very popular in occupational settings. Based on Carl Jung's theory of personality types, the Myers-Briggs classifies people into one of sixteen personality types depending on their scores on four dichotomies (pairs of opposites).

The first dichotomy, extraversion (E) vs. introversion (I), measures the degree to which someone is oriented toward the external, social world or toward their own inner thoughts and reflections. The second dimension, sensing (S) vs. intuition (N), refers to the way people gather information: Do they focus on concrete facts, or do they try to organize information into patterns? The third dimension, thinking (T) vs. feeling (F), relates to the way people make decisions: Do they focus more on facts and principles or on interpersonal concerns? The final dimension, judging (J) vs. perceiving (P), relates to the way that people come to closure: Do they prefer to come to a decision, or do they prefer to keep their options open, continuing to gather new information?

The sixteen personality types are identified by their initials (e.g., ENTJ, INFP, ESFJ) and have been linked to specific occupations. For example, people who score high on extraversion (E) might make good salespeople while people who score high on sensing (S) might make good mechanics. Although this test makes good intuitive sense—that is, it appears to make sense–it has been criticized as lacking adequate scientific validation. Despite these criticisms, the test remains very popular in many settings.

What are the **personality traits** of people who **succeed** in their professions?

Many factors contribute to one's degree of success in a career. Some of these are external, such as opportunity, education, economic conditions, and professional connections. However, there is evidence that certain personality traits also contribute to success. In a 2001 study of 291 Romanian engineers by Marcela Rodika Luca, creativity and self-management were better predictors of success than intelligence. Moreover, intelligence was more closely related to academic than professional success. Of course, the sample was already self-selected for a high level of intelligence. Therefore, in jobs demanding high intellectual ability, after a certain level of intelligence is met, additional intelligence may not add much to the mix.

Several studies have addressed *success orientation*, suggesting that people who want success aim for it, plan how to achieve it, and are willing to work for it. Additionally, based on the many studies that highlight the importance of human relations, *good interpersonal skills* are clearly important in the workplace. Finally, *internal locus of control*, the tendency to believe one has the power to affect one's situation, also contributes to success. Research has shown that when people believe they have control over their life circumstances, they are more likely to take action to reach their goals. In contrast, people with an *external locus of control* tend to be more passive.

What are some **dos and don'ts** for **employees**?

Drawing from the research literature, here is a list of survival tips for employees:

- **Remember you are part of a system.** You do not exist in isolation; you are part of a large network that exists to serve the interests of the organization, whether that be making widgets, serving meals, or cutting hair. Your behavior affects other people just as their behavior affects you.

- **Understand what is expected of you and do it to the best of your ability.** This may seem obvious but it is surprisingly easy to forget.

- If there is a problem with completing your responsibilities, let your supervisor know. Don't hide your deficits out of fear of looking bad. Most supervisors will be willing to work with you if you need extra support or education, or if there's a problem in the system that interferes with your job. But no one likes unnecessary surprises.
- Try to see situations from other points of view. This will reduce conflict with co-workers and supervisors.
- Address your needs, preferences, and complaints from the point of view of a member of a system. You need X, Y, or Z in order to do your job and be a productive member of the group. Do not say you need them because you're you, you're special, or you're smarter than everybody else.
- Address conflict in behavioral terms. "When you don't return my e-mails, I am unable to complete my assignments on time." Try not to personalize, scapegoat, or practice character assassination. Just the facts, Ma'am.
- Try to keep conflict between you and the co-worker in question or take it to your supervisor. Try not to triangulate in your buddies so you can all make snide comments about your new enemy.
- In the face of office politics, try to separate out the temporary noise from your job responsibilities. If you stick to doing your job, you will most likely end up all right.

PSYCHOLOGY IN THE PUBLIC SPHERE

What **role** can **psychology** play in the **public sphere**?

Traditionally, psychology focused on the private life of the individual, but over time the field has broadened its scope. From Wilhelm Wundt's (1832–1920) studies of perception in the late nineteenth century, psychology has moved to the study of the group, as seen, for example, in social and organizational psychology. More recently, psychology has moved into the public sphere, conducting studies on the personalities of politicians, voting behavior, and even ballot design.

Do **politicians** have particular **personality traits**?

Although there has not been much empirical research into the personality traits of politicians, there has certainly been a lot of commentary on this topic from psychoanalysts and other clinicians. The extensive media coverage of the lives of politicians provides ample opportunity for clinicians to make inferences about their psychological traits. The information in the media shares many similarities with the kind of information that psychotherapists gain from their patients during the course of treatment. Notably, the conclusions that different clinicians draw are quite similar. One of the most common traits that clinicians talk about is that of narcissism, maybe because the most active media coverage of politicians follows scandals.

What is **narcissism**?

In effect, narcissism refers to a very fragile and unstable sense of self. In order to compensate for their fragile self-esteem, narcissistic people become preoccupied with their self-image and intensely sensitive to perceived shame or humiliation. Typical narcissists have a grandiose sense of self, with an inflated sense of self-importance and an elevated need for attention, status, and recognition. More recent research has focused upon a kind of reverse narcissism, in which people are tormented by poor self-esteem, but harbor grandiose expectations of themselves. *The Diagnostic and Statistical Manual*, fourth edition (DSM-IV or DSM-IV-TR) lists nine criteria for the diagnosis of narcissistic personality disorder.

A 1998 study suggests that politicians may have a higher level of narcissistic traits than the general population (*iStock*).

What are the **DSM-IV-TR criteria** for Narcissistic Personality Disorder?

Published in 2000 by the American Psychiatric Association, the DSM-IV Text Revision (DSM-IV-TR) is the latest version of the DSM. In order to meet DSM-IV-TR criteria for Narcissistic Personality Disorder, an individual has to display a pervasive sense of grandiosity, excessive need for attention, and lack of empathy across a broad array of situations. Five of the following nine criteria need to be met:

1. Grandiose sense of self-importance.
2. Preoccupation with fantasies of unlimited success.
3. Belief that he or she is special and only can be understood by other special, high status individuals or groups.
4. Need for excessive admiration.
5. Sense of entitlement—assumption that others should accommodate to the person's needs and desires.
6. Interpersonally exploitative.

333

7. Lacking in empathy.

8. Often envious of others or believes others are envious of him or her.

9. Arrogant, haughty attitudes or behaviors.

What is the **Narcissistic Personality Inventory** (NPI)?

The Narcissistic Personality Inventory is a self-report questionnaire that assesses a person's narcissistic personality traits based on criteria from an earlier version of the DSM. Published by Raskin and Hall in 1979, it has become a widely used test of narcissistic traits. In 1984, Robert Emmons divided the total NPI score into four distinct dimensions: leadership/authority, superiority/arrogance, self-absorption/self-admiration, and exploitativeness/entitlement. Emmons found that the first three subscales were correlated with adaptive personality traits, such as self-confidence, extraversion, initiative, and ambition, while the fourth subscale was correlated with measures of psychopathology. This study suggests that narcissistic traits can have both positive and negative implications.

Do **politicians score higher** on the **NPI** than people in other professions?

In one of the few studies to empirically investigate narcissistic traits in politicians, Robert Hill and Gregory Yousey administered the NPI to 123 university faculty, forty-two politicians (state legislators from four states), ninety-nine clergy (both protestant ministers and Catholic priests), and 195 librarians. Their 1998 study found a statistically significant difference in total scores, with politicians scoring higher than the other three professional groups. In terms of the four subscales, politicians scored the highest on the leadership/authority subscale, and clergy scored the lowest on the exploitativeness/entitlement subscale.

In other words, politicians did score higher than the other three groups in total narcissism, but the differences seemed mainly due to their high scores on the leadership/authority scores. Interestingly, although the differences did not reach statistical significance, politicians also had the highest scores on superiority/arrogance and exploitativeness/entitlement subscales and professors had the highest scores on self-absorption/self-admiration. Without statistical significance, however, these last differences could be due to chance.

Does **narcissism create** the **politician** or does **politics create** the **narcissist**?

This is an important question. While there is little to no research investigating this question, most clinicians believe that the personality and the job interact with each other. The traits necessary for success in politics have to be there from the beginning. It takes considerable self-confidence, extraversion, and ambition to wage a successful political campaign. But the experience of political power also has very potent psycho-

What did former preidential candidate John Edwards say about his own narcissistic attitudes?

After the 2008 presidential election, John Edwards, a serious contender in the Democratic presidential primaries, was revealed to have had an extra-marital affair. In a television interview on ABC News, Edwards attributed his behavior to narcissistic attitudes that had mushroomed during his very high-profile campaign. "In 2006, I made a serious error in judgment and conducted myself in a way that was disloyal to my family and to my core beliefs. I recognized my mistake and I told my wife that I had a liaison with another woman, and I asked for her forgiveness.... In the course of several campaigns, I started to believe that I was special and became increasingly egocentric and narcissistic." He stated that his experiences on the campaign trail "fed a self-focus, an egotism, a narcissism that leads you to believe you can do whatever you want. You're invincible. And there will be no consequences."

(Note: Quotes are from the *New York Times,* August 8, 2008, and the *New York Post*, June 19, 2009.)

logical effects. The power and public attention can be intoxicating, leading people to feel they are entitled to special treatment and should not be held back by any limits.

This dynamic can also hold true for celebrities. Clinicians have further commented that the need for a managed and massaged public image can make politicians feel unaccountable for their private behavior. Their public persona becomes entirely cut off from their authentic private selves. All that matters is the image, not the actual beliefs or behavior. In fact, the psychiatrist Robert Millman has coined the term *acquired situational narcissism*, referring to the explosive impact of fame, power, and celebrity on narcissistic tendencies.

Why do so many **politicians** get trapped in **scandals**?

It seems almost every other week we hear of some new political scandal. Politicians get in trouble for financial shenanigans, abuse of power, and sexual indiscretions. Over and over again, we wonder how such politically astute people can act so recklessly. Don't they realize they are bound to get caught? As discussed above, politicians may have a higher level of narcissistic traits than is found in the general population and these traits are only strengthened in the seductive spotlight of elected office. The perks of power can create a semidelusional sense of entitlement and invincibility. In addition, when it comes to sexual scandals in particular, the theory of evolution may have something to add.

335

Who are some American politicians who have been caught in sex scandals?

The list of politicians caught in sex scandals is remarkably long and thoroughly bipartisan in nature. While many other countries expect extra-marital dalliances from their politicians, American political culture is still highly punitive of politicians whose behavior strays from monogamous family values, despite the frequency of such behavior among politicians. Gary Hart was a Democratic candidate for the 1988 presidential primary when a sex scandal caught up with him. Elliott Spitzer was the Democratic Governor of New York, brought down by a sex scandal in 2008. Republican

New York's Governor Eliot Spitzer resigned in 2008 after a scandal involving prostitution (*AP/WideWorld*).

John Tower was denied senate confirmation for a cabinet post in 1989 after revelation of an extra-marital affair. Mark Foley, a Republican congressman from Florida, resigned in 2006 after the exposure of inappropriate contact with adolescent congressional pages.

According to the *theory of sexual selection*, men gain an evolutionary advantage from pursuing multiple mates. In many species, males pursue social dominance in order to gain access to a harem of females. In short, these alpha males maximize their evolutionary fitness by seeking out youth, variety, and quantity in their sexual encounters. While such behavior among humans is certainly not universal, neither is it unprecedented, or even that unusual. Thus, there may be inherent contradictions between the personality traits of people who succeed in the competitive and aggressive arena of electoral politics, and the public façade of pious self-control that many politicians feel compelled to adopt.

Are **celebrities narcissistic** in the same way that politicians are?

In a 2006 study, Mark Young and Drew Pinsky administered the Narcissistic Personality Inventory (NPI) to 200 celebrities. They found that celebrities scored significantly higher on the NPI than both the general population and a comparison group of MBA students. They also found that female celebrities scored significantly higher than male celebrities, which is the opposite pattern found in the general population. Further, reality television celebrities produced the highest NPI scores, followed by comedians, actors, and musicians. Interestingly, they found no correlation between NPI scores and years of experience in the entertainment industry. This suggests that the celebrities' narcissistic tendencies may have predated their entrance into the industry.

What do we know about **celebrity worship**?

One area that has received some attention in the research literature is that of celebrity worship. Several studies have looked at it from an absorption-addiction model, suggesting that extreme forms of celebrity worship may reflect a kind of addiction. Other research has found that mild forms of celebrity worship are quite common and unrelated to psychopathology, while more extreme forms do seem correlated with emotional disturbance.

In a 2003 study, John Maltby, James Houran, and Lynn McCutcheon administered the Celebrity Attitudes scale and a personality measure known as the Revised Eysenck Personality Questionnaire to 219 students and 390 community residents. They found modest but statistically significant associations between different kinds of celebrity worship and different personality traits. People who engaged in celebrity worship for social and entertainment purposes were more likely to score high on extraversion, an adaptive personality trait. People who had an intense and personal investment in celebrity worship scored high on neuroticism, which reflects an anxious and depressive emotional reactivity. Finally, people who scored high on the borderline pathological form of celebrity worship, the most disturbed form, scored high on psychoticism. In Eysenck's scale, psychoticism is less about psychosis than about aggression, psychopathy, and social alienation.

VOTING BEHAVIOR

Why do people **vote**?

Because voter turnout is essential to a democracy, psychologists have joined with political scientists to study the factors that motivate people to vote. If you look at it from a classic rationalist view of costs and benefits, you can argue that it doesn't make much sense to vote. Voting takes time, energy, and even money if you have to miss a day of work to get to the polling place. And any single person is unlikely to feel that his or her vote will change the outcome of an election. Nonetheless, people do vote and their participation in electoral politics remains critical for the survival of the democratic system. Psychologists and their colleagues in other fields have considered the possible motivations for voting. Among other factors, they have suggested the role of habit, social pressure, altruism, and even genetics.

Do people **vote** out of **habit**?

Research into voting records shows that some people vote regularly in every election, while some others seem to target their votes to "issue elections", where there are issues at stake that the voter cares about. Regular voters, or "habitual voters," are more likely to have lived in the same house over several election cycles, according to Wendy Wood, John Aldrich, and Jacob Montgomery.

Does **social pressure** cause people to **vote**?

Researchers have also looked at the impact of social pressure on voting behavior. Not surprisingly, fear of public exposure can motivate people to get to the polling place. A political scientist named Donald Green mailed out letters to about 90,000 Michigan households before the 2006 primary election. An additional 90,000 households received no letters. Four different letters were sent out. One letter simply reminded people of their civic duty to vote, the second letter reminded the recipients that voting records (whether or not people voted) were publicly available. The third letter included information on recipients' previous voting behavior and the fourth letter listed the past voting behavior of recipients' neighbors. It also stated that the recipients' own voter turnout would be reported in another letter sent out to their community. Recipients of the fourth letter showed the greatest increase in voter turnout (8.1 percent), followed by recipients of the third letter (4.9 percent), and the second letter (2.5 percent). Recipients who were simply reminded of their civic duty to vote only increased their turnout by 1.9 percent.

Does **genetics** play a role in **voting behavior**?

James Fowler and Laura Baker have conducted a series of studies on voting behavior in families. They found that the party affiliation of adopted children tended to be similar to that of their adopted parents and siblings, suggesting that party affiliation was culturally transmitted. When the authors compared the voting behavior of a large sample of identical and fraternal twins, they found that identical twins were more similar than fraternal twins in regard to whether or not they voted, but no more similar in their choice of candidate. In sum, this work suggests that voter turnout is related to genetics, while party affiliation is related to environment.

What role does **altruism** play in **voting behavior**?

Other researchers have suggested that altruism plays a role in voter turnout. In an experimental manipulation called "the dictator game," subjects are given money and told to share it with another person who will not know their name. In a 2007 study by James Fowler and Cindy Kam, people who shared their money were significantly more likely to vote than those who did not. Moreover, Richard Jankowski found that people who agreed with altruistic statements were more likely to have voted in the 1994 elections. Perhaps altruism is related to a sense of social commitment, specifically to a sense of connection to the social group and a feeling of responsibility for its well-being. Additionally, we can speculate that altruism may have some genetic component, perhaps accounting for the apparent genetic influence on voter turnout.

Voting behavior is certainly not a purely intellectual activity; researchers have found that other factors, including social pressure, feelings of altruism, and even genetics can play a role (*iStock*).

How do people make **decisions** on how to **vote**?

Candidates are very interested in the psychology behind candidate selection. The classic rational tradition would hold that people determine which candidate best represents their interests or their values and then vote accordingly. However, the psychologist Drew Westen has argued that people rely on far more than rational analysis when choosing how to vote. Careful analyses of candidates' qualifications, voting records, and positions on the issues is time consuming and difficult, especially for people who do not follow current events. Therefore people tend to fall back on shortcuts, basing their decisions on personal liking of candidates, identification with candidates, hot button issues, and simple messages that stimulate strong emotional responses. It is important to realize that much of this emotional information processing can be unconscious. As with many other kinds of choices, people may think their choices are based on rational analyses, when they are actually more emotionally driven.

How do **politicians use psychology** in their campaigns?

Given the emotional influences on voting behavior, it is hardly surprising that a whole industry of political consultants struggles to figure out how to best package candidates to appeal to the voting public. In short, many campaigns try to influence voter response by shaping voters' emotional reactions. One powerful way to do this is through *associative conditioning*. Politicians try to create either negative or positive associations with particular issues or candidates. This can be done through careful use of language, meticulously designed visual images, and intentional use of emotionally significant symbols. For example, the colors of the American flag grace almost every national campaign and, though it may be a cliché, politicians are frequently photographed holding babies. These images prod the voter to associate the candidate with patriotism and support of the family.

What does **Frank Luntz** say about the use of **language** to **influence opinions**?

The political consultant Frank Luntz specializes in shaping language to influence public opinion. Through language he aims to attract the listeners' attention, implant ideas in their memory, and stimulate either positive or negative emotional responses. In his 2007 book, Luntz states that the most effective political rhetoric is characterized by repetition, consistency, simple plain language, catchy memorable phrases, and short sentences. The aesthetic quality of the speeches matter too. A politician's words should be pleasant to listen to with a rhythmic flow. While the message should be consistent, some degree of novelty is also important to capture the listener's attention. Moreover, visual images can often have more power than words. While Luntz has been criticized for promoting style over substance (and in effect, manipulation over communication), he states that content is not entirely irrelevant. The speaker must have credibility; if the politician goes too far beyond what is believable, the audience will be turned off.

How can **language affect public perceptions** of political rhetoric?

In Frank Luntz's view, a single word can frame an issue, creating either a positive or negative association in a voter's mind. In a 2005 memo to Republican party members that was widely disseminated in the media, Luntz listed 14 phrases that should never be said. Included below are seven examples from his list. In support of the power of language, Luntz stated that two-thirds of Americans wanted to "personalize" Social Security, while only one-third wanted to "privatize" it. Lutz's 2005 memo on political rhetoric states:

To Promote a Positive Impression

Never Say	Instead Say
Tax Reform	Tax Simplification
Globalization	Free Market Economy
Foreign Trade	International Trade
Drilling for Oil	Exploring for Energy

To Promote a Negative Impression

Never Say	Instead Say
Government	Washington
Undocumented Workers	Illegal Aliens
Estate Tax	Death Tax

Can **psychology** contribute to **ballot design**?

Given its historical interest in perception, cognition, and motor function, there is much that psychology can contribute to the study of ballot design. There are two main problems to consider when designing ballots. For one, ballots should be functional. People should be able to use them with ease. This issue is of particular relevance for elderly voters, who may suffer from cognitive, perceptual, or physical difficulties. In a 2007 study by Tiffany Jastrzembski and Neil Charness, elderly voters were shown electronic voting machines that differed in two ways. Votes were entered via touch screen or key pad, and races were presented either one at a time or all at once. This resulted in four different combinations of ballot design. Elderly voters performed best on the combination of touch screen ballots with races presented one at a time. Additionally, ballot design should not favor one candidate over the other. For example, in a 1998 study by Joanne Miller and John Krosnick, name order was found to significantly affect voter choice in forty-eight percent of 118 races in the 1992 Ohio state elections. On average, the candidate on the top of the list received 2.5 percent more votes than the candidates listed further down the ballot. While that may not seem like a large margin, it is enough to win an election.

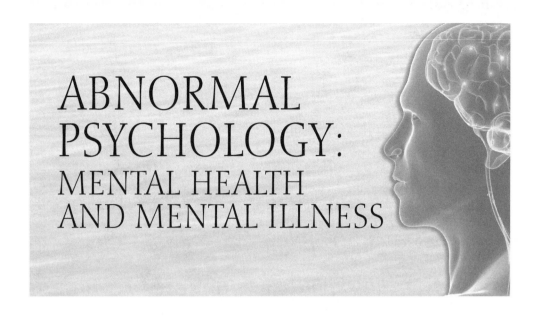

ABNORMAL PSYCHOLOGY: MENTAL HEALTH AND MENTAL ILLNESS

DEFINITIONS AND CLASSIFICATIONS

How do we **define mental illness**?

Some concept of mental illness exists in perhaps every culture on earth and descriptions of it are found in ancient texts dating back to the Greeks and Romans. Those who have confronted mental illness in themselves or someone close to them can appreciate the extreme pain and dysfunction it can cause. Nonetheless, it is difficult to come up with a precise definition of mental illness. In the most recent version of the Diagnostic and Statistic Manual (DSM), a mental disorder is defined as a psychological pattern that causes distress or dysfunction and that is beyond the norms of the individual's culture.

What is the relationship between **abnormal behavior** and **mental illness**?

This is a difficult question. Even though a mental illness must cause distress or dysfunction, to some extent we judge the pathology of behavior by its relationship to cultural norms. Therefore our concept of mental illness is tied in part to our ideas of what is normal. This raises the question of whether all abnormal behavior is pathological and whether all normal behavior is mentally healthy. Clearly, people can engage in unusual behavior that is not pathological. We do not want to diagnose any kind of original or unconventional behavior as mentally ill. Nor is all normal behavior healthy. Drug abuse, violence, and anorexia can be very common in certain social groups, but all cause distress or dysfunction. Thus, although it can be very easy to recognize mental illness in the most extreme cases (such as acute psychosis or severe depression), there are many circumstances where the boundaries between mental health and mental illness are not so clear.

Who are the Lizard People?

Delusions are generally diagnosed as a symptom of a psychotic disorder. A delusion is defined as a fixed, false belief that is considered abnormal within the person's culture. Nonetheless, it is not always easy to separate a delusion from a belief that has become acceptable within a certain subculture. This can be the case even with very bizarre beliefs.

For example, the author David Icke has very successfully promoted the idea that the world is run by a conspiracy known as the Illuminati (a term dating back to earlier conspiracy theories). The Illuminati descend from an alien race of lizard people who came to Earth from

According to one conspiracy theory, prominent politicians and other leaders in the world are actually alien lizard people called the Illuminati (*iStock*).

another planet and are capable of changing shape and assuming human form. Most of the major political and economic figures in the world today, including George W. Bush, Hillary Clinton, and even the late Princess Diana, are actually considered to be lizard people. There are several different branches of the lizard people, including the Grays, the Adopted Grays, the Crinklies, the Tall Blonds, the Tall Robots, and the Annunaki. George W. Bush is reportedly a member of the Annunaki branch of the lizard people.

Are these beliefs delusional? Most of us would consider these ideas to be false beliefs that are culturally abnormal. Nonetheless, David Icke has many followers and his books have sold very well. Within a certain subculture, therefore, these beliefs are not considered abnormal. Situations such as this illustrate how difficult it can be at times to determine what is and is not a symptom of mental illness.

Why do we **classify mental illness**?

All diagnostic systems depend upon classification. What function does classification serve? Imagine if we had no common, standardized classification system for mental illness. With no common language to describe clinical observations, there could be no coordination among clinicians, researchers, or people working in public policy. There would be no way to research the prevalence, etiology (cause), outcome, or progression of the illness. Without a grounding of scientific data, there would be no way to systematically develop and test treatments. Treatments would be fragmented, ad hoc and untested, ultimately based on personal opinion instead of scientific fact.

How do we **classify mental illness**?

Mental illnesses or disorders are classified according to the nature of their symptoms, their causes and their course. The *course of an illness* refers to its progression over time. DSM-IV-TR has sixteen general categories with multiple diagnoses in each category. Examples of these categories include eating disorders, psychotic disorders, impulse control disorders, mood disorders, anxiety disorders, and mental disorders due to a general medical condition.

What is the **DSM-IV**?

DSM refers to the *Diagnostic and Statistical Manual*. DSM-IV is the fourth edition of the DSM, published in 1994. DSM-IV Text Revision (DSM-IV-TR) was published in 2000. This edition made minimal changes to the diagnoses, but updated the literature review in the manual. The DSM system provides a standardized method to diagnose mental illness. It is developed in coordination with the International Classification of Diseases (ICD) which is published by the World Health Organization (WHO). Diagnoses are provided on five axes, the first axis (axis I) lists specific clinical syndromes, such as schizophrenia or major depression. The second axis (axis II) lists personality disorders and mental retardation, chronic conditions that affect the full range of a person's psychological functioning. Axis III pertains to medical conditions that might affect the person's psychological state, axis IV to psychosocial and environmental stressors, and axis V to the person's general level of adaptive functioning (the GAF score), which ranges from one to one hundred.

What is the **history** of the **DSM system**?

Interestingly, the first official psychiatric classification system was developed to help with the U.S. Census. The Census Bureau aimed for an accurate estimation of the U.S. population, including residents of mental hospitals. In 1840, the U.S. Census had only one category for mental illness, idiocy/insanity. By 1880, there were seven categories: mania, melancholia, monomania, paresis, dementia, dipsomania, and epilepsy. In 1917, the official psychiatric professional associations decided it was time to design their own classification system, taking the diagnosis of mental illness out of the hands of the government.

What would soon become the American Psychiatric Association (APA) joined with the National Commission on Mental Hygiene to develop a nomenclature (system of labels) for mental disorders. This system applied mainly to the most severely ill inpatients, those living in mental hospitals. After World War II brought back veterans suffering from the psychological aftereffects of war, the diagnostic systems were expanded to consider the needs of outpatients, those living in the community. The first edition of the DSM was published in 1952, DSM-III came in 1980, DSM-III-R in 1987, and DSM-IV in 1994. The projected publication date of DSM-V is 2013.

Do **psychiatric classifications change** over time?

Because human psychology and culture are so complex and so variable, it is very hard to come up with a foolproof system for diagnosing mental illness. The first editions of the DSM were strongly influenced by prevailing psychological theories and were poorly linked to empirical research. Some of the diagnoses were controversial and what we would now consider culturally biased. For example, homosexuality was listed as a mental disorder until 1974. While more recent versions of the DSM have made much greater use of empirical research, there are still critics who suggest the diagnoses lack adequate scientific validity. Because of the inevitable flaws in any classification scheme, however, it is assumed that each version of the DSM will eventually become outdated and will need to be replaced by a newer edition.

What are the **drawbacks** to **classification systems**?

It is critical to recognize that no matter how complex and sophisticated the classification system becomes, it can only provide guidelines for treatment. Diagnoses are prototypes—they are only ideals—and few patients fit the classification perfectly. In fact, many patients do not quite fit into any diagnostic category. Moreover, it is also critical to remember that the classification system applies to a pattern of symptoms. It does not and can never describe the whole person. For this reason DSM-IV-TR only refers to "individuals with schizophrenia," for example, and not "schizophrenics."

What **changes** will be made in **DSM-V**?

DSM-V is scheduled to come out in 2013. However, in early 2010, the American Psychiatric Association published their proposed revisions in order to solicit comments from readers on these changes. Along with changes to the criteria and classification of specific diagnoses, some very general changes were also proposed. For one, the first three axes of the five-axis diagnostic system will be collapsed into one axis. In DSM-IV, axis I is for clinical syndromes, axis II for personality disorders and mental retardation, and axis III for medical disorders that might be relevant to the mental condition. In DSM-V, that will all be coded on one line. Also DSM-V puts much more emphasis on dimensional ratings than any previous DSM edition. In other words clinicians will rate patients in terms of the *severity* of various clinical traits (such as depression, anxiety, etc), and not just categorize them as either *having* or *not having* a particular disorder. Diagnostic categories will be retained in DSM-V, but there will be more room for dimensional ratings. Because the DSM-V system has yet to be finalized, we will focus here on the diagnostic system of DSM-IV and DSM-IV-TR.

What are some examples of culture-bound syndromes?

DSM-IV-TR includes a section on culture-bound syndromes, which are distinct patterns of emotional or behavioral disturbances that are found only in specific cultures.

- *Ataque de Nervios:* This is commonly found among Latin Americans, particularly those from the Caribbean. Ataques serve as a means of expressing intense emotional distress often following a disturbing event. Symptoms include uncontrollable shouting or crying, trance, aggressive verbal or physical behavior, trembling, or fainting. While ataques may be misdiagnosed as a psychotic episode, they are probably more akin to a panic attack or a conversion disorder, which involves the expression of emotional distress through physical symptoms.

- *Bouffee delirante:* This syndrome is found in West Africa and in Haiti. It involves a sudden outburst of agitation and excitement, in which the person is confused, disoriented, and may complain of visual or auditory hallucinations (seeing or hearing things that are not there). This may be most similar to the DSM IV diagnosis of brief psychotic disorder.

- *Koro: Fear of a Retracting Penis:* This rather bizarre syndrome is found in South and East Asia, including China, Thailand, and India. The word *koro* is believed to be of Malaysian origin, but the syndrome has several different names across the region, including *shook yang, shook yong,* and *suo yang* in China, and *jinjinia bemar* in India. The syndrome is characterized by acute anxiety that the person's genitals (including breasts in a woman) will retract into the body and even cause death. A somewhat similar fear of penis theft is found in parts of Africa. Although in the United States such a syndrome would be seen as a bizarre delusion, koro would be more accurately diagnosed as a conversion disorder.

What **role** does **culture** play in **mental illness**?

While most of the DSM diagnoses can be found across cultures, people from different cultures do vary in the way that they express psychological distress. In many cultures, depression is less likely to involve conscious feelings of sadness and more likely to involve preoccupation with bodily ailments. Likewise, the content of schizophrenic delusions and hallucinations is strongly influenced by cultural themes. Delusions of being the messiah are frequently found in Jerusalem, while delusions of being tracked by the CIA are more likely to be found in the United States. In addition, some cultures have developed unique forms of expressing emotional distress. DSM-IV-TR includes a section on *culture-bound syndromes*, which refer to distinct syndromes that are

347

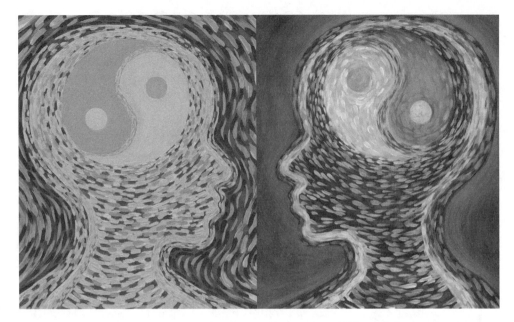

Some people think that schizophrenia means having multiple personalities, a condition which is actually known as Dissociative Identity Disorder. Schizophrenia involves psychotic symptoms like delusions, hallucinations, and disorganized behavior.

found only in specific cultures. Importantly, they are recognized as illnesses or as disturbed behavior within their host culture. Most of these syndromes indicate that the individual is overwhelmed by strong negative emotions. Examples include: Attaque de nervios from Latin American cultures, Koro from Chinese and East Asian cultures, and ghost sickness from Native American peoples.

MAJOR MENTAL ILLNESSES

What is **schizophrenia**?

Schizophrenia is perhaps the most disabling of the major mental illnesses. Although descriptions of similar clinical presentations date back to the earliest periods of written history, the term "schizophrenia" and the current definition of the disorder are relatively recent. The German psychiatrist Emil Kraepelin (1856–1926) first distinguished between manic depressive illness and dementia praecox, or what was later called schizophrenia. The Swiss psychiatrist Eugen Bleuler (1857–1939) coined the actual term "schizophrenia" from the Greek words for "split mind." According to DSM-IV, schizophrenia is characterized by two or more of the following symptoms: *delusions, hallucinations, disorganized speech, disorganized or catatonic behavior,* and *negative symptoms.* These symptoms must have been present for at least one month, and result in significant social or occupational impairment and/or reduction in self-care. Some sign of the disorder must have been present for at least six months, and the symptoms cannot be due to another condition (such as substance-induced psychosis or a medical condition).

How are the **symptoms** of schizophrenia defined?

The DSM-IV diagnosis of schizophrenia describes a range of psychotic symptoms. *Psychosis* refers to a significant break with *reality testing*, or the ability to recognize reality as other people who are in similar circumstances typically see it. There are a number of different types of psychotic symptoms:

- *Delusions* refer to a fixed, false belief that is considered abnormal within the person's culture.

- *Bizarre* delusions are physically impossible, as in the belief that the queen of England is on the planet Mars sending messages to a chip in your brain. A *nonbizarre* delusion is physically possible, such as the false belief that a celebrity is in love with you or that you are being bugged by the FBI.

- *Hallucinations* refer to a perceptual experience of something that is not really there. Hallucinations can be auditory (sense of sound), visual (sense of sight), olfactory (sense of smell), or tactile (sense of touch). Auditory hallucinations are the most common, and often involve one or more voices talking.

- *Disorganized speech and behavior* generally reflect disorganized thought, a breakdown of the coherent, logical flow of thought.

All the symptoms mentioned so far refer to *positive symptoms* or problematic traits that are present. In contrast, *negative symptoms* reflect the absence of healthy traits. Specifically, negative symptoms refer to blunted or flat affect (or emotion) and a dulling of motivation, initiative, energy, and cognitive activity.

What is **thought disorder**?

Thought disorder is one of the most striking and debilitating aspects of severe psychosis. This refers to the way that thought is *organized*. Thought disorder does not pertain to the content of the thought process, to what the person is thinking about, but to the way that the ideas are put together. Does the person display a logical and orderly flow of ideas? Or are the ideas jumbled, only loosely related to each other and ultimately impossible to understand?

There are many kinds of thought disorder:

- *Paucity of ideation* refers to the lack of adequate thought content. The person's mind is more or less blank.

- *Overproduction of thought* is the opposite condition, where ideas are tumbling out of the person's mind.

Other terms refer specifically to the organization of the person's thought and range in severity from mild and fairly normal to entirely incomprehensible.

- *Digressive thought* describes a state where the person drifts from topic to topic, but the speech is still understandable.
- *Circumstantial thought* is roundabout but eventually gets to the point. If you ask a circumstantial patient a question, he or she will go a long way around the point, but eventually answer the question.
- *Tangential thought* is more severe. With effort, you can understand the person, but it takes considerable concentration to identify the connections between the different ideas.
- *Flight of Ideas* is similar to tangential thought, but is also characterized by a highly energized overproduction of thought.
- *Looseness of association* is not intelligible. Fragments of ideas may be recognizable, but the person can lapse into a loose stream of thoughts in which separate ideas bear little relationship to one another.
- *Word salad* is essentially gibberish, with no clear relationship between the words in the sentence.

While thought disorder can be present in many psychiatric illnesses, severe thought disorder is most characteristic of schizophrenia.

Is **split personality** the same as **schizophrenia**?

The popular understanding of psychiatric terminology is often quite different from the technical meaning of the terms. The term "split personality" is is often confused with schizophrenia. Split personality more accurately refers to dissociative identity disorder (DID), formerly known as multiple personality disorder. While schizophrenia is a diagnosis of psychotic symptoms, DID is classified under the category of dissociative disorders. DID generally develops in childhood as a means of coping with extreme traumatic experiences, such as ongoing sexual or physical abuse. People manage the overwhelming emotions occasioned by the trauma by splitting their conscious experience into multiple identities. There may be the cute little girl, the responsible young man, and the rebellious teenager. Outside of their sense of their own identities, however, people with DID are not typically psychotic. In contrast, people with schizophrenia generally have a consistent sense of their own identity, but have ongoing struggles with psychosis.

Is **schizophrenia curable**?

At this point in time, schizophrenia is not curable. It is a lifelong disorder. However, it is definitely treatable. Profound advances in the medication of schizophrenia allow us

What are some examples of thought disorder?

Listed below are quotes taken from writings from individuals suffering from mental illness. Each quote illustrates a specific form of thought disorder.

An example of *looseness of association* (characteristic of schizophrenia) from a woman suffering from this disorder:

- Princess Lella The Hon Dona Sultana Maharajah Imperatrista Malkah Malkahtzedek Anna Renee' Jerusalem Tizyona Shoshanah Shekhinah Shiloh (Shilo, Silo, Shai Lo, Shello) Malkiyah Malkit Tifarah ... Bat David Bat-Rabin Golai Bernadotte, Duchess of Padborg, Duchess of Varmland, holy one of The Most High, wife of Dom Sultan Prince Pasha Maharaja Tzar Melech Maluch Malkitzedek Charles-Philip Edmund Bertil Nikolai Golai Moses (Moshe) Tiferet Maschiach Ben David Bernadotte, Of Sweden, Duke of Varmland, Duke of Padborg, THE ROYAL FAMILY OF ISRAEL, ... THE OFFICIAL ROYAL QUEEN AND KING OF ISRAEL....

A man's writing style indicates mania in an example of *flight of ideas:*

- Court TV, by not covering my story, is clearly telling its viewers that corrupt police officers are more important than the true heroes' families, families of those that gave their lives in the line of duty. Court TV knows that in the same way that two brave officers walked out of the 70th precinct if Court TV gave my story the same amount of time as the chicken's head, that there would be good honest law enforcement officers that would volunteer their own free time to get the evidence to arrest my father, knowing the donation that will be made and the new trend that could get started....

- If you're a bad cop, you've got a friend: Court TV. If you're a good cop, you're worth less than a chicken's head....

- McDonald's employees are for the most part hard-working students who don't carry guns. They are far more likely to be victims like the Wendy's employees than to be a victimizer. Corrupt cops, on the other hand, do carry guns and I suppose that Court TV reporters don't have the backbone that reporters had in the past. One would think given the months I have walked around New York with my picket sign, that some good lawyers and doctors would have approached me and offered their services. One would think that there would be some good honest lawyers and doctors that would want to help the homeless and abused and police and firefighters widow and children fund.

to greatly reduce positive symptoms, such as delusions, hallucinations, and disorganized behavior. Unfortunately, we have fewer tools to treat the negative symptoms. The severity of the illness will vary from individual to individual, however, and some people respond better to treatment than others. Many people with schizophrenia can live in the community, enjoy social relationships, and even perform volunteer or part-time work. The vast majority of people with schizophrenia will need to take psychiatric medication indefinitely, however, to control psychotic symptoms and remain as functional as possible.

Is all **psychosis schizophrenia**?

People can suffer from psychosis without meeting criteria for schizophrenia. Certain medical illnesses and drugs can cause psychotic symptoms. In fact it can be quite difficult to tease apart the relative contributions of mental illness and drug abuse when a substance user has psychotic symptoms. People with mood disorders, such as major depressive disorder or bipolar disorder, can often present with psychotic symptoms. In addition, people under severe stress can sometimes experience psychotic symptoms. The diagnosis of brief psychotic disorder is characterized by quick, transient psychotic symptoms, after which the person returns to normal, generally without need for further medication.

What is **bipolar disorder**?

Bipolar disorder used to be known as manic depression. It is classified as a mood disorder and is characterized by at least one manic episode and typically one or more major depressive episodes. A manic episode refers to a period of at least one week where the person exhibits elevated, euphoric, or irritable mood. The person also displays symptoms of increased activity, with much higher levels of energy, initiative, and impulsivity than normal.

More specifically, three or more of the following symptoms must be present (or four if the mood is only irritable): inflated self-esteem or grandiosity; a decreased need for sleep; an increase in amount of talking or pressure to keep talking; flight of ideas or racing thoughts; distractibility; an increase in goal-directed activity; and an increase in risky, pleasurable behavior. People in manic episodes frequently engage in reckless and excessive spending, sexual activity, or substance abuse. They can also have psychotic symptoms during manic episodes, but the symptoms tend to be mood-congruent (consistent with their elevated, expansive mood). For example, they may have grandiose delusions that they are going to Washington, D.C., to run the State Department. People with bipolar disorder tend to have a higher baseline than people with schizophrenia. Many people are completely symptom-free when not in the middle of an episode and can live entirely normal lives. However, even people who are symptom-free at baseline will need to take medication to maintain their mental health.

What was the mental ailment that tormented the painter Vincent van Gogh?

Vincent van Gogh (1853–1890) was a Dutch-born painter who is now considered one of the greatest artists of the nineteenth century. Little known in his own day, his work currently sells for millions of dollars. Van Gogh suffered from agonizing bouts of mental illness during which he repeatedly tried to kill himself. He eventually succeeded in 1890 at the age of 37. According to all reports, when he was not in the throes of a psychotic episode, he was calm, cooperative and completely focused on his painting.

Over the intervening century, many people have theorized about the nature of the mental illness that eventually killed him. While we can never be fully confident of any diagnosis made in the absence of the actual patient, van Gogh left a treasure trove of letters, mainly written to or by his devoted brother, Theo. From these letters, we can identify several major depressive episodes with psychotic features.

It is well known that the nineteenth century artist Vincent van Gogh suffered from mental illness. The exact nature of his suffering is still a matter of some debate (*iStock*).

However, the psychiatrist Dietrich Blumer noted in a 2002 article that van Gogh also wrote of periods of excitement, increased energy, and excessive religious zeal. Although such symptoms might suggest manic episodes, Blumer concluded that van Gogh suffered from temporal lobe epilepsy, greatly exacerbated by his intake of absinthe, a popular but highly alcoholic beverage. It is also possible that he suffered from both illnesses: epilepsy and bipolar disorder. Tragically, his sister also suffered from mental illness (possibly schizophrenia) and was eventually confined to an asylum.

What is **depression**?

Unlike mania, depression is something many people experience at some point in their life. Therefore the term depression covers a very wide range of experiences. At the most mild end of the spectrum are transient feelings of sadness. Longer periods of sadness following losses or other upsetting events also fall within the normal range of human experience. When feelings of sadness become the constant backdrop of a person's mood, we are moving into depression.

While feelings of depression following difficult life experiences are still very common, severe depression is markedly different from these milder and more transient types of depression. DSM-IV refers to the most severe form of depression as a *major depressive episode*. To meet criteria for a major depressive episode, the individual has to exhibit at least five of the following symptoms over a two-week period and the symptoms have to represent a change from the person's previous state. These symptoms include: consistently depressed mood, diminished interest in activities, significant weight gain or loss (not due to dieting), increase or decrease in sleep (insomnia or hypersomnia), physical restlessness or slowing down (psychomotor agitation or retardation), loss of energy, feelings of worthlessness and guilt, and thoughts of death or suicide. When someone has one or more of these episodes, they are diagnosed with *major depressive disorder*—presuming the episodes cannot be attributed to another mental disorder such as bipolar disorder or a substance-induced depression.

What is the relationship between **mental illness** and **creativity**?

It has been frequently noted that creative people seem to have a disproportionate rate of mental illness. Studies have since borne this out, particularly among writers. Mood disorders may be the most common form of mental disorder among writers, who have an elevated rate of both depression and bipolar disorder. Consequently, there is a disproportionately higher rate of suicide in these artists. For example, the novelists Ernest Hemingway and Virginia Woolf both committed suicide, as did the poets Anne Sexton and Sylvia Plath. It is not clear why creativity and mood disorders are linked to each other, although researchers have speculated that the intense emotionality of a mood disorder heightens the sensitivity of creative people. Additionally, people with bipolar disorder can be extremely productive and creative when in a hypomanic state. *Hypomania* is a milder form of mania, when the elevation of mood and the increase in energy and self-confidence have not yet led to functional impairment.

What is **obsessive-compulsive disorder**?

Obsessive-compulsive disorder (OCD) is classified under anxiety disorders. OCD is characterized by obsessions, which are repetitive, senseless, and intrusive thoughts that generally increase anxiety, and/or compulsions, which are repetitive, senseless behaviors that often serve to reduce the anxiety caused by the obsession. Common obsessions include an unrealistic and excessive fear of danger, of contamination, or of committing hurtful or morally unacceptable actions. Common compulsions include repetitive cleaning, checking, ordering, arranging, and hoarding behaviors.

Although these symptoms can become debilitating—truly taking over a person's life—an individual with OCD always retains some degree of insight into the pathology of their behavior. This differentiates OCD from a delusion, in which the person is convinced of the truth of his or her belief. In a mild case of OCD, a person may need to perform a specific routine when turning off the computer at work every evening, perhaps taking fifteen minutes more than necessary to complete the task. In an extreme case of OCD, someone can take nine hours to finish a shower, washing each body part multiple times in ritualized ways.

What is **autism**?

Autism is a disorder first diagnosed in childhood and is included in the category of *pervasive developmental disorders*. Autism is categorized by deficits or abnormal behavior in three areas: social interaction, communication, and range of interests. Autistic children show avoidance of eye contact and of social interaction in general. They do not develop normal peer relationships and they do not show typical desire to share toys or engage in social play. Their communication skills are also abnormal, with delayed language development, improper use of personal pronouns and stereotyped, or repetitive use of language ("Your parents is coming! Your parents is coming!"). Finally, they show a restricted range of interests, with intense and obsessive focus on particular objects or topics. For example, a person with autism can develop an obsessive interest in trains and memorize the entire schedule of a given transit system. Additionally, there is a rigid adherence to routine and marked distress when the routine is violated. Some of these symptoms relate to another characteristic, one that is well researched but not yet captured in the DSM system.

People with autism frequently suffer from a deficit in *theory of mind*. This refers to the ability to understand another person's subjective experience and is a necessary first step in empathy. Because of their impaired theory of mind, people with autism can have a very difficult time making sense of social interaction and often find social situations extremely stressful.

How is **Asperger's syndrome different** from **autism**?

In recent years there has been increasing interest in the diagnosis of Asperger's syndrome. It is not clear whether Asperger's syndrome is simply a milder form of autism, or whether it is a truly separate syndrome. As with autism, Asperger's syndrome is characterized by deficits in social interaction and a restricted range of interests evident from early childhood. However, there is no delay in language development and verbal skills are generally higher in Asperger's than in autism. Additionally, there is usually no evidence of cognitive delay in Asperger's, whereas mental retardation is fairly common in autism. People with relatively mild forms of Asperger's can be very successful, generally in fields that focus on logical analysis, factual information, or manipulation of objects (for example, computer programming, engineering, or mathematics), but they may still have difficulty negotiating social situations.

What are the **causes** of **mental illness**?

The causes of mental illness are complex and it is not possible to point to one single cause. However, we are aware of many factors that contribute to mental illness; such contributors are known as *risk factors*. We do know that many forms of mental illness have a genetic component to them and specific genes related to the production of *neurotransmitters* such as *serotonin* and *dopamine* have been associated with several forms of mental illness. We also know that early childhood environment plays an important role; stable, loving environments protect against mental illness and chaotic, neglectful, and traumatic environments raise the risk of it. We also know that high levels of stress in both childhood and adulthood contribute to mental illness.

Some reports show a large increase in autism diagnoses in California's Silicon Valley starting in the 1980s (*iStock*).

Particular disorders, such as post-traumatic stress disorder and acute stress disorder, are specifically linked to extremely stressful events. We also know that the physical environment plays a role in mental health and mental illness. Environmental toxins, substances of abuse, and even exposure to substances of abuse in utero can all contribute to the development of mental illness.

So what's the **verdict** when it comes to mental health: **nature or nurture**?

The mental health field has gone through wide pendulum swings with regard to the nature/nurture debate. In middle of the twentieth century, there was an excessive emphasis on environmental causes. Phrases such as the "schizophrenigenic mother" and the "refrigerator mother" put unnecessary blame on mothers for disorders such as schizophrenia and autism. Starting in the 1980s, the pendulum swung back toward a biological and genetic approach, in some cases unnecessarily diminishing the impact of the environment. By the beginning of the twenty-first century, however, an integrative approach to the nature/nurture debate has developed. Now it is widely understood that all psychological processes involve the interaction between genetics and environment. Our genetics affect our environment by influencing how we interact with the environment, which in turn shapes how the world responds to us. Moreover, research has shown that the reverse is also true; the environment affects our genes. More specifically, different environmental conditions (for example degree of maternal touch) can affect whether specific genes are turned on or off.

357

Who are some famous people who suffered from mental illnesses?

Listed below are eight famous people, all highly accomplished, who have suffered from mental illness. Many organizations serving individuals with psychiatric conditions compile similar lists as a way to reduce the stigma associated with mental illness. The National Alliance on Mental Illness (NAMI), which is an advocacy group for people with mental illness, publishes one such list on its website. Note that some of these diagnoses are controversial as many were made after the person in question died.

Many famous people throughout history have suffered from a mental illness or disability. For instance, President Abraham Lincoln endured major depressive disorder (*iStock*).

1. Abraham Lincoln (U.S. president): Major Depressive Disorder

2. King George III (British monarch): Psychotic Disorder Due to Porphyria

3. Howard Hughes (industrialist and aviator): Obsessive Compulsive Disorder

4. William Styron (author): Major Depressive Disorder

5. Vivian Leigh (actress): Bipolar Disorder

6. Vincent van Gogh (artist): Temporal Lobe Epilepsy

7. John Nash (mathematician and economist): Schizophrenia

8. Winston Churchill (British prime minister): Major Depressive Disorder

Can any **one gene** cause mental illness?

As far as we know, the major mental illnesses are not single-gene disorders. Unlike certain medical and neurological disorders (for example, Huntington's disease), psychiatric disorders cannot be attributed to any one gene. While multiple genes have been linked to psychiatric disorders (for example, neureulin–1, catechol O-methyltransferase, and dysbindin genes for schizophrenia), these genes are best understood as risk factors for the disease rather than as definite causes. Not all people with the gene will have the disorder and not all people with the disorder will have the gene. Therefore, geneticists now believe that most psychiatric disorders are related to a whole series of genes, only some of which are currently known. Any one of these vulnerability genes raises the risk of the disorder, but not by a large amount. The greater the number of vulnerability genes that any given person has, the greater the risk of developing the disorder.

Are some psychiatric disorders **more genetically based** than others?

Different psychiatric disorders vary as to the relative importance of genetics or environment. The most severe mental illnesses, such as schizophrenia, bipolar disorder, autism, and obsessive compulsive disorder, are seen to have a strong genetic component with environment playing a largely supportive role. Disorders such as post-traumatic stress disorder, dissociative disorders, and various personality disorders have a much stronger environmental component, with genetics playing a more supportive role.

DISORDERS OF PERSONALITY

What is the difference between **axis I** disorders and **personality disorders**?

The syndromes discussed in the preceding section are known as *axis I disorders*. This refers to specific patterns of dysfunction in thought, emotions, and behavior. But not all psychopathology fits into an axis I diagnosis. Sometimes the problem is more widespread and not just restricted to a specific pattern of behavior. In effect, the problem relates to the person's entire personality. While psychologists and other mental health professionals agree that psychopathology can reflect an ingrained problem with personality, there is less consensus on how to understand personality pathology. In fact, the definition of personality per se is not entirely settled.

How do we **define personality**?

While there are multiple approaches to the study of personality, we can provide a general definition by stating that an individual's personality involves stable patterns of perceiving and interacting with the environment, including the person's cognitive, emotional, and behavioral responses. This includes the individual's self-perception, as well as their typical mode of relating to other people. Personality is largely established by late adolescence or early adulthood. It is conservative and difficult to change. Nonetheless, personality is not entirely fixed and there is possibility for change throughout adulthood.

How do we define **personality pathology**?

In general personality pathology can be defined as any enduring pattern of personality that causes distress or dysfunction and that falls outside the norms of the individual's culture. It is possible to divide the large literature on personality pathology into three overall approaches, *categorical, dimensional*, and *schema*. The categorical approach suggests that different kinds of personality pathology can be classified into specific categories, as is found in the DSM. The dimensional approach suggests that people vary as to the strength of various personality traits, and that each individual will have a unique profile of high and low scores on measures of these traits. Perhaps the best known dimensional approach is the *Five-Factor Model*, as described by Paul Costa and Robert McCrae.

The schema approach is somewhat more complex and comes out of both psychoanalytic theory and cognitive psychotherapy. In this view, our personality is shaped by our expectations of ourselves and other people in relationships. This set of expectations, or schemas, operates largely out of consciousness and guides our thoughts, emotions, and behaviors in meaningful situations.

What causes **personality pathology**?

Personality pathology has both environmental and genetic causes. The schema approach addresses the environmental causes of personality pathology, considering how early relationships with parents and other key figures in childhood shape enduring personality traits. The psychiatrist Robert Cloninger suggested that personality is made up of both temperament and character. Temperament refers to biologically based personality traits that are determined by genetics. Character refers to the parts of personality that are most influenced by the environment. In this way, he integrated both genetic and environmental explanations of personality.

What is the **schema approach**?

The schema approach is used here to refer to any theory that sees personality as derived from a set of *expectations* of self and others that guides cognitive, emotional, and behavioral responses in relevant situations. Depending on the theoretical orientation, such expectations might be termed *schemas, representations*, or *internal working models*. Schemas grow out of early childhood experiences and, by adulthood, they are difficult, but not impossible, to change. For example, if a child's mother is loving, empathic, and emotionally stable, the child will learn that the world is safe, understandable, and benevolent. The child will learn to approach the people he or she encounters in an open and friendly way, which will in turn elicit similarly positive responses. Likewise, if the child is raised in a rejecting, hurtful, and neglectful environment, this will teach the child a suspicious and pessimistic view of the world. Such a negative outlook will guide the child's behavior, thus eliciting negative and rejecting responses from others, further confirming the child's pessimistic schemas.

This general model of personality pathology has received empirical support from a huge range of research and has been integral to the development of many types of psychotherapy. However, it does not lend itself well to diagnosis and so has had little impact so far on diagnostic schemes. Moreover, it only accounts for the learned aspects of personality, and not the inborn or biological aspects.

What is the **history** of the **schema approach**?

The general concept of schemas grew out of psychoanalytic theory. In the beginning of psychoanalysis, in the late nineteenth and early twentieth centuries, the focus was largely on the battles between drives and defenses, between sexual and aggressive instincts, and the need to inhibit them. With time, noted psychoanalysts such as Otto Rank, Melanie Klein, D.W. Winnicott, Harry Stack Sullivan, and W.R.D. Fairbarn expanded that rather narrow focus to include their patients' characteristic ways of engaging with the world around them. To some degree, all of these pioneering psychoanalysts linked the personality traits of their adult patients to their early childhood relationships with parents. This approach later became known as *object relations*, and included an assumption that early childhood relationships impacted adult personality by etching a particular picture of the world into the patient's mind.

What is **temperament**?

One of the controversies that has persisted throughout the history of psychology has to do with the extent to which personality is learned or inborn. Although there is considerable evidence supporting the impact of early childhood relationships on adult personality, there is also solid evidence that many personality traits—such as shyness, extraversion, sensation-seeking, and even impulse control—are genetically determined. In the early 1990s, Robert Cloninger proposed that personality reflected the combination of both *temperament* and *character*. He defined temperament as inborn, genetically transmitted traits that influence the way we process information. He proposed three specific traits of temperament: *harm avoidance, novelty seeking*, and *reward dependence*. He later added *persistence*, which refers to the tendency to persevere toward a goal despite setbacks.

Both harm avoidance, which involves the tendency to avoid risk, and novelty seeking, which involves the tendency to seek out stimulation even if it involves risk, have received considerable support in the literature and do seem to have a genetic component. Harm avoidance may be mediated by the neurotransmitter *serotonin*, while novelty seeking has been associated with both *dopamine* and *norepinephrine*.

What is **Cloninger's concept** of **character**?

Cloninger's concept of character is very similar to the schema approach described above. He believed character to involve learned patterns of interacting with the environment, reflecting concepts of the world that were in large part formed in early childhood. Cloninger proposed three character traits: self-directedness, (initiative, responsibility, and personal agency); cooperativeness (helpfulness, pro-social orientation); and self-transcendance (spiritually-inclined, able to rise above self-absorption). His Temperament and Character Inventory (TCI) is a self-report questionnaire with seven scales measuring the four temperament and three character dimensions.

What **personality traits** are **genetic**?

Cloninger's distinction between temperament and character suggests that some personality traits are learned while others are inborn. This leads to the question of which personality traits fall into which category. Genetic studies suggest that many genes code for either behavioral activation or inhibition. In other words, many of the genes that influence personality seem to code for either sensation seeking, impulsive, and extraverted traits, or anxious, harm avoidant, and introverted traits. Psychiatric disorders such as alcohol abuse, borderline and antisocial personality disorder, and attention deficit disorder are associated with behavioral activation genes, while other disorders or traits such as depression, anxiety, and introversion are associated with behavioral inhibition genes.

What **personality traits** are **learned**?

While personality traits related to behavioral activation or inhibition appear to have a strong genetic influence, traits related to trust, morality, empathy, and capacity for intimacy appear to be more strongly influenced by the environment.

What does Kenneth **Kendler's work** tell us about the **genetics** of **personality**?

The psychiatrist Kenneth Kendler and his colleagues have conducted a series of twin studies to investigate the heritability (or genetic basis) of various personality traits and psychiatric syndromes. Twin studies work by comparing *monozygotic* (identical) twins, who share 100 percent of their genes, with dizygotic (fraternal) twins, who share only half of their genes. If more monozygotic than dizygotic twins have the same diagnosis, we can assume that the disorder has a genetic component. By using very complex statistical analyses on a sample of 2,794 Norwegian twins, Kendler and colleagues determined that the ten DSM-IV personality disorder diagnoses were about 25 percent attributable to genetics and about 75 percent due to non-genetic causes, such as the environment. Moreover, the authors performed *factor analysis* to identify common factors that might influence risk for more than one diagnosis.

Factor analysis works by identifying groups of disorders where twins are similarly alike or different; if twins are alike on personality disorder X, are they also alike on personality disorder Y? In this way, the authors identify *factors* or groupings of disorders that may share either genetic or environmental influence. Three genetic factors were identified in this study: an overall negative emotionality factor, an impulsivity/poor behavioral control factor, and an inhibition/avoidance factor. Interestingly, the environmental contributions did not seem to group together. In other words, the environmental risks appeared to be unique for each personality disorder.

How do we **diagnose personality pathology?**

We diagnose personality pathology by grouping pathological personality traits into categories. The DSM approach to personality disorders is the official diagnostic system of the mental health field. The DSM system defines a personality disorder as "an enduring pattern of inner

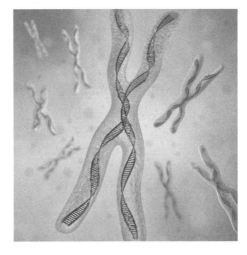

Genes account for some of our personality traits, but environment is also important (*iStock*).

experience and behavior that deviates markedly from the expectations of the individual's culture, is pervasive and inflexible, has an onset in adolescence or early adulthood, is stable over time and leads to distress or impairment." DSM-IV-TR lists ten personality disorders grouped into Clusters A, B, and C. The eleventh diagnosis, Personality Disorder Not Otherwise Specified, is intended as a catch basin diagnosis for people who do not fit the other ten diagnoses.

Two additional personality diagnoses, depressive and passive-aggressive (negativistic), are listed in the appendix as awaiting further study. Cluster A disorders, which include paranoid, schizoid, and schizotypal personality disorders, are characterized by odd or eccentric traits. Cluster B disorders, including histrionic, borderline, narcissistic, and antisocial personality disorders, are seen as impulsive and emotionally erratic. Cluster C disorders include avoidant, dependent, and obsessive-compulsive personality disorders and are associated with high anxiety.

What are the **strengths** and **limitations** of the **DSM-IV diagnoses** for personality disorders?

The DSM-IV diagnoses have shown high inter-rater reliability and internal consistency. In other words, different raters reliably diagnose people in similar ways and the different criteria of each diagnosis strongly correlate with one another. Moreover, they have been shown to predict to many important clinical features (e.g., suicidality, drug abuse, interpersonal problems, criminal activity). In other words, the DSM personality diagnoses are clinically relevant. Nonetheless, there are problems with this system. For one, the categorical approach does not account for severity. It does not say whether you are mildly or severely borderline, which may matter more than the discrete diagnoses. Secondly, the diagnoses are not mutually exclusive, and people may meet criteria for more than one diagnosis. Thirdly, the diagnoses are far from exhaustive and many types of personality pathology are not easily diagnosed in DSM-IV.

What is the **dimensional approach**?

While the categorical approach (as seen in DSM) tries to establish a comprehensive list of personality types, a dimensional approach looks at key personality traits that vary from person to person. The *Five Factor Model* of personality has received considerable attention in the research literature. As presented by Paul Costa and Robert McCrae, the Five Factors include *openness to experience, conscientiousness, extraversion, agreeableness,* and *neuroticism (OCEAN)*. These traits were first identified from factor analytic studies, in which rating scales composed of large lists of emotional words were analyzed to see which words grouped together.

The psychological traits grouped into five different categories. The labels for these categories have varied slightly across different studies, but the OCEAN labels are now widely accepted. Even though there is good evidence that these traits are associated with clinically relevant outcomes, are stable over time, and have some genetic component to them, it is important to note that they are derived from statistical analyses of word lists and not from clinical observations. Therefore, their usefulness in clinical settings may be limited. The Five Factor Model has also been criticized because it is does not provide an actual theory of personality, only a set of empirical findings.

What is **Borderline Personality Disorder**?

Borderline Personality Disorder, in its full form, is one of the most severe of the DSM personality disorders. Classified as a Cluster B personality disorder, it is characterized by highly erratic and tempestuous behavior. To meet criteria for the DSM-IV diagnosis, the person must meet at least five of the following criteria: frantic efforts to avoid real or imagined abandonment; a pattern of very intense and unstable interpersonal relationships with swings between idealizing and devaluing others; identity disturbance reflected in a strikingly unstable sense of self; marked impulsivity in at least two areas (e.g., sex, substance abuse, binge eating); recurrent suicidal behavior, gestures or threats, or self-mutilating behavior (such as cutting or burning the self without intent to die); chronic feelings of emptiness; poorly regulated anger with inappropriate anger outbursts; and transient and stress-induced paranoid ideation or severe dissociative symptoms. Much research has linked Borderline Personality Disorder with a history of severe trauma, such as childhood sexual abuse, although not all people with this disorder report such histories.

What is **Narcissistic Personality Disorder**?

In effect, narcissism refers to a very fragile and unstable sense of self. In order to compensate for their fragile self-esteem, narcissistic people become preoccupied with their self-image and are intensely sensitive to perceived shame or humiliation. Typical narcissists have a grandiose sense of self, with an inflated sense of self-importance and an elevated need for attention, status, and recognition. In order to meet criteria for the DSM-IV diagnosis of Narcissistic Personality Disorder, an individual must meet five of the following nine criteria: has a grandiose sense of self-importance; has a preoccupation with fantasies of unlimited success; carries a belief that he or she is special and only can be understood by other special, high status individuals or groups; need for excessive admiration; displays a sense of entitlement—the assumption that others should accommodate to the person's needs and desires; is interpersonally exploitative; lacks empathy; is often envious of others or believes others are envious of him or her; and exhibits arrogant, haughty attitudes or behaviors.

Is it **necessarily bad** to be **narcissistic**?

Some concern with self-esteem, social status, and accomplishment is a universal part of human psychology. Moreover, there are few people who are entirely free of egotistical or insecure behavior. Thus we can see Narcissistic Personality Disorder as an extreme point on a range of behavior that includes normal human tendencies. Moreover, there is a fair amount of research that shows that some degree of narcissism can be adaptive. In a 1984 study by Robert Emmons, several narcissistic traits were correlated with measures of adaptive personality traits, such as self-confidence, extraversion, initiative, and ambition. Moreover, in a 2008 study by Eric Russ and colleagues, the authors identified three subtypes of narcissistic personality disorder, which they labeled grandiose/malignant, fragile, and high-functioning/exhibitionistic. The third subtype showed significantly less psychopathology and much higher adaptive functioning than the other two groups. Thus, some degree of narcissism may be adaptive with regard to ambition, initiative, and self-confidence. People with severe narcissistic traits, however, have significant interpersonal, emotional, and even occupational difficulties.

What is **antisocial personality disorder**?

People with antisocial personality disorder (ASPD) have a severe deficit in morality. They are characterized by callous and exploitive behavior and by a lack of empathy or remorse. In keeping with the often impulsive and reckless behavior associated with this disorder, ASPD is classified as a Cluster B personality disorder. A related term for this type of personality is psychopathy. Unsurprisingly, people with ASPD are particularly common in prison populations. According to DSM-IV, a person with this disorder demonstrates a pervasive pattern of disregard for the rights of others as evidenced by at least three of the following criteria: repeatedly engaging in illegal behavior; frequently lying, using aliases, or conning others for personal profit; demonstrating impulsivity and lack of future planning; exhibiting irritability and aggressiveness; showing reckless disregard for the safety of self and others; being consistently irresponsible, with repeated failures to sustain employment or fulfill financial obligations;

lacking remorse, as evident in indifference to, or rationalization of, hurting, mistreating, or stealing from others. This definition has been criticized, however, for being too focused on behavior instead of personality traits and also for requiring evidence of conduct disorder (a childhood variant of ASPD) before the age of fifteen.

What is **schizotypal personality disorder**?

Schizotypal personality disorder is quite different from the three personality disorders listed above. Classified as a Cluster A disorder, people with schizotypal personality disorder tend to be inhibited and socially withdrawn, which is in sharp contrast to people with Cluster B disorders. In general, schizotypal personality disorder is characterized by discomfort with social situations and odd, eccentric behavior.

The DSM-IV diagnosis requires five of the following nine criteria: ideas (but not delusions) of reference; odd beliefs or magical thinking (e.g., suspiciousness, telepathy); unusual bodily experiences; odd thinking and speech (e.g., vague or overelaborate); suspiciousness or paranoid ideation; inappropriate or constricted affect (expression of emotion); odd, eccentric or peculiar behavior or appearance; lack of close friends other than close relatives; and excessive social anxiety.

When people have ideas of reference, they believe that events in the environment pertain to them, although there is actually no connection. For example, someone might walk into a room and think everyone in the room is talking about him or her. People with schizotypal personality disorder have an elevated incidence of schizophrenia in their families, and therefore probably share some genetic loading with schizophrenia.

If your **environment supports** your **behavior**, do you still have a **personality disorder**?

By definition, a psychiatric disorder in DSM-IV needs to cause distress or dysfunction and must be outside the norms of one's culture. Nonetheless, there are circumstances when people may meet criteria for a DSM-IV personality disorder, but they are shielded from distress or dysfunction from a protective environment. For example, people who are very powerful, wealthy, or famous may be protected from the negative social consequences of behavior that would not be tolerated in less privileged individuals. In fact the newspapers are full of reports of outrageous behavior on the part of celebrities and politicians. If these people continue to succeed in their lives in spite of such behavior, does their behavior still meet criteria for a personality disorder? Such a question is not easily answered, but we can assume that those individuals who truly do suffer from personality pathology will not be able to modify their behavior when it does start to cause negative consequences. Healthier people will be able to adapt as needed.

What **changes** will be made to the **diagnosis** of **personality disorders** in DSM-V?

The APA is proposing fairly radical changes to the diagnosis of personality disorders. For one, they want to collapse the diagnosis of personality disorders into axis I along with all other psychiatric and even medical disorders. They also remove most of the actual diagnostic categories, leaving only five personality types, specifically antisocial/psychopathic, avoidant, borderline, obsessive-compulsive, and schizotypal. Each patient will also be evaluated in terms of the severity of his or her impairment in self and interpersonal functioning. This will determine the maturity and stability of their understanding of themselves and other people. Finally, patients will be rated on six broad personality trait domains, including negative emotionality, introversion, antagonism, disinhibition, compulsiveness, and schizotypy. Each broad domain has a series of trait facets. For example, under disinhibition, there are the trait facets of impulsivity, distractibility, and recklessness. While this system takes into account much of clinical theory and research, it is also very complex—which might make it hard to apply in real world settings.

SUBSTANCE ABUSE

What is **addiction**?

In general, the term *addiction* refers to a state of obsessive desire or craving for something or some activity, beyond the point of normal use and to the extent of causing

Was Soviet Union ruler Joseph Stalin a psychopath, or just a successful dictator?

One of the key assumptions of DSM-IV is that psychopathology has to cause distress or dysfunction. In other words it has to be self-defeating. But what about behavior that causes gross distress and dysfunction to others? If the individual benefits by his or her behavior but other people suffer, does that count as psychopathology? This quandary shows how difficult it can be at times to determine what does and does not constitute psychopathology. Additionally, it illustrates the difficulty in distinguishing between psychopathology and extreme immorality.

Soviet Union dictator Joseph Stalin committed horrible crimes during his rule. Would his behavior meet criteria for antisocial personality disorder? (*iStock*)

Joseph Stalin (1879–1953) is a case in point. Stalin was appointed general secretary of the Communist party in 1922 and gained complete control over the Soviet Union when Vladimir Lenin died in 1924. He retained absolute power until his death in 1953. Within five years of Lenin's death, he was responsible for the execution of several million people. Stalin brooked no opposition to his regime. Anyone suspected of opposing him or of even having the potential to oppose him might be deported to Siberia, tortured, and/or executed. He has also been accused of causing or at least greatly exacerbating famines that killed millions of people.

Historians now believe that Stalin was responsible for the death of—at minimum—20 million people. Would Stalin meet DSM-IV criteria for Antisocial Personality Disorder? It appears that Stalin met at least five DSM-IV criteria for Antisocial Personality Disorder. He repeatedly broke the law before he was in power; and after attaining power he simply created the law to suit his needs. He lied and conned others to maintain his position of absolute power. As a mass murderer he was clearly irritable and aggressive. He showed reckless disregard for the safety of others; he showed lack of remorse for the mistreatment of others.

Stalin also demonstrated aggressive and illegal behavior in his youth, which may meet criteria for conduct disorder before the age of 15. However, he was a brilliant and immensely successful politician. Despite having murdered tens of millions of people, he was able to hold onto power until his death at age 74. Thus, his genocidal behavior may not have caused distress or dysfunction to *himself*, although it certainly did to others.

harm. As early as 1964, the World Health Organization discouraged the use of the word "addiction" in a mental health context, stating that the word had become too colloquial and was not sufficiently precise. Consequently, the major diagnostic systems, DSM and ICD, diagnose *substance abuse* and *dependence* rather than addiction. Nonetheless, *addiction* remains a widely used term, within the field as well as the popular culture. While use of the word "addiction" generally refers to a chemical substance, such as heroin or cocaine, people also speak of behavioral addictions, such as compulsive gambling or addiction to sex. In fact, a new category of behavioral addictions is being considered for DSM-V.

What do recent statistics say about **drug use** in the **United States**?

The data below come from the 2007 National Survey on Drug Use and Health, conducted by SAMHSA, a division of the U.S. Department of Health and Human Services. Data are based on interviews with 67,870 subjects aged 12 or older. Two main findings stand out. For one, recreational use of substances is extremely widespread, affecting almost half the U.S. population. Nonetheless, use of highly addictive substances, such as heroin and methamphetamine, is far less common than use of less addictive substances, such as marijuana and pain relievers. Secondly, there is a large difference between lifetime use and recent use, suggesting that recreational drug use is either infrequent or temporary for most people.

Percentage of U.S. Population Who Have Used Drugs (2007)

Drug	Lifetime Use	Past Year	Past Month
All Types	46.1	14.4	8.0
Marijuana/Hashish	40.6	10.1	5.8
Cocaine	14.5	2.3	0.8
Heroin	1.5	0.1	0.1
Hallucinogens (e.g., LSD, PCP, Ecstasy)	13.8	1.5	0.4
Inhalants	9.1	0.8	0.2
Non-Medical use of Therapeutics	20.3	6.6	2.8
Pain Relievers	13.3	5.0	2.1
Tranquilizers	8.2	2.1	0.7
Sedatives	3.4	0.3	0.1
Stimulants	8.7	1.2	0.4
Methamphetamine	5.3	0.5	0.2

Is there a difference between **recreational drug use** and **addiction**?

Almost half the U.S. population uses an illicit substance at some point in their life. If we include alcohol, the proportion of people who engage in recreational substance use is far higher. Many people can use psychoactive substances without harm. Addiction, however, is an entirely different animal. Severe addiction, particularly to the most addictive substances such as heroin, cocaine, or methamphetamine, lays waste to peoples' lives. Careers, physical health, families, and even whole communities can be destroyed by drug addiction. Furthermore, approximately 10 percent of people with substance dependence commit suicide, generally in the midst of a substance-induced depression.

What is the difference between **addiction**, **substance abuse**, and **substance dependence**?

The term *addiction* is somewhat of an umbrella term referring to any kind of compulsive use or excessive dependence on a substance or activity. In the DSM-IV, *substance abuse* is characterized by excessive use which continues despite significant negative consequences. More specifically, substance abuse requires recurrent use of the substance, resulting in failure to meet major role obligations; exposure to situations that are physically hazardous (e.g., drunk driving); recurrent legal problems; and continued use despite repeated negative social consequences.

People with substance abuse continue to use drugs despite negative consequences, while people with substance dependence also experience drug tolerance and withdrawal (*Stock*).

Substance dependence is a more severe disorder. In addition to causing social, occupational, and/or financial problems, substance dependence also requires a physiological addiction to the drug. The two most important features involve *tolerance* and *withdrawal*. Additionally, there can be an increase in the amount of substance used over time, a persistent desire to cut down, or unsuccessful efforts to do so, considerable amounts of time spent in pursuit of the substance, sacrifice of important life activities because of substance use, and/or the continued use of the substance despite clear physiological or psychological damage from it.

What do **tolerance** and **withdrawal** mean?

When people develop tolerance, they have become desensitized to the drug and require more and more of the substance to achieve the same effect. Different drugs vary as to how likely they are to cause tolerance. For example, tolerance for amphetamine and opiates is generally stronger than that for alcohol. In fact, people who abuse opiates, such as heroin or morphine, can develop a tolerance for the analgesic (pain-killing) effects that can last for years after the end of the substance abuse. Consequently, people with a history of opiate abuse or dependence often require much more opiates to treat pain than the average person.

Withdrawal refers to physiological symptoms that occur when the substance is discontinued. Because the brain has become adapted to the chemical, removal of the chemical sends the brain into a disregulated state. Withdrawal can be extremely painful as well as dangerous. Depending on the substance, withdrawal symptoms can include changes in heart rate, vomiting, confusion, pain, and even seizures. The effects of withdrawal are generally opposite to the effects of intoxication. For example, people become energetic and euphoric during cocaine intoxication, but experience fatigue and depression during cocaine withdrawal.

Are **addictions pleasurable**?

Few people suffering from substance dependence would say that addictions are pleasurable. Many addicts will say that the use of the drug was initially pleasurable, but that as the addiction set in, the pleasure was counterbalanced by craving. At this point, they used the drug to reduce the discomfort of craving or withdrawal as much as to bring pleasure.

What role does **dopamine** have in addiction?

A growing body of research points to the central role of the dopamine system in chemical, and even behavioral, addictions. Drugs such as cocaine, amphetamine, and nicotine have a direct effect on the dopamine system. Other drugs, such as heroin and marijuana may have an indirect effect on this system. The dopamine neurons originate deep in a region of the midbrain called the *ventral tegmental* area. These dopamine neurons course through the middle of the brain, connecting with a small structure in the forebrain known as the *nucleus accumbens*.

This system is known as the *mesolimbic dopamine tract* and is a central part of the *dopamine reward system*, which seems to be involved in the activation of the organism to pursue rewarding stimuli. In other words, this system is central to an animal's experience of desire and motivation. Activation of the reward system stimulates pleasurable feelings of euphoria, energy, and enthusiasm. Many drugs of abuse directly stimulate this chemical system, providing an immediate and intensely pleasurable experience. In effect, they mimic the brain's natural chemicals.

Unfortunately, nature allows no free lunch. Over time, activating the dopamine reward system by outside chemicals changes the structure of the brain, reducing its ability to regulate the dopamine system.

How does drug **addiction change** the **brain**?

Drugs of abuse act on the brain's *neurotransmitters*, the chemical messengers that coordinate interactions between neurons (brain cells). Because of the direct effect of substances of abuse on neurotransmitters, there is often a dramatic change in neurotransmitter function. For example, in response to foreign chemicals that mimic the activity of neurotransmitters, the neurons may decrease production of their own neurotransmitters. Receptor sites may die off. This change of the actual structure of the neurons contributes to the addictive process. When the brain makes less neurotransmitter or is less able to process it, craving sets in. Drug tolerance, the need for more and more of the same drug to achieve the same psychological effect, is also related to the changes in the neuron's structure. Moreover, changes to the neurons can lead to a reduction in brain volume, in other words, brain shrinkage. This is associated with cognitive, emotional, and physiological deterioration.

Are **some drugs more addictive** than others?

There are at least two ways that drugs can vary in their addictive potential. One is the drug's half-life, which refers to the time it takes for the drug to pass through the body. Drugs with a short half-life often have very quick effects, but also have sharp withdrawal reactions, which can contribute to addiction. Drugs with longer half-lives have a less quick and intense high and cause less abrupt withdrawal syndromes. However, their withdrawal syndromes can last longer as it takes more time for the drug to fully clear the system. The intensity of the dopamine spike that a drug causes also affects its addiction potential. Although drugs such as cocaine, nicotine, and amphetamine all cause an increase in dopamine activity, they vary tremendously in terms of the strength of the spikes they cause.

Why is **methamphetamine** so addictive?

Methamphetamine (also known as meth, crystal meth, ice, and crank) is a fairly new drug of abuse that has swept out from the West Coast, across the center of the United States, and is now moving into the East Coast. Although its popularity in the United States is fairly recent, it was first developed in the nineteenth century and used by the Japanese and the Germans during World War II. It is a devastatingly addictive drug, which can make short shrift of substance abusers in relatively little time.

One of the reasons it is so powerfully addictive is that it causes a dopamine spike much stronger than cocaine and vastly larger than nicotine. This spike is ten to 12 times higher than baseline levels and five to ten times higher than the spikes caused by natural rewards such as food or sex. Moreover, it lasts for hours. Tragically, this greatly enhanced release of dopamine damages the dopamine neurons in a process called *neurotoxicity*. Changes in the dopamine neurons takes place within days of use, both within humans and animals, and the effects can last for months or years.

What are some recent statistics on the **percentage** of the **U.S. population** that **abuses** or is **dependant** on **drugs**?

The table below shows the percentages of the U.S. population that met criteria for substance abuse or dependence for each of the drugs listed during 2007. Consider that each percent of the population (ages 12 and up) is equal to almost 2.5 million people. In other words, in 2007 more than 22 million people had some kind of substance abuse or dependence. These data come from the 2007 National Survey on Drug Use and Health for subjects aged 12 or older conducted by SAMHSA, of the U.S. Department of Health and Human Services. Substance abuse and dependence are based on DSM-IV criteria.

2007 Statistics on U.S. Drug Abuse or Dependence

Drug	Abuse or Dependence	Dependence
Any Type	9.0	4.7
Alcohol	7.5	3.4
Marijuana/Hashish	1.6	1.0
Cocaine	0.6	0.5
Heroin	0.1	0.1
Hallucinogens (e.g., LSD, PCP, Ecstasy)	0.1	0.0*
Inhalants	0.1	0.0*
Non-Medical use of Therapeutics	0.9	0.6
Pain Relievers	0.7	0.5
Tranquilizers	0.2	0.1
Sedatives	0.1	0.0*
Stimulants	0.2	0.1

*Incidence too low to report.

Is there a **genetic basis** to **addiction**?

A fair amount of research in the past few decades has pointed to a genetic component to addiction. Specific genes related to the neurotransmitter serotonin have been linked to early-onset alcoholism, though it is unclear if this is related to alcoholism per se, or to poor behavioral control. In addition, Kenneth Kendler and colleagues have performed twin studies looking at the relative contribution of genes and environment to the abuse of, or dependence on, six different substances: cannabis (marijuana), cocaine, hallucinogens, sedatives, stimulants, and opiates. From their comparison of 1,196 male-male twin pairs, the authors concluded that on average, each form of drug addiction was about 55 percent attributable to genetics and 45 percent attributable to environment.

Drugs and crime are closely linked, partly because people often lose their jobs because of their addiction and turn to crime (*iStock*).

Moreover, there appeared to be a genetic vulnerability to developing drug addiction in general, but not to developing an addiction to any particular drug. Similarly, there was a general effect of environment, influencing the likelihood of any kind of drug abuse/dependence rather than abuse of a specific drug. Interestingly, opiate addiction seemed more heavily influenced by environment (78 percent) than genetics (23 percent). Perhaps opiates are less available than other drugs and, as a result, opiate abuse is heavily dependent on exposure to drugs in the environment.

What is the **relationship** of **childhood trauma** and **addiction**?

There is considerable evidence of an association between trauma and neglect in childhood and addiction in adulthood. In other words, adults with addiction report a higher incidence of childhood trauma and neglect than adults without addiction. Both psychological and neurobiological research show that inadequate parenting and harmful childhood experiences can deeply interfere with the development of mature self-control, including the ability to regulate emotion and behavior. In these circumstances, drug use can be very attractive because it serves (at least at first) to reduce negative emotion and enhance positive emotion. In the absence of effective emotional regulation skills, any shortcut to positive emotion can be very appealing. Moreover, people with poor impulse control are less likely to monitor their drug use. As a result, recreational drug use is more likely to escalate into addiction.

How does **drug use** break down **by age** in the **United States**?

The table below shows the incidence of substance abuse or dependence in 2007, both for illicit drugs and alcohol. As is clear in the chart, substance use disorders start in the early teens, peak at age 21, and then subside after that. The abrupt decline after age 21 is consistent with research suggesting many people conquer their substance problems without treatment. These data come from the 2007 National Survey on Drug Use and Health for subjects aged 12 or older, conducted by SAMHSA of the U.S. Department of Health and Human Services. Classification of substance abuse and dependence is based on DSM-IV diagnostic criteria.

Percentage of U.S. Population in 2007
Abusing or Dependent on Drugs or Alcohol, According to Age

Age	Illicit Drugs	Alcohol	Drugs or Alcohol
12	0.7	0.5	1.1
13	0.9	1.1	1.7
14	3.2	2.9	5.0
15	5.5	7.4	9.8
16	6.9	7.9	12.1
17	8.4	12.1	15.8
18	8.0	12.5	16.4
19	9.6	17.2	21.8
20	9.2	17.7	22.2
21	9.4	20.5	24.6
22	7.5	19.4	23.0
23	7.2	18.1	21.8
24	6.2	15.7	19.1
25	5.9	14.2	17.1
26–29	4.1	12.3	14.5
30–34	3.0	9.4	10.9
35–39	2.4	7.7	9.0
40–44	2.2	7.4	8.9
45–49	1.9	8.2	9.2
50–54	1.0	5.2	5.9
55–59	1.1	4.8	5.9
60–64	0.2	3.2	3.3
65 and older	0.2	1.3	1.4

What is the relationship between **addiction** and **crime**?

For a number of different reasons, drug addiction does contribute to crime. For one, the addiction may destroy the person's ability to hold a job, removing the means to pay for the drug. In this situation, drug addicts may turn to crime in order to obtain the money needed to pay for their drug. Common forms of criminal activity include robbery, drug dealing, and prostitution. Secondly, many drugs of abuse impair judgment and impulse control, which increases the likelihood of reckless and criminal acts. In fact, it has been estimated that 55 percent of car accidents and more than 50 percent of murders involve alcohol intoxication. Thirdly, most Western countries outlaw the most common drugs of abuse. Unfortunately, this fails to erase demand for the drugs (though many argue that it does *decrease* demand). Consequently, the market for illicit drugs goes underground and becomes the domain of criminals. Competition within the illicit drug trade has led to a tremendous amount of violence, dating back to the days of Al Capone in the 1920s.

How much **control** do **addicts have** over their addiction?

Drug addiction is not a psychotic disorder. People are always aware of their drug use and of their choice to use. Thus, we cannot say addicted individuals have no choice and no control over their drug use. Nonetheless, it is important to realize that addiction changes the brain. In the most addictive drugs, the cravings are overwhelming and the ability to inhibit self-destructive behavior is very weak. This is because the parts of the brain that monitor behavior, employ social judgment, and inhibit harmful actions are significantly compromised at the same time that the reward system is on overdrive. Therefore, it is fair to say that addicted individuals have some control over their behavior but far, far less control than a non-addicted person.

What are the **stages** of **change**?

The motivation to change is a major factor in addiction treatment. Some addicts have little to no motivation to change their behavior. Or their motivation may not be sustained. In 1994, James Prochaska, John Norcross, and Carlo DiClemente published their model of the *stages of change*, which describes six different stages that people go through when deciding to change addictive behaviors. This work has been widely integrated into addiction treatments.

The first stage is called *pre-contemplation*. At this point the individual does not believe he or she has a problem and is resistant to suggestions to change. There may be considerable denial about the extent of the problem.

The next stage is called *contemplation*. In this stage, the individual is aware there is a problem and is beginning to consider taking action to change. The third stage is known as *preparation*. The person is now taking steps in preparation of change. For example, he or she may start researching drug treatment options or talking to family and friends about the need to stop using the drug. Nonetheless, there is still ambivalence about giving up the substance.

The fourth stage is termed *action*. At this point, the person takes actual steps to stop the substance use. This may involve joining a twelve-step group, an outpatient treatment center, or even getting admitted for inpatient treatment. The person also recognizes the need to change a broad array of psychological and social patterns associated with the addiction.

In the fifth *maintenance* phase, the person has successfully stopped using the substance. Still, there is ongoing risk of relapse and the person needs to take care to prevent backsliding. There will be need for ongoing support and treatment, often in the form of a twelve-step group such as Alcoholics Anonymous (AA). There is also need for continuing attention to ways of handling emotions, relationships, and responsibilities.

In the final phase, *termination*, the person has successfully mastered the addiction. The temptation to use is no longer a significant danger. Nonetheless, people do not necessarily travel through these stages in a straightforward manner, and there is frequently movement back and forth between the stages.

What kinds of **treatments** are used for **addiction**?

Fortunately, there are many treatments for addiction. Medications are available to treat withdrawal, decrease drug cravings, or reduce enjoyment of the substance. Psychosocial treatments include a wide variety of therapies designed to help the addicted individual choose to stop using the drug, combat cravings, and handle the emotional and interpersonal challenges of daily life without resorting to substances.

Treatments vary from the least to the most restrictive. Depending on the severity of the addiction, including the motivation to stop the drug, the level of functioning in the community, the presence of co-existing psychiatric or medical problems, and the level of family support, the addicted individual may need more or less structure in their treatment. Higher functioning individuals with less debilitating addictions may be successfully treated in an outpatient setting or a twelve-step program such as Alcoholics Anonymous.

People whose addiction has more thoroughly taken over their lives may need greater structure, such as inpatient detoxification (where they are helped through the withdrawal process), inpatient rehab (where their addiction is addressed in a short-term residential setting), or longer term therapeutic communities, where the patient may stay for up to one to two years.

What are the **pharmacological treatments** for addiction?

A number of pharmacological agents (medications) are used to treat withdrawal. In general, withdrawal is treated with a drug that is similar to the drug of abuse. In this way, the individual is weaned off the chemical substance slowly. Common medications for alcohol withdrawal include a class of antianxiety drugs known as benzodiazepines, particularly diazepam (brand name Valium) and chlordiazepoxide (Librium). With-drawal from opiates, such as heroin, opium, morphine, or oxycodone (OxyContin), is often treated with methadone or clonidine. Methadone maintenance is the most com-mon pharmacological treatment of opiate addiction, serving to reduce craving and withdrawal. Naltrexone is also used to reduce craving by blocking the reinforcing effects of both opiates and alcohol.

What is **methadone** and how does it help?

Methadone is a long-acting opiate that is dispensed to opiate-addicted individuals under the supervision of licensed methadone maintenance clinics. Because it is longer acting than most opiates of abuse, it is easier for the individual to maintain steady blood levels of the drug, which reduces the incidence of withdrawal and craving. It also gives much less of a high than other opiates, so it is less likely to be used as a recreational drug. There is considerable research that methadone maintenance reduces the crime, violence, medical problems, and mortality associated with severe opiate addiction. Nonetheless, there is controversy around methadone maintenance because many individuals may stay on methadone for many years rather than becom-ing entirely drug-free. Alternative medications to treat opiate addiction include buprenorphine and LAAM. LAAM, however, is no longer available in the United States or Europe due to rare cardiac side effects.

What is **Antabuse** and how does it help?

Disulfiram (brand name Antabuse) is used to treat alcoholism by causing uncomfortable physical reactions to alcohol. Disulfiram interferes with the metabolism of alcohol. Drinking alcohol after taking disulfiram causes nausea, vomiting, and many other unpleasant symptoms. As the medication stays in the system for at least a week, it can be a potent motivator not to drink. However, long-term use of this medication is not advised because it can cause liver damage. Additionally, drinking while on disulfiram is potentially fatal, so it is not recommended for impulsive patients, those who might drink despite knowledge of the consequences. Finally, this treatment is only useful with highly motivated patients, those who are willing to take the medication and avoid alcohol. Someone who is poorly motivated to stop drinking will simply stop taking the Antabuse.

What **psychological treatments** are most useful for **addictions**?

There are many psychological treatments for addictions. Group therapies are useful in decreasing the stigma of the addiction, confronting denial of the problem, and provid-ing encouragement and support for the struggle toward sobriety. As social animals, we are all highly suggestive to peer influences and tend to conform to group norms. In group therapies, this universal tendency can be put to constructive use. Individual therapies focus on the skills needed to live without substances. Such therapies provide

Group therapy has been proven effective for treating addictions (*iStock*).

education about the effects of addiction, build coping skills to handle cravings and avoid relapse, and help the person to rebuild relationships and handle stress without using substances.

Motivational Interviewing (*MI*) is a relatively recent technique developed by William Miller and Stephen Rollnick. MI addresses clients' ambivalence about changing their behavior. In this brief intervention, clients are asked to consider the pros and cons of substance use and to identify their own personal goals. In a nonjudgmental and reflective manner, counselors aim to guide clients toward greater motivation to change.

What are **twelve-step programs**?

While most treatments of substance abuse depend on mental health professionals, twelve-step programs are entirely member run. Alcoholics Anonymous (AA) was the first twelve-step program. Started in 1935 by Bill Wilson and Dr. Robert Smith, a New York stockbroker and an Ohio surgeon, AA now has over two million members in over 150 countries worldwide. AA offers support groups for alcoholics who wish to stop drinking alcohol. Members can attend daily meetings or even multiple meetings per day, depending on availability of meetings. The original publication, entitled *Alcoholics Anonymous*, was first published in 1939 and is now in its fourth edition. It offers specific guidelines on how to change behavior and maintain sobriety, including the twelve-step program toward recovery. The twelve steps include such measures as admitting that one is powerless over alcohol, asking for help from a higher power, taking an honest moral inventory of oneself, and making amends for past misbehavior. Numerous other twelve-step programs have arisen, such as Narcotics Anonymous, Overeaters Anonymous, Sex Addicts Anonymous, and Gamblers Anonymous.

PSYCHOTHERAPY

What is **psychotherapy**?

Fundamentally, psychotherapy involves talking. Patients bring their psychological difficulties into treatment. Therapists aim to reduce a patient's suffering via verbal discussion. Granted, psychotherapy involves far more than just conversation, but it is distinguished from other kinds of therapies—such as physical, speech, occupational, or medical therapy—by its emphasis on *talking*. In fact, Anna O., one of the world's first psychotherapy patients, described it as the "talking cure." Anna O. (a.k.a. Bertha Papenheimer) was one of Sigmund Freud's case histories, written up in his 1895 *Studies on Hysteria*.

How does **psychotherapy work**?

There are at least three mechanisms through which psychotherapy helps people feel better: *social support, insight*, and *skills building*. A large body of research shows the powerful effect of social support in just about all aspects of psychological health. When people are under stress, it is extremely helpful for them to talk out their problems with another person. Nonetheless, psychotherapy provides more than just social support. Otherwise, there would be no need for trained professionals—friends and family would do just as well. Psychotherapy also helps people gain insight. It helps them learn about their motivations, emotions, and behavior, along with their effect on others.

With greater self-understanding, people are better equipped to handle life's challenges. Additionally, some people lack the necessary psychological skills to function well in life. For example, they could have difficulty managing anger, negotiating conflict, maintaining positive emotion, confronting anxiety-provoking stimuli, or controlling self-destructive impulses. Psychotherapy can teach people new skills to better handle these challenges.

Does **psychotherapy work**?

Originally, there was little scientific data to back up psychotherapists' claims about the effectiveness of psychotherapy. People had to rely on the testimony of psychotherapists which, for many skeptics, was not particularly convincing. The empirical study of psychotherapy started in the 1950s, however, and within a few decades grew into a

What did a 1995 *Consumer Reports* survey say about the effectiveness of psychotherapy?

In 1995 the magazine *Consumer Reports* published a large study on the effects of psychotherapy. The mental health questionnaire was sent out as part of a larger study polling readers on their opinions of appliances and services. Out of the 180,000 people sent the questionnaire, 22,000 responded and 7,000 answered the mental health questions. Of these, 3,000 people had discussed emotional problems with family, friends, or clergy; 4,100 had turned to some combination of mental health professionals, support groups, or family physicians; and 2,900 had consulted a mental health professional, most frequently a psychologist (37%), psychiatrist (22%), or social worker (14%).

The survey showed very positive results for psychotherapy when provided by a trained mental health professional. Ninety percent of those who felt very poor or fairly poor at the start of treatment reported feeling very good, good, or at least so-so at the time of the survey. Moreover, people who stayed in therapy longer did better. People treated by psychologists, psychiatrists, and social workers did better than those treated by other professionals, and the difference was larger over time. No specific type of therapy worked better than any other.

It is important to note, however, that this is a very different kind of study than most psychotherapy research. Most psychotherapy studies are highly controlled *efficacy* studies, with fixed length therapies, manualized treatments, and specific criteria for selecting patients. This *effectiveness* study is much less controlled but much more representative of the real world. Patients pick their own therapists, present with all manner of problems, and stay in therapy as long as they and their therapist agree to continue. Moreover the therapist can tailor the treatment to the patient, which might account for the lack of difference between types of treatments. If a treatment is not working, the therapist may have switched to another approach.

large movement. There now exists an entire field of psychotherapy research and there is substantial data supporting the positive effects of psychotherapy. Consequently, we can now state with confidence: Yes, psychotherapy does work.

What are the **major schools** of **psychotherapy**?

Although new types of psychotherapy are constantly arising, there are perhaps three major schools of psychotherapy: psychoanalytic or psychodynamic approaches, cognitive-behavioral approaches, and humanistic approaches. Additional schools of psychotherapy include family systems approaches and group psychotherapy.

What is **psychoanalysis**?

Psychoanalysis started under Sigmund Freud (1856–1939). Although there have been many developments since his death in 1939, certain pillars of the discipline remain. Psychoanalysis aims to alleviate emotional distress by bringing unconscious patterns of thought, emotion, and desire into awareness. This is done through long-term exploration of the person's mental processes in a one-to-one relationship with the psychoanalyst.

Classical psychoanalysis involves three to five sessions per week, during which the *analysand* (patient) lies on a couch with the psychoanalyst sitting behind, out of view. This arrangement is intended to create a relaxed and reflective state of mind, in which the analysand can access the depths of his or her mind. The analysand is instructed to express whatever thoughts pop into awareness, a process known as *free association*. Psychoanalysts also believe that early childhood experiences and relationships have profound influence on adult relationships. Through the process of free association, unconscious childhood feelings and beliefs can emerge to be understood and reworked with the tools of a mature adult mind.

What is **psychodynamic therapy**?

While psychoanalytic theory has had tremendous influence on the mental health field as a whole, the practice of classical psychoanalysis has become far less common than it was in its heyday in the first half of the twentieth century. *Psychodynamic psychotherapy* has adjusted to the financial and schedule constraints of modern life. In typical psychodynamic therapy, there are one to two forty-five- to fifty-minute sessions per week. Both therapist and patient sit up and face each other. There is no couch. The emphasis on unconscious patterns of thought, emotion, and desire is retained, however, as well as the belief that patterns learned in childhood influence adult emotional experiences and ways of relating to others.

As with psychoanalysis, psychodynamic therapy tends to be of indefinite length (often for many years) and relatively non-directive. The therapist aims to guide self-exploration, rather than provide answers or educate the patient in new modes of behavior. In other words, both psychoanalysis and psychodynamic therapy provide social support and promote insight, but neither one teaches specific skills.

What are **transference** and **countertransference**?

Transference and counter-transference are central concepts to both psychoanalysis and psychodynamic psychotherapy. Early in the development of psychoanalysis, Freud realized that analysands can develop inappropriately intense feelings about their analysts. He quickly recognized this *transference* to be part of the clinical material, believing the patient is likely to "transfer" his or her psychic conflicts onto the analyst. Through exploring the analysand's feelings about the analyst, much can be learned about the inner workings of the analysand's mind.

Counter-transference occurs when the analyst develops inappropriate and intense feelings about the analysand. In the early days of psychoanalysis, counter-transference was seen mainly as a negative, reflecting childish responses on the part of the analyst that were best suppressed and controlled. In current approaches to psychodynamic work, counter-transference is now incorporated into the therapeutic work. When working with either transference or counter-transference, however, it is extremely important that the analyst proceed with tact and care. Direct discussion of the relationship between therapist and patient can be awkward and stressful, and the therapist must introduce such topics carefully and in a constructive manner.

What is the difference between a **one-person** and a **two-person model** of psychoanalysis?

In the last few decades, newer schools of psychoanalysis, such as the interpersonal and relational schools, have moved from a *one-person* to a *two-person psychology*. This means that contemporary psychoanalytic therapists no longer believe in the *blank screen model* of psychoanalysis. In this model, the patient's experience within the therapy is seen solely as a product of the patient's mental processes. The therapist is simply a blank screen onto which the patient projects his or her own feelings and thoughts. The therapist makes no contribution to the patient's experience.

Contemporary psychoanalytic thinkers now believe that both therapist and patient contribute to the therapeutic relationship. The therapist is a living, feeling, and reacting human being. No matter how controlled the therapist's behavior may be, it is impossible to remove the human element from a therapist's technique.

Moreover, the emotional experience of the therapist can be a very valuable source of information, both about the interpersonal process within the therapy and the patient's emotional experience. For example, if the therapist starts feeling annoyed and irritated during the session, this might reflect passive-aggressive behavior on the part of the patient. Likewise, if the therapist starts feeling sad, this may reflect unacknowledged sad feelings on the part of the patient. Clearly the therapist's counter-transference needs to be interpreted with caution, so the patient is not unfairly held accountable for the therapist's emotional state. Consequently, both psychoanalysis and psychodynamic therapy require years of training.

What do psychoanalysts mean by **defense mechanisms**?

According to psychoanalytic theory, we use *defense mechanisms* to protect ourselves from feelings and thoughts that make us anxious. Through these mental manipulations, we keep ourselves blissfully unaware of uncomfortable information. In her classic 1936 book, *The Ego and the Mechanisms of Defense*, Anna Freud (1895–1982) listed ten defense mechanisms. Anna Freud was the youngest of Sigmund Freud's six children.

Types of Defense Mechanisms

Defense Mechanism	Explanation
Displacement	Here the person expresses feelings toward one person or situation that are really aimed at another. For example, a child might express anger at her babysitter when she is really angry at the parent who left to go on a business trip.
Introjection	In *introjection*, people internalize the person or action that has caused anxiety, thus moving from the passive to the active role. For example, a child who has been bullied may start to bully other children as a way of mastering his or her sense of powerlessness. This is similar to the process of *identifying with the aggressor.*
Isolation	In *isolation*, the intellectual awareness of an event is disconnected from emotional experience. The person is aware of everything that happened, but is completely out of touch with the emotional meaning of the event.
Projection	When people *project* emotion onto another person, they are attributing their own emotion to that person. In effect, they are saying, "I don't hate you. You hate me."
Regression	In *regression*, a person avoids anxiety by reverting back to an earlier developmental stage. For example, adolescents afraid of their budding sexuality might regress to their pre-sexual childhood.
Repression	Sigmund Freud believed *repression* to be the primary defense mechanism used to ward off threatening mental content. In repression, disturbing emotions, thoughts and memories are pushed entirely out of awareness.
Reaction Formation	Here the person expresses the opposite feeling from what is truly felt. For example, a rageful person becomes overly solicitous of the other person. An unconsciously rebellious person becomes excessively compliant.
Reversal or Turning against the Self	When people cannot bear feeling negative emotions toward another person, they might turn the emotion inward, for example, berating and punishing themselves rather than acknowledging the real source of their anger.
Sublimation	Here the person redirects the forbidden impulse into a socially valued activity. For example, childhood aggression may be *sublimated* into a career as a surgeon.
Undoing	When people are terribly ambivalent about something, they may express one emotion with one action and then *undo* their action as a way of expressing the opposite emotion.

What is **behavioral psychotherapy**?

Behavioral psychotherapy came out of the academic tradition of *behaviorism*. Behaviorism proposed two primary ways by which people learn a new behavior: classical and operant conditioning. These principals were established through scientific research conducted in the early twentieth century. It was not until the 1950s, however, that behaviorist principals were adapted into psychotherapy techniques.

What is **classical conditioning**?

In *classical conditioning*, people learn to respond to a neutral object or event (the *conditioned stimulus* or CS) in a new way when it is paired with an emotionally meaningful object or event (the *unconditioned stimulus* or UCS). For example, we may develop strong feelings about a particular song (CS) because we associate with an emotionally important time in our life (UCS), such as a romantic break up or great vacation. The new learned reaction is known as the *conditioned response* (CR).

How is **classical conditioning** used in psychotherapy?

Classical conditioning techniques are extremely effective in the treatment of anxiety disorders. In these disorders, the people have learned to *associate* various stimuli with fear. To treat the anxiety disorder, it is necessary to dissociate the feared object (e.g., dogs) from the fear reaction. In this way, the conditioned stimulus (dogs) is disconnected from the conditioned response (fear of dogs). Techniques such as flooding and systematic desensitization expose people to their feared objects, either gradually (systematic desensitization) or all at once (flooding). When no harm comes from the exposure to the object, the fear response diminishes. The conditioned stimulus becomes decoupled from the conditioned response and, *voilá*, the person is no longer afraid of dogs. Further, a new association can be created between the formerly feared object and feelings of relaxation and calm. In other words, a pairing is made between the conditioned stimulus and a new (positive) conditioned response. Relaxation training, involving techniques such as deep breathing, visualization of a pleasant scene, and progressive muscle relaxation, can be used to help the person feel relaxed when in the presence of the formerly feared object.

What is **systematic desensitization**?

One of the most commonly used techniques to help people unlearn fear conditioning is called *systematic desensitization*. People are first asked to create a hierarchy of situations in which they might feel anxious. For example, people who are afraid of dogs might first list thinking about a dog, then seeing a picture of a dog, then seeing a dog from far away, then seeing a dog in a cage, then seeing a dog ten feet away, then five feet away, then standing right next to a dog, and then finally petting the dog. Using a scale from 0 to 100, each situation is scored as to how much anxiety it elicits. Imagining a dog might get a rating of 5, seeing a picture of a dog a score of 10, and touching a dog a score of 65.

The client is then taught relaxation strategies, in order to learn to feel calm when in the anxiety-provoking situation. Next the client is exposed to the situations listed on the hierarchy, starting with the least anxiety-provoking (imagining the dog) and gradually moving up the list to the most anxiety-provoking (petting the dog). At each point, clients are instructed to use relaxation techniques until they can tolerate each step on the hierarchy without undue anxiety. This is an extremely effective technique, and it is used to help people overcome all manner of anxiety problems, including the fear of flying, public speaking, heights, or test taking.

How does **operant conditioning** work?

According to the principles of *operant conditioning*, the likelihood that a behavior will be repeated depends upon the consequences of that behavior. Rewarded behaviors are more likely to be repeated, punished behaviors are less so. Therefore, you can change behavior by modifying its consequences.

How are **operant conditioning** principles **applied** in psychotherapy?

Behavioral modification, as championed by B.F. Skinner (1904–1990) in the 1950s, relies on the principals of operant conditioning. It employs carefully designed rewards (or positive reinforcement) to encourage desirable behavior. Likewise, removal of key rewards reduces incentive for *undesirable* behavior. Alternatively, punishment can be used to decrease frequency of undesirable behavior. Punishment is used less frequently than positive reinforcement, however, because it tends to elicit negative reactions. In sum, behavioral modification changes behavior by manipulating the rewards and punishments that motivate people to perform the behavior.

Such techniques are used in child rearing and animal training as well as the treatment of emotionally disturbed children and individuals with mental retardation. Operant conditioning techniques are also widely used in situations requiring some degree of social control, for example in prisons, schools, and even the workplace. They are less frequently used in individual therapy, as such techniques are most useful for people who lack *internal* motivation to change their behavior. For the most part, people seeking out psychotherapy on their own do so because they are already motivated to change.

What is **cognitive psychotherapy**?

Behaviorism dominated American academic psychology well into the 1960s, at which point the cognitive revolution brought the mind back to scientific respectability. Previously, behaviorists had thoroughly dismissed subjective experiences as unworthy of

What are the ABCs of behavioral therapy?

One of the cornerstones of behavioral therapy involves identifying the consequences of various behaviors. If you want to change a person's behavior, you have to consider what is reinforcing that behavior. Are there positive consequences that motivate the person to perform the behavior? Often the answer is not so obvious.

One of the basic techniques of behavioral therapy is *functional behavioral analysis*. In this process the behavior is observed carefully and a log is kept of the *antecedents* (what happened before?), *behaviors* (what exactly did the person do?), and *consequences* (what happened afterwards?), otherwise known as the ABCs.

After the target behavior has been studied this way, it is possible to identify what reinforces the behavior. For example, a toddler may throw up every night and the parents do not know why. Functional behavioral analysis might show that the toddler throws up at night after the parents put the child down to sleep. First the child cries to get her parents back into the room. The parents resist for a while but when the mother gives in, the child vomits. At that point the mother spends up to 45 minutes with the child, cleaning her up and soothing her. This functional analysis makes clear that vomiting is reinforcing for the child because it brings her mother's attention. The treatment for this kind of problem would be to change the *contingencies* of the child's crying. Instead of entering the room to reassure the child in response to the child's crying, the parent should enter the room at a fixed time interval. This way the child's crying loses the power to control the parents' behavior. The parent first enters the room at a frequent rate, so that the child is only left alone for short time periods. The parent then spaces out the time intervals so that the child slowly adapts to falling asleep without the parent. This process is the basis of the Ferber method, a well-known technique for conditioning babies to sleep through the night.

scientific attention. Taking advantage of this movement, psychologists such as Aaron Beck (1921–), Albert Ellis (1913–2007), and Martin Seligman (1942–), developed a new form of psychotherapy, known as *cognitive psychotherapy*.

All three branches of cognitive therapy start from the premise that psychological distress can be linked to maladaptive *thoughts*. Negative thoughts stimulate negative emotions, which in turn motivate self-defeating behavior. The negative consequences of these patterns reinforce the problematic thoughts, creating a vicious cycle. Unlike psychoanalytic treatment, which explores psychological distress in an open-ended, nondirective way, cognitive therapists actively identify unhealthy thought processes, and train patients to restructure their thoughts into healthier responses.

What are **cognitive distortions**?

In cognitive therapy, therapists point out how patients experience the world through the filter of *cognitive distortions*. These are habitual ways of thinking that contribute to a depressive mindset. Information is distorted to maintain a negative and pessimistic world view. In his book *Feeling Good: The New Mood Therapy* the psychiatrist David Burns listed the following cognitive distortions.

- *All-or-Nothing Thinking:* Life is seen in black and white. If you are not completely successful, you are a total failure.

- *Overgeneralization:* You generalize from a single negative event to a much larger pattern. One bad experience means a lifetime of disappointment.

- *Mental Filter:* You hone in on one negative detail and let that detail cloud your view of the larger picture. After giving a wonderful party, you focus on the one guest who seemed to be in a bad mood.

- *Disqualifying the Positive:* You find reasons to discount positive information. You passed the test because it was easy. The cute girl next door was nice to you because she felt sorry for you. This type of cognitive distortion allows you to maintain your negative view of the world despite contradictory evidence.

- *Jumping to Conclusions:* You jump to negative conclusions in the absence of any evidence.

- *Mind Reading:* You assume you know what someone else is feeling or thinking about you and that their thoughts are necessarily negative.

- *Predicting the Future:* You predict that things will end up badly and then treat your predictions as if they were already fact.

- *Catastrophizing or Minimizing:* In catastrophic thinking, you exaggerate the negative impact or significance of an event, blowing it up into giant proportions. When minimizing, you reduce the importance of something, generally something positive.

- *Emotional Reasoning:* You don't distinguish between your emotions and outside reality. Just because you feel something, you assume it must be true.

- *Shoulding:* You feel you can only motivate yourself with a constant sense of guilt or obligation. You "should", "must", or "ought to" do all sorts of things. You cannot trust yourself to act appropriately unless you are forced to do so.

- *Labeling:* A negative event or behavior is generalized to the person's entire character. For example, your husband is a selfish lout, you are a pathetic wreck, and your neighbor is total snob.

- *Personalization:* You assume that you were the cause of something that may have had nothing to do with you. Your boss shuts himself in his office because he's mad at you. Your best friend is depressed because you weren't sensitive enough when she broke up with her boyfriend.

What are **humanistic therapies**?

Humanistic therapies arose in the middle of the twentieth century, to some extent in reaction against the two reigning pillars of American psychology. Behaviorism dominated academic psychology, and psychoanalysis dominated clinical psychology. Humanistic therapies—as championed by psychotherapists such as Carl Rogers (1902–1987), Fritz Perls (1893–1970), Victor Frankl (1905–1997) and Rollo May (1909–1994)—were considered the third force in psychology, providing an alternative to the two earlier movements. While psychoanalysis focused on the relief of psychological conflict, and behaviorism focused on changing behavior, humanistic psychology emphasized the potential for growth. Concepts such as *self-actualization, unconditional positive regard*, and the *search for meaning* highlighted the basic human need to find fulfillment, happiness, and meaning in life.

The aim of humanistic therapy is less the reduction of psychopathology, than the realization of human potential. Emphasis is less on the past, as with psychoanalysis and psychodynamic therapies, and more on the present. Moreover, there is a spiritual side to humanistic psychotherapy that is completely absent in the two other movements

There is a fair amount of overlap between humanistic and psychodynamic psychotherapies, however, and many of the pioneering humanistic psychologists were initially trained in psychoanalysis. Both types of therapy engage the patient in one-on-one discussions with a psychotherapist. Both presume that verbal exploration of emotionally relevant thoughts, feelings, and problems can help people improve their lives. Finally, both types of treatment focus on how people deal with emotions and relate to other people.

What is the **empty chair technique**?

The empty chair technique is a popular technique used in Gestalt therapy, a branch of psychotherapy founded by Fritz Perls (1893–1970). Clients are asked to address an empty chair as if speaking to somebody with whom they have some interpersonal difficulty. They are then asked to tell that person everything that they are feeling. In this way, they can figure out what they are actually feeling, practice putting those feelings into words, and identify the fears that keep them from communicating directly with the person in question. Interestingly, the empty chair technique has similarities with the behavioral technique of systematic desensitization. By practicing a feared conversation without the actual person present, the client is asked to confront something anxiety-provoking at a lower level of anxiety. If the person can master the anxiety at that lower intensity, presumably he or she can move from there onto the more challenging situation. Hopefully, the person can progress from talking to the empty chair to a conversation with the actual person.

What is **family therapy**?

The second half of the twentieth century was a time of considerable innovation in psychotherapy and many new branches of psychotherapy broke off from their origin

The theory behind family therapy is that individuals do not operate in isolation but, instead, are part of a complex family system. It is therefore important for the therapist to understand the entire family in order to treat one of its members (*iStock*).

in traditional psychoanalysis. Family therapists challenged the emphasis on the individual, a fundamental part of all earlier forms of psychotherapy. In family systems theory, it is believed that families operate as systems and that no one member of the family can be understood in isolation from the other members of the family. This is particularly true for married couples, or for children who live with and depend upon their parents.

Although there are many strains of family therapy, including the structural family therapy of Salvador Minuchin, the strategic family therapy of Jay Haley, and the experiential family therapy of Carl Whitaker and Virginia Satir, all family therapists believe in bringing the entire family (or key members) into the room. By working with the family as a whole, therapists can achieve very different effects than can be accomplished in individual therapy alone.

Family therapists address the patterns of interaction between family members. Are the mother and the oldest child allying together against the father? Is the child acting out at school to force his estranged parents to talk to each other? Are the parents failing to set adequate boundaries with their children, giving the children too much power? Family therapy works by helping family members gain insight into their problematic patterns and then work together to change. Unlike psychodynamic therapy, family therapy addresses the present patterns of interaction with far less emphasis on the past, although past history is recognized if it has contributed to present patterns.

Which **therapies** are **best** for which **kinds of problems?**

Although there is a fair amount of data that shows that the different types of therapy are equally effective, research also suggests that certain kinds of psychotherapy are best with specific psychological problems. Behavioral therapy is most effective for anxiety disorders such as phobias, panic disorder, and obsessive-compulsive disorder. Cognitive therapy is highly effective in mild to moderate depression. Impulsive and compulsive behaviors, such as pathological gambling, self-injurious behaviors, and poor anger management, respond well to skills-building therapies, using both behavioral and cognitive components.

People with mild to moderate personality disorders respond to long-term, insight-oriented treatments, such as psychodynamic therapy, although people with severe personality disorders may also need skills-building treatments. For example, dialectical behavioral therapy (DBT) is specifically designed to treat borderline personality disorder. It is based on behavioral principles and makes use of functional behavioral analyses, but also addresses the poor emotional regulation and problematic interpersonal relationships associated with this disorder.

How necessary is **training** in **psychotherapy?**

A number of studies suggest that patients are equally satisfied after talking to nonprofessionals as they are after talking to trained mental health professionals. Certainly with short-term problems that are not particularly severe, many people can provide reassurance and support without years of professional training. In order to help people with more serious, complex, or entrenched problems, however, training is unquestionably important. The 1995 *Consumers Reports* study showed that, in general, people were happier and improved more from treatment with trained mental health professionals than from treatment with nonprofessionals. Moreover, the difference between the two grew the longer people stayed in treatment.

What **factors matter most** to the success of the **therapy?**

There is a large literature on the predictors to treatment outcome in psychotherapy, in other words, what factors contribute to the success or failure of psychotherapy. Both therapist and patient factors contribute. Among therapist factors, personality variables such as genuineness and empathy (as perceived by the patient) are very important. Positive expectations of therapy outcome are also important. If the therapist believes that the therapy can help, this contributes to a positive outcome. Among patient variables, motivation to change, hope, and positive expectations of the therapy promote positive results. General functioning level and degree of social support also contribute to therapy outcome. Patients who function better in the world and have more supportive relationships tend to do better in therapy. Many studies also stress the centrality of the therapeutic alliance. In other words, when both patient and therapist feel a positive bond and have shared goals for therapy, the therapy is more likely to succeed.

What should someone look for in **choosing a therapist**?

Choosing a therapist is an important decision but there are no hard and fast rules for picking a therapist that will best meet a patient's needs. Because therapeutic alliance is such an important component of treatment outcome, it makes sense to pick a therapist with whom one feels comfortable. As in any relationship, this is to some extent a personal decision. A therapist may provide a perfect fit for one person, but not click as well with his or her friend. When seeking treatment for help with specific problems, it also makes sense to find someone with expertise in that area. As noted above, some problems are best treated with specific types of therapy, for example, anxiety disorders respond very well to behavioral therapy.

In many cases, however, the different types of therapy may be equally effective, so the theoretical orientation of the therapist (for instance whether they are psychodynamic, humanistic, or cognitive-behavioral) may be mainly relevant in terms of patient-therapist fit. For example, people might consider whether they want a therapist who is directive (structures the treatment) or exploratory (promotes open-ended discussion), who does or does not give homework assignments, who talks a good deal or who is more interested in listening, who delves into childhood relationships or who focuses on solving current problems, or who provides short-term or long-term psychotherapy (weeks to months vs. years).

The personality style of the therapist will also affect the type of therapy that is provided. Some therapists are gentle and supportive, while others tend more toward "tough love." Some patients may prefer the first type of therapist, while others may find such a therapist too soft and prefer to be challenged.

How **long** should **therapy last**?

The different schools of therapy have different philosophies about the length of therapy. Cognitive-behavioral therapies tend to be short term, while humanistic and psychodynamic therapies tend to be longer. Psychoanalysis often goes on for many years. Research suggests that minor and relatively recent problems may not require long-term treatment while more severe, complex and long lasting problems will take more time. The length of the treatment also depends on the preferences of the patient.

Some patients are happy with resolution of the presenting symptom and choose to stop treatment as soon as there is symptomatic improvement. Other patients are interested in greater self-exploration and personality development, and stay in therapy much longer. In the 1995 *Consumer Reports* study, patients who stayed in therapy longer tended to be more satisfied with their treatment. Of course, this could reflect a selection bias because people who were more satisfied with their treatment may have chosen to stay in therapy longer.

PSYCHOPHARMACOLOGY

How have **medications influenced** the **treatment** of the mentally ill?

Modern advances in psychopharmacology (psychiatric medication) have radically changed the lives of the mentally ill. Once doomed to a life of anguish, utter dysfunction, and often squalid conditions, many people with mental illness can now live satisfying lives in the community. Although modern psychopharmacology has brought tremendous benefits, it is not without complications.

All medications have side effects, some of which can be quite dangerous. Secondly, the drugs are only effective if they are taken as prescribed. Non-adherence to medication is probably the single greatest reason for treatment failure. Finally, clinical trials (research into the efficacy and safety of certain medications) are extremely expensive. Because of this, they are currently covered primarily by private industry, specifically the pharmaceutical industry, whose profit motive leaves them far from impartial. Consequently, some professionals and patients are concerned about the safety of taking medications, especially for long periods of time.

What are the major **classes** of psychiatric **drugs**?

Although there are quite a few drugs that do not fit neatly into any one category, the main categories of psychiatric drugs are *antipsychotics, antidepressants, antianxiety* drugs, and *mood stabilizers*. For each class of drug, specific neurotransmitters are involved.

What are the **antipsychotics** and how do they work?

Antipsychotic drugs treat psychotic symptoms. These drugs are divided into two general categories, *typicals* and *atypicals*. Typicals date back to the early 1950s when chlorpromazine (Thorazine) was developed in a Parisian laboratory. These medications—which include such drugs as haloperidol (Haldol), thioridazine (Mellaril), and fluphenazine (Prolixin)—operate on the dopamine neurotransmitter system, specifically on the D_2 neurotransmitter receptors.

Typical antipsychotics are highly effective drugs, but have a range of problematic side effects. Anticholinergic effects, including dry mouth, blurred vision, and confusion, are found in low potency typicals, such as chlorpromazine and thioridazine. Extra-pyramidal side effects (EPS) are more common in high-potency typicals, such as haloperidol and fluphenazine. Symptoms of EPS include muscle tremors and stiffness.

Atypical antipsychotics include risperidone (Risperdal), olanzapine (Zyprexa), quetiapine (Seroquel), ziprasidone (Geodon), and aripiprazole (Aricept). The atypicals entered the market in the 1990s, although the first atypical, clozapine (Clozaril), was introduced considerably earlier but fell out of favor due to the risk of agranulocytosis, a potentially fatal disorder of the white blood cells. Atypicals work on a range of neurotransmitters, including serotonin, dopamine, and norepinephrine. While atypicals are less likely to cause the kinds of side effects associated with typical antipsychotics, they bring their own side-effect profile. Most importantly, atypicals have a higher risk of *metabolic syndrome*, characterized by insulin resistance, high blood pressure, weight gain, and high blood sugar. Metabolic syndrome raises the risk of diabetes and heart disease. With the advent of atypicals, clozapine received new attention. It is now considered perhaps the most effective antipsychotic medication. Because of its side effect profile, however, it is only used after other drugs have failed.

What are some **commonly prescribed psychiatric drugs**?

All drugs are given a generic name, which is a unique name for their chemical structure, and a trade name, which is essentially a brand name. When the drug's patent runs out, other manufacturers can produce the drug but only under its generic name. The table below lists commonly used drugs and their uses.

Commonly Prescribed Psychiatric Drugs

Trade Name	Generic Name	Class of Drug	Key Neurotransmitter
Prozac	fluoxetine	antidepressant	serotonin
Celexa	citalopram	antidepressant	serotonin
Zoloft	sertraline	antidepressant	serotonin
Klonopin	clonazepam	antianxiety	GABA
Ativan	lorazepam	antianxiety	GABA
Valium	diazepam	antianxiety	GABA
Haldol	haloperidol	antipsychotic	dopamine
Risperdal	risperidone	antipsychotic	mixed
Zyprexa	olanzepine	antipsychotic	mixed
Eskalith/Lithobid	lithium	mood stabilizer	?
Depakine	valproic acid	mood stabilizer	GABA?
Neurotin	gabapentin	anticonvulsant/mood stabilizer	GABA?

What is the **CATIE study**?

With the arrival of atypical antipsychotics, it was widely assumed that the new generation of drugs was superior to the old generation. Not only did the atypicals have a more

Although some psychologists are licensed to prescribe medications, psychiatrists or primary care doctors prescribe most psychiatric drugs (*iStock*).

benign side effect profile than the typicals, atypicals were assumed to be more effective in treating both the positive and negative symptoms of schizophrenia. (Positive symptoms refer to the active psychotic symptoms, and negative symptoms to the social withdrawal, reduced energy, and emotional flattening associated with schizophrenia.)

The CATIE study is a landmark study published in 2005 that challenged assumptions about the superiority of atypicals over typicals. This study showed no difference in efficacy between three atypical antipsychotic medications (quetiapine, risperidone, ziprasidone) and perphenizine (Trilafon), a mid-potency typical antipsychotic. While olanzapine (Zyprexa) proved superior to perphenizine, it also had the highest rates of metabolic side effects. Of note, this study was funded by the National Institute of Mental Health, a government institution. The study received no funding from pharmaceutical companies.

What are the **antidepressants** and how do they work?

Antidepressant medications treat depression. Currently, the most popular antidepressants are the *serotonin reuptake inhibitors* (*SSRIs*), which work on the serotonin neurotransmitter system. Commonly prescribed SSRIs include fluoxetine (Prozac), sertraline (Zoloft), citalopram (Celexa), and paroxetine (Paxil). SSRIs are very effective and safer than other classes of antidepressants but they do have side effects, the most bothersome being sexual side effects. SSRIs are also helpful in the treatment of anxiety conditions and obsessive-compulsive disorder.

Prior to the arrival of the SSRIs in the 1980s, *heterocyclics* were the most frequently prescribed class of antidepressants. Commonly used heterocyclics include imipramine (Tofranil), amitriptyline (Elavil), and nortriptyline (Pamelor). Heterocyclics, which get their name from the ring structure of the drugs' molecules, hit both the serotonin and norepinephrine neurotransmitter systems, with an emphasis on norepinephrine. They also impact the histaminic and and acetylcholine neurotransmitter systems. Heterocyclics have more dangerous side effects than SSRIs. They are more lethal on overdose and can have notable cardiac side effects.

Another class of antidepressants is *monoamine oxydase inhibitors (MAOIs)*. MAOIs were discovered in the early 1950s and their potentially lethal effects came to light in the early 1960s. MAOIs can cause a hypertensive crisis, in which blood pressure shoots up high enough to cause a stroke.

These crises can be brought on by mixing an MAOI with another medication, such as opioids or SSRIs, or by eating tyramine-rich foods. Aged cheese, cured meats, sausage, and liqueurs are all rich in tyramine. Although MAOIs are the most dangerous of the antidepressants, they are also extremely effective. For those patients with treatment-resistant depression who can follow a low tyramine diet, MAOIs may be a reasonable option. Examples of MAOIs include phenelzine (Nardate) or tranylcypromine (Parnate).

What are the **antianxiety drugs** and how do they work?

There are at least two classes of antianxiety medications, *barbituates* and *benzodiazepines*. Both drug classes act on the GABA neurotransmitter system. Barbituates, such as secobarbitol (Seconal) and pentobarbital (Nembutol), are the older class of drugs. Today, they are rarely prescribed as conventional antianxiety medications because of their problematic side-effect profile. Barbituates have a high risk of addiction and high lethality on overdose. They also have cardiac effects at high doses and can dangerously depress respiration (suppress breathing). Barbituates are still found to be useful in controlled settings, however, as when sedating a patient before an invasive procedure.

Benzodiazepines have largely taken the place of barbituates in the treatment of anxiety. Medications such as alprazolam (Xanax), lorazepam (Ativan), clonazepam (Klonopin), and diazepam (Valium) have far lower risk of death on overdose and tend to be less addictive than barbituates. Nonetheless, benzodiazepines can still be addictive and abrupt discontinuation of the drug can put a person into withdrawal. The drug's half-life (amount of time needed for the drug to clear the body) influences the addiction potential. Benzodiazepines with a short half-life, such as alprazolam, have higher risk of withdrawal and addiction than those with longer half-lives, such as clonazepam.

What are **mood stabilizers**?

Mood stabilizers help patients with bipolar disorder avoid the highs of mania and the lows of depression. They literally stabilize the mood. The most common mood stabilizers are lithium, valproic acid (Depakine), and carbamazepine (Tegretol). It remains a bit of a mystery how mood stabilizers work. Unlike the other classes of psychiatric drugs, mood stabilizers are not clearly linked to specific neurotransmitters. Some mood stabilizers alter the sodium channels in the cell membrane and some seem to work on the GABA neurotransmitter system. Most mood stabilizers also function as antiseizure medications (anticonvulsants), including carbamazepine and valproic acid. Additional antiseizure medications that are used to stabilize mood include gabapentin (Neurontin), lamotrogine (Lamictal), and topiramate (Topamax). Mood stabilizers also treat agitation and impulsivity.

Will **drugs** ever **replace psychotherapy**?

In the late 1980s during the explosive growth of the SSRIs, there was idle talk of drugs replacing psychotherapy. Today, few people think that medications will ever replace psychotherapy. Medications treat symptoms and they are enormously helpful with the most severe mental illnesses. However, they cannot replace the human element that is so central to the effectiveness of psychotherapy. Moreover, medications and psychotherapy treat different problems. Medications are extremely effective with psychosis, mania, severe depression, anxiety, and agitation. Alternatively, psychotherapy is effective with problematic personality traits, disturbed self-image, and impaired interpersonal skills. Specific psychotherapies are also effective in the treatment of anxiety disorders and mild to moderate depression. Although medications generally work more quickly on depression and anxiety, psychotherapy tends to have more long-lasting effects and certainly has fewer side effects.

How are **new drugs developed**?

The process of developing drugs and bringing them to market is long, complex, and expensive. Basic biochemical research, which may take place in universities or in government or industry laboratories, can suggest directions for drug development. Most actual drug development takes place in industry laboratories, paid for by the extremely large and wealthy pharmaceutical industry. Once a drug is developed, it must be tested for efficacy, safety, and tolerability. Efficacy reflects how well it treats the target symptoms. Safety relates to the absence of dangerous side effects, otherwise known as *adverse events*. Tolerability reflects a patient's ability to tolerate the drug. A drug may be safe—that is not dangerous—but still intolerable. For example, it may cause nausea or headaches.

What are the stages of **FDA testing**?

In the United States, the Food and Drug Administration (FDA) requires several phases of testing before a drug can be *FDA approved* for the treatment of a particular condition. In Phase I studies, the drug must prove tolerable and safe in a small sample of healthy volunteers (twenty to eighty subjects). In Phase II studies, the drug must prove tolerable and safe in a larger sample of patients (100 to 300 subjects) with some evidence of efficacy. In Phase III, the drug must show efficacy, tolerability, and safety in a larger sample of patients (1,000 to 3,000 subjects).

How do we **know** that a **drug works**?

The standard method for testing the efficacy of a new drug is through the use of *randomized controlled trials (RCTs)*. In an RCT, a large sample of patients are randomly assigned to receive either the test treatment or a comparison treatment. The comparison drug may be another active drug or may be a placebo (sham treatment that looks like an active drug). Studies must also be *double-blinded*, that is neither doctor nor patient should be able to tell whether the patient is taking the drug or the placebo. At the end of a set period, symptom improvement is compared across groups. The efficacy of the drug reflects the improvement of symptoms in patients taking the active treatment, rather than the placebo.

Why are **drugs compared** to **placebos**?

Placebo controls are necessary because many patients improve just by suggestion. The *placebo effect* refers to the improvement seen in patients on placebo. It can be enormously reassuring just to see a doctor and receive pills, even if there is no active ingredient in the pills. The placebo effect is a real phenomenon and can reach 30 to 40 percent in some treatment studies. Therefore, it is necessary to include a placebo control in a treatment study in order to prove that patient improvement is due to the active ingredient in the drug and not just to the placebo effect.

How do we know **which drugs** work **best**?

FDA regulations ensure that each drug brought to market has shown safety and efficacy compared to a placebo or a comparison drug. FDA regulations do not require comparisons among multiple drugs to determine which drug works best. Pharmaceutical companies have financial incentives to show their own medications in the best light. Consequently, they have no incentive to spend millions of dollars on high quality, objective studies that could potentially reflect badly on their own product. It is no coincidence, therefore, that the CATIE study, which punctured the illusion that newer is necessarily better, was financed by the National Institute of Mental Health and not by private industry. Clearly independent sources of funding are needed to support high quality and impartial drug-to-drug comparisons.

What **impact** does the **pharmaceutical industry** have on the practice of **psychiatry**?

The pharmaceutical industry has had a profound effect on the practice of psychiatry. Ever since the 1980s, the U.S. government has moved more toward deregulation of industry. With this philosophical and political shift, the pharmaceutical industry has gained more freedom to market directly to consumers and engage in joint research with academic centers.

Along with the tremendous advances in psychiatric medications, the pharmaceutical industry has grown extremely profitable and has become integrated into all aspects of psychiatric research, publishing, and training. While there has been some reaction against this in recent years, the pharmaceutical industry still wields enormous influence on prevailing opinion about which drugs are most useful for which conditions.

Unfortunately, there is little in the way of independent investigation, such as the CATIE study, to give unbiased information about the relative effectiveness of different medications. This is not to suggest that clinical research sponsored by the pharmaceuticals is invalid, only that it is far from impartial and few companies are likely to publish studies that might adversely affect their bottom line.

In his 2006 study by Robert Kelly and colleagues (see illustration), the authors looked at 301 articles involving data on 542 drugs (many studies looked at the same drugs). Whether the outcome of the study was favorable or not favorable for each drug was recorded along with the source of research funding. As is shown above, for drugs in studies funded by the drug manufacturer, 78 percent of the studies showed favorable results. For drugs in studies funded by the manufacturers' competitors, only 28% of the studies had favorable outcomes. Finally, for drugs in studies that received no funding from pharmaceutical companies, 48 percent of the outcomes were favorable.

In other words, when a drug company did not fund the study, the likelihood of a positive outcome was about 50/50. In the other situations, however, it appears the dice

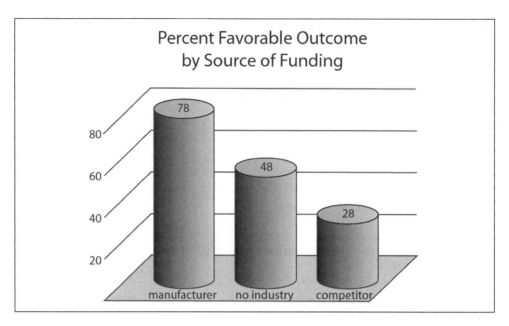

Percent Favorable Outcome by Source of Funding

Drug studies tend to show more favorable outcomes when research funding comes from the drug's manufacturer.

were loaded. How does this happen? Does this mean that the research by pharmaceutical companies is not valid? Most authors believe that the problem is less due to poor science than to selective publication. Drug companies are more likely to publish studies that support their product and less likely to publish studies that fail to do so.

What is **E.C.T.**?

ECT stands for *electroconvulsive therapy*, otherwise known as *shock therapy*. Electrodes are placed at several locations on the skull and a small pulse of electricity is sent through the electrodes into the brain. This causes a seizure, generally of twenty to thirty seconds in duration. Despite its scary reputation, ECT is very effective in severe depression. It is particularly effective in *melancholic* depression or depression with a lot of *neurovegetative* symptoms. This refers to the physical symptoms of depression, such as loss of energy, sleep and appetite disturbance, impaired concentration, and physical slowing. The side effect profile of ECT is reasonable, especially if done infrequently. The most common side effect is loss of memory from around the time of the treatments. ECT is frequently used in the elderly.

Why does **E.C.T.** have such a **bad reputation**?

Compared to many biological treatments used in psychiatry, ECT is quite old, dating back to the 1930s. Over its long history, the use of ECT has been considerably refined and it is now used much more carefully than it was fifty years ago. In the past, ECT was commonly used with a much wider range of disorders than it is now. Sometimes it was used simply for behavioral control. Today it is mainly used to treat depression, although it can also treat mania and psychosis.

Much higher dosages of electricity were used in the past than are used today. Bilateral ECT, in which electrodes are placed on both sides of the head, was the norm, while unilateral ECT is frequently used today. Unilateral ECT tends to have fewer side effects though it is not as powerful as bilateral ECT.

Finally, muscle relaxants were not commonly used, so patients could get hurt during seizures, even breaking bones. Currently, patients are given muscle relaxants and put under general anaesthesia prior to ECT. When they wake up they have no memory of the procedure. Additionally, electronic monitoring machines help ensure that breathing and heartbeat remain normal throughout the procedure.

POPULAR PSYCHOLOGY

What is **popular psychology**?

Popular or *pop psychology* is aimed at a popular audience and communicated through the mass media. It addresses topics related to psychology—such as romantic relationships, stress management, child rearing, and sexuality—and can be found in magazine articles, radio or television talk shows, popular books, and various Websites. The benefit of pop psychology is that it is accessible to a very wide audience and can be an effective vehicle for translating psychological knowledge to the general public. The downside is that there is little to no quality control. The information may or may not be backed by solid psychological science or clinical experience.

What is the **history** of **popular psychology**?

While the term "pop psychology" is relatively new, the concept is certainly not. As long as there have been human beings, there has been interest in human behavior. Along with this comes a pervasive desire to obtain advice from those who seem to know more about life's challenges than the ordinary person. In ancient Greece, people consulted oracles for such advice. For many centuries, religious figures filled this function, although soothsayers, fortune-tellers and other occult figures also came into play. In more recent times, advice columnists have made use of the mass media to provide advice to the lovelorn, the depressed, or people who are otherwise troubled. Since the rise of the professional mental health fields, speakers with academic or medical credentials have gained in popularity. Unfortunately not all people in the popular psychology industry who present with medical or academic credentials actually have training related to the topic they are discussing.

How do **popular psychologists** differ from **licensed professional psychologists**?

No credentials are necessary to become successful within the field of popular psychology. While licensed psychologists need to complete many years of rigorous training before they are legally able to call themselves a psychologist, a talk show host need only master the (admittedly very difficult) art of popular entertainment before giving advice to the general public. Some psychologists or mental health professionals do enter the field of popular psychology, but there is nothing stopping someone with a doctorate in French literature from using the appellation "Dr." and appearing on a daytime pop psychology television show. Thus, much of popular psychology functions more as entertainment than as scientifically based psychological knowledge.

Who is **Dr. Joyce Brothers**?

Dr. Joyce Brothers (1929–) was one of the earliest popular psychologists, an actual psychologist who brought her expertise to the general public through various mass-media outlets. She began her career on a television talk show in 1958, entitled *Dr. Joyce Brothers*. Over the next forty-five years, many other television and radio shows followed. She also wrote at least thirteen books with titles such as *What Every Woman Ought to Know about Love and Marriage* and *Dr. Brothers' Guide to Your Emotions*. Dr. Brothers was trained as a psychologist, holds a Ph.D. in psychology from Columbia University, and has been licensed in the state of New York since 1958.

Who are **Ann Landers** and **Abigail Van Buren** (Dear Abby)?

Ann Landers and Abigail Van Buren are the pen names of twin sisters who ended up as enormously successful advice columnists from the 1950s into the 1990s. Born in 1918 in Iowa, neither sister had any formal training in psychology or a related field. Esther "Eppie" Friedman Lederer (1918–2002) assumed the Ann Landers advice column for the *Chicago Sun-Times* in 1955. She continued until 1987, at which point she switched to the *Chicago Tribune*. Married to a wealthy businessman named Jules Lederer, who was also the founder of Budget-Rent-A-Car, she had amassed a wide range of contacts, which she mined for her column. Her plain-spoken, common sense advice appealed to a great many people and her column was eventually syndicated to over 1,000 newspapers. In 1956, her twin sister Pauline "Popo" Friedman Philips, began a rival column, "Dear Abby", in the *San Francisco Chronicle* under the pen name Abigail Van Buren. Although neither sister had any training in the mental health field, they took care to clarify the limits of their knowledge and abilities, and often advised their readers to seek professional help if their problems seemed beyond the scope of a newspaper advice column.

Who is **Dr. Phil**?

Phillip McGraw (1950–) is a widely known television personality, best known as Dr. Phil. He received a Ph.D. in clinical psychology from the University of North Texas in 1979. Dr. Phil was licensed in Texas and opened a practice for a short while, but moved out of the business of psychotherapy into both popular and forensic psychology. In the mid-1990s, he met the famous talk show host Oprah Winfrey through his work in forensic psychology, a branch of psychology involved with the legal system. He was hired to help with her defense against a lawsuit by cattlemen who claimed she defamed the beef industry on one of her shows. Soon he was appearing regularly on her television show. In 2002 he started his own talk show, which was named *Dr . Phil*. While still living in Texas, Dr. Phil allowed his psychology license to lapse. When he moved to California to pursue his television career, he did not obtain a license in California as the state licensing board determined that his show was more entertainment than psychology and, therefore, his current practice did not require that he be licensed.

Who is **Dr. Laura**?

Dr. Laura is another popular media personality. She works primarily in radio but has also published a number of books. Laura Schlessinger (1947–) has a doctorate in physiology from Columbia University but also obtained a post-doctoral certificate in Marriage, Child, and Family Counseling from the University of Southern California. She states she was in private practice for twelve years. Dr. Laura is known for her socially conservative views and for combining moral, religious, and mental health considerations into her responses to viewers. This departs from the official practice of professional psychologists, who must distinguish between their personal and professional views when dealing with patients.

THE
PSYCHOLOGY
OF TRAUMA

THE PSYCHOLOGICAL
IMPACT OF TRAUMA

What is **psychological trauma**?

Psychological trauma refers to any event that threatens extreme psychological or physical damage, including severe bodily harm or death. Traumatic events evoke feelings of terror, horror, and helplessness. A traumatic event can involve direct threat to the self, but people can also feel traumatized after witnessing harm or threat of harm to someone else. Traumas can include natural disasters, such as an earthquake, tsunami, or hurricane, but traumas can also stem from human behavior, as with war, assault, or rape.

Why do we **study trauma**?

Ever since the first psychoanalytic case histories of the late nineteenth century, it has been recognized that severe trauma can have long-lasting impact on psychological functioning. An enormous body of research shows us that trauma can cause severe psychological distress and that a history of trauma is a risk factor for a very broad range of psychiatric and psychological disturbances.

What kinds of **psychological problems** are associated with **trauma**?

It is important to distinguish between acute trauma in adulthood, such as a natural disaster or an assault, and chronic trauma that occurs in childhood, such as ongoing sexual or physical abuse. Trauma in general has been associated with anxiety, depression, increased drinking, anger outbursts, suicidal behavior, and a syndrome known as

405

post-traumatic stress disorder (PTSD). While personality in adulthood is largely formed, personality is still developing in childhood. Thus, chronic trauma in childhood can have extremely pervasive and long-term effects on personality development.

People with histories of serious childhood abuse can develop severe personality disorders. They can also develop self-injurious behaviors, in which they may cut or burn themselves. Dissociative symptoms are also fairly common. These involve feelings of unreality and disconnection from mental and physical experience. There is a striking lack of awareness of certain feelings, thoughts, or actions. In extreme cases, people might develop dissociative identity disorder (previously known as multiple personality disorder), in which they literally believe that they have several different personalities within their own body.

How did **Freud's seduction theory** account for the **childhood trauma**?

Sigmund Freud's early work on the *seduction theory* set the stage for many of the later developments in trauma psychology. Freud was initially interested in the problem of *hysteria*, which was a fairly common disorder in Victorian Europe. People would complain of various bodily problems that had no basis in actual physiology. We would now diagnose such complaints as *conversion disorders*. After interviewing numerous patients, Freud came up with the seduction theory, which stated that hysteria was caused by seduction in early life. In other words, hysteria stemmed from early experiences of childhood sexual abuse.

Within a few years, Freud abandoned this theory, believing that hysteria was too common to have been solely caused by sexual abuse. This would have meant that far more children were sexually abused than he believed was likely. He replaced his focus on actual experience with an emphasis on fantasy. The child may not have actually been seduced, but instead had repressed fantasies of seduction by the mother or father. With this turn from actual traumatic events to traumatic fantasies, the study of childhood trauma went underground for more than half a century, not to re-emerge until the 1970s and 1980s.

What **role** did **war** play in the development of **trauma studies**?

Although Freud's abandonment of the seduction theory turned the budding mental health field away from the psychological effects of trauma, returning soldiers from World War I brought attention right back to the effects of trauma. The war was tremendously traumatic. Young men were sent away from home and exposed to the constant threat of their own death and to the violent and bloody death of their comrades. They were also forced to perform violent and murderous acts themselves, sometimes against civilians.

Many soldiers returning from WWI exhibited the emotional distress we now know as post-traumatic stress disorder. At the time it was known as "shell shock." But there was little validation of these soldiers' suffering at the time, and it was often seen as a sign of moral weakness. In World War II, the problem recurred (sometimes referred to as "battle fatigue") and there was some progress in the study, treatment, and recognition of post-traumatic psychopathology.

It was not until the Vietnam War, however, that the mental health field truly mobilized to study and develop treatments for the emotional aftereffects of trauma. In 1980, five years after the end of the Vietnam War, the diagnosis of post-traumatic stress disorder was published in DSM-III. (The Diagnostic and Statistical Manual (DSM) is the official diagnostic manual for the mental health field. DSM-III was the third edition.)

What is **post-traumatic stress disorder**?

Post-traumatic stress disorder (PTSD) is a particular condition that follows experience of a severe trauma. There are three clusters of symptoms: persistent avoidance of reminders of the event (*numbing symptoms*), persistent re-experiencing of the event (*intrusive symptoms*), and *autonomic hyperarousal*. With numbing symptoms, there is a blunting of emotional reactivity. There is flat affect, avoidance of various activities, loss of memory for traumatic events, and lack of motivation or interest in activities that used to engage the person. With intrusive symptoms, the opposite happens. Instead of a lack of memory for the traumatic events, there is a flood of memories that cannot be turned off. There may be nightmares or flashbacks, in which the trauma returns as if it is happening all over again. There may also be intrusive emotional storms, such as crying spells, rage outbursts, or panic attacks. With autonomic hyperarousal, the autonomic nervous system is on overdrive. The body is continually on guard, ready to spring into action at any sign of danger. There can be an exaggerated startle response, difficulty concentrating and difficulty sleeping, as well as rapid heartbeat, sweating, and continued muscle tension.

What factors in the event **increase** the **risk** of getting **PTSD**?

Not everyone will get PTSD after a trauma. There are many different kinds of traumas, and different people respond to the same event in different ways. A number of factors within the trauma affect the risk of developing PTSD. Whether the trauma was natural or man-made, and whether the human-induced trauma was accidental (e.g., a car accident) or intentional (e.g., a mugging) all affect a person's response. The more intentional, the more disturbing. Naturally the severity of the trauma is very important. How much danger was involved? How much physical pain was suffered? How much violence? Did anyone die? All these questions influence the impact of the trauma. The duration of the trauma is important as well—was it quick or did it last over time? Whether the trauma was a one-time event or ongoing (e.g., a mugging vs. a war) also factors in. Longer, more chronic, more severe, and intentionally malicious traumas cause greater psychological damage than shorter, milder, single-episode, and unintentional traumas.

Although living through a natural disaster, such as a fire or earthquake, can result in emotional trauma, trauma that is inflicted by other people is much worse emotionally (*iStock*).

How does the **emotional impact** of **human traumas** differ from that of **natural disasters**?

While a natural disaster such as Hurricane Katrina or the tsunami of 2004 can have profound emotional impact on the survivors, there is a uniquely destructive effect from trauma that is caused by other people, specifically if there was intention to cause harm. We are profoundly social animals and a good deal of our psychology is devoted to the negotiation of interpersonal relationships. If we suffer significant harm at the hands of another person, that can throw our entire worldview into doubt. Are people still good? Can other people be trusted? While the loss of a sense of safety regarding our physical surroundings can be enormously frightening, we do not expect morality from the weather. A natural disaster does not in itself threaten our fundamental belief in the decency of humanity. When people lose trust in other people, they can suffer from deep depression and social alienation.

What **factors** in a **person** increase the **risk** of **PTSD**?

Not all people are equally traumatized by the same incident. What kinds of personal factors influence the risk of developing PTSD? Research suggests that people with a previous history of trauma, those with pre-existing psychiatric problems or personality disorders, those with less social support, and those with an *external locus of control* are more likely to develop PTSD in response to a traumatic event. People with an external locus of control believe that outside forces determine the events in their life. They do not believe they have much control over their life. In contrast, people with an *internal locus of control* believe they have significant control over their life. They tend to be more optimistic and more proactive about solving problems. Finally, people who react with dissociation at the time of event are shown to be likely to develop PTSD.

What are the **biological effects** of **trauma**?

Trauma has considerable impact on our neurobiology, and there are actual physiological changes that can accompany trauma. To start with, trauma involves an intense activation of our stress response. The HPA axis (hypothalamus, pituitary gland, adrenal gland) mediates our brain's stress response. In the face of stress, the HPA axis is activated. It sends out stress hormones, known as glucocorticoids. These serve to activate the autonomous nervous system, making our heart pump faster, our breath more rapid and shallow, and blood rush to our large muscle groups from our small muscle groups. This allows our body to respond rapidly to threat.

In normal circumstances, our *parasympathetic nervous system* acts to restore this system to a resting state, allowing our body to recover from the stress reaction. However, with trauma, the whole stress system can be thrown out of whack, causing abnormalities within the HPA axis, and keeping our autonomic nervous system (specifically the *sympathetic nervous system*) on overdrive. This has the effect of wearing down the body, compromising the immune system, and putting undue stress on many parts of the body's regulating systems. In childhood when the brain is not fully developed, severe trauma can interfere with the brain's actual development, causing long-term damage.

What is **dissociation**?

Dissociation involves an alteration in attention and awareness. People cut off awareness of feelings, thoughts, or even memories of actual events. Sometimes people remember all of the events but feel entirely emotionally detached from the memories. Alternatively, they may feel detached from personal experience, as if they are not a real person, but a robot. This is called *depersonalization. Derealization* occurs when people feel that the world around them is not real. Dissociation is similar to a trance state, which is an altered state of consciousness in which awareness of the surrounding world is changed.

Dissociation is fairly common among people who have undergone trauma and it serves to protect the person from becoming overwhelmed by intolerable emotions. During the trauma, some people remember slipping into dissociative states. "That wasn't me down there on the bed. I was floating somewhere up on the ceiling." Although dissociation may help people survive trauma, dissociative symptoms can cause problems after the trauma is over, interfering with the person's ability to process the trauma and return to normal life.

Are **traumatic memories** really **repressed**?

There has been a good deal of controversy over the issue of repressed memories. Many researchers and clinicians have written about patients who lost access to their memories of abuse, only to recover them years later. Often the recovery of memories is associated with a surge of intrusive post-traumatic symptoms, such as nightmares, emotional outbursts, and even suicidality. In the 1980s and 1990s this concern with repressed memories of trauma exploded into a hysterical craze in which accusations flew and innocent people were charged with crimes that were suddenly "remembered" in psychotherapy. Partly in response to this excess, there are factions within the mental health field that discount the possibility of recovered memories at all. Professionals who work with adult survivors of childhood trauma, however, often encounter patients who recover childhood memories long after the traumatic events have occurred.

Can **false memories** be suggested to people?

Elizabeth Loftus (1944–) is a researcher who has long studied the vagaries of memory. She became well known for challenging the idea of recovered memories. Her work showed that memory is extremely malleable, that people are highly suggestible, and that false memories can be implanted by suggestion. In other words, it doesn't take that much to convince people that they remember things that never actually happened. Loftus's work highlights the risk of eliciting recovered memories of childhood trauma in psychotherapy. Clinicians must tread very carefully with patients whom they suspect may have histories of abuse. Clinicians must take pains to avoid leading questions and always keep in mind that the absence of memory may simply mean the absence of abuse.

How do we **treat** the effects of **trauma**?

For the most part, the aftereffects of trauma are treated by psychotherapy, although the acute symptoms of PTSD may be treated by antianxiety or antidepressant medication. Immediately after an acute trauma, people need help in reducing their autonomic arousal. In other words, they need help calming down. They need to be assured that they are safe and that it is safe to let down their guard. Social support is also extremely important at all points of the recovery process, and groups who undergo traumas together often form very strong bonds.

After the immediate crisis has passed, it is helpful for people to discuss what happened, particularly to share their experiences with other people who have experienced the same trauma. This is where support groups or informal debriefings can be helpful. If symptoms of PTSD develop, individual therapy with cognitive-behavioral techniques can help reduce symptoms. Relaxation techniques can reduce the autonomic hyperarousal, gradual desensitization can help people overcome tendencies to avoid any reminder of the trauma, and psychoeducation can help people make sense of their reactions to the trauma. Distorted cognitions about the trauma should also be addressed, particularly excessive self-blame.

Self-blame is a common reaction to trauma as it serves to combat the extreme sense of helplessness. "If it was my fault, I'm not helpless." Likewise, people do need to feel empowered, and constructive actions that grant some sense of control should be encouraged. For example, letter writing to newspapers or government officials, public speaking about the event, and commemoration rituals can all help people feel empowered.

Is **long-term childhood trauma** treated differently than **acute trauma** in **adulthood**?

With more chronic, childhood trauma, the therapy takes more time and needs to move more slowly. The therapy should first address any severe problems with functioning, such as self-mutilation, suicidality, and severe personality pathology. Only when the patient can tolerate talking about the trauma without becoming overwhelmed by painful emotion or developing dangerous symptoms, should the therapy address the trauma directly. With some people this can happen fairly quickly, with others it might take years. Some people with very fragile emotional and behavioral control may never fully process the trauma. Instead, the therapy will focus on shoring up self-control capacities and the general ability to function.

CHILD ABUSE

What is **child abuse** and why is it so important in psychology?

While trauma is defined as any terrifying, life-threatening event, child abuse has a more specific meaning, referring to the maltreatment of a dependent child. Maltreatment can range from failure to attend to the child's fundamental needs to intentionally inflicting harm. Such harm could include violent attacks or sexual molestation. Child maltreatment is generally divided into four categories: *neglect, emotional* or *psychological abuse, physical abuse*, and *sexual abuse*. Child maltreatment has received a good deal of attention within the field of psychology because of its extremely damaging and far-reaching effects—child abuse leaves its mark on almost all aspects of psychological functioning.

How **common** is **child abuse**?

The U.S. Department of Health and Human Services compiles statistics on cases of child maltreatment that are reported to the authorities. According to these statistics, in 2007, there were almost 800,000 incidents of child maltreatment in the United States. Over half the reports involved neglect, 13 percent multiple forms of abuse, 10.8 percent physical abuse, and 7.6 percent sexual abuse. Of course this includes only the cases that were reported. We can assume that the real incidence of abuse is far higher.

What kinds of **abuse** do **children suffer**?

As you can see from the table below, child neglect is the most common type of child mistreatment that comes to the attention of the authorities. These statistics come from the 2007 report on Child Mistreatment by the U.S. Department of Health and Human

411

Services. While psychological abuse is listed as the second *least* common type of abuse reported to the authorities, this probably has little relationship to its frequency in the population. We can presume it is one of the most common forms of abuse, but because it does not put the child in immediate physical danger, it is likely underreported.

Types of Child Abuse Reported in the United States in 2007

Type of Mistreatment	Percentage
Neglect	59.0
Multiple Types of Mistreatment	13.1
Physical Abuse	10.8
Sexual Abuse	7.6
Psychological Abuse	4.2
Medical Neglect	0.9
Other	4.2

Who **commits child abuse**?

According to the U.S. Department of Health and Human Services 2007 statistics, parents were the most frequent perpetrators of child abuse in the cases reported to the authorities. The mother was the perpetrator in 38.7 percent of the cases, and the mother plus another person in 5.7 percent of the cases. The father was the perpetrator in 17.9 percent of the cases, the father plus another person in 0.9 percent of the cases, and the mother and father together in 16.8 percent of the cases. Day care staff accounted for 0.5 percent of the cases, friend/neighbors 0.4 percent, female relatives 1.7 percent, and male relatives 3.1 percent. Unrelated romantic partners of the parents also accounted for a small percent of the cases reported. Male partners accounted for 2.3 percent and female partners 1.7 percent.

What are the **aftereffects** of **child abuse**?

As noted above, trauma in childhood differs from trauma in adulthood. While adults have largely formed personalities, children's psychological capacities are not yet fully developed. Child abuse interferes with the child's psychological development, stunting or distorting the child's growing ability to regulate emotion, control impulses, plan and follow through with goals, negotiate interpersonal relationships, and maintain a stable and positive self-image. Abused children are also more likely to have difficulties with peer relationships and academic performance, and even suffer more medical problems than children who have not been abused. Consequently, child abuse raises the risk of anxiety, depression, impulse control disorders, and severe personality pathology throughout the lifespan. Most tragically, the abuse can teach the child that the world is cruel and uncaring, and that the child is unworthy of love, protection, or respect.

What are the **neurobiological effects** of **childhood trauma**?

In the developing child's brain, trauma can affect the very structure of the brain cells. Trauma can hinder *mylenation*, the growth of a fatty insulation around the neuron's axon. Myelin improves the speed of electrical impulses travelling across the neuron. Trauma can also hinder *synaptogenesis*, the formation of connections between cells as well as the *morphology* or shape of the cell itself. Altogether, this reduces the density and connectivity of the brain. Moreover, brain cells are damaged in areas of the brain involved with emotion, memory, and behavioral control. Such areas include the amygdala, the hippocampus, and the frontal lobe.

What is **complex PTSD**?

Complex PTSD (post-traumatic stress disorder) pertains to the long-term effects of chronic and severe child abuse. This is quite different from normal PTSD, which describes the effects of acute trauma in adulthood. In complex PTSD, there are long-term changes in attention, memory, consciousness, regulation of emotion, and personality characteristics, including unstable, distorted and negative self-perceptions, and problematic interpersonal relationships. These problems can result in the dissociation, self-mutilation, self-destructive behaviors, and emotional storms that are often found with survivors of severe childhood abuse. While chronic PTSD is not an official diagnosis, it is currently being evaluated for inclusion in future editions of the Diagnostic and Statistical Manual (DSM).

What **factors increase** the long-term **damage** of child abuse?

Not everyone who has survived child abuse suffers the same results. Many factors affect the outcome. The first factor is the severity of the abuse. Violent, cruel, frequent and long-lasting abuse obviously has more of an effect than milder abuse. The relationship with the perpetrator is also critically important. The greater the emotional dependence on the perpetrator and the closer the relationship, the greater the damage. Consequently, abusive mothers do the most damage, followed by abusive fathers, other relatives, friends, acquaintances, and then strangers.

What **percentage** of **children** in the United States are **abused** in some way?

The table below shows the breakdown by age and sex of the total number of victimized children in the United States. As the table shows, most of the mistreatment cases occur with children under the age of four (60.2 percent of boys and 58.1 percent of girls). Most of these cases involve neglect. After age four the incidence of mistreatment goes down, only to rise again in adolescence for girls, but not boys. The increase in the mistreatment of teenage girls is probably due to an increase in sexual assaults starting at that time. These statistics come from the 2007 report on Child Mistreatment by the U.S. Department of Health and Human Services.

Percent of Child Abuse Victims (by Age and Sex) in 2007

Age	% Boys	% Girls
< 1 yr.	22.2	21.5
1 yr.	13.2	12.7
2 yrs.	12.8	12.2
3 yrs.	12.0	11.7
4–7 yrs	11.4	11.6
8–11 yrs.	9.2	9.6
12–15 yrs.	6.9	10.5
16–17 yrs.	3.9	7.0

What is the **frequency** of different types of **child abuse** in the United States among different age groups?

This table shows the frequency of different types of abuse across different age groups. For example, 21.8 percent of the total number of mistreatment cases involve neglect of children under the age of four. As you can see, neglect becomes less common as children get older, while sexual abuse becomes more common. All types of abuse decrease by the late teens. These statistics come from the 2007 report on Child Mistreatment by the U.S. Department of Health and Human Services.

Percentage of Different Kinds of Abuse at Different Ages in the United States (2007)

Abuse Type	0-3 yrs.	4-7 yrs.	8-11 yrs.	12-15 yrs.	16-17 yrs.
Neglect	21.8	14.3	10.6	9.0	2.95
Physical Abuse	2.7	2.5	2.1	2.4	0.9
Psychological Abuse	1.14	1.05	0.95	0.78	0.22
Sexual Abuse	0.48	1.8	1.8	2.7	0.8

What is the **generational cycle** of **abuse**?

Tragically, child abuse is often passed down from generation to generation. Frequently the parents of abused children have a history of child abuse in their own families. It is if they have learned automatically to treat children the way they have been treated. It is important to note, however, that the majority of abused children do not grow up to abuse their own children. Moreover, several factors buffer the effect of childhood abuse. For example, victims of child abuse with greater levels of education, social support, and financial security are less likely to abuse their own children.

What factors **protect against** the **after effects** of **child abuse**?

A warm, close relationship with an alternative caretaker, such as an aunt, grandparent, or even a caring neighbor, can soften the damaging effects of child abuse. Likewise, if the abuse is addressed promptly and the child protected from further harm, this can do a good deal to restore the child's faith in the world. This is simplest if the abuser is not a close

Child abuse is often passed down generation to generation, but the cycle *can* be broken. The majority of child abuse victims do not grow up to be abusers themselves (*iStock*).

family member. However, if the child is strongly attached to the abuser—for example, if the abuser is a parent—separation from the abuser can also bring tremendous feelings of loss.

Psychotherapy can help the child victim understand what happened to him or her, correct any distorted views of the abuse (such as self-blame), and work through the complex and sometimes contradictory feelings about the abuse and the abuser. Hopefully, such help can protect against some of the negative psychological effects that often follow experiences of child abuse. Further, connections with institutions that foster relationships with the larger community (e.g., school, church), appropriate discipline in the home, and family stability protect against the negative psychological effects of child abuse.

What do we know about **resilient children**?

As mentioned above, not all survivors of child abuse develop severe psychopathology. In fact, there are estimates that as much as one-third of children from abusive backgrounds grow up to be reasonably healthy and well-adjusted adults. Such children are considered *resilient*, which means they can bounce back and develop well even in the face of tremendous stress. Research has found several factors are associated with resilience in children: intelligence; the ability to make emotional connections with people outside the family; moderate self-control; positive self-image; and an internal locus of control all promote resilience. People with an internal locus of control believe they have reasonable control over their environment and that their actions make a difference. In addition, resilient survivors of child abuse are less likely than their less resilient counterparts to blame themselves for the abuse.

SEXUAL ABUSE

What is **sexual abuse**?

Sexual abuse of children involves inappropriate sexual contact between a child and an adult or a much older child. According to a definition used by Joan Liem, Jacqueline James, and colleagues in a 1997 study, sexual abuse involves any form of coercive sexual contact with an under-age child or any sexual contact between a child thirteen years or younger and someone five or more years older. Although the exact statutes vary state by state, any adult sexual contact with an under-age child is against the law. Sexual abuse ranges from exposure of genitals to fondling of body parts to direct genital contact and, ultimately, to anal or vaginal intercourse. Arguably, sexual abuse may be the most psychologically damaging form of child abuse.

Is **sexual abuse violent**?

The vast majority of incidents of child molestation are not violent. Most child molesters use manipulation or seduction to gain access to their child victims. A sizeable number of child molesters use just enough force to accomplish their goal. Only a small percentage is truly violent. These extreme cases attract the most media attention, however, which unfortunately gives the public a distorted sense of the problem of child sexual abuse.

Who are the **victims** of **child sexual abuse**?

According to government statistics, adolescent girls are the most common victims of child sexual abuse. Sexual abuse of pre-pubescent boys and girls is still widespread, however. In 2007, according to the U.S. Department of Health, there were approximately 56,460 cases of child sexual abuse reported to the authorities, 30,160 (53 percent) involved children under the age of twelve. Most children are abused by someone they know, 34.2 percent by family members, 58.7 percent by friends or acquaintances, and 7.0 percent by strangers, according to FBI statistics.

What are the **effects** of **childhood sexual abuse**?

Although there is a wide range of psychological responses to childhood sexual abuse, problems with low self-esteem, depression, dissociation, lack of trust, and strong feelings of shame are very common. In fact, the diagnosis of complex PTSD was developed largely out of the study of sexual abuse survivors. Borderline personality disorder is also strongly linked to child sexual abuse. Not surprisingly, many sexual abuse survivors also have disturbances in their sexual functioning as adults. Some survivors become over-controlled sexually, with intense fear of and aversion to sexual contact.

Others go to the opposite extreme and become sexually promiscuous, engaging in compulsive, driven, and often reckless sexual behavior. A 2008 study by Beth Brodsky and colleagues showed that the effects of child sexual abuse can reach across generations. Children of mothers who were sexually abused as children had an increased rate of suicidal tendencies compared to children of non-abused mothers.

Is **sexual abuse** transmitted **across generations**?

Like many forms of child abuse, sexual abuse can be transmitted across generations. Adults who were abused as children can grow up to either abuse their own children or partner with someone who will abuse the children. Again, this is not to say that all childhood sexual abuse victims will grow up to abuse their own children. A large proportion of people who were sexually abused in childhood do not pass on their abuse experiences to their own children. Nonetheless, parents of abused children are more likely to have their own abuse histories than are parents of non-abused children.

How does **incest differ** from **other** kinds of **sexual abuse**?

According to FBI statistics, about 34 percent of child abuse cases involve incest. Incestuous abuse occurs when the child is related to the sexual abuser. Victims of incestuous abuse tend to experience more frequent, invasive, and long-term sexual abuse as the perpetrator has ongoing and convenient access to the victim. Research suggests that, on the whole, incest victims suffer greater psychological damage than do victims of other types of child sexual abuse. Not only is the child affected by the sexual abuse itself, the child's entire view of interpersonal relationships is distorted by the incestuous relationship. Particularly when children are abused by a parent or a close caretaker, their ability to trust, to believe themselves worthy of care, and to value or even recognize their own needs and boundaries can be profoundly damaged. The abuser is not acting as a caretaker but as a user and exploiter of the child. In this context, it is often difficult for the child to understand that this is neither normal nor acceptable and that it is the adult who is at fault, not the child.

What is **pedophilia**?

Pedophilia is a psychiatric disorder characterized by persistent sexual attraction to pre-pubescent children. Not all child molesters are pedophiles, however. For example, some child molesters sexually assault children not because they are sexually attracted to children, but because the child is a convenient target, because they are intoxicated, or for some other reason. Further, not all pedophiles are child molesters. Some people with strong and persistent sexual attraction to children may never act on their urges. Additionally, adults who molest adolescents are not necessarily pedophiles, as pedophilia refers only to the attraction to pre-pubescent children. The term *hebephile* is sometimes used to describe adults who are attracted to adolescents.

Are there different **kinds** of **pedophilia**?

There have been several categorizations of pedophilia, but perhaps the most useful involves the distinction between true pedophiles and opportunistic pedophiles. Similar terms include fixated vs. regressed pedophiles and preferential vs. situational pedophiles. True pedophiles have persistent sexual attraction to pre-pubescent children. Opportunistic pedophiles have less of a focused sexual attraction to children. Their sexual engagement with children may depend on circumstances, such as the convenient availability of a child victim, loss of normal inhibitions due to substance abuse, or difficulty feeling comfortable with an adult sexual partner. In this way, opportunistic pedophiles may overlap with non-pedophilic child molesters.

What **causes pedophilia**?

At this point, there is no clear answer to this question, although quite a few possible causes have been proposed. Three possible causes include inadequate social skills, neurological impairment (or brain damage), and the pedophile's own history of childhood sexual abuse.

Do **pedophiles** lack mature **social skills**?

Researchers and clinicians have suggested that pedophiles have poor self-esteem and inadequate social skills and turn to children out of fear of pursuing adult relationships. While this may be true for some pedophiles, it is clearly not true for many others, as there have been many high functioning, socially competent, and even married pedophiles.

Is **pedophilia** caused by **neurological damage**?

There is also research suggesting that pedophiles suffer from some sort of neurological disturbance or brain damage. Again, there is some evidence of this. Several brain imaging studies have suggested abnormal brain function. There have also been cases of people developing pedophilia after suffering brain damage. However, this research is complicated by the samples used in pedophile studies. Most studies obtain their subjects from the criminal justice system. In other words, we study the ones who get caught. We rarely study the ones who have never been caught or have never acted on their urges. We know that, on the whole, convicted criminals tend to have lower intelligence, more problems with impulse control, and higher levels of psychopathic personality traits than the general population. Therefore, it is not clear if the biological findings are related to pedophilia per se, or to other problems common with a criminal population.

Were **pedophiles sexually abused** as children?

There does seem to be a clear relationship between sexual abuse in childhood and the development of pedophilia in adulthood. Many studies have shown a much higher rate of childhood sexual abuse in pedophilic samples than in the general population. Moreover, pedophiles have a higher rate of childhood sexual abuse than do non-sexual criminals and even sexual offenders against adults. As we are learning more and more about how early trauma affects the brain, it is possible that early sexual abuse disturbs the parts of the brain that regulate sexuality, contributing to the later development of pedophilia in some victims.

What are the **signs** that a **child** has been **sexually abused**?

Children frequently do not tell anyone that they are being sexually abused. Even if the child has a close and trusting relationship with a parent and the abuse is by someone outside the family, the child may keep the abuse a secret out of shame, confusion, fear of retribution by the abuser or, if the child is young enough, lack of understanding about what is happening. In these cases, clues may be found in the behavior of the child. There may be a marked change in the child's behavior, including a sudden onset of anxiety, depression, social withdrawal, reduced self-esteem, or sleep disturbances. A previously well-adjusted child may suddenly start acting truant, perform poorly in school or lose or gain a good deal of weight. Unusual or predatory sexual behavior in the child can be another clue that the child has experienced sexual abuse. A sudden fear or aversion to a particular adult may also be a clue. Of course, behavioral changes like these can be due to many other causes besides sexual abuse. There is no need to assume a child who has developed some emotional problems has necessarily been sexually abused. Nonetheless, it is important to recognize that children cannot always verbalize that they have been abused and may express their suffering through marked changes in their behavior.

DOMESTIC VIOLENCE

What is **domestic violence**?

Domestic violence refers to any kind of violence between intimate (or romantic) partners. Generally this refers to a husband and wife, but it can also apply to unmarried couples that do or do not live together. Domestic violence can also occur between homosexual couples, either gay men or lesbians. The severity of violence can range from mild aggression, such as a slap or a shove, to severe aggression (punching, kicking), to extreme aggression (long assaults, burning, or breaking bones), and even to murder.

What is the difference between **domestic violence** and **wife battering**?

Domestic violence is a very general term that does not specify the perpetrator, the severity of violence, or the duration of violence. Wife battering is a more specific term and refers to a systematic pattern of intimidation, control, terror, and physical violence inflicted upon a woman by her male partner. The intent of such behavior is to gain total control over the woman.

What is the **history** of **attitudes** toward **domestic violence**?

The problem of violence between people in intimate relationships has received shockingly little attention until quite recently. As part of the wave of civil rights movements starting in the 1960s, feminism brought attention to the profound problem of battered women, and the disturbing neglect that society has shown the victims. Several researchers and activists interviewed dozens, if not hundreds, of women who told dramatic stories about years of violence and abuse that were minimized, rationalized, and dismissed by the larger society. Police would brush off domestic violence as a private family matter, the clergy would emphasize the need to keep the family together over the women's safety, and the courts would fail to prosecute the cases. Starting in the 1970s, a movement began to bring attention to the profoundly destructive effect of domestic violence and wife battering. Shelters for battered women were set up, new laws were written, and police, clergy and other authorities were educated about the seriousness of the problem.

What **role** did **feminism** play in the **understanding** of **domestic violence**?

The feminist movement played a central role in developing awareness of domestic violence. Feminist writers were the first to describe in detail the psychological, physical, economic, and cultural aspects of wife battering and to insist on bringing public attention to the problem. But as the feminist movement was essentially a political movement, the approach to domestic violence emphasized the political roots of the wife battering. More specifically, wife battering was seen as an outgrowth of the larger societal oppression of women. In a patriarchal (male dominated) society, women were seen as property and wife battering a quasi-legitimate means to keep women under control.

How has the **study** of **domestic violence changed** from the early feminist approach?

More recent work has taken a broader approach to the problem of domestic violence than was taken by the initial feminist writers. There is greater emphasis on empirical research instead of open-ended interviews and clinical histories. There is also interest in same-sex violence, the impact of domestic violence on children, the psychological features of anyone engaging in intimate partner violence, and the role of female-initiated violence. Importantly, empirical research has shown that not all of domestic violence can be explained by patriarchal oppression of women. Although classic instances of wife battering certainly do occur, women themselves are not always helpless victims of an abusive partner. Sometimes women are violent themselves and/or display some of the psychologically abusive tactics of a classic batterer. Additionally, violence between same-sex couples cannot easily be explained by societal oppression of women. Nonetheless, although later research shows a more complex picture than the earlier feminists described, the nature and frequency of domestic violence is undeniably influenced by the cultural, economic, and legal position of women in society.

What are some of the **key concepts** of the **battering syndrome**?

Even though the study of domestic violence has broadened beyond the political vantage point of the 1970s, several key ideas introduced by feminist writers illuminate the psychological mechanics of battering relationships. Regardless of the gender of the people involved, a battering relationship has specific psychological characteristics that have long-lasting and very destructive effects on anyone caught in it. Three important concepts include the *cycle of violence, coercive control*, and *traumatic bonding*.

What is **Lenore Walker's model** of the **cycle of violence**?

The psychologist Lenore Walker has written extensively about battered women. In an influential book entitled *The Battered Woman*, published in 1979, she introduced the concept of the *cycle of violence* to describe a consistent pattern in the violent behavior of batterers. Based on in-depth interviews with battered women, Walker described three phases of the cycle of violence: *the tension-building phase*, the *acute battering incident,* and the *honeymoon phase*. The tension-building phase precedes the acute battering incident. In this period, the batterer grows increasingly explosive and aggressive. There may be verbal abuse, temper explosions at minor frustrations, and an unpredictable building of tension. At this point, the battered woman knows that a serious explosion may occur at any moment, and she works overtime to appease her partner and avert what she ultimately knows is inevitable. She tiptoes around her partner, constantly walking on eggshells.

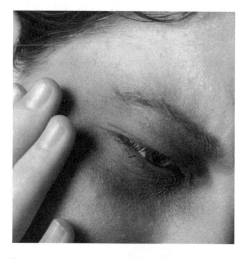

Over a period of time—the length of which can vary from a matter of days to several years—the tension escalates until it finally explodes into a violent assault, known as the acute battering

Both men and women can commit spousal abuse, but violence against women is more common whenever women have less economic or legal power in a society (*iStock*).

421

incident. There can be punching, kicking, hitting with objects, and throwing down stairs. There can also be forced sexual activity. The abuse can go on for hours, sometimes ending only when the abuser is exhausted and has successfully released all his tension. In the honeymoon phase, the batterer expresses remorse, promises to change, and works hard to win back the woman's love. Alternatively, he may threaten suicide if she wants to leave, or try to woo her back with heightened affection, gifts, and romantic attention. This continues until the tension-building phase begins anew. While Walker's theory has been quite influential in the study and treatment of domestic violence, it has also been criticized as overly simplistic and not applicable to all cases of domestic violence. Nonetheless, most clinicians would agree that it is descriptive of some cases of domestic violence.

What is **Evan Stark's model** of **coercive control**?

In 2007, Evan Stark published a book entitled *Coercive Control: How Men Entrap Women in Personal Life*. Stark's ideas about coercive control were not new; in fact, they dated back to the 1970s. But after thirty years of working with battered women, Stark felt that the field of domestic violence had abandoned its feminist roots for an overly narrow focus on physical violence. In his view, it is the psychological aspects of the battering relationship that are the most damaging. *Coercive control* refers to the systematic attempts to psychologically dominate the battered women. Stark felt that this is at the core of all battering relationships.

Batterers use a broad range of tactics, which can include: micromanaging of the most intimate details of the victim's life (e.g., dress, personal appearance, diet), paranoid levels of possessiveness, suspiciousness and sexual jealousy, verbal abuse and name calling, unpredictable outbursts over minor or even imaginary infractions, isolating the battered woman from all sources of social support, and continuous low levels of physical aggression (e.g., hair pulling, arm grabbing, shoving, pushing). These tactics create a climate of fear and self-doubt which, in turn, serves to break down the victim's self-esteem, sense of autonomy, and capacity to resist the batterer's domination. The serious assaults, when they come, only reinforce the victims' helplessness. The violence does not stand on its own; it is part of a larger program to break down the victim and to effectively hold her hostage.

How is **domestic abuse similar** to other forms of **coercive control**?

As several writers have noted, the tactics of coercive control used in battering relationships are remarkably similar to tactics used in other situations of captivity and terror. Political prisoners, cult members, and young girls "seasoned" into prostitution are frequently exposed to tactics of coercive control. The goal is always the same, to break down the self-confidence and autonomous sense of self of the victims, and leave them at the psychological mercy of their captors.

Who is Patty Hearst and why is she still remembered today?

On February 4, 1974, 19-year-old Patty Hearst, granddaughter of the newspaper magnate William Randolph Hearst, was kidnapped off the campus of the University of California at Berkeley. A group calling themselves the Symbionese Liberation Army took responsibility for the crime. For months, Patty was locked in a closet, beaten, and raped. In April 1974, she was photographed taking part in a bank robbery. In September 1975, she was arrested for armed robbery. Prosecutors argued that she had willingly engaged in criminal behavior because she had failed to escape her abductors, even though she had ample opportunities to do so. Patty Hearst was found

The dramatic case of Patty Hearst has become a textbook example of a kidnapping victim who comes to sympathize with her abductors. Hearst went so far as to commit armed robbery in 1974 at the behest of her kidnappers (*Shutterstock*).

guilty and sentenced to 35 years in jail, which was later shortened to seven years. After only 21 months in prison, her sentence was commuted by President Jimmy Carter. Years later she would write of her ordeal and describe how the psychological effects of torture and captivity led her to identify with and then cooperate with her kidnappers' demands, even when she was technically free to escape.

What did **Judith Herman** say about the **psychological effects** of **captivity**?

In 1992 Judith Herman (1942–) published a book entitled *Trauma and Recovery*, which looked at the psychological effects of traumatic abuse from domestic abuse to political terror. Her chapter on the effects of captivity has particular relevance to the discussion of domestic violence. In effect, captivity can produce a form of brainwashing. In a severe battering situation, the batterer holds the victim captive. By controlling the victims' entire world—their sleep-wake cycle, their diet, their physical safety and, most importantly, their access to other people—batterers can gradually take over their victims' mind. Through constant verbal abuse and through the degradation of the physical abuse, the victim loses any sense of self-worth. Her confidence in her ability to control her environment is shattered. Her very sense of what is real is destroyed as the batterer controls the information that is available to her, and constantly denies

423

her own sense of reality. Moreover, by keeping other people away, batterers remove any outside reality check on their distorted worldview.

A particularly powerful way to break down victims' sense of self is to make them betray their own moral values. The victim may be forced to engage in emotionally disturbing sexual behavior or to participate in the abuse of another victim. Similar techniques are used in the brainwashing or "breaking down" of prisoners or cult members. A critical implication of this work is that, under the right circumstances, anyone can suffer the same psychological effects. Likewise, anyone can get into a battering relationship. Of course, certain people are more vulnerable to abusive relationships than others. People with a history of child abuse or domestic violence in childhood may be more vulnerable to entering into and staying in a battering relationship. Similarly, younger people and people with significant psychological problems may also be more vulnerable.

What is **traumatic bonding**?

Traumatic bonding is another concept that helps us understand the power of the battering relationship. When people are under extreme stress, there is an intensified need to form powerful emotional bonds with other people. For example, soldiers in battle often form lifelong ties to other soldiers in their unit. Because of the acute trauma of the battering relationship, the victim also feels an intensified need for social bonds. But because of the victims' social isolation, they have no one to turn to besides their batterers. In this way, victims develop great emotional dependency on the very person who is causing them such pain.

Why do **battered women stay**?

There are many reasons that battered women stay in a relationship, even though it can seem unfathomable to outside observers. First, there are often practical reasons, such as legal, economic, financial, and cultural considerations. Secondly, they have good reason to fear for their safety, and even their life, if they leave. Thirdly, the psychological effects of the battering relationship serve to break down self-confidence to the point that it can feel impossible to leave.

What are the **practical reasons** that **battered women stay**?

Although this is less true now than it was several decades ago, on a purely practical level it is often very difficult for a battered woman to leave her abuser. Inadequate financial means, inadequate legal protection, and lack of support by family and/or clergy can all hinder a battered woman's escape. Although there is now much greater public awareness of domestic violence than there was in previous decades, battered women still may not have the resources or support they need to survive on their own, particularly if they have children. Additionally, battered women have good reason to fear for their safety or for the

Who were Hedda Nussbaum and Joel Steinberg?

Hedda Nussbaum came to national attention after the 1987 beating death of her illegally adopted daughter, Lisa Steinberg. In 1989 her live-in companion, Joel Steinberg, was convicted of manslaughter in the child's death. Initially, Nussbaum was also charged in her death, given her failure to take action to protect her daughter. However, Nussbaum was also a victim of Joel Steinberg's abuse. Eventually, the court agreed that years of physical, sexual, and psychological torture rendered Nussbaum both psychologically and physically incapable of taking action against him, even to save her child's life. Steinberg's constant and brutal battery left Nussbaum permanently disfigured.

safety of their family. Batterers often threaten to kill the woman or to harm her family if she leaves. These are not idle threats. Murder by an intimate partner is the most common form of female homicide and the point of separation is a particularly dangerous time.

What are the **psychological reasons** that **battered women** stay?

The whole aim of coercive control is to break down the independence of the victim. The verbal abuse, terror, unpredictability, and enforced social isolation all powerfully serve to crush a victim's sense of self and even her sense of reality. A psychologically broken woman may not feel she is capable of living without her batterer. This is why so many women return to their batterer after they have left him.

How does **domestic violence** affect the **children**?

There is no question that domestic violence has terrible effects on children. Children experience similar forms of psychological damage from witnessing domestic violence as they do from being a victim of it. Both child victims and child witnesses of physical abuse report higher levels of depression, aggression, problems in relationships, and problems in school. In sum, children who witness domestic violence are victims of it too. Moreover, children who are raised in violent homes can grow up thinking that violence in intimate relationships is normal. As adults, they are more likely to physically abuse their own partners, or to marry someone who will physically abuse them.

Do **only men** batter?

Early feminist scholars insisted that spousal battery was an overwhelmingly male phenomenon. However, a number of studies investigating couples in the community suggest that women were actually more likely than men to commit violence, especially

How did a famous 1994 murder trial draw attention to the issue of domestic abuse in the United States?

The 1994 murder of Nicole Simpson and Ronald Goldman caused an enormous scandal. O.J. Simpson, a popular former football player and Nicole's estranged husband, was arrested for the murders after a dramatic, televised car chase. There was a documented history of domestic violence in the Simpson family, with police records of multiple 911 calls made by Nicole during O.J.'s violent outbursts. There were also graphic photographs of Nicole's bruised face taken years before the murder.

O.J. Simpson (right) with attorney Robert Shapiro during his August 1994 trial (*AP Photo/Nick Ut, Pool*).

Despite what the prosecution described as an airtight case, O.J. was acquitted. His attorney, Johnny Cochran, skillfully turned the jury's focus from the guilt or innocence of O.J. Simpson to the credibility of the Los Angeles Police Department. Simpson was later found guilty in a wrongful death civil suit. After the trial, considerable media attention was given to the ongoing racial divisions in the United States revealed by public response to this inter-racial scandal. Unfortunately, this highly publicized case brought little attention to the problem of domestic violence.

mild forms of violence. In a 2007 study of 607 college students, Rosemarie Cogan and Tiffany Fennell found that 53 percent of women and 38 percent of men reported committing physical aggression toward an intimate partner. In a 2006 study by Susan O'Leary and Amy Slep, 453 cohabitating couples with young children reported similar results. Women admitted to a median of three acts of mild physical aggression and two acts of severe physical aggression in the past year, compared to men, who admitted to two mild acts and one severe act in the past year. Additionally, both males and females perceive female-initiated violence to be less dangerous and problematic than male-initiated violence.

Criminal statistics, however, tell a different story than the research quoted above. Men are far more likely to be involved in criminal assaults against a partner than are women and female homicide by an intimate partner is far more common than the reverse. In fact, murder by an intimate partner is the most frequent form of female homicide. Taken together, these findings suggest that American women are equally if not more likely than men to engage in mild to moderate aggression, but that men are still much more likely to engage in serious and life-threatening violence against their intimate partners.

What are the **criminal statistics** about **intimate partner violence?**

According to the U.S. Department of Justice, from 2001 to 2005, 0.4 percent of women and 0.09 percent of men reported an assault by an intimate partner to the police per year. This accounted for 21.5 percent of all nonfatal assaults for women and 3.6 percent for men. Further, in 2005, 1,181 women and 329 men were murdered by intimate partners. Between 1976 and 2005, 30.1 percent of female murders and 5.3 percent of male murders were committed by intimate partners. Thus women are 3.6 times more likely than men to be murdered by an intimate partner and 4.4 times more likely to suffer nonfatal intimate partner assaults. The good news, though, is that the incidence of all violent crimes by intimate partners has decreased dramatically over the last few decades.

Does the **rate** of **domestic violence** vary across cultures?

Rates of domestic violence, particularly violence against women, appear to vary drastically across cultures. According to a 2009 report by the World Health Organization, the lifetime rate of spousal battery among ever-partnered women ranged from 15 to 72 percent. Rural areas had much higher rates of spousal abuse than urban areas. The lifetime rate of sexual or physical violence from an intimate partner was 72 percent in rural Ethiopia, 69 percent in rural Peru, and 62 percent in rural Bangladesh. The rate was 15 percent in urban Japan, 24 percent in urban Serbia and Montenegro, and 29 percent in urban Brazil. Although the annual rate of spousal abuse was much lower than the lifetime rate, abuse was rarely a one-time thing. If it happened once, it was likely to occur again.

What **affects** the **prevalence** of **violence** against women?

Poverty, war, and political and economic instability lead to increased rates of violence against women. Additionally, alcohol abuse and exposure to domestic violence as a child both increase the likelihood of domestic violence. Arguably, however, the most important factor is the cultural attitude toward domestic violence and the rights of women. When women have no rights and men feel entitled to treat women as property, domestic violence can become endemic.

How do **women's rights vary** across countries?

The widespread acceptance of the equal rights of women is a fairly new phenomenon, arising only in the last four decades. While women now make up almost half the workforce in the United States and account for about 50 percent of law, medical, and doctoral degrees, only thirty-five years ago women accounted for a small fraction of the professions. According to the U.S. State Department's 2003 report on international human rights, the movement toward equal rights for women in the developing world is only just beginning.

In many Islamic countries, for example, the role of women is still extremely constricted, and religious conservatives believe that women should be entirely subordinate to men. Consequently, legal rights for women vary drastically across countries. In most developed Western countries women have essentially the same legal rights as men. In other countries, many things are forbidden to women: the legal right to work; to have access to credit; to own property; to initiate a divorce; to have custody of the children; and even to have one's testimony in court carry as much weight as a man's testimony. In some developing countries, such as South Africa, new, progressive laws support many rights for women. However the enforcement of such laws is often quite lax, and popular acceptance, particularly in rural areas, is very low. In other countries, such as Saudi Arabia, women are not allowed to drive or to travel without a man accompanying them.

How do **attitude** towards **domestic violence vary** across cultures?

The feminist movement brought the problem of domestic violence to public attention only within recent decades. Most industrialized countries now recognize the problem and have laws against it. For example, in Canada there were 524 shelters for battered women by 2002. In other developing countries, such as South Africa, there are laws prohibiting domestic violence but enforcement is a problem and there is little government support for public education against domestic violence or for shelters for battered women. Still other countries, such as Bulgaria or Zimbabwe, have no laws against domestic violence. In many cultures, popular attitudes promote a tolerance of domestic violence. The problem is minimized by the family and community as well as by judicial and medical systems, and both men and women believe a man has the right to physically "discipline" his wife.

What is **forensic psychology**?

The word "forensic" refers to the legal system. Forensic matters include anything related to the application and enforcement of the law, as well as the prosecution of those who violate the law.

Forensic psychology is a relatively new field but it is growing rapidly. Forensic psychologists are involved with many aspects of both civil and criminal law. In matters of civil law, they are involved with competency and disability evaluations, as well as divorce mediation and custody evaluations. In criminal cases, they perform evaluations of the mental state of the defendant (particularly in insanity pleas), and provide expert testimony on relevant psychological factors.

Forensic psychologists may also provide psychotherapy for prison inmates, including specific programs for violent or sexual offenders. They also work directly with law enforcement officials. They screen applicants for the police force and can provide stress management, grief work, and trauma counseling to police officers and other members of law enforcement. Finally, forensic psychologists perform scientific research on such topics as the reliability of children's testimony, recidivism of sex offenders, impulsivity and aggression, and juvenile delinquency.

What is **criminal profiling**?

Criminal profiling involves the attempt to identify psychological, demographic, and behavioral features of the criminal solely from crime scene evidence. Over the past thirty years or so, criminal profiling has become very popular in law enforcement and is now a widespread practice in many different countries. Its popularity is reflected in the NBC-TV show called *Profiler*. While there have been a number of attempts to develop theories and systems of criminal profiling, there is very little actual scientific evidence to show that it works. There is even debate among researchers whether criminal profiling can even be scientifically validated if appropriate research were done. In a 1990 study by Anthony Pinnozotto and Norman Finkel, profilers were more accurate than other groups (composed of detectives, psychologists, and students) when identifying demographic characteristics of sex offenders, but less accurate than detectives with regard to homicides.

THE PSYCHOLOGY
OF CRIMINAL BEHAVIOR

What can **psychology tell** us about **criminal behavior**?

Any kind of criminal behavior involves a conscious choice to violate the law—if the behavior is accidental or unintentional, it is not criminal. While we know that many environmental factors—including poverty, neighborhood crime rates, social norms, and lack of opportunities for legal employment—contribute to the incidence of criminal behavior, psychological factors also play an integral role in the choice to commit criminal acts.

Do **all law-breakers** have **abnormal psychological traits**?

Not everyone who breaks the law has abnormal psychological traits. Illegal behavior can be motivated by many different factors. However, there are certain psychological features that make some people more likely to engage in criminal behavior than others.

Is there a **criminal mind**?

For quite a few decades, the mental health field has attempted to classify and study the personality traits of people most likely to engage in criminal behavior. In other words, they have tried to diagnose the criminal mind. In the latest edition of the official Diagnostic and Statistical Manual of mental disorders, DSM-IV and DSM-IV-TR, the diagnosis of *antisocial personality disorder* describes people who habitually violate social norms and moral codes.

What is **antisocial personality disorder**?

People with antisocial personality disorder (ASPD) are characterized by callous and exploitive behavior and by a lack of empathy or remorse. According to DSM-IV, a person with this disorder demonstrates a pervasive pattern of disregard for the rights of others as evidenced by at least three of the following criteria: repeatedly engaging in illegal behavior; frequently lying, using aliases, or conning others for personal profit; impulsivity and lack of future planning; irritability and aggressiveness; reckless disre-

Do Mafia bosses have abnormal psychological traits? Would they be diagnosed with either antisocial personality disorder or psychopathy, the personality disorders characterized by criminal behavior? Their criminal behavior would certainly meet some criteria for both antisocial personality disorder and psychopathy, but the fact that they operate within a subculture distinguishes them from the kinds of criminals that act alone. Within the culture of organized crime, they would probably not be considered psychologically abnormal (*Library of Congress*).

gard for the safety of self and others; consistent irresponsibility, with repeated failures to sustain employment or fulfill financial obligations; lack of remorse as evident in indifference to, or rationalization of, hurting, mistreating, or stealing from others. This definition has been criticized, however, for being too focused on behavior instead of personality traits, and for requiring evidence of conduct disorder (a childhood variant of ASPD) before the age of fifteen.

What is **psychopathy**?

The concept of psychopathy should be distinguished from the DSM-IV concept of antisocial personality disorder. While diagnosis of antisocial personality disorder is heavily dependent on a record of criminal behavior, psychopathy is more geared to the actual personality traits associated with criminal behavior. Such traits include callousness, superficial and shallow emotion, lack of empathy, irresponsibility, lack of remorse or guilt about harming others, and the tendency to exploit, manipulate and engage in predatory behavior toward others.

Psychopathic prisoners commit more serious and violent crimes than non-psychopathic prisoners. They are also more likely to recidivate (commit another crime) after they are released from prison. Moreover, psychopaths are more likely to commit premeditated rather than impulsive crimes. In Michael Woodworth and Stephen Porter's 2002 study of 125 prisoners convicted of homicide, the thirty-four psychopathic prisoners were much more likely than the ninety-one non-psychopathic prisoners to have committed premeditated murders (93.3 percent vs. 48.4 percent).

How is **psychopathy measured**?

The foremost expert on psychopathy today is a psychologist named Robert Hare (1934–). He has developed an intensive interview to measure psychopathy named the Hare Psychopathy Checklist. His first version was published in 1980 and the revised version (PCL-R) in 1991. The PCL-R is a twenty-item clinical rating scale that is scored based on information from a semi-structured interview and available legal files and medical records. Collateral interviews with someone who knows the subject well are also conducted, as psychopathic individuals are not always reliable informants. Although the maximum possible score is 40, the average scores in both male and female offender populations range from about 22 to 24. Hare uses a cut-off score of 30 to distinguish psychopaths from non-psychopaths. He believes that psychopathy is more of a category than a dimension. This means that someone either is or is not a psychopath. Notably, some other researchers disagree and believe that psychopathic traits fall on a continuum.

How **common** is **psychopathy**?

Hare estimates that about 50 to 75 percent of the prison population meets criteria for antisocial personality disorder, but only 15 to 25 percent exceed the cut-off point for psychopathy. Hare also estimates that psychopaths make up about one percent of the general population. Thus, psychopathy appears to be a more severe disorder than antisocial personality disorder, but fortunately a less common one.

What are the different **dimensions** of **psychopathy**?

In Hare's initial research, he conducted a factor analysis on a large sample of prisoners who had been administered the PCL-R. Factor analysis identifies scale items that cluster together and is used to create subscales of a measure. Two factors were identified, the interpersonal/affective factor (factor 1) and the socially deviant lifestyle factor (factor 2). In 2003, Hare modified his original model with a new 4-factor model. Factor 1 was divided into an interpersonal factor (impression management, grandiosity, pathological lying, and manipulativeness) and an affective factor (lack of remorse, shallow affect, callous/lacking empathy, and failure to acknowledge responsibility). Factor 2 was divided into a lifestyle factor (stimulation seeking, parasitic, lacking goals, impulsive, and irresponsible) and an antisocial factor (aggressive, early behavior problems, serious criminal behavior, engagement in different types of crimes). Other authors have proposed a 3-factor model, dividing Factor 1 as Hare did, but keeping Factor 2 as a behavioral factor. Over the years, new instruments similar to the Hare PCL-R have been developed and have yielded similar factor structures.

Who was Ted Bundy?

The serial killer Ted Bundy (1946–1989), is a perfect example of a psychopath. Handsome, educated, and intelligent, he was actively involved in politics and on close terms with the Washington state governor. Bundy also had long romantic relationships with two women who had little reason to believe he was anything other than what he presented himself to be. Eventually, he admitted to murdering 30 women, but it is likely there were many more victims. He conned, manipulated, and lied to women to get them into his car or some other secluded place, where he would rape, torture, and murder them. He would often approach women wearing a sling, a leg cast, or crutches and ask them to help him carry his belongings. Clearly, his murders were planned and calculated and not at all the result of impulsive outbursts. The dramatic split between his polished public image and his murderous rampages speaks to the callous, sadistic, manipulative, and emotionally disconnected personality traits of a classic psychopath.

What is the difference between **antisocial behavior** and **antisocial attitudes**?

One of Hare's most important findings involves the distinction between Factor 1 and Factor 2. This research suggests that psychopathy is made up of two relatively distinct personality traits, antisocial attitudes and antisocial behavior. The first trait reflects cold, callous personality features. The second trait reflects impulsive-aggression and poor behavioral control. These traits may have different causes, differ in their underlying neurobiology, and predict to different types of behavior. Although the two factors correlate at 0.5, suggesting about 25 percent overlap, they are really quite distinct.

What does **Hare's Factor 1** correlate with?

Factor 1 includes the emotional and interpersonal aspects of psychopathy, the callous, manipulative and egocentric qualities—in other words, the core personality traits. Factor 1 is correlated with measures of narcissistic and histrionic personality disorder and Machiavellian traits. Factor 1 is also correlated with level of violence, risk of recidivism (repeat crimes), and abnormal emotional processing (low anxiety, low empathy). Factor 1 is not correlated with age, education, or socioeconomic status (SES).

What does **Hare's Factor 2** correlate with?

Factor 2 relates to antisocial behavior and the deviant lifestyle. Factor 2 is correlated with measures of substance abuse, criminal behaviors, and antisocial personality disorder. It is also negatively correlated with IQ, education, SES, and age. In other words, people with low SES, education, and IQ are more likely to engage in antisocial behavior. This also means that as people get older, their antisocial behavior decreases. However, core psychopathic personality traits do not appear to be related to age, nor are they necessarily related to other demographic features, such as SES and education.

What role do **narcissistic traits** play in **antisocial attitudes** and **behavior**?

Antisocial individuals have a good deal of narcissistic features and there is some overlap between the two personality types. Nonetheless, it is important to distinguish between the two. Narcissism is not the same as antisocial personality and many highly narcissistic people do not show antisocial traits. As is shown in Hare's scale, grandiosity, lack of empathy, and a tendency to use others for one's own ends are common among psychopathic individuals. And the DSM-IV definition of narcissistic personality disorders lists grandiosity, lack of empathy, and the expectation that others will accommodate to the individual's desires as criteria for the disorder. In true psychopathy, however, there is little room for interpersonal relationships. Other people simply do not matter; they are solely means to an end. In narcissism, on the other hand, there is often a strong emphasis on interpersonal relationships, along with great dependence on others' approval and validation. Narcissists may be self-obsessed but they are not necessarily cold, cruel, or sadistic. Nonetheless, under the proper conditions, highly narcissistic people can veer into criminal behavior. The desire for riches, fame, and power, along with the grandiose belief of being above the limits of normal people, can lead such individuals to cross over legal and ethical lines.

What role does **intellectual ability** play in **criminal behavior**?

The majority of criminal behavior is related to impulsivity and impulsive aggression, and intellectual ability is strongly related to impulsivity. A large literature shows a strong correlation between antisocial behavior and lowered performance on a range of cognitive tests. In effect, impulsivity means acting without thinking. Therefore, the ability to reason through situations is a critical component of behavioral control. This entails the ability to consider alternative explanations of events and alternative solutions to problems. Most importantly, one must be able to anticipate future consequences. It is worth noting that reduced cognitive abilities are related to *behavioral* problems, as measured by Hare's Factor 2.

Less is known about the relationship between cognitive function and the core psychopathic *personality* traits of Hare's Factor 1. Certainly there have been very brilliant psychopaths throughout history, and many have risen to positions of great power. Such people are not impulsive and are very capable of planning ahead. Nonetheless, there is some evidence of subtle cognitive abnormalities in psychopaths, specifically with regard to attention. Several studies have revealed over-focused attention in psychopaths; they only attend to their goal and are relatively unresponsive to peripheral information.

Was the Enron scandal an example of psychopathic traits on the part of corporate executives?

Enron was an enormous energy company based in Texas that quickly rose to national prominence in the 1990s. CEO Ken Lay was a major contributor to political campaigns, and a warm acquaintance of U.S. presidents and other high-level politicians. Enron collapsed in 2001 due to a vast web of fraudulent accounting. This cost tens of thousands of jobs and billions of dollars. Lay, along with executive Jeffrey Skilling and his protégé Andrew Fastow, were all convicted of fraud and sentenced to prison.

Were these men typical psychopaths? Would they meet criteria for antisocial personality disorder?

While the greed of some corporate titans might seem psychopathic, it is unlikely they would meet the full criteria for antisocial personalitry disorder (*iStock*).

Although we can only guess outside of an in-person clinical interview, it is more likely that all three men fell victim to their own narcissism. Seduced by the power, wealth, and glory of their enormous success, they chose to keep their profits growing, even if they had to cross ethical and legal lines in the process. The life savings of thousands of Enron employees became less important than their own ambition. We can also question the societal values that place such priority on financial success, ultimately encouraging the kind of financial misbehavior uncovered in the Enron scandal.

Do criminals **"age out"**?

There is clear evidence that criminals tend to age out. Most serious and violent crimes are committed by people under the age of forty. According to Cathy Widom and Michael Maxfield, the core age for criminal behavior is from twenty to twenty-five. Moreover, Factor 2 on Hare's Psychopathy Checklist, which measures antisocial behavior, is negatively correlated with age. Thus, there is a general reduction of impulsive-aggressive and reckless behavior as people get older. This reduction may also relate to the fact that older people have less energy and physical vigor than younger people. However, *planful* criminal behavior that makes minimal physical

435

demands on the criminal is less likely to diminish with age. As Hare's data shows, the psychopathic personality traits (Factor 1) do not decrease with age but are stable over time. That is why psychopathic people who have underlings to carry out their antisocial behavior, such as murderous dictators and kingpins of organized crime, can continue to engage in criminal activity well into their eighties.

CAUSES OF ANTISOCIAL TRAITS

What are the **causes** of **antisocial traits**?

There is a large literature on the risk factors for criminal behavior. Research points to a multitude of risk factors, including genetic, cognitive, personality, family, and community influences. Of note, however, this research does not distinguish between antisocial behavior and psychopathic personality traits.

What **role** does **environment** play in the development of **antisocial traits**?

Environment plays an extremely important role in the development of antisocial traits. It is no coincidence that most of the people in jail for violent crimes come from lower socioeconomic levels and disadvantaged communities. Even though we are continually learning more about the biological and genetic contributions to antisocial behavior, it is critical to keep in mind that environment greatly shapes all aspects of human behavior. Environment even shapes much of human biology, including gene expression.

What **role** does **neurobiology** play in the development of **antisocial traits**?

The explosion in neurobiological research of the past few decades has shed more and more light on the neurobiology underlying antisocial behavior. We now know much more about the brain areas involved in antisocial behavior, the kinds of biological conditions that contribute to antisocial behavior, and even genes that raise the risk of antisocial behavior.

Is there an **interaction** between **neurobiology** and **environment**?

Current research shows that nature (genes and biology) and nurture (environment) interact throughout life. Our genes prime us toward certain personality traits and psychological abilities (for example, intelligence, verbal skills, risk tolerance). In effect, our genes set the parameters, or the outer limits, of our mental capacities. Our environment then determines whether we will meet our potential or fall below it. Our environment also tells us what kinds of behaviors are socially acceptable and likely to be rewarded or punished. Moreover, when both genetic/biological and environmental risk factors are present, antisocial traits are significantly amplified. For example, children with both biological vulnerabilities and high-risk environments show much more severe antisocial traits than children with either biological or environmental vulnerabilities alone.

What **social factors** contribute to the development of **antisocial behavior**?

The relationship between individual and social risk factors is critically important. Poverty, poor education, inadequate community institutions, lack of appropriate social support systems, antisocial peers, and dangerous and violent neighborhoods can all have a devastating effect on an adolescent's social and psychological development. Together, these factors greatly raise the risk of the child growing up to engage in criminal behavior.

In a 2002 study, Magda Stouthamer-Loeber and colleagues examined risk and protective factors for severe and persistent delinquency over a six-year period in a sample of 871 boys. In particular, they looked at the impact of the general socioeconomic status (SES) of the neighborhood. Neighborhood SES was based on information from the 1990 census, including data on median household income, number of single-parent families, and percentage of families below the poverty line. Neighborhoods were divided into four groups: high, medium, and low SES, and low SES with the majority of residents in public housing. In the boys aged thirteen to nineteen there was a clear relationship between neighborhood SES and criminal behavior. The results showed that 17.7 percent of the high SES group, 32.4 percent of the medium SES group, 41.7 percent of the low SES group, and 69.4 percent of the low SES/public housing group engaged in serious delinquent behavior. In other words, boys from the lowest SES neighborhood were almost four times more likely to engage in serious delinquent behavior than boys from the highest SES neighborhood.

What **role** do **social norms** play in the determination of **criminal behavior**?

Criminal behavior involves the violation of the law, which in most cases also involves violation of social norms. However, in subcultures in which criminal behavior is socially acceptable, such as adolescent gangs, terrorist groups, and organized crime, an individual's participation in criminal behavior may be less a function of abnormal psychology than of the identification with and desire to fit into a social group. In other cases, people join violent social groups not out of free choice but because of coercion from the particular group or a perceived need for protection from other violent, predatory groups. In disadvantaged, low SES neighborhoods where violent gangs are more likely to flourish, this can have a devastating effect on the social development of young people, and young men in particular.

Teen gangs are typically well-structured social groups with clear codes of acceptable behavior. When trying to understand gang members' behavior, it is probably more useful to consider the social environment where gangs tend to flourish than to focus on the psychological traits of individual gang members. In other words, it is likely that gang members become violent because they have been socialized to become that way in the gang (*iStock*).

What **factors** in the **family contribute** to juvenile **delinquency**?

Faulty, inept or abusive parenting, parental psychopathology (such as depression), and antisocial behavior in the siblings all increase the risk of a child engaging in antisocial behavior.

What **role** does **gender** play in **antisocial traits**?

One obvious fact about criminal statistics is that criminals are predominantly male. In a 2001 study by Cathy Widom and Michael Maxfield, there was a 2.5–1 male to female ratio for any arrest among a sample of 667 young adults. For violent crime, the male to female ratio increased to 6.7–1. In FBI statistics for 1998, women accounted for 22 percent of all arrests, 8 percent of convicted violent felons, 23 percent of property felons, and 17 percent of drug felons. Moreover, when female criminal behavior does occur, it is often in the company of a male.

Finally, female antisocial behavior may be more strongly linked to trauma and abuse. For example, in a Widom and Maxfield's study, abused women were 227 percent more likely to commit a violent crime than non-abused women, while the rate of violent crime only increased by 17 percent for abused men vs. non-abused men. We can-

438

not know the extent to which this gender difference is due to cultural or biological influences. Given the predominance of male criminals across history and cultures, however, it is likely there is a strong biological component, possibly involving male hormones such as testosterone.

Does **child abuse** cause **antisocial traits**?

There is considerable evidence that a history of child abuse increases the likelihood of criminal activity in adolescence and adulthood. In their 2001 study, Cathy Widom and Michael Maxfield examined the arrest records of 1,575 individuals, including 908 individuals with documented histories of child abuse or neglect and 667 non-abused controls who were matched to the first group for age, sex, race, and family socioeconomic status. All abuse cases occurred between 1967 and 1971 when the children were eleven years of age or younger. By 1994, 27.4 percent of the abused/neglected group had arrests as a juvenile compared to 17.2 percent of the non-abused group. In addition, 41.6 percent had arrests as adults compared to 32.5 percent of the non-abused group, and 18.1 percent had been arrested for a violent crime vs. 13.9 percent of the non-abused group. Thus, abused children were about 60 percent more likely to be arrested as a juvenile and 30 percent more likely to be arrested as an adult than non-abused children.

Do **all** abused children **develop antisocial traits**?

It is important to stress that the majority of abused children do not grow up to develop antisocial traits. According to some estimates, in fact, as much as one-third of abused children grow up without significant psychological damage. However, the risk of the child developing antisocial traits increases with more severe abuse and with the presence of other risk factors, such as poverty, poor schools, etc.

What psychological **characteristics raise** the **risk** of juvenile **delinquency**?

There are a number of psychological characteristics that raise the risk of later criminal behavior. Poor cognitive and language ability, problematic and irritable temperament, poor self-control and self-regulation, low self-esteem, and inadequate social and interpersonal skills can all raise the risk of an individual engaging in criminal behavior.

What **biological factors** contribute to **delinquency**?

Poor nutrition, inadequate health care, prenatal exposure to illicit substances, and inadequate sleep all interfere with proper brain maturation, hindering social and cognitive development. Moreover, a number of genes have been identified that are associated with reckless, poorly controlled behavior. Finally, biologically based mental conditions, such as attention deficit disorder and various learning disorders, also interfere with behavioral control and raise the risk of criminal behavior.

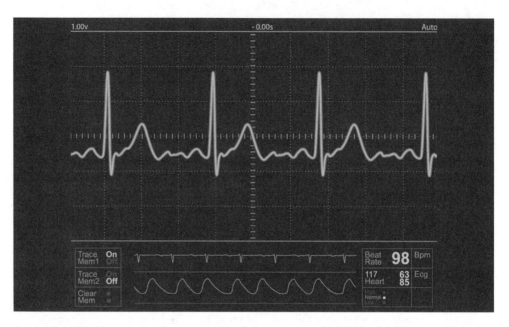

One study found that violent men whose heart rate went down during an argument with their wives had higher levels of aggressive-sadistic tendencies (*iStock*).

What do we know about the **neurobiology** of **psychopathic criminals**?

Psychopathic individuals appear to be hyporeactive to emotional stimuli. In other words, the emotional parts of the brains do not react as strongly to emotional stimuli as the same parts of the brain in healthy people and even in non-psychopathic prisoners. Likewise, a large body of literature shows that psychopaths have difficulty processing emotional information. Compared to non-psychopathic criminals, they are less able to identify emotions as expressed in vocal tone, facial expression, or spoken sentences. Moreover, they may be particularly insensitive to sadness. Also, the two halves of their cortex, the left and right hemispheres, are not well coordinated during cognitive tasks, and the left hemisphere may be less active than is typical for most people. This suggests that the emotional processes of the right hemisphere are not well coordinated with the verbal processes of the left hemisphere. This difficulty making sense of emotion may relate to the lack of empathy that is characteristic of psychopaths.

What do we know about the **neurobiology** of **antisocial traits**?

Modern research has taught us a good deal about the neurobiology of antisocial traits. It is important, however, to distinguish the neurobiological traits associated with *impulsivity* and those associated with *psychopathy*, as they may be quite different. We know that people with high levels of impulsivity and impulsive aggression have less activation in their *orbital frontal* region. This part of the frontal lobe lies just above

440

What does heart rate tell us about psychopathy?

We may be able to distinguish psychopathic individuals from impulsive-aggressive individuals by measuring their heartbeat when they are angry. In an important 1995 study by John Gottman and colleagues, 61 wife batterers were divided into two groups according to their heart rate during disagreements with their wives. One group showed *lowered* heart rates during the disagreement, while the heart rates of the other group went up. In other words, the first group became *less* aroused during the disagreement rather than more aroused.

Compared to the second group, however, the low-heart-rate men displayed more verbal aggression and anger during the discussion, while their wives showed more sadness and possibly more fear. Further, more of these men had a history of violence outside the family and of witnessing domestic violence as children. Finally, they scored higher on measures of antisocial and aggressive-sadistic personality disorder than the high-heart-rate men. In sum, the low-heart-rate batterers looked more typically psychopathic, while the high-heart-rate batterers looked more impulsive-aggressive.

the eye sockets and is associated with behavioral control. Some researchers suggest that the orbital frontal cortex links planned behavior with memories of punishment. In other words, the person is more likely to reason, "Oh oh, if I hit this person, I might get hit back." When the orbital frontal cortex is compromised, the fear of punishment is not strong enough to deter the person from impulsive and reckless actions.

There is also evidence of decreased function in the *dorsolateral frontal cortex* in impulsive aggression. This area is involved in abstract and complex thought, abilities that are often compromised in impulsive-aggressive people. The serotonin system may also be abnormal in impulsive people. The neurotransmitter serotonin also seems to be involved in behavioral control. People with hyperactive serotonin systems may have over-controlled behavior, while the opposite appears to be true with impulsive people, whose serotonin system is underactive.

How can we **explain** the **biological findings** on psychopathy?

To summarize, biological research into psychopathy has shown us that psychopaths have overly focused attention, are under-responsive to emotions, and become less aroused instead of more aroused when they are angry. How might we understand these findings? One possibility is that psychopathic individuals grew up in very threatening and violent environments. As a consequence, they learned to down-regulate their emotional responses and narrow their attention in order to focus solely on getting what

441

they want and on surviving in a brutal, dog-eat-dog world. Unfortunately, what may have started out as a way to survive brutality ultimately serves to perpetuate it.

Is there a **genetic basis** for **antisocial** traits?

There is growing evidence of a genetic basis for antisocial traits. In a 2008 twin study by Mats Forman and colleagues, all 1,480 twins born in Sweden from 1985–1986 were administered the Youth Psychopathic Traits Inventory. By comparing correlations between identical and fraternal twins, the authors concluded that psychopathic traits have a strong genetic basis and that this is especially true for the impulsive/irresponsible subscale versus the grandiose/manipulative and callous/unemotional subscales. Some authors estimate that genetics account for 40 to 50 percent of antisocial behavior. However, it is difficult to know for sure how much of antisocial behavior is due to genetics and how much is due to environment. For one, estimates of *heritability* (or genetics) rely heavily on twin studies, in which the genetic differences are carefully measured but the environmental differences are not. Moreover, twins tend to have quite similar environments. Thus, environmental contributions are probably underestimated.

What **specific genes** have been linked to **antisocial** traits?

One gene that has received a fair amount of attention is known as monoamine oxydase A (MAOA) and codes for an enzyme (also called MAOA) involved with the metabolism of key neurotransmitters involved with emotion and behavior, specifically *serotonin,*

norepinephrine, and *dopamine.* A variant of this gene reduces MAOA enzyme activity and is more common in antisocial individuals than in controls. It is likely, however, that this gene codes for impulsivity rather than antisocial behavior per se. Another gene, called-G1438A, is related to the 5HT2A subtype of the serotonin system. One variant (or *polymorphism*) of this gene, known as the G-allelle, is associated with increased rule breaking in adolescent boys, as shown in a 2009 study by S. Alexandra Burt. The other variant, known as the A-allelle, is associated with lower levels of rule breaking, and incidentally, lower levels of popularity with peers. In other words, boys with the G-allelle were both bigger rule breakers and more popular.

Because of the criminal nature of the drug industry, competition between rival drug dealers is often a horribly violent affair, resulting in countless drug-related deaths. Some analysts believe that drugs should be made legal in order to reduce crime. Others believe legalizing drugs would only increase drug addiction (*iStock*).

What is the **relationship** between **addiction** and **criminality**?

Drug addiction is strongly correlated with impulsivity and many people with antisocial traits also abuse illicit substances. Unfortunately, drug abuse and addiction also *promote* antisocial behavior. For one, drug addiction can destroy an addicted individual's ability to hold a job, removing the means to pay for the drug. In this situation, drug addicts may turn to crime in order to obtain the money needed to pay for their drug. Common forms of criminal activity include robbery, drug dealing, and prostitution. Secondly, many drugs of abuse impair judgment and impulse control, which increases the likelihood of reckless and criminal acts. In fact, it has been estimated that 55 percent of car accidents and more than 50 percent of murders involve alcohol intoxication. Thirdly, most Western countries outlaw the most common drugs of abuse. Unfortunately, this fails to erase demand for the drugs. Consequently, the market for illicit drugs goes underground and becomes the domain of criminals. Competition within the illicit drug trade has led to a tremendous amount of violence, dating back many decades.

SPECIFIC FORMS OF CRIMES

What do we know about the **psychology** of **violent criminals**?

Most violent crime involves impulsive aggression. It is no surprise, then, to find that, on average, violent criminals have many of the characteristics associated with impulsive aggression. They are largely male, young, have problems regulating their aggression, and tend to have lower IQs, less education, and lower SES than the general population. They are also more likely to have childhood histories of physical abuse and neglect. Cognitively, they have difficulty anticipating the consequences of their actions, and tend toward a narrow, rigid, and essentially paranoid interpretation of others' intentions. Ambiguous gestures are interpreted as threatening and hostile, setting off a hair-trigger aggressive reaction. Non-impulsive violent criminals are more likely to have psychopathic traits; that is, they have the callous, exploitive, and unemotional traits of a psychopath.

What do we know about the **psychology** of **nonviolent criminals**?

Perpetrators of nonviolent crimes, such as property and drug offenses, are obviously less violent than violent criminals. Likewise, they have less difficulty with controlling their aggression. These crimes are also associated with impulsivity, however, and nonviolent criminals, on average, have many features associated with impulsivity, such as younger age, lower IQ, and less education. Proportionately, females are considerably more likely to be convicted of a nonviolent than a violent crime. About 20 percent of nonviolent felons are female according to FBI statistics, whereas only about 8 percent of violent felons are female.

What do we know about **child molesters**?

Perhaps because of the extremely damaging effects of child sexual abuse, forensic psychologists have put a fair amount of effort into studying sexual molesters of children. Child molesters tend to be older than other criminals and are probably not as impulsive, although there is likely a subset of highly impulsive child molesters. Most child molesters use bribery, manipulation, and seduction to access their victims, although a sizeable proportion use instrumental force, that is, only enough force to attain their goals. Although there is a small fraction of highly violent child molesters, the vast majority are not violent. While most child molesters are heterosexual males who molest girls, the men who molest boys tend to have far more victims, hundreds or thousands in some instances. In general, the majority of child molesters have only a few victims, while a small fraction with persistent pedophilic tendencies can molest hundreds or thousands of children over a lifetime.

Are there different **types** of **child molesters**?

All professionals who work with child molesters are struck by the variety within this population. There is clearly no one type of child molester. In a 2008 article, Robert Prentky, Raymond Knight, and Austen Lee proposed several subtypes of child molesters, based on their own clinical experience and the research literature. The most important distinction is between *fixated* and *regressed* child molesters. Fixated child molesters have a long-standing sexual attraction to pre-pubescent children. They have a higher rate of reoffending, show greater sexual arousal to pedophilic stimuli, and have a much larger number of victims than other types of child molesters.

Regressed child molesters are not primarily pedophilic, but turn to children for situational reasons. They might have impulse control problems, poor social skills, psychopathic tendencies, or a substance abuse disorder. A second dimension involves social competence. Some child molesters turn to children because they have inadequate social skills to engage with adults. Together, this results in four categories: high fixation/low social competence; high fixation/high social competence; low fixation/low social competence; and low fixation/high social competence. Child molesters are then further differentiated according to the amount of contact, physical injury, and sadism involved.

Are **homosexual child molesters** really homosexual?

Male offenders against boys seem to be quite different from male offenders against girls. Nonetheless, it is unlikely that homosexual pedophiles have much in common with other homosexuals, that is, adult men who are sexually attracted to other adult men. For one, a good percentage of homosexual pedophiles also molest girls, over 60 percent in one study. Secondly, in an important 1988 study by William Marshall and colleagues, about two-thirds of sexual offenders against boys showed greater sexual arousal to pictures of adult women than they did to pictures of adult men.

Were most **child molesters molested** as children **themselves**?

Adults who sexually molest children have a disproportionately high rate of sexual abuse in their own childhoods. Child molesters are more likely to have a childhood history of sexual abuse than are nonsexual offenders and even sex offenders against older victims. According to a 1995 study by Christopher Bagley and colleagues of a community-based, nonforensic sample, men who reported multiple events of sexual contact in their own childhood were almost forty times more likely to report having sexual contact with children than men who reported no sexual abuse in childhood (7.7 percent vs. 0.2 percent).

How do **sex offenders against children differ** from those against adults?

In a 2007 study by Lisa Cohen and colleagues, data on 392 sexual offenders against children and 209 sexual offenders against adults were taken from the New York State Sex Offenders Registry. Offenders against children were older, more likely to have male victims or victims of both sexes, and less likely to use force or a weapon. They also had less invasive offenses and were less likely to have sexual intercourse with their victim. In other words, compared to adult rapists, child molesters are older, less violent, and less focused on female victims.

What can **psychology** tell us about **child testimony**?

Sometimes children are called upon to testify in court. This is particularly relevant in child abuse cases. How reliable is a child's testimony? Research shows that children are just as capable as adults at recalling specific events accurately. Their memory, however, is highly susceptible to suggestion. In other words, they are easily led to recall things that did not actually happen, and then become convinced their new memories are accurate. Because of this, the reliability of the testimony of children is heavily dependant on the interviewer's technique. Interviewers who ask leading questions, repeat the same question numerous times, or communicate a preference for one answer over another are more likely to extract inaccurate testimony from children. Additionally, children are easily intimidated by adult authority figures, particularly those in uniform, and may say what they believe the adult wants to hear rather than what they actually remember. The Kelly Michaels case is a tragic illustration of what can happen when child testimony is misused.

How do **white-collar criminals** differ from **other** forms of **criminals**?

Most white-collar crimes take a higher level of planning, cognitive sophistication, and occupational success than other crimes. Accountants, bookkeepers, or investment bankers who siphon off tens of thousands of dollars tend to do so over a period of months or years, all the while hiding their behavior from their colleagues. Moreover, their ability to attain a position of responsibility in the first place generally speaks to better impulse control, planning, and ability to delay gratification than is found in the typically impulsive criminal. Likewise, white-collar criminals tend to be more educated and come from a higher SES background than other criminals. We can also speculate that many white-collar criminals have a high degree of narcissistic traits and find the allure of the money and the status that it can bring overwhelming. An inflated sense of entitlement dampens their guilt at stealing from other people. Consequently, they fail to inhibit their illegal behavior. However, some white-collar criminals may also have antisocial or psychopathic traits, but are simply less impulsive than other types of criminals.

What do we know about the psychology of **serial killers**?

Luckily, serial killers are quite rare but they tend to get intensive media coverage when they come to public attention. Unfortunately, this may serve to encourage the behavior. It is hard to determine exactly when a murderer becomes a serial killer. One definition includes any one who commits at least four murders. Serial killers tend to act alone or with an accomplice and they generally kill strangers. Importantly, they kill for their own psychological gratification, rather than for money, power, or political purposes. Most derive sexual pleasure from their crimes, which tend to be ritualistic and sadistic.

Forensic psychologists say that serial killers are motivated by the sense of absolute power over their victims, and that they spend a good deal of time fantasizing about and planning their crimes. Not surprisingly, most serial killers are profoundly emotionally disturbed and many report traumatic and painful childhoods. In one small study from 1988, 69 percent reported a history of alcoholism in their family and 74 percent reported psychological abuse in childhood. Nonetheless, serial killers do not tend to be very impulsive. In fact, the most successful serial killers can effectively plan their crimes and escape capture for decades.

What is the difference between **organized** and **disorganized serial killers**?

A popular theory among criminal profilers is that serial killers can be divided into two types according to their crime scene evidence. The first type is organized and has a planful, thought-out approach to the crimes. These serial killers position the body, attempt to hide the body, tamper with the evidence, and take the weapon with them. Disorganized criminals are less careful and methodical. They use an improvised murder weapon, leave the body uncovered, leave a trail of clothing to the murder scene, and leave the victim's belongings scattered about. The two types of serial killers are also assumed to use different modes of torture, rape, and murder.

Surprisingly, this theory has had little scientific evidence to back it up. In a 2004 article, David Canter and colleagues tested the organized/disorganized classification by studying the records of one hundred different serial killers. They found that all of the serial killers were predominantly organized in their approach. This makes perfect sense, given that serial killers are repeat murderers who manage to evade arrest for years. Disorganized features were less common, but present to some degree in almost all subjects.

The authors suggested a new way of classifying serial killers, dividing them into four new categories: those concerned with mutilation, execution, sexual control, or plunder. The first type mutilates the victim's body, often after death. The second type executes their victims quickly after they are finished with them. The third type sexually tortures the victims while they are alive, presumably giving the killer a sense of complete control over another person. The fourth type ransacks and plunders the victims' belongings.

MENTAL ILLNESS AND THE LAW

What is the **relationship** between **mental illness** and **criminal behavior**?

The relationship between mental illness and criminal behavior is a complicated one. Can mentally ill people be judged by the same standards as the rest of the population? Is it fair to punish someone who is incapable of rational thought the same way as

What do we know about the psychology of serial killers John Wayne Gacy and Jeffrey Dahmer?

Serial killers tend to get intense media coverage. Both Jeffrey Dahmer and John Wayne Gacy are well known serial killers. Dahmer was arrested in the early 1990s, and Gacy in the late 1970s. Gacy was a mild mannered, apparently law abiding man who sexually assaulted and murdered at least 30 young men. Interestingly, Gacy was also an artist, and painted bizarrely innocent and child-like pictures of nature scenes and of children's cartoons, such as Disney's seven dwarves. The planned and organized nature of his crimes, as well as the psychopathic split between respectability in public and murderous perversion in private, is characteristic of serial killers. Dahmer, on the other hand, showed extreme psychological disturbance from early on and had problems with alcoholism and sexual offenses from a young age. Both men died in prison.

someone who makes a conscious and rational decision to perform a criminal act? On the other hand, should we excuse people from accountability just because they are psychologically disturbed? How do we balance the right of the individual for fair treatment with the right of society for protection from antisocial acts? The legal system addresses these philosophical questions through the concepts of competence, culpability, and mitigating factors.

What is the **relationship** between **mental illness** and **competence**?

The issue of mental competence comes up far more frequently than the problem of mental illness and culpability. When people are competent, they are intellectually and emotionally capable of acting in their own best interest. In a criminal setting, this may mean being competent to stand trial or to participate in one's own defense. On a civil level, this may mean competent to manage one's own finances, make medical decisions, or otherwise manage one's own affairs. When someone is deemed incompetent to care for him or herself or to perform some specific task, a legal representative is charged with making decisions for the incompetent person and is legally responsible to act in the person's best interest.

What is the **relationship** between **mental illness** and **culpability**?

In order for someone to be responsible, or *culpable*, for a criminal act, it is necessary to have criminal intent. In other words, the person must have intentionally chosen to act in a criminal way. As intention is a psychological state—and one that is not always easy to prove—the individual's mental state is relevant to the proof of criminal intent.

Therefore, someone who is mentally ill, or "insane," may not have the psychological wherewithal to have criminal intent. Such a person may not understand what he or she is doing, or may not be able to control himself or herself. While most people agree that profoundly mentally ill people should not be held to the same standard of accountability as the rest of the population, it is difficult to tell when mental illness justifiably excuses criminal behavior. Can someone be mentally ill and still culpable? How do we define mental illness?

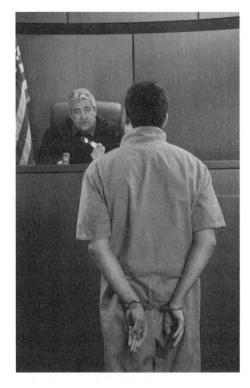

Although a mentally ill person might not have the psychological capacity to form criminal intent, it is not easy to prove legal insanity (*iStock*).

What does **not guilty by reason of insanity** mean?

Not guilty by reason of insanity is a legal defense that means that the individual is not criminally responsible for an act he or she committed because he or she is unable to form criminal intent due to insanity. Insanity is a legal term that is quite different from the clinical term. In the United States, the legal definition of insanity varies from state to state. Most states specify that a person must be unable to appreciate the nature and implications of their behavior or to understand that it was morally wrong. Other states include the inability to resist one's impulses is the definition of insanity. Some states have no insanity defense at all. Under federal law, an insane person cannot "appreciate the nature and quality or the wrongfulness" of the criminal acts.

What does **guilty but insane** mean?

Within the last few decades, several states have adopted a *guilty but mentally ill* verdict. The person is not excused from criminal liability due to insanity, but the court recognizes that mental illness played a role in the crime. Defendants with a guilty but mentally ill verdict are typically remanded to a psychiatric facility or provided with psychiatric treatment while in prison.

How often is the **insanity defense successful**?

Surveys show many people view the insanity defense as an overused tactic exploited by wily criminals and unethical attorneys. Actually, it is used very rarely. An estimated

> ### Was Andrea Yates legally insane
> ### when she killed all five of her children?
>
> **B**y all accounts, Andrea Yates was a devoted wife, a devout Christian, and a conscientious mother of five small children. Unfortunately, she was also mentally ill. She had been hospitalized several times for psychosis and depression and treated with both antidepressant and antipsychotic medication. She had also twice attempted suicide.
>
> On June 20, 2001, Yates drowned each of her five children in her bathtub and then called the police to report what she had done. Yates claimed that Satan had possessed her and that she needed to kill her children before Satan possessed them as well. If they died while they were still pure they would get into heaven. Otherwise, they would be damned to hell for all eternity.
>
> Although her defense attorneys entered a plea of not guilty by reason of insanity, she was found guilty of murder in a 2002 verdict and sentenced to life imprisonment. Her verdict was overturned in 2006, after it was revealed that one of the prosecution's expert witnesses had given false testimony. She was then found not guilty by reason of insanity and remanded to a state hospital.

0.85 percent of cases—that is less than one in 1,000—enter an insanity defense and less than a third of these are successful.

Who was **the Unabomber**?

Ted Kaczynski was strange even as a young child. As a six-month-old infant, he suffered a severe allergic reaction, breaking out in hives all over his body. He was in and out of the hospital for the next eight months, separated from his mother. From the time he returned home, he was unresponsive to human interaction. Throughout his childhood, he was extremely shy and painfully averse to human contact, especially with strangers and other children. At the same time he was extremely talented at mathematics, and single-mindedly focused on mastering mathematical problems.

Although he was never diagnosed, this description is certainly suggestive of autism or Asperger's syndrome. Evidently, his mother considered this possibility as well, and thought of sending him to Bruno Bettelheim, a famous psychoanalyst who specialized in autism.

Kaczynski entered Harvard at age 16, received his Ph.D. in mathematics at the University of Michigan, where he performed brilliantly, and then accepted an academic position at the University of California at Berkeley. Unfortunately, the teaching requirements were too much for him; he was simply incapable of managing the interpersonal demands. He left Berkeley and, with his brother, bought a cabin in the Montana woods. He moved in there alone and became increasingly isolated, even cutting off contact from his mother and brother.

As he cultivated the skills to become entirely self-sufficient in the wilderness, he also developed his anti-technology ideology. For years he had become disillusioned with technology and disgusted with human destruction of the natural world. He came to believe that the only way to destroy the "techno-industrial system" was by violent resistance, so in the late 1970s he began a bombing campaign against people linked with technology, including science and engineering professors, computer store owners, and the airline industry. The FBI named him UNABOMB: university and airline bomber.

Over the next 18 years, he sent 16 bombs, injuring 23 people and killing three. In 1995, he published a manifesto, outlining his anti-technology ideology. His brother David recognized Kaczynski's writings from the manifesto and eventually contacted the FBI. Ted Kaczynski was arrested in 1996. His defense attorneys entered an insanity plea and a court-appointed psychiatrist diagnosed him with paranoid schizophrenia. Kaczynski vigorously rejected this diagnosis, as he did not want his political mission to be dismissed as the rantings of a psychotic man. He plead guilty and was sentenced to life imprisonment without parole but was spared the death penalty because of his brother's intervention.

Was Kaczynski insane? He almost certainly had a diagnosable psychiatric disorder of some kind. However, he was very clear about his intentions and could rationally argue the merits of his violent acts. Whether or not he was mentally ill, he clearly had criminal intent.

What does **mitigating factor** mean?

Evidence of psychological disturbance is effectively used to prove mitigating factors. In this case, the defendant is found guilty of the crime, but evidence of mental disturbance is taken into account during sentencing. The burden of proof in these cases is much lower than in an insanity defense.

How does **neurobiological research** into criminality **affect** the **law**?

The remarkable advances in brain imaging technology in recent years have allowed us to discover much about the neurobiology of antisocial personality traits and behavior. For example, on average, violent felons have reduced functioning in the *frontal lobe* and psychopathic prisoners have under-responsive *amygdalas*. But what does this mean for responsibility? Are violent criminals less culpable if their brains are abnormal? Are psychopaths less accountable if their brain is less able to process empathy?

Presumably small differences in brain function should not be a "get out of jail free" card. Most psychologists agree that people need to be held accountable to the extent that they have choice and control over their actions. On the other hand, brain abnormalities can be used as evidence of mitigating factors. For example, a nonviolent first offender might receive a lesser sentence if there is evidence of recent head trauma. Most importantly, however, neurobiological research can help with treatment and prevention of antisocial behavior, to protect society from future crimes.

What is the relationship between **personality disorders** and **culpability**?

Personality disorders are defined as persistent patterns of thought, emotion, behavior, and interpersonal relationships that are abnormal for the person's culture and cause distress and dysfunction. With 11 separate personality disorder diagnoses in the fourth edition of the Diagnostic and Statistical Manual of Mental Disorders (DSM-IV), personality disorders are recognized as valid psychiatric conditions. Does the presence of a personality disorder remove culpability for criminal behavior? This is especially of concern, given that some personality disorders are associated with, or even defined by, antisocial behavior. In other words, the use of a personality disorder diagnosis in a criminal defense could lead to absurdly circular thinking: *I am not responsible for my criminal behavior because I have antisocial personality disorder, which is defined by my criminal behavior.*

Personality disorders differ from psychotic disorders, however, in that the cognitive abnormalities are mild. The problem is more one of motivation and disturbed interpersonal relations. Therefore, there is no reason that a personality disorder would leave someone *incapable* of forming criminal intent. In sum, the diagnosis has much more relevance for clinical settings than for legal ones.

GLOSSARY

Accommodation—A term from the work of Jean Piaget describing the way that schemas change by adapting to new information.

Action potential—When a neuron fires, it sends an electrical impulse down the length of the axon to the axon terminals. This firing is known as an action potential.

Addiction—Compulsive use or excessive dependence on a substance or activity.

Alzheimer's disease—Alzheimer's disease is an age-related brain disease in which abnormal growths called neurofibrillary tangles and amaloid plaques destroy the brain's ability to function properly.

Amygdala—The amygdala is a small, almond-shaped structure buried deep in the middle of the brain. It seems to be an early responder to emotionally significant signals from the environment and is particularly reactive to fearful stimuli.

Analytical psychology—Carl Jung's theory of mental life, which he developed after he split from Sigmund Freud's school of psychoanalysis.

Androgens—Male sex hormones. Testosterone is a well studied androgen.

Anterior—Refers to the front portion of the brain or a brain region.

Antisocial personality disorder—A personality disorder characterized by a severe deficit in morality as manifested in callous and exploitive behavior and a lack of empathy or remorse.

APA—Abbreviation of the American Psychological Association, American psychology's professional organization.

Archetypes—A concept developed by Carl Jung. Archetypes are patterns of experience and behavior that reflect ancient and fundamental ways of dealing with universal life situations, e.g., the mother archetype, the child archetype.

Artificial intelligence—A computer-based model of intellectual processes.

Asperger's syndrome—A disorder similar to autism that is possibly a less severe variant of autism. Unlike autism there is no deficit in language development and often no intellectual impairment.

Assimilation—A term from the work of Jean Piaget describing the way that schemas shape new information to fit pre-existing ideas.

Associative conditioning—Another term for classical conditioning. A means of shaping behavior by pairing it with an emotionally meaningful stimulus.

Attachment—A biologically based, evolutionarily adaptive drive for the infant to seek protection from the mother.

Attachment theory—A scientifically based theory about the nature and importance of the mother–infant bond. One of the first movements to provide empirical support for the psychoanalytic notion that early childhood relationships with caregivers have profound impact on later personality development.

Atypical antipsychotics—A relatively new class of antipsychotic medication, which includes medications such as olanzapine (Zyprexa), risperidone (Risperdal), and quetiapine (Seroquel). Also known as second generation antipsychotics.

Autism—A disorder first diagnosed in childhood and characterized by abnormalities in social interaction, communication, and range of interests.

Autonomic nervous system—This whole body system gears the body up for action by mobilizing the body's cardiovascular, respiratory, muscular, and gastro-intestinal systems.

Axon—Axons are the output section of the neuron (brain cell) and carry electrical information from the cell out to other neurons.

Basal ganglia—The basal ganglia are a group of brain regions, including the putamen, globus pallidus, and caudate nucleus, which are centrally involved with action and motor behavior.

Behavioral economics—A multi-disciplinary field, linking economics, psychology, and neuroscience that focuses on the psychology of financial decision making.

Behavioral modification—A form of psychotherapy involving the application of behavioral principles to change people's behavior.

Behavioral psychotherapy—A form of psychotherapy based on the principles of classical and operant conditioning.

Behaviorism—A school of psychology that holds that observable behavior is the only valid object of psychological study. Behaviorism largely focused on the way new behavior is learned via the process of conditioning.

Bipolar disorder—A psychiatric disorder formerly known as manic depression that is characterized by at least one manic episode and typically one or more major depressive episodes.

Black box theory—The behaviorist view that the mind is no more than an opaque black box inserted between stimulus and response.

Borderline personality disorder—A personality disorder characterized by highly erratic and tempestuous behavior.

Brain Stem—The oldest and most primitive part of the brain, which regulates basic physiological processes necessary for life, such as breathing, temperature regulation, sleep-wake cycle, and cardiac function.

Brodman areas—In 1909, Korbinian Brodman created a map of the cortex. He divided the cortex into 52 distinct regions based on the way neurons were organized (cytoarchitecture). Only 45 Brodmann areas are found in the human brain; the other 7 are found in the monkey brain.

Caudal—The Latin word for tail, the word is generally used to refer to the back portion of the brain or a brain region.

Cerebellum—The cerebellum, which is Latin for little brain, is the large, bulbous structure located below the back of the cortex. The cerebellum mediates motor coordination, posture, and the smooth flow of movement.

Cingulate gyrus—The cingulate gyrus is a long structure that wraps around numerous other subcortical regions and has attentional, emotional, and cognitive functions, including decision making.

Classical conditioning—A form of conditioning in which behavior is shaped by pairing it with an emotionally meaningful stimulus. Also known as associative conditioning.

Cognition—Thought or intellectual processes, such as attention, memory, and the ability to form concepts.

Cognitive psychotherapy—A form of psychotherapy that assumes psychological problems are caused by maladaptive thoughts. Negative thoughts stimulate negative emotions, which in turn motivate self-defeating behavior.

Cognitive revolution—The explosive shift in academic psychology during the 1950s and 1960s, when the black box model of psychology was rejected and cognition became the object of intense interest.

Cognitive science—A fairly new scientific field that borrows from evolutionary psychology, linguistics, computer science, philosophy, and neurobiology. Cognitive scientists often attempt to model psychological and brain processes with complex computer programs.

Collective unconscious—The Jungian collective unconscious holds the entire, evolutionary heritage of humanity. It is not limited to the individual's life but encompasses the great, impersonal truths of existence.

Concrete operational stage—In the work of Jean Piaget, this stage takes place from about age 7 to about age 11. By this stage, children have mastered the basic rules of the physical world and understand the laws of space and time.

455

Conditioned stimulus—The conditioned stimulus is a formerly neutral stimulus that now elicits a response because of its pairing with the unconditioned stimulus.

Conditioning—The form of learning in which behavior is shaped according to the events with which it is associated or the effects it produces.

Confound—An outside variable that interferes with the results of a study, making its results invalid.

Constructivism—A view of knowledge, championed by Jean Piaget, that holds that knowledge of the world up is actively constructed out of our direct experience with our environment.

Correlation—A statistical measure that shows how much two variables either increase or decrease together.

Cortex—The outer layer of the brain, the wrinkled surface that covers the top and sides of the brain.

Counter-transference—A psychoanalytic term referring to intense and inappropriate feelings that therapists develop toward their patients, which may reflect either the therapist's own emotional conflicts or the patient's unconscious emotions.

Cross-sectional study—A study that assesses behavior at one point in time.

Crystallized intelligence—This refers to learned skills, including fund of information, verbal knowledge, and knowledge of social conventions. In contrast to fluid intelligence, crystallized intelligence stays relatively intact well into late life.

Death instinct—A psychoanalytic concept referring to the motivation behind violence and aggression. Also known as thanatos.

Defense mechanisms—A psychoanalytic term referring to the mental manipulations we unconsciously use to protect ourselves from feelings and thoughts that make us anxious.

Delusion—A fixed false belief. Delusions are seen as symptoms of psychosis.

Dementia—Dementia involves the loss of intellectual abilities, generally memory, spatial skills, and executive functions (planning, abstract thought, self-monitoring, etc.).

Dementia praecox—Emil Kraepelin's term for what would later be called schizophrenia.

Dendrites—Dendrites are the tree-like extensions that reach out from the brain cell body. They are the input section of the cell and carry electrical information into the cell body from other neurons' axons.

Depression—A mental state characterized by enduring sad mood. Although most people experience some kind of mild depression at some point in their lives, more severe depression is considered a psychiatric disorder.

Barnes & Noble Booksellers #2932
395 Route 3 East
Clifton, NJ 07014
973-779-5500

STR:2932 REG:006 TRN:6137 CSHR:Chris M

BARNES & NOBLE MEMBER   EXP: 03/30/2013

Dhammapada: The Teachings of the Buddha
  9781435116528   T1
  (1 @ 6.98) Member Card 10% (0.70)
  (1 @ 6.28)   6.28
His Holiness The Dalai Lama Speaks: Peac
  0727994752899   T1
  (1 @ 19.99) Member Card 10% (2.00)
  (1 @ 17.99)   17.99
Buddha's Brain: The Practical Neuroscien
  9781572246959   T1
  (1 @ 17.95) Member Card 10% (1.80)
  (1 @ 16.15)   16.15
Handy Psychology Answer Book
  9781578592234   T1
  (1 @ 21.95) Member Card 10% (2.20)
  (1 @ 19.75)   19.75
APA Dictionary of Psychology
  9781591473800   T1
  (1 @ 59.95) Member Card 10% (6.00)
  (1 @ 53.95) Item Cpn 15% (8.09)
     #701041
  (1 @ 45.86)   45.86
Complete Illustrated Encyclopedia Of Bud
  9781451347692   T1
  (1 @ 9.98) Member Card 10% (1.00)
  (1 @ 8.98)   8.98
Issue Member   T2
  (1 @ 25.00)   25.00
  Card#:   XXXXXX9309

Subtotal   140.01
Sales Tax T1 (7.000%)   8.05
TOTAL   148.06
VISA   148.06
  Card#:   XXXXXXXXXXXX7115
  Expdate: XX/XX
  Auth: 010225
  Entry Method: Swiped

MEMBER SAVINGS   13.70

Thanks for shopping at
Barnes & Noble

101.27B   03/31/2012 01:46PM

CUSTOMER COPY

fficial guide to the diagnosing of mental
-IV-TR was published in 2000. DSM V is

hotherapy that treats self-destructive
nality disorder.

ransmitters. Dopamine is involved with
vement.

al fin of a shark. It is generally used to
region.

ce to a drug, they have become desensi-
e of the substance to achieve the same

known as shock therapy. Electrodes are
are pulsed into the brain. An effective

hat mediates between the id and reality.
nd recognizes that the world does not

wentieth century to limit the reproduc-
r.

out how species develop over time into

e's genes to the next generation. If there
nt generation than in the previous one,
ted evolutionary fitness.

associated with the frontal lobes, which
rnative actions, abstraction, and chang-

en the association between the stimulus
or between the behavior and the rein-
to erode, the conditioned behavior gets

n Jungian theory. The extrovert attends
nd objects. Extroverts are typically out-

hows how different items group together

457

Fluid intelligence—Immediate information processing skills, such as memory, processing speed, and the amount of information that can be processed at a time. Fluid intelligence reduces with age and is sensitive to illness and injury.

fMRI—Functional Magnetic Resonance Imaging. This technology allows us to get a picture of the brain's activity over time.

Forebrain—The part of the neural tube that develops into the evolutionarily newest parts of the brain, such as the neocortex and the limbic system.

Forensic—The word forensic refers to the legal system. Forensic matters include anything related to the application and enforcement of the law as well as the prosecution of those who violate the law.

Formal operational stage—In the work of Jean Piaget, this stage begins around age twelve and involves the ability to effectively reason about possible or hypothetical events and not just actual events.

Frontal lobe—The frontal lobe is a brain region which comprises the front half of the cortex. It extends from the central sulcus forward.

Functionalism—A school of psychology, pioneered by William James, that focused on the way the mind functions. It arose in reaction to Wilhelm Wundt's structuralism.

GABA—An inhibitory neurotransmitter; it calms the nervous system. GABA neurotransmitters are targeted by antianxiety medications that also act as tranquilizers.

Generalizeability—If the results of a study can be applied to a larger population, we say the study is generalizeable.

Gerontology—The field of study that focuses on aging and late life.

Gestalt—A gestalt refers to a perceptual whole. It is created out of the relationships between the parts.

Gestalt psychology—The core idea behind Gestalt psychology is that the mind actively organizes information into a coherent whole or a gestalt. The mind is not a passive recipient of sensory stimuli but an active organizer of information.

Gestalt psychotherapy—A school of psychotherapy founded by Fritz Perls in the 1940s. Distinct from Gestalt psychology, it is the body of research derived from Max Wertheimer's experiments with perception.

Glutamate—The main excitatory neurotransmitter in the brain; it activates the nervous system and appears to be involved in learning and memory.

Grey matter—The brain tissue made up of dendrites and cell bodies (as well as glial cells and capillaries).

Gyrus—The outer surface of the brain's folds are referred to as gyri. Gyrus is the singular form of the word.

Hallucination—A perceptual experience of something that is not really there.

Hindbrain—A section of the neural tube that will develop into the brain stem and cerebellum.

Hippocampus—A caterpillar-like structure on the medial (inner) side of the temporal lobe that is heavily involved with memory.

Hominids—A group of species related to humans. Hominid species include *Homo sapien sapiens* (humans), *Homo sapien neanderthalensis* (neanderthals), *Homo erectus*, *Homo habilis*, and the Australopithecus genus.

HPA axis—The HPA axis includes the hypothalamus, pituitary gland and adrenal glands. This triad is centrally involved in the body's stress response.

Humanistic psychology—A group of psychological theories and practices that originated in the 1950s and emphasized free will and the importance of choice.

Humanistic psychotherapies—A branch of psychotherapy that arose in opposition to the dominance of psychoanalysis and behaviorism. Humanistic therapies focus on personal growth as opposed to psychopathology.

Hydraulic model—Sigmund Freud's view of the instincts, or motivating forces, as a fluid-like substance. The hydraulic model dates back several centuries before Freud.

Hypothalamus—A brain structure involved with motivational drives such as hunger, sex, and thirst, which also serves as a coordinator of the physiological centers of the brain. The hypothalamus is the master control center for the autonomic nervous system.

Hypothesis—The prediction made before a study is conducted, spelling out what the researchers expect to find.

Hypothetico-deductive reasoning—A form of reasoning found in Piaget's formal operational stage, in which the individual can imagine many possible solutions to a problem and then plan ways to test each of those hypotheses. This kind of reasoning from the hypothetical is the same kind of reasoning used in scientific experiments.

Id—Translated literally as "the it," Freud's concept of the id refers to the part of the mind that contains the animalistic passions that must be subdued in order for civilization to function.

Impulse control—The ability to control potentially destructive behavior by considering the negative consequences of the action.

Inferior—Refers to the lower portion of the brain or a brain region.

In-group—A group of which one is a member

Insecure attachment—A child who is insecurely attached feels insecure about the mother's emotional availability or responsivity to the child's attachment cues.

Insula—A brain area located on the inside of the cortex, sandwiched between the temporal, frontal and parietal lobes. It processes sensory information from inside our bodies, specifically the processing of aversive food tastes and the experience of disgust.

459

Intermittent reinforcement—A schedule of reinforcement in which the behavior is only rewarded intermittently.

Internal working model—A term from attachment theory referring to a kind of mental map, or script, of the caregiver and the self developed out of repeated attachment experiences with the caregiver.

Introversion—A personality trait derived from Jungian theory. The introvert is turned inward, preoccupied with internal, subjective experience.

IQ test—A test of cognitive skills that produces an IQ score, or an intelligence quotient, which is an estimate of general intelligence.

Lamarckian evolution—An eighteenth century theory of evolution promoted by Jean-Baptiste Lamarke, which states that genetic change takes place in response to the animal's behavior. An animal adapts to the environment and these changes are then somehow passed onto the animal's offspring.

Latency period—Freud proposed a psychosexual stage, generally occurring from about 7 to about 12 years of age, in which the passions of the earlier psychosexual stages calm down and go underground, only to re-emerge in adolescence.

Lateral—Lateral means away from the body's midline, while medial means close to it. Lateral is generally used to refer to the outside portions of the brain or a brain region.

Law of Effect, The—A law derived by Edward Thorndike that states that the effect of an action will determine the likelihood that it will be repeated.

Learning theory—The behaviorist view of how learning occurs—when a new behavior is repeatedly and consistently performed in response to a given stimulus.

Libido—The primary motivating instinct behind all love and desire according to psychoanalytic theory.

Limbic system—A group of brain structures in the middle of the brain that serve as the seat of our emotions. The definition of the limbic system varies, but commonly includes the amygdala, hippocampus, septum, fornix, mammilary bodies, anterior nucleus of the thalamus, and cingulate gyrus.

Locomotor abilities—The ability to walk, run, or physically move about on one's own.

Longitudinal study—A study in which behavior is observed over a period of time, sometimes over decades.

Magical thinking—A kind of reasoning, often found with preschool children, that involves faulty reasoning about causation.

Major depressive disorder—A severe form of depression characterized by two weeks of depressed mood and symptoms such as sleep and appetite disturbance, feelings of worthlessness, loss of energy, and thoughts of death.

Mania—A psychiatric disorder characterized by elevated, euphoric, or irritable mood. The person also displays symptoms of increased activity, with much higher levels of energy, initiative and impulsivity than normal.

Mean—The statistical average.

Medial—Medial means close to the body's midline (as opposed to lateral which means away from it). Medial is generally used to refer to the inner portions of the brain or a brain region.

Median—The number that falls in the middle of the sample; half of the scores lie above it and half lie below.

Metabolic syndrome—A disturbance of metabolism with symptoms such as high cholesterol, high blood sugar, and weight gain, which is caused by some atypical antipsychotics.

Metacognition—The ability to think about thought, to reflect on one's own thought processes.

Midbrain—The midbrain is a section of the neural tube which develops into the tectum and the cerebral peduncle. The cerebral peduncle includes several brain areas that contains neurons that produce important neurotransmitters.

Mirror neurons—A group of neurons found in the premotor cortex that respond both to witnessed movements in other animals and to the analogous movement in the self.

Mode—The mode refers to the most common score in a sample.

Motor behavior—Physical action taken by the body, bodily movement.

Myelin—Axons are coated by a fatty sheath known as myelin that speeds up the rate that the action potential travels down the axon.

Myelination—The process by which the axons of the brain's neurons become coated with a fatty sheath known as myelin. The myelin sheath increases the speed that electrical impulses travel down the neuron.

Narcissistic personality disorder—A personality disorder characterized by inflated sense of self-importance and an elevated need for attention, status, and recognition.

Natural selection—The effect of the natural environment on the transmission of genetically based traits from one generation to the next.

Negative reinforcement—Involves the removal of a negative condition as a consequence of the targeted behavior with the intent of increasing the frequency of that behavior.

Negative symptoms—Symptoms of mental illness characterized by the absence of healthy behavior, such as lack of motivation, initiative, and emotional expression. Negative symptoms are generally associated with schizophrenia.

Neocortex—The six-layer tissue that forms the outer layer of the human brain. Also known as the cortex.

Neural tube—A long tubular structure that develops from the outer layer of the initial plate of embryonic cells. The brain and spinal cord develop out of the neural tube.

Neuroeconomics—The study of the parts of the brain that are involved in our responses to money.

461

Neurogenesis—The growth of new neurons in the brain.

Neuron—A brain cell, the basic building block of the brain.

Neuroscience—The science about the brain and the functions of the brain.

Neurotransmitters—The chemical messengers that neurons use to communicate with each other.

Norepinephrine—A major neurotransmitter system involved in attention, mood, arousal, and the fight/flight reaction.

Nucleus accumbens—A central node in the dopaminergic reward system in the brain.

Object constancy—The psychoanalyst Maragaret Mahler's concept referring to the ability to hold onto love for another person even in the face of anger towards him or her.

Object permanence—A term from Jean Piaget referring to the ability to hold an image of an object in mind even when the object is no longer physically present.

Obsessive-compulsive disorder—A psychiatric disorder characterized by obsessions, which are repetitive, senseless, and intrusive thoughts that generally increase anxiety, and/or compulsions, repetitive, driven and senseless behavior.

Occipital lobe—The occipital lobes are at the lower back end of the cortex.

Oedipal complex—According to Freudian theory, around the age of four to seven, the little boy goes through the Oedipal crisis, which results in the formation of his superego. The little boy falls in love with his mother. Recognizing his father as his rival, he feels murderous rage towards his father, which is only resolved by his acceptance of his father's authority and identification with the male role.

Olfactory bulbs—The parts of the brain involved with smell. In humans they are two tiny little orbs sandwiched between our limbic system and the bottom of our frontal lobe.

Operant conditioning—A form of conditioning in which the consequences of a behavior are used to shape the likelihood of its recurrence.

Operation—In Jean Piaget's work, the term operation refers to the ability to act upon an object in one's mind.

Operationalize—To translate an observed trait or behavior into a variable for scientific research.

Opiates—Synthetic or plant versions of opioids. When ingested, opiates bind to the opioid receptors in the human brain. Thus the brain responds to opiates the same way that it responds to our own endogenous (internally created) opioids.

Opioids—A brain chemical that serves to dampen our pain response. They are our home-made analgesics, our natural pain killers.

Orbital frontal cortex—This brain region lies on the underside of the frontal lobe, just above the eyes. It is particularly important for impulse control, for the inhibition of dangerous or reckless actions.

Organizational psychology—The branch of psychology that studies the behavior of people in the workplace.

Out-group—A group of people who do not belong to the in-group.

Outlier—An extreme value in a sample, one that falls far apart from the other values.

Oxytocin—A brain chemical that has been linked to a wide range of social behaviors both in humans and other animals.

Paraphilias—The technical term for abnormal sexual desires and behaviors.

Parietal—The parietal lobes cover much of the back surface of the cortex, extending from the central sulcus back to the border with the occipital lobe (the parietooccipital sulcus).

Peak experience—A term used by Abraham Maslow to refer to a state of total awareness and concentration in which the world is understood as a unified, integrated whole where all is connected and no one part is more important than another.

Pedomorphy—Pedomorphy refers to an evolutionary process in which adult animals maintain the traits of juveniles.

Perception—Perception follows sensation. The raw sensory data is synthesized in our brain into more complex patterns so that we can ultimately recognize objects in our environment.

Personality disorder—DSM-IV defines personality disorders as "an enduring pattern of inner experience and behavior that deviates markedly from the expectations of the individual's culture, is pervasive and inflexible, has an onset in adolescence or early adulthood, is stable over time and leads to distress or impairment."

Phrenology—A popular movement, outside of academic psychology, that tried to link personality characteristics to the shape of the skull.

Phylogeny—Phylogeny refers to the development of a species across evolution.

Placebo—A non-active treatment that cannot be differentiated from the active treatment, for example a sugar pill that looks identical to a real pill. Placebo conditions are routinely used as a comparison against the active treatment in clinical trials.

Positive psychology—A branch of happiness studies championed by Martin Seligman.

Positive reinforcement—Also called reward, this refers to the positive consequence of a behavior which increases its likelihood of recurring.

Positive symptoms—Symptoms of mental illness that involve the presence of a pathological behavior, such as auditory hallucinations or delusions.

Posterior—A posterior region of the brain lies towards the back.

Post-traumatic stress disorder (PTSD)—A psychiatric condition that follows experience of a severe trauma. PTSD is characterized by numbing symptoms, intrusive symptoms, and autonomic hyperarousal.

Pre-operational stage—The second of Jean Piaget's intellectual stages, which takes place between the ages of two and seven. In this phase, children have learned to symbolize; they can think about an event when it is not immediately happening.

Projective tests—A type of psychological test in which subjects are asked to complete a task (e.g., to tell a story based on a picture) that is intended to reveal characteristic ways of thinking, feeling and behaving. The subject is unaware of the information being revealed.

Prospective studies—Studies that collect data at several points over a period of time. In this way it is possible to observe how various traits develop over time without having to worry about the data being distorted by memory.

Psychoanalytic theory—The body of theory about abnormal mental processes pioneered by Sigmund Freud.

Psychodynamic psychotherapy—A type of therapy derived from psychoanalytic schools of psychotherapy which is less time-intensive and more flexible than orthodox psychoanalysis.

Psychology—The systematic study of mind and behavior.

Psychopathy—A personality style characterized by callousness, superficial and shallow emotion, lack of empathy, irresponsibility, lack of remorse or guilt about harming others, and the tendency to exploit, manipulate and engage in predatory behavior towards others.

Psychopharmacology—The study of drugs that affect psychological processes, such as mood, cognition and behavior.

Psychosexual stage—In Sigmund Freud's theory of child development, children pass through five psychosexual stages as they develop from infancy into adulthood. The five stages are the oral, anal, phallic, latency and genital stages.

Psychosis—A mental state characterized by a loss of reality testing, or the ability to understand reality as others see it.

Psychosocial stages—Erik Erikson's adaptation of Freud's psychosexual stages into a theory of child development that emphasizes interpersonal relationships over sexual desire.

Punishment—A method of decreasing the likelihood of a behavior by creating a negative consequence for it.

Quantitative study—In a quantitative study, behavior is translated into numbers.

Reality testing—The ability to see reality as others see it, or to check one's own perceptions against conventional perceptions of reality.

Reinforcement—In operant conditioning, a behavior is reinforced when the consequences of performing it increase the likelihood of it being repeated.

Reinforcement contingencies—The conditions of the reinforcements of behavior in operant conditioning, such as the frequency and predictability of reinforcement.

Relativism—The view that knowledge is not absolute, but rather is shaped by the individual's personal perspective.

Reliability—The reliability of a test refers to its ability to measure a given trait consistently.

Representation—A mental map, idea, or concept of an event. This can refer to an object, a daily routine, or an interpersonal relationship.

Reproductive fitness—The degree to which an animal's traits enhance its ability to pass its genes on to the next generation.

Reproductive success—Those organisms that pass their genes onto the next generation have succeeded; their genes and the traits associated with them have survived into the next generation.

Retrospective studies—Studies that use data based on memories or reports of past behavior.

Reward—A positive consequence to a behavior that increases the likelihood that it will be repeated.

Reward system—The reward system refers to a tract of dopamine-containing neurons that are centrally involved in the experience of desire. This all-purpose motivation machine is active in drug craving (cocaine, methamphetamine, alcohol, and cigarettes) and in gambling, eating, and sex.

Rorschach inkblot test—A well known projective test that consists of 10 cards with images of inkblots, some in black and white and some with color.

Rostral—A Latin word for head, generally used to refer to the front portion of the brain or a brain region.

Sample—The group of people selected from a larger population to be included in a study. In psychological research, we try to draw conclusions about a larger population from observations of a small sample.

Schema—A map or representation of commonly occurring events. Schemas are used in Piagetian theory and also cognitive psychotherapy.

Schizophrenia—A mental illness characterized by psychotic symptoms such as delusions and hallucinations.

Secure attachment—A securely attached child feels secure in the mother's availability and responsivity to his or her attachment needs.

Self-actualization—A term, popularized by Abraham Maslow, which refers to a state of full self-expression, where one's creative, emotional, and intellectual potential is fully realized.

Self-reflective functioning—The ability to reflect upon one's emotional experiences in a thoughtful and coherent way.

465

Self-report questionnaire—A form of psychological test in which a subject answers a series of questions that gives information about one or more psychological traits.

Sensation—Sensation is the immediate mapping of raw sensory data, such as light patterns, sound waves, or tactile stimulation.

Sensory-motor stage—In Jean Piaget's theory of intellectual stages, the sensory motor stage covers the first two years of life. In this stage, the child only knows the world through direct physical contact, that is through sensory experience (e.g., touch or sight) or motor action (e.g., kicking or grasping).

Separation-individuation—Maragaret Mahler's theory of the process by which a child develops an independent sense of self.

Septum—The septum is a small brain area that is involved with the experience of pleasure among other functions.

Serotonin—A major class of neurotransmitter. Serotonin is involved with mood, impulse control, sleep, appetite and sexual function.

Sexual selection—A type of natural selection specifically related to sexual behavior, such that any physical trait or behavioral pattern that increases access to mates will be evolutionarily advantageous.

Shamanism—A practice in traditional, pre-modern societies in which special individuals (shamans) mediate between their community and the world of the spirits. In order to do so they enter a trance-like state, often by dancing, music or a psycho-active plant.

Social psychology—The branch of psychology that studies how people behave in social groups.

Sociobiology—The field of sociobiology explicitly applies the principles of evolutionary theory to the understanding of social behavior.

Somatosensory strip—The primary sensory area for touch is called the somatosensory strip in the anterior (front) region of the parietal lobe.

SSRIs—Selective serotonin reuptake inhibitors, a class of antidepressant medication that works primarily on the serotonin system.

Standard deviation—The standard deviation measures how much the individual scores vary from the average score. Are all the scores clustered tightly around the mean or are they more spread out?

Statistics—A mathematical technique to measure the relationships between two or more variables (traits of interest such as intelligence, aggression, or severity of depression).

Stereotype—When we stereotype people, we attribute a series of traits to them based on the one trait that signals their membership in a particular group.

Strange situation, the—A 20-minute procedure, used to classify the infant's attachment status, in which 12- to 18-month-old infants and their mothers are observed across a sequence of separations and reunions.

Structural model—Freud's theory of mental structure that included the id, ego and superego.

Structuralism—A school of psychology pioneered by Wilhelm Wundt that aimed to identify the components of the mind.

Subcortical regions—The subcortical regions are the brain areas that lie underneath the cortex. These include the cerebellum and brain stem at the very base of the brain, the thalamus and related regions towards the middle of the brain, and the limbic system which wraps around the thalamus.

Substance abuse—IN DSM-IV-TR substance abuse involves the repeated use of a mind-altering chemical substance despite significant negative consequences.

Substance dependence—The DSM IV and IV-TR term for a serious substance abuse problem. In addition to causing social, occupational and/or financial problems, substance dependence involves physiological addiction to the drug.

Sulcus—The inner fold of the brain's surface is known as a sulcus; sulci is the plural form of the word. A sulcus is like a crevice.

Superego—In Freudian theory, the superego is the source of our morality. It is formed through our internalization of our parents' rules and discipline.

Superior—Refers to the upper portion of the brain or a brain region.

Survival of the fittest—Survival of the fittest means that those genes that produce traits that are best adapted to the particular environment are most likely to be passed on to the next generation.

Symbolic thought—The ability to think about objects in terms of symbols. For example, the use of language, in which words symbolize objects or events, depends on the capacity for symbolic thought.

Synapse—The contact point between the dendrite of one cell and the axon terminal of another is called the synapse.

Synaptic cleft—This refers to the space between the pre-synaptic and post-synaptic neuron.

Synaptogenesis—The creation of new synaptic connections in the brain.

Systematic desensitization—A behavioral therapy technique used to treat anxiety disorders. The person is exposed to progressively more anxiety provoking situations, in order to extinguish the connection between the feared object and anxiety.

Temperament—Personality traits that are inborn and genetically based as opposed to learned.

Temporal lobes—The two thumb-like segments of the cortex are known as the temporal lobes.

Thanatology—The study of death and dying.

Thanatos—Freud's term for the death instinct, which he believed to be a primary motivating force behind violence and aggression.

Theory of mind—The ability to understand the nature of the mind, to recognize that people experience the world through their beliefs.

Thought disorder—A symptom of psychosis in which the organization of the person's thought breaks down.

Topological model—Freud's theory of mental life that focused on the unconscious, preconscious, and conscious layers of the mind.

Transference—A psychoanalytic term referring to intense and inappropriate feelings based in childhood emotional conflicts that patients develop towards their therapist.

Triune model—Paul Maclean's division of the brain into three general regions—the reptilian, palio-mammalian, and neo-mammalian—which he believed to correspond with different periods of evolution.

Typical antipsychotics—The class of antipsychotic drugs that preceded the atypical antipsychotics. Also known as first generation antipsychotics.

Unconditioned stimulus—The unconditioned stimulus is the stimulus that elicits a natural and unlearned response.

Unconscious, the—The unconscious refers to any mental content of which the person is not aware; any thoughts or feelings that are out of awareness. The unconscious is a central focus of psychoanalytic theory.

Validity—Scientific validity refers to the accuracy of the study; how much do the results of an experiment give an accurate picture of the topic of study?

Variable—A variable is the fundamental unit of psychological research. Any trait or behavior that we wish to study is translated into a variable so that we can measure it with numbers. We use the term variable because we are studying traits that vary across individuals or across time.

Ventral—A Latin term which refers to the belly of a body. It is used to describe the lower sections of the brain or brain regions.

White matter—Because myelinated axons are white in appearance, brain tissue made up of these fibers is called white matter.

Withdrawal—The physiological syndrome that occurs in drug addiction when the drug is discontinued. Because the brain has become adapted to the chemical, removal of the chemical sends the brain into a disregulated state.

BIBLIOGRAPHY

Administration on Children, Youth and Families, U.S. Dept of Health and Human Services (2009) *Child Maltreatment 2007*. Washington, DC: U.S. Government Printing Office.

Ainsworth, M.D.S., Blehar, M., Waters, E., and Wall, S. (1978). *Patterns of Attachment*. Hillsdale, NJ: Erlbaum.

Alcoholics Anonymous World Services (2002). *Alcoholics Anonymous: The Story of How Many Thousands of Men and Women have Recovered from Alcoholism,* 4th edition. New York: AAWS.

Alderfer, C.P. (1972). *Existence, Relatedness, and Growth: Human Needs In Organizational Settings*. New York: Free Press.

Allman, J. (2000). *Evolving Brains*. New York: Scientific American Library.

American Psychological Association (1994). APF Gold Medal Award: Bernice L. Neugarten, *American Psychologist, 49,* 553-55.

American Psychiatric Association (2000). *Diagnostic and Statistical Manual of Mental Disorders, Fourth Edition, Text Revision*. Washington, DC: American Psychiatric Press.

Andersen, R.A. (1997). "Multimodal Integration for the Representation of Space in the Posterior Parietal Cortex," *Philosophical Transactions of the Royal Society London, 352:* 1421-28.

Andreiessen, E.J.H, and Drenth, P.J.D. (1998). "Leadership: Theories and Models." In P.J.D. Drenth, H. Thierry, and C.J. de Wolff (Eds.) *Handbook of Work and Organizational Psychology,* 2nd edition. Volume 4: *Organizational Psychology*. East Sussex, UK: Psychology Press, pp. 327-55.

Ariely, D. *Predictable Irrationality: The Hidden Forces that Shape Our Decisions*. New York: Harper Collins.

Armstrong, D., Lawrence, W.G., and Young, R.M. (1997). *Group Relations: An Introduction*. London: Process Press.

Aron, A., Fisher, H.E., and Strong, G. (2006). "Romantic Love." In Anita L. Vangelisti and Daniel Perlman (Eds.). *The Cambridge Handbook of Personal Relationships*. New York, NY: Cambridge University Press, pp. 595-614.

Aronson, V. (2000). *Ann Landers and Abigail Van Buren. Women of Achievement*. Philadelphia: Chelsea House.

Asch, S.E. (1956). "Studies of Independence and Conformity: I. A Minority of One Against a Unanimous Majority." *Psychological Monographs, 70*(a), 1-70.

Ausubel, L. (1999). *Adverse Selection in the Credit Card Market,* Working paper. College Park, MD: Department of Economics, University of Maryland.

Bagley, A.D., Abramowitz, C.S., and Kosson, D.S. (2009). "Vocal Affect Recognition and Psychopathy: Converging Findings across Traditional and Cluster Analytic Approaches to Assessing the Construct." *Journal of Abnormal Psychology, 118* (2), 38-398.

Bagley, C., Wood, M., and Young, L. (1994). "Victim to Abuser: Mental Health and Behavioral Sequels of Child Sexual Abuse in a Community Survey of Young Adult Males." *Child Abuse & Neglect.* 18: 683-69.

Bai, M. (2005). "The Framing Wars." *New York Times,* July 17.

Bailey, J.M., Dunne, M.P., and Martin, N.G. (2000). "Genetic and Environmental Influences on Sexual Orientation and Its Correlates in an Australian Twin Sample." *Journal of Personality and Social Psychology, 78* (3), 524-36.

Bailey, J.M., Gaulin, S., Agyei, Y., and Gladue, B.A. (1994). "Effects of Gender and Sexual Orientation on Evolutionarily Relevant Aspects of Human Mating Psychology." *Journal of Personality and Social Psychology, 66* (6), 1081-93.

Bailey, J.M., and Zucker, K.J. (1995). "Childhood Sex-typed Behavior and Sexual Orientation: A Conceptual Analysis and Quantitative Review," *Developmental Psychology, 31* (1), 43-55.

Barash, D.P. (1982). *Sociobiology and Behavior,* 2nd edition. New York: Elsevier.

Barrett, L., Dunbar, R., and Lycett, J. (2002). *Human Evolutionary Psychology.* Princeton, NJ: Princeton University Press.

Barlett, D.L., and Steele, J.B. (1979/2004). *Howard Hughes: His Life and Madness.* New York: W.W. Norton.

Baron-Cohen, S. (2006). "The Hyper-systemizing, Assortative Mating Theory of Autism." *Progress in Neuro-Psychopharmacology & Biological Psychiatry, 30,* 865–72.

Bartol, C.R., and Bartol, A.M. (Eds.) (2008). *Current Perspective in Forensic Psychology and Criminal Behavior,* 2nd edition. Thousand Oaks, CA: Sage Publications.

Baumeister, R.F. (2000). "Gender Differences in Erotic Plasticity: The Female Sex Drive as Socially Flexible and Responsive." *Psychological Bulletin, 126* (3), 347-74.

Baumrind, D. (1991). "The Influence of Parenting Style on Adolescent Competence and Substance Use." *Journal of Early Adolescence,* 11, 56-95.

Berk, L.E. (2008). *Exploring Lifespan Development.* Boston, MA: Allyn and Bacon.

Berkowitz, L. (1989). "Frustration-aggression Hypothesis: Examination and Reformulation." *Psychology Bulletin, 106,* 59-73.

Blumer, D. (2002). "The Illness of Vincent van Gogh." *American Journal of Psychiatry, 159,* 519-26.

Bordnick, B.S., Thyer, B.A., and Ritchie, B.A. (1994). "Feather Picking Disorder and Trichotillomania: An Avian Model of Human Pathology." *Journal of Behavior Therapy and Experimental Psychiatry,* 25: 189-96.

Bownds, M.D. (1999). *The Biology of the Mind: Origins and Structures of Mind, Brain, and Consciousness.* Bethesda, MD: Fitzgerald Science Press.

Bowlby, J. (1969/1999). *Attachment,* 2nd edition, *Attachment and Loss,* Vol. 1, New York: Basic Books.

Bowlby, J. (1973). "Separation: Anxiety & Anger." In *Attachment and Loss,* Vol. 2 (International Psycho-analytical Library, no. 95). London: Hogarth Press.

Bowlby, J. (1980). "Loss: Sadness & Depression." In *Attachment and Loss,* Vol. 3 (International Psycho-analytical Library, no. 109). London: Hogarth Press.

Brent, J. (2008). *Inside the Stalin Archives New York: Discovering the New Russia.* New York: Atlas & Company Publishers.

Bretherton I (1985). "Attachment Theory: Retrospect and Prospect." In *Monographs of the Society for Research in Child Development,* Vol. 50, no. 1/2, pp. 3-35.

Brickman, P., Coates, D., and Janoff-Bullman, R. (1978). "Lottery Winners and Accident Victims: Is Happiness Relative?" *Journal of Personality and Social Psychology, 36,* 917-27.

Breuer, J., and Freud, S. (1955/1895). *Studies on Hysteria.* New York: Basic Books.

Brewer, M.B., and Campbell, D.T. (1976). *Ethnocentrism and Intergroup Attitudes: East African Evidence.* New York: Sage Publications.

Brodsky, B.S., Mann, J.J., Stanley, B., Tin, A., Oquendo, M., Birmaher, B., Greenhill, L., Kolko, D., Zelazny, J., and Brown, R. (2000). *Group Processes.* 2nd edition. Malden, MA: Blackwell Publishing.

470

Bruce, C.A. (2007). "Helping Patients, Families, Caregivers, and Physicians, in the Grieving Process." *Journal of the American Osteopathic Association,* 107, 7 supplement, 33-40.

Bucks, B.K., Kennickell, A.B., Mach, T.L, and Moore, K.B. (2009). "Changes in U.S. Family Finances from 2004–2007: Evidence from the Survey of Consumer Finances," *Federal Reserve Bulletin, 95,* A1-A56.

Bureau of Democracy, Human Rights and Labor (2004). *2003 Country Reports on Human Rights Practices.* Washington, DC: U.S. Department of State. (http://www.state.gov/g/drl/rls/hrrpt/2003/index.htm). Accessed 10/17/2009.

Bureau of Justice Statistics (2007). *Criminal Offender Statistics.* Washington, DC: United States Department of Justice. (http://www.ojp.usdoj.gov/bjs/crimoff.htm# women). Accessed 12/1/2009.

Bureau of Justice Statistics (2007). *Intimate Partner Violence in the U.S.: Victim Characteristics.* Washington, DC: United States Department of Justice. (http://ojp.usdoj.gov/bjs/intimate/victims.htm). Accessed 10/17/2009.

Burke, A.K., Melhem, N.M., and Brent, D. (2008). "Familial Transmission of Suicidal Behavior: Factors Mediating the Relationship between Childhood Abuse and Offspring Suicide Attempts." *Journal of Clinical Psychiatry, 69* (4), 584-96.

Burlingame, G.M., and Barlow, S.H. (1996). "Outcome and Process Differences between Professional and Nonprofessional Therapists in Time-limited Group Psychotherapy." *International Journal of Group Psychotherapy, 46* (4), 455-78.

Burns, D. (2000/1980). *Feeling Good: The New Mood Therapy.* New York: Quill, Harper Collins.

Buss, D.M. (1989). "Sex Differences in Human Mate Preferences: Evolutionary Hypotheses Tested in 37 Cultures." *Behavioral and Brain Sciences, 1,* 12-49.

Campbell, D.P., and Borgen, F.H. (1999). "Holland's Theory and the Development of Interest Inventories." *Journal of Vocational Behavior, 55,* 86-101.

Canter, D.V., Alison, L.J., Alison, E., and Wentink, N. (2004). "The Organized/ Disorganized Typology of Serial Murder: Myth or Model." *Psychology, Public Policy and Law, 10,* 293-320.

Center for Disease Control (2006). *National Vital Statistics Report.* 54 (20), 1-7.

Chase, A. (2004). *A Mind for Murder: The Education of the Unabomber and the Origins of Modern Terrorism.* New York: Norton.

Chiacchia, K.B. (2000). "Insanity Defense." In B.B. Stickland (Ed.) *Gale Encyclopedia of Psychology.* Detroit, MI: Gale Group.

Churchland, P.S. (2002). *Brain-Wise: Studies in Neurophilosophy.* Boston, MA: Massachusetts Institute of Technology.

Christensen, A., Jacobson, N.S. (1994). "Who (or What) Can Do Psychotherapy: The Status and Challenge of Nonprofessional Therapies." In *Psychological Science.* 5 (1), 8-14.

Clark, K.B. (1988). *Prejudice and Your Child.* 2nd edition, Middletown, CT: Wesleyan University Press.

Coalson, D., and Raiford, S. (Research Directors) (2008). *Wechsler Adult Intelligence Scale—4th Ed. (WAIS-IV).* San Antonio, TX: Pearson.

Cogan, R., Fennell, T. (2007). "Sexuality and the Commission of Physical Violence to Partners and Non-partners by Men and Women." In *Journal of Consulting and Clinical Psychology, 75* (6), 960-67.

Cloninger, R.C., Svrakic, D.M., and Prsybeck, T.R. (1993). "A Psychobiological Model of Temperament and Character." *Archives of General Psychiatry, 50,* 975-90.

Cohen, L.J. (2005). "Neurobiology of Antisociality." In C. Stough (Ed.) *Neurobiology of Exceptionality.* New York: Kluwer Academic/Plenum Publishers, pp. 107-124.

Cohen, L.J. (2007). "Psychological Tests in Inpatient Psychiatry." In Lydia S. Boyar (Ed.) *New Psychological Tests and Testing Research.* New York: Nova Science Publishers.

Cohen, L.J., and Galynker, I.G. (2002). "Clinical Features of Pedophilia and Implications for Treatment." *Journal of Psychiatric Practice, 8* (5), 276-89.

Cohen, L.J., and Galynker, I.G. (2009). "Psychopathology and Personality Traits of Pedophiles: Issues for Diagnosis and Treatment." In *Psychiatric Times, 26* (6).

471

Cohen, L.J., and Slade, A. (1999). "The Psychology and Psychopathology of Pregnancy: Reorganization and Transformation." In Zeanah, C. (Ed.) *Handbook of Infant Mental Health.* New York: Guilford Press, pp. 20-36.

Cohen, L.J., Stein, D., Galynker, I.I., and Hollander, E. (1997). "Towards an Integration of Psychological and Biological Models of OCD: Phylogenetic Considerations." *CNS Spectrums, 2:* 26-44.

Cory, G.A., and Gardner, R. (2002). *The Evolutionary Neuroethology of Paul MacLean: Convergences and Frontiers.* Westport, CT: Praeger Publishers.

Costa, P.T., Jr., and McCrae, R.R. (1992). "Normal Personality Assessment in Clinical Practice: The NEO Personality Inventory." *Psychological Assessment, 4,* 5-13.

Crain, W.C. (1985). *Theories of Development.* Upper Saddle River, NJ: Prentice-Hall.

Crary, D. (2007). "U.S. Divorce Rate Lowest since 1970." *The Associated Press.* (http://www.Breit bart.com). Accessed May 10, 2010.

Cummings, J.L., and Trimble, M.R. (2002). *Concise Guide to Neuropsychiatry and Behavioral Neurology.* 2nd edition. Washington, DC: American Psychiatric Publishing, Inc.

Dahmer, L. (1994). *A Father's Story.* New York: William Morrow & Co.

Daley , D.C., and Marlatt, G.A. (1997). *Managing Your Drug and Alcohol Problem. Therapist Guide.* San Antonio, TX: The Psychological Corporation.

Damasio, A. (2003). *Looking for Spinoza: Joy, Sorrow, and the Feeling Brain.* New York: Harcourt.

Davidson, R.J., Kabat-Zinn, J., Schumacher, J., Rosenkranz, M., Muller, D., Santorelli, S.F., Urbanowski, F., Harrington, A., Bonus, K., and Sheridan, J.F. (2003). "Alterations in Brain and Immune Function Produced by Mindfulness Meditation." *Psychosomatic Medicine, 65* (4), 564-70.

Davis, K.E., and Roberts, M.K. (1985). "Relationships in the Real World: Descriptive Approaches to Personal Relationships." In K.J. Gergen and K.E. Davis (Eds.). *The Social Construction of the Person.* New York: Springer-Verlag.

DeMartino, B., Kumaran, D., Seymour, B., and Dolan, R.J. (2006). "Frames, Biases and Rational Decision-making in the Human Brain." *Science, 33,* 684-87.

Diamond, L.M. (2003). "What Does Sexual Orientation Orient?: A Biological Model Distinguishing Romantic Love and Sexual Desire." *Psychological Review, 110* (1), 173-192.

Diener, E., Lucas, R.E., and Scollon, C.N. (2005). "Beyond the Hedonic Treadmill: Revising the Adaptation Theory of Well-being." *American Psychologist, 60,* 305-314.

Dodman, N.H., Moon-Fanelli, A., Mertens, P.A., Pflueger, S., and Stein, D.S. (1997). "Veterinary Models of OCD." In E. Hollander, D. Stein, (Eds.) *Obsessive-Compulsive Disorders: Diagnosis, Etiology, Treatment.* New York: Marcel Dekker. pp. 99-145.

Dollard, J., Doob, L.W., Miller, N.E., Mowrer, O.H., and Sears, R.R. (1939). *Frustration and Aggression.* New Haven, CT: Yale University Press.

Dubin, M.W. (2002). *How the Brain Works.* Malden, MA: Blackwell Science, Inc.

Dubovsky, S.L., and Dubovsky, A.N. (2007). *Psychotropic Drug Prescriber's Survival Guide: Ethical Mental Health Treatment in the Age of Big Pharma.* New York: Norton.

Dunne, K. (2004). "Grief and Its Manifestations." *Nursing Standard, 18,* 45-53.

Dutton, D.G. (2007). "The Complexities of Domestic Violence." *American Psychologist, 62* (7), 708-9.

Edwards, A. (1977) *Vivien Leigh: A Biography.* New York: Simon & Schuster.

Emmons, R.A. (1984). "Factor Analysis and Construct Validity of the Narcissistic Personality Inventory." *Journal of Personality Assessment, 48,* 291-300.

Epstein, H. (2009). "Dreams from the Monster Factory: A Tale of Prison, Redemption and One Woman's Fight to Restore Justice to All by Sunny Schwartz, with David Boodell." *New York Review of Books, 66* (10), 30-33.

Erikson, E.H. (1950). *Childhood and Society.* New York: Norton.

Exner, J.E. (1997). *The Rorschach: A Comprehensive System. Vol. 1, Basic Foundations and Principles of Interpretation.* 4th edition. Hoboken, NJ: John Wiley and Sons.

Fallon, J. (2006). "Neuroanatomical Background to Understanding the Brain of the Young Psychopath." (http://law.osu.edu/osjcl/Articles/Volume3_2/Symposium/Fallon-PDF-03-29-06.pdf). Accessed June 1, 2010.

Ferber, R. (2006). *Solve Your Child's Sleep Problems.* New York: Fireside.

Festinger, F.E. (1957). *A Theory of Cognitive Dissonance.* Evanston, IL.: Row, Peterson, & Co.

Fisher, Helen E. (1998). "Lust, Attraction and Attachment in Human Reproduction," *Human Nature, 9* (1), 23-52.

Flores, E., Cicchetti, D., and Rogosch, F.A. (2005). "Predictors of Resilience in Maltreated and Non-maltreated Latino Children." *Developmental Psychology, 41,* 338-51.

Fonagy, P., and Target, M. (2003). *Psychoanalytic Theories. Perspectives from Developmental Psychopathology* (Whurr Series in Psychoanalysis). New York: Brunner-Routledge.

Forman, M., Lichtenstein, P., Larsson, H., and Andershed, H. (2008). "Genetic Effects Explain the Stability of Psychopathic Personality from Mid- to Late-Adolescence." *Journal of Abnormal Psychology, 117,* 606-17.

Fowler, J.H., and Kam, C.D. (2007). "Beyond the Self: Social Identity, Altruism, and Political Participation." *Journal of Politics, 69,* 813-27.

Fowler, J.H., Baker, L.A., and Dawes, C.T. (2008). "Genetic Variation in Political Participation," *American Political Science Review, 102,* 233-48.

Franzoi, S.L. (2007). *Psychology: A Journey of Discovery.* (3rd ed.) Cincinnati, OH: Atomic Dog Publishing.

Freud, S. (1965/1966). *Introductory Lectures on Psychoanalysis.* New York: Norton.

Gangestad, S.W., Bailey, J.M., and Martin, N.G. (2000). "Taxometric Analyses of Sexual Orientation and Gender Identity." *Journal of Personality and Social Psychology, 78* (6), 1109-21.

Gao, G. (2001). "Intimacy, Passion and Commitment in Chinese and U.S. American Romantic Relationships." *International Journal of Intercultural Relations. 25* (3), 329-42.

Gardner, H. (2000). *Intelligence Reframed: Multiple Intelligences for the 21st Century.* New York: Basic Books.

Gay, P. (1988). *Freud: A Life for Our Time.* New York: W.W. Norton.

Geier, A., Rozin, P., and Doros, G. (2006). "Unit Bias: A New Heuristic that Helps Explain the Effect of Portion Size on Food Intake." *Psychological Science, 17,* 521-27.

Geraerts, E., Schooler, J.W., Merckelbach, H., Hauer, B.J.A., Ambadar, Z., and Jelicic, M. (2007). "The Reality of Recovered Memories: Corroborating Continuous and Discontinuous Memories of Childhood Sexual Abuse." *Psychological Science. 18* (7), 564-68.

Gerber, A.S., Green, D.P., and Larimer, C.W. (2008). "Social Pressure and Voter Turnout: Evidence from a Large-Scale Field Experiment." *American Political Science Review, 102,* 33-48.

Gerner, L. (2006). "Exploring Prenatal Attachment: Factors that Facilitate Paternal Attachment during Pregnancy." *Dissertation Abstracts International: Section B: The Sciences and Engineering, 66(7-B),* 3934.

Gibbs, N. (2009). "What Women Want Now: A Time Special Report." *Time,* October 26, 2009, 25-29.

Giedd, J.N., Blumenthal, J., Jeffries, N.O., et al. (1999). "Brain Development during Childhood and Adolescence: A Longitudinal MRI Study." *Nature Neuroscience, 2* (10): 861-63.

Gillespie, J.F. (1999). "The Why, What, How, and When of Effective Faculty Use of Institutional Review Boards." In G.D. Chastain and R.E. Landrum (Eds.). *Protecting Human Subjects: Departmental Subject Pools and Institutional Review Boards.* Washington, DC: American Psychological Association, pp. 157-77.

Ginsburg, H., Opper, S. (1979). *Piaget's Theory of Intellectual Development,* 2nd edition. Englewood Cliffs, NJ: Prentice Hall.

Glad, B. (2002). "Why Tyrants Go Too Far: Malignant Narcissism and Absolute Power." *Political Psychology, 23* (1).

Goldberg, E. (2001). *The Executive Brain: Frontal Lobes and the Civilized Mind.* New York: Oxford University Press.

Goldstein, R. (2006) *Betraying Spinoza: The Renegade Jew Who Gave Us Modernity.* New York: Shocken Books.

Goleman, D. (1997). *Emotional Intelligence: Why It Can Matter More than IQ.* New York: Bantam.

Gottman, J.M. (1993). "A Theory of Marital Dissolution and Stability." *Journal of Family Psychology, 7* (1), 57-75.

Gottman, J.M., Fainsilber Katz, L., and Hooven, C. (1996). "Parental Meta-emotional Philosophy and the Emotional Life of Families: Theoretical Models and Preliminary Data." *Journal of Family Psychology, 10* (3), 243-68.

Gottman, J.M., Jacobson, N.S., Rushe, R.H., Shortt, J.W., Babcock, J., La Taillade, J.J., and Waltz, J. (1995). "The Relationship between Heart Rate Reactivity, Emotionally Aggressive Behavior, and General Violence in Batterers." *Journal of Family Psychology, 9* (3), 227-48.

Gould, R. (1980). "Transformational Tasks in Adulthood." In S.J. Greenspan and G.H. Pollock (Eds.). *The Course of Life: Psychoanalytic Contributions toward Understanding Personality Development.* Vol. III: *Adulthood and the Aging Process.* Bethesda, MD: National Institute of Mental Health.

Gould, S.J. (1985). *Ontogeny and Phylogeny.* Cambridge, MA: Belknap Press.

Gould, S.J. (1996). *The Mismeasure of Man.* New York: W.W. Norton.

Graham, J., Haidt, J., and Nosek, B.A. (2009), "Liberals and Conservatives Rely on Different Sets of Moral Foundations." *Journal of Personality and Social Psychology, 96* (5), 1029-46.

Green, E.G.T. (2005). "Individualism in Cross-Cultural Psychology: Separating Self-Reliance and Success Orientation / L'individualisme en psychologie interculturelle: Séparation de l'autosuffisance et de l'orientation vers le succès." *Revue Internationale de Psychologie Sociale. 18* (1-2), 11-34.

Greenberg, J.R., Mitchell, S.A. (1985). *Object Relations in Psychoanalytic Theory.* Cambridge, MA.: Harvard University Press.

Greenberg, M. (2008). "Just Remember This." *New York Review of Books,* December 4, pp. 10-14.

Greene, J. (2007). "Why Are VMPFC Patients More Utilitarian?: A Dual-Process Theory of Moral Judgment Explains." *Trends in Cognitive Sciences, 11* (8), 322-23.

Greene, J.D., Sommerville, R.B., Nystrom, L.E., Darley, J.M., and Cohen, J.D. (2001). "An fMRI Investigation of Emotional Engagement in Moral Judgment." *Science, 293*, 2105-2108.

Gurman, A., and Kniskern, D.P. (1991). *Handbook of Family Therapy,* Volume II. Bristol, PA: Brunner/Mazel.

Gurr, T.R. (1970). *Why Men Rebel.* Princeton, NJ: Princeton University Press.

Hagedoorn, M., Van Yperen, N.W., Coyne, J.C., van Jaarsveld, C.H.M., Ranchor, A.V., van Sonderen, E., and Sanderman, R. (2006). "Does Marriage Protect Older People from Distress?: The Role of Equity and Recency of Bereavement." *Psychology and Aging, 21* (3), 611-20.

Hales, S., Zimmermann, C., and Rodin, G. (2008). "The Quality of Death and Dying." *Archive of Internal Medicine. 168*, 9, 912-18.

Hall, C.S. (1979/1954). *A Primer of Freudian Psychology.* New York: New American Library.

Hare, R.D. (2008). "Psychopathy: A Clinical Construct Whose Time Has Come." *Current Perspective in Forensic Psychology and Criminal Behavior,* 2nd edition. Thousand Oaks, CA: Sage Publications.

Hazan, C., and Diamond, L.M. (2000). "The Place of Attachment in Human Mating." *Review of General Psychology, 4* (2), 186-204.

Hearst, P., with Patricia Campbell Hearst (1982). *Her Own Story* (originally published as *Every Secret Thing*). New York: Avon.

Herdt, G.H. (Ed.) (1998). *Rituals of Manhood: Male Initiation in Papua New Guinea.* Piscataway, NJ: Transaction Publishers.

Herman, J. (1992). *Trauma and Recovery: The Aftermath Of Violence—From Domestic Abuse to Political Terror.* New York: Basic Books.

Herzberg, F., Mausner, B., and Snyderman, B.B. (1959). *The Motivation to Work.* New York: John Wiley.

Hettema, J.M., Neale, M.C., Myers, H.M., Prescott, C.A., and Kendler, K.S. (2006). "A Population-based Twin Study of the Relationship between Neuroticism and Internalizing Disorders." *American Journal of Psychiatry, 163,* 857-64.

Hill, R.W., and Yousey, G.P. (1998). "Adaptive and Maladaptive Narcissism among University Faculty, Clergy, Politicians, and Librarians." *Current Psychology: Developmental, Learning, Personality, Social, 17,* 163-69.

Hogg, M.A., and Cooper, J. (Eds.) (2007). *The SAGE Handbook of Social Psychology.* London, UK: Sage Publications.

Hoberman, H.M., Lewinsohn, P.M., and Tilson, M. (1988). "Group Treatment of Depression: Individual Predictors of Outcome." *Journal of Consulting and Clinical Psychology, 56,* 3, 393-98.

Horn, J.L., and Cattell, R.B. (1966). "Refinement and Test of the Theory of Fluid and Crystallized General Intelligence." *Journal of Educational Psychology, 57,* 253-70.

Horowitz, J.E. (1985). "Sexual Abuse of Children: A Review of Victim Symptomatology, Offender Behavioral Patterns, and Treatment Methods." *American Mental Health Counselors Association Journal, 7* (4), 172-79.

Hovland, C., and Sears, R.R. (1940). "Minor Studies in Aggression: VI. Correlation of Lynchings with Economic Indices." *Journal of Psychology, 9,* 301-10.

Hulsker, J. (1971). "Vincent's Stay in the Hospitals at Arles and St.-Remy: Unpublished Letters from the Reverend Mr. Salles and Doctor Peyron to Theo van Gogh," *Vincent. 1* (2), 24-44.

Hunt, D.M. (1999). *O.J. Simpson Facts and Fictions.* Cambridge, MA: Cambridge University Press.

Hunt, M. (2007). *The Story of Psychology.* 2nd edition. New York: Anchor Books.

Hyde, J.S. (1990). "Meta-Analysis and the Psychology of Gender Differences." *Signs, 16,* 55-73.

Ickes, D. (2001). "Children of the Matrix: How an Interdimensional Race Has Controlled the World for Thousands of Years—and Still Does." Wildwood, MO: Bridge of Love Publications.

Insel, T.R., and Collins, F.S. (2003). "Psychiatry in the Genomics Era." *American Journal of Psychiatry, 160,* 616-20.

Insel, T.R. (1997). "A Neurobiological Basis of Social Attachment." *Journal of American Psychiatry, 154,* 726-35.

Jacobi, J. (1942/1973). *The Psychology of C.G. Jung.* New Haven, CT: Yale University Press.

Jankowski, R. (2007). "Altruism and the Decision to Vote: Explaining and Testing High Voter Turnout." *Rationality and Society, 19* (1), 5-34.

Jastrzembski, T., and Charness, N. (2007). "What Older Adults Can Teach Us about Designing Better Ballots." *Ergonomics in Design, 15* (44), 6-12.

Jeffery, K.J., and Reid, I.C. (1997). "Modifiable Neuronal Connections: An Overview for Psychiatrists." *Archives of General Psychiatry, 154* (2), 156-64.

Johnson, W., and Krueger, R.F. (2006). "How Money Buys Happiness: Genetic and Environmental Processes Linking Finances and Life Satisfaction." *Journal of Personality and Social Psychology, 90,* 680-691.

Joint Committee on Standards for Educational and Psychological Testing of the American Educational Research Association, the American Psychological Association, and the National Council on Measurement in Education (2004). *Standards for Education and Psychological Testing.* Washington, DC: American Educational Research Association.

Jones, James H. (1997). *Alfred C. Kinsey: A Public/Private Life.* New York: Norton.

Judge, T.A. (2009). "Core Self-Evaluations and Work Success." *Current Directions in Psychological Science, 18* (1), 58-62.

Kaplan and B.J. Saddock (Eds.) *A Comprehensive Textbook of Psychiatry-II.* Volume 1, 2nd edition. Baltimore: Williams & Wilkins Co.

Kaslow, N.J., and Thompson, M.P. (2008). "Associations of Child Maltreatment and Intimate Partner Violence with Psychological Adjustment among Low SES, African American Children." *Child Abuse & Neglect, 32* (9), 888-96.

Kelly, R., Cohen, L.J., Semple, R.J., Bialer, P., Lau, A., Bedenheimer, A., Neustadter, E., Barenboim, A., and Galynker, I.I. (2006). "Relationship between Drug Company Funding and Outcomes of Clinical Psychiatric Research." *Psychological Medicine, 36,* 1-9.

Kemp, S. (1998). "Medieval Theories of Mental Representation." *History of Psychology, 1,* 4, 275-88.

Kendler, K., Aggen, S.H. Czaijkowski, N., R̄yhsamb, E., Tambs, K., Torersen, S., Neale, M.C., Reich-born-Kendler, K., Jacobson, K.C., Prescott, C.A., and Neale, M.C. (2003). "Specificity of Genetic and Environmental Risk Factors for Use and Abuse/Dependence of Cannabis, Cocaine, Hallucinogens, Sedatives, Stimulants, and Opiates in Male Twins." *American Journal of Psychiatry, 160* (4), 687-95.

King, D.B., Viney, W., and Woody, W.D. (2008). *A History of Psychology: Ideas and Context.* 4th edition. New York: Pearson Education.

Kjennerud, T. (2008). "The Structure of Genetic and Environmental Risk Factors for DSM-IV Personality Disorders." *Archives of General Psychiatry, 65,* 1438-46.

Klaus, M.H., and Klaus, P.H. (1985). *The Amazing Newborn: Making the Most of the First Weeks of Life.* Reading, MA: Addison-Wesley Publishing Company.

Knutson, B., Scott, R., Wimmer, G.E., Prelec, D., and Loewenstein, G. (2007). "Neural Predictors of Purchases." *Neuron, 53,* 147-56.

Knutson B., Adams C.M., Fong, G.W., and Hommer, D. (2001). "Anticipation of Increasing Monetary Reward Selectively Recruits Nucleus Accumbens." *Journal of Neuroscience, 21,* RC159, 1-5.

Koffka, K. [1924] (1980). *Growth of the Mind.* New Brunswick, NJ: Transaction Books.

Koslow, S.H. (1995). *The Neuroscience of Mental Health II. A Report on Neuroscience Research. Status and Potential for Mental Health and Mental Illness.* Rockville, MD: National Institute of Mental Health.

Lee, J.A. (1977). "A Typology of Styles of Loving." *Personality and Social Psychology Bulletin, 3,* 173-82.

Lehrer, J. (2009). *How We Decide.* New York: Houghton Mifflin Harcourt.

Leiblum, S.R. (Ed.) (2007). *Principles and Practice of Sex Therapy,* 4th edition. New York: The Guilford Press.

Lemonick, M.D., and Park, A. (2001). "The Nun Study: How One Scientist and 678 Sisters Are Helping Unlock the Secrets of Alzheimer's." *Time.* May 14, 2001.

Levinson, D., With Darrow, C.N., Klein, E.B., Levenson, M.H., and McKee, B. (1978). *Seasons of a Man's Life.* New York: Ballantine Books.

Levinson, D. (1987). *Season's of a Woman's Life.* New York: Ballantine Books.

Lewis, M. (1997). "The Self in Self-conscious Emotions." In J.G. Snodgrass and R.L. Thompson (Eds.) "The Self across Psychology: Self-Recognition, Self-Awareness, and the Self Concept." *Annals of the New York Academy of Sciences, 818,* 119-42.

Lezak, M.D., Howieson, D.B., and Loring, D.W. (2004). *Neuropsychological Assessment.* 4th edition. New York: Oxford University Press.

Lieberman, J.A., Stroup, T.S., McEvoy, J.P., Swartz, M.S., Rosenheck, R.A., Perkins D.O., Keefe, R.S.E., Davis, S.M., Davis, C.E., Lebowitz, B.D., Severe, J., and Hsiao, J.K., for the Clinical Antipsychotic Trials of Intervention Effectiveness (CATIE) Investigators (2005). "Effectiveness of Antipsychotic Drugs in Patients with Chronic Schizophrenia." *New England Journal of Medicine, 353,* 1209-23.

Liem, J.H., James, J.B., O'Toole, J.G., and Boudewyn, A.C. (1997). "Assessing Resilience in Adults with Histories of Childhood Sexual Abuse." *American Journal of Orthopsychiatry, 67* (4), 594-606.

Linnoila, M., Virkkunen, M., Scheinen, M., Nuutila, A., Rimon, R., and Goodwin, F. (1983). "Low Cerebrospinal Fluid 5-Hydroxyindoleacetic Acid Concentration Differentiates Impulsive from Nonimpulsive Violent Behavior." *Life Science, 33,* 2609-14.

Loftus, E.F., and Ketcham, K. (1994). *The Myth Of Repressed Memory: False Memories and Allegations of Sexual Abuse.* New York: St. Martin's Press.

London, K. (2008). "Investigative Interviews of Children: A Review of Psychological Research and Implications for Police Practices." In *Current Perspective in Forensic Psychology and Criminal Behavior*, 2nd edition. Thousand Oaks, CA: Sage Publications.

Lopez, M., Kosson, D.S., Weissman, D.H., and Banich, M.T. (2007). "Interhemispheric Integration in Psychopathic Offenders." *Neuropsychology, 21* (1), 82-93.

Lucas, R. (2007). "Long Term Disability Is Associated with Lasting Changes in Subjective Wellbeing: Evidence from Two Nationally Representative Longitudinal Studies." *Personality Processes and Individual Differences, 92* (4), 717-30.

Luntz, F. (2007). *Words that Work: It's Not What You Say, It's What People Hear.* New York: Hyperion.

Luria, A.R. (1966/1980). *Higher Cortical Functions in Man.* 2nd edition. New York: Basic Books & Consultants Bureau Enterprises, Inc.

Lyubomirsky, S., King, L., and Diener, E. (2005). "The Benefits of Frequent Positive Affect: Does Happiness Lead to Success?" *Psychological Bulletin, 131,* 803-55.

Lyubomirsky, S., Sheldon, K.M., and Schkade, D. (2005). "Pursuing Happiness: The Architecture of Sustainable Change." *Review of General Psychology, 9,* 111-31.

Maciejewski, P.K., Zhang, B., Block, S.D., and Progerson, H.G. (2007). "An Empirical Examination of the Stage Theory of Grief." *Journal of the American Medical Association, 297,* 7, pp. 716-23.

MacLean, P.D. (1974). *Triune Conception of the Brain and Behaviour* (The Clarence M. Hincks memorial lectures). Toronto, ON: University of Toronto Press.

MacLean, P. (1982). "On the Origin and Progressive Evolution of the Triune Brain." In *Primate Brain Evolution: Methods and Concepts.* E. Armstrong and D. Falk (Eds.). New York: Plenum 1982, 291-316.

Mahler, M.S., Pine, F., and Bergman, A. (1975). *The Psychological Birth of the Human Infant: Symbiosis and Individuation.* New York: Basic Books.

Maikovich, A.K., Jaffee, S.R., Odgers, C.L., and Gallop, R. (2008). "Effects of Family Violence on Psychopathology Symptoms in Children Previously Exposed to Maltreatment." *Child Development, 79* (5), 1498-1512.

Main, M., Kaplan, N., and Cassidy, J. (1985). "Security in Infancy, Childhood, and Adulthood: A Move to the Level of Representation," *Monographs of the Society for Research in Child Development, 50,* 1/2, pp. 66-104.

Maltby, J., Houran, J., McCutcheon, L.E. (2003). "A Clinical Interpretation of Attitudes and Behaviors Associated with Celebrity Worship." *Journal of Nervous and Mental Disease. 191* (1), 25-29.

Marangell, L.B., and Martinez, J.M. (2006). *Concise Guide to Psychopharmacology.* 2nd edition. Washington, DC: American Psychiatric Publishing.

Markstrom, C.A., and Kalmanir, H.M. (2001). "Linkages between the Psychosocial Stages of Identity and Intimacy and the Ego Strengths of Fidelity and Love." *Identity, 1* (2), 179–96.

Marshall, W.L., Barbaree, H.E., and Butt, J. (1988). "Sexual Offenders against Male Children: Sexual Preferences for Gender, Age of Victim and Type of Behavior." *Behavior Research and Therapy, 26,* 383–91.

Maslow, A.H. (1987). *Motivation and Personality,* 3rd edition. New York: Harper & Row.

Maslow, A.H. (1964/1987). *Religions, Values, and Peak-Experiences.* New York: Penguin Books.

Mayo Clinic Health Solutions (2008). "Alzheimer's Disease: New Research Brings Hope. Special Report," *Mayo Clinic Health Letter.* Supplement. October, 1-8.

McCrae, R.R., and Costa, P.T., Jr. (1996). "Toward a New Generation of Personality Theories: Theoretical Contexts for the Five-Factor Model." In J.S. Wiggins (Ed.). *The Five-Factor Model of Personality: Theoretical Perspectives.* New York: Guilford, pp. 51-87.

McGowan, P.O., Sasak, A., D'Alessio, A.C., Dymov, S., Labont&ecute;, B., Szyf, M., Turecki, G., and Meaney, M.J. (2009). "Epigenetic Regulation of the Glucocorticoid Receptor in Human Brain Associates with Childhood Abuse." *Nature Neuroscience, 12,* 342–48.

McMahon, D. (2006) *Happiness: A History.* New York: Grove Press.

Michaud, S., and Aynesworth, H. (1999). *The Only Living Witness: The True Story of Serial Sex Killer Ted Bundy.* Irving, TX: Authorlink Press.

Miller, G.A. (2003). "The Cognitive Revolution: A Historical Perspective." *Trends in Cognitive Sciences. 7,* 141-44.

Miller, J.M., and Krosnick, J.A. (1998). "The Impact of Candidate Name Order on Election Outcomes." *Public Opinion Quarterly, 62* (3), 291-330.

Miller, W.R., and Rollnick, S. (1991). *Motivational Interviewing: Preparing People for Change.* New York: Guilford.

M.I.N.D. Institute (2002). *Report to the Legislature on the Principal Findings from the Epidemiology of Autism in California: A Comprehensive Pilot Study.* Davis, CA.: University of California, Davis. (http://www.ucdmc.ucdavis.edu/mindinstitute/ newsroom/study_final.pdf) Accessed October 17, 2010.

Minuchin, S., and Fishman, H.C. (1981). *Family Therapy Techniques.* Cambridge, MA: Harvard University Press.

Mitrushina, M., Boone, K.B., Razani, J., and D'Elia, L.F. (2005). *Handbook of Normative Data for Neuropsychological Assessment,* 2nd edition. New York: Oxford University Press.

Moffitt, T.E. (2005). "The New Look of Behavioral Genetics in Developmental Psychopathology: Gene–Environment Interplay in Antisocial Behaviors." *Psychological Bulletin, 131* (4), 533-54.

Moffitt, T.E., Gabrielli, S.F., Mednick, S.A., and Schulsinger, F. (1981). "Socioeconomic Status, IQ and Delinquency." *Journal of Abnormal Psychology, 90* (2), 152-56.

Mora, George (1975). "Historical and Theoretical Trends in Psychiatry." In A.M. Freedman, H.I. Muller (2008). "Criminal Profiling: Real Science or Just Wishful Thinking?" *Current Perspective in Forensic Psychology and Criminal Behavior,* 2nd edition. Thousand Oaks, CA: Sage Publications.

Munsey, C. (2008). "Why Do We Vote?" *Monitor on Psychology, 39,* 60-63.

Murray, H.A. (1943). *Thematic Apperception Test Manual.* Cambridge, MA: Harvard University Press.

Myers, Isabel Briggs, McCaulley, Mary H., Quenk, Naomi L., and Hammer, Allen L. (1998). *MBTI Manual (A Guide to the Development and Use of the Myers Briggs Type Indicator).* 3rd edition. Menlo Park, CA: Consulting Psychologists Press.

Nair, J. (2004). "Knowing Me, Knowing You: Self-Awareness in Asperger's and Autism." In B.D. Beitman and J. Nair (Eds.) *Consulting Psychologists Press Self-Awareness Deficits in Psychiatric Patients: Neurobiology, Assessment, and Treatment.* New York: W.W. Norton.

Nasar, S. (1998). *A Beautiful Mind: The Life of Mathematical Genius and Nobel Laureate John Nash.* New York: Touchstone.

National Institute of Health (2008). "Alcohol's Effects on the Adolescent Brain." *eNotAlone* (http://www.enotalone.com/article/11157.html). Accessed June 1, 2010.

Nussbaum, H. (2005). *Surviving Intimate Terrorism.* Baltimore: PublishAmerica.

O'Leary, S.G., and Slep, A.M.S. (2006). "Precipitants of Partner Aggression." *Journal of Family Psychology, 20* (2), 344-47.

O'Malley, S. (2004). *Are You There Alone?: The Unspeakable Crime of Andrea Yates.* New York: Simon & Schuster.

Ozer, E.J., Best, S.R., Lipsey, T.L., and Weiss, D.S. (2003). "Predictors of Posttraumatic Stress Disorder and Symptoms in Adults: A Meta-Analysis." *Psychological Bulletin, 129,* 52-73.

Panksepp, J. (1998). *Affective Neuroscience: The Foundations of Human and Animal Emotions.* New York: Oxford University Press.

Patterson, C.L., Uhlin, B., and Anderson, T. (2008). "Clients' Pretreatment Counseling Expectations as Predictors of the Working Alliance." *Journal of Consulting Psychology, 55,* 528–34.

Piaget, P. (1951/1962). *Play, Dreams and Imitation in Childhood.* New York: W.W. Norton.

Pickvance, R. (1986). *Van Gogh in Saint-Remy and Auvers.* New York: The Metropolitan Museum of Art.

Pinker, S. (2008). "The Moral Instinct." *New York Times Magazine,* January 13.

Plato (1999). *Phaedrus.* B. Jowett, Trans. Seattle, WA: The World Wide School.

Plassman, H., O'Doherty, J., Shiv, B., and Rangel, A. (2007). "Marketing Actions Can Modulate Neural Representations of Experienced Pleasantness." *Proceedings of the National Academy of Sciences, 105,* 1050-54.

Prelec, D., and Simester, D. (2001). "Always Leave Home Without It." *Marketing Letters, 12,* 5-12.

Prentky, R.A., Knight, R.A., and Lee, A.F.S. (2008). "Child Sexual Molestation: Research Issues." *Current Perspective in Forensic Psychology and Criminal Behavior,* 2nd edition. Thousand Oaks, CA: Sage Publications.

Price, M. (2008). "Building a Better Ballot: Psychologists' Research Seeks to Make Voting Methods More Fair and Accessible." *Monitor on Psychology, 39,* 64-65.

Prochaska, J.O., Norcross, J.C., and DeClemete, C.C. (1994). *Changing for Good.* New York: William Morrow.

Quinones-Jenab, V., Ed. (2001). "The Biological Basis of Cocaine Addiction." *Annals of the New York Academy of Science,* 937.

Rachman, I.M., Unnerstall, J.R., Pfaff, D.W., and Cohen, R.S. (1998). "Estrogen Alters Behavior and Forebrain c-fos Expression in Ovariectomized Rats Subjected to the Forced Swim Test." *Proceedings of the National Academy of Science, 95,* 13941-46.

Raine, A. (2002). "Biosocial Studies of Antisocial and Violent Behavior in Children and Adults: A Review." *Journal of Abnormal Child Psychology, 30* (4), 311-26.

Raskin, R., and Hall, C.S. (1979). "A Narcissistic Personality Inventory." *Psychological Reports, 45,* 590.

Rawson, R.A. (2006). *Methamphetamine: New Knowledge, New Treatments. Clinician's Manual.* Center City, MN: Hazelden Publishing, pp. 1473-81.

Renard, John (2002). *The Handy Religion Answer Book.* Detroit, MI: Visible Ink Press.

Rieger, G., Linsenmeier, J.A.W., Gygax, L., and Bailey, J.M. (2008). "Sexual Orientation and Childhood Gender Nonconformity: Evidence from Home Videos." *Developmental Psychology, 44* (1), 46-58.

Robbins, J. (1998). *Diet for a New America.* Tiburon, CA: H.J. Kramer.

Röhl, J.C.G., Warren, M., and Hunt, D. (1998). *Purple Secret: Genes, "Madness" and the Royal Houses of Europe.* London, England: Bantam Press.

Ronson, Jon (2001). "Beset by Lizards." *Guardian.* (http://www.guardian.co.uk/books/2001/mar/17/features.weekend). Accessed July 18, 2009.

Rothbart, M. (1981). "Measurement of Temperament in Infancy." *Child Development. 52,* 569-78.

Russ, E., Shedler, J., Bradley, R., Westen, D. (2008). "Refining the Construct of Narcissistic Personality Disorder: Diagnostic Criteria and Subtypes." *American Journal of Psychiatry, 165.*

Sachs-Ericsson, N., Blazer, D., Plant, E.A., and Arnow, B. (2005). "Childhood Sexual and Physical Abuse and the 1-Year Prevalence of Medical Problems in the National Comorbidity Survey," *Health Psychology, 24,* 32-40.

Sadeh, N., Verona, E. (2008). "Psychopathic Personality Traits Associated with Abnormal Selective Attention and Impaired Cognitive Control." *Neuropsychology, 22* (5), 669-80.

Sadock, B.J., Sadock V.A. (2003). *Kaplan & Sadock's Synopsis of Psychiatry: Behavioral Sciences/Clinical Psychiatry,* 9th edition. Philadelphia: Lippincott, Williams & Wilkins.

SAMHSA. (2007). *Results from the 2007 National Survey on Drug Use and Health: National Findings.* Rockville, MD: Office of Applied Studies, Substance Abuse and Mental Health Services Administration, United States Department of Health and Human Services.

Sandburg, C. (1954/2002). *Abraham Lincoln: The Prairie Years and the War Years.* Boston, MA: Mariner Books.

Savin-Williams, R.C., and Diamond, L.M. (1997). "Sexual Orientation as a Developmental Context for Lesbians, Gays and Bisexuals: Biological Perspaectives." In N. L. Seqal, G.E. Weisfeld, and C.C. Weisfeld (Eds.), *Uniting Psychology and Biology: Integrative Perspectives on Human Development.* Washington, DC: American Psychological Association Press, pp. 217-38.

479

Sbarra, D.A., and Emery, R.E. (2005). "Coparenting Conflict, Nonacceptance, and Depression among Divorced Adults: Results from a 12-Year Follow-up Study of Child Custody Mediation Using Multiple Imputation." *American Journal of Orthopsychiatry, 75* (1), 63-75.

Schaie, K.W. (1994). "The Course of Adult Intellectual Development." *American Psychologist, 49,* 304-13.

Seligman, M.E.P. (2005). "The Effectiveness of Psychotherapy: The Consumer Reports Study." *American Psychologist, 50,* 12, 965-74.

Seligman, M.E.P., Rashid, T., and Parks, A.C. (2006). "Positive Psychotherapy." *American Psychologist, 61,* 774-86.

Seligman, M.E.P., Steen, T.A., Park, N., and Peterson, C. (2005). "Positive Psychology Progress." *American Psychologist, 60,* 410-21.

Sell, R.L., Wells, J.A., and Wypij, D. (1995). "The Prevalence of Homosexual Behavior and Attraction in the United States, the United Kingdom and France: Results of National Population?-?based Samples." *Archives of Sexual Behavior, 24,* 235-48.

Sevecke, K., Pukrop, R., Kosson, D.S., and Krisher, M.K. (2009). "Factor Structure of the Hare Psychopathy Checklist: Youth Version in German Female and Male Detainees and Community Adolescents." *Psychological Assessment, 21,* 45-56.

Sherif, M. (1936). *The Psychology of Group Norms.* New York: Harper & Row.

Sherif, M., and Sherif, C.W. (1953). *Groups in Harmony and Tension: An Integration of Studies on Intergroup Relations.* New York: Octagon Books.

Shiv, B., and Fedhorikhin, B. (1999). "Heart and Mind in Conflict: The Interplay of Affect and Cognition in Consumer Decision Making." *Journal of Consumer Research, 26,* 278-92.

Siegel, D.J. (1999). *The Developing Mind: How Relationships and the Brain Interact to Shape Who We Are.* New York: Guilford Press.

Slade, A., Cohen, L.J., Sadler, L.S., and Miller, M.R. (in press). "The Psychology and Psychopathology of Pregnancy: Reorganization and Transformation." In Charles Zeanah (Ed.), *Handbook of Infant Mental Health,* 3rd edition, New York: Guilford Press.

Snook, R., Eastwood, J., Gendreau, P., Goggin, C., and Cullen, R.M. (2008). "Taking Stock of Criminal Profiling: A Narrative Review and Meta-analysis." *Current Perspective in Forensic Psychology and Criminal Behavior,* 2nd edition. Thousand Oaks, CA: Sage Publications.

Snowdon, D. (2001). *Aging with Grace: What the Nun Study Teaches Us about Leading Longer, Healthier, and More Meaningful Lives.* New York: Bantam Books.

Soubrie, P. (1986). "Reconciling the Role of Central Serotonin Neurons in Human and Animal Behavior," *Behavioral and Brain Sciences, 9,* 319-64.

Sowell, E.R., Thompson, P.M., Holmes, C.J., et al. (1999). "In Vivo Evidence for Post-Adolescent Brain Maturation in Frontal and Striatal Regions." *Nature Neuroscience, 2* (10): 859-61.

Spreen, O., and Strauss, E. (1998). *A Compendium of Neuropsychological Tests,* 2nd edition. New York: Oxford University Press.

Stark, E. (2007). *Coercive Control: How Men Entrap Women in Personal Life.* New York: Oxford University Press.

Steadman, H., McGreevy, M.A., Morrisey, J.P, Callahan, L.A., Robbins, P.C., and Cirincione, C. (1993). *Before and After Hinckley: Evaluating Insanity Defense Reform.* New York: Guilford Press.

Stein, D.J., Shoulberg, N., Helton, K., and Hollander, E. (1992). "The Neuroethological Approach to Obsessive-Compulsive Disorder." *Comprehensive Psychiatry, 33,* 274-81.

Stern, D.N. (1985). *The Interpersonal World of the Infant: A View from Psychoanalysis and Developmental Psychology.* New York: Basic Books.

Sternberg, R. (1986). "A Triangular Theory of Love." *Psychological Review, 93* (2), 119-35.

Sternberg, R. (1987). "Liking vs. Loving: A Comparative Evaluation of Theories." *Psychological Bulletin, 102* (3), 331-45.

Sternberg, R., and Gracek, S. (1984). "The Nature of Love." *Journal of Personality and Social Psychology, 4* (2), 312-29.

Stouthamer-Loeber, M., Loeber, R., Wei, E., Farrington, D.P., and Wikstron, P.O.H. (2002). "Risk and Promotive Effects in the Explanation of Persistent Serious Delinquency in Boys." *Journal of Consulting and Clinical Psychology, 70* (1), 111-23.

Storr, A. (1988). *Churchill's Black Dog, Kafka's Mice and Other Phenomena of the Human Mind.* New York: Ballantine Books.

Styron, W. (1992). *Darkness Visible: A Memoir of Madness.* New York: Vintage Books.

Sullivan, T., and Maiken, P.T. (2000). *Killer Clown: The John Wayne Gacy Murders.* New York: Pinnacle.

Swartz, A. (1997). "What Is Mirror Self-recognition in Non-human Primates, and What Is Not?" In J.G. Snodgrass, R.L. Thompson (Eds.). "The Self across Psychology: Self-recognition, Self-awareness, and the Self Concept." *Annals of the New York Academy of Sciences, 818,* 65-71.

Swedo, S.E. (1989). "Rituals and Releasers: An Ethological Model of Obsessive-Compulsive Disorder." In *Obsessive-Compulsive Disorder in Children and Adolescents.* J.L. Rapoport (Ed.). Washington, DC: American Psychiatric Press, 1989.

Task Force for the Handbook of Psychiatric Measures (Eds.) (2000). *Handbook of Psychiatric Measures.* Washington, DC: American Psychiatric Association.

Taylor, S.E., Klein, L.C., Lewis, B.P., Gruenewald, T.L., Gurung, R.A.R., and Updegraff, J.A. (2000). "Biobehavioral Responses to Stress in Females: Tend-and-Befriend, Not Fight-or-Flight." *Psychological Review, 107,* 441-29.

Tennov, D. (1979). *Love and Limerence: The Experience of Being in Love.* New York: Stein and Day.

Thaler, R. (1992). *The Winner's Curse.* Princeton, NJ: Princeton University Press.

Thompson, P.M., Hayashi, K.M., Simon, S.L., Geaga, J.A., Hong, M.S., Sui, Y., Lee, J.Y., Toga, A.W., Ling, W., and London, E.D. (2004). "Structural Abnormalities in the Brains of Subjects Who Use Methamphetamine." *The Journal of Neuroscience, 24,* 6028-36.

Twenge, J., Konrath, S., Foster, J.D., Campbell, W.K., and Bushman, B.J. (2008). "Egos Inflating Over Time: A Cross-temporal Meta-analysis of the Narcissistic Personality Inventory." *Journal of Personality, 76* (4), 875-902.

U.S. Bureau of the Census (2007) Current Population Survey. *Marital Status and Living Arrangements.* (http://www.census.gov/population/www/socdemo/ms-la.html). Accessed June 1, 2010.

U.S. Bureau of the Census, Current Population Reports, P23-180 (1992). *Marriage, Divorce, and Remarriage in the 1990's.* Washington, DC: U.S. Government Printing Office.

Vanneman, R.D., Pettigrew, T.F. (1972). "Race and Relative Deprivation in the Urban United States." *Race, 13,* 461-86.

Van Ijzendoorn, M.H., and Kroonenberg, P.M. (1988). "Cross-cultural Patterns of Attachment: A Meta-analysis of the Strange Situation." *Child Development, 59,* 147-56.

Veen, P., and Korver, T. (1998). "Theories of Organization." In P.J.D. Drenth, H. Thierry, and C.J. de Wolff (Eds.) *Handbook of Work and Organizational Psychology.* Vol. 4: *Organization Psychology,* 2nd edition. East Sussex, UK: Psychology Press, pp. 5-37.

Veenhoven, R., "Average Happiness in 145 Nations 2000-2008, *World Database of Happiness, RankRepport 2009-1a.* (http://www.worlddatabaseofhappiness.eur.nl). Accessed June 1, 2010.

Veenhoven, R. (2005). "Is Life Getting Better?: How Long and Happily Do People Live in Modern Society?" *European Psychologist, 10*(4), 330-43.

Veenhoven, R., and Kalmijn, W. (2005). "Inequality-Adjusted Happiness in Nations: Egalitarianism and Utilitarianism Married in a New Index of Societal Performance." *Journal of Happiness Studies, Special Issue on Inequality of Happiness in Nations, 6,* 421-55.

Veenhoven, R., and Hagerty M. (2006). "Rising Happiness in Nations 1946-2004: A Reply to Easterlin." *Social Indicators Research, 79,* 421-36.

Viamontes, G.I., Beitman, B.D., Viamontes, C.T., and Viamontes, J.A. (2004). "Neural Circuits for Self-awareness: Evolutionary Origins and Implementation in the Human Brain." In B.D. Beitman and J. Nair (Eds.). *Self-Awareness Deficits in Psychiatric Patients: Neurobiology, Assessment, and Treatment.* New York: W.W. Norton.

481

Vinokur, A., and Bernstein, E., (1974). "Effects of Partially Shared Persuasive Arguments on Group-induced Shifts: A Group Problem Solving Approach." *Journal of Personality and Social Psychology, 29,* 305-15.

Vitebsky, Piers (1995). *Shamanism.* London, UK: Duncan Baird Publishers.

Vroom, V.H., and Yetton, P.W. (1973). *Leadership and Decision Making.* Pittsburgh, PA: University of Pittsburgh Press.

Walker, L.E. (1979). *The Battered Woman.* New York: Harper & Row.

Watson, J. (1913). "Psychology as the Behaviorist Views It." *Psychological Review, 20,* 158-77.

Weinberg, S.S. (1997). "Joyce Brothers." In P. Hyman and D. D. Moore (Eds.). *Jewish Women in America.* New York: Routledge.

Weinberger, D., Elvevag, B., Giedd, J.N. (2005). *The Adolescent Brain: A Work in Progress.* Washington, DC: The National Campaign to Prevent Teen Pregnancy (http://www.thenationalcampaign .org/resources/pdf/BRAIN.pdf). Accessed June 10, 2010.

Westen, D. (2007). *The Political Brain: The Role of Emotion in Deciding the Fate of the Nation.* New York: Public Affairs.

Whiteside, M.F., and Becker, B.J. (2000). "Parental Factors and the Young Child's Postdivorce Adjustment: A Meta-analysis with Implications for Parenting Arrangements." *Journal of Family Psychology, 14* (1), 5-26.

Widom, C.S., and Maxfield, M.G. (2001). "An Update on the 'Cycle of Violence.'" *National Institute of Justice: Research in Brief.* Washington, DC: Office of Justice Programs, U.S. Department of Justice.

Wilson, T., Lisle, D., Schooler, J., Hodges, S.D., Klaaren, K.J., and LaFleur, S.J. (1993). "Instrospecting about Reasons Can Reduce Post-choice Satisfaction." *Personality and Social Psychology Bulletin, 19,* 331-39.

Wolf, G.K., Reinhard, M. Cozolino, L.J., Caldwell, A., and Asamen, J.D. (2009). "Neuropsychiatric Symptoms of Complex Posttraumatic Stress Disorder: A Preliminary Minnesota Multiphasic Personality Inventory Scale to Identify Adult Survivors of Childhood Abuse." *Psychological Trauma: Theory, Research, Practice and Policy, 1,* 49-64.

Wofford, J.C., and Srinivasan, T.N. (1983). "Experimental Tests of Leader-Environment-Follower Interaction Theory of Leadership." *Organizational Behavior and Human Performance, 32,* 35-54.

Woodworth, M., and Porter, S. (2002). "In Cold Blood: Characteristics of Criminal Homicides as a Function of Psychopathy." *Journal of Abnormal Psychology, 111* (3), 436–45.

Woolsey, T.A., Hanaway, J., and Gado, M.H. (2003). *The Brain Atlas: A Visual Guide to the Human Central Nervous System,* 2nd edition. Hoboken, NJ: John Wiley & Sons.

World Health Organization (2009). *Violence against Women by Intimate Partners.* Geneva, Switzerland: WHO. (http://www.who.int/gender/violence/who_multicountry_study/summary_report/ chapter 2/en/index2.html). Accessed 10/17/2009.

Wright, S.C., Aron, A., and Tropp, L.R. (2002). "Including Others (and Their Groups) in the Self: Self-expansion and Intergroup Relations." In J.P. Forgas and K. Williams (Eds). *The Social Self: Cognitive, Interpersonal and Intergroup Perspectives.* Philadelphia, PA: Psychology Press, pp. 343-63.

Wright, D., and Taylor, D.M. (2003/2009). "The Social Psychology of Cultural Diversity: Social Stereotyping, Prejudice and Discrimination." *The SAGE Handbook of Social Psychology, Concise Student Edition.* M. Hogg and J. Cooper (Eds.) Los Angeles, CA: SAGE Publications, pp. 361-87.

Wyatt, G.E., Guthrie, D., and Notgrass, C.M. (1992). "Differential Effects of Women's Child Sexual Abuse and Subsequent Sexual Revictimization." *Journal of Consulting and Clinical Psychology, 60,* 167-73.

Young, S.M., and Pinsky, D. (2006). "Narcissism and Celebrity." *Journal of Research in Personality, 40* (5), 463-71.

Zweig, J. (2007). *Your Money and Your Brain.* New York: Simon & Schuster.

Index

Note: (ill.) indicates photos and illustrations.

M